DRESS

DRESS

FOURTH EDITION

Eleanor Jerner Gawne, Ed.D.
Professor
Framingham State College
Framingham, Massachusetts

and

Bess V. Oerke

Chas. A. Bennett Co., Inc.
Peoria, Illinois 61614

ISBN 87002–069–2

Library of Cong. Cat. No. 74–83–969

PRINTED IN THE UNITED STATES OF AMERICA

75 76 77 K 6 5 4 3 2 1

Preface . . .

When DRESS appeared, it was enthusiastically received by teachers and students who were pleased to discover a book that was appealing to high school girls and was concerned with all aspects of clothing and personal appearance. The revised edition is planned to meet the same needs—to help high school students to select appropriate and attractive clothing for many occasions, to plan one's clothing purchases in relation to personal and family goals and resources, to understand textiles and garment construction so as to buy fabrics and clothes intelligently, to keep clothing looking like new, and to learn when and how to construct and alter garments for personal and family use.

Since the first revision of this book was made, there have been many changes in society. Today, both men and women are not only working outside the home in a career for much of their lives, but they are also sharing in homemaking responsibilities.

The basic approach is similar to the first edition, so that teachers will be at home with this revision. Learning activity suggestions have been increased; more experiments are included to help students discover principles for themselves. Summary statements for each chapter are followed by questions planned to reinforce them. Selected references for student use are listed at the end of the book. More extensive references will be found in the Teacher's Guide.

Emphasis is placed on basic principles of clothing construction and renovation rather than on exact procedures for specified projects.

Although the course may follow the sequence of chapters, each chapter is complete by itself so that the book will meet the needs of teachers with varying curriculum plans. Because of this, there is planned repetition. Cross references are also used.

This revision is directed to young men and young women with the realization that both men and women will share in wage earning and homemaking. Stress is also given to the importance of clothing and grooming for part-time jobs held by high school youth and for success in future vocations.

Most of the book will be of equal value to young men and young women. Chapter 9 is concerned solely with clothing for boys and men and parallels the second section of Chapter 5, which is concerned more specifically with clothing for girls.

I wish to extend personal appreciation to Paul Van Winkle and Marion Cronan, who have patiently and intelligently guided me in this revision. Grateful acknowledgment is made to the clothing and the textile concerns whose agents provided photographs and other educational material. Credit lines are given in the text. Special recognition is made to the late Bess Oerke for her vision in initiating a book with the appeal and educational value of DRESS.

E. J. G.

5

Contents

Part 1. PERSONAL CLOTHING NEEDS

Contents

Part 2. CLOTHING THE FAMILY

Part 3. TEXTILE FABRICS

Part 4. CLOTHING CONSTRUCTION AND ALTERATIONS

7

Part 5. LOOKING AHEAD

List of Color Illustrations

Dame Fashion . . .

Who is Dame Fashion?
  Why, nobody knows;
Or where she may come from
  Or whither she goes.
She merely says "Presto!
  Go alter your clothes."
And we all obey her;
  Why, nobody knows.

She's always a ruler
  Without any throne;
She comes in a breath,
  In another she's gone;
I know I despise her
  And so, too, do you,
We scold her, scorn her
  (And follow her, too).

She looks at your dress
  And she says it won't do;
It's too—too—well, you know,
  It's just simply too—
Too what? It doesn't matter.
  Too why? I can't say.
Dame Fashion decrees it,
  That makes it O.K.

Your hat is too fussy,
  It ought to be plain,
'Twas fussy last summer,
  It may be again.
But that doesn't alter
  The fact that today
Dame Fashion decrees that
  Your hat is passé.

So it's off to the tailor
  To buy some new clothes.
Why? It's no matter
  For nobody knows.
Dame Fashion has spoken:
  "Go, alter your clothes!"
And lo! We obey her
  Why, nobody knows.

Oh, skirts may be skimpy
  Or skirts may be full;
And skirts may be silken
  Or skirts may be wool.
"It's style," so they tell you
  It's style—and it GOES!
Who made it? Don't ask me
  For nobody knows!

—JAMES FOLEY, *North Dakota Poet*

PART 1

PERSONAL CLOTHING NEEDS

CHAPTER ONE

The Many Meanings of Dress— And You

O F COURSE you are interested in dress or you would not be enrolled in a clothing course. People have always been concerned about dress for many reasons. You are probably interested in your own dress in order to appear more attractive and to be more likeable. Did you know that our dress has more meanings than most of us realize? One man, when asked why people wore clothes, said that he wore them "to keep warm and to keep out of jail!" True, but he would be most unusual if he did not have many additional reasons.

In this chapter you will read about the meaning of clothing so that you can understand better what it means to you. Until you understand your needs and desires, you will not be able to make wise decisions about dress.

THE MEANING OF DRESS

We are inclined to judge a person by the clothing he wears, as clothes are often the first thing we notice. We recognize that a good appearance is important. In order to appreciate the true importance of dress, we need to discover how we feel about the clothes we wear.

SELF ADORNMENT

In all cultures dress provides a means of adornment and decoration. The physical self can be made to seem more desirable and more attractive by the use of certain clothing, hair styles, cosmetics, and even posture.

Primitive man adorned himself with colored clay and inserted jewelry in his nose, ears, and lips. The urge to adorn himself and his family led man to a search for furs and fibers all over the world. Read about the desire for silk in Chapter Ten. Have you seen pictures of people who seem beautiful to themselves and their countrymen, but who would not seem so in your community? Small feet were considered beautiful in much of the Orient; therefore a little girl's feet were bound tightly to restrain their growth. What other examples can you think of?

PROTECTION

It is obvious that clothing can protect from rain and wind and hot sun as well as the winter cold. In some sections of this country footwear is necessary as protection from hookworm, and in other places protection is needed from poisonous plants and insects. Well-fitting shoes can be protection against improper development of feet. Can you think of other clothing items that can protect one from poor physical development or can hinder one's good development? Is fashion more important than protection? Can you think of clothing that is popular for rainy or cold weather but does not offer sensible protection? See page 70 for an illustration of how color in clothing can be a means of safety.

CIBA CORPORATION, SUMMIT, NEW JERSEY
Early man liked to decorate himself. Berry juices were often rubbed over the body, and feathers and colored stones added to brighten simple clothing items.

STATUS AND PRESTIGE

Prestige can be obtained from various methods . . . some people prefer clothing. Have you ever met a person for the first time and thought he was "somebody" just because of the way he was dressed? Or perhaps you were not impressed because he was dressed in a way that did not seem correct to you? A new fur coat for a businessman's wife makes people think that his business is succeeding. Do some girls feel "better" because their sweaters are cashmere and not just wool? Through fashion, men and women attempt to achieve and maintain their goal of social approval and rank.

Everyone needs a feeling of status or prestige and manner of dress is one way this can be accomplished. Clothing may not be too important to people who have hobbies or vocations or talents that are very satisfying to them. There are times in everyone's life when one's dress may not be as important as some other aspect of life . . . but all happy, well-adjusted individuals recognize the need to be reasonably well dressed, and to gain recognition from others in this manner.

Why do college graduates wear distinctive robes and mortarboard hats? And why do robes and hats worn by those who have received advanced degrees differ? Such clothing is a means of showing one's academic rank or status. The student nurse who is "capped" enjoys a higher status than the nurse who has not reached this stage. Today, boys can never reach the status of a man by wearing their first long pants—toddlers wear them all the time. What type of clothes indicate adult status for either men or women in your community?

SIMMONS COLLEGE SCHOOL OF NURSING

A nurse's uniform can show if she is a graduate nurse or a student nurse. These girls are wearing the cap and white uniform of a graduate nurse, not the colored ones usually worn by student nurses. As part of their graduation exercises, they are receiving pins which bear the seal of the nursing school where they have trained.

INSTITUTE OF LIFE INSURANCE

Do you think this little girl feels more "grown-up" wearing clothes that belong to an older person? Do you remember wearing mother's or big sister's clothes? How did you feel?

As similar kinds of clothing become available to all ages and economic levels, clothing is a less reliable indicator of social class or age. In small communities where people rarely move, fashion may not be so important. Everyone knows everyone else and his business. Fashion cannot be used as a prestige device. In large cities where people are constantly moving, fashion is considered important. First impressions often count and one way to judge a person is by what he is wearing. Is it more important for a student who is new to your school to be well dressed than for one who has grown up in the community and whom everyone knows? Why?

Not only can clothing indicate status but it is also important in group identification. If a person wears a uniform you can easily identify his job. Can't you often tell whether a person is a member of some organization or school by what he wears? Perhaps the group is more of a clique or "in-group" but clothing can indicate to others that one belongs and can also make the person feel that he belongs.

All people need to have a feeling of belonging someplace, somewhere. Clothing can meet this need. How do you feel when you discover that you are dressed differently from others at a party or special occasion? When people wish to conform, they often wear similar clothes. Children have a desire to look like their peers, and

14

When you were little do you remember feeling grown-up when you wore certain clothes? What were they? Why did you feel as you did?

Have you ever worn a uniform? Does it make you feel different? Do you know someone who has just received a school band uniform? How does he act?

Do any of your classmates have jobs or hold offices in clubs that require the wearing of uniforms or distinctive clothing? Have them form a panel and tell the class how they feel when in uniform. Perhaps they can study the meaning of the various parts of the uniform and tell the others.

Have you ever had a garment that fit and was in good condition and which you liked but which you would not wear because it was no longer in style? Why could you no longer wear it?

DEPARTMENT OF DEFENSE

A uniform not only contributes to the "esprit de corps" or sense of belonging to a branch of the armed forces but it also identifies such a person to others.

adults do not want to be too different. To be "out-of-style" is dreadful for many people.

One high school girl known for her sense of humor said that "we could end wars easily . . . by requiring that all those fighting be nudists. If no one knew who the enemy was, no one would know who to fight and there would be no war." This may be an extreme theory but clothing is important in war—to identify which side one is on and also to identify the leaders and the members of the different groups. In sports this is also true—imagine a football game if both teams had identical uniforms.

Collect pictures of shoes that you would expect an older woman to wear. Compare them with shoes you believe a young woman would choose. How do they differ?

If you were applying for a job in an office and you wanted to appear as an efficient office worker, what type of clothing would you wear?

How would your clothing differ if you were planning to attend a senior prom?

Have you ever formed a first impression of a person that later proved to be wrong? Describe how clothing may have influenced you.

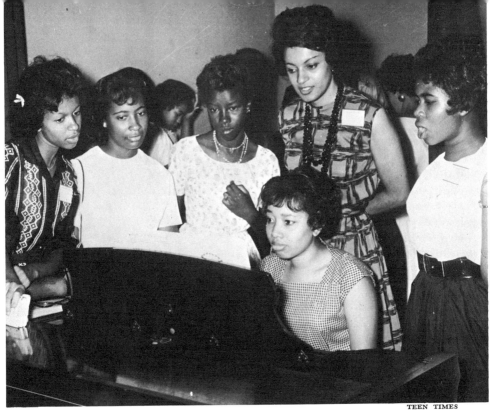

Joining in the group singing is fun when you are dressed like the others. The girls here have all chosen to wear informal dresses suitable to the Future Home-makers of America social meeting.

ROLE IDENTIFICATION

The word **role** may seem strange but it simply means the part one plays at a particular time. You have many roles; that of daughter, a big sister, a student, a date, and a business woman if you have a job. Your role on a date will differ for a tennis game or at a prom. Do you use clothing to indicate your role? Probably you do. Would you dress in a different manner if you were helping in a hospital, cutting grass at home, or going to a special dance? Would you feel and act differently because of your dress?

Society has certain expectations about the way people should dress for certain roles. Men are expected to dress differently from women and when fashion is such that it is hard to tell the sexes apart, concern is felt by many. There has been a considerable change in recent years concerning the rigidness with which people are expected to dress for their role.

"Since the beginning of nursing as a profession around 100 years ago, the desirability of some kind of common uniform was recognized, as the same pride in uniform which helps to maintain the spirit of an army is applicable in the training of nurses. But it was also learned long ago that people are happier when they like what they are wearing; therefore, uniforms of all kinds continue to change and keep step with fashion and new living habits." [*] Some hospitals are experimenting in having their nurses wear colored uniforms or regular street clothes.

---

[*] From a release issued by Virginia Dickson and White Swan Uniforms, Inc.

Collect pictures of persons dressed in various ways. Describe a "first impression" of each person. Think about the impression each person may have been trying to create through her dress.

Analyze your own dress. What impression does it probably make on others? Is this the impression you wish to give?

Interview the employment officer of a large company near you. Ask him how he judges the dress of a person applying for a job. Does this company also interview the wife of an applicant? If so, what do they look for in her appearance?

Is it a compliment to a hostess to dress up for her party? How would she feel if you said, "I didn't feel like dressing."

HORN/GRINER

This attractive and functional uniform identifies the teen who volunteers her services as a "candy striper" to help the ill in hospitals. Patients and nurses know that they can rely on a girl who wears this uniform.

Today some grandmothers can wear styles identical to their teen-age granddaughters with approval from everyone. Despite these few exceptions, clothing is important in helping identify your role and in helping you fit into the accepted behavior of your role.

In an emergency, would you have more faith in an airline hostess in uniform than some one in a silk dress? Are you more apt to ask directions from a policeman in uniform than someone else? Do you suppose a bandage applied to a hurt child by a woman in white is more calming than one applied by his classroom teacher? Will you listen to the advice of a saleswoman dressed neatly in the latest fashion or someone wearing last year's style? Have you ever mistaken a school principal for a custodian during vacation because he was wearing a simple sports shirt? It has happened! Clothing tells others who we are and what we do.

Confident for a job interview because she feels well dressed and well groomed.
BOSTON SUNDAY HERALD AND KATHERINE GIBBS

EFFECT ON BEHAVIOR

Clothing can tell others about your expected behavior but it can also influence you. Do you think policemen feel braver in uniform? Do nurses feel more capable in uniform? Do girls feel more feminine in a long dress? How do young men feel in a suit and tie? Will you act differently if you wear neat clothes to school rather than faded jeans, run-down loafers, and a top that has seen "better days"? Although schools no longer have dress codes, it has been found that youths behave more appropriately in school when suitably dressed.

Not only your appearance is affected by the clothes you wear but your self image is also. A girl who may not be too secure usually feels much more capable and likeable when dressed becomingly in a current style. Boys who feel they haven't a chance to succeed have been known to mature quickly when they obtain clothes acceptable to others.

SELF-EXPRESSION

You have read how people are often judged by their clothing. Do you realize that one way you tell others who you are and what your values are is by the clothing you select and wear?

If you value craftmanship and high standards of work, you will want clothing carefully constructed with handmade or other distinctive touches. A person who is modest will dress in that manner. One who wants to look older or younger will select clothes for the desired age group. If you want people to think you are like a certain group of girls, you will dress as that group does.

Clothes can also *affect* your mood. Do you have a dress or coat that

How do some young people today dress to show rebellion against convention? How may this type of dress affect the wearer?

makes you "feel good"? And another one that you seldom wear because you just don't feel happy in it? Explain.

Clothes can also *tell* your mood. Do you ever select a certain dress for no reason except that you "felt like it"? Perhaps you did not know what mood you were in but others knew by looking at your clothes. Are you apt to choose bright and gay designs when you feel outgoing and in a party mood? Do pastels appeal to girls when they feel feminine? Solemn occasions call for darker colors. Progress in some mental illness is judged by the type of clothing selected. An inhibited, shy person who has felt secure in dull colors is on the road to recovery when brighter or lighter colors are desired.

Clothing can tell how a person feels about himself. Someone who does not feel very worthwhile may select quiet clothes so as not to be noticed or poor clothes because one does not feel worth anything better. On the other hand, if one does not feel worthwhile, the more expensive, latest clothes may be needed in an attempt to be popular. Do you know anyone who fits these descriptions?

Just as clothing can indicate belonging to a group, it can indicate a rebellion against a person or a group. Teens often select clothing that they know is not approved by others, especially older people. Why is this?

SEARS, ROEBUCK AND CO.

This young man expresses his personality with a well-coordinated outfit.

CREATIVITY AND INDIVIDUALITY

Just as we all need to feel we belong and are like others, we also need a feeling of individuality. Clothing can accomplish this by the use of details and colors that are different and still within the accepted mode.

Many people enjoy applying their creative ability to clothing. Instead of painting or writing poetry, they apply the art elements to articles of dress. In Chapter Two, this is described in greater detail.

CHANGE AND ADVENTURE

Clothing can help one escape from the routines of daily living and provide a relief from boredom. All persons have the need for novelty to add interest and zest to life, and fashion can help meet this need. Fashion results from a desire for change on the part of the consumer because we tire of clothing more frequently than we do many other things. One reason for the large sale of accessories is that people cannot always afford new garments, but a change can be effected with a scarf, beads, or accessories.

Party clothes can help one achieve a feeling of adventure. The woman who spends most of her time in her home doing housework may feel the need for fancy party clothes as a change. The woman who has many different daily experiences may select simpler party clothes.

SIMPLICITY PATTERN CO.

One means of expressing individuality. A high school girl selected a pattern similar to those of her friends but tie-dyed the top (see page 423) and added a distinctive braided string belt.

Choosing ready-made clothes to suit you and your needs are one way of expressing creativity. Another way is creating clothes, by sewing or other means. This young lady made her two-piece sweater set using a simple but interesting classic pattern that can be worn for many seasons.

A Means of Achieving a Sense of Well-Being

When we are physically well and comfortably dressed, we have a better chance to enjoy life. A charming girl is one who is well dressed in such a satisfying manner that she can forget herself and be interested in others. She will have a feeling of inner security and can be friendly and out-

going. You may not be as attractive as you wish but by wise clothing selection, you can help yourself achieve a sense of well-being. Dress reflects what we think we are and what we want to be.

Fashion and Ads

Fashion advertisers use a knowledge of the psychology of fashion when they plan their ads. Some appeal to one's need for protection while others appeal to one's desire to fit in with the "right" people. Have you seen advertisements that stress the adventure you will have if you wear certain clothes? Other ads stress low cost, long wear, or ease of care.

Appeal to the Same or Opposite Sex

Do we dress for the opposite or our own sex? Some people believe that clothes are selected to appeal to the opposite sex but others believe that women wear clothes to arouse envy or comment in other women. They believe that fashion is a battle within rather than between the sexes. What do you think?

Clothing and Family Values

The term "values" may seem abstract and unrelated to clothing but "value" means anything that is important to you. Clothing is very important in some families. Have you heard it said of some people that "they put all their money on their backs"? Being well dressed with many changes of the latest styles is uppermost in their values and they tend to judge others by the clothing they wear. Other families select clothing only for comfort, economy, and ease of care, and prefer to use their money for travel, or school-

Collect advertisements of clothing that appeal to various emotions. Label sections of your classroom tack boards with such reasons as *protection, status, change, safety, economy, adventure* and others listed in this chapter. Place the ads under the correct term. Do ads for children's clothing differ from those for women, men, young people? Explain.

ing, or to improve the family business or farm.

Many families value only a certain type of clothing—mother must have a fur coat, or the children must have the best quality shoes, or the son away at college must have an expensive and varied wardrobe. There is no right way. Each family, and each individual in it, must think through his needs and values to decide where to put the emphasis. It is essential to be well dressed and well groomed but this can be accomplished without undue emphasis on clothing.

Values change just as one's needs change throughout life. The young mother who used to cherish cashmere sweaters and delicate fabrics now prefers drip dry clothes as she finds little time or money for herself with the growing demands of the family. When her children are grown she may again become very clothes conscious in an effort to regain her individuality.

Before you can make wise decisions about your clothing, you need to give serious thought to the meaning of clothing to you. What needs does it meet? Should it be more important or less important? What changes do you need to make in your dress in order to become the attractive and secure person you can be?

FASHION, STYLE, AND FAD

Comments such as "that's high fashion," "that is not in style," "that coat is a fad," are common. What is the difference between these three terms? A *style* is a term that describes an object or art form that has certain distinguishing characteristics. A shirtwaist dress is a style of garment as is the middy blouse or the A-line skirt. It implies something that has come to be approved over a period of time. *Fashion* is the current mode. It is a style that is popular at the time. It reflects a change in style but it is not so extreme or short lived to be called a fad. A *fad*, therefore, is something that has enormous appeal for a short time but soon passes. Like flaming paper, a fad burns high and then burns out. Usually a fad is some detail in decoration, accessory, or fabric.

Some fads do become fashions if they are well designed and meet a need. Many years ago the small neck scarf came in as a fad but continues to be fashionable in most seasons. It meets the need for flattering color and texture near the face.

Can you remember when something you wore was criticized by your family or friends? How did you react? Did you change your manner of dressing?

How do you react when you receive compliments on your clothing? Do you think that your clothing choices are influenced by what others think?

Denim pants and jackets once were traditionally worn just for heavy work. Almost overnight, they became popular clothes for school, leisure, and other occasions for both men and women of almost all ages. What do you think are some of the reasons for this popularity?

High style or high fashion is a term of the fashion world to describe whatever is the newest fashion. Usually it refers to materials and workmanship of fine quality.

A *classic* is a style that can be worn year after year. A simple cardigan, pleated skirts, and loafer shoes are examples.

Not all fashions are revivals of past styles. Designers are constantly trying to find inspiration from historical sources and also from nature, art, costumes used in other countries, and new materials.

How many current fashions can you find that have been adapted from sailors' clothing, from oriental dress, from designs from India, from current space explorations?

Select pictures of garments that are high fashion or are an accepted style. Notice how many past styles have become fashionable again with some adaptations.

Can you think of clothing fads that were uncomfortable but were worn by many because it was the "thing" to do? List them. Are there fads that are not flattering to the average person but are still accepted? And what about ease of care—can you remember fads that were impractical but that you and others liked?

Oklahoma FHA'ers promote international good will while learning to understand and appreciate the differences in dress, as well as customs and living, of other peoples.

22

People in prestige positions often start fashions. The leaders in a country, whether a monarchy or democracy, play an important role in determining fashion. If they adopt a certain style, it is chosen by others and may become fashionable. As soon as the leaders feel their exclusiveness and individuality is being threatened, they will change. Remember the Eisenhower jacket? Would it have gained such prominence if developed and worn by an army private . . . regulations permitting? What other fashions can you think of that have been started by well known people?

THE HISTORY OF DRESS—INFLUENCE OF HISTORIC COSTUME TODAY

Fashion results from the thinking of each generation. Economic and political conditions have changed habits of living and fashions of dress. The history of fashion is also the history of man.

"As good be out of the world as out of fashion," Shakespeare said, and the great Bard has many who agree with him.

By studying clothing of the different periods, one can understand political, social, and economic standards of the era. The ideas and events of the time will take on meaning. Even

Collect pictures of current fashions. Analyze their sources. Can you find a picture to illustrate each source?

Choose a country you have been studying in history, or literature, or geography. Prepare a report on the native clothing and how it is affected by location, economics, and other national characteristics.

A national election inspired the designs on these shirts.

the climate and the amount of heating in the homes will be understood. As more English homes are built with central heating, their tweeds are becoming lighter in weight. No longer do American school children wear heavy underwear to poorly heated schools—warm snowsuits are used for outdoor play but indoor clothing is suitable for heated rooms. As Japanese women have become more active in the life of their nation, they have abandoned the kimona and shoes that forced them to move slowly and kept them close to home. See illustration on page 26.

During World War II women took over men's jobs and their clothing became mannish in appearance. Skirts became short and narrow because fabrics were scarce due to large demands for military purposes. Soon after the war, as a reaction, skirts dropped many inches in length and became very full.

23

When there is little change in customs or ideas in a country, there is apt to be little change in style of dress. In some areas of the East where civilization has remained constant for centuries, fashions have remained quite stable. Women today wear almost the same style clothing worn by their great-great-grandmothers. In our country there has been a constant mingling of nationalities and new developments, and thus fashions change frequently.

EGYPTIAN FASHIONS
The history of Western fashion begins in the Mediterranean area, where the Egyptians wore a tightly fitted garment. A dress of an early Egyptian woman consisted of a simple, very narrow, straight garment which reached from the breasts to the ankles. It was held in place by two straps over the shoulder. How did climate influence this design?

GRECIAN FASHIONS
Greeks believed that the beauty of the human body could not be surpassed. They also believed that the clothing should follow the lines of the human body in order to be beautiful. Their dresses were draped on the person and held in place by means of pins. The desired length of the dress from the floor was determined by pulling the dress up above the girdle, which formed a blouse. Sometimes a cord or gold-embossed leather strap passed over the shoulders and under the arms. What did climate have to do with this kind of costume?

METROPOLITAN MUSEUM OF ART, NEW YORK

Egyptian dress has influenced our dress design at various times.

ROMAN FASHIONS

The Romans wore loose-fitting, simple clothing. The tunic consisted of two pieces of woolen fabric sewn at the sides and top to form a shirt-like garment with short sleeves. Roman women often fastened their garment along the upper arm with brooches, which formed a sleeve.

MIDDLE AGES

In Europe styles changed slowly up till the 12th century. For example, it required 300 years for a bodice to be buttoned up the front instead of the back, and tight sleeves instead of loose sleeves to be worn! The center of civilization shifted from mild, Mediterranean areas to the north and the Atlantic coast. This greatly affected styles. Clothing became heavier and more garments were worn.

FRENCH RENAISSANCE

Kings and queens have originated styles, sometimes for trivial personal reasons. It is said that Henry II of France adopted the ruff in 1540 to conceal a scar on his neck.

In the 16th century, also, Catherine de Medici, queen of France, introduced the hoop skirt. Queen Elizabeth of England made the 13-inch waist fashionable. With a few exceptions, women were slaves to these cumbersome, uncomfortable fashions until the 19th century.

When Rousseau, during the second half of the 18th century, urged that children no longer be dressed as adults, a radical change occurred in the attire of French children. Marie Antionette is said to have initiated a new custom by dressing her three children in garments that were simple in texture and trim but retained much

METROPOLITAN MUSEUM OF ART, NEW YORK

A portrait of a lady painter showing the Greek influence on early 19th century dress.

the same cut as that of their parents. During the middle of the 1700's silk was a popular fabric, and deep lace ruffles trimmed the sleeves.

The French Revolution freed women of hoops and corsets. The simpler, high-waisted dress, known as the Empire gown, came into fashion in Napoleon's time at the beginning of the 19th century.

Fashion's pendulum soon swung back to tight corsets and the crinoline period with its multitudinous petticoats, broad shoulders, and ruffled fichu of the Romantic period of the 1860's.

The costumes did not follow the lines of the body; however, they had a feminine fascination, which made up for their inconvenience and discomfort. The attractiveness of the crinoline dress has caused its reappearance in modified form repeatedly up to the present time.

A showcase of history—each shoe was fashionable in its time. Can you decide why?

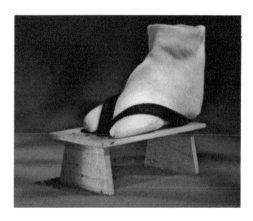

In Japan monks for centuries favored these simple wooden clogs with black fabric thongs. To this day they are still worn in Japan.

These Roman senator's shoes immediately marked their wearer as a man of power and wealth. The square upturned toes, thick leather soles, and metal crescent fastenings at the sides indicated "fashion."

ALL PICTURES THOM MC AN SHOE CO.

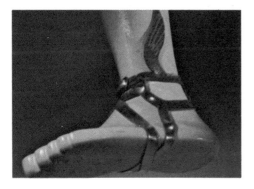

Gold sandals such as this one were worn in Greece about 1000 B.C. Their purpose was strictly decorative since they had no soles.

In 10th century France the fashion setters of the time considered these leather half-boots an important part of their dress.

In 14th century England the sweeping curved forms were popular for wide lace collars, cuffs, long hair, and also splay-foot shoes.

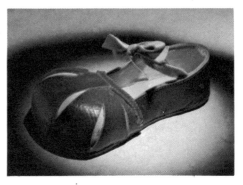

A trend toward broad toes went to the extreme in northern Europe. These 16th century English shoes were called "Duckbills." Soon this style gave way to the round toe, and then to the pointed toe.

The ladies of 17th century France combined a rounded toe and a medium height leather heel. Can you notice any similarities between a modern woman's pump and its 17th century counterpart?

One factor was function. These 18th century raised wooden American shoes were ideal for walking on the unpaved and often muddy streets found in most cities at that time.

Marie Antoinette's neckline and full skirt still influence design. Gone are the days when children dressed like this!

INFLUENCE OF SOCIAL EQUALITY

For centuries laws were made regulating the dress of people by classes. The Roman Caesars decreed: "Each class shall wear robes of different colors." The effect was amazing. The purpura, a native shellfish in the Mediterranean Sea, produced a deep purple dye. When the supply of the shellfish was almost exhausted by the people of Tyre, the king decreed that the use of purple was restricted to his family and his court. Consequently, at one time in Rome, it sold for $10,000 a pound!

In the 19th century an English law ruled: "Furs of ermine and embellishment of pearls, excepting for a headdress, are strictly forbidden to anyone not of the Royal family or a noble having upwards of 1,000 pounds a year . . . wearing of silks and embroidered garments is prohibited to persons without rank."

By the 19th century in America many class distinctions in dress were gone. The sewing machine did much to promote equality in dress. When Sarah Bernhardt, a great European stage star, made her last visit to America, she noted: "It is difficult to tell which is the shop-girl and which is the society belle, all dress so much alike."

Madame Favarat, a painting by Drovais. Notice the use of lace at neckline and sleeve edges and the neck ruffle.

Mrs. Jay Gould's costume, 1880, has features, including numerous petticoats, which are repeated in fashion from time to time.

There are no fabric or color restrictions today except those Dame Fashion and personal choice dictate. A combination of the machine age and scientific production has revolutionized the fabric world. Vast quantities of good quality synthetics and blends in unusual weaves, designs, and finishes are produced at a minimum cost which makes it possible for fabrics of "luxury" texture to be enjoyed by practically all American families.

20TH CENTURY STYLE TRENDS

By 1890 American women were ready for a fashion that would express their freedom and independence. Charles Dana Gibson made famous for the first time a "typical American girl," who dared to ride a bicycle. As the 20th century approached, skirts became ankle length and the number of petticoats was reduced to one.

Early 19th century Gibson costume. Note collar and pleated sleeves at the shoulder. Have these been in style in recent years?

29

The "typical American girl" dress, early 19th century, for a thirteen-year-old. With minor changes at the sleeves and in the skirt length, could it be a modern dress? What details are still being used? Note skirt fullness, cut of bodice, and neckline.

For many years Paris was the center of style trends. Americans followed the fashion dictates of Paris as early as the American Revolution. The influence of such French designers as Chanel, Lanvin, Mainboucher, and Schiaparelli was observed in the creations of dress designers for many years.

When the first world war in Europe caused the fall of Paris and a ban on trade, American designers were developed out of necessity. This made America a source of fashions for the future. The fresh, new American-born fashions appealed to lively American people.

During World War I a one-piece dress that hung from the shoulder instead of the waist was introduced in America. After the war came the boyish flapper with her waistline at her hips and her skirts up to her knees. About 1922 a new silhouette had become established. It was a one-piece costume with the waistline about the hips, and the skirt about eight inches from the floor. The garment hung straight with no suggestion of a waistline. Narrow belts often held low waistline fullness in position. Satins, velvets, silks, and elegant serges were favorites. Beads and braid decorated glistening fabrics. The hats were average in size, close fitting, covering the ears and hanging over the eyes. Formal gowns, dinner dresses, and street garments all appeared in the same straight silhouette, until about 1925, when slightly full skirts were gathered to long, slim bodices.

Costumes of the 1920's have had some influence today. The simple shoulders and drop waistline are examples. During periods of "good times" people try almost anything to be different!

Shorter skirts, continued emphasis of the hipline, and simple shoulders mark 1925 fashions.

After the popularity of the mini length in the late 1960's, the midi look was promoted by the fashion industry. How successful was the promotion?

Note the two-piece outfits at the right which are not as extreme as the other dresses shown. This marks the height of the fashion trends in the late 1920's.

31

About 1928 to 1930 the straight silhouette was being replaced with pleats to give fullness. Skirts were knee length and the waistline remained low. Many combinations of color and fabrics were high fashion. For variety a new hemline was introduced with the front at the usual knee length and the back lengthened. In the thirties a tailored suit garment with padded shoulders and slim-hip effect held a foremost position.

In 1935 the new silhouette had a fitted waistline. Street, dinner, and evening dresses were above the ankle.

About 1940 the silhouette made another change. Waistlines and bodices became fitted and skirts became shorter.

After World War II, skirts became long and full, often only eight inches from the ground for school dress. Full, ruffled petticoats were popular but were hard to store since they crushed easily.

Men's clothes did not change much. However, brightly printed shirts, worn outside of pants, were popular for summer wear and sports events. Crewcuts were in style.

In the 1960's the sack dress was introduced. Soon the idea of a waistless dress was accepted—belts almost disappeared. Dresses fit loosely, a look achieved by darts and A-line cuts. High school girls wore white "bobby socks" of bulky yarns and penny loafers. Hair rollers were used for a looser, bouffant hair style. Girls often wore hair rollers to school so their hair would look nice for the evening. School rules were introduced against this.

Skirts became shorter and pants tighter. School dress codes were developed to ban shorts, tight pants, and mini skirts.

By early 1970, dress codes were ruled a violation of individual rights in most communities. Students adopted a uniform look of pants, mostly denims, with tops of various styles and colors. Young men wore their hair long, either straight or curly. Girls wore theirs long and straight. Many schools banned bare feet as unsafe and unsanitary but left clothing to students' choice. Knee-length boots were worn for most occasions.

Pants styles changed from very tight ones to "flares" or bell-bottoms. Wide pants with cuffs, short shorts, and halter tops made their first appearance since the 1940's.

The early 1970's introduced the natural look—no girdles, simple make-up, and straight or softly waved hair. Shoulder pads and padded bras were a thing of the past. Students enjoyed wearing ethnic clothes from many countries. Handmade articles became desirable.

What is in style now? What do you predict will be the usual student attire in the next few years? Why?

Collect pictures of current dresses and other clothing articles that bear the names of well-known fashion designers. Arrange a display for a bulletin board. You may wish to group them under the country in which they work.

Have a conference with a fashion designer or a successful dress buyer in your community concerning fashion trends. Give a report to your class.

Career apparel today offers many choices. Colors indicate specific job assignments.

LADIES' HOME JOURNAL,
COPYRIGHT, CURTIS PUBLISHING CO.

The beginning of a complete style change, marked by the uneven hemline. This led to longer skirts and the high waistline of the 1930's.

Some elements of the 1920's flapper look were revived in the late 1960's, combined with mini-length skirts.

SIMPLICITY PATTERN CO.

Summary with Check-Up Questions

Dress has many meanings.
- *Besides making one appear more attractive, for what other reasons do people wear clothes?*

In all cultures, dress provides a means of adornment and decoration.
- *How did primitive man make himself appear attractive?*
- *How did the desire to appear more attractive lead to the development of world trade?*
- *What examples can you give where dress considered attractive for people of other countries would not be favored in our country?*

Clothing can provide protection from the elements and also help in good physical development.
- *What clothing items are worn to protect from rain, cold, wind, or hot sun?*
- *What clothing items help in good physical development? Which can hinder physical development if not fitted properly?*
- *What clothes are currently popular for rainy or cold weather wear which do not offer sensible protection?*

A person is expected to dress suitably for his role at a specific time.
- *If you were helping costume a school play, how would you dress a girl playing the part of a college student? How would you dress the girl who plays the grandmother? If the grandmother were at home cooking a meal, what would she wear? If she were working as a nurse in a hospital, would her clothing be different? How would a college man's clothing differ from that of the college girl?*

Clothing has an effect on behavior.
- *Do you feel more capable and secure when you know you are "well-dressed" for the occasion?*

- *Does a policeman or soldier feel braver when he wears his uniform?*
- *If you were not dressed as well as you would like to be, would you be more apt to keep quiet and stay in the background, or would you speak up in class or join in an activity at the time?*

Clothing is a means of self-expression.
- *How can clothing meet one's need for belonging and also express one's individuality?*
- *Why is the wearing of clothing not approved by parents or others in authority a means of rebellion?*
- *How would the clothes you select to wear differ if you are feeling happy or if you are feeling sad?*

Clothing can provide a feeling of change, adventure, relief from boredom and routines of daily living.
- *Why is a masquerade party a fun affair?*
- *Have you ever felt like a "different" person because of some new clothes you wore? Why?*
- *Why do mothers who are busy at home with household responsibilities usually enjoy dressing up for social occasions?*

Fashion advertisements often reflect the many meanings dress has for people of differing needs and desires.
- *What would you stress in an advertisement for an expensive, unusual suit?*
- *What appeals would be made for a moderate-cost suit of good quality fabric that is easy to care for?*
- *What other needs that people have are stressed in advertisements of clothing items?*

Clothing must conform to current fashion so that the wearer may meet her need for belonging but it must also express her individuality.

- *How can a current fashion worn by many people be adapted to express your personality?*
- *What changes would be made by a friend of yours who has different interests?*

One's choice of clothing is influenced by his own and his family's attitudes toward fashion, comfort, style, conformity, status, and other interests.

- *How will a family who feels it very important to have the latest in everything select clothing compare with a family who believes that comfort and economy are very important?*
- *Will clothing be more important to a freshman entering college or to a junior who is returning to the same college? Why?*
- *What problems may arise in a family when the parents are very concerned about saving money for a daughter's further education and she feels the need to have a large and fashionable wardrobe?*

Style refers to the characteristic or distinguishing features, cut, design, or type of article. **Fashion** is the accepted, prevailing style at any time. **High style** is a new fashion, generally costly and unusual, which is accepted by fashion leaders. It may change slightly and become popular for many. A **fad** is a short-lived fashion, usually extreme, quickly accepted and quickly dropped. A **classic** is a style that can be worn year after year with simple changes such as hem length, belt placement, or accessories.

- *What items are high fashion now?*
- *How many fads can you list that are popular now with high school girls? What was everyone wearing a year ago that is no longer in style?*
- *What classics that you wear now were also worn by your mother when she was your age? In what ways do the classics of today differ from past years?*

Studying the clothing of different periods of history can help one understand political, social, and economic standards of the era.

- *How did World War I and World War II affect the dress of American women?*
- *Compare the dresses worn in the 1880's with those worn today. What are some of the reasons for changes you have observed?*

Clothing can help establish a group to which one belongs.

- *How do you feel if you are wearing clothes different from others at school or a party or sports event?*
- *Why are uniforms usually worn by members of a band or a sports team?*
- *Are there certain types of clothing you do not want to wear because they are often chosen by girls from a group with whom you do not wish to be identified?*

Clothing is one means of providing status and prestige.

- *Which clothing items indicate status or prestige to you?*
- *What are the reasons that some people have for buying very expensive clothing?*

Can You Explain These Terms?

style	high style
fashion	or high fashion
fad	classic

CHAPTER TWO

Design

Naturally you want to select clothes that make you as attractive as possible. An application of the principles of design will help. Have you ever heard one of your friends say that you look as if you had lost weight when you wear a certain dress? At another time someone may ask you if you have grown taller. It is probably the design of your clothes that makes you appear different. Or have you found yourself noticing for the first time what pretty blue eyes a friend has? No doubt she was wearing a color that accentuated them.

Or perhaps you have heard someone say, "Such a pretty dress," when she was simply being kind to the person inside it, *whom it did not make more attractive.* How much better for her to be able to say, "My, how nice you look!" If she says this, you know that she sees what the dress does for *her* rather than just a pretty dress hanging on the wrong person.

Well-chosen clothes can bring out your best personality traits and physical features and make you feel your very best. Well-designed garments also will not go out of style so quickly

and you will not tire of them as soon as clothes designed for the moment without thought to enduring style.

In this chapter you will read about certain general design principles. Then you will study various figure types and learn how your good points

TEEN TIMES

Because of their study of clothing design principles, these national officers of the Future Homemakers of America have selected clothes which suit their own personalities and figure types.

Find pictures of three or four fashionable dresses of different styles. Which do you think will go out of style first? Explain.

Combining stripes and checks with a novelty belt and hair style creates an effect suitable for fun clothes.

can be emphasized and your less desirable ones minimized so as to create the appearance that enhances you.

WHAT IS A WELL-DESIGNED DRESS OR COSTUME?

A well-designed garment has beauty and appropriateness which makes it right for the wearer and for the occasion. *Fashion* is the prevailing mode which cannot be ignored but which can seldom be used as a guide for attractive clothes for everyone. *Fads* are extremes of fashion which are usually short-lived. When you understand the principles of good design and your own figure and personality, you can adapt the fashion and fads of the year to your own particular needs.

BASIC DESIGN FEATURES

The selection of clothes and accessories is both an art and a science. In order to improve your taste in clothing you will find that a study of the principles of design will help. It is best not to use them as rules or laws that you must follow but as guides to help you. These guides are the results of centuries of study and observation of well-designed clothes and other works of art. Yes, whether you design an entire costume or decide what items of clothing to wear together, you are using the elements and principles of design. All art is concerned with the organization of the basic elements, *line, form* or *space, color,* and *texture.*

In order to arrange these elements well, we need to apply the principles of *unity, emphasis, balance, proportion,* and *rhythm* so that the entire design has *harmony* with some *variety* or *interest.*

These are not abstract art terms but specific guides to help you select attractive garments.

Unity

Let's look at the first principle— unity. When all the parts of the design go together, when the art elements of line, form, color, and texture suit the personality and the characteristics of the wearer as well as the occasion, we say the design is unified.

37

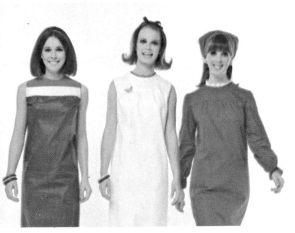

These girls have used the elements and principles of design to create dresses that suit the personality and the figure of each girl.

Balance

Balance implies pose, equilibrium, steadiness, security. When important details or decorations are designed for a dress, they should be grouped in such a way that there seems to be equal interest or weight on each side of an imaginary center. If both sides are alike to achieve this interest, it is called *formal* or *symmetrical* balance.

Balance may also be obtained when the design elements on both sides are different but are placed in such a way that the effect is pleasing,

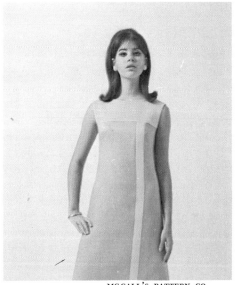

The dress on the left is an example of formal balance. The one on the right uses masses of color to create informal balance. The smaller amount of an intense yellow balances a larger amount of a neutral blue.

The arrangement of the pockets is an example of informal balance. Blue and white striped ticking makes an attractive shirtwaist dress in a pleasing combination of vertical and horizontal lines.

as when large and small persons balance on a seesaw. This is called *informal* or *asymmetrical* balance.

Formal balance is easier to create but may not be as interesting as informal balance. If a dress has more interest on one side than the other, it is said to be unbalanced in design. Such clothes usually have a short fashion life. Sometimes a pin, flower, or other accessory can create a balanced or restful feeling.

Balance can also be achieved through the use of color. Dark colors, warm colors, and bright colors have a feeling of more weight than light colors, as you will read in Chapter Three.

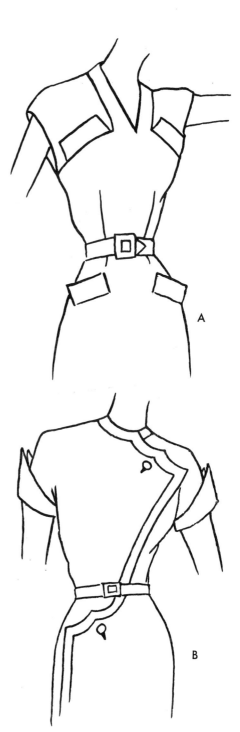

Balance. (A) formal; (B) informal.

39

Pattern books show many styles of garments. Some dresses are alike on both sides and some are not. How can you tell if a style is well-balanced?

Secure pictures of dresses that illustrate formal or informal balance. Be able to explain how balance is achieved in each dress design.

Find pictures of dresses that are not well-balanced. What changes would you make so that these dresses would be appealing for a longer time?

A well-balanced dress is balanced from top to bottom as well as across. A long dark tunic and a white skirt may give the appearance of top-heaviness to a person and may not be very attractive.

A casual style and medium-large plaid are suitable for a rather tall, easy-going personality with many sports interests.

COUNTRY MISS

Proportion

Whenever two or more parts of a garment are assembled, there is *proportion*. Proportion is the principle of design that involves a relationship between all parts in relation to each other and to the whole.

Articles of apparel worn together should not show too great a difference in size relationship to the wearer and to each other. This means that the separate parts of the ensemble—a hat, bag, and jewelry—should be consistent to the scale of the wearer. It also means that the individual parts of the garment—such as collars, cuffs, pockets, sleeves, trimming details, and surface patterns and textures—should be in relation to the size of the wearer and to each other. A small, petite type girl could be overpowered with a big picture hat and a large purse. A heavy girl of average height would look out of place in a dainty print dress and a tiny handbag. What other examples can you give?

A 19th century toile fabric of Jouy, France. The design is considered an example of formal balance. Although the pictures are not identical on each side of the center, the visual weight is similar.

Which is your preference, the mini-length skirt or a mini tunic over pants?

Only a tall man of good proportions can wear an outfit with a design that cuts the figure at both the hip and the chest lines.

Contrasting trim is used in this pants suit to lead the eye upward. Doesn't it have a slenderizing effect?

The most interesting divisions of a costume are those that divide the body unequally and have the larger space division at the bottom. Most designers agree that the Greek theory of proportion of 2 to 3, 3 to 5, and 5 to 8 is desirable. Stand before a long mirror and put your hands at your natural waistline. How does this divide you? Does your belt divide you so that approximately ⅗ of your height is below your waistline? The figure of a normal person is an example of good proportion.

Sometimes the body is visually divided at midpoints by a current fashion. If a style distorts the figure or makes one part appear grotesque or out of proportion, it goes out of fashion quickly and looks awkard in a short time. Garments that flatter the natural figure and bring out its good proportions are always pleasing.

The girls' wardrobe of separates can be interchanged. Do you prefer the effect of a plaid worn with a matching plain color garment or would you prefer all plaid and all plain combinations? Notice the different neckline effects. The stripes around the young man's sweater neck match his shirt and trousers.

When you study shape or form, you will find that the most interesting shapes are those with irregular ratios of width to length. An oblong that has a length exactly twice its width is seldom as interesting in shape as one where the length is more or less than twice the width. Can you explain why some purses appear awkward in shape and others seem "right"?

Collars that are a little narrower or wider than half the shoulder width are more interesting than those exactly half the shoulder width. You will also notice that an uneven number of buttons is more pleasing than an even number. Stripes of even width are seldom as interesting as those that vary in width.

Secure pictures of dresses that illustrate good proportion for the size of the persons wearing them. Find pictures of dresses with parts such as the collar or pockets that are too small or too large for the whole garment. Sketch the improvements you would make.

Select a current fashion trend or fad that is not flattering to all figures. Plan how this could be adapted or changed for girls who like it but do not find it attractive for them.

Find two pieces of striped material as alike as possible, yet one with a more pleasing combination of lines. Explain why you prefer your choice.

Cut belts of various widths from a light colored paper or a non-woven fabric. Place them on a basic dress at the waistline, above it, and below it. Decide which is the most becoming location and width for you, also for girls of other figure types. Why? Follow the same procedure for collars and cuffs. Which call attention to the upper part of the body? To the hip area?

Cut pockets of various sizes and shapes. Pin them in various positions on a basic dress and notice the effects.

Experiment with placement of braid or similar trim on the lower part of a skirt or apron. Make a drawing of a pleasing arrangement.

Select pictures of two costumes— one with pleasing design proportions, one with awkward proportions. Suggest changes that will make the awkward design more pleasing. Justify your decisions.

Bring to class some article of clothing or fabric which has a rhythmic pattern. This could be a piece of lace, embroidery, fabric, or an actual dress showing repetition of lines, colors, or designs. Describe the type of rhythm. How is rhythm obtained in the dress pictured on this page?

Rhythm

Rhythm, the final principle of design, is the arrangement of line, color, or decoration to control the movement of the eye over the object. It is a related movement leading the eye from one part of the design to another in an easy, flowing manner. Rhythm can be achieved by *repetition* of lines, colors, or shapes; by a *graduation* such as a change in colors or sizes; or by *radiation* as when lines converge at a central point, like the spokes of a wheel.

Lines evenly spaced may be repetitious but may also be monotonous if the principles of good proportion are not followed. See the illustration on page 42.

Emphasis

All parts of a costume must go together, but for true beauty, one central theme is needed. The less important details should be harmonious and contribute to the dominant idea.

Sometimes fashion places the emphasis so as to make the figure appear grotesque but, with a knowledge of good design, you can adapt current fashion to make yourself attractive. A focal point near the face makes *you* more important than your clothes.

You may want to detract attention from an undesirable feature. For instance, you can use your knowledge of the design elements while you have a temporary facial blemish that disturbs you by wearing simple necklines and attracting attention away from your face. Unusual belts, skirts of novelty fabrics with plain blouses, and no jewelry near the face are some ways of doing this.

There are many ways of creating emphasis. You can use a strong contrast of colors and values, novel details, grouping of objects, directional lines, repetition, or unusual balance.

PFAFF AMERICAN SALES CORP.

The machine embroidered design on the dress of this young miss is an example of pleasing rhythm by means of repetition with enough variety to avoid monotony.

43

PENDLETON WOOLEN MILLS

A family enjoying a holiday in look alike clothes. Notice how the mother's pin attracts attention to her face. Big sister's blouse has a different appearance because it is cut on the bias.

COUNTRY MISS

*A simple black pants suit worn by this young lady complements
the stylish red cape. Even the black trim serves to accentuate
the scarlet color.*

*Neckline emphasis is achieved by contrast-
ing colors of the jumper and the blouse or
sweater, and also by contrasts between
clothing and facial coloring. Would the
emphasis be as noticeable if the girls ex-
changed the blouse and sweater? Why?*
SIMPLICITY PATTERN CO.

45

Select a student with an average figure to wear a basic dress or a simple dark sweater and skirt to class. Try various accessories on her to see how attention can be detracted from the hips, the waist, the face, or how various parts of the body can be emphasized. If you can't do this on a real person, perhaps you can use a tack board outline figure, or sketches of a basic dress with accessories.

With a basic dress, use one lovely accessory, such as a pin or necklace. Show how you can attract attention away from it by the use of other accessories. How can you repeat its design to emphasize it?

How would you use the principles of design to emphasize a slender waist? Graceful hands? A lovely neck? How would you detract from a skinny, angular figure or heavy hips or a large bust? Illustrate with pictures from magazines and pattern books.

Show how one poorly selected accessory could destroy the line of a harmonious costume.

Collect pictures of dresses that show ways of attracting interest to the face.

But remember, don't try to repeat distinctive elements too often. For example, the impact of a lovely red necklace on a white dress is lost if you wear red shoes, a red belt, a red hat, and a bracelet to match.

ELEMENTS OF DESIGN

Did you realize that whenever you design anything, whether it be a painting, a fabric, or an arrangement of dishes on a table, you are using the tools or elements of design such as *color, line, shape* or *form,* and *texture?* Each of these tools can create a pleasing, interesting design. The rules for using these elements described in the first part of this chapter are called the principles of design. NOTE: Color is so important that the entire next chapter will be devoted to it.

Line

You have seen the way lines can play tricks on our eyes. Notice how the lines in the illustration on page 47 appear different in length even though they measure the same. When your eye reaches a crosswise line as in B, it stops and moves from side to side. Because your eye has been stopped, the line appears shorter than it is. In line D your eyes are forced to look upward, thus making the line appear longer. The lines of a garment or a hat or any part of your costume can fool the eye and attract attention to some aspect of your appearance or, on the other hand, lead the eye away from something you wish to minimize.

Lines may lead the eye vertically, horizontally, or diagonally. Since *vertical lines* are those that go up and down, they suggest height. Usually, but not always, vertical lines will lengthen or slenderize a figure as they carry the eye up. Hats with pointed crowns or upstanding feathers, clothes with center front closings, narrow lapels, vertical tucks, and rows of buttons up the front of a dress can create the illusion of height.

The direction in which lines carry the eye may be deceiving since vertical stripes do not always lead the eye up and down but may lead the eye across, depending on the spacing and color of the stripes. See the coat on page 47.

A student explains how vertical lines placed closer together have a slimming effect. The other chart shows the effect of crosswise lines.

A tall slender woman may find that lengthwise stripes create a broadening effect as in this coat. The bold vertical stripes placed far apart lead the eye across the body from stripe to stripe rather than up and down. The binding of the lower sleeve edges also adds to the feeling of breadth.

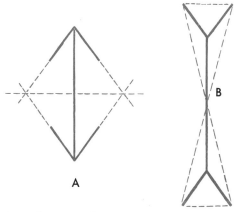

Hats that turn down, and thus deflect the upward motion, help achieve a diamond effect as in (A), whereas hats that have an upward turn increase the hour-glass effect, as in (B). Note in trying hats on yourself how they affect your height. Hairstyles can create the same effects.

47

Horizontal lines which carry the eye around the figure add apparent weight and make a person appear shorter. A wide brimmed hat will make a wearer appear broader and shorter. Jackets of colors that contrast with skirts also have this effect, as do contrasting yokes, pockets, belts, and other decoration.

There are a few exceptions that many people do not understand. Horizontal stripes can help a short, slender girl appear taller if the narrow to medium crosswise stripes extend across the full width of a straight sheath-type garment. The stripes are of short length, horizontal, and are extended over a relatively long space from shoulder to hem. Here the result is a ladder effect so the eye tends to "climb" upwards instead of moving crosswise. If the stripes are uneven, the widest should be at the bottom of the skirt.

However, if a short, plump person wears broad crosswise stripes, the emphasis is more on the crosswise direction of the stripes than on the illusion of height caused by the repetition of the lines. Therefore, a broad person can expect crosswise stripes to cause her to appear wider.

Which diagram appears broader? Which one appears longer? Narrow vertical stripes give the appearance of more height than widely spread stripes.

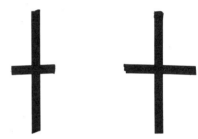

Which vertical line appears shorter? How would a wide crosswise belt or a double-breasted jacket affect the apparent height of a person?

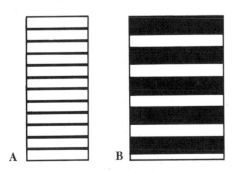

(A) *Ladder effect of narrow crosswise stripes worn by a slender girl.* (B) *Increased width due to wide crosswise stripes on a broad person.*

A kiltie-moccasin and a pigskin flat with heavy front zipper. Which shoe would you suggest for a girl with a long, narrow foot? Which shoe would be a better choice for a girl with a short, wide foot?

Have these girls made a wise use of line for their particular figures? Why or why not?

Diagonal lines and long V opening. Is the effect slim or broad?

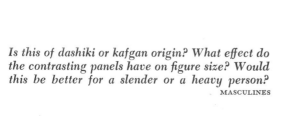

Is this of dashiki or kafgan origin? What effect do the contrasting panels have on figure size? Would this be better for a slender or a heavy person?

49

Remember that you can use lines to help you emphasize height, conceal weight, or attract attention to a desirable feature.

Diagonal lines are those that slant. Usually diagonal lines appear to lengthen or to slenderize a figure. The more nearly vertical a diagonal line is, the more slenderizing it will be. If the diagonal line is almost horizontal, the figure will appear broader.

Diagonal lines add interest to an object and produce a dramatic sense of motion as well as adding either length or width, depending upon their angle of direction.

Curved lines usually add softness, grace, and femininity. But even straight lines appear somewhat rounded by the figure under them. Curved lines are most effective if used sparingly. Too many will become confusing.

V-shaped lines are two diagonals brought to a point. Long V's are slenderizing but if they are wide and flattened, they will broaden a figure. In the illustration, notice how one yoke would be fine for a thin girl and the other would be good for a heavy-set girl.

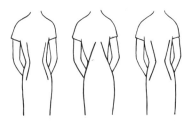

The direction of such structural lines as darts can affect the apparent size of the wearer's waist and hips. What effect do the different type darts have on body shape?

Select pictures of dresses that illustrate each of the different kinds of lines—vertical, horizontal, diagonal, and curved. Choose one that is especially suitable for you and tell why. Be able to explain the apparent effect of each type of line on the height and weight of the person wearing the garment.

Find a picture of a costume where a serious mood is created by the use of lines and one where a gay, party mood results from the use of different lines.

Find pictures of clothing that illustrate the principles of the lines illustrated on page 47. What effect do the lines have on the appearance of the wearer?

A long V such as the yoke on the right is slenderizing, but a wide flattened V is broadening.

Form or Shape

The outline of your clothes and not the details are noticed when you are seen at a distance. This is called the *silhouette* and refers to form and shape. Women's costumes appear to have many shapes but fashion authorities say there are only three: the straight or tubular, the bell-shaped or bouffant, and the bustle silhouette with skirt fullness brought to the

BOBBIE BROOKS

The wide panel which gives a double-breasted effect and the broad neckline adds a broadening effect to a slender girl.

back. Look back to Chapter One to see examples of these silhouettes in the straight Egyptian clothes, in the mid-Victorian crinolines, and in the late Victorian back fullness.

Shapes that are as tall as they are wide are not as pleasing as those that vary in vertical and horizontal measurements. No one wants to look like "Mr. Five-by-Five." An application of design principles, especially the wise use of line, can create illusions so that shapes appear less square—or less long and thin.

Look at several purses. Which are the most interesting in shape? The most novel? Which are uninteresting? Which probably will be acceptable after a long time?

Find pictures of dresses in current fashion that illustrate each of the three basic silhouette shapes.

Texture

Another basic art element you can use to create an effect in your clothes is *texture*. Texture refers to the surface quality of a fabric such as smooth, rough, shiny, or dull. The feel or "hand," such as soft, crisp, or hard, also is determined by the texture of a material. You will find that textures can be used along with color, shape, and lines to create the effect you desire. This is discussed in detail on page 61 of this chapter.

Other Requirements of Good Design

One of the first requirements of good design is *harmony*, a combination of shapes, textures, and colors that are similar to one another or get along with each other. However, some *variety* is needed for contrast and interest and to provide needed emphasis. In an attempt to provide interest, you may be tempted to use too many shapes or colors so that you end up with a confused and cluttered design.

A jumper may be worn with several blouses. The machine stitching is in harmony with the lines of the plaid blouse. The tiny collar accents the face.

BUCK'S, WICHITA, KANSAS

51

Top stitching with a heavy contrasting thread emphasizes the structural lines of this pants suit and adds decorative interest. Would it appear better balanced if the front closing were made with a vertical band and both edges outlined?

The anchor on the girl's shirt is purely decorative. It serves no functional purpose in the construction of the garment but does identify her as a person who enjoys boating. Both outfits can be made easily from knit fabrics in a short time.

Structural and decorative design. You may read of structural design and decorative design as you study clothing. *Structural* design is formed when the garment pieces are joined together, for example, by seams, darts, and pleats. *Decorative* design is a surface enrichment added after the basic structure is made, such as buttons, lace, and trims. For many purposes structural design is all that is needed for an attractive garment. When decorative designs are added, it is important that they are in harmony with the basic structural lines.

Realistic and stylized design. A fabric printed with roses that look so real one wants to smell them is said to be a *realistic* design. Roses may also be designed in such a way that they do not look real but still give the impression of roses. This design would be called *stylized.* An *abstract* design has no resemblance to a real object but it takes its charm from color and line contrasts.

Reading about design cannot take the place of continuous observation

52

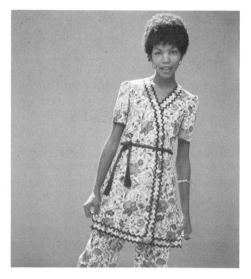

and actual experimentation. Now that you have studied the basic principles of good design, you will find that the following activities will help you to understand better how to achieve good design in your dress.

Make a tracing of the picture of a garment you like. Identify the structural lines such as seams and darts. In a different manner identify the decorative design.

How would you improve on a dress with scalloped opening down the front, a pointed collar, square pockets, and diamond-shaped buttons?

Look for pictures of dresses using only structural lines as decoration. Find some with the decorations in violation of the structural lines. Find others with the applied decoration in harmony with structural lines.

Find samples of textiles with natural, stylized, and abstract designs.

Structural lines are emphasized on this stewardess uniform by the use of contrasting braid and buttons.

53

This tunic design is abstract—it takes its charm from line and value contrasts, not a representation of a real object.

Observe the most attractively dressed people you see during the next two weeks (or find pictures to illustrate such persons). Explain why their costumes attracted you. Select one costume and analyze it in detail, applying the principles and elements of good design to your analysis.

Observe and note how emphasis is used to attract attention to one particular feature.

How did the wise use of line minimize figure faults and help the person appear attractive?

What evidences of good proportion did you observe in the use of accessories such as purses, hats, and jewelry?

THE REAL YOU

Every figure is a blend of good and less desirable characteristics. You will find that by accenting your own individual good points, you can achieve an attractiveness you may not have known you had. A style that looks good on someone else may not be right for you at all. Of course, you want to be one of the crowd, but you also want to be an individual.

Few people have ideal figures. Study yourself carefully. This should not make you self-conscious, as few girls have perfect proportions. This is why you need to have an understanding of the tools of design such as line, color, shape, and texture to help you to create the illusion of a well-proportioned figure. Is the area above your waist about $\frac{1}{3}$ of your total length? A girl who has almost perfect proportions has about $\frac{1}{3}$ of her height above her waist and about $\frac{2}{3}$ below. (Some experts believe that $\frac{2}{5}$ and $\frac{3}{5}$ are truer figures.) Her length will be divided in half at the hipline. The mid-point of the top half of her body is at the underarm line. The mid-point of the bottom half is at her knees. How do men's proportions differ?

Look at yourself in the mirror again. Are your shoulders slightly wider than your hips and is your waist just narrow enough to complement both? If not, you will need to select clothes that will make your figure appear nearer this proportion. (Perhaps wise food selection can also help alter your proportions.)

POSTURE

Maybe what you think is a figure problem is really one of posture. You cannot change your body structure but you can change your posture. For many years you have read about good posture, listened to lectures on it, and have seen demonstrations. Yet many

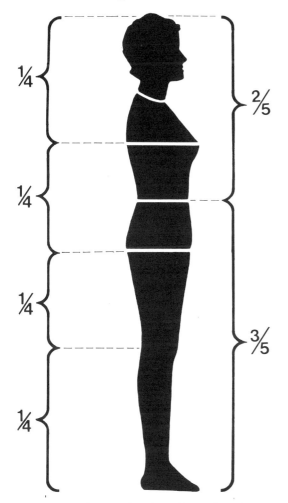

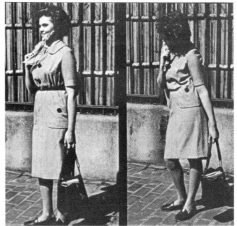

Good posture makes the same dress appear very different than poor posture.

Proportion—a pleasing relationship of space.

girls continue poor posture habits. Perhaps all these instructions have been too involved and difficult to follow.

Here is a simple formula for good posture: (1) *Lift up in front;* (2) *Pull down in back;* (3) *Stand as tall as you can,* with your feet on the floor, head erect, and abdomen in. As you stand in this position, a straight line can be drawn from your ear to your ankle. It will pass through the joint of your shoulder and hip.

When you sit, have the base of your spine resting against the back of the chair and your body will be in good balance. *As you descend stairs,* reach forward with the toes of one foot, bend the other knee, and keep your head up.

Posture contributes so much to a lovely appearance that it is important that you do everything you can to make a good alignment of your body.

Helpful exercises are described in Chapter Six.

FIGURE ANALYSIS

You may have a mental picture of how you would like to look. Your mirror will show you how you really look. Analyze your figure. Study yourself in a full-length triple mirror. Is your figure type short plump, short thin, tall plump, tall thin, or average?

To check your physical features *write the word or words which apply to your figure on an extra sheet of paper:*

Is my figure average, plump, slender, short, tall?

What is the shape of my face— round, oval, long, thin, angular?

Instead of a big check and bright plaid pattern that exaggerates size, a stout girl looks better in an up and down stripe pattern that adds height, making her look taller and slimmer.

Have these young men selected jackets suited to their figure types? What suggestions would you make for improvement?

The tall girl should wear styles that take advantage of her height, yet provide added fullness to her figure. Skirts that move away from the body are especially good if the tall girl has large hips she wishes to hide.

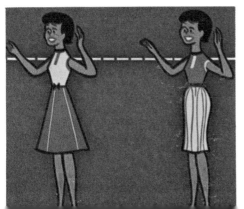

Is my neck long and thin, short and thick, average?

Are my shoulders narrow, sloping, broad, square, round?

Do I stand erect?

Are my shoulder blades too prominent?

Do I have a "tummy" bulge?

Through the bust am I extra full, medium, shallow?

Do I have a long, average, or short trunk?

Am I long, average, or short "waisted"?

Are my arms long and thin, long and full, short and fat, short and thin, normal?

Do I have a large, medium, small waistline?

Are my hips too large, medium, small?

Do I have a prominent derriere?

How would I describe my legs?

Are my ankles thin, thick, medium?

What other figure problems or assets do I have?

These physical features of yours must be taken into account when considering a costume design. You don't want your face to look broader, if it is already too broad. Nor do you want to look shorter if you are already the smallest person in your group.

How to Modify Your Figure

If your figure is average—not too tall or too short, not too thin or too heavy, not too busty or hippy—you are fortunate, as you can wear almost any style of garment with almost any fabric texture and still have an attractive, balanced silhouette. Most individuals are not so lucky.

If you want to appear taller or shorter, thinner or plumper, the following chart gives suggestions.

Two · Design

Choose	*Avoid*

To Look Taller and Thinner

Dress or suit of one color	Top and bottom of contrasting colors
Matching sweater and pants	
Narrow belt of same fabric as dress or pants	Broad collars and horizontal trim
	Full sleeves
Tapering V neckline	Tight waist and wide belts
Diagonal lines	Design at the hip line
Emphasis on the face	Large prints or wide stripes
Narrow vertical tucks	Shiny fabrics

To Look Taller and Plumper

Vertical and princess lines	Tailored garments
Frilly collars	Too much fullness
Narrow belt that matches	Large pockets and cuffs
Light, bright colors; Small prints	Wide stripes or big plaids or prints
Empire style dresses	
High round necklines	

To Look Shorter and Thinner

Grayed colors	Bows and ruffles
Simple lines	Fullness at hips
Softly tailored garments	Large full sleeves
Slightly full skirts or pants	Wide belts
No belt or a narrow matching belt	

To Look Shorter and Plumper

Contrasting shirts and skirts or pants	Vertical unbroken lines
	Long narrow skirts or pants
Full sleeves and wide cuffs	Many ruffles
Plaids, checks, and bright colors	Clinging fabrics
Hip-line belts and pockets	Long tight sleeves
Horizontal design emphasis	Hats with an upward emphasis
Double-breasted effects	Deeply V'd necklines

To Look Less Hippy

Wide collars or yokes	Tightly fitted skirts or pants
Bright blouses, neutral skirts	Accents at the hip as large pockets
Slightly flared skirts such as A-line or flared pants	Plaid skirts or pants with plain tops
	Skirts that taper toward the hem such as sheaths or pegged pants
Boxy short jackets	

To Make a Short, Heavy Neck Appear Longer

Scoop necklines	Turtlenecks
Deep V necklines	Mandarin collars
Stand away necklines	High rolled collars
Hats with an upward sweep	

THE MAGIC OF THE RIGHT LOOK FOR YOU

If you search for the right look for you, there is the magic of tops and bottoms, knowing how to put different skirts and pants with a variety of blouses, sweaters and jackets to get the most costumes, and to combine the styles that look best on you.

With the magic of tops and bottoms, you can almost be your own designer, mixing up necklines, collars, shoulder lines and skirt styles.

And this magic applies to fit, too. A top in one size and a bottom in another size can be the magic answer for a figure that isn't "perfect."

Select collars and necklines that will do the most for your face. A round face looks best above a pointed collar or simple V-styled neckline. A slender, angular face will gain softness with a rounded collar or banded Chinese cut.

The cut of sleeves is important, too. Narrow shoulders are at their best in raglan or bat-wing sleeves—that avoid the set-in armhole. The added bulk of a jacket or cardigan can do a lot for your figure if you're tall and slender.

And don't forget sweaters. There's a sweater for every occasion—from active sports to dress-up wear. And every wardrobe needs at least one slip-over with its own matching cardigan that can do double duty as a lightweight topper with dresses.

Pants

Pants seem to come in greater variety with every season. And to wear them well, it's important that you take an utterly honest look at your figure and pick the length and style most becoming to you.

If your figure is good—no matter what your height—you can indulge in all the newest cuts and colors, patterns and gimmicks. But if you're looking for a bit of camouflage, stick to the solid colors—(and not too shouting-loud). Or if you insist on patterns try tiny checks, muted plaids or designs with indefinite outlines.

Pick the length that makes your legs look their longest and slimmest. But whatever the length, remember that only the perfect figure can afford a tight-tight fit.

Skirts

Skirts can give you lots of "looks." Knife pleats sway and should never "break" open. If they do—try a skirt in a size larger.

Hip-stitched pleats mold you below the waist, then swing out. Unpressed box pleats are soft and less figure-identifying, but are best on the girl with slender waistline and a bit of height. Try the hip-stitched pleat if you're not so slim. It will give you the freedom of fullness at the hemline with the straight smooth look where it does the most figure-whittling.

The A-line skirt is flattering to most figures. It has enough fullness for comfort and a feminine appearance without causing hips to look too large.

Look at the blouse details pictured on page 59. Describe a blouse or dress top which is suitable for you and give reasons.

Study the styles shown on page 60. Write a paragraph stating which skirt style you prefer and why. Describe the styles which are less flattering to you.

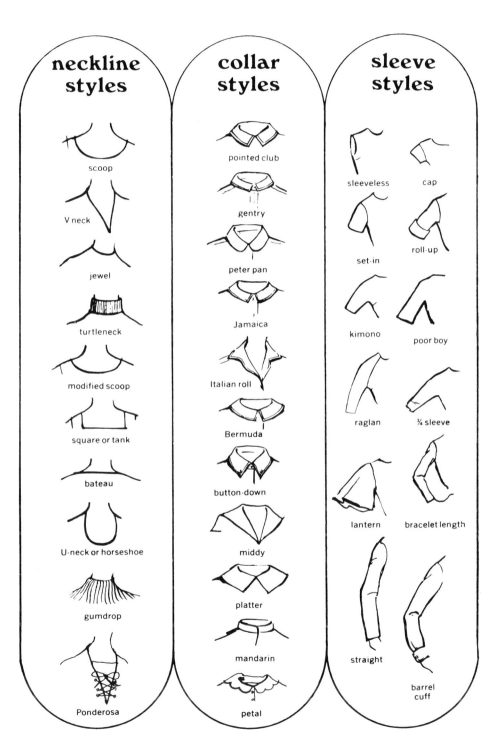

neckline styles

scoop

V neck

jewel

turtleneck

modified scoop

square or tank

bateau

U-neck or horseshoe

gumdrop

Ponderosa

collar styles

pointed club

gentry

peter pan

Jamaica

Italian roll

Bermuda

button-down

middy

platter

mandarin

petal

sleeve styles

sleeveless

cap

set-in

roll-up

kimono

poor boy

raglan

¾ sleeve

lantern

bracelet length

straight

barrel cuff

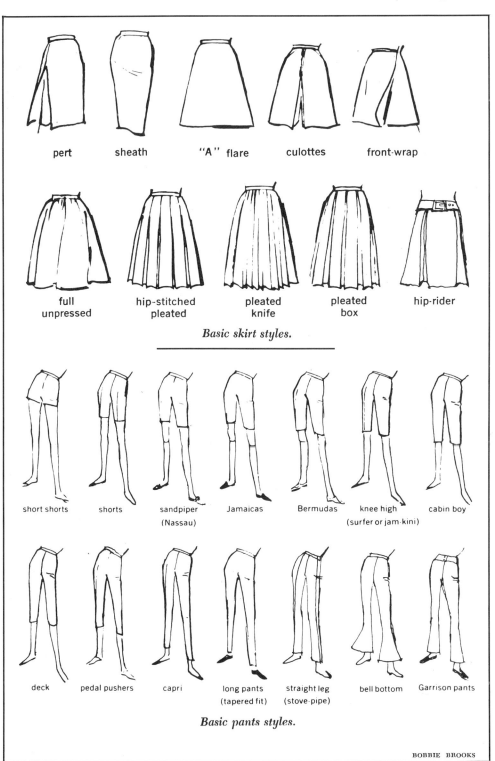

pert   sheath   "A" flare   culottes   front-wrap

full unpressed   hip-stitched pleated   pleated knife   pleated box   hip-rider

Basic skirt styles.

short shorts   shorts   sandpiper (Nassau)   Jamaicas   Bermudas   knee high (surfer or jam-kini)   cabin boy

deck   pedal pushers   capri   long pants (tapered fit)   straight leg (stove-pipe)   bell bottom   Garrison pants

Basic pants styles.

BOBBIE BROOKS

Fabric Textures and Design Can Influence Your Figure

Each fabric has specific characteristics which determine its appearance, feel, and the way it may be used. The design and texture may control the lines of a pattern, deceive the eye, and change the apparent size and proportion of a figure.

Texture. As previously noted, texture refers to the surface appearance of a fabric as well as its feel or "hand." The fibers used, types of yarns, the finishes and design processes applied—all affect the texture of a fabric. Some materials fall into the dull, rough, harsh, or heavy group; others are soft, smooth, fine, and shiny. Many are in-between, described as medium textured.

It is important to consider the principles of design when one selects fabrics for their texture. Related textures are needed for harmony, but variety is also needed for interest. Usually a medium texture goes best with fabrics of either of the other groups. Extreme texture contrast is often used for fads such as sequins and jewels on a burlap skirt, but these combinations do not maintain interest long.

Shiny or *glossy* textures reflect light and thus increase the apparent size of the person wearing them. They also reveal the true shape of the person as the highlights on the shiny surface reveal contours. Harsh light may be reflected on the skin, so the average or blemished skin is not flattered by such fabrics close to it. The slender, well-proportioned person can wear satins and other shiny-surfaced fabrics, but both the too-thin and the stout person may not find them attractive.

Dull fabrics absorb light and thus

SPRINGS MILLS

The nubby texture of the vest adds interest to a simple school costume. The plain colored fabrics permit the design of the military buttons to be seen to advantage.

SIMPLICITY

Both shirts are in shades of blue. However, the light blue of the girl's shirt tends to make her appear larger while the duller blue of the young man's has a slenderizing effect.

An all-over print design can disguise many figure faults. A large-waisted person may prefer a matching belt. Try covering up this belt with your hand—is the girl's face more noticeable or not? Explain why.

A multi-colored velour fabric makes a poncho that is striking on a tall slender girl. Plain textured skirt or pants makes an effective contrast.

tend to decrease the apparent size of the wearer and to conceal the true silhouette. Nearly all types of figures can wear dull surfaced fabrics.

Stiff or crisp fabrics increase size but conceal the true figure, as they hang away from the natural contour of the body. A person only slightly larger than desired may wear stiff fabrics which tend to hide her true size. A person with large hips and average bust may wear a soft fabric blouse which reveals the upper slenderness and a skirt of firm texture that will conceal the outline of too-heavy hips. Stiff fabrics should be avoided by heavy girls and used carefully by slightly heavy people who are attempting to disguise actual contours.

Heavy fabrics also increase the size of the wearer and conceal the actual outlines of the figure. Pile and fuzzy textures tend to add bulkiness if of heavy weight and used in large quantities. They tend to make the figure seem larger and to emphasize angularity. Tall persons who are not too thin or too heavy can wear heavy fabrics. The average figure can wear moderately heavy fabrics but may be more flattered by medium weights.

Transparent fabrics neither increase nor decrease the apparent size of a figure, but they reveal the true shape so definitely that a thin person may look thinner and a stout person may look stouter. Only a person of good proportions will find transparent fabrics becoming. A sheer fabric over a carefully made slip or several layers of a fabric such as chiffon may be softening for a not-too-perfect figure.

Clinging fabrics reveal the silhouette and emphasize bulk. They can reveal even minor figure defects if fitted too closely. These fabrics should be used only on very good figures and then only over correctly-fitted foundation garments.

Designed or *patterned fabrics.* A few simple principles make it easy to select fabric designs that are wearable and becoming. First of all, notice whether the design has a strong crosswise movement, or if it leads the eye in a vertical manner. Many overall prints have the same effect as stripes. Some prints have a swirling-'round feeling which increases the rotund look of the wearer. Angular, geometric designs may make the figure seem more stiff and angular than it is. Some prints are spotty, so that the eye jumps from spot to spot in an unsettling way.

Designed fabrics may be beautiful or unattractive, depending upon how good the designs are! The light and dark areas, as well as large and small spaces, need to be balanced. The designs should all be related in shape and type to be harmonious. *Stylized designs* usually indicate better taste than natural or realistic ones. See page 52.

There are so many variations in fabric designs that everyone may find becoming ones, regardless of figure type. Fabric designs with *indefinite outlines* break up the space and make the figure appear smaller. Fabrics with definitely prominent patterns make a figure appear larger. They are striking for the tall, slender figure. *Large* designs on a contrasting background increase the apparent size of the wearer. Prints with *long* designs, or curves and dots, soften the figure outline and decrease size. Plaids add apparent width. (See chart on page 57 for figure flattening ideas.)

BOBBIE BROOKS

The effect of this striking print is lost when it is used for an entire garment without sufficient plain contrast.

BOBBIE BROOKS

The tucked detailing adds interest to this plain fabric. Its design effect would be lost on a fabric with a large print. Wide, lengthwise stripes would also create a confusing pattern.

The design of a garment is influenced by the kind of fabric you choose. Do not plan to use a figured fabric exactly the way you use a plain one. Figured fabrics should not be cut into so many pieces that the effect of the design is lost or confused. Figured and plaid fabrics are decorative in themselves; therefore a simple pattern is suitable, with a trimming of a plain color. The lines of a well-designed garment may not be noticed if the pattern of the fabric is too elaborate.

Look through pattern books and find patterns that are suitable to be used with the following types of fabrics: (a) plain colors, (b) stripes, (c) small prints, (d) large prints, (e) plaids, (f) border prints. Explain your choice.

APPEARANCE OF YOUR FIGURE MAY BE INFLUENCED BY:

1. The shape of the face.
2. The width and shape of shoulders.
3. Location of the waistline.
4. Width of belt.
5. Fullness.
6. Length of garment.

1. Face. What is the shape of your face? The shape of your face determines the types of necklines that are most becoming. The face is emphasized by the shape of the neckline or collar. A V-shaped neckline or large oval neckline is becoming to a broad round face. A round neckline softens a pointed chin. The neckline of your dress should make an attractive frame for your face.

2. Shoulders. When the space between the armholes is narrow, the width of the shoulders will seem to decrease. Your shoulders will look broad if the armhole lines are placed far out. For stooped shoulders, place the shoulder line slightly back of its

---

SUMMARY OF FABRIC DETAILS

Fabrics That Seem to Decrease Size	Fabrics That Seem to Increase Size
Dull textures	Transparent fabrics
Sheer woolens and crepes	Stiff fabrics
Smooth-finished fabrics	Heavy fabrics—tweeds or fleece
Indistinct prints	Shiny textures

Set-in sleeves exaggerate wide shoulders since they define the actual end of the shoulder line. Kimono sleeves, which are cut in one with the dress, slide easily over the shoulder line so problem shoulders are not easily seen. Raglan sleeves can exaggerate rounded or narrow shoulders.

normal position. Raglan sleeves are becoming on erect shoulders.

3. Waistline. Low waistlines are becoming for tall people because they cut height. However, if the waistline divides the figure in half, it produces an uninteresting appearance. High waistlines give the appearance of added height.

4. Belt. Since narrow belts do not attract attention, they are good for most types of figures. A narrow belt of self-material is especially becoming for a person with broad hips and a large waistline because it does not attract attention.

5. Fullness. Since fullness adds bulk to a figure, it is not becoming to anyone large. Also much fullness is not good for a thin person because it makes one appear thinner in contrast to the bulky garment. If you are slightly swaybacked, a belt may be located just below the waistline. The waist will then blouse at the back and balance the swayback.

6. Length. The length of your dress affects the appearance of your figure. A short skirt on a stout girl will make her appear shorter and heavier. How-ever, a short skirt on a very tall, slender girl will have the opposite effect, because her slender legs will be more noticeable. Dame Fashion may decree that skirts will be short this season and long next season. However, an alert modern woman will adapt the style to suit her.

A man can also adapt the current pants length and width to that which is most flattering to him.

A basic jacket can be suited to individual needs with varying necklines. One girl has selected a V-shaped opening to lengthen a short face, the middle girl has softened the V opening with a rounded sweater vest, and the third girl has chosen a high neckline to shorten a long neck.

AMERICAN AIRLINES

65

With the help of your teacher and the commercial patterns available in your school, cut various shapes of necklines and collar patterns from a suitable fabric (non-woven interfacing is good). Experiment with them on yourself and your classmates. Why are some shapes becoming to some people while others are not flattering?

Collect pictures of costumes good for a person who is:
    too tall
    too short
    too heavy
    too thin
    too large in the hips
    too large in the bust
    too small in the bust
    round shouldered
    too sway-backed
who has:
    too long arms
    too large arms
    too short a neck
    too long a neck
Mount these pictures with an explanation of why your selections are good ones.

Summary with Check-Up Questions

All art is concerned with the organization of the basic elements: line, form or space, color, and texture. When you select what to wear, you are using these tools to paint the picture of yourself that others will see.

In order to arrange these elements well, the principles of unity, emphasis, balance, proportion, and rhythm must be applied so there is harmony with some variety or interest.

A well designed garment will enhance an individual's appearance and be suitable for the occasion for which it will be worn.

- *For what reasons do many garments appear beautiful in store windows but lose their attractiveness when tried on?*
- *Have you borrowed a friend's coat or other article and found that it did not look as nice on you as on your friend? Why?*

When all parts of a design are in harmony, we say the design is unified or goes together.

- *Why is a lace trim more suitable for a velveteen blazer than one of denim?*
- *Would you prefer sneakers, suede pumps, or platform sandals to wear with jeans to a picnic? Why?*

Lines can be used to emphasize attractive features and also to de-emphasize unattractive features.

- *How can lines be used to make one appear taller or shorter?*
- *What is the effect of diagonal lines? How does the effect change as the diagonal moves from the vertical to the horizontal?*
- *What effect will vertical lines have if placed closely together? If placed farther apart?*

The texture of a fabric can affect the appearance of a person.

- *What effect do fabrics of shiny textures have on apparent size?*
- *Why do dull textures seem to make a person appear more slender?*
- *What effect will heavy textures such as pile and plush fabrics have on the apparent size of a person?*

Proportion is the relationship between all parts of a design to each other and to the whole.

- *Is a large hat on a tiny girl generally suitable? Why?*
- *Why are dresses with a belt worn at the hip line in style for brief periods of time, but dresses with belts at the normal waistline in style for long periods of time?*
- *Would a dainty floral design or a medium sized print be better for a large girl? Why?*

Although every part of a design must be harmonious, some contrast or variety is necessary for interest.

- *What effect will a design have if there is no contrast—if every part is the same in color, line, and texture?*
- *How would you improve an outfit of brown suede shoes, a brown velveteen dress, brown suede gloves and purse, and a brown felt hat?*

- *If there is too much variety in a design, will the effect be disturbing?*

A design is said to be balanced when the important details or decorative designs are grouped in such a way that there appears to be equal weight on both sides of an imaginary center.

- *How does formal balance differ from informal balance?*
- *Why is informal balance harder to achieve than formal balance?*
- *How can a costume be balanced from side to side, yet still not be balanced from top to bottom?*

The wise use of the elements of design can be learned and applied, by study and practice, so that you can select clothes to bring out your best personality traits and physical features.

- *What new knowledge have you acquired from the readings and activities in this chapter which will help your appearance?*

Can You Explain These Terms?

unity	*form*
balance	*texture*
formal or symmetrical balance	*harmony*
informal or asymmetrical balance	*variety*
proportion	*structural design*
emphasis	*decorative design*
vertical line	*realistic design*
horizontal line	*stylized design*
diagonal line	*abstract design*

CHAPTER THREE

Color

H AVE you ever really looked at color? Of course you have, you say, as you choose colors to wear every day. But have you really *seen* color, the effect colors have upon each other and, most important, upon you? In this chapter you will study the selection and combination of colors that will do the most for you— that will make you feel good all over, that will make the most of your natural beauty and will create the optical illusions to make your figure appear more nearly as you wish it.

But first you may need help in learning to *see* and *understand* color. Then you may better understand your own natural coloring, how to select the exact tones that are right for you, and how to combine colors easily and effectively to improve your appearance.

THE MEANING OF COLOR

Did you know that color has an effect on you whether you are conscious of it or not? It can make you feel happy or depressed, make you hurry or move quietly. It may make you appear dull and withdrawn, dignified and serious, or gay and sparkling.

Colors create mental associations. This means that some girls will like a color that others will dislike. Are there some colors that you dislike because you associate them with someone you do not like? Perhaps your favorite is that of a dress you wore when you had an especially good time. Most people are cheered by bright clear colors and are depressed by dark, dull, and drab ones.

The results of experiments on the psychology of color can help you understand the effect colors have on you. *Yellow* appears cheerful, warm, and sunny to most people. *Red* seems exciting, aggressive, and enlivening. *Orange* strikes us as lively, cheerful, and joyous. *Green* is friendly, pleasant, and calming. *Blue* seems serious, peaceful, and quieting. *Purple* is dignified, dominating, and rich. *White* appears clean, pure, and young; whereas *black* seems more dignified, somber, and old.

*Which of these color combinations would make you feel gay, quiet, feminine,
vibrant, or depressed? Are there any colors you would not feel happy wearing?
Can you explain why these colors affect you as they do?*

What are your favorite colors? Can you explain why? Do you know why you dislike others? Really try to decide by writing down reasons for each.

Find a picture of a dress or suit of suitable color for a job interview. Why do you think the color is right? How would you change the color if you were going to wear this suit to a party? Why?

Not everyone feels about color as Americans do. Study the meaning of color in other countries, especially for special occasions. Talk with people who have lived in other places and find out what colors are used for weddings, for parties, for anniversaries, funerals. What colors are considered suitable for baby boys? For baby girls?

Color is also associated with safety. Red stop lights attract attention before other colors. Notice the little girl and her father shown here. Which one will be seen first by drivers at dusk or on a rainy day?

DU PONT

Notice how yellow stands out in dreary weather. If this little girl wore a brown raincoat as her father does, would she be seen easily by motorists? Does she probably feel more cheerful in this color on a rainy day?

SCIENCE OF COLOR

To understand color, it helps to know that sunlight is "made" of many colors. When light falls on an article, some of the rays are absorbed and some are reflected. For example, a blue dress absorbs all light rays except the blue ones, which are reflected back to your eyes. Therefore this dress appears blue to you. A red article absorbs all the light rays except the red ones, and thus you see it as red.

White combines all colors and therefore a white object reflects all colors. But since black absorbs all colors, no hue is reflected back. Can you see why a white roof on a house will keep the house cooler in the hot sun than a black roof? Why is white used so much for clothing in the tropics? Most artificial light is like sunlight but some lamps do not give off white light. Mercury vapor lamps, often used for highway lighting, give off light with no red rays in it. Therefore, in this light, red clothes and even red lips will not appear red, as there are

70

no red rays to be reflected. They will usually appear blue or purplish. Some lights—such as infra-red heat lamps—give off only red rays; articles seen in this light look very different from those seen in the usual sunlight or white light.

A rainbow shows that sunlight is made up of many colors. Tiny drops of water in the air, after a rain, may separate the rays in sunlight and reflect them. Next time you see a rainbow, or by using a prism, take time to notice the order in which the colors appear.

DIMENSIONS OF COLOR—
HUE, VALUE, AND INTENSITY

When you describe an object, you mention its length, width, and breadth. Did you know that color also has dimensions which are called hue, value, and intensity?

Hue is the *name* given to a color family such as red, blue, or yellow.

Value refers to the amount of *lightness* or *darkness* in a color, such as a light green or a dark green. Those hues with more lightness are called *tints*. Those hues with less light are called *shades*. Thus pink is a light red or a tint and maroon is a dark red or a shade.

If you half close your eyes when you look at a color, you can see the true value easier. Look at a pure yellow and a pure purple. You can see that yellow is a lighter value than purple. Every hue can be seen in values which range from almost white to almost black. Look around you and try to describe the values of the various hues you see. Color values can be classified as *very light, light, medium light, medium, medium dark, dark,* and *very dark.*

Intensity is the strength of a color—its *brightness* or *dullness.* A bright green is a color of high intensity; a dull green is a soft, grayed green. There are many ranges of intensities but most colors can be described as *very bright, bright, medium bright, medium, medium dull, dull,* or *very dull.*

Neutrals and chromatic colors. Although we often speak of black, white, and gray as colors, they are really neutrals. The true hues—such as blue, red, and yellow—are called chromatic colors.

COLEBROOK

This knit suit so suitable for a tall, slender girl is all of one hue, a red-violet. However, the blouse is a light value and the skirt a darker value. The bands at the waist are more intense or brighter than the other tints and shades.

Select several varying samples of one hue, either in paper or fabric. Arrange them in order from the lightest value to the darkest value.

With the same samples or with another group, arrange them in order from the brightest intensity to the dullest. Have a classmate or classmates check your arrangement.

Find a tint and a shade of each of the common colors. Perhaps you could arrange a display, properly labeled, on the tack board in your room.

THE COLOR WHEEL

As you begin to work with colors, you will need to know how they are related to each other, if you have not studied this in other courses. The color wheel is a helpful guide. Keep referring to the wheel as you read about colors.

Would you agree that brown is a warm color of the same chroma as orange? This shade is flattering to girls with brown and other hair colors.

BERNARD ALTMANN

Primary colors. One generally accepted color system is based on three *primary* or entirely different colors —red, yellow, and blue. These are called primary colors because all other colors may be mixed from their pigments. As you may know, they cannot be made from a combination of any other colors.

Secondary colors. The *secondary* colors are orange, green, and purple. Each combines two primary colors. Perhaps as a child you discovered that if you spilled some blue paint into yellow paint, you had a green color. You were discovering the principle of secondary colors. Red and blue mixed together make purple, which is often called violet. Orange results when red and yellow are mixed together.

Intermediate colors. There is another group called the *intermediate* colors which result when a primary and secondary color are mixed. They are yellow-green, blue-green, blue-violet, red-violet, red-orange, and yellow-orange. NOTE: It is customary to state the name of the primary color first.

By using more of one hue than another you can obtain many variations of color. Thus yellow-yellow-green is lighter than a yellow-green.

Brown. But what about brown, you may ask? Where does it fit on the color wheel? Look carefully at a true brown and you will be able to see that it is a low or grayed value of orange. Some browns are closer to red-orange; others to yellow-orange. Some browns may have much black added, as in chocolate brown. Does chocolate seem to favor yellow or red? Compare with the brown of cedar bark or an autumn oak leaf.

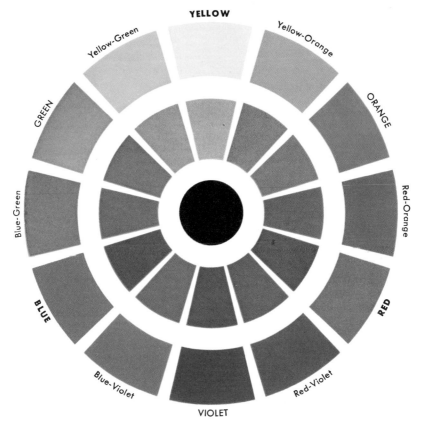

The outer circle shows the primary and secondary colors, separated by six intermediate colors. The inner circle shows darker colors obtained by mixing two colors that lie opposite each other in the outer circle.

From *The World Book Encyclopedia.* © 1968
Field Enterprises Educational Corporation

A useful color chart, showing: three primary colors—yellow, blue, and red; secondary colors—green, violet, and orange; and tertiary hues—yellow-green, blue-green, blue-violet, red-violet, red-orange, and yellow-orange. Note the grayed inner circle where complements are blended.

"New" fashion colors. Every year "new" colors are in fashion. They are old colors that have new names and are featured in the latest styles. The names given them may be very attractive but are not helpful if you want to know what a color is really like. You can study the dimensions of any fashionable color and, with development of a good eye for color, you can see a hue for what it really is.

No longer will a marlin blue belong just to a fish but you can find it in a good color chart as a dark value of a grayed blue which is more useful in identifying it. The "new" astronaut blue will be seen as an intense shade of blue. When you have learned really to "see" color, you will be able to select the exact tone you want for your purposes. The ability to use colors in harmony is important.

Can you secure cellophane paper in red, blue, and yellow hues? If so, you will find that it is interesting to overlap different colors against a white background. See what secondary colors you can create this way. By using several thicknesses of one color and just one thickness of another, you can make the intermediate hues.

Another way to discover for yourself how secondary and intermediate colors are formed is to prepare a glass jar of red dye, one of blue dye, and one of yellow dye. Probably you have done this earlier in school. Pour some yellow dye into an empty jar. Carefully add some blue to it. What color do you see? Experiment to produce all of the secondary colors and also some of the intermediate colors.

While you have the jars of dye available, take a cotton print fabric

The blues are considered to be cool colors and the reds and purples are considered warm. The center group ranges from cool greens to warm yellows and oranges.

with a light background and dip it into the yellow dye. How are the original colors changed? Can you explain why? Try this experiment with other color dyes.

Find several samples of green hues, either paper or fabric. Sort them into pure greens, yellow-greens, and blue-greens. Arrange as a tack board display. Perhaps your class could divide into six groups and each group work with a different primary or secondary color for this activity.

Secure a glass prism (if you do not have one in your classroom, your science teacher will probably lend you one.) Look at the light reflection on a white surface. What colors do you see? In what order are they? How does this compare with the color wheel? You may want to report to your class the reasons for the color pattern.

What are the most popular colors for this season? List them by their names; then look at them carefully and describe them correctly as to hue, value, and intensity.

WARM AND COOL COLORS

On a hot day, do you select a red-brown dress to wear, or do you reach for a white or a pastel dress to make you feel cooler? Colors really do make a person feel warm or cool. Long before scientists discovered that white reflects light rays and black absorbs them, some people in desert areas wore white clothes because they felt and looked cooler in them. This was notably true where people had lived for many generations on the desert, as in North Africa.

Because colors have such properties, some are considered warm and others cool. *Yellow, orange,* and *red* are *warm* and the colors represented on the other side of the color wheel, *blue, green,* and *violet,* seem *cool.* Blue is the coolest color and orange is the warmest. Although violet tends to be cool, a very red-red violet can be warm. We also speak of a warm shade of green when we mean a yellow-yellow green. A tint of a warm color, such as pink, is cooler than the pure color, such as red. But tints of warm colors are not as cool as tints of cool colors. Therefore, a pink dress seems warmer than a pale blue dress. Brown is warm because of its relation with orange.

These qualities are meaningful for dress in many ways. Warm colors tend to convey a feeling of gaiety and cheerfulness, but if overdone they may create a "jittery" or nervous impression. Cool colors appear dignified but too much in one costume makes one look and feel depressed. Such an outfit may need the pick-up of a gold accent or other warm color.

Warm color areas appear to advance towards you and seem larger than cool color areas, which seem to recede. Clothes of warm colors tend to make a person appear larger. Which colors will you select if you want to appear smaller?

Color Harmonies

Not only are colors beautiful by themselves, but any two can be combined *if* the correct values and intensities are selected and *if* they are used in the right proportions. But if you just mix any two colors together, you may have a combination that clashes and is jarring rather than beautiful.

In the illustration on page 78, which of the prints shown have cool colors? Which have warm colors? Which prints are mostly cool with some warm accents? Are there any prints which are warm in feeling but which have cool accents? Which ones?

Prepare or purchase equal sized sheets of paper in pure red, yellow, orange, blue, green, and violet hues. Place them against a neutral background. Stand back from them. Which seem to advance towards you? Which seem to recede? Which seem largest and which smallest? Does a grayed red have the same effect as a pure red? Explain. What effect does a pale value of a color have?

Contrast can result in restful, pleasant color harmony if neutral hues are used.

COUNTRY MISS

A monochromatic color harmony that is striking because of the contrast of intense blue and a large amount of white.

Harmony in color gives pleasure to our eyes just as harmony in music gives pleasure to our ears.

An understanding of the well-known color harmonies may help you to combine colors effectively. If you are already familiar with them, you have been better able to create your own color combinations to enhance your appearance.

Related Color Harmonies

Harmonies of related colors usually produce restful costumes because of their unity. Also exciting contrast can be created with related color harmonies when extreme value contrasts are used.

Monochromatic. The simplest color scheme is the monochromatic or one-hue harmony. A navy blue suit with a powder blue blouse is an example of a monochromatic color scheme. (Monochromatic comes from

mono, meaning one, and **chroma,** the Greek word for color.) When combining tones in this way, be certain that the values are different enough so that it does not look as if you tried to match them and just missed!

Neutrals such as black, white, or gray may be used in this harmony as desired.

Analagous. Another color harmony of related color combinations is made by combining hues occurring next to each other on the color wheel, such as blue-green, blue, and blue-violet. This harmony is called adjacent or analagous. Remember, to avoid monotony, you may provide a contrast by a difference in the intensity and the values.

Notice how the gold pin calls attention to the face and hair color of this attractive girl who is wearing a dress of subtle stripes of analogous colors.

DAN RIVER

Accented neutral. An accented neutral harmony is produced when white, black, or gray is used with a bright color accent. An example is a gray dress with a red scarf and other accessories of black.

Contrasting Color Harmonies
Complementary. Complementary colors are those shown opposite each other on the color wheel. Can you see why a combination of complementary colors is called a contrasting color harmony? Look at red and green which are across from each other in the color circle—green is composed of blue and yellow but has no color in common with red, its complement. Yellow and its complement, purple, share no common color and therefore they contrast.

Complementary color schemes can be vivid and exciting but care is needed in developing such combinations. A large area of one color and a small area of its complement is good; an equal amount of each of two complements is usually jarring unless relieved by a large amount of neutral tones. For example, bright blue and orange may be attractive as accents to a white dress.

The soft tint of one color and a deep tone of the complement creates an attractive color combination, as a soft pink blouse with a dark green skirt.

Notice that complementary colors tend to make each other look brighter. This is a very important characteristic to remember in selecting colors, and will be further developed in this chapter.

Split-complementary. Another similar harmony is the split-complemen-

A complementary color harmony of red and green could be clashing but in this costume the shades of rose and a soft green create a lovely feminine effect.

tary. Here a color is combined with colors that lie on each side of its complement on the color wheel. To create a split-complementary harmony with yellow, first find its true complement, which is purple. Then take the colors on each side of it, or red-violet and blue-violet.

Which colors would you use with green to create a split-complement harmony? Check with the color wheel to see if you are correct.

Triad. A triad color harmony combines three hues that appear equally distant from each other on the color wheel. The primary colors red, yellow, and blue are an example; also the combination of orange, green, and violet.

Clothing is available in almost any color imaginable. Thus a well-dressed person needs to understand how color affects an individual's appearance and how it coordinates with the rest of the wardrobe.

Find pictures of costumes in color that appear restful and of others that are striking and exciting. What types of color harmonies are shown in each? What types of value contrasts are shown?

Which of the fabric prints, in the illustration on page 69, are examples of a monochromatic color harmony? Which are examples of an analagous harmony? Are any complementary, triad, or accented neutral color harmonies shown?

Select a printed fabric that you enjoy. Choosing bias tape or another trimming that would make a good accent for this print, form a *related* color harmony. Select another trimming color that will produce a *contrasting* color harmony. Be able to explain your choice.

DESIGN PRINCIPLES AND COLOR

Just because colors are selected from certain locations on the color wheel is no guarantee they will always result in a beautiful harmony. Principles of good design, as discussed in Chapter Two, must also be applied to the combination of colors.

Proportion. In the previous chapter it was stated that unequal space divisions are generally more pleasing than equal ones. This also applies to the distribution of colors in your clothes. (Equal areas of color are tiresome and uninteresting.) When combining two colors, use more of one than the other.

If you are using three colors, the trick is to use a lot of one color, a moderate amount of the second, and just a "smidgen" of the third. For many years designers followed the rule that a color harmony is most pleasing when one color predominates, when there are both light and dark values, and when bright colors are used in small amounts. They noted that nature uses large areas of quiet colors such as blue and green and reserves bright colors for accents, as in flowers and the plumage of small birds. Today these rules are still good ones to follow, but we also enjoy bright colors for special occasions.

Balance. Colors have a kind of weight, as stated before. Warm colors and dark colors appear heavier than light and cool colors. Even different hues of the same intensity cannot balance each other. For example, pure yellow is lighter in feeling than pure blue, and therefore a small amount of bright blue can balance a large amount of yellow. See the dress on page 38.

Thus colors, as well as lines and shapes, can also be used to achieve balance in a costume. A collar that is too small will appear larger if bright-hued. A bright red tie that may seem too large for a small person could look just right if it were a cool blue or a greyed color.

Rhythm. Balance in color may be achieved by distributing the color in an interesting manner according to the principles of rhythm as explained in Chapter Two. A lovely, soft green necklace may seem too pale, but if the same green is repeated elsewhere in the costume, the necklace color may be just right.

Wise use of color repetition can give unity and color balance to a costume, as well as add interest. Too much repetition of color, or line, can prove monotonous or result in a jumpy, disorganized feeling. Many students in their first attempt at using color creatively decide to match all accessories. This was referred to in Chapter Two. A girl may want accessories in red for a blue and white dress. She selects red shoes, a red belt, red gloves, and a red purse. Does her costume appear harmonious or does it seem jumpy? A young man may try to match his belt, tie, watch strap, and sweater. Three accents of any one strong color are enough; two are often better.

Variety and emphasis. You have read that to provide interest some contrast is necessary for an attractive costume. Also, the greater the contrast the more exciting and dramatic the combination. With too much contrast, however, the result is confusing and lacking in unity. Did you ever walk on a floor with large black and white squares? These and other extreme color contrasts can create an insecure feeling.

Aside from using contrasting hues, emphasis may be secured by the use of a different value or intensity of the same color. The dress shown on page 71 is an example of both variety and emphasis, with the use of different values of one hue.

Harmony in a color arrangement can only be achieved when there is a feeling of unity, when the colors seem to belong together. It takes practice to be able to combine colors so that you have both harmony and interest. After you have confidence in your own ability, you find pleasure and pride in combining colors in your wardrobe.

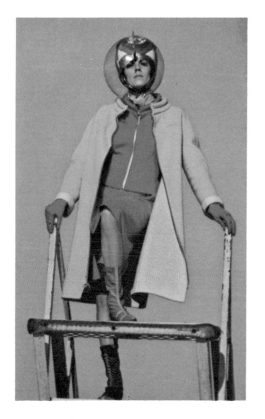

BRANIFF AIRLINES

In keeping with the excitement of air travel, one American airline has adopted new color combinations for their air hostesses. The basic uniform is a hot pink suit with a wrap-around skirt and a jacket which zips off to reveal a blue culotte working suit worn when serving meals en route. For cold weather, a zip-front reversible coat of shades such as apricot and chartreuse is worn with a combination scarf hat. A plastic bubble hat provides excellent protection against strong airport winds. Soft shoes are worn on the plane and boots for outside wear.

Collect pictures of costumes that exhibit too great a variety of color to please you. Mount them and tell how you would improve the color combinations.

Find a picture of a beige suit that you like. Select colors for a hat, shoes, shirt, and other accessories that would go well with this suit. Now, find a picture of a suit of bright blue or plaid of similar style. How would the accessory colors that you would select for this suit differ? Why?

Select two examples of plaids or checks, one that has large even checks of white and a color and another with uneven amounts of white and a color. Which is more interesting? Why? Find examples of striped fabrics, some with colors evenly distributed, and others with an uneven distribution of color. Which is more pleasing? Why?

COUNTRY MISS

Is this color combination better for a person with large hips and a small chest or for a person with very narrow hips? Explain your answer.

How Color Affects Other Design Elements

Shape. In the previous chapter it was noted that a shape could appear to change in length or width by changing the lines within it. Colors also influence the appearance of a figure. Dark, cool colors make a form seem smaller than do light, warm ones. A person with large hips and a small chest would look better balanced in dark pants or skirt and a light top because the dark bottom would minimize the hip size and the light top would make the chest seem larger.

However, a dark object against a light background will not seem small because it will "stand out." Therefore, even though a black garment should make you look smaller than a light one, it will not have this effect if the room where you spend most of your time has light walls. However, an object that is similar to its background in hue, value, and intensity will be less noticeable and will thus appear smaller. Actually, this information is more important for room decoration than for clothes selection, as in a room the backgrounds stay put but people move about! In a room with light green walls, a large chair will appear much smaller in a light green slip cover than it will with a dark green one.

If you are scheduled for a stage appearance and know the color of the backdrop, you might plan to wear colors that will create the appearance you desire.

A

B

Which of these blouse and skirt combinations would you select for a girl with prominent hips and a small bust? Which for a girl with a tiny waist, small hips and average bust? Which would be good for a large busted girl with small hips? Which would be suitable for most figures?

C

D

SHIP'N SHORE

Try a black shoe on one foot and a white shoe of similar style on the other foot. Which foot looks smaller? Compare one hand in a black glove and the other hand in a white glove. Which one looks larger? Why?

A shape will look longer and narrower if it is of one color rather than two colors. A wide belt or waist band of a sharply contrasting color will also make a person look wider.

Try on a basic dark dress or a dark, close-fitting sweater and skirt. Add a wide, bright belt. How does your shape appear to change? Change to a light or bright sweater. How does your appearance change now? Why?

Texture. Have you ever noticed how much darker a color looks in the folds of a fabric? This is because of the shadows. Shaggy or rough weaves also cast shadows that dull colors. Smooth, firmly woven fabrics or those with shiny surfaces reflect light and make a color look brighter or lighter. Look at a red tweed and contrast it with a red satin. Extremely shiny fabrics, like satin, reflect light and call attention to complexion faults. White satin is especially difficult to wear, as it reflects all light.

Some fabrics, like velveteen, can be worn in bright colors by those who usually do not look attractive in these shades. The texture softens the color and is more flattering. A bright color in a rough texture will be more subdued and therefore will not add as much apparent size as the same color in a shiny or smooth surface.

Any large person should avoid a shiny fabric, such as satin or taffeta, especially in bright intensities.

EFFECTS OF COLORS ON EACH OTHER

Value and intensity contrasts. You may have noticed how much browner a tanned skin looks when a white dress is worn. An extreme contrast will make the colors involved appear brighter. Against a light background, a color appears darker than if used alone or against a dark background. A light pink, lovely by itself, may look washed out if used with an intense color but may be pleasing if used against a dull, light, or dark color.

A shade always looks darker against a tint and lighter against a dark color. Some colors will blend together if used in nearly equal proportions. At a distance red and white striped material may appear pink and a plaid of yellow and blue may appear green. This blending may be used to your advantage, but it may also create a problem if, for example, your accessories are matched to the color of the stripe.

Repeat the first experiment on this page, but this time try on a dull black shoe such as suede and a bright black shoe such as patent leather. How do the sizes of the feet seem to differ? Why?

Collect samples of fabrics in various textures. Try to find samples similar in hue, value, and intensity but different in texture. How do the colors appear to differ?

Experiment with fabrics in similar colors but in dull, average, and smooth textures. Which textures look best on you? Why?

This young man has matched his turtle neck top to one of the colors in the plaid shirt. The effect is one of casual "put-togetherness."

Effect of complements. When two colors are used together, they may cause their complement to appear in each other. When white, gray, and even a solid black are placed next to an intense color, the complement of the color will appear in a neutral. Stare at a bright red sheet of paper for a few minutes. Then look at a white background. Don't you see a greenish square? Our eyes need relief from bright colors and the "after-image" is a common phenomenon. Place a neutral gray next to an intense green color and the gray will appear pink. (Red is the complement of green.) Bright blue will make a gray appear yellow but yellow next to gray causes it to appear bluer.

While white contrasts a tanned skin because of value differences, wearing medium blue will make the

skin appear even more brown. Remember, blue is the complement of orange, which is a high value of brown. A delicate lavender dress will emphasize any yellow in the skin and a blue-green dress will bring out pinkness in the skin.

Effect of reflection and repetition. A color looks brighter if placed next to the same hue of a duller intensity but it will look washed out if placed next to an intense shade of the same hue. Blue eyes are not noticed if a bright blue is worn near the face, but a dark grayed blue or a medium blue is reflected in the eyes and makes them look bluer.

EFFECT OF LIGHT ON COLOR

Colors may appear one way in the daylight and another way under artificial light. Some colors are softened by artificial light so that brighter colors may be worn at night than during the day. Therefore, colors that are flattering at night may be unbecoming in the daylight. On the other hand, artificial light may cause some grayed colors to lose part of their tone so they are not nearly so pretty at night. Artificial light, especially the fluorescent type, usually fades pinks, violets, and reds.

Select a grayed blue fabric or sheet of paper. Place it next to a bright blue. What has happened to the first blue? Now take away the bright blue and use an orange piece of paper. What has happened?

Find samples of fabrics that appear to have a different hue from a distance than from close-up. Be able to explain the reasons.

If you are going to wear a color only at night, then try it on under artificial light. Otherwise it is best to look at a color in daylight. Avoid strong sunlight, which does not give a true impression of colors as they will appear in everyday use.

COLOR AND YOU

When you are young, you are able to wear brighter and a greater variety of colors than an older person. However, there will always be some hues that are more becoming to you than others. If you know which colors go well together, you can understand which ones look well on you. Select colors that enhance your skin, hair, eyes, or figure—not just because they are fashionable.

Your Personality

Youths in their teens are changing in personality but have developed traits that make some colors right for certain types. If you are full of pep and energy, with strong coloring, you can wear and probably enjoy bright colors and striking contrasts. If you are quiet and delicate, such colors can overpower you, make you appear washed out and drab. Your choice should be lighter colors and medium contrasts. If you like bright colors but they do not do anything for you, try wearing them in small amounts as accents or for at-home wear as in robes and pajamas. Remember to emphasize "you" and your coloring rather than the colors in your dress.

Your Personal Coloring

Everyone is born with a very personal coloring. Your complexion or skin tone, color of eyes and hair affect the colors you can wear well. Have you noticed that some colors make your skin appear clearer and pinker while others bring out any yellow there may be? Some colors will make your hair drab, others make it appear full of life. Even your eyes, as previously noted, can be made sparkling or dull by the use of colors.

- Look at yourself carefully in a mirror in clear daylight.
- Wear a white shirt or top.
- Pull your hair back to get a true look at your skin.

Now that you are beginning really to see color, you may notice overtones in your skin that you were not aware of before.

Complexion colors. Skin tones are basically red and yellow combined about equally to make an orange which, when lightened, becomes a creamy white with pink tones or, when darkened, a lovely brown. Between the light and the dark there are many tints and shades.

"CHARM BY CHOICE," NATIONAL URBAN LEAGUE
The selection of color depends on your skin tone. There is a color that will add facial beauty to every skin tone from very white transparent skin to the darkest brown.

"CHARM BY CHOICE," NATIONAL URBAN LEAGUE

Find the color that complements not only your size and skin tone but also your personality, since color selection can make you feel happy, sad, outgoing, or quiet.

In choosing colors it is not so important to consider the color of your eyes and your hair as it is to determine your skin color. When Mother Nature worked out your own personal color harmony, she saw to it that the color of your hair and eyes blended in with that of your skin. This is the reason that people with tinted or dyed hair may look as if their skin doesn't quite go with the rest of them. So always select colors that make your skin look fresh and alive.

Make-up can help you look better in a color that is becoming to you but seldom can it make an unbecoming color really flattering.

Eyes. Eyes are brown, blue, or greenish gray. Some have violet overtones.

Hair. Hair colors range from almost blue-black to brown to pale yellow to red-orange tones to white. When you look at ordinary hair carefully, you may see yellows or reds in what you thought was "just brown."

COLOR TYPES

It is impossible to classify people into definite color types as we are all of mixed heritage which has produced a variety of characteristics. However, most of us fall into one of six basic types.

1. The BLOND may be a pure blond with light yellow hair, blue eyes, and very fair skin. Some girls are more of a semi-blond with medium brown hair, fair skin, and blue or gray eyes. Almost all colors are good for blonds except the very intense ones, which overpower them, and very pale, drab hues, which make them look washed out.

Intense yellow will appear to fade blond hair, but soft gold and pale yellow will make golden hair lovely. Black and white, dark colors, and clear pastels are usually flattering. Blues, greens, and turquoises are often spectacular on blonds.

2. The REDHEAD may have hair that ranges from almost blond to an intense "carrot" red. Her skin may have a fair, bluish cast or warm tones with freckles. Eyes are usually blue, hazel, gray, or brown.

Vivid blues and greens will emphasize freckles, bleach out the warm skin color and make the hair look almost brassy bright. All other greens such as dark and light clear greens, blue-greens, and yellow-greens are attractive, as are cool blues. Blue-red tones should be avoided as well as pure red, but some peach pinks are lovely. Jewelry in amber, copper, and gold is flattering.

High school girls trying on color "bibs" to determine which colors are most flattering to each girl's own personal coloring.

3. The true BRUNETTE is usually striking in color contrasts with fair skin, dark brown or black hair, and blue, hazel, or brown eyes. Bright colors, black, and beige are becoming.

Least attractive are subdued pastels.

4. You can notice many shades of brown-haired people between the brunette and the blond who are called BROWNETTES. Some have light skin with light brown hair and others have olive skin tones with light or medium brown hair.

Brownettes can usually wear almost any color that flatters their skin tones.

5. LATINS or ORIENTALS usually have skins with a yellow bronze cast, dark brown hair and eyes. A creamy white tone is striking. Warm, slightly grayed colors are good.

Warm yellow-green may be flattering, while blue-green is not.

6. The skin tones of the DARK BRUNETTE may range from olive tan to very dark brown. Some skins have a blue cast. The hair is an intensely dark brown, but not true black, and the eyes are usually brown.

People of warm coloring look well in warm colors so beige and tan are attractive but may be uninteresting without appropriate accents. Other warm colors that are not too intense such as rose and apricot or creamy white can be lovely. Cool blues and greens are often good choices.

Black is not a flattering color and neither are dull browns or yellow-greens. Bright, glaring colors are to be avoided and tints may be too weak for skins with considerable pigmentation.

How to determine your best colors. The best way to determine your own most becoming colors is to stand in front of a mirror in good clear daylight and drape different colored fabrics around your shoulders. You will easily see which colors make you more attractive and which ones lessen your own natural beauty, either by throwing an unbecoming tone onto your skin or by overpowering your own coloring by the intensity of the color itself. This is the way great couturiers select colors for their clients; no color chart can ever take the place of this time-tested method.

Although you will want to know the general group of colors your type can wear, you must look at yourself carefully and find out your own best colors.

After you have looked at yourself carefully and analyzed your own skin, hair, and eyes for their true color, you can decide what you want color to do for you. Do you want your skin to appear lighter or darker? Do you want to subdue too much pink or yellow in your skin? Do you want to emphasize your eyes or subtle tints in your hair?

MEN'S FASHION ASSOCIATION

Although attractive the year 'round, the dark plaid pants and blue shirt are especially suitable for cold-weather wear. The plaid is colorful but not so extreme that it cannot be worn by the average figure.

SIMPLICITY PATTERNS

Has each girl chosen a color suitable to her personal coloring? Both of these attractive outfits were made from the same pattern.

88

Your class can be divided into groups of 4 to 6 girls each for laboratory work. Try swatches of color in various hues, values, and intensities on each member—one at a time—to discover what colors are especially becoming and which are least becoming. Try to find the answers to the following questions for each girl. NOTE: You will want to keep a record for yourself of your own findings.

Which colors:

- Make you feel good when you use them?
- Overpower you, are more noticeable than you?
- Make your skin seem clearer and fresher?
- Make your skin appear duller, not as fresh and clear?
- Attract attention to any skin blemishes?
- Make your eyes appear more noticeable?
- Make your eyes appear less noticeable?
- Bring out desirable tints in your hair?
- Dull your hair?

Be sure that you describe the colors accurately as to hue, value, and intensity.

Prepare a summary stating your most flattering colors, those that are fairly becoming, and those that you should avoid.

EFFECTS OF COLORS ON YOUR PERSONAL COLORING

A desirable hue in one's personal coloring may be emphasized by contrast with its complement. Remember how complementary colors emphasize each

"CHARM BY CHOICE," NATIONAL URBAN LEAGUE
White next to the face is too great a contrast for girls with very dark skins. This creamy white is lovely on this girl of medium brown coloring.

other? Therefore, if your skin is yellowish to brown-toned, avoid bright blue and purple, which emphasize their complement, yellow. If quite dark, avoid brown and dark shades of blue or purple. If your skin is too reddish or florid, avoid clear green, and blue-greens which make a florid skin look more purple. If it is sallow or pale, never wear red-purple which will give it a sickly, greenish-yellow cast. Pink skin tones are made more lovely with greens or blue-greens.

A desirable hue in one's personal coloring may be emphasized by repeating that hue, but not in an intense form. Blue eyes will appear bluer if one wears such colors as blue-green, green, blue-violet, and light violet. Gray eyes will appear bluer if worn with blue or blue-green.

89

Select students in your class who are the opposites in shade and contrast of coloring, perhaps one with very dark hair and dark skin and one with fair skin and blond hair. Hold up various color swatches and see which ones are becoming to the dark person and which to the light. Try to tell why.

Perhaps you could find students who represent each of the basic coloring types. Your own ability to choose colors wisely for yourself can be improved by noticing colors that others can and cannot wear well.

Select from a fashion magazine or pattern book a garment design that you think is suited in line and proportion for you. Choose the colors that you think are suitable for the design and becoming to you. Which colors have you selected? Why do you think these colors are good for you? Use samples of colored paper or fabric for your report.

Black drains color and white reflects light. Black fabrics absorb light and color rays and thus drain the color from your skin and make it look paler. Only those clear, near white skins with a healthy color look good in unrelieved black. Navy blue is more flattering than black to most skins, if a deep shade is desired. White and light tints reflect light and make your face appear to have more color. Florid skins seem flush-red with pastels.

COLOR AND YOUR FIGURE

If you have a figure problem, let color help you disguise it. As you remember from your study of warm and cool

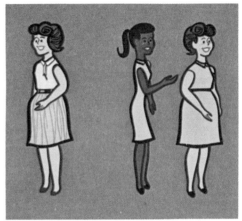

"CHARM BY CHOICE," NATIONAL URBAN LEAGUE
Bright colors, though they are generally vibrant and attractive, do very little for the large girl but are a good choice for the tall or average. Large girls will look much better in toned down, yet pretty shades.

tones, colors can make your figure look smaller or larger. Also, warm colors, as red and yellow, seem to come toward you and therefore are called advancing colors. If you want to look larger, you will wear these colors. Remember, the cool hues—green, blue, and purple with bluish tones —seem to recede; they make you look smaller. Bright colors and those light in value appear to increase the size of the object, while colors dark in value and grayed in intensity seem to decrease the size of an object.

Anyone with very large hips should not choose a bright-colored skirt or pants and a pale top. A top-heavy person, however, might find this a good combination.

Black or any very dark hue will outline a figure and produce a decided silhouette which will reveal either a good or a poor figure. So, although dark shades usually slim, they will make your outline stand out and are not good for problem figures.

BOBBIE BROOKS

Attention is drawn to the small waist of this girl by the use of light colored buttons at the waist and insets in the skirt. Notice the stitching around the neckline as well as the waistline.

COUNTRY MISS

The muted shades in this pants suit make it suitable for travel. Soil and wrinkles will be difficult to see. The colors are not ones you will tire of easily if you vary your accessories. What color scarfs and tops would you suggest to "perk up" this suit?

Grays and medium value colors make a figure appear part of the background, as do many prints.

Remember the power of an accent! A colorful accent can draw the eye away from a bulge and force attention on a pretty face, a tiny waist, or attractive legs and ankles.

Bright shoes and a bright hat will make a person seem less tall, but a grayed color costume with the hat as the only bright accent will add height. Notice how your eye is attracted upwards.

A colorful purse and gloves will draw attention to the hipline, which will make the wearer seem heavier there. Experiment with a white flower on a dark dress. Place it high at the neckline, lower at the waistline. Notice how the eye follows it.

COLOR FOR VARIOUS OCCASIONS AND SEASONS

Occasions. Even though pink may be one of your best colors, you wouldn't want to select a pale pink coat as your only coat for a long trip or for a hike in the country. It would soon be soiled and then it would not be attractive.

Attractive all year around, the brown and yellow tones in this blouse are especially suited to the autumn of the year. Basically a monochromatic color scheme, the variation in values and intensities used with white create an interesting effect.

cold, dreary winter. During spring, pastels remind us of flowers soon to come. During the summer you want to feel and appear as cool as possible, so white and tints are appropriate, although you may select bright colors to blend with active vacation fun. In the northern fall when the leaves are changing and the air turns crisp, the earthy fall colors seem just right—browns, dull reds, and dull greens. When winter comes, you are interested in looking and feeling warm. Dark and warm colors appear at their best then.

There will always be a time when a change is welcome and you will find that a dark color will be a relief in the middle of light summer colors, just as white may look refreshing at New Year's time. But even then, accessories will probably reflect colors suitable to the season.

Don't get in a rut about colors. Just because a color is good for you, you don't have to wear it always. In late summer when your skin is tanned, light colors will look better on you than when your skin is paler. As you grow older and your skin color changes, you may find that your becoming colors will change also.

Don't be afraid to experiment with colors. Each year different shades and tints are featured; you may discover a fresh color combination that is very flattering to you.

• In addition, colors should suit the occasions for which they will be worn —as well as being practical.

Planning clothes for a job? Today we see every possible color in the wardrobes of business people but you will look more businesslike and make a better impression if you wear dark or muted shades with bright accents that suit you.

Seasons. There are certain colors that just seem to belong to each season of the year. In the early spring, bright prints look cheerful after a

Summary with Check-Up Questions

Color has an effect on how you feel, whether you are conscious of it or not.

• *Which colors make you feel quiet and calm?*

• *Which colors make you feel excited and raring to go?*

• *Which colors make you feel depressed?*

Color is a factor in safety.

• *Why is red used as a warning light rather than blue?*

• *Why should children's play clothes contain some bright colors?*

• *What colors are worn by most policemen for traffic duty on rainy days?*

Light is made up of many colors. When light falls on an article of clothing some rays are absorbed, others reflected.
- *Why does a blue dress appear blue?*
- *Why does a black dress make most girls appear pale?*
- *Why is white used for clothing in hot countries?*

White brings out all the colors in a skin.
- *Why is pure white seldom considered a good choice for a dark-skinned person?*
- *What effect will a white collar on a dark dress have for a person with a small amount of pink pigment in her skin?*

Color has three dimensions—hue, value, and intensity.
- *What is the hue of a scarlet color? Of a golden color?*
- *Is pink a light or dark value of red?*
- *Is baby blue called a tint or shade? Which is navy?*
- *How does an intense color differ from a dull color?*
- *List the neutrals.*

One of the properties of color is described as warmth or coolness.
- *Which colors appear cool?*
- *Which colors appear warm?*
- *Which colors can be warm or cool, depending upon their exact shade?*

Two major types of color harmonies are *related* and *contrasting*. Related harmonies are usually restful as the colors share a common hue. Contrasting harmonies are often exciting.
- *Why is the combination of blue and green restful, while that of blue and orange is not?*

Monochromatic color schemes are usually mellow and pleasing to the eye.
- *What is meant by the word "monochromatic"?*

- *Why is a monochromatic color scheme often dull if not carefully planned?*
- *How would you achieve a striking monochromatic color harmony? (Would a contrast of values and intensities help?)*

Colors have weight, just as objects do.
- *Are warm colors heavier or lighter than cool colors?*
- *Would a large travel bag appear heavier in beige or dark blue?*
- *What effect do warm colors have on apparent size?*
- *Would you suggest that a girl with very large feet wear shoes of warm or cool colors? Why?*

A single color with a neutral for accent or vice versa is an easy way to achieve color harmony.
- *How would you describe the type of harmony of a rose dress with white accessories?*
- *Suggest an accented neutral harmony for a gray suit.*

Analogous color harmonies are usually restful because the colors used share a common hue.
- *What colors would you use with blue to achieve an analogous harmony?*
- *What colors would you select to go with pink and red for an analogous harmony?*

Complementary color harmonies are vivid and exciting if colors are used at full intensity. They can be subdued if a tint of one color and a shade of its complement are used.
- *What effect would an equal amount of orange and blue have?*
- *Why is beige and navy a restful combination?*
- *What colors would you select to wear with a green skirt if you wished to create a complementary combination?*

Bright colors reflect light and usually make you appear larger than life! Cool, retreating colors and dark colors minimize size.

- *Would you select bright orange pants if you are hippier than desired?*
- *What effect will dark navy clothing have on a large person?*
- *If you wanted to distract attention from your broad shoulders and the rest of your figure was in good proportion, what colors would you select?*

The principle of proportion is applied to the distribution of color in your costumes as well as to other art elements.

- *What effect does an equal amount of two colors have?*
- *If you are using three colors such as dark blue, green, and yellow, how much would you use of each one? Why?*
- *What is the effect of a white dress with red shoes, belt, jewelry, purse, and hat? Why?*

The appearance of a color may differ if combined with different colors.

- *How will a pale pink differ in appearance placed next to dark blue, bright green, or pale cream?*

There are so many colors and shades and tints to select from that color study is important. Everyone has some colors which are more becoming to her than others.

- *Which colors have you discovered that you can wear well? Describe them, stating hue, value, and intensity.*

Colors in your skin, hair, and eyes can be emphasized by wearing the complementary color or by repeating the same color in a duller intensity or a different value.

- *What effect will a rose shirt have on a skin? Will such a color be more flattering to a person with a slightly pale skin or one whose skin is too florid?*
- *What effect would a bright yellow shirt, compared with a honey beige sweater, have on golden hair?*
- *What colors will make blue eyes appear bluer?*

The texture of a fabric affects the appearance of the color. Some colors may appear flattering in rough textures that would be harsh in smooth finishes.

- *Why is velvet flattering to many complexions?*
- *What effect has white satin when worn next to the face? How will a white crepe fabric differ?*

Because of variations in skin tones, rules can give you suggestions for flattering colors but your final decision should be based on the effect the color has on you. Try on the color in clear daylight rather than brighter sunlight or artificial light unless you plan to always wear the garment in such light.

- *What effect does artificial light have on colors? Will bright colors appear brighter or duller?*
- *Why may a garment color that appears lovely in a store window appear unattractive when you try it on?*

Can You Explain These Terms?

hue

value

tint

shade

intensity

neutrals

chromatic

color wheel or circle

primary colors

secondary colors

intermediate colors

warm colors

cool colors

related harmonies

monochromatic harmony

analagous harmony

accented neutral harmony

contrasting harmonies

complementary harmony

split-complementary harmony

triad

CHAPTER FOUR

Wardrobe Planning

Have you ever looked in your closet and said, "I haven't anything to wear?"

Of course, you had *something*— your closet wasn't empty. What you really meant was that you didn't have a suitable item for a certain occasion. Perhaps it was because some garments needed cleaning or repair but probably it was because you had been buying clothes without a plan. Even if a garment is attractive and suits you in color and line, it may not be a wise choice for you if it doesn't fit in with your other clothes and if it isn't suitable for your activities.

Many people do not like to take the trouble to plan ahead but if you do, you may be able to have the clothes you *want* and *need* for your activities within the money you have to spend for clothing. Through wise planning you can choose a few garments that go together and look like many. You will also be able to anticipate your needs and avoid last minute shopping which is often expensive. When you have time, you can shop carefully to get what you want, or you may have time to make some of your clothing.

HOW TO PLAN A WARDROBE

Some people like to plan their clothing needs for an entire year, but this is a long time span. At least we can plan for one season at a time, although some usually find it best to plan for both autumn and winter clothes before they start to school in the fall.

There are two major ways to plan a wardrobe; one is to take inventory of your present wardrobe and then determine what additional clothes you will need for your activities. The other way is to consider first your activities and the clothes you need for them, then determine what clothes you already have that are suitable for your needs. Later, you can plan what new items you must have. In this chapter we will use this approach.

For a little while, forget about the clothes you already own. No, of course we are not suggesting you throw them all away and start from scratch. But if you think first of the type and amount of clothes you need for YOUR life, you will be more honest with yourself and not confuse needs and desires too often, nor will you tend to justify keeping some of the clothing in your present wardrobe that may be useless to you.

It is not easy to decide what is a need and what is a desire. You really only "need" one sweater to keep you warm, or perhaps two, so one can be cleaned while you are wearing the other. But some people "need" many sweaters because it is important to them to have a variety for many changes or because one of their interests and hobbies is clothing and fabrics. Others may find they have more interest in other articles; perhaps they "need" a variety of shoes, or they may not be interested in clothing at all but prefer to spend time and money on other things as music, education, drama, travel, or special family concerns.

Perhaps reading Chapter One can help you decide which clothing items are necessary for your activities and interests so you can be as honest as possible in deciding the clothes that belong in your wardrobe.

Only after you have decided the types and amount of clothes that are important for your activities should you inventory what you already have in your wardrobe. While you are checking what you have, you will also be deciding how each article can fit into your life. Perhaps you also will discover uses for some garments you never thought of before. You may also face up to the fact that some articles you own are not worth the space they take in your closet or drawers and could be better used by someone else.

After determining what you need and what you have, then the major planning job comes—that of figuring out what additional items you need and how you can acquire them. This will be discussed in detail in the last part of this chapter.

CONSIDER YOUR ACTIVITIES

Before you start to buy even one item for the coming season, think carefully about your activities.

- For what occasions will you need special clothes? Of course you will need them for school, for dress such as church and social affairs, for certain sports, and for lounging and sleeping.
- What are your other activities? Perhaps you have a job that requires special clothing. Do you participate in such sports as riding, swimming, skiing for which particular clothing is needed? What types of parties do you attend?

What about the future? Look ahead to the next year, as many of your new clothes should last for several years. Will you be starting a new job or will you go on for further study? Your future needs may affect the more expensive clothes you buy now, such as a coat. If you plan to start working next year, you may not want to spend much for an informal school jacket this year. Will you be moving to another location where the climate is different? This will affect your future and the clothing you buy now.

To determine the relationship of your environment and activities to your clothing needs, make a list of all the activities in which you participate regularly. Copy the chart, page 98, on another sheet of paper.

MY ACTIVITY CHECKLIST AND CLOTHING NEEDS

ACTIVITY	TYPE OF CLOTHING NEEDED				
	Indoor	Outerwear	Garments	Shoes	Accessories
School Five days a week—wear same outfit from 7 a.m. until 4 p.m. or later. Are six to seven changes right for you?					
Job What type of job do you have? What type of clothes are suitable?					
Church, Special Events Do you need more than two complete outfits?					
Parties and Social Gatherings Can you wear the same clothes as worn for church? What other types of social occasions do you attend?					
Sports and Other Leisure Time Activities In what types of sports do you participate? What are your hobbies and other leisure activities?					
After School, At Home, and Shopping Do you change clothes when you get home from school? Do you do anything at home that requires special clothes?					
Sleeping and Lounging Nightwear, robe, slippers, of course. Anything else?					
Winter Extras Does your climate require boots, scarfs, mittens?					
Summer Extras Will you need swim wear, casual shoes, shorts?					
Travel Will you be traveling this season? Where are you going? Will you drive, go by plane or how?					

As you read this chapter, fill in the right-hand columns with your *own* answers. NOTE: Be sure to list any other activities that you may have that require special clothing.

School clothes. Why not start first with your school needs? You probably spend more waking time there than any other place. What clothes are suitable for your school? If your school has a uniform, you will consider only shoes, coats, and accessories. Otherwise, several pants or skirts to be worn with tops are the usual choice. These are wonderful because they can be "mixed or matched" for many changes. A wise student knows that "three and three can equal nine" clothing outfits.

On warm autumn days you may need lightweight clothes that don't look summery. In most climates a school coat or heavy jacket is needed for many months of the year.

Shoes need to be comfortable, durable, and easy to keep clean. In some communities nylon hosiery is worn daily by girls. In others knee socks or anklets are popular. Only in very warm climates is it fashionable to go without some hosiery and even then foot socklets are desirable for comfort and to protect shoes.

Bare feet and shorts are usually frowned upon in school except for special sports events.

Headwear is needed if your weather is not always sunny and warm.

Will you need gloves, mittens, or rainwear for the school year? Will one pair of boots serve for both rain and colder weather or will you need two? Of course, you want a purse to carry your many necessities.

A special school occasion may require something a little less casual than jeans and a shirt—perhaps a well-coordinated outfit.

RECOMMENDATIONS FOR A "DRESS RIGHT CODE" FOR SCHOOL

Based on recommendations originated by the Inter-High School Student Council of Buffalo, New York, and subsequently adopted by thousands of High School student groups throughout the United States in the 1960's. **How would you change this code to suit today's dress practices?**

Girls

RECOMMENDED:

1) Blouses, sweaters, blouse and sweater, jacket with blouse and sweater.

2) Skirts, jumpers, suits, or conservative dresses.

3) Shoes appropriate to the rest of the ensemble.

NOT RECOMMENDED:

1) V-neck sweaters without blouse.

2) Shorts, kilts, party-type dresses, slacks of any kind.

3) Ornate jewelry.

4) T-shirts or sweat shirts.

AMERICAN INSTITUTE OF MEN'S AND BOYS' WEAR

*Casual coats suitable for schoolwear in most sections of our country and also
for many sporting events. The double-breasted coat is of heavy corduroy with a
pile lining. The center coat is also corduroy and features an interesting use of
a second color which pipes the pockets and lines the collar. The wool fleece coat
has a harmonizing wool scarf. Can you name the three types of pockets?*

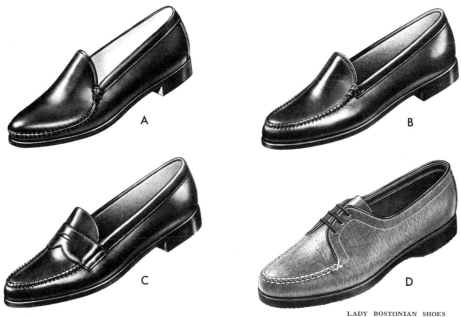

LADY BOSTONIAN SHOES

Flats suitable for school activities. Although A and B appear similar, A would be more flattering to a narrow foot and B would be better for a wide foot. The cross piece on the traditional "loafer," C, makes the foot appear shorter. D is a classic oxford with crepe sole.

Raincoat of water-repellent cotton poplin with large "industrial size" zippers. Those at the cuff are primarily decorative but they permit the sleeves to be rolled back to form cuffs for fair-weather use.

DAN RIVER

A pair of plastic boots is a necessity for most parts of this country because they can be folded up and easily carried for sudden downpours. There is a heel shape for almost every shoe made. The flat sole is most practical as it fits all but the highest heel.

101

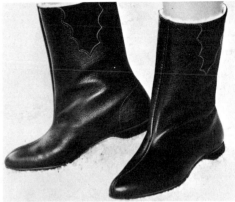

THE WOLVERINE SHOE COMPANY

Winters in northern states can be snowy. Warm, waterproof boots, short or long, are necessities for everyday wear.

THE WOLVERINE SHOE COMPANY

Lined with warm pile fabric, often made with acrylic, olefin, or other synthetic fibers that can be washed off, these boots are made of water-repellent outer materials to keep one warm, dry, healthy, and attractive in the coldest weather.

Last minute check-up on plans before presenting a school assembly. These FHA'ers from Washington know that such an occasion often calls for a dressier outfit than everyday schoolwear.

"TEEN TIMES"

Jobs. Regular school clothes may often be worn for after school jobs if they are still fresh and neat. Even though your work may not have any special requirements, you will find that you will get ahead faster if you wear clothes that make you appear business-like. It is always wise to ask your employer what type of clothes are preferred for your work.

Uniforms are required for such jobs as hospital helpers and waitresses. Here you will need shoes and hosiery that look suitable and are comfortable for long periods of being on your feet. A sweater that blends with the uniform is desirable for chilly days.

If you are babysitting, you may want to wear slacks or shorts but it is wise to ask the mother if she approves. You will want clothes that can be easily cleaned and that will allow for comfort as you engage in active play with your charges. Little children like colorful touches and will be pleased if you dress for them.

Church. Clothes suitable for church are also suitable for many occasions in the lives of young people. It is best not to put on a fashion show or to be too conspicuous in church. For women, a dress with a coat, or a dressy suit, and a hat or scarf are worn with gloves and purse. A basic suit is always good as it is seldom too dressy and can be varied with accessories to appear different almost every time it is worn.

Social occasions. Parties differ in various communities. Some are very informal to which school clothes or even sport clothes are worn and others call for dressy fabrics and styles. The clothes you wear to church may be suitable depending on the jewelry and other accessories you select.

FIRST NATIONAL STORES

Uniforms are provided by the supermarket for this young girl to wear when working after school as a "checker." She needs to be certain that her shoes are comfortable for standing for long periods of time.

Women who are on their feet a great deal know that the most important item in their wardrobe is shoes. Comfort and support is necessary when standing and walking for long periods of time. Resilient soles cushion the shock of walking on hard floors so common to hospitals, restaurants, and large stores. The wedge effect of this shoe provides both comfort and support.

THE WOLVERINE SHOE COMPANY

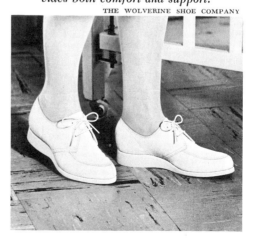

Knit trousers and sweater and an easy-fitting shirt make a comfortable outfit for leisure activities.

Suitable for an informal pizza party. This colorful print blouse and box-pleated skirt is also appropriate for school and many other occasions.

Formal dances usually require sleeveless dresses, either long or short, depending upon the current style and local traditions. Shoes dyed to match your gown are often preferred or else low-cut white or black shoes. Select hosiery made to be worn with low-cut shoes.

A small beaded or cloth bag is essential for carrying your necessities since it is difficult for your date to appear well dressed if his pockets are loaded down with your needs. A dressy wrap is a luxury few high school girls can afford or need. Many classic coats can double as an evening topper and in warm weather a dressy sweater is appropriate.

Sports. When you are a spectator at sports events, you can usually wear school clothes or slightly dressier ones. If you are watching football or other games in a cool climate, be sure that you are dressed warmly with needed foot and head wear as well as a coat. For active sports you need clothes that provide for freedom of body movements. Wear comfortable clothes. It's hard to be a good sport if your feet are tired from improper shoes or if you have to keep tucking your blouse into your skirt or are irritated by a sleeve that binds your arm. Easily cleaned clothes that don't show soil and wrinkles are essential. It is no fun to be worried about getting your clothes dirty when you should be paying attention to your sports activities.

Hiking, bicycling, and picnicking call for slacks or shorts or a walking skirt with some fullness. An extra sweater is good insurance in case chilly breezes develop. Sandals may seem attractive but seldom provide the support or protection needed. Loafers or sneakers are better.

SIMPLICITY PATTERN COMPANY

Special occasions call for special clothes. (a) This is a short version of the baby doll dress, sleeve edges ruffled, in oversized black and white checks with black pique bodice. (b) Unless a man uses formal wear frequently, he may find it better to rent such attire, complete with shirt and other accessories. (c) This simple but glamorous short black crepe dress is accented with a brief, white lace jacket. (d) The floor-length dress of bonded lace is an example of sophisticated simplicity. Wear it with or without its sheer lace jacket.

MASCULINES

DU PONT

Suitable for many active and spectator sports, this pant dress is made of a madras plaid.

MCCALL CORP.

Even in the early 1920's women had special costumes for sports activities. Notice the knicker-dress combination for the tennis player (and her hat!). The lady golfer was very fashionably dressed for that era.

Teamwork is as important in fashion as it is in the game. Deep pleats in the skirt leave room for action, and also keep a neat silhouette. Suspenders will stay in place. They go under the shoulder tabs of the oxford shirt. Notice the neat look of the collar and the double button cuffs.

BOBBIE BROOKS

Smartly dressed for a tandem ride. The total look with matching stockings and pullover in argyle patterned stretch fabrics for comfort. The bicycle skirt is a suitable length for this activity.

DU PONT

Jeans and matching jackets are suitable for most leisure-time activities. Individuality can be expressed by varying the tops.

THE LEE CO.

SEARS, ROEBUCK AND CO.

A casual but well-coordinated outfit for spectator sports. The colors in the cotton-polyester shirt and the sleeveless sweater harmonize with those in the plaid polyester knit pants.

Sailing calls for rubber soled shoes such as these sneakers for secure footing on rolling, wet decks. Shorts or slacks are desired because skirts are not compatible with the wind off the water. This overblouse has the nautical collar which is so appropriate.

BOBBIE BROOKS

107

DU PONT

A new look for the golf course is the button-front golf dress with a swinging skirt that stops above the knees, and comes with its own matching shorts. With it she wears a visored cap for sun protection, an elasticized belt with room for tees, and traditional golf oxfords. Notice how this dress resembles the tennis costume of 1922 shown on page 106.

LADY BOSTONIAN SHOES

Close-up of golf oxford with kiltie tongue. Perhaps the popularity of golf in Scotland explains why the traditional golf shoe has a kiltie tongue.

LADY BOSTONIAN SHOES

Special sole of a golf shoe showing the small cleats that prevent sliding in slippery grass and secure one's stance when swinging.

Tennis players have traditionally worn a one-piece sleeveless white dress, above the knee in length, with white tennis shoes. Shorts and a sleeveless blouse are preferred by others. In cold weather slacks may be more desirable. Absorbent socks and a visor to shade the eyes are needed as well as rubber-soled shoes.

Swimming suits are of two types, one for the girl who swims and another for the girl who takes a quick dip and then prefers to sit on the sand or at the edge of the pool! A one-piece suit of a simple knit or stretch fabric is preferred by the serious swimmer who has the figure for it. A dressmaker suit with pant legs is more flattering to a heavier girl. Two-piece suits are charming on some girls but not all figures are improved by such exposure. A robe is often needed to wear from the dressing room and is handy to have for protection from sun and breezes. Don't forget a bathing cap if you swim in a pool or if you want to protect your hairdo.

Bowling is not easy in a dress with tight sleeves or a blouse that keeps coming untucked. Nor does dangly jewelry help improve your score or that of others in your group. Pants seldom present a very attractive image from the rear unless you are quite slender. A one-piece dress with freedom of movement is preferable, sleeveless or with some sleeve fullness. Shoes may be special bowling ones or flat-heeled shoes with nonstick soles.

Golf also requires freedom of movement. A skirt that isn't so full that it will blow up with every gust of wind or a shirtwaist style dress and a sweater are good choices. Pants and

108

Cut-off jeans and a comfortable knit shirt—suitable for active sports or just relaxing.

What better place to wear pants than in the country? Heavy corduroy pants with harmonizing shirt are suitable for many activities from casual horseback riding to fall picnics. For what other activities would this costume be suitable?

shorts are also suitable for certain weather conditions. Leather gloves may protect your hands and aid your grip. Walking shoes should be water-proofed and may have spiked soles.

Horseback riding is usually enjoyed by high school girls. Long pants are needed to protect one's legs so jeans or slacks are sensible. A formal riding outfit is expensive but it is durable and the style is good for many years. This type consists of breeches or jodhpurs worn with a fitted coat. Breeches are worn with riding boots that come almost to the knee, and jodhpurs are worn with low boots that cover the ankle. The formal fitted coat is worn with a tailored blouse. A hard hat for protection in case of falls and leather gloves are traditional and desirable.

Skiing and other winter sports require freedom of movement but also warmth without bulk. You may be warm if you are bundled up but it will be hard to ski or skate and enjoy these activities. Dressing in layers is a good winter pattern as this takes advantage of the insulating value of air spaces between articles of clothing and also provides an opportunity to shed some clothing when the sun is warmest or to add when it gets chilly.

consider home wear when planning clothing needs. Many old clothes are not comfortable or safe for work at home and one never knows when the door bell will ring or you have to dash away on an errand. It is better to give some serious thought to your home needs. A smock or apron to slip on

DU PONT

The way a girl dresses for a sport is half the fun. This warm sweater of acrylic fibers has an attached hood which keeps the wintry wind off her neck and can also be folded back as a collar. The band of stripes is repeated in the hood.

Against the snow you will find that most colors are attractive—bright colors, clear pastels, and black and white are striking. Be sure to include head protection—scarf, knitted helmet—or some stylish way to keep head and ears warm. Hands and feet need suitable covering. Boots are warmer with two pairs of medium weight socks than with one pair of heavy ones. Sun goggles are also needed. Ice skaters may prefer tights and a short skirt to the usual long pants of winter sportsters.

At home wear. Some girls think they can wear any of their old clothes around the house and do not need to

Washable pants and top are often selected for work around the home by women who want to be comfortable yet still suitably dressed for shopping and other interruptions.

GLAMORENE PRODUCTS CORP.

over school clothes is essential for short periods of work. Do select a pretty one that will really protect you. (Have you ever had to change a shirt the last minute before leaving for school because of some accident which occurred while helping with breakfast?)

When you have much housework to do, a washable outfit such as jeans or shorts, and a top is always suitable. Bedroom slippers seldom provide firm foot support for working. School shoes are suitable but you may want to indulge your desire for unusual shoes at home.

How suitable are blue jeans, a washable cotton jersey, and sneakers for working around the house? Can these garments take heavy wear and the frequent washing needed to maintain a fresh appearance?

What better selection of clothes for helping with the outside work in cool climates in the fall than a V-necked sweater with matching knee socks, Bermuda shorts and a tailored blouse? Do you think this young miss is more efficient with her work than she would be in an "old dress" no longer suitable for public wear, and run-down shoes?
BOBBIE BROOKS

For winter wear, pajamas of flannelette with machine embroidered yoke.

A knee-length nightdress designed for teen-age young women. Made of a polyester fiber and cotton blend, the fabric is washable with easy care and comfort. The ruching which trims the hem and sleeves is durably pleated. Notice the stretch slippers of acrylic knit.

Lounging or bedroom clothes can be whatever you desire—tailored or frilly, lace trimmed garments. Some girls prefer pajamas and others like nighties, either long or short. Today there are so many different styles and even the frilly ones are usually practical as they can be easily washed, need no ironing, and wear well. Gone are the days of an old, beat-up all purpose bathrobe. There are so many new styles of house coats and wraps to slip into to keep you cozy in winter or comfortably covered up in summer. Slippers, of course, and here is the place to feel free to wear styles and colors that you like but which may not seem wise for wear outside the home.

Winter extras. You are unusual if

you live in a climate where winter does not require additional clothing for everyday wear. Perhaps you live in southern Texas where wet weather is your only inconvenience—and you have little of that. But if you live in any of the middle or northern states, you will have to consider boots, gloves, headwear, coats, and even tights or longies to keep you warm. The girl who rides to and from school in a heated car may not need as warm a coat as the one who walks through the wintry cold so give thought to your own situation and needs.

Summer extras. Summer may mean a job for you with business-like dresses needed or it may mean a lazy time at the seashore or in the country where you seldom change from casual shorts and blouses. Surely it will mean cooler clothes, a summer purse, casual shoes, and some change in your usual clothing habits.

Du Pont

Brass-buttoned long dress in clan-plaid fabric is comfortable and attractive for an evening at home.

NATIONAL COTTON COUNCIL

A nightdress that can also be used as a summer robe. Made of a soft cotton fabric, it is trimmed with lace, narrow tucks, and beading. The satin ribbon bow adds another feminine touch.

113

For only a few pennies, it pays to have on hand a small, attractive hat, a pair of short white gloves, a single strand of beads with matching button earrings, and a few colorful scarfs. These accessories can be used with so many outfits they are almost basic in the wardrobe of a well-dressed woman.

Undergarments. Under it all, undergarments. But just because they are underneath does not mean they are not as important as clothing seen by all. Every girl needs bras, panties, slips, or petticoats. Almost every girl needs a girdle. Young men need shorts and undershirts. If you wear a white uniform at work, you will need white undergarments even if you prefer colors for other occasions. Pay special attention to what you wear under summer clothes made of thin fabrics. Bright undershorts seen under light pants detract from the appearance. The same care is needed for sheer dresses.

Travel needs. Weekends, holidays, vacations—it seems as if everyone is going places today. And for happy holidays, clothes must be appropriate as well as good travelers. You will want garments that will pack easily, arrive looking wearable, and that will be suitable for many occasions.

Your first thought for a trip may be to get new clothes but wise travelers find that their present wardrobe is usually suitable with a few additions.

A tie is a very important accessory for a man. It can add the right note of color or make an old suit appear new. Fashion calls for thin ties one year, wide ties other years. However, you can always find colors and patterns that will do the most for your appearance. Which width is in style now?

A scarf of brilliant colors, or interesting subtle effects worn with a flourish creates the effect of a new costume.

Your present clothes will look new to others who have not seen them and they will be more comfortable than brand new ones, especially shoes and girdles. Travel can also age clothes quickly, new things soon look worn.

A good rule for all travelers is to travel light with a small range of clothes that blend together with one set of accessories. One of your dresses may be perfect for traveling but if it requires another set of shoes, purse, and hat because of its color, you would be wise to leave it at home. Most travelers today have to care for their own clothes along the way so take things that wash and dry quickly —packing a wet wool sweater is no fun. Even with travel irons that work on various currents, it is better to be able to wear a dress that needs no ironing or just a quick steaming from the shower. Small prints, checks, and tweeds are wonderful for hiding the soil and wrinkles of travel life.

A purse is a necessity but be sure it can be easily carried, fastens securely, and is large enough for your necessities, but not too heavy.

Plane travel is common today whether you are going across the ocean or to the next large city. In either case, your baggage will be limited, either by weight or size. You will want to wear something that "sits" well so you can be comfortable while you relax and perhaps nap a little. Some skirt fullness is wise so you won't have to keep tugging at your skirt to keep it down. Choose a sweater or blouse that goes over your skirt rather than one that tucks in. After a few hours of sitting, your waist may feel as if it has gained a few inches so keep it unconfined. And remember, what tucks in can slide out—true of scarfs as well as blouses.

GENERAL ELECTRIC

A portable steam and dry iron is handy to have when traveling—this model has adaptors so the plug will fit most foreign electrical outlets. But, be sure to take the water reservoir off before packing!

These travelers are smartly dressed. Notice the lady's suit. It is made of textured fabric which resists wrinkles and stays clean looking. Loose jewelry—sometimes a nuisance when traveling—is not needed with this overblouse which matches the suit lapels.

PAN AMERICAN AIRWAYS

115

All unnecessary, extra pieces should be avoided. A loose sweater or jacket is essential to allow for temperature variations en route. Never wear new shoes on a trip as your feet are apt to swell from sitting and much walking while sightseeing. It is wise to take a pair of soft slippers along in your tote bag and slip them on while sitting. If you wear a girdle, wear your oldest on the plane—you'll feel a lot better.

Plane trips are so short nowadays that there is seldom time to change into something else before landing. Anyway, lavatory space is shared with many others so it is wise to wear clothing that will look fresh when de-planeing.

Ship travel allows for more luggage but there is still the problem of handling it on arrival and while en route. Casual clothes during the day are the rule, slacks and shorts for active sports, but dresses for meals. Evening meals may be very dressy and there are usually parties almost every night. Low-heeled shoes take the rolling that even huge liners experience so carry sneakers or loafers for daily wear. A warm sweater or coat is a necessity for ocean breezes. Few ships have laundry facilities so expect to wash and dry your clothes in your wash basin.

Train or bus travel also requires something "sit-able" and a warm wrap easily available as the air conditioning can be unpredictable. If you spend the night in reclining chairs, you may prefer pants and a top of a crease-

---

Suggested Basic Travel Wardrobe for a Woman
(How would you change this list for a man?)

1 coat suitable for the season of travel (a wrinkle-resistant all-weather coat with a detachable lining is a good choice)

1 suit with some skirt fullness

1 or 2 basic dresses with matching jacket or pants suit

1 or 2 dressy frocks

1 skirt or tailored pants

2 or 3 tops

1 sweater set or cardigan

1 pair of shorts for resort wear (not to be worn in cities)

2 nightgowns or pajamas

1 robe (a combination dressing-beach robe is handy)

2 slips, 2 bras, 6 pairs of panties, 1 or 2 girdles

6 pair hosiery (and socks, if worn for sports)

3 pair shoes (walking, dress-up, and sneakers—all broken in)

1 head scarf or small foldable hat for church visits

2 bathing suits (if swimming available)

1 travel purse

1 smaller dressy bag

6 handkerchiefs or a supply of tissues

1 pair of slippers

• And don't forget:

Sun glasses, facial tissue, cellophane tape, shower cap, cosmetics, rain boots and scarf, jewelry, small cakes of soap, detergent in plastic bag, small clothes line, sewing kit, pocket flashlight, first aid kit, extra head scarfs or bands for windy weather, gloves, scissors, and extra shoelaces.

• Be sure to put your name inside your luggage and carry an extra set of keys with you.

resistant fabric. Train sleeping accommodations today usually have private lavatory facilities so that you can change to nightwear for sleeping and arrive looking rested and well-groomed.

Automobile travel is the most common method of transportation today and yet few people give thought to what to wear when going by car. Tight pants and shorts may be comfortable when riding but may not be acceptable in some restaurants or on some sightseeing trips. Girls often find it convenient to have a skirt available to put on over the shorts, if needed. While comfort is important when traveling, plan to arrive at your destination dressed presentably, especially if you are going to a sophisticated metropolitan area.

Of course, your clothing needs will differ if you are taking a class trip to Washington, D. C., or a motor trip with your family to visit relatives, or

an air trip to Europe. However, this difference will not be as much as you might expect. A smart traveler limits luggage; even a long-tripper finds it wise to travel with a minimum wardrobe. The list at bottom of previous page has been compiled from suggestions made by several travel concerns and is a guide you can use to make your own personal plans.

Packing is almost as important as selecting the clothes you take for traveling. There are so many interesting types of luggage available that one needs to do some serious thinking before buying any. Many experienced travelers find that a 26″ pullman or wardrobe case with one piece of hand luggage such as a tote bag will take them anyplace.

Everyone has a favorite way of packing but a few pointers may help you.

- Be sure all clothes are clean before packing.

Luggage is part of a travel wardrobe as the condition of one's clothing depends upon the manner in which it is carried. Sizes and shapes of bags vary as seen by those in this grouping. Some travelers prefer a wardrobe case with hangers and partitions; other prefer the pullman model which allows for greater flexibility. The 26 inch size is a good choice when buying only one suitcase; however, the 24 inch may be large enough if your trips are of short duration.

LADY BALTIMORE FASHION LUGGAGE

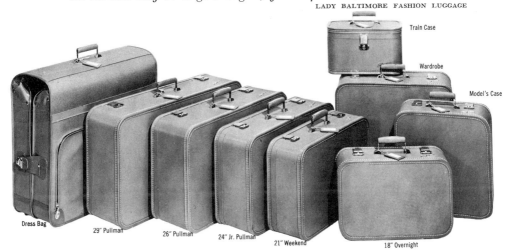

Train Case
Wardrobe
Model's Case
Dress Bag
29″ Pullman
26″ Pullman
24″ Jr. Pullman
21″ Weekend
18″ Overnight

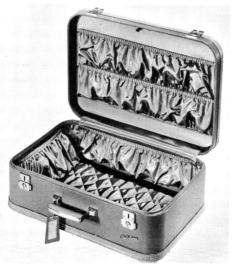

LADY BALTIMORE FASHION LUGGAGE

Interior of 26 inch pullman type suitcase. Notice the pockets in the lid and along the sides for storage of small items.

LADY BALTIMORE FASHION LUGGAGE

Wardrobe case.

- Tighten tops of all liquid containers and place in waterproof bags. It's best to place them in the bag you carry with you as one spilled or broken bottle in your suitcase can ruin an entire trip.
- Shoes need to be wrapped in tissue or placed in shoe bags that can be bought or easily made. Stuff them with hosiery and soft items to help keep their shape and to save space.
- A regular suitcase is best packed with hard and bulky items *on the bottom*. Over this, place a piece of cardboard cut to fit the case. This provides a firm base for soft items and can be lifted out of the case to provide access to bottom items without disturbing clothes on top. Place clothing folded carefully on top of this.
- Lingerie, scarfs, and stockings can be rolled and placed in corners. Clear plastic bags are good protectors for them.
- Always button jackets and close zippers when folding garments.

SAMSONITE

One way of packing clothing into small or large bags is the layer principle. Large garments are folded neatly and placed in alternating direction across the bottom with excess length overhanging the suitcase. Soft articles are placed on top and then the extended sections are folded over these articles. When done carefully, this method results in very few wrinkles as the folds are well cushioned.

118

Secure suggestions of teachers, parents, and students about suitable clothes for school. Can you explain any differences of opinion?

Select an occasion which has special meaning for many class members. Are you going on a senior trip to a large city? Or do you have a special picnic or party that highlights the end of the school year? Plan a suitable wardrobe for the occasion. NOTE: A display in the school exhibit case may be of interest to other students.

What various sports activities are enjoyed by class members? Collect pictures of clothing suitable for each and arrange them on the tack board. Arrange to talk with people who are very skilled in each activity and include clothing suggestions given by them.

Pretend you are going on a trip to one of these places for a weekend: a large city, the country, a small town, the beach, a camp. List the things you will probably be doing and describe the clothing you should plan to wear for each occasion.

Plan a bulletin board showing how Miss or Mr. Right and Miss or Mr. Wrong would dress for the following activities: church, a prom, office work, participation in a school assembly, shopping, housework.

Talk with people who have recently moved to your community from other parts of the country. Find out how clothing patterns differ. Report to the class on regional differences.

Interview an employment officer of an organization which employs high school students for part-time or summer work. Ask about clothing recommended for such workers. Report to the class.

Form committees to find pictures of clothes that would be appropriate for students your age to wear to church, football games, proms, local shopping, big-city shopping, a picnic.

Talk with elderly persons to find out what was worn in the cold weather when they were young. What was worn at the beach? Ask about favorite party clothes. Report your findings to class and compare with choices for wear today.

Plan a basic wardrobe for a young mother at home, a college student, a young secretary, a student nurse. In what ways are they alike? How do they differ? Do the same for a young businessman and a college student. Compare.

TAKE AN INVENTORY OF WHAT YOU HAVE

After you have considered your needs, and completed a chart similar to the one on page 98, you are probably eager to shop for what you need, but *stop*. Unless you can afford to throw away all your clothes (who can?) you will want to consider what you have that is suitable and usable. Only then can you plan wisely so that new clothes will fit in with what you already have.

Do you think you know what clothes you own? You may be surprised to discover clothing items you forgot you had—at the back of the closet or in the bottom of your bureau drawers or even on a hanger under another dress.

It takes time to make an inventory or listing of your clothes, so pick a day when you don't have too much to do. Empty all items out of your closet and your bureau drawers. (Now is a good time, also, to clean the closet.) Place them neatly on your bed or a table. Is there anything at the cleaners or in the laundry that should be considered? Items that are good but suitable for another season should be stored elsewhere or put back in dust-proof bags.

Now you are ready to list the clothes you have. Try on each garment if you haven't worn it recently and ask yourself these questions:

- Is it attractive in itself and becoming to me?
- Is it in good repair and clean?
- Is it in style?
- Does it fit well?
- Will it be suitable for at least one of my activities?

If you can answer "yes," place it back where it belongs and enter it on your inventory chart. Describe its style, color, and fabric. The form on page 121 may be helpful.

You probably have a pile of clothing left over. Some things are good but need repair, cleaning, or simple alteration such as a hemline change to make them wearable. Check for loose buttons, split seams, torn hems, and other minor repairs. Enter these on your inventory list but put a check mark before them so you will know they are not yet serviceable. If you have a sewing kit and ironing board in your room now, you may be able to alter or repair certain garments immediately. Plan to set aside time to get other garments into service as soon as possible.

What will you do with the clothes

still left over? Some can be creatively remade in the latest style. It's amazing what a change in sleeve length can do. A smart jumper can be made by removing the sleeves and collar of a dress. If the color is not attractive, will different accessories help? A white collar or attractive scarf at the neckline can make almost any color tolerable.

Many garments are still usable but the colors are not what you desire or they are faded and sad-looking. Why not experiment with tinting and dyeing such garments? There are several dyes available which are easy to use and quite effective if the instructions are followed. Some can be used in the washing machine. Lingerie, scarfs, and many accessories can be perked up or made to appear entirely new through the use of modern dyes. Remember your knowledge of fibers and the correct dye because not all fibers dye the same. Use your knowledge of colors. You may achieve a lovely effect by "over dying," dipping an article already colored into another color. Consider the effect of a soft blue dye or a clear green on a yellow and white scarf.

Hints for good results with modern dyes

- Material should not be crowded in the dyebath. Use a container large enough so the article is not crowded, and do not dye too many bulky items in the washer at one time. If the article is crowded, it is impossible for the dye to penetrate evenly to all parts of the material, which results in uneven color.
- Before dyeing, remove stains and wash thoroughly. If likely to shrink, trace outline of garment, or meas-

CLOTHING INVENTORY

NOTE: When you list an item, describe it as to color, style,
and occasions for which it can best be worn.

COATS	DRESS OR SUIT	SKIRTS OR PANTS	SHIRTS OR BLOUSES
1 gray fleece 1 plastic rain coat		2 pr. jeans, 1 old, 1 new	1 yellow jersey turtle neck

SWEATER OR JACKET	SHOES	UNDERCLOTHING	ACCESSORIES
1 brown plaid sports jacket (old but usable)	1 pr. brown loafers 1 pr. black boots		1 dark plaid wool scarf 1 pr. warm black gloves

(Notice how a high school student has started to complete the form.)

ure it before washing, so article can be adjusted to tracing or measurements after dyeing.

• It is very important that the article is stirred or kept in motion the entire time it is in the dyebath. Otherwise, uneven coloring will result. This is why the washer helps!

• Dye only washable garments or articles. Items for which "dryclean only" is recommended should not be dyed, washed, or immersed in any water solution because of probable damage to the finish on the material or damage to the tailoring, fashioning, or construction.

• Dark colors require more dye than light colors, so for best results when dyeing very dark colors, double the quantity of dye.

Despite your most creative imagination, there will be some items remaining that you have outgrown, worn out, or that you dislike. In some homes items stored in the attic remain there for many years not used

Bring to class a garment that is "perfectly good" but one you never wear. Discuss the reasons for your failure to wear it. Compile a list of the reasons given by all class members for failure to wear a "good" garment. What rules can you use to prevent such a buying problem in the future? Have other class members suggest their ideas for creative remodeling or remaking so the garments will be wearable.

Survey your community to find organizations that will welcome donations of used but wearable clothing. Be sure to find out if they accept all types of clothing or prefer those for certain age groups.

Have each student bring to class one clothing item that is a "favorite" —something that is worn often with great pleasure. Be prepared to tell why it is a good member of your wardrobe.

Compile a list of repairs and alterations needed for clothing belonging to class members. This will probably include changing hem lengths, sewing on buttons, making simple mends, and restitching seams that have become loose. Select one item and prepare a demonstration for the class. Refer to Chapter Seven for helpful directions.

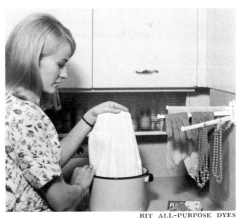

RIT ALL-PURPOSE DYES

One way to stretch your budget is to "make-over" old items by freshening or changing their colors. Gloves, scarfs, blouses, and even some jewelry can be transformed into new ones by tinting with all-purpose dyes.

by anyone. In other homes such material finds its way into hooked rugs, remodeled projects, or other uses. Which home is yours? Before you store away clothing you can't use, consider that there may be others who can find use for it right now.

It may not be an easy task to study your discards but it can be an educational one. Many clothes are simply outgrown, as expected, or have served their time, but were others unwise purchases? Did you find that you bought something and had no occasion to wear it or that it was poorly made and did not allow for normal growth? Study of discards can help make you a better shopper in the future.

CONSIDER YOUR NEEDS

Now, and only now, are you ready to consider what additional clothes you need for the coming season. Sit down with the list of your activities and with your clothing inventory. Prepare a Wardrobe Plan chart like the one on page 124, or perhaps you prefer that pictured on this page.

After each activity listed, select items from the inventory list that can be worn together and that are suitable for the activity. Jot them down in the crosswise spaces of the chart. Cross off the items from the inventory list as you transfer them to your wardrobe plan sheet. Some will be used for more than one activity.

Now write in items that you actually *need*, to complete outfits for your activities. Circle them so that you can easily see your needs and wants.

If you are like most students, you will add many circled items. Look at these carefully and see if you can plan one item to serve two purposes. Perhaps one coat with a water-repellent finish and a zip-out lining can serve for both rain and cold weather wear. Instead of a maroon sweater to match maroon pants and a blue sweater for blue pants, find another color to harmonize with both outfits. It may seem wonderful to have many clothes but well-dressed individuals find it easier and less confusing to have a compact wardrobe with each item well chosen and in harmony with the others.

When planning your wardrobe, try to obtain small swatches of the fabrics of your present clothes. You will find it easier to plan for harmonizing colors and textures. (Most garments have seams wide enough to permit snipping a small piece for such a purpose.)

CRESLAN ACRYLIC FIBER

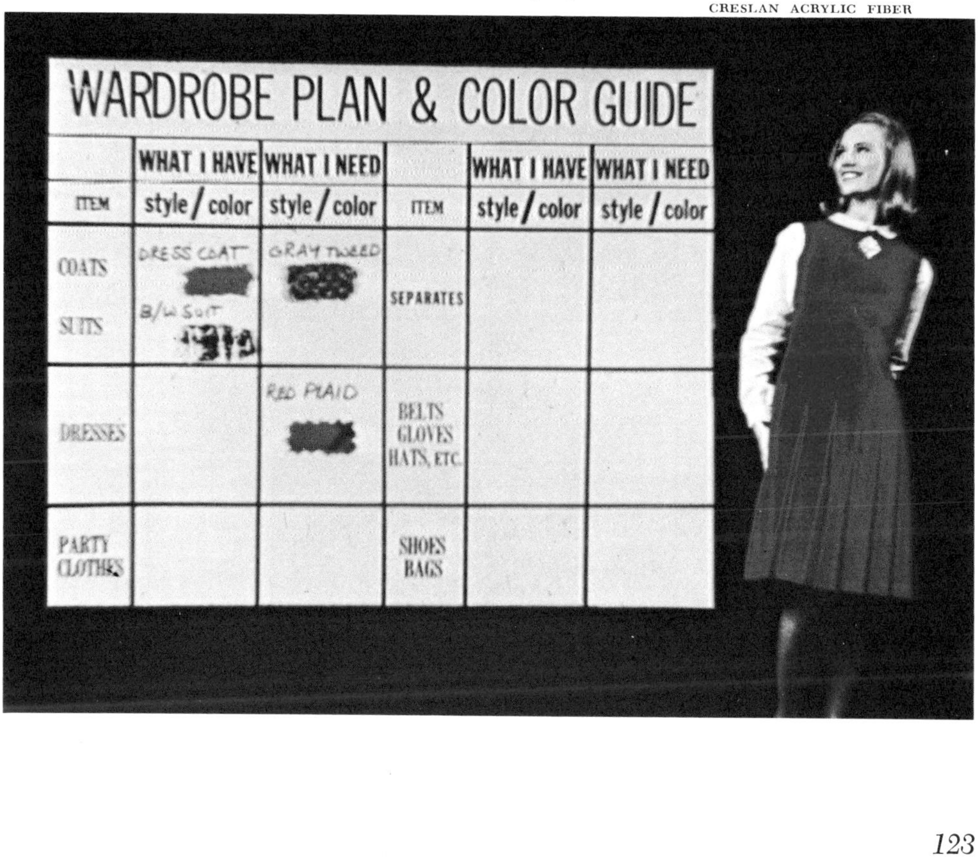

123

MY WARDROBE PLAN FOR ——— SEASON

ACTIVITY (list only those that apply to you)	TYPE OF CLOTHING NEEDED							
	Coats	Dresses or Suits	Skirts or Slacks	Blouses or Shirts	Sweaters or Jackets	Shoes	Underclothing	Accessories
School								
Job								
Church, Special Events								
Parties and Social Gatherings								
Sports and Other Leisure Time Activities								
After School, At Home and Shopping								
Sleeping and Lounging								
Winter Extras								
Summer Extras								
Travel								

- In the left-hand column list those activities you decided need special clothing, as for the chart on page 98.
- After each activity, select items from your inventory list to which can be worn together and jot them down on the same horizontal line of the chart.
- Try several combinations of clothes in order to make outfits that appear different.
- Cross items off the inventory list as you transfer them to the wearing guide.
- Fill in items on the wearing guide which you need in order to complete an outfit. Circle these items.

Before you decide you need a new clothing item, ask yourself these questions:

- Does it fill a need?
- Will it do "something for me" or will it just "do"?
- Will it go with the clothes I now have?
- Will it serve for several occasions or is it very important to me even if of limited use?
- What additional accessories must I purchase to go with it?
- Can I afford it? Is it worth the price to me?
- Will it be worth the upkeep needed?
- How long will it last as far as fashion is concerned?
- Is it a "spur-of-the-moment" idea or is it going to be a "joy" because it is part of a wardrobe plan?

MARY O. BRADFORD H. S., KENOSHA, WISCONSIN
Senior high school girls planning their spring wardrobes.

Consider your color plan. In planning a color scheme for a wardrobe, each costume may have a color pattern of its own but some must also be related to other clothing. In this way your coat from last season will fit into this season's plans without clashing with a recently purchased dress. If you have planned well, separates can be combined in many ways, and accessories will blend.

It is wise to select a basic color, such as blue, brown, or black, and build around it. If your outfits are all bright colors, then you should consider dark or neutral colors for accessories. But if you prefer plain colors for your clothes, you can use bright accessories.

A coat is often the first consideration in color planning a wardrobe as it has to go with so many other items. A coat doesn't have to be a neutral color. Would you love a red coat? Go ahead, but key the rest of the clothes to it. Remember, a bright red coat is lovely over most neutrals and perhaps many bright colors, but it would fight with a magenta red dress or some bright greens. A plaid coat can be distinctive and will go nicely with many colors but, if you like plaids, dots, and floral prints for dresses and skirts, it may not be a good choice.

The *seasons* also have to be considered in planning the color of a coat. A rust or red-brown coat may be lovely in the fall but will it look as suitable on cool spring days? What colors would be suitable for both fall and spring wear? Keep this question in mind. Even in warm climates, we tend to have too many seasonal clothes that are really unnecessary.

Coordinates . . . notice how the skirt, jumper, slacks, blouse, and sweater are interchangeable. How many different outfits can be made from these five clothing articles?

This young family works out its spending plan together. The adults are discussing their clothing needs as well as those of their child. When the child is older, should he have an opportunity to help the family decide which clothing needs take priority?

126

Is your present wardrobe a hodge-podge of colors? Do you find yourself changing purses often to match your clothes or keeping your coat buttoned so it won't clash with what is underneath? Or do you find yourself buying a "different" item and then having to buy other things to go with it? Now is a good time to get yourself out of this mess! It may take a season or so, but plan your purchases carefully so your things will fit in with a master color plan, and so that one-color accessories, at least for the fall and winter seasons, will be attractive with all your clothes.

Look back over your wardrobe plan and see if you can consolidate your needs or change them so that colors will all harmonize together. Of course, if everything matches, you may have an uninteresting wardrobe. However, the colors need to blend, not clash.

Textures and styles also need to harmonize. A beige silk crepe shirt may look lovely with brown but would you want to wear it with brown slacks to a picnic? A variety of textures can be combined but some textures are identified with sportswear and others seem more dressy. You may wish to change a few of the listed needs in your wardrobe plan. Will calf shoes serve more needs than suede shoes? Will a satin blouse be as usable as one of broadcloth?

PLAN YOUR PURCHASES BASED ON MONEY AVAILABLE

Now that you have given serious thought to your wardrobe needs for the coming season, you are ready to make another list of the items needed. Make a chart like that on page 124 and transfer all the circled items from your wardrobe plan to it. Before setting out to buy anything, estimate the costs by studying catalogs, advertising, and by window-shopping.

Written plans may seem a bother but they gradually help you to plan "in your head," and develop skill in wardrobe building.

- Is the estimated total what you expected?
- Can you afford it this season?
- Do some items seem to call for more than their share of money? Perhaps you can delay some purchases until later in the year.

You probably do not have as much money as you would like; few girls do. If you study how to plan clothing purchases it can help to get more of what you need with the money available to you. In other words, a spending plan does not provide you with any more money but it does help you shop within your clothing allotment and plan your purchases wisely so that you will be able to get that which is most important to you.

What others do. Sometimes it helps to know what the average family in this country spends for clothing. Recent studies of the U. S. Bureau of Labor Statistics indicate that most families spend 10.4 percent of their income after taxes on clothing and clothing care. Families in higher income brackets may spend up to 12.3 percent and those with less money spend a smaller amount. The greatest amount of family money is spent for housing. Food takes as much as automobile purchases and upkeep in some homes, and clothing expenditures rank fourth.

Who do you suppose spends the largest part of the family clothing outlay? Yes, the teen girl.

Some families buy clothing items as they need or want them and never give a thought to an overall plan. Others work out a total family budget together and give consideration to spacing major purchases so that each family member does not need to buy a new coat or other expensive item the same year.

How much money should you have for clothing? It depends upon many things. Total family income, the number of family members, other things needed, unusual expenses such as illness, and the values of your family all affect what you will spend for clothing. Some families feel that clothing is very important, while others prefer to use more of their money for better housing, for education, for travel, or other needs. You want to be fair and not take more than your family share. If you feel you must have more clothes than you can manage with your share of money, you can find ways of getting them. A part-time job brings in more income but good care of present clothes can also make money available for other items.

CAN YOU SAVE MONEY BY SEWING?

Can you really save money by making your clothes? It all depends upon you, your skills, and your needs. Many people sew today simply for the fun and enjoyment of it, for the satisfaction of creating a useful and attractive garment, or because they have some special figure problem that makes it difficult to buy clothing.

However, many smart women do save a great deal of money by sewing. Once you have learned to sew with some skill, you should be able to make most garments for half the cost of ready-mades.

A study made by the specialists at the U. S. Department of Agriculture reported that money can be saved by home sewing. The money savings were greater for children's dresses than for simple house frocks and still larger for cotton daytime dresses. More money was saved for festive occasion gowns and for tailored garments. Most garments were made for half of the ready-to-wear cost but savings for home sewing increase with the retail price of the garment. This conclusion is supported by market research showing that labor costs take a larger share of the total manufacturing cost of high-priced rather than low-priced clothing.

In terms of time spent, the money savings were still worthwhile for day-

Making one's own suits can save a great deal of money if one has the necessary skill and enjoys the experience. This suit with matching blouse was made by a 4-H member for much less than the cost of a similar ready-made suit.

MASSACHUSETTS 4-H

time dresses made by skilled sewers. Though the money savings per hours spent were less for lower priced garments, they are probably sufficient to induce homemakers who enjoy sewing to use time for such a purpose. Busy homemakers with little skill in sewing might question their use of time for home sewing.

If you are a canny shopper for fabrics, you can save more, and you may also be able to save by making deeper hems on your clothes so they can be worn longer and by using good quality buttons, zippers, and other items that wear well.

Items such as underclothes and swimsuits can be made easily from the wide assortment of fabrics—sheer to heavy weight—available to the home sewer.

Basic blouses can usually be bought for little more than it costs to make them at home. However, skirts, housecoats, summer dresses, and party frocks can often be made for a fraction of the cost to buy. What about suits and coats? These take skill and time but if you have learned to sew well and enjoy this activity, you will find that you can save a great deal of money with tailoring skills.

Sewing, as said before, can also save you money in repairs and minor alterations so that you can wear your clothes longer. Often an old garment can be given fresh appeal with very little cost and work if you have skill and creative imagination.

You Can Save Money Sewing If You:

- Enjoy creative work.
- Use your ability to learn.
- Have necessary sewing equipment.
- Have time available.

MISSISSIPPI 4-H CLUBS

Individual styling details, usually found only in expensive ready-to-wear garments, can be added at little or no cost to garments you make yourself. This 4-H member made her jacket lining reversible for variety and style.

- Can be a smart shopper for fabrics.
- Have special fitting problems which require a lot of alterations of ready-made clothes.
- Want individual styling, special fabrics, or extra finishing touches.

Impulse Buying

Now that you have a plan, be wary of impulse buying. One splurge can ruin your whole plan. A certain green sweater can be a wonderful "bargain" but what if you have to buy a new skirt to go with it or, if you already have enough sweaters, will you be able to afford other things you must have? Sometimes you can get just what you want at an unexpected moment, but this seemingly lucky purchase is usually the result of having thought out your needs and knowing that this item will fit into your total plan.

A WORD ABOUT FADS

Of course you enjoy the latest fads as most high school students do.

Fads are fun for a short time, but in a very little while they may become boring and out-of-date. So use your fad money for accessories and other inexpensive items only—things that can be replaced easily. Coats, suits, and skirts are better bought in styles that will last through several seasons. A classic skirt and cardigan set will

---

Divide the class into groups of four students each. Select a picture of a basic jacket that is suitable for a high school student. Find pictures of various accessories that can change its appearance and make it wearable for many occasions. Perhaps you can make a display on the tack board.

Act out these situations and discuss several solutions to each problem.

- *A girl asks for money to buy a new dress. Her father says she cannot have it.*
- *A young man wants a new jacket and his younger brother needs a new coat.*
- *A high school girl wants a new dress for a party and her mother says she has a dress that is perfectly good and she should wear it.*

What is the latest, most popular clothing fad? What is the cost of a typical item? How long do you estimate its popularity?

Describe a typical family in your community. Determine the clothing needs and problems of each member. Make a circle chart to represent the entire clothing dollar. Proportion the circle according to the clothing share of each individual in your typical family. How did you arrive at the amounts?

Arrange to have a buyer or fashion coordinator from a local clothing store come to class to speak on selecting a well-coordinated wardrobe.

Plan mix-and-match separates by bringing in actual garments or pictures to show how a few articles can add up to many outfits. How many different outfits can be made from two skirts, two blouses, and two sweaters which harmonize?

Compare the cost of the ready-made garment with one that you (or someone else) has made in clothing class. Consider the quality of the garment, needed alterations and other features which may differ.

What is the average family income in your community after taxes? (You can often get an estimate from the city hall.) If families spend 10.4 percent of this on clothing, how much money do they have available a year for clothing? What part of this do you feel the high school student should have as a share? If there are two children in the family, how will this differ?

Divide into groups of four to six to discuss the following: A girl in your school loses all of her clothing in a fire. How much money is the minimum she needs for a basic wardrobe? Will this differ for a boy? List major clothing items and estimate costs. Compare your results with those from other groups.

look wonderful for years and, with the latest accessories, will stay as up-to-date as a fancy or oddly cut fad that is soon discarded.

BUYING

Chapter Five has suggestions for buying which is the next step after planning to achieve the total wardrobe that will do the most for you.

Having your photo taken? Of course you won't buy a special wardrobe just for this occasion but it is important to select suitable clothing. A natural look is the most important. For example, it is not a good idea to experiment with a new hairdo the day before you have your picture taken. If you feel uncomfortable, it may be revealed in your portrait. So wear something comfortable and flattering. Some studios have dressing rooms so you can change there into something fresh—or if you are not sure, take along a few selections and ask the photographer's advice.

Avoid all prints and frills that attract away from your face. Bare arms tend to photograph heavier than they are so sleeves may be more flattering. Select basic necklines that will not become outdated too soon. Stark black may be too harsh against many light skins. A plain white blouse is often the best choice. Jewelry may be worn but choose simple pieces which will not attract attention nor date the picture too soon.

If you wear make-up, use it as usual but with a lighter touch. Lipstick should be a medium tone. Accentuate your eyes with a little mascara on the upper lashes if you wish, but avoid eye shadow unless you want the appearance of two black eyes. Foundation make-up with a light touch of powder is good but leave off a blusher—it will look like shadows.

Glasses. Yes, if you usually wear them. Without them you will not look like yourself. And when the proofs come back, try looking at them in a mirror. That is the way you look to yourself and you can determine more easily the most natural looking photo.

Summary with Check-Up Questions

A well-planned wardrobe is a thoughtful collection of flattering garments and accessories needed to keep you suitably dressed for all usual occasions at a cost you can afford.

- *Why is a wardrobe of haphazardly selected garments that do not blend with each other, even if each one is lovely by itself, not considered a well-planned wardrobe?*
- *Is a wardrobe well-planned if your clothes are attractive for you but not really appropriate for your activities?*

Planning ahead for your clothing needs helps assure that you have the clothes you need and want at a cost within your budget.

- *What will be the effect of an impulsively bought expensive sweater on the total wardrobe of a typical high school girl?*
- *If you are aware of the need for a new garment some time before actually needed, why will you probably make a better selection than if you must make a hurried purchase?*

- *What is likely to be the result of buying clothing piece-meal, that is, a skirt today, a pretty blouse of the latest style another day, and adorable shoes "on sale" without giving thought to how each item will blend with others you already own?*

A suitable wardrobe is a personal matter; it must be planned for your very own wants and needs and based on the activities in which you engage.

- *How will a wardrobe of a girl who is very interested in winter sports differ from one who prefers indoor crafts and music?*
- *What will be the difference between the wardrobe of a student who goes to school in the city in the southwest from one who lives in Florida? How will their wardrobes differ from that of one who lives in a rural northern area?*
- *How will the wardrobe of a girl who "adores" pretty clothes differ from that of the girl who cares little about clothes except for being suitably dressed?*
- *How will the wardrobe of a high school student who works after school and Saturdays on a job where a uniform is provided differ from one who works as a sales clerk in a store?*

Future plans can affect your present wardrobe planning.

- *What effect will the knowledge that you are moving to another climate next year have on many of your clothing purchases this year?*
- *Will a senior high school student make a different choice of an everyday winter coat if she knows she will attend college next year, than if she knows she will work in an office in a city?*

After deciding your clothing needs, it is necessary to take an inventory of your present wardrobe before making any additional purchases.

- *What types of clothing can be worn for several seasons?*
- *How can "tired looking" garments or articles be made to look new?*
- *In what way can giving away useless garments help your present wardrobe?*

Is it more sensible to spend a lot of money for an everyday purse than for one used for dress wear?

- *Which purse will get the most wear, and so should be durable, to remain nice looking?*
- *Which purse will go out of style first, possibly before showing signs of wear?*

Getting ahead in one's job is helped by dressing suitably.

- *Who will probably be promoted first, a person who is always well dressed or one who appears dowdy, even though each is of similar ability?*
- *For what types of work is clean, appropriate clothing absolutely essential?*

Dual or multi-purpose garments are a wise selection whenever possible. A large wardrobe is cumbersome, hard to store and care for, and may limit purchases of new styles because one already has too many items too good to discard.

- *What type of coats can serve many purposes?*
- *Suggest shoe styles that can be used only for one activity and others that serve many needs.*
- *When is it wise to buy an article that can be worn for only one purpose or occasion?*

Undergarments are as important in a wardrobe as outer garments.

- *How will a sheer top appear if worn over an old, frayed undergarment?*

- *What effect will an improperly fitted girdle (or none) have on a close-fitting garment?*
- *Does it matter how carefully you selected a skirt if it is worn over a slip or pettislip that bunches and sags?*

Sports activities require clothes that are suitable for the physical activity involved as well as the weather.

- *How will clothing worn for roller skating differ from that needed for ice skating out-of-doors? In what ways will they be alike?*
- *How will clothing suitable for bowling differ from that worn for tennis or playing golf? Why?*

After comparing your clothing needs with your clothing inventory, you are ready to plan the additional clothing needed so that your wardrobe will suit your needs.

- *Why will your first list of needs and wants probably be longer than your final shopping guide?*
- *Why should the colors and textures of new articles blend with some of your present clothing?*
- *Why is it a common mistake for girls to buy too many clothes for one purpose and have nothing suitable for other occasions?*

Sometimes it pays to sew, sometimes it doesn't.

- *What types of garments can be easily made by girls who know how to sew and enjoy it?*
- *Unless one is very skilled or enjoys challenging activities, some types of garments are better bought. Which are they and why?*
- *Why is it possible to make many garments for less money than to buy them ready-made?*

Each member of the family must be considered when planning the clothing budget.

- *Why is it seldom fair to divide the family money available for clothing into even shares for each member?*
- *Why do some families spend a larger share of their income on clothing than other families?*
- *Why do some families try to stagger the purchase of large items as coats and suits so that two or more members do not need to buy them at the same time?*

Various moods can be created by using different accessories with the same garment. Accessories need to be coordinated to produce harmonious costumes.

- *Black accessories seem to be a wise choice for a red and black plaid dress. However, what will be the effect if the shoes are black suede, the purse is of a shiny patent, and the belt is a smooth calfskin?*
- *What will be the mood created by wearing a simple pearl necklace and navy suede shoes with a navy piqué dress? How will it differ if the same dress is worn with red sandals and a scarf of red, yellow, and white tucked in at the neck?*

Being able to plan a wardrobe that is suitable for one's needs and wants takes time and effort and often mistakes are made as one is learning.

- *What mistakes will you try to avoid as a result of your study about wardrobe planning?*

Can You Explain These Terms?

wardrobe inventory
wardrobe plan

Shopping Wisely
and Well

PLANNING what you need for your wardrobe is only part of dressing well. Shopping is equally important.

In order to shop wisely and well, you will need to know what stores carry the type of clothing you want, how to compare price and quality, when to buy, how to make a decision, and how to pay for the articles bought. You must be a super shopper to narrow down the many choices available today in order to get what you really need and will enjoy. The art of wise shopping is worth learning so you can be better dressed for less money. You will also have the satisfaction of becoming a wise purchasing agent for yourself and your family.

RETAILING

To become a good shopper, you will need to know how retail stores actually operate.

Retail stores buy clothes and other goods from a manufacturer or a wholesaler and sell to individuals. The amount the retailer has to charge for an item is more than he paid for it, of course, as the selling price must include all the overhead costs plus his profit.

Overhead. The difference between the wholesale price and the retail price is called the *markup*. A little of the markup goes for profit but most is used to cover the expenses of the store. Every store must pay for the cost of the building or rent, heat, light, supplies, insurance, delivery, salaries of salespeople and other workers, advertising, displays, telephones, and many other operating expenses. This is spoken of as *overhead*. Losses from shoplifting, losses on unsold merchandise, and damage from improper handling also must be covered by the markup.

Some stores can make a profit with a small markup only because they do not have as many expenses as other stores. Others sell so many items that they, too, can afford a small markup. A store that sells ten coats a day at $10.00 profit each makes no more money than a store that sells 100 coats a day at $1.00 profit each.

Five · Shopping Wisely and Well

Therefore, one must consider turnover or actual number of sales as well as the overhead or cost of operation. Some stores advertise that they can sell cheaply because they have low rents, but if they are not exposed to large groups of shoppers, they may not sell many items. It may cost them more to exist than a store in an expensive shopping center that is convenient to shoppers.

Markups vary with different items in a store and with different stores. It is stated in an article in "Changing Times" that a report from the National Retail Merchants Association indicates that large department stores add 100 percent of the wholesale price on misses' coats and suits. This means that if a coat costs a merchant $10.00, he must plan to sell it for $16.75. (Some merchants may call this a 50 percent markup. They prefer to state their markup in terms of selling costs, as it appears lower.)

Before he could shop for this outfit, this young man needed to know what stores carried the types of garments he wanted, how to judge the quality of the articles, how to determine if the price was suitable, and what method to use to pay for them.

High school girls visit a large store for a peek "behind the scenes" to learn how retailing works. Can you help arrange such a trip?

Women's shoes average a higher markup, about 77.6 percent, but the markup for boys' clothing is lower, about 61 percent. This is probably because boys' clothing is more stable in style, and it is seldom necessary to clear out-of-style items.

Basement stores and self-service discount houses may not mark up their selling prices as much (often 20 percent of the price you pay), because they have lower expenses. But, as mentioned before, if their location results in a low turnover of items, they may need as high a markup as other stores in order to continue in business.

(Confused? Markup is easy to compute once you know the method. First, determine the difference between the retail price and the wholesale price. To determine the true markup, divide this difference by the wholesale cost. To determine the markup, as usually figured by the retailer, divide the difference by the retail cost.)

What factors affect the price of clothing? The price you pay includes the cost of all the materials used plus the labor cost of production, shipping costs, store expenses, and losses on necessary clearance sales, as well as some profit to all of the people involved.

WHERE DO YOU BUY YOUR CLOTHES?

Where you buy your clothes can make a difference in their cost and quality. Perhaps you have been used to shopping in one local store. It may suit your purposes but a wise shopper knows many sources of clothing and knows when to use each. At how many types of stores do you shop?

A typical suburban branch of a large department store features convenient parking space and attractive landscaping.

In large *department stores,* almost all clothing and household needs are offered. It may be more convenient for you to make all your purchases in one store, even though the price of a garment in a department store must help pay for many services. These stores provide such services as information and complaint desks, rest rooms, check rooms, and delivery. They may also present many interesting fashion shows, educational displays, and special exhibits.

Close-up of the park-like suburban store landscaping. On a warm day a short rest in such a setting should help one be ready for more shopping.

FILENE'S

Large stores may provide the services of a fashion coordinator who will help groups of young people present fashion shows. Here we see a fashion coordinator going over plans for an assembly program on "Tips for Good Dressing and Grooming for Teen Boys."

SEARS, ROEBUCK AND CO.

CARE LABELS FOR HOME SEWING FABRICS

MACHINE WASHABLE FABRICS

 MACHINE WASH WARM

MACHINE WASHABLE FABRICS

 MACHINE WASH WARM
LINE DRY

MACHINE WASHABLE
PERMANENT PRESS

 MACHINE WASH WARM
TUMBLE DRY
REMOVE PROMPTLY

MACHINE WASHABLE
DELICATE FABRICS

 MACHINE WASH WARM
DELICATE CYCLE
TUMBLE DRY LOW
USE COOL IRON

MACHINE WASHABLE FABRICS

 MACHINE WASH WARM
DO NOT DRY CLEAN

ALL HAND WASHABLE FABRICS

 HAND WASH SEPARATELY
USE COOL IRON

DRY CLEANABLE FABRICS

 DRY CLEAN ONLY

PILE FABRICS

 DRY CLEAN PILE FABRIC
METHOD ONLY

VINYL FABRICS

 WIPE WITH DAMP
CLOTH ONLY

*These coded labels, developed for use with over-the-counter fabrics, meet the
Permanent Care Labeling Law of 1972.*

Examples of permanent care labels for ready-made garments.

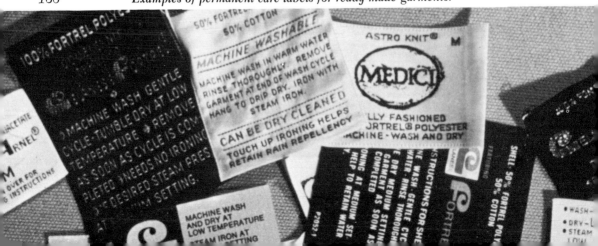

ZOLLINGER-HARNED CO., ALLENTOWN, PA.

Interior of a modern department store. Clothing and other items are displayed so they show off to their best. Lighting is flattering and mirrors are available to help the customer make a wise selection.

Large department stores group clothing items in various ways. Here we see hats and handbags near the coats and suits for which they will be accessories. It helps a shopper to be able to select items which will be worn together at one time.

ZOLLINGER-HARNED CO. ALLENTOWN, PA.

The merchandise carried is usually of medium to high quality, including high fashion items.

Many department stores have branches in smaller communities and in shopping centers. The selection of items may not be so large as in the downtown store, but items may be available on short notice from the main store. Branch stores usually provide convenient parking and shopping hours suited to nearby residents.

Speciality stores sell a limited type of merchandise such as millinery, shoes, or ready-to-wear for men, children, or women only. They may stock a large selection of these particular items. Because these stores are often run by their owners, they can provide many personal services. The cost of clothing may be a little more than in other stores, as the volume of business is smaller but, in return, you may benefit from the personal interest.

Neighborhood stores are provided for the convenience of people in the immediate vicinity. A small independent store may offer a limited selection of articles such as notions, hosiery, dress fabrics, or lingerie. The most important service is convenience to a customer, which makes it possible to shop for minor purchases near home. The extra selling cost may be offset by the time and money saved from travel.

Mail order stores have a large volume of business and few services are involved in their overhead, so they usually can sell the same item for less than a local department store can. Chain discount stores can compete successfully, but in mail-order shopping, one can study the detailed catalog descriptions carefully before buying, and order at home by mail.

Buying by mail may be unsatisfactory because you cannot be sure of the color, quality, or true size of a garment. To compensate, mail-order establishments follow this policy, "Your money back if not satisfied." NOTE: Returns may take considerable time.

You will find it helpful to read mail-order catalog descriptions before shopping even if you plan to purchase locally. This will give you information for comparison shopping.

Variety stores, no longer concerned just with items selling at five and ten cents, are a source for clothing. Merchandise is usually of low price and average quality. This may be fine for items you do not expect to wear long such as beach hats, novelty items, and fad clothes.

Discount houses claim to sell at a discount or lower than the usual retail price. They operate on a smaller profit margin than usual, and their overhead is smaller because they have the self-service system, do not deliver, and generally do not give credit although charge accounts are a feature of a few chains. They carry a limited range of merchandise and expect to sell in large quantities.

Some stores carry only well-known brands, but others carry unbranded items or little known brands and expect to make a larger profit from these as the customer usually has nothing with which to compare prices. For example, when a well-known brand of shirt selling for $5.00 in most stores is offered for $4.00, the customer knows she is getting a "discount." However, a shirt selling for $3.50 may seem to be a better buy, but if it is an unknown brand of poor quality, it may be hard for the shop-

Select a large department store in your community. Keep a record of the special activities they have during the next month. Of what value are they to you? To a homemaker? Visit the main store of a department store and one of its branch stores. In what ways do they differ? When do you think it advisable to travel to the main store and when is the local branch a better source?

Investigate clothing exchanges in your locality. Where do they get the clothes they sell? What is their policy about selling price? Do you see any types of clothes that might be good buys for the average girl?

Comparison shop. Select one item that you can find in many types of stores, such as a man's shirt, a slip, a simple blouse, or a plain skirt. Visit stores of many types to obtain selling prices and information. What conclusions can you draw?

Arrange for a class trip to a department store. Learn how various items are purchased, received, and priced. How are customer complaints handled? What additional services are provided? What are the requirements for a job selling or altering clothing?

Pretend you are planning to go to a discount store or a factory outlet that is ten miles away to buy an item that sells for $10.00 in your own neighborhood. Estimate the cost by automobile or public transportation. What would the garment have to sell for so that your trip would be worthwhile? If you regularly shop at stores some distance from your home, estimate the cost of a trip there and return.

per to determine this until the shirt is worn. When you find a certain brand article selling for less money than the identical one in another type of store, it is a discount.

You can save at discount houses with careful shopping, if you have a good knowledge of quality and current prices of garments available at several types of stores.

Factory outlets can be a good source of clothing if you are an experienced shopper. These stores usually sell merchandise directly from a factory, often overstocked items, slightly imperfects or even seconds. Naturally they can afford to sell such stock at a price lower than usual. NOTE: Some stores call themselves "factory outlets" when in reality they sell poor quality articles or bring in floor samples and older stock from other stores or distributors. If an outlet is a legitimate one for a factory making quality clothes, it can be an excellent source.

Many young people shy away from the idea of used clothing but in many communities *clothing exchanges* and *rummage sales* are economical sources.

Clothing exchanges are often run by charity groups who accept only clean garments in good condition, which they sell at low prices. The previous owner gets a part of the selling cost, often 70 percent, and the remainder goes to run the exchange and for the charity involved. This may be an opportunity to buy party frocks, children's clothes, and even school coats for a fraction of what they cost when new. Also, you may want to sell some clothes that you have outgrown or no longer need at such an exchange.

DEPARTMENT—chain or independent store merchandising a large variety of goods, divided into departments for purchasing, promoting, and selling.

Retail Stores

Business establishments engaged in selling merchandise to consumers.

CHAIN—member of a group of stores with similar goods and policies.

True Chain—owned and operated by one company.

Voluntary Chain—independent stores associated for common buying and promotional activities.

INDEPENDENT—operated by the owner.

SPECIALTY—chain or independent store specializing in a limited type of merchandise, such as children's wear, shoes, women's clothing, hats, men's clothing.

VARIETY—chain or independent store selling a variety of consumer goods usually in a low-price range and with a high amount of self-service and open counter display.

DISCOUNT—chain or independent store selling some known lines of merchandise at consistently low prices.

DIRECT DOOR TO DOOR—selling in the consumer's home.

Non-Store Retailers

A business established to sell goods to consumers on non-store basis.

MAIL-ORDER—selling through orders received and delivered by mail.

VENDING MACHINES—providing goods through a coin-operated machine on a self-service basis.

Clothing Exchanges

Second hand clothing offered for sale; previous owner often retains a major portion of selling price.

USED CLOTHING—sold at low prices, often for benefit of charity group which retains all or part of selling price.

FACILITIES

Advantages	Disadvantages
Many services are usually offered. "One stop" shopping is possible. A wide selection of goods is provided in every price range. Merchandise may be returned.	The size of the store and location of departments may make it difficult to find what you want. Department stores are often located in areas beyond your neighborhood.
There is greater variety within the area of specialty than in general stores. A wide range of prices is available in the specialty items. Salespersons are usually trained and their knowledge of the specialty results in good service and advice.	"One stop" shopping is not possible. Prices may be higher than in larger stores.
Merchandise is openly displayed. Self-service is speedy. The price range is low. Lower quality of clothing.	Salespeople may not be well trained. Shopping traffic may be heavy. Few services are provided.
Parking is convenient. Self-service is speedy. Prices may be lower than other retailers. Stores are usually open for night shopping.	Limited variety of clothing offered. Usually little effort is made to display merchandise attractively. Service is limited. Return privileges are limited. Location may be inconvenient. There are usually few salespeople. Much unbranded merchandise.
Shopping at home is convenient. Often the product is demonstrated for you. Offers the opportunity to see or use items in your home before purchasing them.	There is little opportunity for comparisons of products and price. Investigation of salesmen's qualifications is up to you. Salesmen may come at an inconvenient time. There is limited selection and price range.
Armchair shopping is convenient. Saves time and energy. Return privileges are offered. Prices are usually reasonable. Catalog descriptions are usually accurate and helpful.	There is no opportunity to see and inspect merchandise before buying. You pay the cost of delivery. The time lapse between buying and delivery may be inconvenient.
It is quick and easy. It offers 24 hour service.	There is limited opportunity to inspect products. Machines are impersonal. No returns or services are possible.
Low cost. Chance to receive some money from your own used clothing.	Clothing is used and may show signs of wear. Limited clothing of latest style available. No returns possible.

Adapted from "Money Management, Your Shopping Dollar," Household Finance Corp.

Rummage sales usually last only one day and may not have quality garments. One can get wonderful buys by examining the clothes carefully, especially if you are able to make some alterations. Many wise mothers use this source for children's clothes that are quickly outgrown or for party dresses that are worn only a few times.

Mrs. Smith, a young married secretary, needs the following items for fall wear:
an everyday slip
hosiery for work
a high style dress to wear to a wedding of a friend
shoes and handbag to match
a "good" suit which can be worn to work
slacks for sports wear
a blouse for her suit and a blouse or knit top to wear with her slacks.

Within reasonable shopping distance of her home there are the following types of stores:
a large department store
a "discount" store
a used clothing exchange
a small specialty store for women's shoes
a variety store
several fabric stores
a factory outlet for shoes about 20 miles away.

She also has a charge account at a large mail-order concern. She can sew well and enjoys it. She has a good income but she and her husband are saving for a new house.

After each item listed, suggest where you believe she could best purchase it, or if it should be made. Give reasons for each answer.

GUIDES TO HELP YOU SHOP WISELY AND WELL

Before you go shopping, it pays to know something about the specific things you want as well as about the types of stores in which you may shop. Window shopping and browsing can pay off in a better knowledge of the styles available and the costs of various garments. Before you have done much shopping, you will have learned that advertising, price tags, and the advice of salespersons are not always an adequate or accurate guide to quality. It will be necessary for you to study and do research on your own to be the smart shopper you want to be.

Advertising. Advertising is a source of shopping information that may be either useful and informative or meaningless and indefinite. You can shop more intelligently if you study advertising and learn to recognize helpful information.

Advertising has two purposes—to sell and to inform. The major purpose of the advertiser is to sell, to make his things look so desirable that you must have them whether you need them or not.

You can learn a great deal about styles and materials from ads but you must learn to read them carefully. What do the words mean? If something is *guaranteed*, what does this mean? Who stands behind the guarantee and for what is it guaranteed and for how long? Most TV stations, magazines, and newspapers will not accept advertisements they know are false, but it is up to you to be the judge of the information presented. Learn to read between the lines and to notice the small print as well as the banner headings. Ask others about their experiences before trying every deodorant or beauty soap demonstrated on TV!

Consumer magazines. Giving consumer information is the sole purpose of some magazines. *Consumer Reports* and *Consumer Research* publish monthly magazines which are available from the library and on the newsstands as well as by subscription. "Best buys" in their periodicals may not be suitable for you but you will discover important shopping information by reading them. Some families feel that the information in these magazines more than pays for the yearly subscription.

Women's magazines also provide helpful information on shopping and things to look for on individual clothing items. *Today's Health*, published by the American Medical Association, describes many unnecessary or possibly dangerous cosmetics and other beauty aids.

A little time spent reading about major purchases may save you money by preventing costly mistakes, as well as insuring satisfaction by selecting a product that meets your needs.

Brand names. A brand name can be of help in shopping. If an article of a specific brand has given you good service, you will probably get the same quality again. But brands do change specifications and companies are bought by other manufacturers! New and improved brands come on the market that may be more suitable. Brand loyalty over a period of time without further comparative shopping is unwise.

Labels. Regardless of what an advertisement says about a garment or a fabric, the statements on the label are the important ones. Information provided on labels is usually more exact and regulated by law than that provided by advertisements.

What types of information can you expect to find on a label? Clothing labels may include many of the following: Name of product, manufacturer, guarantee, quantity or size, construction, performance expected in use, brand name, agency approval, quality or grade, selling points, how and where manufactured, and care instructions. (See pages 146–148 for details.)

MACHINE WASHABLE
IN LUKEWARM WATER
DO NOT BLEACH, WRING OR SPIN.
THOROUGH RINSING IMPORTANT.
HOT IRONING RESTORES REPELLENCY

MACHINE WASHABLE
IN LUKEWARM WATER
■ launder under careful commercial or home laundering conditions
■ dry away from heat or sun. If tumble dryer is used, follow the instructions issued by machine manufacturer

Which label will be of more help when the garment is ready for cleaning, the label which is sewn in or the hang tag?

When selecting fabric, look for the label at the end of the bolt and the code number for the care label.

CROMPTON-RICHMOND CO., INC.

KINDS OF INFORMATION
THAT MAY BE FOUND ON LABELS

Name of product or what it is
May be necessary for new products or unusual designs.

Manufacturer or distributor
Name or registered identification number of the manufacturer or someone responsible required by law for textile products.

Guarantees
Be sure to learn for what is it guaranteed, by whom, and for how long

Quantity and/or size
Need for size of many clothing articles necessary. Quantity of prepackaged items helpful.

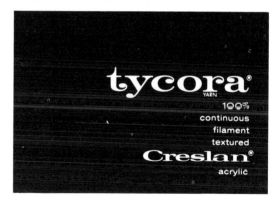

Construction
It helps to know how fabrics are made. For example, ply yarns, thread count, and names of unseen finishes are valuable to anyone who understands their meaning.

Made of
DU PONT
COLOR-SEALED ACETATE LUXURY YARN

The color is part of the yarn, added to the viscous solution while the acetate is being made. Later when the yarn forms, the color is truly SEALED IN.

THE COLOR RESISTS —
Light and gas-fading
• Crocking
• Dry-cleaning
• Perspiration

Du Pont Acetate resists weakening by mildew and does not attract moths. It has beauty of drape, is pleasant to the touch, combining luxury with economy.

Dry cleaning is recommended. Do not wash or send to laundry. Press wrong side, using lowest iron-setting.

ACETATE has been time-proved and improved by DuPont for 25 years.

Performance in use
One of the most important parts of a label and often ignored. How much will it shrink, how will sun affect it, will it need ironing?

Brand name or trademark

Helps in identifying quality if you are familiar with the brand.

Approval by recognized agencies

Does it have the American Institute of Laundering approval, or others? (See page 149.)

Form and variety

Fabrics containing wool fibers must be labeled whether reused, reprocessed, or new wool.

Quality or grade

"Seconds" and "irregular" indicate grade as do such words as Pima, Merino, Mongolian.

Selling points

The manufacturer wants to sell articles, so may include information that is appealing to the customer.

147

Conditions under which produced

The label of International Ladies Garment Workers Union, AFL-CIO, indicates good working conditions. (See page 159.)

Composition

Fiber content essential for most clothing items. Ingredients used in cosmetics need not be listed.

SWISS MINICARE
100% Cotton
WOVEN & EMBROIDERED
IN SWITZERLAND FOR
ALSADA CLASSICS
New York N.Y.

Geographical source

Country of origin of imported fabrics or furs required by law. Optional on other articles.

Direction for use and care

How to wash and iron—should it be bleached? How should beauty aids be used?

A label is all the descriptive information which is attached to or accompanies a product. Labels which describe the proper care should be sewn in or otherwise attached permanently whenever possible. Information necessary for wise purchasing may be on a tag attached to the garment (called a hang tag) or printed on the package. Booklets are part of the label.

Although it will not solve all your shopping problems, the time spent in *reading* labels and in *learning* the meaning of the information on them is time well spent.

When you shop, note the clothing with informative labels. Only as you use them for wise purchasing will manufacturers feel it necessary to put helpful labels on their products.

Seals of approval. Some magazines and manufacturers maintain testing laboratories and employ independent agencies to examine products for advertising.

The Consumers' Guaranty is *Good Housekeeping* magazine's simple promise to the public to replace or refund the purchase price of merchandise advertised in its pages if that merchandise is not as advertised. This unique service is worth mentioning even though it is promoted by a commercial organization. The familar oval symbol provides guidance to consumers in their selection of clothing. The seal tells the public that *Good Housekeeping* has satisfied itself that the product is a good one.

The certified washable seal of the International Fabricare Institute means that any garment bearing this seal can be laundered by any laundry in the country.

The *woolmark* symbol on a garment or fabric means that it is of high quality, pure virgin wool. The mark means more than the legally required label giving fiber content as it assures the consumer of superior quality. Products bearing this mark must meet performance requirements in strength and color fastness. The mark, used internationally, is sponsored in the United States by The Wool Bureau, Inc.

The *woolblend* mark was introduced in June, 1971, to indicate quality in fabrics containing wool and

Woolmark Symbol

Woolblend Mark

another fiber, either natural or synthetic. Like the woolmark, it assures the consumer that samples of the product have been tested by Wool Bureau inspectors for strength, color fastness, fiber content, and level of workmanship.

OTHER SHOPPING AIDS

The Better Business Bureau is a local agency maintained by business firms to help protect consumers and merchants who do their best to maintain good standards. It is affiliated with a national group. You can write or call the local Bureau to report complaints about any advertising or selling practice that you believe is dishonest. The Bureau will check the claims in an effort to protect the consumer against fraud and schemes. It has no legal enforcement powers but can give you advice and will try to have the store involved cooperate.

Of course, you will not be buying from telephone "con" artists, who often are the ones exposed by a Better Business Bureau. Your purchases from a reliable store can usually be returned if not satisfactory and if you do not soil them.

The Federal Trade Commission protects both the consuming public and the business community by preventing and eliminating deceptive practices and unfair methods of competition. The following are among the unlawful activities proceeded against by the FTC: false advertisements; price-fixing agreements; combinations in restraint of trade; discriminations in prices, advertising allowances and services; monopolistic mergers; division-of-market arrangements; marketing of misbranded textiles and furs; marketing of flammable

The pictures shown here describe some of the testing done before a garment is permitted to be labeled with the Certified Washable Seal of the International Fabricare Institute. This testing is very much like that done by many large stores and manufacturers.

This Stoll-Quartermaster Universal Wear Tester is used by A.I.L. to measure comparative resistance of fabrics to abrasion. A sample of the fabric is clamped in the circular holder. A diaphragm below the sample is extended by air pressure so that the sample is pushed up. The platform holding the circular clamp and sample oscillates forward and backward so that the fabric rubs against an abradant (rough substance) held above it. The fabric that takes the most rubs before wearing out should give the best service.

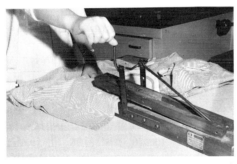

This picture shows the Crock Meter. A wooden "finger" covered with a white fabric is rubbed back and forth over the surface of the fabric to see if the color will rub off.

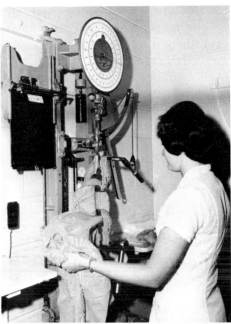

Tensile strength tests are made on the Model J Scott tester using the grab method to be sure that the fabric is strong enough to give good service. This picture shows a strength test across a seam.

INTERNATIONAL FABRICARE INSTITUTE

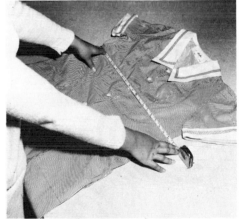

Shrinkage is determined by measuring the garment originally and after laundering. In cottons, shrinkage is usually complete after three washings. Some permanent-press fabrics have shown shrinkage starting after as many as ten launderings (when the finish wears off).

fabrics; and misleading demonstrations. It also gathers and makes available to the Congress and the public factual data concerning economic and business conditions.

The Food and Drug Administration (FDA) is a scientific, regulatory agency of the U. S. Department of Health, Education, and Welfare and is charged with the enforcement of the Federal Food, Drug, and Cosmetic Acts. These are concerned with the safety, wholesomeness, purity, packaging, and labeling of foods, drugs, and therapeutic devices or cosmetics that move in interstate commerce. Because it is believed that an informed consumer is his own best protection, educational materials are made available to school and individual consumers. The work of this agency with cosmetics and other beauty aids is of special interest to readers of this book.

The laws do not require a cosmetic manufacturer to prove the ingredients, other than colors and "new drugs" ingredients, safe before marketing although many manufacturers do this voluntarily. Any product that does prove harmful can be removed from the market. The law does not

---

Collect advertisements that present information about a product that will help you make a wise choice and also collect other ads that appeal only to your emotions. Prepare a bulletin board of informative and non-informative ads.

Collect misleading advertisements and some that cannot be verified. Compare ads from television, radio, magazines, and newspapers.

Write a letter to a company with misleading advertisements and read the reply to your class.

Select a committee to visit the local Better Business Bureau to learn more about its work.

Make a display of recent leaflets available from the U. S. Department of Agriculture which are low cost and which will help girls and other family members be better dressed. Your home economics department probably has some. If you have a county Extension Agent whom you can contact, you may obtain more. Write to references listed at the end of this book for others. If there are adult classes in your school, arrange to have the display seen by members who may find this information helpful.

Select a recent issue of a consumers magazine that contains an article about an item of clothing. Read it and report to the class on the main findings. If you do not have this magazine you will find it in most libraries.

Collect labels of clothing items. Mount those that you consider good, informative labels on one page and those that are of little value on another page. Write a summary of your reasons for mounting them as you did. Rewrite the poor labels so they will be more meaningful for the consumer. Underline the terms found on labels and explain their meaning. For example, sanforized will not shrink more than 1%.

protect the occasional individual who is allergic or sensitive to some cosmetic ingredient, but if a product causes injury to a large number of persons, it can be removed from the market. Therefore it is important that you notify the nearest Food and Drug Administration office if you believe you have been defrauded or injured by a cosmetic. Save the remainder of the product, or the empty container, for evidence in case it is necessary. You should also report your experiences to the manufacturers or distributor listed on the label, and the store from which you bought the product.

Branches of the United States Department of Agriculture (USDA) are concerned with clothing needs of men, women, and children. Research is done to improve the quality of such items and to determine satisfactory shopping methods. Booklets are published on the care, selection, and construction of clothing and related subjects and are made available for a small cost from the Government Printing Office, Washington, D. C., or from local or state Extension Service offices.

Many *sales people* are well trained for selling their merchandise and can give you a lot of help. If you discover such a person who is interested in you or is recommended by friends, get to know her so she can point out things you may not have noticed.

CAN YOU GET A BARGAIN AT A SALE?

A good buy is anything that suits your needs at a price you want to pay. If you can get what you want for less money than usual, or if you can get better quality or a higher fashion for the same money, you have a good buy, or a bargain. But just because you saved money on purchasing an item, it is not a bargain if you cannot use it. Some items in your closet which you seldom wear are there because they seemed like a bargain when you bought them but now they do not fit right, they do not blend in color with other clothes, you do not have any place to wear them, or the quality is so poor they look sad after a little wear.

Can you get a bargain at a sale? Yes, but it does mean that you have to understand what sales really are.

Why do stores sell some items for less than usual?
- Perhaps they need to get rid of clothes that are not moving well. It does not pay the owners of large stores to keep left-over seasonal merchandise, so they usually sell styles or colors that are not too popular at a price less than usual. They may also find themselves with certain sizes left over and will sell them for less.
- At other times stores have special sales to get people to buy, especially when it is a slow season, as after Christmas, Easter, or during August.
- Occasionally a new item is introduced at a low price to get people acquainted with it. At other times, after a fire, for example, things are sold at a low cost. Of course, if a company is going out of business, goods are sold at low prices to clear. Items that are soiled or torn are also cleared at less than the usual price.

It pays to watch the terms used in sales. One often sees a *half price* sale, but is it really half price if you have to buy one item at full price and then

TERMS SMART SHOPPERS KNOW

Irregulars	Manufactured articles with slight imperfections of some kind that are not usually noticeable.
	These items are sold at a discount. Irregular hosiery is perhaps the most common item sold as imperfect.
Seconds	Items that have flaws such as mended runs and tears.
As Is	Damaged articles sold as is—no returns permitted.
Loss Leaders	Special buys to get shoppers into a store in hope they will buy other articles at regular prices.
Job Lots	Special orders from a manufacturer. They may or may not be of inferior quality. At times the manufacturer will give the retailer a good price for sale purposes. Items may be made during a slack season and manufacturers may sell them at cost merely to promote the brand and defray expenses of his plant.
Broken Lot	Lines of items that are being discontinued. Not all sizes or styles are available.
Dog	Inferior merchandise or articles which did not sell for some reason. They may be out of style, an unpopular color, or poorly made.
Damaged	Indicates that the garment has been soiled or torn. (See *As Is.*)
Markdown	Most often at the end of the season. The price is lower than the usual price.
Special Purchase Lot	Often a store buys all a manufacturer has left over at the end of the season at a reduced price, to clear.

buy the second at half price? Have you ever heard of a *penny sale?* Are you really paying a penny for an item if you had to buy one or two at regular cost first?

A *going-out-of-business* sale may offer low prices but who is responsible if the article is not satisfactory? In some communities it is necessary to secure a permit from the local police office to have such a sale; this insures that qualities of cheap merchandise will not be brought in to mislead the customers.

End-of-season sales at department stores usually offer regular stock at a considerable reduction. If you are a larger or smaller size than average you can often get good buys. Be sure you can use the merchandise another season and that it will not be out of style.

Some stores have *store brands* or private labels which they offer at lower prices than other brands. Large stores contract with manufacturers to produce goods for them under the store's own brand name. The stores can arrange to sell for less, as they buy in quantity but do not pay for national advertising. NOTE: You cannot assume that the quality is the same as the advertised brand, for the same manufacturer may change the quality some. Perhaps fewer stitches per inch are used, or a different type of buttons. So, even if it looks the same, only close observation can determine if it is. Many store brands are good buys.

Perhaps you are saying that it is too much trouble to buy at sales. However, it has been shown that many smart women can save almost half their clothing costs by wise shopping at sales, or have twice as many clothes, or garments of better quality. If you can do this, you are contributing to your family income by being a good shopper. Also, if you can afford the time it takes to shop at sales and have the knowledge needed, you have a feeling of satisfaction.

When you are about to buy a "bargain," ask yourself:
- Is this the merchandise I really need?
- How does it compare with regular merchandise in price and quality?
- Does it suit my purpose?

Set aside one portion of a bulletin board in class to display advertisements for "sales" of clothing found in local newspapers. Study them carefully to determine if there are misleading statements. Prepare a summary of the types of sales most common at the time of year you did this project.

Bring to class one clothing item you or a family member has purchased which you consider a "bargain." Explain why. If you have an item which did not prove to be such a good buy, bring that and give your reasons.

List articles you or your parents often purchase, giving the trade name or brand name of each article. Why was the particular brand purchased?

A class committee may want to arrange good and poor clothing advertisements on the bulletin board with statements explaining why each is or is not good from the standpoint of providing information about the article.

Talk with a clothing buyer of a large department store. Find out if they have their own "store brand" of women's hosiery, men's shirts, or other clothing. If so, learn the name used. Compare prices and quality with other well known brands, if possible.

- Will the store stand behind it if necessary, or can I take care of any flaws?
- Do I have the money for it now?

WHEN SHOULD YOU SHOP?

Of course, you have to shop when it is convenient for you. If you are in school mornings, you cannot consider shopping at that time even if the stores are less crowded and the sales people have time to help you. However, even on a busy schedule, you can find some time to shop when the stores are not crowded.

Try to avoid the rush hours and pre-holiday shopping by planning for your needs and shopping ahead of time. You will get better service, the selection will be larger, and you will not become as tired and can therefore be a more intelligent shopper.

Why buy at the last minute? If you need a dress for a party and have to buy it the day before, you will be forced to take something that may not flatter you and that may cost more than you want to pay. A good shopper thinks about her needs in advance, looks at what is being offered, and shops around before making a decision. With such a background, you are ready to buy whenever you see the right thing at the right price.

The time of the year makes a difference, too, in the cost of the items and the selection available. If you have fitting problems and special needs, you may have to shop early in a season when there is a large selection of sizes. Other items can wait until special sales after holidays when you can profit from the savings.

WHAT PRICE SHOULD YOU PAY?

You will want to get the best value for your money but you may not always want to buy the highest quality. You need to consider what an article means to you and its purpose.

- Is it worth it to you to have one cashmere sweater even though it costs twice as much as a wool sweater that will wear as well?
- Do you want the best quality if you are buying a dress that you know is a fad and that you will enjoy wearing for a short time only?

Relation of quality to price. Quality is related to price, but a high price does not always mean the best quality nor does a low price always mean low quality. The cost of an item is often more directly related to luxury features, such as fur trim, than to quality.

High quality implies a standard of excellence with the best workmanship, materials, and design as well as luxury.

Highest quality will be your best buy if:
- The item is a classic design that will not go out of style and it is to be used for a long time.
- Fine points in workmanship, materials, and design are particularly satisfying to you and are related to your use of the article.

Visit several stores at which pupils in your school and their family members frequently shop for clothing. (Perhaps each member of your class can select a store to visit for the report.) Find out from the manager or someone in charge which days are the most crowded and which hours are the busiest. Learn if there are some months when the stores are more crowded than otherwise. Report to the class suggestions for the best time to shop if one wants a good supply of articles and does not want too crowded a store.

- The price of the article does not make it necessary for you to sacrifice other needs.
- The prestige value of owning "the best" is important to you.

Medium quality implies a standard of reliability which includes good workmanship, materials, and design. It is generally in the medium price range and does not have the excellence of high quality merchandise nor the extra features of higher priced goods. However, the utility and durability of medium quality merchandise is well suited for most purposes.

A medium quality item will be your best buy if:
- Utility and durability are of greatest importance.
- "Extras" are not a major concern for you.
- The medium price fits your budget.
- Luxury is not a way of life for you.

Lower quality implies fair standards of workmanship, materials, and design. It is usually in the low price range and has few, if any, luxury or convenience features. Items of lower quality generally meet needs for utility and are fairly durable.

Lower quality is the best buy for you if:
- The item suits your purpose.
- The item is necessary and you cannot afford higher quality.
- The item is for limited or temporary use.
- Superior workmanship and design are not overly important to you.
- The item is "high style" and likely to be out-dated in a short time.

In judging the quality you want for your purchases, it is wise to consider the intended use of each item and your purpose in buying it. A thrifty shopper pays only for the quality she needs and wants. For example, if you are considering a young boy's dress suit which is to be worn only occasionally, you would not demand the same durability that is desired in a man's business suit.*

HOW SHOULD YOU PAY FOR YOUR PURCHASES?

Do you prefer to save your money until you have enough to pay cash for clothing or do you prefer to use one of the many ways of "buying now and paying later"?

Layaway. One of the simplest ways to buy something for which you do not have the money is to put it on a "layaway" plan. In this case the store puts the article away for you and you pay a certain amount each week or month until you have covered the full amount. This service does not usually cost you anything extra, but you do not have the use of the garment until you have paid for it. In the meantime, if you should change your mind or be unable to pay, you will forfeit what you have put down on it.

Charge accounts. There are many types of charge accounts which mean that you can use garments as soon as you buy them and pay later.
- The *regular charge account* customer is billed within a month of buying the article and is expected to pay soon after receipt of the bill. Some sellers add a special charge if payment is not made soon. This type of charge account is available in some stores only to adults who are apt to purchase a great deal.

---

* Adapted from "Home Management, Your Shopping Dollar," Household Finance Corp.

- The *revolving charge account* is newer to department stores. It partially safeguards the stores as charges are limited to amounts that are suited to the customer's ability to pay. At the time the account is opened, the maximum amount that may be owed the store at any one time is determined. Each month a certain amount of the total is due and must be paid to keep the account in good standing. There is an interest charge on the unpaid balance which averages $1\frac{1}{2}$ percent a month. Since the true annual rate is twelve times the monthly quoted rate, this can total 18 percent.

Is easy credit always easy? No, but there are advantages to buying on credit, just as there are disadvantages. With charge accounts you do not need to carry money when shopping and so there is less chance of losing your money. You can also have the use of items sooner than would be possible if cash had to be paid.

The disadvantages appear to be greater than the advantages.

- You are apt to buy only in the store where you have credit and this often prevents getting better values at other stores.
- The additional service charge can, in the course of a year, amount to enough to pay for other desired clothing items.
- If something happens to one's earning power so that income is lowered or stopped, it is serious if one cannot pay. In such cases, merchandise can be taken back by the merchant.

If you charge your clothing, it is important to develop a good credit record, as this will stay with you all your life. A major purchase, like the mortgage on a house, may be affected by your early credit record. Be sure that you give the truth on applications for credit and be certain to ask questions about the type of credit you are getting and its true cost. You have learned to ask questions about the type of clothing you want. It is also important to ask questions about the credit you want.

- Be certain you read the credit application thoroughly and know what you are signing.

Credit can be a wise method for paying for clothing if the answers to the following questions are suitable:

- How much more will it cost me to buy on credit above the cash price?
- Is the credit worth the added cost?
- If I must have this credit, can I get it more cheaply and satisfactorily from another agency such as a bank?
- Will I be able to meet the payments in the future?

What you should expect of a store

You expect stores to provide good quality clothing and accessories at prices suitable for the quality and style. What else do you expect of them?

They should stand behind their merchandise and if it fails because of faulty construction, they should take it back and make a suitable refund or replacement. If the article has been used, you can't expect a full refund.

Although you know that advertisements and labels are planned to make you want to buy, you should expect them to be honest in their claim.

What the stores expect of you

Just as you expect a store's employees to treat you with courtesy, so they expect you to be a courteous shopper. If you want the help of a salesperson, wait your turn and state your needs correctly. If you are just looking, tell her so she can attend to serious shoppers.

Of course, you will want to try on clothes if you are interested in buying them, but take good care of them. Be especially careful of lipstick, as these stains are hard to remove. Put on the clothes carefully so as not to tear the openings, and hang them up correctly when you are through. You wouldn't want to buy a dress that has been soiled or torn by someone and you should take the same care of dresses you try on.

Most stores allow a return of merchandise soon after its purchase if it has not been worn. If it is necessary to make a return, try to do so as soon as possible and in the original wrappings and with the sales slip. If you cannot make a suitable exchange, you may get a refund or a credit slip to be used for other purchases. If you charged the item, seldom will you get a cash refund but the return will be taken off your account.

Never wear a dress and then try to return it as unworn—the store may refund your money but the dress will have to be marked down. They may refuse to extend you credit or sell you anything if you do this repeatedly.

You also have a responsibility to yourself and the store to return any merchandise that is defective or un-

---

Select a clothing item that you or a family member plans to purchase in the near future. Prepare a report stating why it is needed. Then suggest at what type of store it can best be bought and what the best method of payment is for you.

Prepare two skits, one of a girl with good shopping manners and another of a girl with poor shopping manners. Have them presented to your own or another class.

Prepare a debate. One side is to argue that: "It pays to buy the best quality." The other side to argue that: "A wise shopper pays as little as possible for clothing."

Investigate charge accounts and layaway plans in stores where you often shop. Find out the age requirements for starting an account. What is the interest or carrying charge on such accounts?

Write an article that could be used in a magazine for teens. Select one of the following topics: "When is a bargain not a bargain?" "It pays to buy the best." "Shopping tips for teens."

Debate the use of charge accounts versus paying by cash.

Interview a store manager. Find out the estimated yearly loss from shoplifting.

Arrange to bring in a garment and the label that was attached to it. By working in groups, suggest ways the label could be improved. Rewrite it. Find out what information must be on the label due to legislation. Decide what else the consumer needs to know.

Collect bottles, jars, and packages that are misleading in size. Arrange a display of deceptive packaging in grooming aids.

Report on the problems of a store accepting returned goods, from both an ethical and hygienic standpoint.

satisfactory. Stores may not be aware of the inferior merchandise if customers do not tell them. Usually such merchandise can be returned to the manufacturer for credit.

• What should you do if you are aware of someone shoplifting? Ignore it, speak to the person involved, or speak to a salesperson?

Your responsibility to garment workers

Manufacturers once permitted their employees to work overtime at low wages in unsanitary surroundings in their efforts to produce inexpensive garments that the public demanded. The Fair Labor Standards Act set up minimum wages and maximum working hours for both men and women. This has helped improve conditions under which our clothing and textiles are produced. Organizations such as the International Ladies Garment Workers Union also set stand-

ards so that "sweat shops" have been replaced by power sewing machines and good working conditions, neat surroundings, good lighting, and comfortable chairs.

Give a class report on regulations regarding hours of work and minimum wages for women in your state.

Be sure each garment you buy bears a label stating that it has been produced under good working conditions. By doing this your purchases will serve a wardrobe need and you will help provide desirable working conditions for other young women workers in the textile industry.

Should you buy imported garments

Many articles are being made in other countries and imported into the United States. Low labor costs make it possible for other nations to produce goods at a lower cost than we can. The U. S. government has enacted some protective measures such as high tariffs and low quotas. This means that certain items imported from other countries have *tariffs* or taxes applied before they can enter this country. A *quota* means that only a limited number of items can be imported so that competition will not be too great for our own products.

Many people do not approve of this as they feel that free trade is a better policy because we export our products to other countries. You may be interested in talking about this matter with your parents and others.

The Federal Trade Commission does require that fabrics and many clothing items made in other countries be labeled as to the country of origin. Therefore the American shopper knows where the clothing has been made and is free to make his own decision regarding its purchase or to refuse to buy.

SHOPPING FOR CLOTHING FOR GIRLS

What factors should you consider when you purchase ready-to-wear garments?

Review Chapters Two and Three. Study your figure and posture in relation to the fit of your garments. Analyze your figure carefully to select designs that emphasize your good points and minimize your less desirable ones.

When you buy a dress or coat or shoes or any article of clothing, you want your money's worth. Take time to look for:

• Good fit
• Style attractive to you
• Comfort
• Good workmanship
• Easy care
• Cost within your budget
• Color that becomes you and combines with your other clothes
• Smart appearance that will last
• Suitability for your activities

Read the labels carefully so that the fabric will have the qualities you wish for the particular garment.

High school girls looking at workmanship details of a blouse to determine if it is worth the price.

Know your size for correct fit. Many articles of clothing are available in different size ranges. In order to get the best fit, determine the size range that suits you best and ask for those sizes when shopping.

To determine the correct size range for your figure type, have someone take the following body measurements and note them on paper.

Height: Remove shoes and stand naturally against a wall or door. Measure height from top of head to floor.

Bust: Measure around the body at the fullest part. Be sure the tape does not sag when it crosses the back.

Hip: Stand with knees together, hold the tape firmly but not tightly around the fullest part of the hips (usually 7″ below the waist).

Back Waist Length: An important measure to be certain the waistline is right for you. Measure from the prominent bone at the base of neck to the waistline following the curve of the spine.

Look at the chart on page 462 and determine whether your measurements are closest to those of a girl, junior petite, junior, misses', half size, or women's. Some stores carry special clothing for chubbies, petites, and tall girls. For example, junior petite sizes are proportioned for the short girls who are in the junior size range. Probably your needs can be met by one of the special sizes if regular sizes do not fit too well.

Good workmanship. Quality in ready-made garments is much easier to judge if you know the characteristics of good workmanship. The way a garment is cut, sewn, and finished affects its appearance when new but even more important, it predicts how it will appear after wear and cleaning. Points which generally apply to specific garments are described in sections that follow. General points of good workmanship which apply to clothing for everyone—women, men, and children—are listed here.

Fabric grain is one of the most important things to check for. Are all pieces cut on the grain of the fabric? Are the lengthwise threads at right angles to the floor at both the center front and center back? Are the crosswise threads parallel to the floor at chest level? (See page 488 for problems caused by off grain garments.)

Careful matching of designs is a mark of good quality. A manufacturer who takes time to have the designs well matched will almost always take pains with other workmanship details. Look especially at center back seams. Pockets, sleeves, and collars should match and look well in relation to the body of the garment. It is almost impossible to match every seam so don't be concerned if designs do not match under the armhole or at places not easily noticeable.

Stitching, hand or machine, should be small, even in length, neat, straight, and fastened securely. Thread should be of a matching color and colorfast.

Seams should be flat and even in width. Wide seams are usually a sign of quality, provide greater strength, and allow for possible alterations. Raw edges should be finished if the fabric tends to ravel easily.

Pleats should be carefully stitched and deep enough to hang well.

Reinforcements should be made at points which receive much strain.

Would you notice the pocket if the handkerchief were not there? The design matches at the front opening and also at the collar tips. Most other details of this shirt show evidence of good workmanship.

Plaids and checks present special matching problems. Care was taken to match checks at the center front, the pocket, and collar ends. Notice how the sleeves are cut alike.

An inexpensive blouse that is serviceable but not well made. Seams are narrow and pull out easily. Notice the lack of care in matching center-front plaids and the uneven design on the collar.

Extra stitching should be at pocket corners, bar tacks at tops of some pleats and plackets, and metal rivets on jeans.

Hems should be deep enough to allow for some changing of length and to cause the skirt to hang nicely. Stitching should not show on the right side. If seam binding is necessary because of the type of fabric, it should be firmly woven.

Fasteners, such as slide fasteners, should be long enough to allow the garment to go on easily. Loose threads which may catch should be trimmed or the seam finished.

Hooks and eyes, snaps, buttons, and *trimming* should be securely sewn on. Extra buttons, especially if they are of an unusual color or design, are often supplied by quality manufacturers. Buttons need some reinforcement under them unless the fabric is very firm.

Buttonholes should be firmly stitched and should fit the buttons. Buttonholes made along the crosswise grain of the fabric stay closed better than vertical ones, but are not always possible because of the design of the fabric. Bound buttonholes are preferred to machine-made ones for quality garments.

Collars and cuffs that may need to be cleaned apart from the main garment should be easily removable, either snapped or basted on. White collars sewn to dark dresses are not desirable.

Poor quality merchandise can usually be spotted by off-grain sections, shallow pockets, hanging threads, pockets not reinforced, facings not tacked down, poorly finished belts, and narrow unfinished seams.

Not every garment you like will

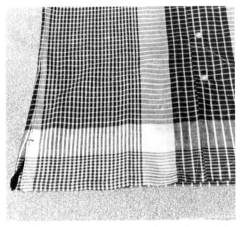

Another indication of good workmanship: this shirt has bartacks at the top of side openings to prevent pulling at the seams.

CRESLAN ACRYLIC

Check to see if a white collar that should be washed separately from the dress is easily detachable.

have all these characteristics. If the fabric, style, and fit are good for you, you may have to improve the appearance and wearing quality yourself. Or if the garment is to be worn for only a few dress occasions or quickly outgrown, high quality is not necessary. But it is a wise person who recognizes signs of quality in clothing and who can decide when certain ones are important.

If possible, visit a garment factory and watch the manufacture of wearing apparel. Give a class report on your experience.

Compare seam details (as stitching and finishes) on several ready-to-wear dresses with those on dresses made in class.

Try to become acquainted with features of better quality garments. Examine the clothes on display in the window and inside displays of better stores. You will be a better shopper even if you buy in a lower-priced department. Summarize your observations concerning design and workmanship of higher priced garments. Are they always better quality?

Prepare a display similar to the chart on page 179. In the center place an actual garment, if possible, or a large picture. Around the edges of the display list signs of quality, good or poor, to look for. String pieces of ribbon or heavy cord from each statement to the place referred to on the garment.

Investigate the insurance coverage most families have on clothing. It is usually included in a fire and theft policy on the total household contents. Speak with an insurance agent to learn what clothing is covered and how claims are made if all clothing is lost in a fire. What happens if clothing is stolen, either from the home or an automobile? Decide whether it pays to have clothing covered by insurance.

If you think the price is right for the quality of the fabric and workmanship, and other features meet your approval, try on the garment. Study it in a full-length mirror. (1) In what ways does it improve your appearance? (2) Are there any features about it that make you less attractive? (3) Is it comfortable as you walk, sit, and bend your arms? A garment should be as smooth fitting as the style trends require; however, it should never be tight or strained. (4) If alterations are necessary, determine how much they will cost. Do not buy anything that will require many alterations. If you cannot find an outfit that fits throughout, choose one that fits the upper part of the body. The skirt is easier to fit than a waist. A person skilled in alterations can often change the fit of a shoulder or neckline, but the cost is seldom worth it.

BUYING THE READY-MADE COAT OR SUIT

A coat that you select carefully can be worn several years. A hastily selected garment may prove unsatisfactory, and you'll wish you could discard it after it is worn a few times. Choose your coat first, and consider its color before you make any other garment selection.

Design

Coats, raincoats, and jackets may be fitted, semi-fitted, or loose in style. Coats range in length from a short topper to full length. Some years fashionable lengths are $3/4$ or $7/8$. These lengths limit the skirts and dresses which can be worn attractively with the coats. Jacket lengths range from above the waist to below the hips. Select a garment with line and length most becoming to you, not just the latest style.

Coats suitable for many climates. The pea jacket is of heavy wool, double-breasted for warmth, and especially attractive when worn with pants. The navy blue raincoat on the left is of polyester and can be used for slightly chilly weather. The red wool worsted coat of identical design, in the center, is made for winter wear over skirts and dresses. Notice the boots, matching leather gloves, and a handbag with adjustable strap so it may be used in several ways.

A classic coat design is a good choice unless you can afford to purchase many coats and replace them whenever styles change. Which coats, pictured on page 164, can be worn for several years (with perhaps a change of hemlength) without looking dated? Less expensive items such as scarfs and blouses can sensibly be chosen for their "latest" style.

If you need a coat or jacket primarily for warmth, be sure it is designed for such a purpose. For a warm winter coat, you will want:

- A neckline that can be buttoned securely.
- Sleeves shaped to the wrist or an inner sleeve lining cuff attached to the sleeve and gathered at the wrist.
- Sufficient lap for coat front and buttons well down the front.
- Check the interlining. A closely woven, napped woolen lining will provide warmth. The air spaces between the outer cloth, the lining, and the interlining are good insulators.
- A fitted waistline or a belt prevents wintry drafts getting close to your body.

Coats with removable linings are desirable in many climates. For less frigid weather the lining may be detached. Often these coats are made water-repellent to serve for rainy weather also.

Tailored coats usually look best on a tall person who has good posture, broad shoulders, and slim waist and hips. However, a young woman whose figure is such that she can wear a tailored suit well may look better in softer dressmaker styles because of her personality type.

Collars that are high or turned up

in the back are for a girl with a long neck. Low rolling collars and collarless styles are better for short necks.

Full sleeves are suitable for a tall person. Set-in sleeves with slightly padded shoulders are becoming to a figure with slightly sloping shoulders and oversize hips.

Fit

A good fit in a coat or suit is essential for comfort, neat appearance, and good service. *No two makes of suits or coats fit the same even though they are labeled the same size!* You need to try on garments in your size range until you discover which one is designed for your figure. When you find a brand in a coat or suit that fits, you can ask for it the next time you buy.

Take plenty of time to examine the fit of a coat or suit before you buy. Try the garment on over the type of clothing you will wear under it. Look at yourself from all views in a full-length mirror. How does the garment look when you walk, sit, and reach?

Points to check in the fit of a coat or suit jacket:
- The *collar* should fit close to the neck at the back and the sides.
- The *shoulder line* should run straight from the neck to the highest point of the sleeve.
- The *lengthwise grain* of fabric must hang straight at the center front of the jacket.
- The *crosswise grain* of the fabric should run straight around the body.
- *Sleeves* should be large enough for clothing worn underneath. Fullness at the elbow, such as darts, should come at the elbow bend. If you drive a car, the fit and comfort of sleeves is very important.

- *Shoulders* and *hips* should have a smooth fit without wrinkles under the arms or across the back.
- The *waistline* in a fitted garment should be slightly below the normal waistline to be most comfortable and to stay in place. The waistline button should be located at the natural waistline.
- *Fasteners* should close without strain.
- In a full-length coat, the lower edge of the *hem* should be slightly longer than the clothing worn underneath.
- The *lower edge* of the jacket or coat should run straight around your figure.

Workmanship

The general principles of good workmanship listed on page 160 apply to coats and jackets also. Look first at the outside. The general appearance should be neat and well-pressed. Good hand tailoring is flexible and made with neat firm stitches; however, good machine work looks and wears much better than poor handwork.

The *lining* should be smooth, comfortable, and neatly fitted, with a pleat at the center back for ease. A closely fitted lining will pull out. A good quality coat or suit is tacked securely around the armholes and along the shoulder and side seams. When a coat has an open lower edge, you can usually check the materials and examine the workmanship. Linings that fray easily should have deep seam allowances with the edges finished to prevent fraying.

If there is an *interlining*, it should be tacked securely in place to the side seams, shoulder seams, and around armholes. As a time saver, sometimes the lining and the interlining are seamed together, which makes bulky seams that pucker on the right side. (See page 168 for lining fabrics.)

Linings for coats and suits

The lining of a coat or suit should be both attractive and serviceable. An

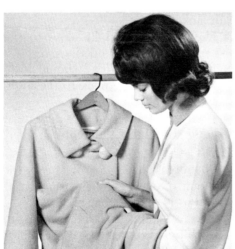

Look first at the outside of a coat. A good one is neatly and evenly stitched with perfectly matched thread.

A pleat at the center back of the lining allows for give and helps make a coat comfortable. It also prevents the lining from being strained.

A coat opened at the lower edge shows the materials and workmanship.

Seams puckered on the right side of the material. This is to be avoided.

inferior quality will soon wear out, pull at the seams, or shrink. The money you may spend relining a coat might be better invested in a garment with a better quality original lining.

Here are a few tips about the lining:

- A lining with a slippery texture, such as satin, will make the garment easy to put on and to take off.
- Be sure the lining you select is pre-shrunk, resistant to perspiration, and colorfast.
- A pleasing color that will blend with the garment fabric makes a lining attractive.
- An *interlining* should be lightweight.

A basic suit with accessories for casual wear. The shoulder bag and the turtleneck ribbed sweater match the line in the plaid of the suit. Knee socks and loafers are also suitable for casual wear.

SEARS, ROEBUCK CO.

167

LININGS IN COATS AND SUITS

Material	Appearance	Fiber Content	Characteristics
Crepe	Plain woven lining with slightly roughened surface. Best qualities are soft, fine, and compactly woven.	Usually rayon or acetate; sometimes silk.	Rayon or acetate crepe of good quality wears well, usually stands more abrasive wear than soft silks.
Satin	Lustrous, smooth, and soft. Shiny on right side, dull on under side. Crepe satins are softer, more supple than plain.	Silk, rayon, or acetate.	The slippery surface of satin makes coats slide on and off easily—helps cloth resist soil. Silk satin is softer, drapes better, is less shiny, and has warmer texture than satins of man-made fibers. Both kinds wear well if firmly woven, good quality. Because lining satins fray they will serve you better if cut edges are finished.
Twill	Diagonal firm weave. Finest qualities look much like satin.	Acetate or rayon.	Wears very well if quality is good. Widely used in tailored suits and toppers. Because twill linings fray, seams need to be generous, or protected with a serging stitch, which serves as secure overcasting. Narrow seams pull out.
Taffeta	Plain-woven; crisp hand. Sometimes taffetas have fine crosswise rib; these taffetas are plain color. Taffetas made of yarns the same size both ways are usually patterned.	Ordinarily rayon or acetate.	Taffeta linings give body to coats—help prevent wrinkling, make coats slide on and off easily. Good qualities wear well, considering cost.
Pile	Looks much like fur. Pile about ⅜ inch deep.	Alpaca pile surface—cotton backing or acrylic pile and backing.	Used chiefly to line and trim storm coats. It is very lightweight, soft, quite warm, and washable if made from acrylic fibers.
Nap-back satin	Lustrous satin on top side serves as lining; dull nap on under side takes place of coat interlining.	Rayon or acetate surface, cotton backing.	Lining and interlining combined in one fabric lacks air space of usual lining plus interlining which contributes to warmth. This material is best suited to coats for moderate temperatures. Seams are bulky.
Metal-insulated lining	Crepe or satin lining with gray metallic backing.	Rayon or acetate with aluminum coating on back.	Keeps in more body heat than usual lining. Does not take the place of warm interlining plus lining. Metal backing flakes off where material is creased. Material wrinkles badly. Stiffer than linings without this finish.
Fur	Usually short-haired fur of lower quality than fur used for outside of coat.		Very warm, but bulky and somewhat stiff.

U. S. DEPARTMENT OF AGRICULTURE "BUYING WOMEN'S COATS AND SUITS"

Woven wool is a loose fabric used as an interlining in dressy and all-purpose coats for moderate climates. Chamois, a soft flexible leather, is good for very cold climates. Plastic foam materials also make lightweight, warm interlinings. Lining fabrics that have a metalized backing, such as Milium—supposed to take the place of a separate interlining—are seldom warm enough for freezing temperatures.

Linings of an acrylic pile which face the body are as warm or warmer than a lining and a separate interlining. In addition, the fabric is lightweight and washable.

Quality

You will find it difficult to determine whether fabrics in a ready-made coat or suit have all the qualities you want. For many years, feel and appearance were the consumer's best guides to quality; however, neither is sufficient or reliable now because manufacturing processes and pressing can improve the appearance of inferior fabrics to the extent that one is deceived. The best source of information about such things which you cannot see or feel is factual tags on fabrics. It is advisable to learn all you can about the fibers and fabrics used in coats and suits, so you can evaluate information on tags to judge the quality, and give your garment the care it needs.

You will save time and cleaning expense if you will choose colors and fabrics that do not show soil readily. If you prefer a dark color, select one that does not show lint noticeably.

Fibers used in coats and suits are natural and man-made. Wool has been popular because it resists wrinkles and is durable and serviceable. The use of other fibers is increasing for special needs.

There is a trend toward *blends of fibers*. One fiber in the right amount will counteract the disadvantages of another, or it may add qualities that make a fabric serve its purpose better. A small amount of nylon (10 to 20%) added to cashmere increases the strength of cashmere and makes it more resistant to abrasion without affecting the appearance or the soft hand. Lightweight washable jackets are often made of cotton. The tendency of cotton to wrinkle and need ironing is lessened by the addition of polyester fibers.

The charts on pages 168, 170 & 171 list facts about natural and man-made fibers that are now used in suitings, coatings, and linings or which are being developed for those uses. These facts may help you decide how well these fibers will serve your needs for linings and coats or suits.

Buttons and Buckles

Buttons and buckles should be sturdy and able to stand dry cleaning. Be sure there are no rough or painted surfaces. Examine the metal shanks on buttons for sharp edges. Cloth covered buttons are inexpensive and will always match your coat or suit; however, they soon wear out. At least one extra cloth button should be supplied with the coat.

Trim

The best quality garments emphasize the *cut, line,* and *fabric*. Simple trim is best. It should follow the construction lines of the garment and be made and attached to last as long as the garment.

COATINGS AND SUITINGS

Material	Appearance	Fiber Content	Properties and Uses
Gabardine	Hard-finished worsted-type twill weave—fine or coarse, lightweight or heavy. Solid color. "Sheen gabardine" is made of very fine yarn, with steep twill, which gives a smooth satiny surface.	Most gabardines are all wool, but many are now made of such man-made fibers as rayon, acetate, polyester, and blends.	Used widely in both suits and coats. Rayon and acetate gabardines are commonly used in storm coats. Tailors well, keeps shape, wears well. Becomes shiny; needs special care when pressed to avoid shine. Colors in lower grades of gabardine may be affected by dry cleaning.
Flannel	Twill or plain weave. Either worsted or woolen type. Full nap often hides weave. Striped or plain.	Originally all-wool. Now flannels of man-made fibers have been developed for clothes in budget price lines.	Good qualities are serviceable in suits, lightweight coats, and coat linings. Flannels made of wrinkle-resistant man-made fibers wrinkle more than do those of good wool, and wrinkles do not hang out as well. However, these flannels cost less and may be pressed quickly and easily.
Sharkskin	Hard-finished worsted-type twill weave with alternate light and dark yarns. May be plain, striped, or patterned.	Wool usually, although man-made fibers are being used to make this material available in less expensive clothes.	Neat, trim-looking in suitings and utility coatings. Wears very well, keeps shape and press. Doesn't show spots, soil, or mends readily.
Tropicals	Lightweight worsted-type plain, open weave—smooth and unnapped.	Wool, or blends of various man-made fibers. Those blended with wool are most common and generally most satisfactory.	Cool, porous, resists wrinkles, and requires little or no pressing. Used for summer or lightweight suits.
Tweed	True tweed has a rough twill weave. May have nubby multicolored yarns, plaid or check patterns. Made in both coat and suit weights.	Wool is true tweed—but other fibers made to look like wool are being used in novelty and low-cost tweeds. Great care needs to be used in selecting tweeds as it is not easy to tell good quality from poor.	Best qualities stand up under harsh treatment—require little care, resist wrinkling, and don't show spots, lint, or repairs. Poor qualities are scratchy and do not wear well.
Jersey	Fine, knit material with soft, very light nap.	Wool usually, but some jerseys are now being made of a blend of wool and man-made fibers.	The most satisfactory jerseys are special suit or coat weights that are guaranteed not to sag. Jersey is lightweight to wear; it resists wrinkling, is an excellent choice for travel.
Homespun	Plain, loosely woven, rough, nubby. Looks much like tweed and may be miscalled tweed.	Coarse wool often mixed with wiry hairs. Like tweeds, the quality of homespun varies much and its appearance can be deceiving.	Good qualities stand a lot of hard wear and do not wrinkle. Used in sports coats.

COATINGS AND SUITINGS

Material	Appearance	Fiber Content	Properties and Uses
Fleece	Bulky coating in plain or twill weave, which does not show on right side because of thick nap. Patterned or plain.	Sheep's wool, or one of the specialty wools such as cashmere, or camel's hair; these also may be blended. Man-made fibers are also used in fleeces; some are backed with cotton.	Appearance and warmth vary greatly with fibers and weight of fleece. Highgrade fleeces are soft, silky, pliable, warm, and do not collect soil readily. Fleeces of inferior quality or fleeces made of fibers that develop static collect soil quickly. Light colors show soil readily so are costly to maintain unless washable. Fleeces often shed; this should be expected.
Chinchilla	Originally heavy pile fabric, but it is now lightweight. Densely napped with tiny nubs over the surface.	Wool	Warm, soft coating for casual wear. Collects lint readily—requires much brushing
Reversible coating (double cloth)	Two separate cloths linked together making outer cloth and lining as one.	Wool	Practical for between-seasons coats. Not warm enough for cold winters unless worn with a warm suit.
Suede cloth	A compact cloth with short cropped nap. Looks much like suede leather.	All wool originally but now it may be made of man-made fibers blended with the wool.	Rich looking cloth used in winter coats. Collects lint, requires much brushing.
Fur fabrics	Resembles such furs as Persian lamb, caracul, leopard, or broadtail. On close examination, particularly from the under side, it is easy to see that these materials are woven or knitted fabrics instead of fur.	The fiber varies; the acrylic and modacrylic blends are common.	Some do not always clean satisfactorily. Often becomes fuzzy and lose curl where coat or suit is rubbed as worn. Others are very warm and light weight and do not wear easily.
Corduroy	A pile weave with lengthwise rib.	Cotton. However, may sometimes be blended with polyester.	Used with shower-resistant finish for storm, and other utility coats. Wears reasonably well if background weave is firm. If loose, the pile gradually works out. Does not keep a neat press. Pile may flatten at elbows and skirt back. Inexpensive.
Linen	Firm, plain-woven, somewhat coarse, summer suiting.	Flax. Many linen suitings have a permanent wrinkle-resistant finish. Some fabrics made to look like linen are of cotton, rayon, or silk.	Long-wearing and practical.
Shantung	Plain-woven spring and summer suiting with thick and thin crosswise yarns. Has silky sheen.	Pure silk in finest fabrics. Rayon and acetate in lower-priced shantungs.	Wears fairly well. Heavy slub crosswise yarns eventually cause lengthwise yarns to split. Becomes shiny. Rayon shantung often dull and lifeless.

U. S. DEPT. OF AGRICULTURE "BUYING WOMEN'S COATS AND SUITS"

Cloth trim can be attractive and inexpensive. It may consist of crosswise or biaswise bands of the same fabric as the outer fabric. *Stitching* is an excellent trim for tailored garments. Even, firm, neat stitching lends dignity. It can strengthen your garment and give body to the collar and cuffs.

Fur trim increases the cost of a garment and the cost of upkeep. Would it be better for you to put your money into a better quality cloth coat? If you do buy a coat or suit with fur trim, look for a soft, thick, lustrous fur. The color should be even and characteristic of the kind of fur it is. Many of the less expensive furs are rabbit, dyed to look like more expensive furs. The label must state the fur used.

Decorations are often added to inexpensive coats to make them more appealing. You may find it wise to discard the one that came with the coat and use one of your own if needed. Your own jewelry will add an individual touch to the coat and will probably be of better quality.

SKIRTS

Buying points for skirts are similar for separate skirts, those that are part of a suit, and the skirt part of a dress.

Narrow skirts can be worn best by a girl with a slim figure. Skirts pleated

SHIP'N SHORE

This straight skirt is suitable for slender girls who are not too tall. The color in the blouse plaid ties the costume together, yet the blouse is suitable for wear with many other skirts and sport clothes. Notice the matching band in her hair.

Act out a shopping scene of two students buying winter coats. One lives in a very cold area and is outside a great deal. The other lives in a moderate climate with considerable rain. What questions will they ask? What points should the salesperson make to each one about the merchandise?

Put on a classmate's coat that is slightly too large for you and one that is about one size too small. Model them for the class. Make notes of the places where the garment does not fit well. Now model a coat the correct size and notice the difference.

A skirt of unpressed pleats is suitable for girls with some hip fullness but may "stick out" in an unflattering manner if worn by girls with full hips. The white blouse has a soft dull texture similar to the skirt.

The sweater and shirt harmonize with the plaid in the trousers. Both could also be worn with solid-colored trousers. Although the sweater is sleeveless, note the drop-shoulder effect.

all around are also best for the slim or average figure. The girl with full hips looks better in a skirt with a slight flare such as an A-line or one with low pleats. A single box pleat is also good for her. Tall, slender girls can wear almost any type of skirt including those that are circular or draped. A straight skirt may emphasize height.

Select a skirt according to your waist measurement or dress size. However, if your waist is much smaller than your hips, you may have to buy a skirt that fits over the hips and alter the waistline. Try on the skirt. Sit down in it. There should be enough fullness to prevent strain, wrinkles, and discomfort.

Narrow and A-line skirts made of loosely woven fabrics should be lined with a firm material such as taffeta. Skirts with both front and back linings will hold their shape better than those with only a back lining.

Points you should check in the fit of a skirt:

- There should be *enough room* in a suit skirt to avoid ripped seams and crosswise wrinkles.
- A skirt should not *pull up* when you sit; neither should it *cup under*.
- The *waist band* should fit snugly to your figure and hold the skirt in place.
- The *hips* should be comfortable with extra ease at the fullest part.
- A *slide fastener* should lie flat and smooth.
- The *lengthwise grain* should hang straight at center front and center back.
- The *crosswise grain* should run straight around your figure on all straight-cut skirts.
- The *lower edge* of a skirt must be straight and an even distance from the floor.

SWEATERS AND BLOUSES

Buying points for sweaters, blouses, and the bodices of dresses are similar. Designs vary and some can do a great deal to flatter the figure and face. If you want to appear taller and more slender, look for U or V shaped necklines that keep the eye moving upward, narrow flat collars that follow the natural neckline, diagonal lines moving more vertically than crosswise, and close fitting long sleeves. To make a figure appear heavier or shorter, select rounded or squared necklines, scarfs and turtlenecks, close or high collars, wide short sleeves, patch pockets, and horizontal yokes and inserts. See Chapter Two for a more complete discussion of the effect of line on your appearance.

SWEATERS

Sweaters are general-purpose garments that provide an opportunity to

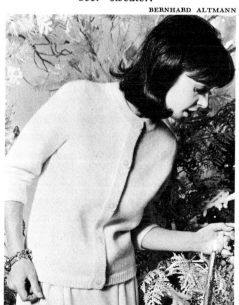

A cardigan sweater of classic style. It has a rounded neckline, buttons down the front with pearl buttons, and has ¾ length sleeves. Other cardigans have shorter or full length sleeves. A cardigan may be worn by itself or over a blouse, dress, or a pull-over sweater.

BERNHARD ALTMANN

A pull-over with a V neck that is flattering to a girl who wishes her face to appear longer and thinner. It is often worn over a blouse with the collar folding back at the neckline or may be filled in with a scarf as shown here.

BERNHARD ALTMANN

BERNHARD ALTMANN

A pull-over with a turtle neck, especially attractive on a girl who wishes her neck to appear shorter. It is also a warm sweater and is often worn under a coat or jacket for cold weather sporting events. Notice the fashion marks along the sleeve seams where stitches were knit together in order to shape the sweater.

add a touch of color to your wardrobe. Two classic styles which remain popular year after year are the *cardigan* and *pull-over* (sometimes called pull-on). A cardigan opens down the center front and is closed with buttons or a zipper; a pull-over is pulled on over the head. It usually has no buttons but may have two or three small ones at the closing of one shoulder seam. Sleeves may be short, $\frac{3}{4}$ length, or long. Pull-over sweaters fit more snugly than cardigans. Which type is best suited to your figure?

Fibers used in sweaters.

Wool is the most popular fiber used in the manufacture of sweaters because it is durable, elastic, and warm. Fabrics knit from worsted yarns are firm, strong, and resistant to rubbing that forms little balls, called "pills." Fabrics made from ordinary woolen yarns are soft and wear well; however, they tend to pill and are not as durable as worsted fabrics.

Cashmere is a very soft and fine silky yarn made from the fleece of Cashmere goats. The fleece is imported and the supply is limited, which keeps the cost high. It cannot take a lot of hard wear.

Lamb's wool is a soft wool from young sheep. It is not as expensive as cashmere and it wears well.

Mohair is a smooth wiry fiber from the Angora goat. Kid mohair is generally used in sweaters because it is fine and lustrous. For softer yarns, mohair is often blended with wool.

A *cotton* sweater is cool, comfortable, and easy to launder. It does not have the elasticity of wool and in a short time it will need reblocking to size it.

Acrylic fibers such as Orlon and Acrilan are popular for easy care sweaters. Because these fibers are not affected by water and do not shrink, they may be washed easily, even by machine. Sweaters made from these fibers keep their shape, need no blocking, and are soft and warm. They do pill, and because the fibers are strong, the little pills or balls cling more tightly than on wool. Research is underway to develop a pill-resistant yarn.

Textured filament yarns of man-made fibers marketed under the trade names of Ban-lon, Taslan, and Tycora do not pill but are not as warm or wool-like in appearance.

Bi-component yarns such as Orlon Sayelle are comfortable and easy to care for but must be machine dried. Garments made from these yarns carry informative labels to help purchasers give them the proper care.

Other animal fibers such as alpaca, vicuna, camel's hair, and man-made fibers like polyester, nylon, rayon, and olefin are used occasionally for sweaters and knitted blouses. Characteristics of these fibers are described in Chapter Ten.

Workmanship of sweaters. Sweaters may be full-fashioned or cut-and-sewn, depending on the method of *shaping. Full-fashioned* sweaters are shaped by increasing or decreasing the number of stitches, which makes little fashioning marks that you will find about the armholes, sleeves, and sides.

In *cut-and-sewn* sweaters, the pieces are cut from knit yard goods. Unless the cutting is done very carefully, these sweaters will sag and twist. If a sweater is cut incorrectly the wales or lengthwise ridges will show it. Consider the lengthwise wales as warp yarns. Check to see that the center front wale is perpendicular to the floor and not slanted.

In full-fashioned sweaters, *seams* are usually joined by looping. In cut-and-sewn sweaters, seams should be stitched securely and covered to keep cut edges of the fabric from raveling. (This is done on a machine that stitches and covers the edges at the same time.) Shoulder and back-of-neck seams in cut-and-sewn sweaters are often covered with straight tape or a strip of knit fabric. If tape is used, be sure it has been "eased on" so that it will give slightly as the fabric stretches.

In the best grade of sweaters, both full-fashioned and cut-and-sewn, *bands* are joined to the sweater by a hand looping process that continues the knitting without a seam.

The *neck* finish of a sweater is very important because it must stand a lot of strain. If the neck stretches out of shape, the fit and general appearance of the sweater is spoiled. A neck may be finished by a *single loop* or a double loop. *Double-looped* means that the ribbing is double, with a fold on the neck edge. A double-looped neck has less stretch than a single-looped one, but keeps its shape better. To make the neck fit snugly, *elastic thread* is sometimes carried along with the knitting yarn into the edge.

A *front opening* should follow one lengthwise rib of the sweater. Openings are usually faced with grosgrain ribbon or knit banding. *Ribbon facing* makes a neat finish and is strong reinforcement for buttons and buttonholes; however, it may fade or shrink and spoil the appearance of a good sweater. A knit banding facing will match the sweater exactly in color and react the same in washing; however, it is more bulky than ribbon.

Pearl or synthetic buttons are popular for sweaters. Often they are dyed to match the sweater. Some buttons are covered with matching yarn. If so, look for one or two extra buttons attached to the sweater.

Good *buttonholes* should last the lifetime of a sweater. A firm reinforcement of either ribbon facing or knit banding is necessary to keep the buttonhole from spreading and pulling out. A well-made buttonhole is cut straight with both the garment and the reinforcement. The stitches are deep enough to prevent pulling out, and close enough together to cover the cut edges. The facing should be a little wider than the buttonhole is long on crosswise buttonholes so that the buttonholes will not run into the knit fabric. *Vertical* buttonholes on closely fitted sweaters do not stay fastened as well as *crosswise* ones do. Be sure the buttonholes are evenly spaced and the same distance from the edge.

Size in sweaters. You may select a sweater two sizes larger than a blouse. A girl who wears a size 34 blouse may prefer a size 38 sweater.

Also, sweaters of the *same style* and marked with the *same size* number *may differ as much as two inches* in bust or chest measurement and *an inch or more* in sleeve length and width! Until sweater sizes are standardized, always try on a sweater.

Remember to try it on over the kind of clothing that will be worn underneath it.

Special finishes. Shrinkage and damage by moths have been wool sweater problems for a long time. Manufacturers have developed moth-resistant finishes which may be temporary or long lasting. It is wise to select wool sweaters with this finish as moths can quickly damage a sweater. Read the label to learn how long the finish can be expected to last and whether it can withstand washing and dry cleaning.

Wool sweaters can usually be washed successfully if directions are carefully followed but too hot water or too much agitation can cause a felting type shrinkage as described on page 257. Research is underway to prevent this shrinkage and wool sweaters which can be washed are available in limited quantities.

Sweaters of man-made fibers are not harmed by moths and seldom shrink or stretch if washing directions are followed.

Some sweaters are classics and in style year after year. Other sweaters go through fashion cycles. Some years the beaded sweater is in high style; other years the Scandinavian ski sweater is a favorite. Prepare a report on the type of sweater which was fashionable in recent years but is losing popularity, and the type of sweater that is becoming most stylish. Observe store displays and advertisements, and talk with retail personnel to gain your information.

Bring to class a collection of sweaters of different fibers. Your family and friends, as well as classmates, may lend you some. Compare the appearance, feel, and warmth. If you know the original cost, compare prices also.

Study sweaters of different fibers for pilling or balling of fibers on the fabric surface. What conclusions can you make concerning the amount of pilling and the fiber content of the sweater?

Survey several women about the sweaters they like best. Include an older person, one of middle age, a young career woman, and a mother of young children. Ask the mother about her preferences for her children. Summarize your findings to determine if there are certain preferences common to different age groups. The survey will have more meaning if several members of your class do the same and you compare your results.

BLOUSES

Blouses may change the appearance of a suit, skirt, or slacks to make it suitable for several occasions. Semi-dressy blouses are usually worn for informal occasions. Some dressy blouses can be worn with formal skirts. Sports blouses, simply tailored and made from gay cotton fabrics are worn with school outfits.

Beware the blouse that goes with "everything" as it may not belong to anything in your wardrobe. A blouse should be coordinated to the skirt or other clothing article with which it is worn, either by color or texture or design. A well chosen blouse will usually harmonize with several items in your wardrobe.

Blouses are bought by bust measurement but they vary in the way they are cut so that a blouse should be tried on to be sure it fits your figure. When the blouse is on, look to see that:

- The collar fits smoothly and does not wrinkle or stand away from the body.
- The fullness at the bust is adequate with no pull wrinkles below the bust.
- The blouse is smooth across the back of the shoulders.
- Sleeves hang straight.
- There is no strain across any center opening.
- The length is suitable for you.

If an overblouse, it should not be so short that it rides up above the

This simple blouse, which is sleeveless, is an essential part of this costume. Made of the same fabric as the collar and lap facing, it also matches the belt. This young secretary has dressed up her suit with pearls so that it is suitable for a date after work.
BOSTON HERALD AND KATHERINE GIBBS SCHOOL

waistline with movement, nor so long that it looks awkward. Needless to say, a blouse that tucks in can seldom be too long!

Signs of good workmanship will be found on page 179.

DRESSES

The points suggested for wise selection of skirts and those for blouses or sweaters can be applied to the selection of dresses. The fit and location of the waistline is an additional consideration. If there is a seam at the waist, it is easy to notice whether or not the fit is correct. However, many dresses without waist seams still have a slight inward curve which must coincide with your waistline to be comfortable and attractive. Waistline alterations can be made but they often involve a change of zippers and relocation of buttonholes, so look carefully at any dress that does not fit properly at the waist.

ANATOMY OF A SHIRT

Things to look for before you buy!

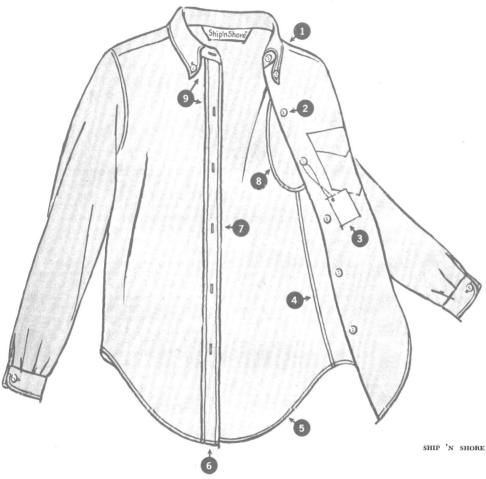

SHIP 'N SHORE

1 Collars should be evenly cut so that both sides match, and sewn smoothly without any puckers.

2 Be sure all the buttons are of fine quality, stitched on securely.

3 The tag should tell you that the shirt won't shrink, colors won't fade.

4 All seams should be fully cut and closely stitched, so they won't "pop."

5 Tails should be tapered evenly and stitched smoothly, with a neatly turned-up hem.

6 All extra details—such as plackets, pleats or tucking should be sewn smoothly and evenly.

7 Buttonholes must be firmly stitched, in order to avoid fraying.

8 Sleeves must be fully cut and set in smoothly to assure good fit. See if cuffs are even all around and sewn neatly.

9 For crisp, lasting "body," features like the collar, neckband, placket and cuffs should be lined with an inner-facing that's soft and pliable for comfort, and shrink-proof to stay smooth and flat after laundering.

Both the top and bottom parts of a pants suit must fit well. The crotch should be long enough not to bind when sitting or bending but not so long as to sag when standing. The waistline of the top needs to coincide with the natural waistline so the top will not ride up when moving.

SPORTS AND CASUAL WEAR

Trouser type garments such as shorts, slacks and pedal pushers are often worn for sports, housework, or lounging. They are sized by regular dress size or by waist measurement and are made in proportioned lengths. Many styles are available in stretch fabrics which allow for freedom of movement, greater comfort, and a trimmer fit.

Shorts vary in length from thigh to

180

knee. Slacks end at the ankle or just above. Pedal pushers stop just below the knee. Legs may be straight or tapered for a close, trim fit. Slacks may have bell-bottoms. See page 60 for other types.

Always try garments on before a full-length mirror. Try sitting down and bending over and notice the crotch. Are you comfortable? Pay particular attention to side and rear views. Is this garment attractive on you?

UNDERGARMENTS

Just because undergarments are "under it all," does not mean that they are not important. The appearance of the outer garment is almost always affected by what is worn under it.

Foundation Garments

History. Foundation garments are believed to have had their origin in Crete about 2500 B.C. Much later, in the early 1600's A.D., Queen Elizabeth wore a corset of steel plate, which is a far cry from present-day spandex and nylons! In 1828, when the research analyst Harvey discovered the circulation of the blood, women decided that the corset stopped the circulation, and was the cause of various aches and pains they had been experiencing. The corset then became more flexible. In about 1893 corset designers made the first straight-front corset, which meant comfort and better health for women. The trend continued, till the girdle finally replaced the corset.

Undergarments protect your body from cold by holding your body heat near the skin. In hot weather they absorb perspiration, which evaporates and cools your body. Also, since undergarments absorb moisture and oil from the body, your outer garments are protected from soil and stain.

There has been a trend for several seasons toward casual corsetry. Lighter elastic or stretch fabrics and less boning are used. The trends of fashion influence the styling of the outer garment lines, because foundations are the beginning of a smart fashion look.

For young girls, brassieres and girdles are light and especially designed for a growing figure. Because figure changes and silhouettes vary, fitting is desirable. Careful fitting will provide the right foundation garments to make your youthful curves smooth, to encourage erect posture, and to make your dresses look more attractive.

Your hips, waist, or bust may be out of proportion to the rest of your body. Foundation garments help to redistribute, to support, and to control muscles and flesh to give more graceful contours. You should, however, have firm muscles developed from good posture and exercise. They will help you attain good proportions. Foundation garments also improve the "set" of clothes and help to give you a well-groomed appearance.

Types of Girdles

There are many types of girdles: panty girdle, step-in girdle, side-opening girdle, and corselets.

A *panty girdle* is made from lightweight fabrics that mold and control. The lengths are for short, medium, and long figure types which require little control and no support. See illustration on this page. Garters are often detachable so the garment may be worn with or without hosiery.

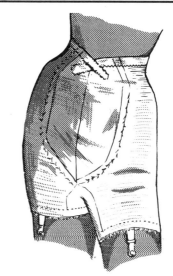

Panty girdle. The front panel is a firm fabric which does not stretch but holds the tummy firm. Garters are detachable, so it may be worn without hosiery.

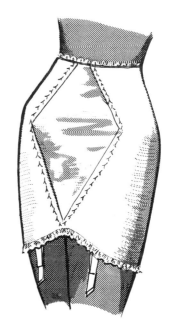

A step-in girdle. This style will not stay in place unless anchored by hosiery.

A *step-in* has no closure. It may be the roll-on type with no boning or the girdle type with some boning. See illustration on page 181. A *side-opening* girdle is usually made of strong firm fabrics and has more boning than other girdle types.

A *corselet* is an all-in-one bra and girdle combination that extends from above the bust to well below the hips; therefore it insures an unbroken torso line from bust to thigh. This garment may have a back or side closing or none at all. A one-piece may be made of thin, fine fabrics with little or no boning and no straps, or of very sturdy fabrics and much boning. A one-piece, two-way-stretch girdle is more comfortable if you have a small figure. A longer panel-type girdle is better if you have a large figure difficult to mold.

Garter belts are suitable for slim figures. Shop for a wide belt because it is more comfortable than a narrow one. Examine the closing; it should be padded so hooks do not dig in. A garter belt is really not a girdle as it gives no support. It is intended only to hold up stockings.

Garters are a most important part of your garment. They hold up hose and keep the garment down. There are usually four to six garters on a foundation garment. Many garters have some means of adjustment.

Sizes of girdles

Take your measurement over the fullest part of the hip. Check the chart below to learn which size is right for you.

Hips under 34″	Petite size
34″ to 37″	Small
37″ to 40″	Medium
40″ to 44″	Large
44″ to 48″	Extra-large

Some girdles are proportioned to height. Check with the salesperson about this if you are shorter or taller than average.

Characteristics of a comfortable girdle. A well-fitted girdle is comfortable and does not need adjusting while being worn. It should be long enough to extend comfortably from the midriff to cover the heaviest part of the thigh. In this way, a girdle can eliminate any fleshy bulge at the thigh and can give a smooth line to the upper leg. Boning aids the fabric to mold, control, and support the abdomen. A girdle should fit snugly into the curve of the back and bend when your body is in motion. It should not bulge or pinch your body as you sit, stand, or walk.

The way a garment is worn affects both your comfort and the lasting qualities of the garment. One of the best ways to prolong the life and keep the original style of a foundation garment is to maintain good posture. The purpose of a foundation garment is to give smooth, firm contours. Remember it cannot do the work of the muscles or correct poor posture

Fabrics for foundation garments. Fabrics which do not stretch are used in panels to provide trim control. Most of the garment is made of elastic fabrics which give with the body but which also have controlling action. Fabrics may stretch because of the use of rubber or spandex yarns. Spandex yarns are lighter in weight and more comfortable to wear. They may also be dyed attractive colors.

How do you put on a girdle? When you try on a girdle, slip into it as you do your stockings. Do not grasp it from the top and pull. Instead fold the girdle in half, turning the top toward the lower edge. Step into your garment carefully, pulling it into proper position. Then roll up the top to the waistline. Remove by rolling it off your body until it is inside out.

Care of the girdle. Two or more garments should be worn alternately to allow frequent laundering and to allow the elastic to rest and regain its full stretch.

To receive the most satisfaction from foundation garments, they must not only be fitted properly, but must have the best of care. Wash your garment frequently in warm soapsuds. Rub soiled spots gently with a soft brush and rinse thoroughly. Squeeze the water out gently, fold lengthwise over a rod, or lay flat to let dry. *Never dry a girdle near heat or in the sun.* Avoid chlorine bleaches on garments with rubber or spandex fibers.

THE SLIP

The forerunner of the modern slip appeared in Italy, as a sheer, washable undertunic, finished with embroidered edges which showed at the neck and wrists.

Your slip is a foundation for your dress. It will help determine the lines of your figure. The full skirts of the last half of the 19th century required many stiffly starched underskirts. When the straight-line silhouette became the fashion, underskirts had to become close fitting and made of soft, unstarched fabrics. Hence the slip was developed.

There are two types of slips, the *full slip* which is a one-piece garment held up by shoulder straps, and the *half slip* or petticoat. Some slips are strapless and used for evening wear or under low-cut sun dresses. A full slip is desirable for wear under a sheer dress or blouse or a dress that does not have a waistline seam. The

bra straps that show through the back of a sheer blouse are not flattering and the waistline elastic of a half slip can destroy the unbroken line of some dresses. Half slips are suited to suits, belted dresses, and separates if the top part is opaque. Pettipants are a cross between a petticoat and panties. They are fashionable and appropriate for wear with very short dresses.

Design and style of slips. A slip should be simple in design with seam lines in harmony with the lines of the dress with which it is worn. Elaborate trimming may be difficult to launder and often wears out before the rest of the garment.

Some slips are tailored with little or no trimming while others are trimmed with lace, net, or embroidery. Tailored slips will probably wear longer but many trimmings of nylon and man-made fibers are very strong despite their fragile appearance.

For wear under a skirt that is not opaque, select a slip with narrow, if any, trimming at the hemline. A deep lace or net trim which can be seen through the bottom of a skirt lessens the appearance of the garment. For very sheer dresses, select a slip with a shadow panel (a double layer of fabric in the front gore or section).

The size of a full length slip is based on the bust measurement and the size of a half slip is based on the waist measurement. Some slips are proportioned for short or tall women.

A satisfactory slip should *fit* with ease, and should be smooth over the bust, underarm, and at the waistline and hips. Try on the slip. Does it fit smoothly over the bust, under the arms, and around the waistline? Does it allow sufficient ease for movement in walking, bending, sitting, and stooping? Does it hang evenly? Is it the correct length? Will it launder easily?

Do not plan to adjust the shoulder straps more than one inch. Otherwise the slip may bind under the arms, bunch around the top, and be strained at the hips.

The length of a slip should be one inch shorter than the outer garment.

To check the fit across the hips, try on the slip and grasp both sides of the slip skirt on each hip. Pull this part up to the waistline. The slip should then fall down easily over the hips without tugging, if not, it is too tight.

Slip fabrics. Slip fabrics are knitted or woven of cotton, rayon, acetate, nylon, and other man-made fibers. The knit or tricot fabrics made of nylon or similar fibers are comfortable because they "give," shed wrinkles easily, do not bunch up under outer garments, feel smooth next to the skin, and need no ironing. These fabrics may build up static electricity which will cause the outer garment to "cling" in cold, dry weather and will gray with casual laundering. A final rinse with a fabric softener will help prevent this. (See page 256.)

Cotton or blends containing cotton are preferred by many women for summer wear. The absorbency of cotton makes the fabric feel comfortable in hot weather when perspiration is normally greater.

Construction. Unless your slip is cut correctly and well-made, it will not prove satisfactory. Check for the following construction features:

- Shoulder straps should be attached to the body of the slip, not just the trimming. A piece of elastic fastening the strap to the slip at the back provides for additional "give."

- Seams should be finished to prevent fraying. Knitted fabrics may have an overcasting that covers the raw edges. Woven slips may be pinked and top-stitched the second time.

- Hems in woven materials should be narrow and held in place with two or more rows of stitching. Knit fabrics are hemmed with close zig-zag stitching which permits the fabric to stretch without breaking the stitches.

- Trimming should be firmly attached.

PANTIES

Types

Panties include briefs, step-ins, and tights. **Briefs** are short, snug-fitting with elastic or bands at the bottom of the legs. **Step-ins** come in various lengths longer than briefs. **Tights** may reach to the ankle or cover the foot.

Sizes

Some panties are sized by hip measurement but most are marked with a number that refers only to panty size.

	Size	Hip Measure
Regular	4	32
	5	34
	6	36
	7	38
Large	8	40
	9	42
Extra Large	10–12	44–52

Because there is no standardized sizing method, it is wise to check with a salesperson to be certain you are getting the correct size.

Construction

Run-resistant knit fabrics are generally used for panties. These fabrics are easy to launder and need no ironing. They are comfortable because

184

they give and are smooth. The fibers may be nylon, rayon, acetate, or cotton. Check for a double thickness of fabric at the crotch and a generous back rise. The back rise is the length of the panty from the bottom of the crotch to the center of the back waistband. Check also the elastic at the waistband. Good elastic stretches almost twice its original length and springs back quickly. The elastic at the waist often wears out before the rest of the panty and is difficult to replace. If you cannot buy nylon panties with an elastic that lasts as long as the nylon fabric itself, you may find it better to buy less expensive panties of acetate or rayon and replace them more often.

THE BRASSIERE

Brassieres are intended to support the bust in a normal position and not confine it. They vary from a narrow bandeau for a figure with a small, firm, upright bust to the long-line type that supports the bust and covers the top of the girdle.

Shoulder straps help hold the garment on the body and uplift and hold the bust-cup sections in their proper positions. If they are too long, the breasts are not lifted. If straps are too short, the breasts are pulled too high. Shoulder straps usually have elastic insets or some means of adjustment. They should be placed so they will not slip off the shoulders. Generally, the strap is attached to the brassiere above the center of the bust. This strap should follow the center of the shoulder and be attached to the back of the garment closer to the center of the back than to the underarm line. Comfortable straps are about ½ inch wide. *Forked straps* give a balanced

distribution of uplift. *Built-up shoulder straps* are more comfortable and generally more satisfactory for larger figure types.

Built-up straps are more comfortable for girls, especially for those who are very active.

TEEN FORM

This brassiere converts from standard type to either a halter or criss-cross type.

185

Lace brassiere tops, unless strapless, may need a reinforcement of net at the place where the strap and garment are joined.

If padding is desired in a brassiere, polyester and similar fibers produce a more realistic appearance and are more easily washed than foam rubber.

How to determine correct size

Manufacturers differ as to how to measure for size so that no one method is accurate for all figures. The only way to be sure a brassiere fits properly is to try it on. Even though you have found a size that fits you, you will need to check it every 3 months while you are still growing and developing.

Brassieres are sized by both the bra-band measurement and the bra-cup size. (The teen's very first bra will not have a cup size as the entire cup section is made of a stretch fabric which stretches as the figure develops.) One method of measuring which may help you determine size follows:

For bra band size:
Take a snug measurement around the diaphragm, just under the bust and add 5 inches.
Underbust measurement ...___
Add 5 inches
Bra band size ....___
For cup size:
Measure fullest part of bust .___
Subtract bra band size .....___
Difference ....___
If the balance is zero (band and cup the same) you are AAA or an AA cup.
If the balance is 1 inch larger than the band, you are an A cup.
If the balance is 2 inches larger than

the band, you are a B cup.
If the balance is 3 inches larger than the band, you are a C cup.
If the balance is 4 or more inches larger than the band, you are a D cup.
Bra-cup size ....___

This is only a guide. It is much better to try on a brassiere to be sure of fit. Do not switch sizes and bust cups. A 36A is not the same as a 34B. An experienced saleswoman is used to fitting many girls and women and can help you get a size that is most comfortable and does the most for your appearance.

There is a way to put on brassieres that will improve their wear. Slip both arms through the straps. Bend over from the hips so that the breasts fall forward and rest comfortably in the cups. While bending over, hook the garment behind you as far down

Collect ads of undergarments from various sources and classify them as to age of wearer, body type, style of garment, price, and claims of advertiser.

Collect slips that are ready to be discarded. Your family and friends can help you. Find out where they have worn out or why they are being discarded. Relate these findings to buying a slip.

Prepare a bulletin board of pictures of types of slips available and the outer garments that should be worn effectively with each. In some stores the lingerie buyer will come to a school and show some of the styles available and discuss their uses. Perhaps you can arrange for such a visit.

your back as you can reach. Stand erect again, place both forefingers inside the bottom of the brassiere, and run your fingers around the garment. As you do this, pull the garment down in the front and in the back.

Ask yourself: (1) Are the shoulder straps comfortable? (2) Are the bust cups in the correct positions? (3) Is the underbust portion comfortable?

Remember, brassieres should be washed after each wearing to be fresh and to prevent perspiration damage to the fabric and elastic.

SHOES

How to Buy Shoes

The satisfaction you derive from shoes is most important for your health, as well as for your appearance and the limits of your clothing budget!

Your shoe wardrobe should include shoes for every occasion. Your inventory should show the shoes in your wardrobe that are wearable and that need repair, as well as the kind yet to be purchased. Before you go shopping for shoes, decide the *purpose* they are to serve, the *type, lines,* and *colors* that will harmonize with your wardrobe, and the *price* you can afford. Your money goes further when you purchase shoes that will serve several purposes—for school, sport, and street wear. You may also need shoes for formal, warm weather, and leisuretime wear.

The *price* you can pay for shoes is determined by your activities, the care you give them, and the condition of your feet. Well-fitted shoes of good quality may be expensive, if you are hard to fit. Therefore decide on the

price you can afford to pay and begin looking for shoes before you need them. Your purchase will then meet your needs and fit your feet and your pocketbook.

The *comfort* of your shoe is more important than looks and price. An uncomfortable, ill-fitted shoe is expensive because it may cause malformation, corns, bunions, and flat arches and will result in an unhappy expression on your face.

Points to look for in a good shoe
- The sole should be heavy enough to protect your foot from hard surfaces; however, the shoe should be pliable and not too heavy.
- Correct proportion in length from the heel to the ball of the foot and from the ball to the toe, in relation to the overall length, is very important.

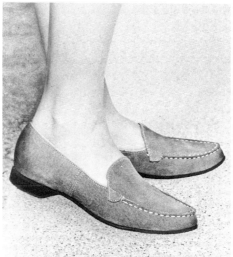

WOLVERINE SHOE CO.

Do your shoes fit this well? The shoe fits snuggly but not tightly at the heel, does not gap along the side, and is about 1 inch longer than the end of the big toe. In addition, the widest part of the shoe corresponds with the widest part of the foot (the ball), an important place to check fit.

187

- The heel should be a comfortable height and wide enough to support the foot. High heels (over 2″) place the foot on an incline from heel to toe, causing more weight to be carried on the front part of the foot. Movement of the toes is hindered and added strain is placed on the metatarsal arches. Narrow heels give an unstable base which cause the foot to twist.

Buying shoes that fit

Shoes are one of the few items that cannot be altered to fit and can actually cause physical damage if fitted improperly.

Do not buy shoes by previous size, but have your feet measured each time you buy shoes. Sizes vary with different makes. Feet grow until one is about 20 years old. A weight change may increase or decrease your shoe size. As one enters middle age, the foot often lengthens.

Shoe sizes are computed on two size ranges. The first size range is used for infants and small children and ranges from size 0 to 13½. The second size range begins at 1 and goes up to 15. This range is used for older children and for adults. (Sizes 7, 7½, and 8 are the most frequently sold women's sizes.)

Sizes in width run from quadruple A (AAAA) to E. A is the narrowest and E is a very wide width. (AA is narrower than A and wider than AAA.) Most shoes for women range from a narrow—A, medium—B, or wide—C. There is no exact number of inches that determines a size in width. The entire circumference of the foot at the ball varies about ¼ of an inch between each width. Size AA is therefore about ¼ of an inch nar-

rower than A, but the sole may appear to be only 1/12 to 1/16 of an inch narrower.

Shop for shoes after walking awhile to allow for normal foot expansion. Shoes bought the first thing in the morning may never be comfortable for all-day wear. Shoes should be fitted to the longer foot. Try on both shoes and walk around. Stand with your weight on both feet to judge shoe length and width. Study your total appearance in a mirror.

How can old shoes serve as a guide for shopping?

- SOLE. If the sole is worn more in the front, your shoe is too short from heel to ball. The sole should wear through at about the center.
- SOLE LINE. When the uppers bulge over the sole line, your shoes are too narrow.
- HEEL. A slight wear at the back or outside line is normal. If new lifts are needed often, or if the heel pushes under, the shoe is too short. When the heels wear on the inside, the arch is weak.
- THE TIP. If a shoe wears at the tip, it is too short.
- TIGHT SHOES. If the inside sole of a shoe has worn pockets for your toes, the shoe is too tight. Shoes that are out of shape mean that the size is not correct.
- SHOES PUCKERED OR WRINKLED. When a shoe is puckered or wrinkled behind the ball along the arch, this shows that it is not long enough from ball to heel.

How to buy shoes to ease foot ills

- WEAK OR FLAT FEET. Choose a sturdy, well-built shoe to support you. A built-up arch holds the foot firmly and gives aid to muscles and ligaments.

- CORNS, CALLOUSES, BLISTERS. Shoes should be made of soft, pliable leather, shaped and cut so there will be no pressure or seams on tender areas.
- INGROWN TOENAILS. A broad toe style provides room. Good depth in the vamp will give added comfort.
- SWOLLEN FEET. Shoes and hose should not be tight. Shoes of porous leather, perforated styles, or open toes permit feet to dry quickly.

Testing your shoes for a good fit

Shoes should be ½ to ¾ inch *longer* than your foot to allow for the lengthening of your foot when you stand. Be sure that you are not fitted too short. The overall length may be right yet the shoe too short because of the proportion from the toes to the ball and from the ball to the heel.

Shoes should have sufficient *width* to prevent crowding and overlapping of your toes. Bend your foot. Is the shoe comfortable?

Be sure the *instep* of the shoe fits smoothly in the "waist." A shoe that is cut too high may cause pressure on the instep and stop circulation. One too tight may cut into your instep.

The shoe *heel* must be broad and deep enough to give you sufficient support. Can you walk easily with the heel height or does it tend to throw you off balance? Does the heel slip? If so, constant rubbing may cause a blister. Does the back of the heel cut into your tendon? If it does, the heel is too deep.

How does the shoe feel as you walk? Does it fit comfortably at the heel, under the arch, over the instep and ball, and with plenty of toe

room? If you wear properly fitted shoes you not only will feel better but your posture will be more graceful.

Correct *lines* for shoes can add or subtract inches from your height, minimize the width of your ankles, or make your feet appear larger or smaller than they are. Always study

AMERICAN AIRLINES

High boots are often worn with very short skirts for appearance as well as protection. Panty hose are a better choice than stockings and garters for miniskirts. Notice how the beret and scarf add interest to a basic dress and coat.

189

U. S. KEDS

Shoes of cotton or polyester and cotton blend uppers and thick rubber soles are sensible for sports wear. Originally called tennis shoes, they are more often called sneakers today. Always available in white, they are often made from plaid and corduroy fabrics for added style.

the effect of your shoes on your figure in a full length mirror. You may find the following suggestions for selecting shoe styles of help to you:

- Wide feet look best in shoes of simple style and all one color.
- Ankle straps call attention to heavy ankles. They also cut the illusion of height.
- A wide foot appears more slender in shoes with V throats or short vamps (portions of shoes from toe to instep).
- A buckle or other decoration may make the foot appear shorter or wider.
- A short foot looks best in a plain line shoe or one with a V or U throat.

NOTE: Heels should be repaired as soon as they become worn. An uneven heel will twist the shoe out of

shape and make you uncomfortable. It will also look shabby.

Materials Used for Shoes

Leather is used for the uppers, linings, soles, and heels of good quality shoes. It is also used for the outside and outer sole of medium quality shoes. For the purpose of fashion, leather may have many finishes—smooth, textured, suede, patent, or metallic. Leather provides a healthy foot covering as it is a sturdy, protective material and it "breathes" or allows normal foot moisture to pass out of the shoes.

Man-made substitutes for leather have been used for style purposes and for less expensive shoes for many years. Vinyls are used for less expensive shoes and different styling effects. **Duck, canvas,** and even **corduroy** made of cotton or blends of cotton and polyester are used for sneakers and shoes for casual wear. Many of these can be washed if directions are followed.

HOSIERY

Buying Hosiery

You now wear hose much better than those designed for queens a few hundred years ago. In 1561 Queen Elizabeth was given her first pair of knitted silk stockings. Then they were so rare and beautiful that for a very long time only she wore silk stockings. Yet your beautiful sheer nylons would seem like a fairyland veil spun from sunbeams, compared with the coarse, uneven hose of England's queen in 1561. Ever since the first nylon hose were sold in Wilmington, Delaware, in October 1939, they have been improving in fit, in construction, and in sheer beauty.

Both men and women wore leg coverings in the early times; however, it was not until the late 18th century that the skirts of women were shortened and they displayed their stockings. Perhaps the improvement in appearance of stockings had something to do with this!

Hosiery may seem to be an insignificant wardrobe item but your total appearance is affected by your choice of leg covering. In addition, you probably spend more money for hosiery than you realize. Research shows that the average woman spends 10 percent of her clothing budget on hosiery. According to home economists at the U. S. Department of Agriculture, the average female (15 years and older) purchases 19 pairs of full-length seamless nylons a year, in addition to other hosiery. The wide variety of styles, fibers, and

Panty hose. Notice the use of finer yarns for the stocking and heavier yarns for the panty section. The solution of what to wear under short, full skirts.

DU PONT

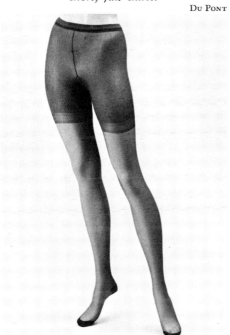

Hosiery for casual or sports wear. Knee socks of a cable design.

BONNIE DOON

191

colors available make it necessary to understand common terms about hosiery in order to make wise decisions.

Types of Hosiery Available

Socks are usually ankle or knee length and are made from medium-weight to heavy yarns. *Stockings* are full length and are usually made of lightweight, fine yarn. In seasons when long skirts are fashionable, knee length sheer hosiery is popular. *Panty hose* are a combination of stocking and panties and are made from fine yarn for the leg portion and heavier yarn for the panty part. *Tights* are also a combination of stockings and panties but are made from heavier, stretch yarns.

Fibers for Hosiery

Stockings are made of silk, nylon, cotton, rayon, or olefin fibers. Nylon is the most popular because it is elastic, easy to wash, dries quickly, and because of its strength, it can be made into very sheer, yet durable hosiery. Olefin fibers are used for long stockings but are not liked too well because they do not feel as soft and often bag at the knee. Silk hosiery was in great demand before the 1941 embargo on silk because of their beauty, elasticity and feel. However, since World War II, they have been very scarce on the market due to their high price and the competition of nylon. Cotton is used for heavy hosiery, usually worn only in very cold weather.

Knee length socks are made from wool or acrylic or other man-made yarns that have the appearance of wool. Cotton is more often selected for ankle length socks.

BONNIE DOON

Long stockings of heavy yarns in a rib pattern. This design is flattering to larger legs.

BONNIE DOON

Sports hosiery of a diamond knit pattern. Suitable for girls with slender legs as the design will give the impression of added size.

Full-fashioned hosiery with seamed back and fashion marks showing where the stitches were knit together for shaping purposes at the calf and the thigh.

Styles

The two types of knit construction used in nylon hose are *full-fashioned* and *circular-knit* or *seamless*.

Full-fashioned hose are knit flat and shaped or proportioned as stitches are decreased or knit together near the calf of the leg. Fashion marks are formed where stitches are combined. The two edges are seamed together along the bottom of the foot and up the back of the leg. Full-fashioned hose fit better than circular knit. They also retain their shape better during wear and after washing.

Circular-knit or seamless hose are knit in tubular form from the welt in one continuous operation. Seamless hose are made with standard heel reinforcement or in the nude style.

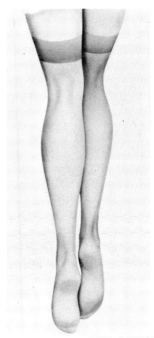

Seamless hosiery suitable for wear with low-cut shoes.

Since circular-knit hose have no seams over the ball of the foot, some people consider this style more comfortable than full-fashioned hosiery.

The fabric of stockings is knitted with two-way stretch. The types of knitting are *plain* and *mesh*. Plain knitting may be recognized by lengthwise loops on the right side and crosswise loops on the wrong side. This results in a sheer hose that is elastic. The disadvantage is that a break in any loop can cause a run. Some stockings are knit with two threads used together as one. This results in longer wear because if one thread breaks, the second thread will hold the fabric together.

In **mesh knitting** the interlocking yarns produce a variety of tiny patterns. Frequently the fabric is of a run-resistant construction in which the loops are interlocked.

The individual yarns can snag as in plain knit, but a broken yarn develops only a hole in the fabric rather than a run. Some mesh knits only run above a thread break. Most mesh knit fabrics are less elastic than plain knit. It is wise to choose a half size larger stocking to make up for the lack of stretch and to avoid strain.

Stretch hosiery are made from yarns made by special patented techniques so that yarn has lasting stretchability. These stockings provide comfort and close fit without binding. Because of their stretchability, these stockings are made in fewer sizes.

The Weight of Hosiery

The size or weight and thickness of nylon yarn is called **denier** (den-yer). The lower the denier number, the thinner the yarn and the sheerer the stocking. The higher the number, the thicker and heavier the yarn and the stronger the stocking. Yarns for hosiery start as low as 7 and may run as high as 80 denier. Most hosiery worn for dress occasions are 15 denier.

You may hear the term **gauge** used as a measurement in hosiery also. It tells you how close and fine the stitches are. The term describes the number of stitches across 1½ inches of a stocking. The higher the gauge number, the greater the strength and stretch, and the less chance of snagging. Stockings will look coarser with lower gauge numbers.

Because the terms denier and gauge are confusing to most consumers, hosiery is often labeled for its purpose: evening sheers, daytime sheers, business, walking, and service weights. You may find that for school

use a business sheer (about 30 denier) will last much longer than the 15 denier most girls wear, and will not appear noticeably heavier.

Determining the correct size and fit of hose

To secure the correct *size* of stockings, consider your foot length and width, and your leg length. The length of your foot in inches is your foot size. A size 9½ stocking should fit a foot 9½ inches long. You may buy comfortable stockings according to your shoe size if the proportion of your legs is about average. Most stockings today are made from stretch yarns and come in small, medium, and large sizes. Some come in extra-large. Consult the chart on the package—it suggests sizes in relation to height and weight.

If the standard stocking size does not fit your foot, or if it does not fit your leg, then ask for *proportioned* stockings. A correct fit for you will depend on the length and shape of your leg and the length of your foundation garment. Flat measurements do not tell how a stocking will fit the fullness of your leg. In each foot size there is a choice of short, medium, and long lengths and three proportions: slender, average, full. Manufacturers have also produced many combinations of ankle, calf, and thigh measurements. When a stocking is on your foot, full-fashioned hose should be ½ inch longer than your foot, and circular knit one inch longer.

Grades of hosiery

The government recognizes the following grades of hosiery: *first quality,* *irregulars,* and *seconds.* As previously said, manufacturers of well-established brands inspect all stockings before shipping them to stores. Those with the slightest flaw in knit, color, or dimension are labeled "irregular" and must be marked down in price. "Seconds" are stockings that have repaired runs or mends or obvious flaws that may affect wear, and naturally they are also sold cheaper.

Care of stockings

When putting on a pair of stockings, gather together the leg portion in both hands and slip your foot into the toe; then gently draw the stocking over your leg, keeping the seam straight. To take them off, do the same thing in reverse. Never pull the extra fullness from the toe of a stocking back up to the heel and over. Smooth it forward and give your toes room to flex.

When fastening garters, flex your knee slightly. This eliminates too-tight gartering and assures enough flexibility for normal leg bending without exerting strain on the stocking. Fasten the back garter first, to make sure that the seam is straight. With the knee still slightly flexed, fasten the front garter last at the top of the stocking. Garters should hang straight and not twist the stocking.

Handle hose carefully at all times. Be sure your hands and nails are smooth. Keep your feet and legs smooth with a body lotion. Wash new hose before wearing them. They should be washed as soon as possible after each time they are worn to remove soil and to restore them to their original shape.

Some hosiery fitting problems

When a stocking is *too long* in either the foot or leg, the wear is increased at the points not reinforced and the loose fabric is more easily snagged. It usually wrinkles at the ankle, bags at the knee, and the seam twists around the leg. If stockings are too long, you will need to fasten them below the safety welt.

A stocking that is *too short* is most annoying because stretching it over the foot or leg uses up its reserve elasticity. Such stockings may bind and make it uncomfortable for you to sit, bend, or reach. If stockings are too short, there will be too much strain on them and they may "pop" and run at the knee.

Stockings that are *too tight* may cause your feet to burn. When an undersized stocking is stretched to get it on your foot it constantly tries to return to its normal shape, and the circulation in the foot is restricted.

Other helps for wise hosiery buying

Always buy two or more pairs of hose alike. You will get at least three times the wear than if you bought two different pairs. If one stocking develops a run, its mate may be used as a spare for the other pair.

If your shoes are open and low cut, sandals, or heel-less, select hosiery without heel and toe reinforcements. Wrong hosiery selection can ruin the effect of these shoes.

In very cold weather, try wearing two pairs of sheer nylons. Be certain the under pair is seamless. You will find the additional pair hardly noticeable but the insulation value and the air space between the two pairs will keep you very warm.

Fashionable colors change from season to season. Dark shades make heavy legs look slimmer and lighter shades add "weight" to thin legs.

However, because a shade of different value than one's other clothing attracts attention, you may want to wear light hose with light clothing even if your legs are heavier than you like. A grayer tone of hose blends best with blue, gray, or black and a beige tone looks best with warm colors as reds, yellows, and browns. Gay colored hose add size to one's legs, for example, red knee socks are seldom flattering on girls with heavy calves. A shade about the same as one's legs attracts less attention and blends well with most dress clothes.

SHIP'N SHORE

How would a pair of these gaily patterned hose look on you? They are a novelty item for the girl with slender, attractive legs. This girl sensibly combines them with a plain colored blouse and shorts of harmonizing colors.

Secure a catalog from a large mail-order company. Study the pages showing hosiery. Make a list of the various sizes carried. What denier hosiery is available? When is gauge mentioned? What colors are featured? How many mesh and how many plain knit are offered? How many are seamless and how many have seams? What is the price range? Are different lengths available? Are there stockings advertised that are of a style new to you? Select the stocking which best suits your needs for everyday wear and state in detail why you selected this one.

Survey your class, or another group of young girls, to learn what they look for when they select hosiery. Perhaps you can develop a short questionnaire that does not need to be signed. Find out the price they usually pay, where they buy, and what styles they prefer. Summarize. Add your own opinions concerning how these girls could be better shoppers of hosiery.

Obtain samples of hosiery of different weights. Ask family members and friends to save worn out stockings for you. Wash them thoroughly and bring them to school. Notice the difference between 10, 15, 30 denier, and heavier weights. Try to determine why each item was discarded.

Sports hose or socks vary in style from season to season. Report to the class the latest styles and fibers used. A visit to a store selling sports hose will be of help as well as a study of advertisements. Talk with the store buyer, if possible, to learn of new trends.

HANDBAGS

In ancient Greece and Rome the weathly citizens carried their coins in a leather drawstring purse. During the Middle Ages, the coin purse was made of other materials and decorated with tassels, beads, and embroidery for a decorative effect. However, it wasn't until the 19th century that all women started to carry handbags. Before then dresses were cut with large, full skirts and had many deep pockets which served as carrying places. When dresses were made to fit the body and pockets largely disappeared, the separate handbag became widely used.

Today most women consider a handbag a necessity but also an accessory that may contribute to the appearance of their entire costume. It may blend with other clothing or it may contrast to provide a needed touch of color or design interest. Texture, color, and design of the bag must harmonize with the entire costume.

Types of bags. Handbags are classified into four basic types: a good sized sports or casual carry-all for school and everyday wear; a tailored daytime bag, somewhat smaller than the carry-all; a bag for luncheons, church, and not too dressy affairs; and a bag for dress-up such as the theater and dances. You may find that with careful selection one bag can serve all your needs except for very dressy occasions. See page 198.

Workmanship. It is difficult to judge the workmanship of a handbag by appearance. However, you should check the fastening. Be certain that it will not come open by itself. Seams should be securely stitched. Gay linings add interest but if they are of a

This girl is checking the fastening of a handbag before purchasing it. She wants to be sure that the bag will not accidentally open in use.

light colored fabric, they may show soil easily. Be sure to select a bag large enough to carry all your needs; the easiest way to ruin the shape and appearance of any handbag is to stuff it too full.

HATS

There is a wide variety in shapes, sizes, colors, and trim in hats. You will find a becoming one among the many styles.

A hat makes a background for the hair, face, and eyes. A hat will be adapted to your figure and suited to the occasion. There has been a fashion for wearing a tiny band or flower in place of the usual hat. These are usually becoming because the hairdo instead of the hat serves as a frame for the face.

HANDBAG STYLES

ATTACHE OR VANITY
- often framed or with center zipper divider
- opens into two equal halves

BOX
- rigid shell, often lid-opening

CHANEL
- distinguished by chain handles
- frequently quilted

CLUTCH
- adaptable round-the-clock depending on material
- disappearing handle or no handle at all

POUCH
- generally soft, roomy and easy to carry

SATCHEL
- large and spacious
- wide, flat bottom
- luggage type handle

SHOULDER STRAP
- casual, ideal traveler
- generally has adjustable strap

SWAGGER
- outside pockets surrounding an interior frame or center zippered pocket

VAGABOND
- enlarged envelope with flap opening

TOTE
- open-top sometimes tab-closed

NATIONAL AUTHORITY FOR THE LADIES' HANDBAG INDUSTRY

The material and workmanship determine the quality and control the price of a hat.

When you know the type of hat you need, much time can be saved. A felt casual hat may be worn for many occasions and for several seasons. Velvets and straws can be worn for only a short time each year.

In Chapter Two in the discussion on line, it was shown that the eye can be carried upward or downward depending upon the type of hat. Decide upon a becoming hairdo; then select a hat that harmonizes with it. Wear the costume which you plan to wear most frequently with the hat. Stand before a full-length mirror as you try it on. Study the hat and your costume from every angle to see if the lines are becoming to your *face* and your *figure*.

Sometimes the way you wear a hat makes it unbecoming. Experiment with placing the hat on your head. Notice that your facial expression will change as you move the hat. Hats tilted at a slight diagonal seem flattering to the average face.

Buying Gloves

Gloves give you a well-dressed and well-groomed appearance. They should harmonize with the costume.

Gloves are made of leather or fabric. Leather gloves are usually more expensive than fabric gloves. Gloves made of kid, lambskin, and novelty fabrics are worn for dressy occasions. Capeskin, pigskin, and tailored fabrics of cotton, wool, rayon, or nylon are suitable for school, street, or sports wear.

Have your hands measured and try on gloves at a counter. Glove sizes may vary with the nature of the material and with different manufacturers.

The manner in which gloves are put on for the first few times influences their fit. Work each finger on carefully with fingers of your opposite hand.

Sizes in women's gloves range by quarter inches from 5½ to 8, with the average of 6½. To determine the size, measure around the knuckles, the widest part of the hand. (Do not include the thumb.) Because most gloves stretch, the measurement is usually one size larger than the glove needed. For example, a girl whose hand measures 7 inches around the knuckles will probably wear a glove size 6¾.

When you buy gloves, the sales person may ask you what glove length you wish. Lengths are referred to by button lengths. This term dates back to the time in France when gloves were fastened with buttons 1 inch apart, starting with a button 1 inch above the thumb. So today, whether the glove has buttons or not, a 2-button glove measures 2 inches from the base of the thumb to the top edge. The most popular length which is suitable for almost every occasion is the 2-button glove. The shorter version, a 1-button, is used for daytime wear or for evening wear except for very formal occasions. A 4-button glove is chosen to wear with ¾ length sleeves. An 8-button glove is usually dressy and is worn with short sleeves. A 16-button glove comes between the elbow and shoulders and is used only for very formal occasions when the gown worn is sleeveless.

As a general rule, gloves should meet the sleeve if it is ¾ length or longer. Very short gloves are correct with short-sleeved or sleeveless dresses except for very formal evening wear.

Check the *workmanship* of the gloves. The seams should be straight and evenly stitched. A *gusset* inserted at the base of each finger will make gloves fit better and wear longer.

HANDKERCHIEFS

Handkerchiefs have been made of many fabrics, from the silk tissue of the early Chinese to the many natural and man-made fabrics of the present.

Since sheer-weight linen absorbs moisture readily, dries quickly, and can be washed and bleached, it is the most satisfactory material. Linen handkerchiefs are made for every occasion, depending on the woven design, print, or trim, and are selected to harmonize with the costume.

Women's handkerchiefs may be decorated by initialing, embroidering, drawnwork, and lace. A handkerchief may be used to supply a bit of color or design needed to complete a costume. A fresh, crisp handkerchief indicates a well-groomed appearance.

SCARFS

The season and the style of garments influence the popularity of scarfs. Fashion determines the shape, size, and texture. Regardless of the type or how worn, scarfs should be selected to harmonize in color and texture with the remainder of the costume. For casual wear, select wool, rayon, or firm silk scarfs. They may be knitted or woven in plain or unusual designs. Silk chiffon and sheer nylon are appropriate for dressy occasions. Scarfs give the correct touch to complete a costume. They may provide warmth as a *head covering* or worn about the neck to protect collars from soil. The *neckerchief* may substitute for beads.

JOHN HANCOCK INSURANCE CO.

A colorful scarf can add a flattering touch of color near the face and also individualize a plain outfit.

Scarfs, like costume jewelry, may add an interesting note of color to a costume as an accent or contrast.

COSTUME JEWELRY

Select costume jewelry in proportion to your figure and suitable to your personality and age. If you are small, select small jewelry. A girl, average in height and weight, will have a greater choice of accessories. A large girl should not wear accessories that are too small. A tailored, dignified type of girl, or the "bombshell" type, can wear striking effects in designs, colors, and textures. Her designs in jewelry may be bold. A feminine, dainty type should wear small jewelry, delicate in design.

Use as little costume jewelry as needed. Unless you can have the right jewelry it is better to do without. The costume jewelry you wear depends to a great extent upon the current fashion in ready-to-wear garments. Necklines decorated with lace and embroidery do not need jewelry. When plain necklines are the fashion, jewelry for the throat and neck, such as beads and necklaces, usually increase in popularity. Costume jewelry worn near the face and neck should enhance the beauty of personal coloring. Never hide your individuality with jewelry but try to bring out your personal type of beauty. Beads may add an interesting note of color to your costume as an accent or contrast.

A *pin* worn in the center front gives a slender appearance to the face and neck. Two pins, one at either side of the neck, give an impression of increased width. One pin or two pins placed on one side of the neckline is more slenderizing than one on each side. When worn high on the shoulder, pins give an added impression of height.

Select bracelets suited to your type. Several narrow bracelets are becoming to most types.

Colorful scarfs worn on the head can help keep the hair in place and also add design and color interest. The design of this scarf is different from the plaid of the skirt but repeats the colors and shapes.

Do you consider your umbrella an accessory? This one is of red and white taffeta and matches the scarf worn at the neckline. Long gloves are worn because of the mid-length sleeves of the all-weather coat of water-repellent polyester and cotton.

Choose your earrings with the shape of your face in mind—large, round earrings accentuate a plump face and long dangling earrings can make a thin face appear more so. Stout girls should avoid wearing large, round beads in a choker effect. This arrangement is for a slender, youthful neck. Long strands, perhaps with an ornament low on the chest, give a more slenderizing effect. "Glitter" such as rhinestones is usually reserved for evening wear.

REMINDER: Being well-groomed is as essential as being well-dressed. A clean well-pressed outfit, polished shoes, straight hose seams, and fresh gloves do more to influence your appearance than a new, expensive outfit. Your posture is important for health and general appearance. Stand tall, chin in, and back straight. Put a song in your heart and a sparkle in your eye, as you go about your activities.

Giving much thought to your clothes and accessories may seem like too much work, but it is really worth the effort.

Paul Poiret, the great French designer of the past, said, "Those who are really well-dressed enjoy a sense of satisfaction equal to the triumphs of any other art."

Prepare a bulletin board or exhibit to illustrate button length of gloves. Show the relationship between lengths and occasions for wearing.

Practice combining accessories with garments. Select pictures of several types of garments. Mount with pictures or descriptions of accessories to be worn with each garment. State the occasion for which you are planning.

Read reference books for information on costume accessories worn in different periods of world history. Study pictures of these accessories from the standpoint of habits of living in that period and of possible influence of these accessories on those of today. List modern accessories with the periods that influenced their reproduction.

Collect pictures of accessories that might be worn by the following figures: (a) short thin, (b) short plump, (c) tall thin, (d) tall plump, (e) average.

Make a collection of pictures showing accessories that might be worn for the various occasions listed in Chapter Four.

Have you purchased satisfactory and unsatisfactory clothing articles because of emotional appeal? Name some.

Watch shoppers for techniques used. Report to the class specific examples of buyers who are shopping without a purpose.

Answer the following questions concerning one of your recent purchases:
   a. Was it satisfactory?
   b. Did you make use of all available informative advertising?
   c. Was the quality of the article worth the price you paid?

Choose a clothing article that is sold by brand name. Check the price of the same article in three stores if possible. Explain why you found the prices the same or different.

Can You Explain These Terms?

overhead	*rummage sale*	*loss leader*
markup	*clothing exchange*	*job lots*
department store	*brand name*	*broken lot*
specialty store	*labels*	*dog*
neighborhood store	*seals of approval*	*markdown*
mail-order store	*bargain*	*lawaway*
variety store	*store brand*	*regular charge account*
discount house	*end-of-season sale*	*revolving charge account*
factory outlet	*irregular*	*tariff*
seconds	*as is*	*quota*

Summary with Check-Up Questions

In order to be a wise shopper, a consumer needs to understand how retail stores operate.

- *What is the difference between a markup and profit?*
- *Why can some stores operate at a lower markup than others?*
- *Why can stores afford to sell some items at little, if any, profit?*

A good buy is anything that suits your needs at a price you want to pay.

- *If you can get what you want for less money, is it a bargain?*
- *If you can get a better quality for the price you expect to pay, is it a bargain?*
- *If an item does not really suit your needs but it costs much less than the usual price, is it a bargain?*

Consumers cannot depend entirely on legal regulation for quality or safety.

- *What information is legally required to be on garment labels?*
- *Are cosmetics tested for safety before being marketed?*
- *Is it illegal to charge more for a clothing item than it is worth?*

Shopping at sales can sometimes save money:

- *Is it worth it to drive 20 miles to a sale to buy a pair of shoes for a dollar less than the usual price?*
- *Why can stores sell articles for a small profit at sales?*
- *Does it pay large stores to keep merchandise for another season?*

A good shopper handles merchandise carefully.

- *How do stores dispose of merchandise that has been damaged or soiled?*
- *How can the cost of all merchandise in a store be affected by the loss a merchant takes on damaged goods?*
- *How do you feel if you purchase an article and find it soiled or torn?*

A good shopper returns unsatisfactory garments.

- *Why do retail stores want to know if their merchandise proves defective?*
- *Retail stores buy in good faith; most stores do not have testing laboratories of their own. How will they discover if some items are not as claimed?*

203

A high priced item may not be the best quality.

- *What effect does fancy trim such as fur, sequins, or an unusual braid have on the price of a garment?*
- *Do retailers mark up garments of classic style more or less than those apt to lose their popularity at any time?*
- *What effect does the decoration and the services offered by a store have on the price of merchandise carried?*

A wise shopper saves labels and sales slips for a reasonable time.

- *If a garment needs to be returned because it did not wear as expected, of what value is the label and sales slip?*
- *When it is time to have a garment of a new fiber or finish cleaned, how will you know the best method?*
- *If you want to buy another article similar to one which has given you good service, how will you describe it to the salesperson?*

Comparison shopping at several sources can save money.

- *Why do prices differ for the same merchandise at different stores?*
- *Why do prices differ at the same store from time to time?*
- *If you find an article that you think is just what you want, how will you know if it is worth the price asked?*

A wise consumer evaluates her past purchases in terms of price, amount of care required, and wearing qualities in order to get helpful information for future purchases.

- *How will a study of worn shoes help one in selecting new ones?*
- *What can you learn from looking at your "perfectly good" garments which you seldom wear?*
- *What are the reasons for evaluating the appearances of a clothing article you are discarding?*

Reading and heeding labels can help consumers make satisfactory clothing purchases.

- *Why does a manufacturer state washing instructions on clothing labels?*
- *How can one tell if a fabric has been treated for water repellency, shrink resistance, or no ironing after laundering?*

The best quality may not be as wise a choice as the medium or lower quality for some clothing purchases.

- *What quality would be best for a coat to be worn several seasons?*
- *Why would the best quality of workmanship not be necessary for a gown to be worn as a guest at a wedding?*
- *An unusual style blouse is the latest fad. What quality would you suggest for such a purchase?*

A high quality outer fabric is of little value if the other parts of the garment are of poor quality.

- *What will be the effect of an interfacing material that shrinks on a firm, good quality cotton suiting?*
- *Why is it often wise to remove the belt and buttons from a lower quality garment and replace them with your own selection?*
- *What will happen to a lovely well-made dress if the thread used is not colorfast?*

A wise shopper knows how to determine the quality of clothing items or is able to understand the meaning of labels.

- *Is price always a guide to quality?*
- *Can you assume that all clothing sold by a store with a good reputation will be of top quality and free from defects?*
- *What information is needed about garments and fabrics that cannot be determined from appearance and feel alone?*

Advertising can be of value to a consumer if used with understanding.

- *How can one learn of new items available on the market?*
- *How can advertising cause you to buy something you do not really need or want?*
- *How can you get needed information about clothing items needed before going on a shopping trip?*
- *What means do stores use to let customers know of special sales?*

Buying on credit has both advantages and disadvantages.

- *What is the cost of a garment purchased on a revolving credit plan?*
- *What happens if you do not complete payment on a layaway item?*
- *When can you wear a garment bought on the charge plan?*

Shoes are one of the few items that cannot be altered to fit and that can cause actual physical damage if fitted improperly.

- *What can be done with shoes that are too narrow?*
- *How are corns and calluses caused?*
- *What is the appearance of shoes fitted too large?*

There are advantages and disadvantages of each type of store.

- *If personal attention is needed, what type of store or stores will you choose?*
- *When a large choice of items is desired, where is it wise to shop?*
- *If one needs to buy as economically as possible, what are suitable sources?*

Sometimes it pays to sew; sometimes it pays to buy ready-mades.

- *Is it wise for a person to sew her own clothing if she is very busy and has very little free time?*
- *What are the advantages of sewing for a woman whose figure requires many alterations?*
- *Why do mothers often find it worthwhile to sew for their families?*
- *What garments are better bought by all but the most skilled seamstresses?*
- *What garments can be satisfactorily made by most sewers?*

A good shopper avoids buying garments that require alterations other than such simple ones as a change of hemline.

- *How much do stores charge for alterations of women's clothing?*
- *What is the effect on the lines of a garment if alterations are poorly made?*

Shopping for undergarments is as important as shopping for outer wear.

- *How will a lovely sheer dress look worn over an ill-fitting brassiere?*
- *What effect will a tight girdle have on a sheath dress?*
- *How can a slip or pettislip affect the appearance of the dress worn over it?*

A wise shopper needs to know where to shop, how to understand advertisements and labels, which method to select for paying for purchases, and how to judge quality.

- *As a result of your study of this subject, what improvements will you make in your shopping techniques?*

CHAPTER SIX

Grooming

To BE well groomed means to be suitably dressed, poised, and clean and neat. A handsome man who is not well groomed does not look his best. Even a girl of rare beauty lacks charm if she is untidy. Anyone can achieve distinction through proper grooming! It is much more important to your success, happiness, and health to be well groomed than good looking. Good grooming and personality are far greater assets than perfect features.

THE MIRROR TEST

As you stand before your mirror, take an inventory of yourself. What needs to be done to give you a fresh, immaculate appearance? Perhaps your hair has lost its sheen, your clothes could be more tidy, or your skin is not well kept. Check on yourself. Use the following rating sheet for this purpose.

After you have filled out the self-evaluation form, study it carefully. What areas need most improvement? Set a date for a few weeks from now,

perhaps a special holiday or family celebration. Decide on a plan for self-improvement and check yourself again on that date. You will be surprised and pleased what a little consistent effort can do to improve your general appearance.

A nutritious lunch helps this young miss maintain her well-groomed and charming appearance.
SIMPLICITY PATTERN CO.

SELF-EVALUATION FUN QUIZ

How I Rate Now	How I Will Rate
DATE _____	DATE _____

<table>
<tr><td>

FUN-DAMENTAL STATISTICS:

Height _____
Weight _____
Age _____

</td><td>

FUN-DAMENTAL STATISTICS:

Weight lost _____
Weight gained _____
Same _____

</td></tr>
<tr><td>

MY GENERAL APPEARANCE IS:

Good looking _____
Average _____
Due for a change _____

</td><td>

MY GENERAL APPEARANCE IS:

Excellent _____
Improved _____
Same _____

</td></tr>
<tr><td>

MY FIGURE IS:

Good _____
Like a drinking straw _____
Like a butterball _____

</td><td>

MY FIGURE IS:

Excellent _____
Improved _____
Same _____

</td></tr>
<tr><td>

MY HAIR CONDITION IS:

Shiny as an apple _____
Average _____
Drab, drab, drab _____

</td><td>

MY HAIR CONDITION IS:

Excellent _____
Improved _____
Same _____

</td></tr>
<tr><td>

MY HAIR STYLE IS:

Becoming _____
Tidy _____
Like a mop _____

</td><td>

MY HAIR STYLE IS:

Excellent _____
Improved _____
Same _____

</td></tr>
<tr><td>

MY NAILS ARE:

Clean _____
Brittle as a peppermint stick _____
Rippled as a clamshell _____

</td><td>

MY NAILS ARE:

Excellent _____
Improved _____
Same _____

</td></tr>
<tr><td>

MY POSTURE IS:

Erect _____
Average _____
Pretzel-shaped _____

</td><td>

MY POSTURE IS:

Excellent _____
Improved _____
Same _____

</td></tr>
<tr><td>

MY WALK IS:

Graceful _____
Average _____
Clump, clump _____

</td><td>

MY WALK IS:

Excellent _____
Improved _____
Same _____

</td></tr>
<tr><td>

MY LIPS ARE:

O.K. _____
Too thin _____
Too full _____

</td><td>

MY LIPS ARE:

Excellent _____
Improved _____
Same _____

</td></tr>
<tr><td>

MY SKIN IS:

Smooth _____
Oily as tossed salad _____
Dry as a wishbone _____

</td><td>

MY SKIN IS:

Excellent _____
Improved _____
Same _____

</td></tr>
<tr><td>

MY SPEECH IS:

Pleasant _____
Harsh _____
Too soft _____

</td><td>

MY SPEECH IS:

Excellent _____
Improved _____
Same _____

</td></tr>
<tr><td>

MY MAJOR PROBLEMS ARE:

_____
_____

</td><td>

THIS IS WHAT I WILL DO IN THE FUTURE:

_____
_____

</td></tr>
</table>

(Why not check the clothes care chart on page 239 also?)

ADAPTED FROM KNOX GELATINE

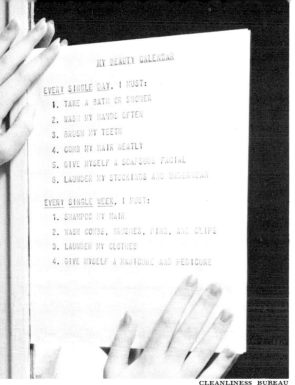

MY BEAUTY CALENDAR

EVERY SINGLE DAY, I MUST:

1. TAKE A BATH OR SHOWER
2. WASH MY HANDS OFTEN
3. BRUSH MY TEETH
4. COMB MY HAIR NEATLY
5. GIVE MYSELF A SOAPSUDS FACIAL
6. LAUNDER MY STOCKINGS AND UNDERWEAR

EVERY SINGLE WEEK, I MUST:

1. SHAMPOO MY HAIR
2. WASH COMBS, BRUSHES, PINS, AND CLIPS
3. LAUNDER MY CLOTHES
4. GIVE MYSELF A MANICURE AND PEDICURE

Don't trust your memory with even the best planned beauty schedule—especially in the beginning. Make up a beauty chart, listing all the things you plan to do daily and weekly. Place this where you are sure to see it—preferably on a bedroom or bathroom mirror.

Careful grooming is essential to your health and happiness. It will help you increase your self-respect, keep your friends, and make new acquaintances.

Perhaps earlier in your school career you kept a health score card. Recall a few of the important things that were listed, such as: cleanliness, eating wisely, beauty sleep and rest, fun and exercise in the fresh air, and regular elimination. In this chapter you will continue to study more about making yourself attractive.

A few minutes of personal attention each morning and evening will get the habit formed so that beauty will become a part of you. Beauty is acquired and kept by constant care of your body.

Find a picture of a well-groomed person and another picture of a person who is not well-groomed. What are the characteristics of each? Perhaps you could make a collection over a period of time of pictures of people who are not as well-groomed as desired (the newspapers are a good source) and mount them on a tackboard with suggestions for improvement. Add pictures of well-groomed people for comparison.

Discuss the difference in the way one feels when well-groomed and when not well-groomed.

Have a panel discussion on what makes a person attractive and admired; consider posture, health, cleanliness, manners, general behavior, becomingness and condition of clothes.

YOUR SKIN

A clean, smooth skin usually accompanies good health. The skin of a healthy and well-nourished person is smooth, slightly moist, and tinged

These FHA national officers are good examples of careful grooming that add to one's attractiveness.

with pink. The skin of a poorly nourished person is likely to be dull and dry.

Your skin expels about two pints of perspiration each day through its pores. The water in perspiration is evaporated but oily secretions and body impurities are left on the skin. Frequent bathing is necessary to remove body wastes, dirt, and loosened scales of skin. *Cleanliness* is your first step in good grooming. A well-groomed person has a well-scrubbed appearance at all times. This has been true with many before you, even in ancient times. Earliest written records mention bathing for pleasure and cleanliness in the river Nile in ancient Egypt and later in the municipal baths of ancient Rome.

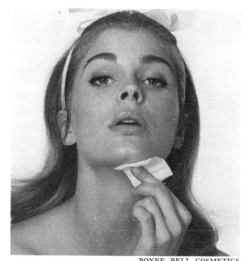

BONNE BELL COSMETICS

This girl's skin shows the good care she takes of it. It is smooth, slightly moist, and clear. Also she is lucky because her skin is free of blemishes.

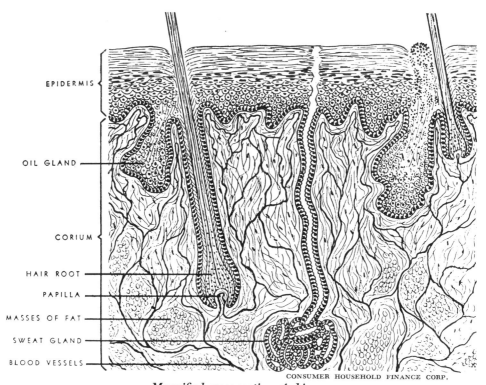

EPIDERMIS

OIL GLAND

CORIUM

HAIR ROOT

PAPILLA

MASSES OF FAT

SWEAT GLAND

BLOOD VESSELS

CONSUMER HOUSEHOLD FINANCE CORP.

Magnified cross-section of skin.

A daily bath in warm water with a generous lather of *mild soap* will provide cleanliness. Strong soaps will dry out the oils from your body and make the skin rough. Be sure to rinse well after your bath. Dry your body thoroughly to help prevent *chapping*. The soothing effect of warm water helps to release muscular tensions. Remember to keep your back and shoulders thoroughly clean *all* year so they won't show neglect when you decide to wear low-cut party clothes or swim suits.

A sponge bath can be a good substitute for a tub or shower. A cold shower in the morning is stimulating to the circulation of the blood, if followed by a brisk rub with a coarse towel.

Depilatories, deodorants, and antiperspirants are essential to a well-groomed appearance. Short sleeves require that your underarms be clean and free from excess hair. Do not use a deodorant immediately after removing hair, because it may irritate your skin.

A strap-type scrubber of rough material gets every inch of the back clean. A rough towel will serve the same purpose but may be harder to use.

"CHARM BY CHOICE," NATIONAL URBAN LEAGUE

A leisurely bath is fine if you have time. But if other family members must use the same facilities, a quick shower or thorough stand-up sponge bath is adequate to remove dust and grime from clogged pores so they can breathe freely.

FACIAL CARE

Your face and neck require special care. A few minutes every morning and night spent caring for your face can prevent many hours of corrective care later.

Cleansing. If you use cosmetics, they should be removed with cleansing cream before you wash your face and neck. One method of facial care consists of a thorough cleansing twice a day. Soap your hands or use a warm sudsy cloth and go over your face and neck. Use an upward motion as you stroke your face. Give special attention to the oily areas around your nose and chin and remember to wash around your hairline. Rinse the face in warm water, then with cooler water, always stroking upward. Several rinses with cold water will stimulate the circulation. Pat dry with an absorbent towel. If you rub, do it gently. To keep a smooth skin, never go to bed without thoroughly cleansing your face and neck.

A skin that is clean will seldom have clogged pores that result in blackheads and whiteheads. Should blackheads appear, squeeze them with care to prevent an infection. Some authorities recommend softening blackheads with hot water packs. With very clean hands, and a disposable tissue, gently press out the material. When the pores are freed of clogged material, close them by sponging with cold water. The regular use of an astringent cream often brings the little deposit of a whitehead near the surface where it can be washed away.

Chapped face. Does your skin feel rough, flaky, and taut after washing? If so, it may be dry or chapped. If your face is chapped, you may prefer cleansing it with cleansing cream just before washing it. An application of a cream before going out in cold, windy weather may prevent skin chapping. Good cold creams will help to make it soft and cleanse more deeply than will soap and water. Cold creams do not nourish the tissue where they are applied. The skin is nourished only through the blood. Your face condition depends largely upon your general health and cleanliness.

Wrinkles may be caused by facial habits such as frowning or squinting. A change of habits may help prevent their increase. Take proper care of your skin when you are young, and you can help prevent lines and wrinkles from appearing on your face.

Blemishes. During adolescence, oil glands are likely to be more active than at any other stage of life. Many chronic cases of pimples are the result of an oily skin. When the condition of the skin improves, pimples are likely to disappear.

Acne (prolonged eruptions) is common to many young people during adolescence. Although it is not certain if it is directly related to nutrition, a well-balanced diet and adequate rest helps to maintain a healthy condition of the skin and, together with special cleanliness, may keep acne under control. Many young people have found that it helps to eat less fatty foods such as fried potatoes, rich pastries, and chocolates. If the skin eruptions are persistent, a dermatologist (a doctor who specializes in skin problems) should be consulted.

This smart young miss covers her hair with a towel to protect it. Notice that she gives special attention to her elbows, and also how the waterproof pillow helps her relax as she soaks for a little while.

CLEANLINESS BUREAU

This high school student is as conscientious about removing make-up as she is about applying it. Her good-grooming schedule includes a soapsuds facial daily, and an occasional gentle scrubbing with a complexion brush for thorough cleansing and extra stimulation.

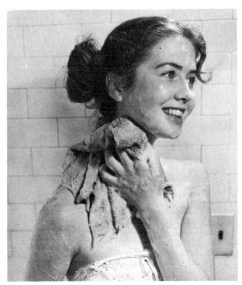

When your face is washed, finish with a cold splash to tighten facial muscles and close pores. Pat your skin dry with a soft towel or gently wipe upward.

You may feel that you can hasten the cure of a pimple by squeezing it, but this action may spread the matter in it and contribute to spread of more pimples and possibly result in an infection. Apply a hot pack with a clean washcloth to help bring the pimple to a head and dry it up quickly. NOTE: A cotton square which can be discarded after use is even better than a washcloth.

Even though you may feel that a blemish stands out like a spotlight on your face, you will find that your friends seldom notice it if you are cheerful and well-groomed. Perhaps some of the tricks described in Chapter 2 will help attract attention away from your face until the blemish clears up.

Exposure to the sun. A suntan is flattering to many people but tough,

blackened skin is not. So don't overdo it. Continued exposure to the strong sun can dry out skin and make it look old before its time. If you must be out in the bright sun, wear a large hat or use a special sunburn preventative. Suntan preparations are intended ei-

Read a consumer's magazine such as "Consumer Report" or "Consumer Digest" on the effectiveness of various types of deodorants and antiperspirants. Summarize the findings for the class.

Prepare a report on the value of various types of sunburn lotions and suntanning preparations from references listed at the back of the book. Summarize for the class.

Interview the school doctor concerning his suggestions for avoiding acne and treating pimples.

Only clean, well-brushed hair could appear as glowing as this girl's. Notice how natural her make-up looks.

Oily and blemished skins are common to teenagers, so a thorough and stimulating cleaning is necessary. Rinse with plenty of water to remove any traces of soap which may help dry out the skin.

ther to screen out the burning rays of the sun or to soothe skin already sun-burned. Suntan preparations are of two types: (1) oils or greases that hasten the development of natural tan in the skin; (2) creams and lotions, that, when applied on the skin, simulate the color of tanned skin.

CLOTHING TIP: White is flattering to your suntan. Pale blue accentuates it and solid, bright colors are striking.

Make-up. Girls in the lively teens usually have sufficient coloring in their faces. They need very little make-up. If you wish to use it, use only enough to look natural or *like yourself at your very best*. Make-up, like hair styling and hand care, should bring out your best points and conceal your least desirable ones.

At work or school you can work up a suds from available soap to wash away smudges acquired during the day. Only a few minutes during free periods or lunch time will keep your skin clean and pretty.

213

Cosmetics can never cover up the lack of proper skin care. Study your complexion to determine the tone of powder or foundation base you require. Powder may be used to protect your skin and make it smooth.

Powders are either rosy to harmonize with skins that are pink, or beige to harmonize with yellowish skins. Select a powder in a color group that harmonizes with your skin and is just a trifle deeper than your own skin tone. Bronze and dark brown shades are available for similarily colored skins, but a colorless, transparent powder which adds no tint but cuts down on shine and leaves a soft, smooth look to the face, may be preferred. Young girls seldom need the liquid or pancake make-up that covers up the flaws of older skin.

If you care to use a "complexion aid" such as rouge, lipstick, or blusher, be sure they match. To insure the exact tones, some girls use their lipstick as rouge. Experiment in daylight in front of your mirror. You should not be able to detect where your rouge or "complexion aid" stops and starts. Wear deeper tones of lipstick at night. More rouge may be used for nighttime activities. (Remember always to be *natural looking*.) In selecting cosmetics, give thought to the color of your clothes as well as your skin. You would not wear a blue-red dress with orange-red cosmetics.

Lipsticks come in many, many colors but they can be classified into three groups—a clear red, red-orange, and a red with blue-violet tones. Orange-red lipsticks may have brown undertones which are flattering to bronze skins.

Clear reds and pinks go well with almost any skin tone. At times, frosted tones are popular. Reds and pinks with a blue tone are flattering to fair and pink skins and go well with clothes of rose, blue, purple, wine, and navy. They are also attractive on dark skins with a red-violet overtone. Red-orange and coral are stunning on girls with red hair and golden tanned skins. These colors harmonize with costumes of brown, green, yellow, orange, and pink with a yellow overtone.

Do not permit yourself, through the use of make up, to appear to be something you are not. Make-up, when used, should make you look like yourself at your prettiest. It should never be so startling that it attracts attention.

After tweezing stray eyebrows, especially the fine hairs that grow over the nose, apply a small amount of cream or lotion to smooth the skin.

Remember to blot your lipstick carefully with a tissue after applying it. No girl is well-groomed with lipstick stains on her teeth.

Eye make-up may be used in the evening to make your eyes more noticeable, *not* to attract attention to the make-up. Some seasons it is in style to use a "smidgen" of eye make-up during the day.

Eye make-up can provide an attractive frame for the eyes—making them seem larger, more radiant. It emphasizes and lends importance to eyes that would otherwise pass unnoticed, and is a boon to girls who wear glasses. It can also attract so much attention to the eyes that the girl herself goes unnoticed, or else she looks so made-up that she seems ready for a party, not for school or work. In most offices eyebrow pencil and a light touch of mascara are permissible.

If your eyebrows are wild and shaggy, a shaping job is needed. Tweeze away stray hairs at the bridge of your nose and beneath the arch. Tiny, feather-like strokes of an eyebrow pencil or brush, not a straight line, can help your appearance if your eyebrows are light or sparse. Avoid black unless your hair is truly jet-black, as it will look harsh and unnatural. Select a brown pencil if you have dark brown hair; otherwise, a light or reddish brown pencil is flattering.

Mascara will darken eyelashes so eyes may seem larger and more radiant. If your lashes are very light, select a brown shade for a natural look. Brownish-black or black is effective for darker lashes. Blues, greens, and other exotic shades are suitable for evening wear. Apply mascara only to the upper lashes; keep your touch light so the lashes do not stick together—each lash must be separate when you finish.

A Reminder

Watch your manners. Touch-ups of powder and lipstick, and hair combing are not in good taste at a dinner table, in a classroom, or in a friend's living room. If you must refresh your make-up in public, do it as quickly and as inconspicuously as possible.

Some students in your class probably have clear skin while others have oily or dry skin. A few may have a combination of both oily and dry. Form committees for each type of skin. After the members of each group have read references to determine the proper care for their type of skin, report to the class.

Why not classify the lipsticks your classmates are wearing now as to red, blue-red, or orange-red? Have each girl draw a line on white paper with her current lipstick and then group the samples into the correct groups. From fabric swatches, notice how certain lipsticks "go with" some colors and clash with others.

How much do cosmetics cost the average girl each year? Try to keep an account of what you spend during the next month.

Prepare an experiment to determine the difference in results in the look of face powder directly on the skin, over a foundation base, and over a moisturizing lotion. The back of the hand is a suitable place for such a demonstration.

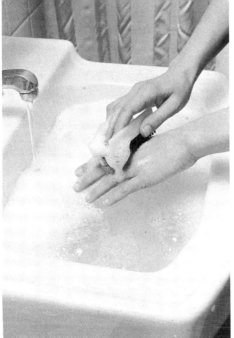

A thorough hand scrubbing with a nail brush and suds at least once a day will help slough off dry skin cells and remove grime. Always scrub downward like doctors do so the soil and bacteria are carried safely away.

HANDS

You may not possess hands with well-shaped fingers; however, you may have well-groomed, attractive hands at the expense of a little thought and daily care. Your hands often attract as much attention as your face. Therefore, you owe them special care.

Cleansing and softening. Rough hands are difficult to keep clean. Protect them with gloves when doing house or yard work. Wear rubber or plastic gloves when your hands are in water or a cleaning solution for a long time.

Brush the nails with a nail brush. Rinse your hands in clear water and wipe them, gently pushing back the cuticle around each fingernail. How would you like a professional-style manicure? Would you like to practice

on each other's hands using cosmetics from home? You may wish to follow the suggested instructions or perhaps you could plan a manicure session at a club meeting.

Manicure. Remove all the old nail polish with an oily base remover, as it is not as drying to your nails and cuticle as one without oil. Wash hands well and scrub the nails with a brush. Trim away the uneven and rough edges with an emery board. A metal file may be suitable for a young man's nails but it is too coarse for girls.

Cuticle remover helps keep the cuticle where it belongs. Follow the directions on the bottle as brands vary.

Your nails may be filed round, oval, square, or pointed. The shape that is chosen depends upon the contour of your fingers and your preference.

You may wish to buff your nails to give them a gloss. If you decide to apply liquid polish, apply it evenly with wide strokes, being careful not to let polish spread onto the skin around the nail. Should this happen, remove with the tip of a file or with your finger and then wipe the polish off quickly with a tissue.

A coat of nail base will prevent the polish from chipping. Apply a thin coat of polish and let it dry, then apply a second coat. With a tissue, remove a tiny edge at the end of the nail. Your polish will not chip so easily.

Clear polish is always attractive and makes nails look clean and attractive. If you use color, select the same tone as your lipstick.

TIPS ON POLISHING: If your nail polish needs repair, do not try to patch or recoat. Remove the old polish and apply fresh. Fresh polish applied over old gives the nails a scarred look.

This teen combines her urge to chat on the phone, with her weekly nail beauty treatment—finger soaking and brushing with soapsuds, shaping, cuticle care, and nail polish for special occasions.

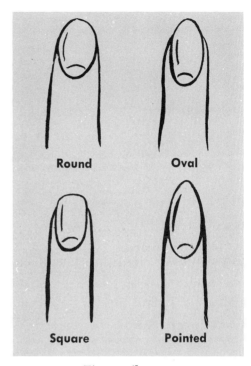

Round   **Oval**

Square   **Pointed**

Fingernail types.

In putting on nail polish, provide time for it to dry and prevent smearing. Polish is not necessary if nails are well groomed.

Polish is the last step for a manicure—soak in warm soapsuds to thoroughly cleanse skin and nails and to soften the cuticle is the first step.

217

For hands that have become rough, stir some glycerine into thick soapsuds, massage the mixture over your hands, and put on plastic mitts while the lubricant penetrates. Rinse thoroughly. Used as a weekly treatment, skin will be softer and nails cleaner.

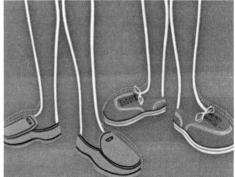

"CHARM BY CHOICE," NATIONAL URBAN LEAGUE
Care for your feet the way you care for your hands to be sure they are not neglected. For lasting foot health, wear proper shoes that fit well. Soft sneakers and flat open loafers are great for occasional wear but when worn every day will allow your foot to spread.

FEET

If your feet are bothering you, perhaps it is because you haven't treated them right. Girls do not always realize that many foot troubles are caused by poorly fitted shoes or stockings. Corns and bunions often develop during the late teen-age years. How can the care of your feet improve your personal appearance? The way you look often depends upon the way your feet feel. It is hard to smile and have a pretty face when your feet hurt.

Comfortable shoes help you to move with natural grace. You will find information on selection of shoes in the chapter entitled "Shopping Wisely and Well."

Foot troubles. A *callous* is caused by pressure over an area. A *corn* is caused by pressure at a point. The

"CHARM BY CHOICE," NATIONAL URBAN LEAGUE
Excessively high heels, in addition to being uncomfortable, can do damage to your posture. One and two inch heels are comfortable and you will look better when you walk.

outer layers of skin are separated from the blood vessels and nerves. The greater the pressure the heavier the layers of callous or corn. *Soft corns* form between the toes; *hard corns* form where skin is dry.

Ingrown toenails are caused by shoes which are too narrow and too short. Trim the nail straight across as

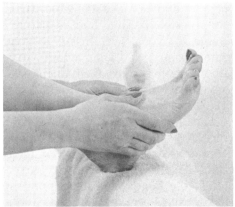

Cold cream or hand lotion rubbed on your ankles and backs of your heels will help prevent roughness.

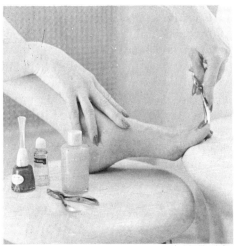

Cut the toenail straight across.

Ivory foot with sandal—Roman imperial era.

Modern sandal with two straps back of toes, nothing over heel.

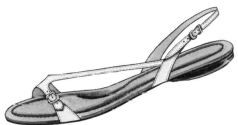

Delicate stripping and banded sandals focus attention on a pretty foot or a trim ankle.

a preventive measure before trouble develops.

Your feet require almost as much time and the same equipment for a pedicure as your hands, if you keep them well-groomed. Heels with rough, scaly skin are not attractive under sheer hosiery. The frequent use of hand cream will soften heels. The style of wearing thongs, sandals, or open-toed shoes and no stockings is not attractive if your feet are not well kept.

How do the sandals of long ago differ from those worn today? According to the Bible, as Abraham sat in his tent during the heat of the day, he looked up and saw three strange men. He went to meet them and asked them to rest under a tree while his servant went for water so they could wash their feet. These men wore sandals which gave no protection from dust and dirt; thus it was necessary to wash the feet after every walk.

CLEANLINESS BUREAU

Homework deluxe! This student keeps her feet in shape by soaking them in a basin of warm soapsuds. After 15 minutes of soaking—along with homework—her calluses and pump bumps will soften enough to be scrubbed away with a brush or well-lathered pumice stone.

Pedicure or nail care. Scrub your toenails during a bath. An orange-wood stick may be used to clean around and under the toenails during the foot bath. Dry the toenails thoroughly and push the soft cuticle back with an orange-wood stick. Cut toenails straight across and almost even with the end of the toe. File the rough edges with an emery board.

Dry carefully between the toes, as a moist area is a potential hazard for infection often called athlete's foot. When you walk in your bare feet at a beach or in any public place, you may pick up this fungus, which is irritating and difficult to eradicate.

HAIR

Hair is known as a person's crowning glory. Whether it be red, blonde, black, or brown, you can be attractive if you keep it well-groomed. Most people appreciate soft, glossy hair, simply styled. Your hair is nature's frame for your face. Just as a good complexion is fed from within, so is shining hair the result of cleanliness, a balanced diet, good health and regular care.

Clean hair can also help your complexion as medical authorities believe that oily hair is the cause of many skin blemishes. Very oily locks that touch the face and drifting dandruff flakes can cause skin blemishes. If you wear your hair down on your face and you are bothered with skin eruptions, try keeping it away from your face and see if you notice an improvement.

Brushing the hair. Your hair requires constant care because it accumulates and holds dust. As you brush and comb your hair, you help to remove dust and keep it glossy; you also stimulate circulation and permit your scalp to "breathe." A stiff brush is best because it stimulates your scalp. Brushes with synthetic bristles are harsh on delicate hair. As you

"CHARM BY CHOICE," NATIONAL URBAN LEAGUE

Defuzzing legs and underarms is important. Either a hair removing cream or a razor can be used.

220

brush your hair every night, lift the scalp each time you make a stroke. Massaging your scalp will help. Begin at the back of your neck by pressing upward with both hands, and continue the circular motion over your

Brush your hair away from the scalp, lifting it each time you take a stroke. You will find the blood circulation improved and your hair will be better nourished.

Long hair needs regular brushing to distribute the natural oils and help prevent dry ends.

entire head. Remember to keep your hair brush clean—wash it whenever it appears dirty and *always* when you shampoo your hair. Why should you not lend your comb or borrow one from a friend?

Dry hair is improved by brushing as the scalp is stimulated to secrete more oil and the hair becomes softer. Oily hair is also helped as the hair oils are distributed evenly. A piece of gauze placed over the brush often absorbs excess oil.

Shampooing. Shampoo your hair as often as it becomes dirty. How often and the method you use will depend upon your hair. If your hair is oily, you may need to shampoo it once or twice a week. On the other hand, too frequent washing makes it seem lifeless. To shampoo your hair, first brush it; them massage your scalp. Finally, wet your hair with warm water, work a liquid soap into the scalp, rub well, and rinse with warm water. Repeat the soaping and rinsing about three times or until the scalp is clean. It is a good idea to use a soft sudsy brush all around the hairline to remove stale cosmetics and neckline grime.

Massaging the scalp and shampooing the hair at the same time.

221

A lemon rinse is suggested for blondes; brunettes may use about two tablespoons vinegar to a quart of water. Then rinse your hair in clear water. Your hair is clean when it makes a squeaky sound as you rub it in rinsing. You may wish to rub your hair dry with a towel or you may set it while wet.

Special hair problems. Special hair problems need special attention. To help control *dry hair,* massage a very little warm olive oil into your scalp. Then, just before washing it, wind a towel wrung out of hot water around your head to "steam" the oil into your scalp. Shampoo as usual. You may need to repeat this treatment several times before achieving results.

To help control *oily hair,* wash it twice a week. Expose your hair to lots of sunshine and brush it frequently.

Dandruff is a nuisance that almost everyone has at times. Usually it is a sloughing off of the dry skin of the scalp and can be controlled by thorough brushing to remove the excess skin particles from the hair. A special dandruff treatment shampoo may help. If you have an extremely scaly scalp or one with sores, a dermatologist should be consulted.

Hair Styling. Selecting a hair style is like selecting a new dress. You want one that accentuates your good features and is also suitable for your activities. Just as fashion styles change, so do hair styles. One year "everyones" hair must be short and a few seasons later long hair is more stylish. Also, like fashion in dress, you need to discover a style that is current but especially flattering to you.

Girls with oval-shaped faces and regular features can wear almost any hair style, but very few people have oval faces! Many more girls have faces that are either long and narrow, round or square, diamond or heart shaped. Other girls are concerned about suitable styles for a high forehead or perhaps an overly long or short neck or a receding chin. Even eyeglasses can influence the way you wear your hair.

GEORGETOWN UNIVERSITY HOSPITAL

Hair styles suitable for nurses—well away from the face and no loose strands to disturb patients.

JORDAN MARSH AND CO.
CHARM AND BEAUTY WORKSHOP

Deciding on a becoming hair style is often easier if a friend helps.

Set aside a time in an activity period for girls to help others discover new hair styles suitable for them. You may discover a method you never thought of that is both becoming and suited to your activities.

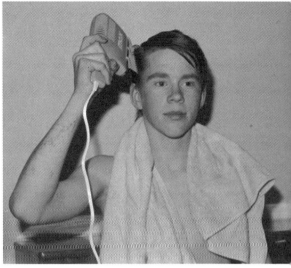

A hand-held hair dryer will dry your hair quickly and also help style it the way you prefer. The same dryer can be used by both girls and young men.

The oval face. If you have an oval-shaped face, you are fortunate, as it is considered the ideal type. It suits all styles of hairdress equally well because the proportions of the face are nearly perfect.

The long face. You may reduce the apparent height of the forehead on a long face by dressing the hair with curls or bangs. Style the hair so that it is flat on top and full behind your ears. Sometimes a center part will broaden a face and help to give it the appearance of being shorter. Avoid too-short or too-long hair.

The round face. The width of a round face may be apparently decreased by parting the hair high on the side, with a soft, loose arrangement. A high up-sweep hairdress (when in style) decreases the apparent width of the face. Keep sides smooth and away from the face.

Heart-shaped face. You may give more width at the jawline by having

curls or waves over the ears. Break the forehead span with a side dip.

Square face. Shorten the lines with a short bang; keep hair short and brushed away from the temples. Avoid cutting hair just at the angle of the jaw.

Side effects. What side effect in hairdress is most becoming to you? Should your hair be close to your head or flare out, and how much? Should the wave start close to your face, or how far away? The settings shown here are for the same general side effect; however, the wave placement can be varied. When you have in mind the result you want, then choose a type of setting to suit you.

Front. The height of the hair in front will flatter different-shaped faces. Which is your type of face?

Neck types. Five general types of necks are: (1) short and thin, (2) long and thin, (3) short and fat, (4) masculine, (5) "perfect."

223

Your HAIR makes your FACE!

ROUND FACE
Lengthen by revealing off-side triangle of skin on forehead; narrow with hair on cheeks. You need irregular lines. Try high bangs, too, but split in a triangle, not solid.

LONG FACE
Lines curving outward near the eye and on cheeks widen face. Bangs cut length. Ear-tip fullness helps. Avoid hair that falls too straight; bare forehead.

SQUARE JAW
Soft curves both above and below ear attract attention from jaw and provide needed roundness. Bared brow also helps balance jaw. Avoid hair behind ears and upward lines.

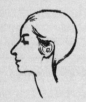 

LENGTHENED NOSE
Back height does a wonderful balancing job. You can wear long or short hair, provided it rises at tip of crown, not on top. If you wear hair behind ears, it should slant up.

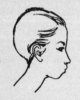

SLOPING CHIN
Cut hair jaw length with height at back of crown. All lines should go underneath and in a forward direction, curving toward chin. Bangs are good if they're lifted.

GLASSES
There is no one hairdo for glasses. Just make sure that the hairdo is wider than glass frames. Here bangs balance a triangular face, and glasses follow same horizontal lines. Watch frame color.

JOHN H. BRECK, INC.

"CHARM BY CHOICE," NATIONAL URBAN LEAGUE

For an oval face, almost any style will be suitable. Be sure that hair is clean.

"CHARM BY CHOICE," NATIONAL URBAN LEAGUE

For a round face, short hair combed back and up will add a definite longer line. A soft suggestion of a bang sitting to one side will add length to a face—especially if the forehead is short.

"CHARM BY CHOICE," NATIONAL URBAN LEAGUE

For a square-shaped face, hair softly lifted and combed back will add length.

"CHARM BY CHOICE," NATIONAL URBAN LEAGUE

For a long, rectangular face, fullness at the sides will shorten the face line.

The *short, thin* neck requires a hairdress with the hair brushed up off the neck into a flare effect, giving the appearance of length and width. The *long, thin* neck requires a hairdress that will produce an appearance of shortness and width. The hair extends behind the ears on the sides, providing necessary width. The *short, fat* neck needs a back hairdress that will create an appearance of length. Short, swirled hair and vertical waves will achieve it. The *masculine* neck needs a soft back with an oval effect. The *"perfect"* neck can wear any type of back hair styling, depending upon your desire.

Which type of neck do you have?

Hairsetting to wave straight hair. It takes skill to learn to set your hair for the effect you want, but it is a skill that you know is worth learning. Most girls shampoo and set their own hair, using a hairdresser only for special occasions. Even girls who have their hair done frequently need to know how to care for it between sets. Many girls are proficient in giving each

225

other home permanents, with results that are usually good if the directions are carefully followed for the specific type of permanent used.

A good cut is essential for any hair style. This should be done by a skilled hairdresser. Trimming is especially important before a permanent. No longer are permanents considered only to achieve curly hair. Most of the current hair fashions including straight hair, need the "body" a permanent gives. Hair still needs setting. A permanent merely makes the hair hold its set.

Remember, as the hair grows, so does the permanent. Hair grows about ½ inch a month, which may not seem much to you; but think how three months growth or 1½ inches can change your appearance. It is not unusual to cut an inch off one's hair every two months, so that before long, most of the hair treated with a permanent is cut off.

Rollers and pincurls. Hair can be set in many ways—even sticky tape is good for holding bangs in place. But most hair styles use a combination of rollers and hair pins. *Rollers* are better for setting high, loose curls or for deep, soft waves. They will also smooth out hair that is kinky from too tight a permanent. Small rollers make tight curls and large rollers create loose curls or hair body. *Pin curls* don't create the height that rollers do but are necessary for soft waves and many types of curls.

Specific directions for attractive hair styles are available from references at the end of the book. Why not send for some and practice with your friends?

To straighten curly hair requires professional help if the hair is very

MISSISSIPPI 4-H

Notice how the use of bangs attracts attention to the eyes.

Hair spray applied in small amounts will control excess curl, stray wisps and keep your hair-do in place. Too heavy an application will give an artificial look to the hair.

curly. Strong chemicals are needed which may harm the hair if used improperly. Frequent blunt cutting and shaping is also necessary to make the hair behave as desired. If your hair is only moderately curly, there are home kits for straightening which may be helpful. These suggestions may also be of help: Stretch your hair over jumbo rollers when wet and use a setting lotion with extra holding power. (Avoid getting your hair wet

226

How to SET like a professional . . .

HOW TO SET ROLLERS
First comb the setting lotion well through hair. Then section hair by parting from forehead to nape; from ear to ear; or diagonally, depending on direction of hairdo. Clip all hair except first section to be rolled out of way. Part first strand.

Strand should be narrower than roller; no more than an inch deep at scalp. Don't try to put too much hair on roller. Comb strand smooth in opposite direction from way you're going to roll. Lift and give gentle tug to create tension. Apply end tissue if needed.

Now hold strand straight out, if it is front or back of head; straight up if it is on top. Roll in direction hair will go. Don't twist. Roll all the way so that roller is firm but not tight against scalp. Clip at bottom of roller. Roll section by section, starting from top.

HOW TO SET PINCURLS
Section hair. Part off strand for first pincurl, the wider the strand, the bigger the curl. Comb strand smooth, and hold so that stem of curl, the part nearest scalp, is directed in the way the finished curl will go: upward for up curls, downward for down curls.

Next press finger against scalp at base of curl to create hollow to fit curl into. Now hold strand about 1½ inches from tip with one hand, and with thumb and index of other hand wind strand in circles as you would roll ribbon, from tip to scalp.

Fit curl into hollow. Clip flat against scalp. Set pincurls in rows in same direction, or in alternating directions for fluffier curls. To make stand-up curls on top of head, wind in same way, from top. Clip at base only, so that curl is erect rather than lying flat.

JOHN H. BRECK, INC.

227

as dampness may cause the curl to jump back.) Always use a cream rinse to make your hair more manageable. Try taping cheek curls, nape hair, and bangs so they will dry just the way you want them.

The hot pressing method is widely practiced to straighten hair. After the hair is shampooed and towel dried, a small amount of oil is rubbed on the hair. The oil serves as a heat transfer medium for the combing step which follows. A metal comb, heated to a temperature of 300 degrees to 500 degrees, is passed quickly through the hair. The high temperature breaks certain structural bonds within the hair and this permits the hair to straighten under the tension of combing. The effect from this procedure is temporary as high humidity or even scalp perspiration may cause the hair to revert to its natural curly state.

Some girls with long hair try ironing it themselves. Unless carefully controlled, the heat can damage the hair temporarily, making it fragile and dry, so that it breaks easily.

Determine the shape of your face if you do not already know it. Pull your hair back tightly (a good time is when you are shampooing it and there are thick suds on it). Perhaps your classmates can help you determine your facial shape if you are not certain. Make a collection of current styles which are suitable for your facial shape.

Arrange to have a professional beautician come to class and demonstrate the correct way to set pin curls, use rollers, and straighten overly curly hair. Have her supervise students as they try these processes.

Investigate the requirements for becoming a professional beautician in your state. What training is required? How long does it take and what does it cost? Where may such training be obtained? What tests are taken to be licensed in your state? Report to the class your findings.

Prepare a class tackboard. Cut out basic facial shapes from magazines and place on the board with hair styles suitable for each shape.

After school or during an activity period conduct a hair-styling clinic. In small groups, work with your classmates and find out how each one looks with a different part, with bangs, with hair loose or pulled up. If you can borrow some hairpieces, such as falls, experiment to see the effect of different hair lengths. Men's short wigs might be of interest to young men with long hair.

Study a consumer's magazine such as *Consumers Reports* concerning shampoo and other hair preparations. Prepare a report for the class on the relative merits of each type.

Secure the reports available from the Food and Drug Administration concerning drugs and cosmetics. Prepare a report on the safety of various cosmetics. If you are near a large city, you may be able to obtain a representative of this department to meet with your class.

There is always a danger the scalp will be accidentally burned also.

Chemical hair straighteners are available for home use but are not recommended unless one has had considerable experience with such chemicals. These products act by partially disrupting the chemical bonds of the hair protein. The hair is then set in a straightened position and the bonds reform. The action of the curl relaxers is fast and a great deal of judgment is needed to know when to apply a neutralizer to stop the straightening process. The scalp should be covered with a protective oil or cream because chemical burns can occur if not used properly.

NOTE: Do you think you will look glamorous to your friends at an evening party if they have seen you all day with your hair in rollers? A well-groomed, poised girl is never seen on the street (or at school!) with her hair up. If it is a real emergency and you must go out on an errand, cover the hair fixings with an attractive scarf, but try to plan ahead so you won't get caught!

Posture

No matter how well-groomed you are and how stylish your clothes, you may not look attractive if you slouch or have poor posture. When you look in the mirror, what do you see? You cannot change your bone structure but you can do something about the way you carry yourself. For many years you have read about good posture, listened to lectures on it, have seen demonstrations, and have probably been nagged to "sit up straight." Yet many girls continue poor posture habits. Perhaps all these instructions have been too involved to follow.

Here is a simple posture formula: (1) *Lift up in front.* (2) *Pull down in back.* (3) *Stand as tall as you can,* with both feet together on the floor, head erect and abdomen in. As you stand in this position, imagine a straight line being drawn from your ear to your ankle. It will pass through the joint of your shoulder and hip.

Sit with the base of your spine resting against the back of your chair and your body will be in good balance. When you use the stairs, hold your head erect. Use your thigh muscles rather than pulling on the bannister. As you descend, reach downward with the toes of one foot and bend the other knee.

Whenever you find yourself ambling along in a slouch, think of these three points—*lift up in front, pull down in back*, and *stand as tall as you can*. Practice them until they become automatic. You will be amazed at how much better your clothes, and you, look when you improve your posture.

OXFORD PAPER CO.

Walking with a book on your head may be one way of achieving good posture but active exercises can help more.

HEALTH AND BEAUTY HABITS

All of your life you have heard about the need for a good diet, careful tooth care, outdoor exercise, and sufficient rest to make you healthy. But did you know that these things also make you more attractive and help you appear well groomed?

Diet. A healthy skin and a good figure must be nourished by a well-balanced diet that provides enough food eaten regularly so that you enjoy your daily activities. A good daily diet includes foods from each of the four basic food groups. Also drink plenty of water each day—it assists in the elimination of body wastes.

As you check your diet habits, learn to eat *fresh fruit, fruit juices, and milk desserts* rather than rich desserts and candy. Learn to like the foods you should eat to retain a beautiful skin, to keep your body trim, and to make your clothes look better. You will then be rewarded with admira-

Which of these "Beauty Helpers" do you feel essential to have? What additions would you make to this list?

soap	emery board
clean towels	nail scissors
clean wash-cloths	shower cap
	toothbrush
shampoo	toothpaste or
deodorant	powder
cream or	hair brush and
lotion	comb
orange-wood	rollers or bobby
stick	pins
nail brush	hair net
tissues	mirror

tion from your friends and you will have more pep and energy.

Teeth. Is your smile accented by pretty teeth? A clean mouth and teeth are not only necessary for an attractive appearance, but they assist in keeping your general health good. *Brittle teeth* may be due to a faulty diet. The responsibility for keeping them attractive and in good working order belongs to you!

Exercise. Activity in the fresh air and sunshine is like medicine for keeping well and looking beautiful. It stimulates your body organs, increases the pace of your circulation, and gives you a good appetite and sparkling appearance. Exercises help get your muscles in shape and keep you fit for all your activities. Study the ones described on page 235. Perhaps you and some friends would be interested in doing them together.

On extremely bright, sunny days wear tinted glasses to protect your eyes and to prevent tiny squint lines around them. Be sure the glasses are designed to keep the glare of the sun from your eyes.

Sleep. Plenty of sleep is necessary for your good health, and either physical or emotional fatigue detracts from a well-groomed appearance. You probably still need from eight to ten hours of sleep, even though you are entering womanhood. To relax quickly upon going to bed, take a bath using water at body temperature just before retiring, go to bed about the same time each evening, have plenty of fresh air, and forget your problems of the day.

Beauty care and treatments are not substitutes for a *good diet, daily teeth care, exercise in the fresh air,* and plenty of *sleep.*

SHAVING

Shaving is something you'll probably do every day of your life. Knowing the right way to shave can make this morning task easier and more enjoyable for you.

There are three big steps to a good shave:

1. Prepare your beard well. Take *two full minutes* to wash your face, rinse it, and apply shaving cream. The longer your whiskers are wet, the easier they will be to shave because the warm water softens the beard. Shaving cream keeps the water from evaporating and provides just the right amount of lubrication to allow the razor to glide smoothly across your face.

2. Use the right razor for your skin type. Your razor should exert minimum pressure on your skin. If you have a sensitive skin or other skin problems, try an adjustable razor which permits the blade exposure to be varied for a gentler or a closer shave.

As you shave, use light, gentle strokes—and as few strokes as possible. Save the chin and upper lip for last, because these are where the coarsest whiskers grow and those extra seconds of water contact mean they'll be easier to shave off.

3. Be sure your shaving edge is sharp and clean. An inferior blade or a dull, overused blade won't cut whiskers cleanly and easily. Instead, it causes needless pulling and tugging of hairs. New technology permits blades to be used much longer than previously possible, but even the new blades do not last forever.

A morning shave is an important part of a young man's good grooming routine.

So check to be sure your shaving edge is sharp and clean at all times.

After shaving, rinse your razor with hot water. If you use a double-edge razor, loosen it slightly before rinsing. Never remove the blade to wipe it as this may damage the edge.

Men's facial hair styles seem to go in cycles and right now we are in the lots-of-facial-hair era. This means mustaches are popular. Even though they're fun to wear, they take time to keep well groomed. Nothing is more unattractive than an unkempt mustache.

If you wear a mustache, trim straggly hairs regularly with a small scissors. Set aside a few extra minutes each morning to groom your mustache during your regular shave. The same goes for sideburns.

FOR GIRLS ONLY

Though there are many ways for removing excess leg hair, shaving is usually preferred by most women. Shaving is usually chosen for underarm areas as well.

Your razor should have a special blade setting for women's shaving needs and a long handle for easier use.

Leg and underarm shaving causes blade edges to deteriorate six times faster than if used in male facial shaving. Therefore be sure your skin surface is properly prepared and that a sharp blade is used.

To avoid skin irritation, never shave dry. Make certain hair is moistened with warm water. This softens it and makes it easier to shave. A woman's hair is finer and needs less time for softening than a man's. You may want to shave while your skin is still wet after a shower or bath.

Soap lather or shaving cream should be applied to the moistened skin. Either one keeps the moisture from evaporating. At the same time, it softens the hair even more than just moisture alone and also lubricates the area to be shaved. Thus your razor can work smoothly and easily with little chance of nicking or scraping.

When shaving legs, don't bear down—the weight of the razor is all you need. Shave legs with long, light strokes. If you begin to shave upward from the ankle against the direction of hair growth, you will have a closer, smoother result. If you work downward from the knee in the direction the hair grows, you'll get an easier, more comfortable shave. Choose the direction that suits you best. Be careful in shaving the delicate areas around your ankles and shins and behind your knees.

After shaving legs, use a good dry-skin moisturizer or cream to lubricate the skin and leave it soft and smooth.

When shaving underarms, for best results stand in front of a mirror with your arm raised to keep the skin taut. Moisten underarm hair with warm water and apply soap lather or shaving cream to soften hair and keep it moist and to lubricate the area to be shaved. Use very little pressure and let the razor glide across the skin. Experiment for best shaving direction. You may find a combination of both upward and downward strokes gives you the closest underarm shave. Do not use a deodorant or anti-perspirant right after shaving as they may irritate the skin.

Always rinse your razor when you finish shaving so that it will be fresh and ready when you need it again.

How often should you shave? Establish a regular grooming routine. Shave at least once a week, oftener in warm weather when sleeveless dresses and stockingless legs are in season. To be always well groomed, keep arms and legs smooth and stubble-free.

THE GILLETTE CO.

When shaving underarms, stand in front of a mirror with your arm raised to keep the skin taut.

A GUIDE TO GOOD EATING

Use Daily:

Milk Group

3 or more glasses milk — Children
smaller glasses for some children under 9

4 or more glasses — Teen-agers

2 or more glasses — Adults

Cheese, ice cream and other milk-made foods can supply part of the milk

2 or more servings

Meats, fish, poultry, eggs, or cheese — with dry beans, peas, nuts as alternates

Meat Group

Vegetables and Fruits

4 or more servings

Include dark green or yellow vegetables; citrus fruit or tomatoes

4 or more servings

Enriched or whole grain
Added milk improves nutritional values

Breads and Cereals

This is the foundation for a good diet. Use more of these and other foods as needed for growth, for activity, and for desirable weight.

The nutritional statements made in this leaflet have been reviewed by the Council on Foods and Nutrition of the American Medical Association and found consistent with current authoritative medical opinion.

NATIONAL DAIRY COUNCIL

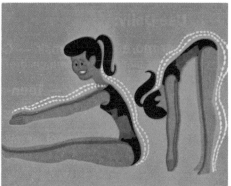

"CHARM BY CHOICE," NATIONAL URBAN LEAGUE

After a few preliminary stretches and waist bends, try a few easy exercises that are more fun than work. Sitting on the floor feet together, hands over head, bend to the beat of some lively music and touch your toes.

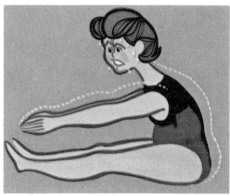

"CHARM BY CHOICE," NATIONAL URBAN LEAGUE

The first try is the hardest. Do ten of these the first week and increase gradually afterward. You will be amazed how this will tone your back and stomach muscles.

Suggest snacks that are tasty and good for one's skin and figure. Perhaps students in a foods class could prepare some for a display.

Select a picture of a girl or young man who you think is very attractive. Mount it and state why you chose it. List what you believe a grooming routine might be daily, weekly, and monthly.

Prepare a chart that you can hang in your closet or by your mirror to remind you of check-up activities needed for good grooming.

Prepare a display of the basic items needed for good grooming. What other items would it be nice to have but are not absolutely necessary?

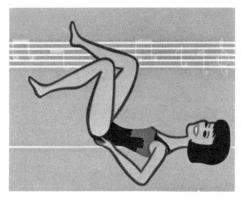

You can cover a lot of mileage in the reducing department with the bicycle ride. Lie flat on your back, support your hips in the palms of your hands with elbows resting on the floor. Then, ride the bicycle and leave extra weight in the stomach and hips far behind.

"CHARM BY CHOICE," NATIONAL URBAN LEAGUE

234

LIMBER UP by trotting in place, done to 32 counts. Right foot hitting the floor is one count. Exercising to music is both inspiring and fun.

KICK OFF to the goal of a best possible figure. Improve posture with this exercise. Shoulders back, stomach muscles tight, spine straight—lift (do not swing) each leg eight times. Point toes.

JUMP FOR JOY and top form. Condition your body for sports or dancing by alternating a straight jump with the tuck jump shown bending and lifting your knees to the chest, back straight.

FACE UP to figure problems. Sit with one leg extended forward, knee straight, the other knee bent, with inside of leg on floor, as far behind you as comfortable. Place hands on floor on each side of hips for support. "Bounce" forward four times, trying to touch chin to knee. Arch back four times. Stretch forward four times, trying to put top of head on knee. Arch back four times. Do twice on each leg.

Grooming Your Wardrobe

To be happy and comfortable, you need to be at ease, with a feeling of poise and confidence. The *little things* in the grooming of your wardrobe need your constant attention. Of course you never have run-down heels on your shoes. Neither do you substitute pins for buttons or for mending a shoulder strap! Soiled, untidy clothes and clothes that are inappropriate and unattractive in style and color cannot give you a feeling of confidence or assurance.

Before you leave the house in the morning, check up on yourself.

- Is your hair neat, orderly, and becomingly arranged?
- Is your shirt tucked in your pants?
- If you are a girl wearing a dress, are you sure your slip doesn't peek out below the hemline?
- Are your shoes polished and the heels in good condition?
- Are your teeth brushed? Did you use a mouth wash if needed?
- Did you clean your face this morning as well as before going to bed?
- Did you take special precautions to guard against body odors?
- Are your nails neatly manicured?
- Do you stand and sit tall at all times?
- Do you smile rather than frown?
- Is your make-up flattering to you and not noticeable in itself?
- Did you use hand lotion after washing your hands or helping with the dishes?
- Did you eat a healthful breakfast?

BOBBIE BROOKS

If you keep excess weight off by wise eating and exercise, you'll be able to wear the latest styles without fear of unsightly bulges.

Are the clothes you plan to wear tomorrow in condition to wear? Even your handbag should be tidy! Provide enough time for dressing to present that well-groomed appearance; then you can be sure that your buttons are not missing, your belt is not twisted, and there is no dandruff noticeable on your shoulders.

What precautions should you observe if you comb your hair after you dress? As you take off your clothes, how can you avoid unnecessary wrinkling? Take a careful look at yourself in your mirror. Are your clothes always appropriate and well groomed? Chapter Seven, Caring for Your Clothes, describes the many ways for keeping your clothes attractive and well groomed.

Can You Explain These Terms?

acne	callous	dandruff
anti-perspirant	corn	emery board
deodorant	pedicure	nail file
athlete's foot	chapped skin	manicure
	dermatologist	

Summary with Check-Up Questions

Any person can be attractive if well-groomed—if clothing is clean and neat and suitable for activities and if the complexion glows, hair is glossy, eyes are sparkling, teeth are sound and clean, and vitality from proper care of the body is evident.
- *What effect does a girl with pretty features make if her hair is dirty, straggly, and her make-up left over from the day before?*
- *Can a young man be attractive if his clothes smell of body odor and are torn in places?*
- *Does a tired person who is dragging along do justice to clothes or body care?*

In order to be well-groomed, one must work at it. A plan for daily, weekly, and monthly activities is of help.
- *Will you "forget" to care for your hands or toenails if you do not have a regular time for such care?*
- *What will result if you "forget" to care for your hair and skin for several days because you are too busy? How long will it take to get yourself back in condition?*
- *What activities do you suggest for daily, weekly, and monthly grooming?*

Skin reflects the general health of the body as well as care given it.
- *What can cause a sallow, lifeless complexion?*
- *How can you delay wrinkles and deepening frown lines from happening?*
- *In what ways are skin blemishes related to one's general health?*

Frequent bathing is necessary to remove dirt, perspiration, body odors, and loosened skin scales.
- *How can bathing be accomplished if one does not have access to a tub or shower?*

- *What are ways of keeping the back clean?*
- *What effect besides cleansing can a leisurely warm bath have on your appearance?*

A beautiful complexion begins with a healthy, clean skin.

- *What effect will improper diet have on the appearance of a complexion?*
- *How does a skin appear that has been gently soaped and then toned with a cold water rinse?*
- *What effect has make-up applied over an unwashed face?*

Make-up colors must be keyed to a girl's own coloring and the clothes she is wearing.

- *What colors of lipstick are suitable for girls with tan skin coloring?*
- *What shades of skin look well with purplish-red lipsticks?*
- *Why do clear reds look well on almost every skin coloring?*
- *For what skin colors would you suggest a pinkish powder? A beige powder?*

Water is constantly evaporated from the skin through perspiration but the oily secretions and odors remain.

- *What is the purpose of a deodorant?*
- *What is the purpose of an anti-perspirant?*
- *Why is thorough washing seldom enough to keep one dainty and inoffensive?*

Feet require special care similar to that given hands.

- *Why is it wise to soak hands and feet for several minutes in warm, sudsy water before shaping nails?*
- *How are toenails shaped differently from fingernails? Why?*
- *What is the effect of chipped polish, either on toes or hand nails?*

Cleanliness of hair is most important in good grooming.

- *How can oily, soiled hair affect one's complexion?*
- *Will hair that is not clean hold a set well?*
- *"A young man's or girls crowning glory"—can it be that way without being clean?*

Hair needs to be brushed often to remove surface dirt, stimulate circulation of the scalp, and increase the sheen of the hair.

- *What is the difference between combing and brushing in overall effect on hair beauty?*
- *How should hair be properly brushed?*
- *Mild cases of dandruff can often be controlled with frequent hair brushing. Why is this?*

Hair styles should be suited to the facial shape and accentuate one's good features.

- *What is the effect of a suggestion of a bang on one side of the forehead for a girl with a round face?*
- *What hair styles can a girl with an oval, well-proportioned face wear?*
- *How can sideburns affect the shape of a man's face?*

Even though clothes are attractive and one is well-groomed, one will not look well dressed if posture is poor.

- *What effect has slumping on the appearance of clothing?*
- *What is the simplest posture rule that does the most for one's appearance?*
- *How can poor posture affect one's health?*

After studying this chapter on grooming, what plans do you have for improving your grooming procedures?

CHAPTER SEVEN

Caring for Your Clothes

A WELL-GROOMED LOOK is the result of careful attention to yourself and to what you wear. When you made a wardrobe inventory, you probably found some garments that were still attractive and fit well but which could not be worn because they needed cleaning or some small repair. Regular care helps you have a well-groomed appearance every day.

It also saves time and money spent on excessive cleaning and replacement of clothing that is not well cared for.

In this chapter you will read about ways to take care of your clothes every day as well as the special care that needs to be given at the change of seasons. You will discover ways to clean, launder, and press garments and how to remove spots and stains.

Daily Care

Before you start off for school or work each morning, ask yourself these questions:

- *Are my undergarments and hosiery as clean as my outer garments?*
- *Are buttons and other fasteners sewn on securely?*
- *Are my shoes polished, heels straight and not run over?*
- *Is the collar of my coat or jacket clean and well brushed?*

What about the clothes I took off last night—are they put away carefully instead of lying on a chair or even the floor?

- *Are holes and tears, even the tiny ones, mended so that safety pins are not needed?*
- *Are my pockets empty instead of being stuffed with my lunch, gloves, scarfs, or yesterday's snack wrappers?*
- *Are all my clothes pressed well?*

Do you think the girl who left her room looking like this when she dashed off to school is as well-groomed as she could be? Why?

When job hunting, an immaculate tip-to-toe wardrobe is important. This smart miss carries an extra pair of white gloves in a plastic envelope, and changes to clean gloves just before her interview.

CLEANLINESS BUREAU

CLEANLINESS BUREAU

This new graduate of a business school glows over her good marks and good job— an immaculate appearance was one of her highest recommendations in landing that new position as well as good marks.

Simple repairs that extend the life of your clothes and make them look better, as well as some remodeling ideas, will be discussed.

If you have many no's, chances are that your clothes (and you) do not always look as well as possible and that often you cannot wear a desired garment because it needs something done to it . . . chances are also that a big chunk of your weekend time could be spent pressing, cleaning, and straightening your room.

What other suggestions can you add that may prevent *unnecessary* clothing care?

240

AN OUNCE OF PREVENTION

Helpful Hints to Avoid Unnecessary Clothing Care

✓ Change to washable clothes or wear an apron or cover-up when working in the kitchen, around the house, or out-of-doors.

✓ Prevent perspiration stains and damage by using deodorants, anti-perspirants, or underarm shields.

✓ Wear rainwear—raincoat, boots, and carry an umbrella to prevent clothing from being ruined by bad weather.

✓ Apply cosmetics or other skin aids after finishing dressing to prevent stains on garments, or protect your lips with tissues when dressing.

✓ Use a towel to protect your clothes when brushing and combing hair.

✓ Put clothes on the correct way to prevent bursting seams or popping buttons.

✓ Hang up clothes after each wearing—at home or away from home.

✓ Mend small tears or loose buttons as soon as noticed. Searching for a missing button or replacing an entire set takes time.

✓ Put on pins and other jewelry carefully, to avoid making holes in clothing.

✓ Watch that newspaper—newsprint comes off on many fabrics.

✓ Remove stains before pressing—stains and soil may be permanently set by heat.

DAILY ROUTINES

Perhaps you have never given thought to how to keep your clothes in "working order." If you are willing to take the time and effort to learn how to take good care of your clothing now, it will become a habit so that you can do it easily in the future.

Practice wise daily clothes care until it becomes routine.

Hanging clothes properly. When you take off your clothes, don't toss them on a chair or the floor. Think how much more time and effort it will take to pick them up later, get them in good shape, and put them away where they belong.

A shirt or a sweater hung on a hook may develop an unsightly shape or even be torn. Clean clothes should be hung on suitable hangers with shoulders eased in place, zippers closed, and buttons (at least the top one) fastened.

Skirts and pants may gap if zippers are left open and necklines can stretch with buttons left open.

It is wise to take off a belt and hang it by the buckle on a hanger. This relieves the strain on the side seams of the garment and the belt won't crush as much. If you can't find a skirt hanger, don't fold the skirt and toss it over a regular hanger. It will take more time to press it later than it will to find a correct hanger or suitable substitute now.

Knits should be folded and placed in a drawer or on a shelf so they won't stretch. Remember that crowded fabrics can't breathe and wrinkles won't hang out, so allow adequate room for your clothes, either on a closet rod or in drawers.

Brushing and airing. Many fabrics need to be aired or brushed before being put away. Wool fabrics hold onto dust and odors because of the scaly structure of the fibers. A few hours hanging in front of an open window, outside in the shade, or ten minutes tumbling in an automatic dryer at the fluff setting can result in a tired fabric bouncing back like new.

Sweaters stay fresher if turned wrong side out and hung over the back of a chair to air overnight. Next morning, turn them right side out and fold gently to fit your storage space.

Frequent brushing prevents dust and grime from penetrating fabrics . . . it also helps restore the surface appearance. Brush with the grain of the fabric and the direction of the nap, using long strokes.

- Use a whisk broom for coats and heavy fabrics.
- Use a fine bristled clothes brush on softer, more delicate fabrics.
- A bit of velvet is a good brush for fine fabrics.
- Sticky tape removes lint that is hard to dislodge.

Remember that wearing a plastic cape when combing hair and applying cosmetics prevents the need for much clothes brushing.

Bathroom steaming will remove many wrinkles without pressing. Hang clothes in a closed bathroom. Then run hot water in a tub or shower until the room is slightly steamy. Allow time for wrinkles to hang out and be sure to dry clothing thoroughly before wearing.

How to put on and take off clothes properly. Did you know there is an art to putting on and taking off clothing? Many lovely garments become shapeless, saggy, and even torn because their owners make a daily struggle of getting them on and off.

- Put a dress on over your head instead of stepping into it, unless it has a long opening. Be sure all fasteners are completely opened and that belts are not twisted or binding.
- Shoes will hold their shape if all fasteners are loosened before being put on. A shoe horn helps prevent the back of the shoes from breaking down.
- Girdles go on easily if you fold down the top 3 inches. Step into the garment, pull it up around the hips and then unroll the fold. Sharp fingernails tugging at a girdle can easily make holes in elastic.
- Be sure your nails are smooth when putting on hosiery. Roll the leg of the stocking down past the heel so the toes slip into the toe section easily. Adjust the foot correctly and then unroll the leg part of the stocking. It is best to fasten garters while sitting down to allow for strain on the knees. Socks also last longer if the tops are rolled down before the feet are slipped into them.
- Pullover sweaters need special attention. First insert your arms in the sleeves and gently ease the sweater over the head. Never tug. If it does not slip on easily, ease it gently with both hands on the inside of the sweater at the neckline. *Take off eyeglasses and jewelry* before removing a sweater, to prevent snags. (If one does occur, pull the snagged yarn to the inside and fasten it with matching thread.)

Everyday wearing of clothes. If you are wearing a full skirt, learn to slide one hand along your lower back to smooth out any obvious wrinkles when you are sitting down. The heat and the pressure of your body on a wrinkled fabric can create long-lasting creases. A tight skirt will have less strain put upon it if you pull it up slightly at both sides before sitting down.

Always loosen the lower buttons of a fitted coat before being seated, to avoid unnecessary strain on them.

Shoulder bags and books carried always on one hip will quickly spoil the surface appearance of most fabrics.

Wet clothes. If you are caught in a shower or snowstorm without proper precautions, remember that wet clothes need special care. Dry them slowly, as too much heat can dry out fibers, creating steam damage and long-lasting wrinkles. Allow knits to dry flat; stuff shoes with paper to help absorb moisture and keep their shape. Place other garments on well-shaped hangers. Many fabrics need brushing after drying to restore the natural luster and feel.

Soiled clothes. Clothes that are soiled or need repairs should not be put back in a closet as they are usually "lost" there until needed, and then there may not be time to repair or clean them. If you must put them back, place a colored piece of cardboard over the hanger loop so that you are reminded of a needed repair.

Your soiled clothes may be put in two places—a personal laundry bag for clothes you wash yourself or the family hamper for clothes laundered with the family wash.

• Some fabrics develop wrinkles or the colors may run if tossed in with damp bath towels.

• Garments with "easy-care" finishes

Practice putting on and taking off a pullover sweater. When you have mastered the art, demonstrate to the class.

Study the references and demonstrate how to put on gloves properly.

Prepare a demonstration of the proper ways to shine shoes and clean suede shoes. Can boots be made waterproof? Show how.

Do you have wool garments that are clean but look "tired?" Brush them and notice the improvement in appearance. If you have an automatic dryer, place them in it at the fluff setting for 10 to 15 minutes. Compare with those that you brush by hand.

Prepare a skit of a person getting ready for bed. Show do's and don'ts of clothing care.

are best left on hangers until washing, if you have the space.

Other daily routines for clothing care. A handy pincushion on your dresser or pinned to a bedroom curtain with needles threaded in basic colors can make that "stitch in time" an easy one. Refer to page 276 for help with common mending problems. It also helps to get in the habit every day of removing any spots you may have picked up. You can read how to do this on page 265.

CLOTHES CLOSETS AND OTHER STORAGE

Everyone needs suitable places to store clothes—a closet or place to hang some garments, and shelves or drawers for other articles.

DRAWER SPACE

Knitted garments such as sweaters and jerseys will not stretch out of shape if stored flat. Underclothes, night garments, hosiery, scarfs, gloves, and handkerchiefs are usually kept in drawers also. If you have more closet space than drawer space, you will want to hang your tops and shirts. Otherwise they should be folded and placed in drawers. If there is not enough room in your chest for sweaters, you may find room for a sweater box or bag on a closet shelf. Or will a low chest fit in your closet under your short clothes?

Compartments help keep things neat. You can buy drawer dividers or use containers such as shoe boxes to separate items. The things you use daily are best stored in the top drawers so they are easy to get.

Instead of keeping all items of a kind together, would it be more convenient to keep scarfs, gloves, and hosiery worn daily in one place, and those worn only for dress occasions together in another drawer?

Have you tried rolling scarfs, underwear, and hosiery? They take less space than folding and are easier to see than if stacked.

CLOSETS

Housing experts state that an ideal closet provides 8 feet of pole space per person. This includes out-of-season clothes as well as ones in current use. Very few homes can provide this amount of space but you may be surprised to find that closets can be made to expand without increasing their size one single inch. Your closet may seem crowded to you but there is probably a lot of waste space that can be used.

First of all, must you keep everything in it that is there? Can you store out-of-season clothes or seldom-worn party clothes elsewhere—in the attic, a dry basement, or a general family storage room? Perhaps a portable closet for the attic would be a good investment. Have you tried a special chest that fits under a bed for seldom-worn items?

How do you hang your clothes? Most students have enough short garments such as jackets and skirts that can be placed together to free space for a small chest below. Is there a shelf above the closet pole? Perhaps there is room for another shelf way up for seldom used things. Look at your closet door. Can you use the back for hooks to hold belts, night clothes, shoeracks, and small items?

The Attractive Closet. Everyone likes a nice closet. If your room has plain walls, perhaps you could line the closet with a designed wallpaper. Or paint it a contrasting color. Remember that a light color makes it much easier to find things in the corners than a dark color, even if you are fortunate enough to have a light in the closet. You can buy all sorts of colorful accessories but you can also create them yourself. Boxes can be easily covered with wallpaper, plastic backed paper, or leftover fabric and then varnished or shellacked so they will be easy to clean. Not only will your clothes stay fresher with such accessories but you will get a "lift" whenever you look in your closet.

Closet Accessories. Good clothing care may mean investing in some closet accessories—hangers of proper sizes and shapes, garment bags, sweater bags, and other items. Take your time before you buy too many.

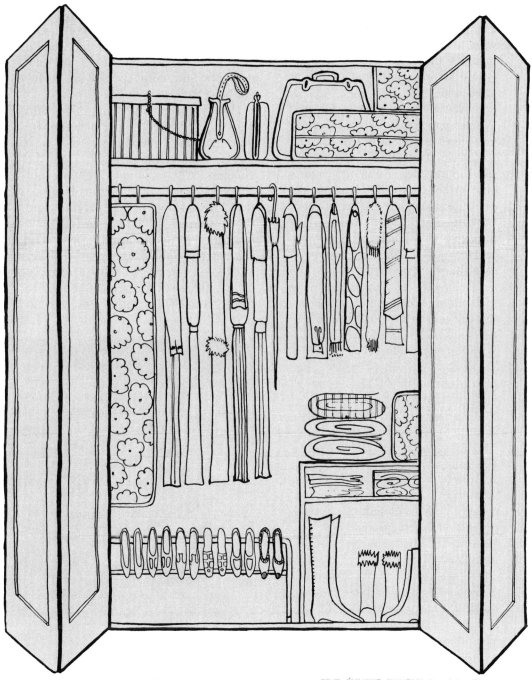

PINE CLEANER INFORMATION CENTER

One method of organizing a closet. Notice the shoe rack which keeps the shoes off the floor, the dust-free cover for seldom worn garments, the use of space under short articles for additional storage, and the way the double-fold doors open to allow easy access to the entire closet including the overhead shelf. What other good ideas can you see?

245

Form a panel of class members who share closets. Discuss the methods they have found helpful.

Collect advertisements of closet accessories. Which ones would help you in your clothes storage? Which may create clutter because you won't use them much?

List closet accessories you would like to have. Select one or two you can make from easily available materials. Complete the project and bring to class to show others. Keep a record of the cost of materials and compare with a similar item available in a store.

Plan a day in class when each girl brings one or more closet or drawer accessories that she finds helpful. Be prepared to tell others why this item helps you.

Draw a diagram of your closet as it is now, listing all hooks, poles, shelves, and other articles in it. Study references on closet planning listed at the end of this book. Make a plan for improvement of the space available to you.

If there is a closet in your home economics room that is inefficiently arranged, form committees to study it and make suggestions for improvement. What storage accessories could be made?

Prepare an exhibit of inexpensive household articles which can be used as storage accessories, for example, plastic bags, boxes, and clothespins for skirt hangers. What other ideas can you add?

Some bedrooms don't have closets. How could one be created? The industrial arts teacher can tell you ways this may be done.

Quite a few can be made inexpensively at home. Other gadgets may look grand in the stores but create only a clutter in your closet, as they may not suit your special needs for clothing storage.

Hangers are important. The thin wire hangers used by dry cleaners are intended for temporary use—as a means of carrying garments from the cleaners to your home. They are not shaped correctly and clothes hung on them for a long period of time lose their shape. Wooden and plastic hangers are more appropriate. The shaped wooden hangers with thicker ends keep top coats and suit coats in shape. Skirt hangers are convenient to have. NOTE: Clip clothespins work as

Piggy-back skirt hangers make it possible for several skirts to be hung in a small space.

A   B

C

Skirts and trousers need special hangers. Here are favorites of high school students. (A) Trouser hangers with self-locking clamps hold pants firmly in place. (Wider ones are available solely for skirt use.) (B) Suit hangers with metal spring clamps adjustable for the width of the skirt. The hanger holds a matching jacket. (C) For closets with limited pole space, three or four skirts can be hung in the space of one. (D) A plain metal hanger works well if bent back and the skirt attached with pins so it remains firmly in place.

D

well as special hangers with clips to hold the waistband. You can also bend up the ends of ordinary wire hangers and hang skirts by the waistband loops, or use ordinary pins as shown in the illustration. Plastic hangers won't rust, so they are used for drip drying or where the humidity is often high.

Shoes left on the floor gather dust and make cleaning more difficult. They are better stored in shoe bags or on a shoe rack or shelf.

Seldom worn clothes need dust-proof covers to protect at least the top parts. With see-through plastic, you have the advantage of knowing what you have.

Sharing a Closet. Many teenagers share a closet with another family member. Decide on a fair section for each of you. (It may not be half-and-half if one roommate is older and works and has greater need for clothes storage.) After deciding on a fair share, stick to your part.

Perhaps you may want to paint the closet in two colors—one for you and one for your roommate so that you can both easily keep to your section.

Students should take time in the spring to put away their winter clothes carefully just as they take time before school starts in the fall to get ready for the new season and to put away summer clothes. There are very few places in our country where the same clothes can be worn all the year around and even then a seasonable check-up is advisable.

Storage Places. Your out-of-season clothes may be stored in your regular closet if there is enough room so they and other clothes will not be squashed to wrinkles. They should be placed in dust-free bags or boxes so they will remain clean. Any closet or storage area that is dry and not in direct sunlight that could fade colors may be used. Avoid warm, damp places if at all possible.

Protecting Stored Garments. Cotton and linen garments should be *clean* because dirt particles may weaken fibers, attract insects, and are hard to remove if allowed to remain for any time. Clothes should be free of starch because mildew is more apt to form on starched garments in warm, damp weather. *Mildew* is a thin, grayish white growth produced by molds which are always present in the air but which need moisture, warm temperature, and starch or other food to grow. Mildew not only leaves a musty odor but discolors and rots fabrics.

If you use *bluing*, rinse it completely from garments to be stored. Bluing contains an iron compound that sometimes oxidizes during storage, developing rust spots.

Man-made fabrics are usually resistant to mildew and insect damage. They should be cleaned before storage, as soil can weaken the fibers. Otherwise, they need no special care.

A HELPFUL IDEA. Do you change hem lengths every season? If so, let down the hem before having the garment cleaned for storage. Then it will be all ready to be put up at the correct length when you need it.

WOOL BUREAU
Moth larva of the clothes-destroying type.

Woolens and furs must be protected from moth damage unless they have been mothproofed with chemicals which make the cloth unappetizing to moths. If your garments are labeled *mothproofed* or *moth resistant*, you may store them in any clean place protected from dirt and dust.

Moths lay eggs and the eggs hatch into worms or larvae which will eat any fabric available that contains wool. Carpet beetles do similar damage but the means of protection is the same. Dry cleaning and washing destroys any eggs, live moths, or larvae in fabrics. If you store clean clothes in containers which will not allow moths to enter, your clothes will be protected.

If you do not launder or dry-clean certain garments before storage, careful brushing—especially the folds, pockets, under the collars, and other hidden places—will usually dislodge any eggs or larvae present.

Woolens wrapped in heavy paper and sealed securely with tape will be safe from moth entry as will clothes stored in sturdy plastic bags. The moth worm or grub can pass through a hole $\frac{1}{25}''$ in diameter, so play it safe by sealing cracks and crevices in containers with gummed tape, which is quick and easy to use. *Large glass jars* with tight lids are good for storing mittens, scarfs, and small objects, as you can easily see the contents. *Cedar chests* are not always tight enough to keep out moths, nor is the cedar oil strong enough to repel them. NOTE: Sandpaper the inside of a cedar chest or closet every few years to freshen the odor.

Moth flakes (napthalene or paradichlorobenzene) will repel moths if the fumes are strong enough. You

One way of storing woolen articles when not in use. Large glass jars, well sealed, keep moths out and allow you to see what's inside.

must use enough so that the odors seem strong to you. Follow the directions on the package carefully. If you store garments in a garment bag, place the crystals at the top as the vapors are heavier than air and will penetrate down throughout the clothing. *Caution:* Here is one place not to use plastic hangers—some plastics will soften and melt from the fumes of moth crystals and may stain clothing.

Washable garments can be mothproofed at home by soaking them in solutions available at drug stores. As many people are sensitive to these substances, be sure to wash the treated garments before wearing.

Clothes can also be mothproofed by sprays, but be sure to use enough to moisten the entire garment, especially inside areas.

Remember, clean clothes stored in containers sealed tightly so no moth or other insects can enter are protected from damage and shouldn't need the addition of moth repellents.

CLEANING METHODS

Clothes become soiled because of dust in the air, perspiration oils on the body, and contact with other staining materials. Cleaning your clothes may not seem very exciting but it is essential to keep them looking like new.

Care Labels. Since 1972, almost all clothing articles must have a permanently attached label that states how to care for each. The Federal Trade Commission (FTC) ruled that these labels must be attached by sewing or some other permanent means in a prescribed place. (See page 251.)

Attached labels have one drawback —because space is so limited, the instructions must be minimal. Further explanations of the prescribed terms are given on page 252. Directions found on hangtags are usually more complete and should be saved whenever possible. Remember that care instructions are written for the majority of consumers. It is possible, for example, that you could hand wash a woolen garment that is labeled "Dryclean Only" and obtain excellent results. However, because many consumers would not do this properly, the manufacturer must use the more cautious directions.

When you buy a fabric for home sewing, you should be given a care tag to sew into your garment. The end of each fabric bolt carries a code number from 1 through 9, which matches the code number of the proper label for your fabric. They are described on page 138. Be sure to ask for this care tag when you buy fabric.

It is important to save tags with directions for washing, drying, and finishing clothing items, and keep them handy for ready reference on washdays. Make your own file of laundering instructions by attaching each hang tag or label to a card, identifying it with the appropriate garment. Keep these in a file box near your washer so you will always know how to handle special fabrics and finishes.
CLEANLINESS BUREAU

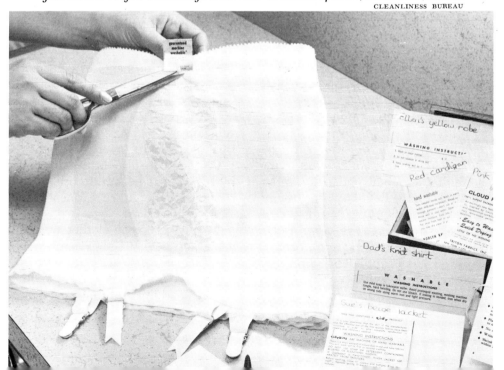

There was a time when only sturdy household fabrics went into the regular wash. Anything delicate was painstakingly washed by hand or sent out for dry cleaning. Today more and more fabrics are washable because of modern fibers and washing aids.

NOTE: Because wool fibers have a tendency to felt as well as shrink in water, it is wise to have wool articles drycleaned unless labeled washable or unless you are willing to take the special care needed. Garments with linings and interlinings can seldom be washed successfully. Loosely woven and spongy or crepe-like fabrics may shrink a great deal in water but can be handled safely by drycleaning. If in doubt, ask a reliable drycleaner how to best clean a garment.

HOME LAUNDERING

LAUNDERING EQUIPMENT

Women all over the world wash clothes in streams or in lake water, many pounding the garments without soap to get the dirt out. Others wash everything by hand with the aid of scrub boards. Anything can be washed by hand but a machine, of course, makes it easier to get soiled articles clean. Most families in our country have access to a washing machine, either their own or in a coin-operated center.

RECOMMENDED PLACEMENT OF PERMANENT CARE LABELS

Packaged or Folded Apparel. If the label is not visible through the package or on the folded item, the identical instruction must appear on the outside of the package in addition to the permanent label on the garment. This can be done by printing on the package, or by a paste-on label on the package or by a printed insert in a clear package, or by hangtag on folded apparel.

Coats, Jackets. The label should be affixed to right-hand front facing below waistline or at the neckline.

Multipiece Garments such as suits, coordinates or sets, sold as a unit, require only a single label, provided the identical care instruction applies to all pieces. If individual pieces of a multipiece unit require different care, each piece must be individually labeled.

Blouses, Dresses, Jackets Robes, Knit Tops, Loungewear, Vests, Nightgowns, Undershirts, Slips, Shirts, Sweaters. The label should be affixed at center back neckline in such a way that it will be permanent.

CELANESE FIBERS MARKETING CO.

CONSUMER CARE GUIDE FOR APPAREL

When Label Reads:	It Means:	When Label Reads:	It Means:
Machine Washable		*Home Drying*	
Machine wash	Wash, bleach, dry, and press by any customary method including commercial laundering and drycleaning.	Tumble dry	Dry in tumble dryer at specified setting—high, medium, low, or no heat.
Home launder only	Same as above but do not use commercial laundering.	Tumble dry Remove promptly	Same as above, but in absence of cool-down cycle, remove at once when tumbling stops.
No chlorine bleach	Do not use chlorine bleach. Oxygen bleach may be used.	Drip dry	Hang wet and allow to dry with hand shaping only.
No bleach	Do not use bleach of any type.	Line dry	Hang damp and allow to dry.
Cold wash Cold rinse	Use cold water from tap or cold washing machine setting.	No wring No twist	Hang dry, drip dry, or dry flat only. Handle to prevent wrinkles and distortion.
Warm wash Warm rinse	Use warm water or warm washing machine setting.	Dry flat	Lay garment on flat surface.
Hot wash	Use hot water or hot washing machine setting.	Block to dry	Maintain original size and shape while drying.
No spin	Remove wash load before final machine spin cycle.	*Ironing or Pressing*	
Delicate cycle Gentle cycle	Use appropriate machine setting; otherwise wash by hand.	Cool iron	Set iron at lowest setting.
		Warm iron	Set iron at medium setting.
Durable press cycle Permanent press cycle	Use appropriate machine setting; otherwise use warm wash, cold rinse and short spin cycle.	Hot iron	Set iron at hot setting.
		Do not iron	Do not iron or press with heat.
Wash separately	Wash alone or with like colors.	Steam iron	Iron or press with steam.
		Iron damp	Dampen garment before ironing.
Non-Machine Washing			
Hand wash	Launder only by hand in lukewarm (hand comfortable) water. May be bleached. May be drycleaned.	*Miscellaneous*	
		Dryclean only	Garment should be drycleaned only, including self service.
Hand wash only	Same as above, but do not dryclean.	Professionally dryclean only	Do not use self-service drycleaning.
Hand wash separately	Hand wash alone or with like colors.	No dryclean	Use recommended care instructions. No drycleaning materials to be used.
No bleach	Do not use bleach.		
Damp wipe	Surface clean with damp cloth or sponge.		

AMERICAN APPAREL MFRS. ASSOC.

In tropical countries women may spread clothes upon the grass to dry. Hot sun does this in a short time. But our weather is not always dependable for quick drying of clothes. Automatic dryers heated by electricity or gas, dry clothes in all weather at any time, day or night. Many fabrics come from a dryer looking and feeling better than if line dried. Clotheslines are used for airing clothes and for drip drying as well for general laundry by those who do not have access to a mechanically heated dryer.

Even with the development of easy care and durable press garments, many need some pressing after laundering. A good iron is a wise investment and needs to be taken care of properly. See section on page 263 for helpful ironing suggestions.

It is predicted that in the future the cleaning of clothing will take place by rays which will pull out the soil by ionic attraction. There will be no shrinkage, no fading, no need to dry or iron later. Others predict that much of our clothing will be disposable . . . worn until soiled and then thrown away. But until that time comes, if it does, every smart young miss needs the knowledge and skill to clean clothes successfully.

LAUNDERING SUPPLIES

Water. Did you ever stop to think how important water is for cleaning your clothes—not just the temperature but the type of water? If you live in a soft water area, you may not have thought of this, but if your water is hard, you are probably aware of the problems it can create in laundering. Soft water, such as rain water, contains little or no minerals. Hard water contains dissolved minerals, usually calcium or magnesium, which unite with soap and make a scum which is difficult to remove from clothing. Because some of the soap unites with the minerals, more soap is needed for cleansing action.

The follow table lists the categories of water hardness:

    0 to 3 grains—soft
    4 to 9 grains—medium
    10 to 15 grains—hard
    over 15 grains—very hard

People at your local water department can inform you about the hardness of your water. Hard water can be softened by using a water softener or conditioner in the wash water or by installing equipment in the home which separates the minerals out before the water reaches sinks and washers.

The laundry specialists at the United States Department of Agriculture state that water of 140 to 160 degrees F. provides most soil removal and sanitizing action and is desirable for white cottons and linens and heavily soiled articles of wash-fast colors. Man-made fabrics and lightly soiled clothes can be washed satisfactorily in cool water which prevents wrinkles from forming. If your supply of hot water is limited, you will find laundering heavily soiled items more difficult.

Soaps and Synthetic Detergents. SOAPS are made from fats and oils carefully selected to obtain desired color, hardness, and other properties. When these materials are brought into contact with lye in the proper proportions, a chemical reaction occurs called saponification which produces soap and glycerine. The glycerine is removed, purified, and used in

253

many industries including pharmaceuticals and explosives. The excess lye and other impurities are separated from the soap which is then finished, perfumed, and made into powders, bars, flakes, or liquids.

DETERGENTS are made from chemical compounds. Until a short time ago they were referred to as "synthetic detergents" or syndets for short. This differentiation was made because soaps are also detergents, as they deterge the soil from fabrics. However, today the word "soap" is commonly used to refer to the natural product and the word "detergent" for the synthetic product.

Soaps work best in soft water where scum is less likely to form. Detergents work equally well in soft and hard water. You may prefer to use soaps for hand washing if your water is not too hard as detergents remove body oils so effectively they may be harder on your skin than soaps.

Built and unbuilt cleaning aids. Both soaps and detergents are made in mild form for light soil removal and for delicate fabrics, and in all-purpose form for the majority of family washing. The all-purpose products (also called heavy duty) contain alkaline salts that increase their cleaning ability. These added salts make the product alkaline in solution which improves cleaning ability but may also be hard on woolens, silks, and other delicate fabrics. These products are called "built" because ingredients have been added to them to improve

Collect empty containers of soaps and detergents used in your community. Arrange a display, sorting them into four groups: light duty or mild soaps, light duty or mild detergents, all-purpose soaps, and all purpose detergents. You may wish to subdivide the last group into low- and high-sudsing products.

Talk with the chemistry teacher in your school and try to arrange a demonstration of the making of a simple soap.

Compare the effect of soap in hard and soft water. Put a cup of hard water in one bottle and a cup of soft water in another. Add soap to each bottle until there is one inch of suds. Keep accurate measurements of the amount necessary. How do the amounts compare? (If you live in a hard water area, collect rain water, as it is very soft. If your local water is soft, you may be able to find hard water from wells nearby, or arrange to have friends bring some back from a trip to a hard water area.)

Demonstrate the effect of water softeners and conditioners when soap is used in hard water. Put a cup of hard water in each of two bottles. Add one teaspoon of soap to each. In one, put the amount of water softener recommended on the package for that amount of water. Shake and observe the difference in suds level.

Do you have iron, sulphur, or other heavy minerals in your water? If so, ask the home economist from your local utility company to come to class and discuss the best ways to overcome such laundering problems.

their cleaning ability. "Unbuilt" or mild cleaning agents do not contain these additional salts. They are called light-duty detergents for light soil. Most all-purpose detergents contain agents which:
• Reduce surface tension to help the water to "wet" the fabric and soil.
• Aid in soil removal and prevent it being deposited again on the fabric.
• Inactivate water hardness.
• Protect metals used in washing machines (a corrosion inhibitor).
• Stabilize or suppress sudsing.
• Brighten fabrics.
• Add a pleasant fragrance to the finished wash.

High- and low-sudsing detergents. Both high-sudsing and low-sudsing detergents are available. The latter are recommended for use in certain types of automatic washers where high suds interfere with mechanical action. Otherwise both types clean effectively.

How a soap or detergent works. The main steps in cleaning a fabric are wetting it, removing the dirt from the fabric, and keeping the removed dirt in suspension so that it can be rinsed away. Water has very little cleaning power in itself. When the soiled fabric is agitated during the washing process, oily dirt is broken up into small particles, each of which is surrounded by a film of the detergent solution. As the dirt is lifted out of the fabric, the detergent holds it in solution. Clothes which are soaked too long reabsorb dirt which is then more difficult to remove. Therefore, quick and thorough rinsing is as essential to getting clothes clean as is the actual washing.

Bleaches. Both the chlorine type bleach and the oxygen or perborate

Fabrics Which Can Be Safely Bleached with Chlorine Bleaches	
NO	**YES**
wool	acetate
silk	acrylic
spandex	cotton
leather	linen
some resin-	modacrylic
finished	nylon
fabrics	polyester
non-colorfast	rayon
colors	

type help whiten clothes, brighten fast colors, remove many stains, and kill some household germs. A chemical reaction known as oxidation takes place which removes grayness or yellowness of fabrics due to aging, and many staining materials.

The most common type of bleach is the chlorine type which is safe for all white and colorfast fabrics except those made from protein fibers (wool, silk, and leather) and spandex. Unfast colors may be lightened or streaked by its use. NOTE: Some resin finishes applied to cellulose fabrics for easy ironing and for design purposes are chlorine retentive; they hold onto the chlorine and turn the fabric yellow. Retained chlorine may also cause the treated cellulose to scorch and decompose in the presence of heat as in ironing.

Oxygen or perborate bleaches are safe for any fabric but are not effective for whitening heavily grayed fabrics. They need to be used for every washing.

Caution: Chlorine bleach must be diluted before being added to the wash water. Follow the directions carefully. Never pour chlorine bleach directly on fabrics as stained or weakened areas may result.

Authorities of the United States Department of Agriculture state that chlorine bleach helps disinfect clothing. Therefore its use is wise for handkerchiefs, bedclothes, and other items, especially during family illnesses. See the references at the end of the book for other suitable disinfectants.

Disinfectants. Research shows that the addition of a suitable disinfectant to family wash can prevent or reduce the spread of bacterial infections by clothing and household textiles.

Disinfectants are necessary because bacteria can remain alive through laundering in individually owned or coin-operated washers

---

Determine the effect of chlorine bleach on various fibers. Obtain small samples of fabrics made of wool, silk, cotton, nylon, and other fibers. Place a drop of chlorine bleach on each sample. Rub between your fingers. Which samples are weakened by the bleach action? Remember, the bleach may have an effect on the dyes used but may not weaken the fibers.

Collect samples of white cotton or rayon fabrics with resin finishes. They will be labeled "Wash and Wear," "Easy Care," "Little or No Ironing," or other terms that indicate the use of resins. Soak them in a solution of chlorine bleach and water. Why do some turn yellow?

Compare the cost of liquid and pre-packaged powdered chlorine bleaches for a wash load.

Demonstrate the effect of fabric softeners. Secure two similar items, either towels, cotton blouses, or handkerchiefs. Wash together, using the usual wash and rinse cycle. Remove one item and place the remaining item in a rinse with a fabric softener added. Dry and compare the appearance and feel of each item.

---

when water temperatures are not high enough to kill bacteria. It is wise to use disinfectants if colds or other infections are going around your family or if you use public machines. Follow the directions on the labels of the disinfectant you select. A reference at the end of the book gives specific directions.

Fabric Softeners. Do your clothes cling in cold, dry weather? Do they seem less soft than when they were new? Perhaps the use of a fabric softener could help. A fabric softener is not a water softener; its function is quite different. It is a lubricating agent added to the last rinse to soften fabrics, make them fluffy, reduce static electricity, and make clothes easier to iron. A thin, invisible coating forms over the surface of each fiber which makes closely woven yarns slip easily over each other. As a result, softer, more wrinkle-free clothes are obtained.

Reducing static electricity. Synthetic fabrics and finishing agents are poor conductors of electricity. When there is no moisture to carry away the static charge, it remains and even increases. The fabric softener, basically a quaternary ammonium salt, surrounds the fibers with a film of moisture from the air, so that the static charge drains out by way of absorbed moisture.

The continued use of fabric softeners cuts down on absorbency of moisture, so it is wise to skip their use every four or five launderings.

Starch. A crisp, fresh finish can be added to cottons and linens by starch if they have not already been so treated. Starched clothes also stay clean longer. Spray starches are the most expensive type available but save time and effort and are very good if you want to stiffen only part of a garment such as the collar and cuffs. Dry starches are the least expensive but are not as convenient as the liquid type. If you have a lot of clothes to treat, you can starch them in a washing machine. Be sure to read the directions for whichever type of starch you select.

Bluing is a kind of dye that counteracts the yellow cast which may develop as a result of the aging of the fabric or from soap left in it. Most detergents today contain optical brighteners which give the same blue-white effect.

SHRINKAGE OF FABRICS

Many fabrics shrink unless specially treated. Shrinkage takes place in dry-cleaning as well as washing, although usually not as much. There are several reasons for fabric shrinkage.

Relaxation shrinkage is the term given to fabrics which relax or return when wet to the size made. During the finishing process, fabrics are often stretched and dry in that form. When washed, they "relax" to their unstretched shape. Fabrics are often preshrunk before sewing for this reason.

Swelling shrinkage is due to fibers that absorb moisture and swell in thickness, remaining in a slightly swollen state even after drying. Yarns going the other direction must draw up in order to cover the greater diameter of each yarn and thus the total fabric is shorter in length, or shrunk. Ironing while damp can correct much of this.

Felting shrinkage occurs only with wool and hair fibers that have scales on the surface of the fibers. The scales overlap like shingles on a roof or like scales on fish. All the scale edges point in one direction only. When the fabric is subjected to heat and moisture, the scales are softened. The addition of friction such as rubbing during hand washing or the agitation from a washing machine causes the scales to move together, interlock, and pile up into a denser and heavier fabric. Sometimes the fabric "felts" so much that the weave is no longer noticeable.

The thermoplastic fabrics seldom change size as they have been heat-set to shape during manufacture and do not absorb enough moisture to create problems.

Look for meaningful labels on cotton, linen, rayon, and wool fabrics. Be sure to find out what is the remaining or residual shrinkage. A fabric which has been preshrunk may still shrink 3 to 5 per cent more.

Shrinkage may not happen all at once. There may be a small amount each cleaning which you do not notice until the third or fourth time when it affects the fit. Some fabrics have finishes which hold the fabric stable and when that finish disappears (usually through improper washing), shrinkage will begin.

GENERAL HINTS FOR LAUNDERING

• Wash clothes before they are too soiled. Vigorous washing is harder on clothes than more frequent gentle laundering.

• Proper sorting is important. One dark sock of a nonfast color can leave its mark forever if washed with whites. Consider the colors, the water temperature, and the amount of agitation needed.

• Examine clothes before putting them in the washer. Check pockets—a cleansing tissue can ruin a whole load with lint and a crayon or lipstick can cause even more serious damage. Close zippers and fasten hooks to prevent snags. Tie apron strings and sashes together loosely or else the entire load will get tangled.

• Darn or repair little tears—small ones become big in washing. Lost buttons and fasteners can clog machines.

• Remove nonwashable trim, such as belts and fancy buttons.

• Pretreat soiled areas, especially collars and cuffs, by brushing with a liquid detergent or a paste made of granulated detergent and water.

Cotton and linen articles such as handkerchiefs, aprons, household linens, blouses, pajamas, and sportswear can be washed with hot water and all-purpose soap or detergent. Read labels carefully, as some cottons have had finishes added which require cool water washing. Heavily soiled or greasy clothes need hot water (at least 140 degrees) to release embedded dirt and remove perspiration odors.

Synthetics which are heat sensitive and other fabrics with special finishes should not be washed in hot water or dried in hot dryers. Wrinkles may be-

CLEANLINESS BUREAU

By wearing white gloves while sudsing and rinsing nylons, you'll protect the hose against nail damage—and the gloves also come clean.

come set, finishes may disappear, and the fabric may become harsh. These fibers are strong and can take regular agitation in a machine. However, if the seams tend to fray or if delicate laces are used as trim, you may have to hand wash.

Hosiery must be washed by hand unless you have a special mesh bag for the machine. Squeeze the suds through, don't scrub or wring. Roll in a towel to remove excess moisture and dry in the shade away from excess heat.

Lingerie is usually made of sturdy synthetic fibers and can be machine washed in warm water with all-purpose soap or detergent. Garments with elastic or spandex fibers should not be chlorine bleached. White ny-

258

Another way to wash nylon hose without snagging them with your fingernails is to shake them clean in a plastic juice shaker half full of lukewarm soap or detergent suds. Then flush-rinse them under running water until all soil and suds are removed.

lons must not be washed with other colors. Nylon is a scavenger and may pick up colors from other garments that do not seem to "run."

Woolens usually need to be washed by hand, not with the family laundry, so many wise girls care for their own sweaters. Wool fabrics are subject to a felting as well as relaxation shrinkage. In the presence of heat and water, agitation can cause felting. Tests have shown that it is the mechanical action that causes shrinkage more than the type of soap or water temperature. Nevertheless, cool to lukewarm water and mild soap are preferred.

• Dissolve the soap first. Special soaps for wool are available which dissolve readily in cool water but any mild soap or detergent is suitable.

• Soak the garment for two to three minutes. Squeeze the solution through the garment gently to remove dirt.

• Support the fabric while wet with your hands to prevent it from stretching from the weight of the water.

• If very soiled, rinse and then suds again. Rinse thoroughly in cool water. Roll in a towel to remove excess moisture.

• Do not wring. Place on a flat surface for drying. Dry indoors or outside in the shade. Avoid direct heat.

Many woolen scarfs, skirts, and even sweaters can be machine washed with cool water and a delicate agitation cycle. Machine directions must be followed carefully. Experiment with a skirt or sweater you do not care too much about and you may be pleasantly surprised.

Sweaters of *synthetic fibers* are usually washed in the machine. To prevent excessive pilling, turn inside out and put through a short, delicate agitation cycle. Machine dry at a low setting. Some bicomponent yarns (two-fiber), such as Sayelle, must be machine dried to prevent shrinkage. These special knits are usually well labeled as to care needed.

The Corduroy Council of America recommends that all corduroy items be turned inside out before washing to avoid any lint clinging to the fabric. Never twist or wring as this will set creases in the pile. Colorful new garments should be put through a series of clean suds and rinses to flush away excess dye to keep further bleeding at a minimum. A fabric softener in the final rinse water eliminates most ironing and maintains the "loft" of the pile.

SEARS, ROEBUCK AND CO.

Acrylic sweaters such as these can be machine-washed in warm water and tumble-dried at low-heat settings.

Outline the shape of a sweater, which may shrink before it is washed. After washing you may be able to ease it gently back to the original size.

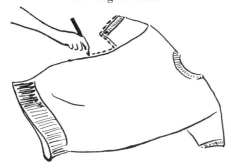

Sweaters with fancy decorations should be washed before becoming very soiled. Use well-lathered fingers to "massage" soil lines or spots, and a soft complexion brush to work the suds in and around beading and other decoration.

CLEANLINESS BUREAU

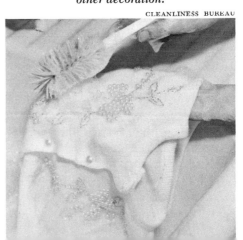

260

Washing Guide For Everyday Fabrics

Fiber	Washing	Ironing or Drying	Other Information
Cotton Linen	Use very hot water for white articles—boil if needed. Use warm (120 degrees) for colored.	Iron while damp with hot iron at cotton or linen setting.	Avoid chlorine bleaches or extreme heat on many wrinkle-resistant finished cottons.
Silk Acetate	Wash in warm water 100 to 120 degrees by hand or delicate machine cycle.	Do not tumble dry. Use low setting on iron.	Many colored silks are not colorfast, so wash separately if uncertain.
Wool	Use cool water. Wash by hand or keep agitation to a minimum.	Do not tumble dry. Use steam iron for pressing.	Avoid chlorine bleach.
Nylon Acrylic Polyester Olefin	Use warm to hot water (not over 140 degrees), cool rinse.	Avoid very hot drying temperatures.	Fabric softener in rinse prevents static electricity problems. Wash white nylons with only white clothes.
Rayon	Lukewarm water and mild agitation as fibers are weaker when wet.	Iron at steam or cotton setting.	High modulus rayons can be handled like cotton.
Spandex	Use warm water with any suitable detergent.	Avoid hot drying temperatures.	Avoid chlorine bleach, which will cause yellowing.

Wash leather gloves on your hands, using warm suds. Rinse well and remove carefully from your hands to dry flat.
CLEANLINESS BUREAU

To wash especially soiled areas on a girdle or panty girdle, use a soft brush with plenty of warm water and suds, and scrub spots gently. Squeeze more suds through the entire garment after using the brush, then rinse in clear water several times.
CLEANLINESS BUREAU

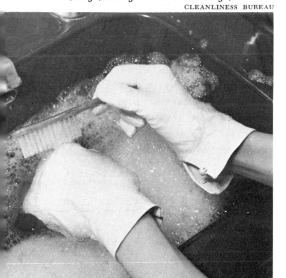

To whiten grayed nylon garments, wash thoroughly with soap or synthetic detergent by machine, if construction of garment and trim permits; otherwise wash by hand and rinse well. Then dissolve one package of color remover, from a drugstore or a variety store, in an enamel pan with a gallon of hot water (about 140 degrees). Immediately add the wet garments. Stir occasionally, keeping the temperature about 140 degrees for 30 minutes. Check, and if white enough, rinse thoroughly in hot water. If not as white as desired, leave another 30 minutes.

Caution: A temperature higher than 150 degrees may set in wrinkles which will be very hard to remove later.

For further whitening, dissolve 2 tablespoons of detergent and 2 tablespoons of a chorine bleach in a gallon of warm water. Let garments soak 20 minutes. Rinse very thoroughly.

To whiten clothes that have yellowed because of a chlorine bleach reaction, use a commercial color remover following directions on the package. Or dissolve 1 tablespoon of sodium hydrosulphite or sodium bisulfite (obtainable from any photo supply store) in a quart of water. Submerge the garment for 30 seconds or until yellowing disappears. Remove immediately and put through a complete wash cycle in a machine, using an all-purpose synthetic detergent. Avoid all chlorine bleaches in the future; use only sodium perborate bleaches.

To recondition fabrics grayed from hard water. Unless minerals in water and dirt are counteracted, film or hangover dirt will build up layer by layer with repeated washings. This scum clings to fabrics, causing yellowing and graying. You can get rid of hangover dirt by using a water conditioner as directed on the package. Add one-half cup of borax or household ammonia to this solution. Put clothes through a complete washing cycle *without* any soap or detergent. You may need to put them through two cycles.

Uniforms of Nylon, Orlon, Dacron or other acrylic or polyester fibers maintain their fresh appearance if washed after every wearing, even if the soil appears slight. In the case of white uniforms, wash them only with other white garments. Treat heavy stains as soon as possible. Rub a liquid detergent or a paste made of water and all-purpose soap or detergent into the stain and allow it to remain for 10 minutes or more. Then wash as usual. You may also want to pretreat soil at necklines and cuffs. If touch-up ironing is required, use a steam iron. The use of fabric softener in the last rinse prevents uniforms from clinging and may lessen soiling due to static electricity problems. The use of a bleach occasionally may be of value.

Water-repellent fabrics such as those used on raincoats and jackets are often washable. However, remember that soap must be thoroughly rinsed out to restore the repellency, as soap naturally makes it easier for water to penetrate fibers. Put these clothes through an additional cycle of the machine without any soap or detergent to be certain of a thorough rinse. A light ironing often helps increase repellency.

IRONING

Automatic dryers and "wash and wear" garments have reduced the

A portable steam and dry iron is handy for travel and for touch-up pressing in one's own room.

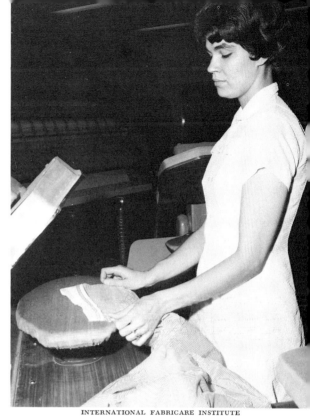

Commercial laundries use presses as shown here with a padded buck (base) and a steam-heated pressing surface which is lowered onto the fabric. The temperature of the steam heating the press head used on this cotton dress is 338 degrees F.

amount and difficulty of ironing. A steam iron with a good heat control will handle the touch-ups needed by the treated fibers as well as regular ironing. Steam makes it easier to iron heat-sensitive fibers. Heat control is extremely important as thermoplastic fibers can be glazed and actually melted with an iron that is the right temperature for a plain cotton blouse. *Never* put a hot iron on a fabric you are not sure of; test it first on a seam allowance.

Most cottons and linens need to be dampened before ironing. If you can't iron all you have dampened, don't leave the clothes for another day unless you put them in a refrigerator or freezer, which will inhibit mildew from forming.

Iron on the right side if a shiny finish is desired—for example, polished cottons or linen damasks. For a dull finish, iron on the wrong side or use a press cloth on the right side. NOTE: Iron marks show less on dark fabrics if ironed on the wrong side.

Iron all fabrics with the grain or direction of the threads, to avoid stretching. To keep the raised appearance of monograms on a blouse or any embroidery, place the fabric face down over a towel or pad before pressing. Avoid ironing over a zipper. Metal zippers leave marks on the fabric, and nylon ones are sensitive to hot irons.

Velvet, corduroy, and other pile fabrics stay their loveliest if they are steamed rather than ironed. Sometimes a steaming in the bathroom is

263

all that is needed. Otherwise, place the fabric pile side up. Cover with a dampened cloth. Move a steam iron or a regular hot iron over the cloth slowly and lightly, barely making contact with the press cloth. Let dry before wearing. If you have a velvet board, place the cloth on it, pile down, and go over it with a steam iron.

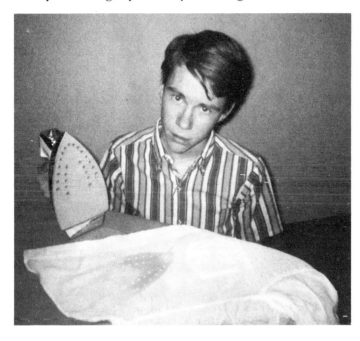

If an iron is too hot for the fiber or left on the fabric too long, it can result in a scorched area. A faint scorch mark may often be removed by bleaching but a scorch as heavy as this one has probably damaged the fabric permanently.

CLEANLINESS BUREAU

Cotton clothes dampened but no time to iron? Place in a plastic bag in the refrigerator. Cold prevents mildew from forming and clothes will iron crisp when you are ready.

CLEANLINESS BUREAU

Ironing should go easily with this arrangement—stand to hold finished garments, adjustable ironing board for suitable height, basket to hold work ready for ironing, and mending materials easily at hand for simple repairs.

Collect labels which give directions for washing and care of fabrics. Sort them into two groups: one that is helpful and clear and another that is meaningless or confusing. Prepare a display for others to see.

Make a list of types of garments that must be drycleaned, of those that are better drycleaned but may be washed, and of those that should be washed.

Ask the representative of an equipment dealer or a home economist for a utility company to come to class and demonstrate how to use a washer and dryer and how to care for fabrics in style.

Bring to class one article which you or your mother dislike washing or which never seems to come out nicely. Share your problems with others in the class and seek suggestions. Prepare a report on a better way to care for this garment. Compare the cost of washing a sweater at home and having it drycleaned commercially.

Visit a local drycleaner and find out which garments he does not recommend drycleaning. Perhaps you may wish to compile a list of questions class members have about cleaning clothes and report his answers after your visit.

Visit a local market. List the different types of laundry aids shown there, plus the claims made for each. How many are essential for routine clothes care? Are there any which are unnecessary?

Select samples of acetate, rayon, wool, cotton, and linen fabrics. Set the iron at the lowest setting. Press it on each sample for 30 seconds. Observe the effect. Raise the iron setting to cotton. Press again and notice the effect. What conclusions can you draw from this experiment? Now set the iron at the highest setting (linen). Dampen one half of the linen fabric thoroughly. Iron the entire sample and compare the two sections. What conclusion can you make?

Visit a commercial laundry and observe the methods used for washing and ironing.

Secure a large sample of a fabric made from cotton and polyester fibers. Wash it, using a normal washing procedure. Cut the sample in half. Line dry one section and dry the other in a dryer. Observe the difference.

Investigate the cost of drying an average load of clothes in a dryer heated by gas and one heated by electricity. Local utilities can give you this information.

SPOT AND STAIN REMOVAL

What do you do if you are ready for school or for a big date and you notice an unsightly spot on the dress you plan to wear? Knowing how to remove spots and stains can save many dollars as well as keep your clothes ready for use. Laundering removes many stains but the heat of the water and drying may make others almost impossible to remove later.

Spots should be removed *before* laundering.

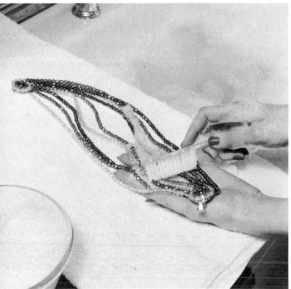

CLEANLINESS BUREAU

Cushioned by a folded towel, this multi-strand necklace gets a sudsy treatment to restore its highlights. Gentle "scrubbing" with a soft brush pulls out gummy make-up and perspiration film often lodged along the beads.

GENERAL STAIN REMOVAL DIRECTIONS

The sooner you remove a stain, the easier it will come out and the less damage will be done to the fabric. A gentle sponging with cool water will remove many fresh spots that require complicated removal methods if "aged" with time and improper care.

No one can remember the specific directions for each type of stain. An instruction booklet or chart should be kept by the washing center for easy reference. Such guides are available from the government and other sources listed in the references at the end of the book.

Keep common stain removal supplies ready for use at the laundry center.

There are times a stain is so com-plex or the fabric so delicate that you should seek the help of a trained spotter at a professional cleaning business before you have complicated matters with the wrong method. Don't expect miracles as there are some stains that can only be removed with a scissors!

• Do not iron a stained fabric. The heat of pressing causes many stains to become permanently set.

• Test the stain remover on a hidden part of the fabric, such as an inside seam, pocket, or even inside the hem. Sometimes the appearance of the fabric will be seriously changed or the color altered. Other fabrics may fade, shrink, bleed, or stretch. Materials such as satins, crepes, velvets, gabardines, moires, and taffetas are easily affected by stain removal.

• Some stains are invisible when fresh but turn brown during cleaning, as pictured on page 274. This is usually the result of common foods that contain reducing sugars, such as soft drinks, because the heat needed in cleaning caramelizes the sugar.

• Fabrics treated with stain-repellent finishes release stains easily if blotted when fresh. However, a stain rubbed in and set will be very difficult to remove, so act quickly.

• Ignore old stain removal methods. Modern day ink is not removed by milk, and milk stains are difficult to remove from some fabrics. Ginger ale may remove a spot but will leave a sugar stain, noticeable at a later date.

• Before starting to remove a stain, know what it is. If you can't determine the cause, find out if it is greasy, non-greasy, or a combination of both. Fiber content is also important, as some stain removers dissolve certain fibers.

USDA

Stain removers. Notice the four types: absorbent materials, detergents, solvents, and chemical stain removers such as bleaches.

Miscellaneous supplies used in removing stains. A small syringe and a medicine dropper are helpful along with absorbent paper towels, cloths, cotton, and containers.

USDA

267

STAIN REMOVERS

Solvents. CAUTION: Naphtha, benzene, and carbon tetrachloride are solvents which dissolve the staining matter, especially oily substances. All of these are dangerous in some manner. The fumes are highly volatile and can be poisonous if inhaled. Some solvents are flammable if used near a flame or electrical equipment. Always use these cleaners outside or in a well-ventilated place, away from flames.

Other solvents are acetone which dissolves nail polish (also acetate and triacetate fibers!), turpentine, and alcohol. Water is also a solvent which, used promptly, releases and frees staining material before it has a chance to set.

USDA

Applying a grease solvent. Place fabric stained side down on a pad of absorbent material. Sponge back of stain with pad dampened with grease solvent. Apply only a small amount at a time. Work from center of stain toward the outside edge, using light brushing or tamping motions.

To use solvents, turn the fabric right side down on a blotter or soft, absorbent cloth. Starting at the center of the stain, use a pad of cloth moistened with the solvent, and pat and stroke the stained area gently. As the stain is absorbed by the blotter or absorbent cloth, change to fresh ones. Feather out the cleaning fluid so there is no definite edge. See page 269 for information on rings.

Detergents. Oily and non-oily stains are often removed by detergents in water, suspending and floating them out of the fabric. Liquid detergents penetrate easily.

Absorbent Materials. Talcum, chalk, and cornstarch absorb some stains from a fabric. A blotter, paper towels, and soft cloths can also absorb moisture, grease, and oil which is softened with heat.

Chemical Stain Removers. Other substances react chemically with stains used. Bleaches, oxalic acid, ammonia, and pepsin are examples.

OILY STAINS

Many stains are made by butter and other fats, chocolate, chewing gum, sauces, and gravies. If there is solid matter, first remove as much as possible.

Ice will congeal gum, chocolate, or tar so it can be gently scraped off with a dull knife.

Washable fabrics can have liquid detergent or a paste made of granulated detergent and water applied directly to the spot. Work it in with the fingers and then rinse with as hot water as appropriate for the fabric. If stains remain, apply a grease solvent as described on this page.

Simple oily stains can be removed by placing the stained area over a blotter or soft absorbent towel and pressing with a fairly hot iron to force the oily material to the padding underneath.

Non-washable fabrics are best treated with a grease solvent according to the directions on the container. On light colors you may sprinkle on an absorbent powder such as cornstarch, talcum, or chalk. Allow to dry and brush off gently.

NON-OILY STAINS

Washable fabrics should be soaked in luke-warm water for at least a half an hour. Then work in a detergent and rinse well. Persistent stains may be made unnoticeable with diluted solutions of bleaches if colors will not be affected.

Non-washable fabrics that will not be damaged by a small amount of water respond to running a fine stream of water through the stain. If this does not work, try a grease solvent.

COMBINATION STAINS

Stains which are a combination of both oily and nonoily substances are common. Start by sponging the stain with cool water; then let soak for 30 minutes or longer. Work detergent into the stain and rinse thoroughly. After it is dry, if the stain remains, sponge with grease solvent one or more times. If a colored stain still remains, use a chlorine or perborate bleach.

TO REMOVE SPECIAL STAINS

Blood, egg, meat are protein materials which harden with heat. Scrape off the excess. Soak in cool water. A little ammonia added helps loosen the stain. If it is not removed, apply powdered pepsin (meat tenderizer),

keeping the area moist and warm until rinsed out with lukewarm water. (Pepsin is an enzyme which digests protein.) Dried and aged stains may need repeated treatments.

Chewing gum can often be easily removed if hardened with an ice cube or by placing in a freezer. A grease solvent will remove any remaining stain.

Cola and other soft drinks seldom show a stain when fresh but turn yellow or brown on aging. Sponge immediately with cool water.

Ball point ink of one type can be removed by washing but another type is set by the same treatment. To determine if stains will wash out, mark a scrap of similar material and wash it. Acetone removes ink safely on all fabrics except acetate, Arnel, Dynel, and Verel. Use amyl acetate on these fabrics.

Fruit juice is easy to remove if fresh but may be invisible until aged. Sponge immediately with cool water. Follow directions for non-oily stains. If safe for fabric, pour boiling water through the spot from a height of 1 to 3 feet.

Scorch may be washed out if mild. Heavy scorch may penetrate the fabric and cannot be removed. Bleach may remove some of the color.

If in doubt, sponge with cool water and use a grease solvent.

A *ring* is a circular spot left around the outer edge of the spotted area after it has dried. When a liquid remover is applied to a stain, it loosens any solid particles where it wets the fabric. These solid particles may be tiny specks of dye, finish, or dirt. They are not noticeable on the original fabric because they are uniformly distributed. But when wet, they move from the wet center to the dry outer edge of the stain and form a "ring." The final rubbing of the spot should be with strokes going away from the

With your classmates, make a list of stains common to your age group and your activities. Form committees to demonstrate the removal of these stains on various scrap fabrics.

Make a "first aid" kit for stains to be available in your home economics room. Study the references at the end of the book and obtain the basic equipment and supplies needed for removing common stains. Put them together in a suitable box with a chart or booklet containing directions.

Visit a reliable drycleaner and talk with the spotter. Find out how he determines the types of stains and how he removes them. Are there any stains that are more difficult to remove than others? Report back to your class.

Visit a local fire station. Ask the fire fighter in charge his opinion of the improper use of cleaning fluids. Have there been any fires in your community recently as a result of their improper use?

Check garments and household articles at home for stains. If there are some that you can remove, follow the directions given in this chapter and record the results as follows: (1) kind of fabric, (2) kind of stain, (3) equipment used, (4) methods used, (5) results.

Demonstrate various types of commercial spot removers. Include cost, purpose, and precautions needed for their use.

center to the outside of the spot ending in an irregular design. If a ring remains, rub the material against itself; then with your fingernail or the edge of a coin rub the ring. If it still remains, try holding the spot over the spout of a steaming kettle. Cleaning the entire garment may be necessary in some instances.

Perspiration odors may not appear as stains but the odor is just as noticeable and objectionable. Many fabric finishes hold onto these odors even after washing. Try soaking your garment in a solution of baking soda and water (two tablespoons in a basin of water). It will usually emerge sweet smelling with no fabric damage.

DRYCLEANING

The idea for drycleaning is supposed to have started when a servant in a French home tipped over a turpentine lamp onto a tablecloth. After the cloth dried, spots of soil had disappeared from the area. The owner of the home, who ran a dyeing establishment in Paris, started using this method to clean fabrics.

Drycleaning is a method of cleaning fabrics by immersion and agitation in "dry" solvents, either petroleum distillates or hydrocarbons, with the addition of appropriate soaps and detergents. This method loosens the insoluble dirt and dissolves soil of a greasy nature with little change of size, shape, appearance, and details such as pleats.

There are over 40,000 drycleaning plants in the United States operating under a variety of conditions. Machines vary in design, different types of solvents are used, and even the soil content of the clothing handled

Seal of International Fabricare Institute

differs. The International Fabricare Institute (IFI) is a voluntary organization to which many firms belong. Members display the seal and receive up-to-date information on proper care of new fabrics. Many reliable firms do not belong to the IFI but the seal is an indication that the member firm has high standards.

When garments are received for drycleaning, they are marked for identification purposes and are carefully inspected. The marker must be on the lookout for rips and damages to the garment that the customer may not know exist. The marker must also look for unusual stains that will need prespotting before cleaning to ease removal. Buckles, buttons, and ornaments that would be damaged in the cleaning process must be removed, put in an envelope, and attached to the ticket in order to be replaced after finishing.

Pockets, cuffs, and seams are brushed to remove lint and to prevent its transfer to other garments. All pockets are carefully searched for customers' valuables and for items that can cause damage and expense to the drycleaner, such as ball point pens, lipstick, and knives. The garments are then sorted by color, texture, and finish.

Any soil spots or stains that have a water base are removed before cleaning by prespotting. Some stains are actually set in drycleaning when they

INTERNATIONAL FABRICARE INSTITUTE

Identification tags are attached to the garments to prevent them from being lost or misplaced while in the drycleaning plant.

have not been spot removed before cleaning. Stains such as paint, gutter splash, mustard, and grass are more difficult to remove if they have gone through the drycleaning cycle without being prespotted. It is because of this that you are asked to help in identifying stains you know about.

A load of soiled clothes is placed in a drycleaning "washer" containing a petroleum or synthetic solvent. After the correct length of time, the solvent is removed and clothes are tumble dried with warm air and then deodorized with clean, fresh air.

271

If the garment is not one that needs special care (such as a wedding gown), it has gone through these processes with a number of other garments of the same type and texture. After being extracted, the garments are handled individually by the spotter, who inspects them and removes remaining spots and stains. He must have a knowledge of textile fibers, fabric construction, dyestuffs, and chemicals as well as the special skills necessary to remove stains.

From the spotter the garment is sent to the proper finishing depart-ment. The term "finishing" is used because no mechanical pressure is used as in home pressing. Only steam and air are used. Presses are built in various sizes and in the shapes of some garments. Some garments are finished or partly finished on a garment form that inflates with air. Hard-to-get-at areas, such as shoulder and folds and frills, are pressed over "puff irons." These consist of perforated metal forms which are padded and covered.

After finishing, the garments must have a final inspection and repairs are made.

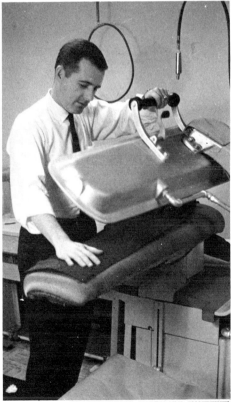

INTERNATIONAL FABRICARE INSTITUTE

Steam is used to soften the fabric, remove the wrinkles, and restore the original shape and style of the garments. This is done by using presses of various sizes and shapes in combination with hand steam irons.

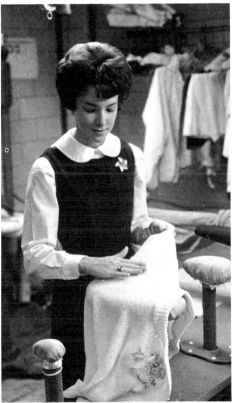

INTERNATIONAL FABRICARE INSTITUTE

This young miss who enjoys working with fabrics and clothing has found employment in a drycleaning shop where she uses the wool finisher and helps restore garments to an appearance like new.

A seamstress makes simple hand or machine repairs, such as sewing open seams, attaching linings that have become loosened, replacing or securing buttons and trimming, or sewing hems that need it.

Coin Operated Drycleaning

In the coin-operated cleaning establishments, a load of garments can be cleaned by placing it in a machine and dropping in the correct amount of money. Garments can be cleaned much less expensively than at a professional drycleaners, but they do not receive any special attention. You can clean most clothes this way successfully if you will follow the same procedures used by the drycleaners.

Sort clothes so that your load contains either light or dark colors. Brush lint from pockets and cuffs and *check pockets* carefully for items that should not go into a cleaning machine. *Get out spots* before cleaning, especially if they are a non-oily type. Don't overload the machines. Most machines have a weight limit but crowding of clothes is more serious. Garments should move freely in the

Invite a representative from a drycleaning establishment belonging to the IFI to discuss procedures used. Ask him to bring some of the bulletins from the IFI to show to the class.

Compare the cost of cleaning an average load of sweaters and skirts in a coin-operated machine and at a traditional shop.

" 'Tis not the cost but the upkeep." Be prepared to tell the class about some item you or a friend purchased that costs more to care for than expected.

solvent for best success, so underload rather than try to put in one more item. NOTE: You can use a heavier load of small articles than large ones, as small ones move more freely.

Remove immediately when finished and place on hangers to prevent wrinkles from developing. Air outdoors or in a well-ventilated area if any solvent odor remains.

Home drycleaning is extremely hazardous; therefore it is never recommended.

CLOTHING REPAIRS

"A stitch in time saves nine" is as true today as when some wise unknown first said it. Repairing simple tears and rips when first noticed can prevent more lengthy repairs or the actual replacement of an article. It is a thinking person who knows how and when to mend and when to discard a garment. Some garments are too worn and the fabric too weak to be repaired, but others can be made better than new.

Every year garments that have developed problems in drycleaning are sent to the International Fabricare Institute for study. Some of the common problems are shown here.

INTERNATIONAL FABRICARE INSTITUTE

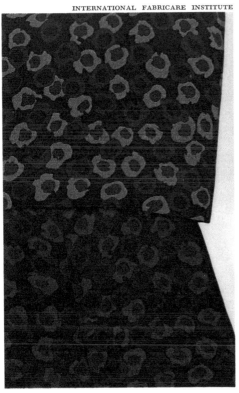

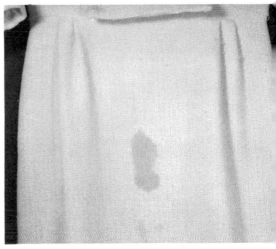

Reducing sugars are found in fruit juices, soft drinks, and alcohol. When these liquids are spilled on clothing, the stain often disappears when it dries. But when the residue it leaves is subjected to heat as in pressing or drying or even storage in a hot attic, these sugar residues may decompose to form brown stains. The heat or aging caramelizes the sugars. Some of these stains cannot be removed—be sure to tell your drycleaner if you have spilled any of these liquids on clothing to be cleaned.

Resin-bonded pigments. The top part of this dress is the way it appeared when bought. After drycleaning, the light blue changed and the dress appeared a different color.

Textured acetate may deluster or become dull during wear or during spot removal or in pressing the garment. The lower half of this garment became dull with steaming. If you press a textured acetate garment between its trips to your drycleaner, remember: (1) Turn inside out and press on the wrong side; (2) do not tug or pull while the fabric is moist or damp with steam; (3) avoid too much pressure; (4) do not press over a wet spot; (5) do not brush or rub the fabric too hard if you attempt to remove a stain.

REINFORCE BEFORE WEARING NEW GARMENTS

A few stitches when a garment is brand new may mean longer wear and a more attractive appearance. Manufacturers produce so many items at a time that it is difficult to inspect for all the loose buttons and dangling threads.

Seams which are narrow or loosely stitched may pull out during washing and wearing. One day you will find yourself with an embarrassing split seam. Stitch over long stitches with a medium to small stitch. A narrow seam can be reinforced by machine stitching about 1/16-inch deeper than the original seam line.

Underarm seams of raglan or ki-mono-type sleeves receive strain and should be reinforced. One way is to press the seam open and apply seam or bias tape along it on the wrong side. Stitch by hand or machine.

Dangling threads can be fastened by pulling to the inside and tying securely. Fasten chain stitching carefully so it won't unravel.

Slide fasteners can be prevented from catching if loose seam edges are overcast or the loose threads clipped so they don't obstruct the zipper.

Pocket corners may need reinforcing if they will get much use.

Loose buttons should be secured and frayed or weak buttonholes reworked. Check any snaps, hooks, and eyes and secure if necessary.

The curved underarm seam is pressed open and tape applied along it on the wrong side. Notice how the tape takes the strain off the stitching of this kimona sleeve.

USDA

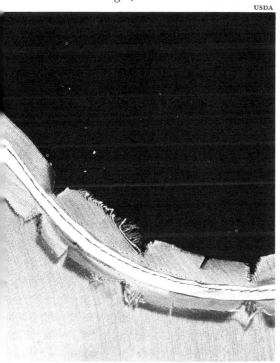

The top of the pocket has been reinforced so it will not pull loose or tear the fabric.

USDA

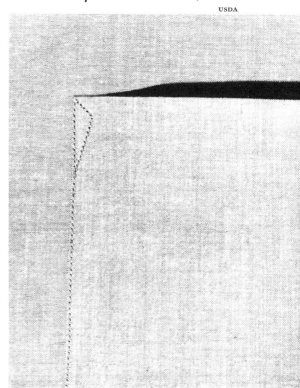

275

SUGGESTIONS FOR MENDING

Consider the garment when choosing the repair method. Iron-on patches may last on a garment with little wear but seldom last on anything that is washed often. If the needed repair is at a place that gets much strain, you may have to sacrifice appearance for durability. In other places you may prefer to make a repair that is not as strong but will be inconspicuous.

• Match the repair fabric as closely as possible. Fabric from a worn garment that is still sturdy may be a better choice for patching than new material.

• Use thread that matches or blends. A shade darker than the fabric itself is less noticeable. For hand darning, try to use thread pulled from seam edges of the garment itself.

• Use the sewing machine as much as possible. Tears, holes, and thin places in work and play clothes as well as in household linens can be quickly mended this way.

The professional services of a reweaver may be required to repair some garments. His work may seem expensive but can often keep a garment wearable. Home insurance policies may cover the cost of burned holes, so read your policy carefully. The classified ads list reweavers in almost every large city.

Keep a well-stocked mending kit easily available. Most homes can use three—one in the bedroom to catch a snag noticed when dressing, another one by the ironing board for quick repairs there, and a third more complete kit for mending that takes a longer time. You will want needles and thread of various colors in all the kits and also small scissors. Extra snaps and hooks and eyes as well as simple buttons and scraps of twill and hem tape should be included. What other items would you want?

DARNING

To prevent holes increasing in size, darn garments before they are washed. Select thread that matches the color and fibers of the item. Use one or two threads, depending upon the size of yarn in the fabric but do not tie a knot. Work over a darner, or over your hand on the right side of the fabric.

Before you darn a stocking, be sure the hole is not in such a place that it could irritate the foot of the wearer.

A plain weave **_hand darn_** is the best way to mend small moth-eaten or burned holes. Large holes are better repaired with a patch.

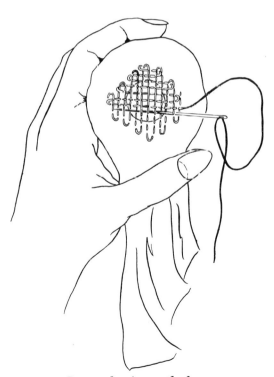

Correct darning method.

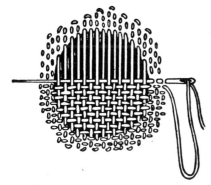

Close-up of darning method.

• Trim away all frayed edges.
• Put running stitches about ½ inch from the edge of the hole.
• When the hole is reached, continue the running stitches to the top of the hole. The rows are irregular in length.
• Make running stitches at right angles to the first stitches. They cross under one thread and over the next as in plain weaving.
• When darning is completed, cut the thread; do not tie a knot.

Machine Darning is suitable for work clothes and household linens. Tears in blouses can be almost unnoticeable if repaired this way:
• Place the fabric to be mended in an embroidery hoop to hold it taut.
• Release the feed dog (teeth under needle of machine). Check the instruction book of your machine for directions.
• Check the tension before darning to see that it is loose. If the fabric is soft or the hole large, baste a backing of lawn or organdy on the wrong side.
• Place the fabric in the hoop under the needle, fabric down. Lower the presser bar. Move the hoop slowly to make short stitches. Stitch backward and forward over the area to be darned, following the lengthwise threads of the fabric. Avoid stiffness

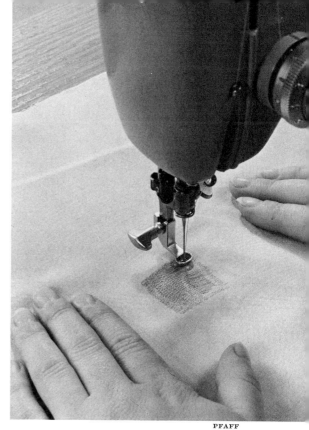

PFAFF

Machine darning is fast and strong.

by keeping the stitching lines from touching. Turn the hoop and stitch crosswise, following the crosswise threads in the same manner. Fasten threads by retracing.

PATCHING

Holes too large to look neat when darned may be patched. A large hole would require too much time to fill by interlacing threads, as in darning. A piece of patch fabric will fill the hole more quickly. The patch should be of the same material as the garment. When new material is used for a patch it should be faded either by sunlight or laundering to correspond with the garment. The threads of the patch should match those of the garment. In printed fabrics, the designs should match after the patch is in place.

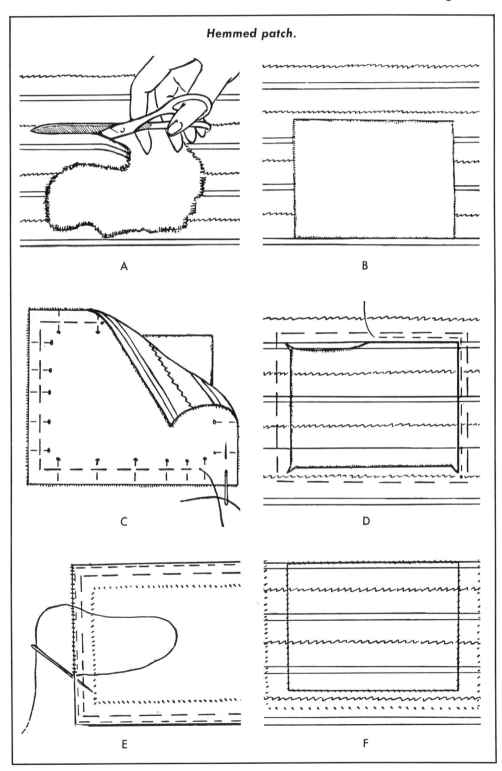

Hemmed patch.

A

B

C

D

E

F

Hemmed Patch. The kind of patch used is determined by the fabric and the location of the patch. A hemmed patch is suited to fabrics that are laundered frequently.

Trim the hole to be patched along the lines of warp and filling threads, making the hole either square or rectangular in shape (A and B).

Cut the patch one inch larger each way than the hole, and place it on the wrong side of the garment matching designs (C).

Pin so that the patch edges extend about one inch past the edges of the hole. Baste about ½ inch from the edge of the hole.

Turn the garment to the right side and clip corners of the hole diagonally ¼ inch. Turn under each edge and baste; then hem (D).

Turn the garment to the wrong side and turn under the edges of the patch about ¼ inch on all sides. Baste to the garment; then hem (E).

Remove basting and press (F).

Darned Patch. Large holes in wool fabrics can be repaired inconspicuously with a darned patch. Follow the directions for the hemmed patch except that the raw edge of the hole is secured to the patch with tiny hand stitches. Try to use thread from the fabric to be repaired by raveling from inside seams.

Machine Set-in Patch. Jeans and Levis are popular for at home and sports wear but the knees wear out quickly. If you have younger brothers, you will find this patch a helpful one for their clothes. The set-in patch is done quickly on the machine from the wrong side. (See next page.)

1. Cut away worn material. Trim to a square or rectangular hole following the straight threads of the cloth. Cut diagonally ½ inch into each corner.

2. Turn the garment inside out. With a hot iron crease back a seam allowance of ½ inch along the four cut edges.

3. Cut a patch of matching material on the grain. Make it at least 2 inches longer and 2 inches wider than the hole to be patched.

4. Pin the patch material to cut edges along the crease fold, which is now the seam line.

5. With the patch down, sew along the pressed edges. Begin in the center of one side and stitch to the corner. Leave the needle in the cloth, raise the presser foot, and turn the garment. Lower the presser foot and sew to next corner. Repeat.

6. To strengthen, make a second line of stitching near the raw edges of the seam, stitching diagonally across each corner as you come to it. This may make a slight pucker as you stitch across. Turn the garment right side out and press well. A row of top stitching along the patch will provide extra reinforcement.

Knit Stitch Patch. This patch is used on plain knit garments to duplicate the original stitch. It is almost invisible and stretches in use. Sweaters are often mended with this patch. (See the next page.)

A. Make two horizontal cuts—one above the hole and one below.

B. Ravel knit to end of these cuts. A thread may be run through the loops as a guard against further raveling.

C. With a needle, thread loose ends of yarns at sides of patch and pull ends back to under side of knit. Follow drawings B and C to complete patch.

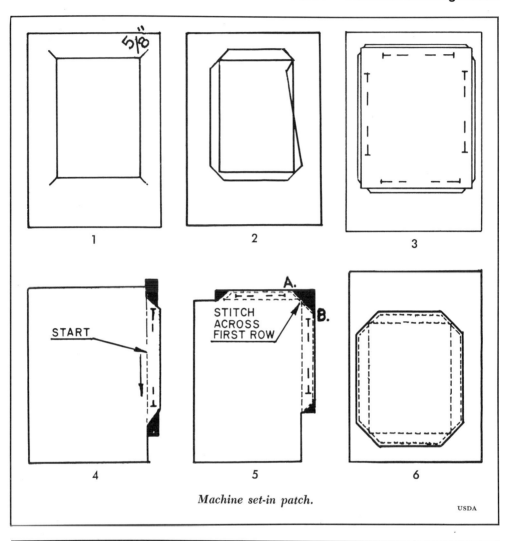

Machine set-in patch.

USDA

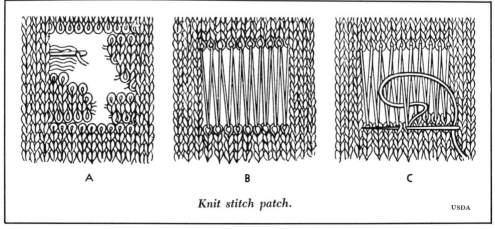

Knit stitch patch.

USDA

OTHER REPAIRS

Have you ever considered replacing the torn lace at the bottom of an otherwise good nylon slip? Or adding new straps if the present ones are broken? Both are easy repair jobs, as you can buy new lace and straps in variety and department stores and quickly attach them with nylon thread.

Do you have a brassiere that is good except for the stretched elastic in the back? Elastic replacement closures can be easily set in place and the bra will be as good as new.

When you have learned to sew simple garments, you will find it an easy matter to replace broken zippers, lost buttons, and even alter waistlines that no longer fit. Directions in Chapter 17 will help you.

ALTERATIONS

Some garments are clean and in good repair but no longer stylish or suitable for your activities. Consider altering them before you decide to give them away. A sleeveless jumper is easily made from many old dresses. Too-tight sweaters can be changed into cardigans and sleeveless sweater vests by removing the sleeves and facing armholes.

Elastic thread sewn into baggy sweater cuffs and necklines makes a sweater pert again. See page 621 for more ideas.

DYEING AND TINTING

Faded and unattractive garments can often be tinted with all-purpose dyes available in drugstores and variety stores. Large garments can be tinted in washing machines but it is hard to make colors fast without boiling them. Time spent experimenting with simple items now will pay off in years to come as you become proficient in freshening clothing and household items. (Review page 120.)

281

Men's shirts worn without the collar or sleeves make good painting smocks for young artists. This FHA'er decorated the bottom on one smock with eyelet trim and left the other one tailored.

OKLAHOMA FHA

Freshening the color of faded garments or changing them to new shades is a project easily undertaken with the use of liquid dyes and an automatic washer.

RIT DYES, BEST FOOD CO.

Dyeing in olden days was a long and physically hard process.

Bring to school a new ready-to-wear garment and complete any unsatisfactory construction features which may cause trouble. Examples: Sew on a loose button; stitch or finish a narrow seam. Show the other class members what you have done and explain why you felt it necessary.

Keep a record for one or two weeks of all mending problems you encounter. You may want to ask your mother to list problems arising in clothing care of other family members so you will have a more realistic account of the repairs a homemaker makes for family clothing. Share your list with other class members and compile a total list.

Select one type of repair from the class list and prepare a demonstration for the class of one effective method of doing the work.

Summary with Check-Up Questions

A well-groomed look is the result of keeping clothes neat and clean as well as careful body grooming.

- *What impression will be made if one is clean, has shining hair, but is wearing clothes that are soiled and smell of perspiration, have splitting seams, and safety pins where other fasteners should be?*

Clothing kept in good condition is ready to wear when wanted and seldom needs frequent clothing care.

- *What is the effect of tossing garments wet from rain or snow carelessly on chairs or hooks?*

- *What may happen if you struggle into a garment without releasing the zipper and opening all buttons?*

- *Will a blouse hurriedly shoved into a drawer be ready to wear?*

Storing garments in planned places saves time and energy locating them and helps preserve their wearability.

- *Why is the floor of a closet not a good place to store shoes?*

- *What will happen to pants that are doubled up and stored over the lower part of a wire hanger?*

- *What will result from hanging a sweater on a hook behind a door?*

Clothes become soiled because of the dust in the air, perspiration oils of the body, and contact with other staining and soiling material.

- *Why will clothes need to be cleaned less often if they are brushed frequently?*
- *Why should clothing be stored in dust-free bags, closed closets, or drawers?*
- *What effect will result from wearing a washable scarf at the neckline of a winter coat?*

Clothing should be clean when stored for a long period of time.

- *Will mildew form more easily on clean or soiled material?*
- *Are stains easier to remove when fresh or when aged?*
- *How can soil particles weaken a fabric?*

Many cleaning and clothing repairs are the result of carelessness and are unnecessary.

- *Why is it wise to wear an apron or smock when working in the kitchen?*
- *What will be the result of forgetting to use an antiperspirant or shields?*
- *How can wrinkles carelessly be put in fabrics that will result in needed ironing?*

Few closets are as efficiently arranged for clothing storage as possible.

- *How can grouping short clothing in one section result in more storage space?*
- *What can be done to the back of closet doors that open out to help relieve clutter?*
- *What closet accessories may prove of value to many girls?*

Moths will not eat woolens that are clean and are stored in containers too tight to permit moth entry.

- *What effect has washing or dry cleaning on moth life?*

- *How can garments be freed of moths if they do not need to be cleaned?*
- *What are several ways to store woolen garments to protect them from infestation from moths?*

Proper laundering methods are essential if equipment and supplies are to be used effectively. Techniques will vary according to the equipment, water available, and type of fabric.

- *Why is it important to save labels and hang tags?*
- *What problems are caused by hard water?*
- *What can happen to clothing items if washed improperly?*

The type of water must be considered in laundering.

- *Why is more soap needed for laundering in hard water than in soft water?*
- *What is the scum often seen in wash water or on the washing tub?*
- *What is a common source of soft water?*

Soap or detergent must be selected for the type of water and the amount of soil.

- *What type of soap or detergent would you select for a heavily soiled garment?*
- *Why is a mild detergent recommended for a lightly soiled sweater?*

Bleaches help to whiten clothes, brighten fast colors, remove stains, and kill some household germs. They must be used according to directions.

- *What will result if chlorine bleach is poured directly on clothing without being diluted?*
- *Should perborate or chlorine bleaches be used on spandex undergarments?*

Fabric softeners are helpful when washing synthetic fabrics, especially if dried in tumble dryers.

- *Why is static reduced?*
- *What effect do fabric softeners have on fluffiness and necessary ironing?*

283

Shrinkage of fabrics is common unless specially treated for nonshrinkage.

- *What type of shrinkage results from heat, moisture, and agitation applied to most woolen fabrics?*
- *What is meant by relaxation shrinkage?*
- *Why do thermoplastic fabrics maintain their shape?*

The temperature for both washing and ironing is important to preserve the appearance of a fabric.

- *What effect will a hot iron have on thermoplastic fabrics?*
- *Why is steam necessary for proper wool pressing?*
- *Why is a cool rinse desirable for many man-made fabrics?*
- *What temperature is needed for ironing linen garments?*

Spots and stains should be removed as soon as possible and definitely before cleaning.

- *What effect will the heat of washing and drying have on protein stains?*
- *What effect will heat have on sugar stains such as fruit juices and soft drinks?*

To remove stains effectively, it is necessary to know what causes the stain, the fiber content, and any special finishes on the fabric.

- *Acetone removes some ball-point ink, but what would happen if used on an acetate taffeta dress?*
- *What would be the result if you tried to remove a stain from wool fabrics with chlorine bleach?*
- *A red fabric turns pink when a stain remover is applied to it. Why?*

A self-service, coin-operated drycleaning service is effective for garments that do not need special care, if used wisely.

- *Why should garments be brushed and pockets emptied before being placed in the cleaning drum?*
- *What may happen if light and dark colored clothes are washed together?*
- *What is the reason for removing garments immediately after drying and carefully placing them on hangers?*
- *Why is it unwise to overload the cleaning drum?*

Before wearing a new garment check for needed repairs and reinforcements.

- *What may happen to seams stitched with very long stitches?*
- *Why should pocket corners be checked?*
- *What are common problems with buttons and fasteners of new garments?*

Everyone can improve in clothing care. As a result of your study of this chapter, what improvements do you plan to make?

Can You Explain These Terms?

bleaches	drycleaning	stains
chlorine type	fabric softener	greasy
oxygen type	hard water	non-greasy
detergents	mildew	combination
built	moth larva	stain removers
unbuilt	shrinkage	solvents
low sudsing	felting	absorbents
soap	relaxation	water softeners
synthetic detergent	swelling	

PART 2

CLOTHING THE FAMILY

CHAPTER EIGHT

Clothing for Children

CLOTHING can play an important part in a child's development. Everyone likes to see babies and children in cute dresses and suits but, in addition to appearance, it is important to remember health and comfort features when selecting clothing for little ones. Care required and durability, as well as cost, are important features to parents. In this chapter general requirements for children's clothing will be discussed. Later specific requirements for infants, toddlers, preschool children, and the young school child will be considered in greater detail.

GENERAL REQUIREMENTS FOR CHILDREN'S CLOTHES

A small child soon acquires definite likes and dislikes. For him to develop socially as well as physically, his clothes must be *suitable for his activities* and *similar to those of his playmates*. He is conscious of clothing other children wear and wants to look like them. A little boy will not enjoy

wearing a new jacket when his playmates are all wearing sweaters. A little girl cannot enjoy herself in pretty, dressy clothes in which she cannot run and play and get dirty, while her playmates are dressed in play clothes. A child may suffer from being overdressed, or feel inferior because he is not as well dressed as his friends.

COMFORT

The most important clothing consideration for children is comfort. They want to be able to run, climb, jump, and squat without being aware of clothes hampering them. They want to play without being afraid of getting their clothes dirty.

Tight clothes which restrict activity and which may even interfere with natural circulation should be avoided. Elastic bindings should be loose, not tight enough to cause red marks. It is better to have elastic in only part of an opening such as a waistline or leg. Many underpants have a plain band in front and elastic in back.

Heavy, bulky clothes are tiring and hard to handle. Select lightweight clothes. Acrylic and nylon fibers have made it possible for snowsuits and other winter apparel to be warm and cozy and also light in weight.

Ample *ease* in the crotch is essential to allow for bending and stooping. Not only is a tight garment uncomfortable but it may actually cause an unpleasant rash to develop in sensitive areas.

Clothes which hang from the shoulders are usually more comfortable than those that hang from the waistline. Be sure the neckline is big or loose enough so there is no strain across the throat. Also, puffed sleeves with bands at the bottom are very binding if a young girl wants to move freely; they can make a little one irritable.

Soft, absorbent *fabrics* are essential, as a child's skin is sensitive. Few little girls can be happy in organdy collars, or little boys in heavily starched shirt collars. Seams which are flat are a wise choice for children's garments.

Clothes that are too large can be as uncomfortable as those that are too small. To avoid this, select garments that fit but which allow provision for growth as explained later. To make sure of the correct size, *always try on the garment* and check the fit carefully. Children's clothes may not be sized consistently.

Raglan sleeves provide for more freedom as well as growth than set-in sleeves. NOTE: Set-in sleeves may be used if the sleeve bands are loose enough and the armhole large enough so it does not bind.

Shoulder straps on trousers, sunsuits, and skirts can be very annoying if they are constantly slipping off. There should be a sturdy chest bar in the front or shoulder loops on the shirts to hold them in place.

Active children need comfortable play clothes.

Well designed dress for a little girl's comfort. It hangs from the shoulder line, has a low cut neckline so there is no strain across the throat, has loose sleeves and an easy-to-get-into front.

USDA

287

Safety

Comfort and safety go hand in hand for children's clothing. Clothes which are too large may be uncomfortable and may also cause awkwardness. Loose garments can catch on fire more easily around an outdoor grill or range. Dangling sashes and trims can get caught on objects and in moving parts of a tricycle. Remember that bright colors are more easily seen by motorists than dark or grayed colors. (See page 70 for advantages of such colors.) Buttons and loose trim are unsafe for babies and little children who put everything in their mouths.

Self-Help

Being able to dress and undress themselves gives children a feeling of confidence and self-reliance. Many of the most attractive children's clothes are too difficult to put on or take off by young children. Having to be dressed is frustrating to a child who wants to dress himself.

Openings must be large enough so that a child can get in and out of the garment easily. Front openings are easier to use. There should be enough buttons to make a secure closing and large enough so they can be easily grasped by a child's hand. Sturdy slide fasteners with large pulls can usually be handled by little children.

A front that looks different from the back is important. If this is not possible, mark the front so that the child knows which is which.

The following fastenings will retard self-help in dressing: small snaps, hooks and eyes, bows tied at the waist or tied at the neck, small buttons, and thread loops.

CARTER'S

Little children enjoy colorful garments with self-help features. Notice the easy-to-manage front zipper and the wide shoulder straps that will stay in place. Gripper fasteners make diaper changing easy. The narrower cuffs might prevent some falls caused by feet catching in wide pants legs.

When the weather gets warm what is a mother to do? The baby needs an undershirt with diaper tapes, yet mother wants the child to look dressed up. A shirt of the type shown here may be the answer. It is made of soft, absorbent fabrics and holds diapers up with anti-wicking tapes, yet has the look of outerwear with crew neck snap fastened at the shoulder to go over the head easily. Shoulder loops keep trouser straps in place.

WILLIAM CARTER CO.

Although one-piece coveralls don't allow for easy growth alterations, they are comfortable if cut roomy enough. Shirts do not pull out and straps do not slide off shoulders. This one has a large zipper for easy entry and also a snap fastened crotch for diaper changing when necessary.

WILLIAM CARTER CO.

EKCO PRODUCTS

A special place for her clothes helps a child develop a sense of ownership and neatness. Everyday clothes are hung on the lower bar and garments for special occasions are hung higher for mother to select. The closet pole height can be adjusted as the child grows.

Side openings are easy to fasten if buttons are large.

USDA

289

This handsome coat is sensibly constructed with a zip-out pile lining and as a result can be worn from early fall through late spring. Raglan sleeves allow for shoulder growth. The matching Eton cap has ear flaps to turn down on chilly days.

Room for Growth

Make allowance in children's clothing for growth, especially in length. It is not always wise to buy a larger size. Too large clothes are not comfortable or safe and may be worn and faded by the time a child grows to fit them. It is better to choose clothes to fit, with provisions for lengthening.

• Look for fabrics that will not shrink noticeably.

• Knit pajamas and some underclothing are not always finished to prevent shrinkage. Then it is necessary to buy one or more sizes larger and wash them before wearing.

• Deep hems or tucks in the hem area are essential. Some trousers are made with cuffs that can be let down to lengthen the leg length.

• Adjustable straps on overalls and skirts are a must.

• Raglan sleeves allow for growth better then set-in sleeves. Some clothes are made with tucks and pleats at the shoulder line to allow for increased width.

Everyday clothes may be worn out before they are outgrown but dress coats and seasonal items such as snowsuits should last for two seasons, if possible, and growth features here are desirable.

Avoid waistline seams for girls' dresses. A set-in band across the front two or more inches in width, with a sash in the back, accomplishes the same effect but allows for growth.

A jumper with a lowered waist can be worn during several stages of growth. Changes in blouses or sweaters worn underneath suit it to almost all weather conditions and change the appearance.

ECONOMY

Because children grow out of or wear out some garments so fast, it does not always seem wise to select the best quality. However, other garments get such hard wear that good quality is necessary to prevent constant replacement.

For the rapidly growing toddler and preschool child, buy fewer clothes to serve many purposes, and keep them in continuous wear. Coats with zip-in linings can be worn year-round. Light-weight jackets may serve in cold weather if warm sweaters are worn underneath. Clothes with adjustable features have possibilities for longer wear. Take advantage of after-season sales *only* if you are sure clothing bought will fit next year and be suitable for the child's activities. Clothing exchanges are often a good source of used clothing at reasonable cost. (See page 141.) Hand-me-downs also help stretch clothing dollars. NOTE: Hand-me-downs adjusted to fit and with a new trim or other personal touches make a child feel they are really his.

Shoes are one item of clothing which should not be passed from one child to another because foot shapes may be very different. Children's foot bones are in a soft, formative stage and can be misshaped by shoes that fit another child or are poorly made.

APPEARANCE

Children have definite ideas about the appearance of their clothing and they should be allowed to express a preference whenever reasonable. Some choice at a young age will help them develop their ability to select appropriate clothing. The same factors that influence the attractiveness

Notice how the bright caps and mittens worn by these boys bundled up against winter's cold are easily seen even though their snowsuits are of more practical colors.

of adults' clothing applies to children's. Colors should suit personal coloring as well as be liked by the child. A favorite color that is not flattering can be used in trim or other accents. Bright colors for outerwear make it much easier to spot a child on the playground, the street, or the yard. Have you ever tried to keep an eye on a child in a beige or pale blue swimming suit at a beach? Red or other gaily colored suits make it much easier. If you cannot obtain bright snowsuits and jackets, select head coverings and scarfs in gay, easily seen colors.

Lines should emphasize desirable features and camouflage undesirable ones. Chubby children and bean poles, alike, can be made to appear different through wise selection of clothing. (See Chapter 2.)

Clothing should be chosen to flatter the figure of an elementary school age girl.
Which of these dresses would you prefer for this chubby miss? Why?

Fabric designs should be in scale with smaller figures. Usually dainty floral prints and small scale checks, stripes, and plaids are best. Large scale designs may be interesting but often overpower the child.

Easy Care

Children are happier if they do not have to be worried about getting their clothes dirty. Mothers appreciate clothes that wash easily, stand the strain of wear and frequent laundering, need little or no ironing, and do not need continual mending. Look for reinforcements at such points of strain as knees, pocket corners, and elbows.

French or flat fell seams wear longer than plain seams. Double knees are almost essential on play trousers for young boys.

Fabrics

Soft, firmly woven or knitted fabrics which are easy to care for, comfortable to the skin, do not wrinkle easily, and do not show soil readily are desirable for children's clothing. Whenever possible avoid clothing which must be drycleaned. It is better to pay more for a washable jacket or snowsuit. Dress suits for little boys are often washable. NOTE: Delicate fabrics which must be washed by hand and colors which may run into others are not wise choices for a child with a busy mother.

Printed fabrics show wrinkles and soil less, as do corduroy and textured fabrics.

Cotton is widely used for children's clothing, as it is easily washable and comfortable to wear. Wool is warm but requires some special care and may irritate delicate skins. Garments made from nylon, acrylics and polyester fibers wear well and are cared for easily. A blend of cotton and polyester is often more comfortable for a child than all polyester, as it is more absorbent. Sweaters of Orlon or Acrilan and other acrylic fibers may pill but are warm and machine washable, requiring no special care.

Check labels carefully as it is easy to get "carried away" by a cute garment only to find that it is an unwise purchase because special care is needed.

WILLIAM CARTER CO.

What could be more feminine than this knit dress with machine embroidery trimming? The bands at the sleeve edges stretch for comfort, as does the entire garment. Washable, with no ironing needed, it is also appreciated by mother.

Du Pont

Would you believe this dainty dress to be washable with little or no ironing needed? Made of acrylic, the three bold candy stripes end in floral appliques.

293

Trim is common and attractive on children's clothing but should be selected with thought. Some braids may shrink more than the fabric itself, causing puckering. If trim is not colorfast, it ruins a garment.

UNDERWEAR FOR CHILDREN

Underwear must be washable, durable, and comfortable. Knit underclothing is suitable because it stretches and fits the body without binding. Be sure that there is room enough in the crotch for easy movement. Any elastic used should not be tight enough to leave red marks.

SLEEPING GARMENTS

Sleeping garments should be loose enough to permit a child to turn and stretch in his sleep. The shoulder width should be enough to prevent any binding at the arm or across the back. A one-piece garment prevents gapping, but two-piece garments allow for growth. Some two-piece pajamas for little children have adjustable gripper fasteners which keep the parts together but do allow for growth. Sleepers with feet are warm for cold weather while a short-leg, short-sleeve type is better for warm weather.

It is difficult to keep blankets or any covers on many children. "Blanket-sleepers" of warm acrylic fabric are made to serve the purpose of a blanket and a sleeping garment.

Avoid bright red fleece pajamas, often sold around holiday time, unless you are sure the color will not rub off on sheets.

Planned for a summer sleeper, this cool cotton knit garment has snap fasteners at the waist and the top front opening. It can also be worn comfortably in the daytime by little ones learning to crawl.

WILLIAM CARTER CO.

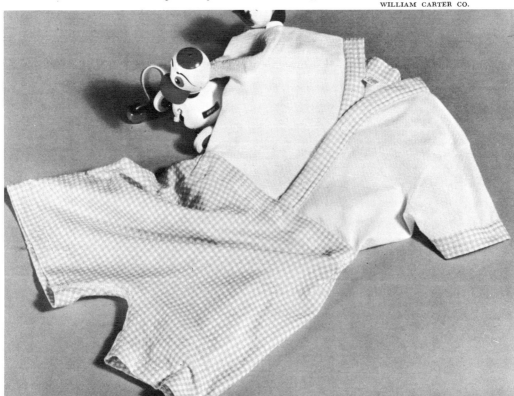

Eight · Clothing for Children

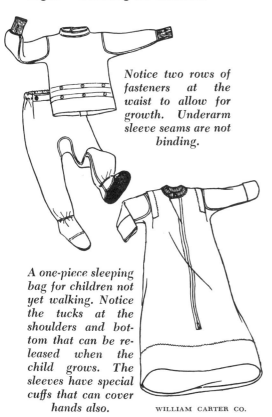

Notice two rows of fasteners at the waist to allow for growth. Underarm sleeve seams are not binding.

A one-piece sleeping bag for children not yet walking. Notice the tucks at the shoulders and bottom that can be released when the child grows. The sleeves have special cuffs that can cover hands also.

WILLIAM CARTER CO.

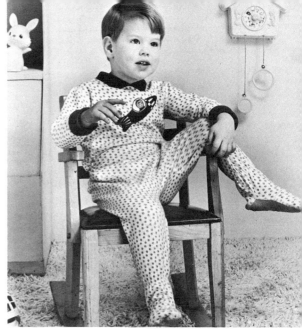

WILLIAM CARTER CO.

A two-piece pajama with attached feet to keep a child cozy all over as he sleeps and roams the house in the wee hours. There are two rows of waistline snaps to allow for growth. Additional bottoms can be purchased so the entire garment does not have to be changed in case of "accidents."

It's hard to stay awake in a comfortable "Jama-Blanket." A one-piece garment with attached feet that eliminates the need for blankets keeps a child warm all night long.

WILLIAM CARTER CO.

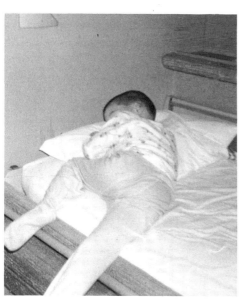

Children often assume unusual sleeping positions so all-in-one pajamas are needed for warmth.

295

SNOWSUITS

Snowsuits have become popular as outdoor protection for a child in snow or cold weather. These need to be lightweight and also warm. Because snowsuits get heavy wear, they need to be of good quality. Two suits may be necessary unless an automatic dryer is available to dry a snowsuit, damp after morning play, so it will be ready for wear again in the afternoon.

A one-piece, unbelted, loose-fitting snowsuit allows freedom of movement and meets the needs of an active child. There should be plenty of room for climbing, stooping, and bending. If there is not sufficient width and length in the seat, stooping

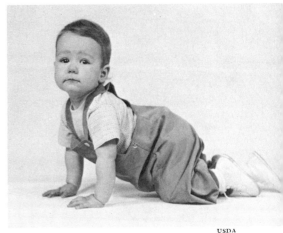

USDA
Snug worsted or elastic cuffs prevent entanglement with the toes.

USDA
A knitted cap fits any head and is warm in cold weather.

and bending will cause the suit legs to draw up and the neckline to pull back against the throat of the child. A two-piece suit allows for growth but may gap at the waist and not be warm. The upper front of the trousers of some two-piece suits extend over the chest of the child and adjustable shoulder straps allow for growth.

A suit with a long opening that extends from the neck down near the crotch permits a child to sit down, put his feet through the legs, and pull up the suit without any help.

• Knitted bands at the neck and wrists help to keep out cold.

• Some suits have mitten grippers sewn in the sleeves so that mittens can be clipped on and always be available.

• Pockets placed at hand level with slanted openings are enjoyed by children.

• An attached hood prevents drafts on the neck. Some hoods can be adjusted into collars for milder weather. Berets, knitted caps, or some other ear covering is desirable for cold weather.

Eight · Clothing for Children

OVERALLS

Overalls are popular with both boys and girls because they are designed for freedom in play and are easy to put on and take off. They are suitable for most weather conditions by varying the shirt worn underneath. They also protect legs when crawling and playing.

Full-length, heavy slide fasteners are better than buttons and drop seats. Shoulder straps should be wide and built into the garment. Legs need to be wide enough for easy knee bends but not enough to cause the child to trip and fall. Cuffs collect dirt and can be tripped on but they also allow for length adjustment. Double knees prolong wear, as little children spend a lot of time sliding on the knees.

Corduroy fabrics are washable, need no ironing, and are soft and warm. Denim is also a good choice for overall fabric.

SHIRTS

A cotton knit polo or T-shirt with enough stretch in the neck to go over the head easily is practical and comfortable. A T-shirt does not work up, is not bulky, requires no fastenings, and seldom needs ironing. Inexpensive knitted shirts may shrink in length and stretch in width excessively during laundering so check labels for shrinkage control before purchase. The typical shirt with collar and button front is a better choice for dress than for daily wear as it is not as comfortable and requires more care.

SHOES AND HOSE

The correct fit in shoes and hose for a small child may mean foot comfort and health during his entire life. If the first stocking is too short or too

KEDS BY U. S. RUBBER

For big and little girls, what could be more fun or more comfortable than matching sneakers?

small, it may cause as much harm as a shoe that is too short. Stockings should be large enough to provide free toe action but not so long that there are folds of fabrics to cause blisters. Buy several pairs of the same stocking or sock for everyday wear, then if one wears out or is lost, the remaining socks can be matched. When stockings are outgrown, discard them. Whenever there is a change of shoe size, new stockings are usually needed. Properly fitted stretch hosiery may be most comfortable.

Shoes should be selected and fitted carefully, because the soft bones of a child's foot may be injured by wrong-fitting, badly shaped shoes. Be sure to consider the *length* and *width*, the height of *toe space,* and the fit of the *heel.* Draw an outline of the child's foot while he is standing on paper. Shoes should follow the natural shape of the feet and be $\frac{1}{4}$ inch wider than the outline. To make sure that shoes fit correctly, they should be fitted on the child by a person experienced in fitting children.

297

WILLIAM CARTER CO.

These slippers have safety non-skid soles and are also machine washable. The girls' version has a pompom for its trim and the boys' style is trimmed in a masculine manner.

W. C. RUNDER, ST. LOUIS, MO.

An assortment of shoe styles for the well-dressed younger lad.

A child's first shoes should be selected for safety, balance, and support. *Laced shoes* are best for infants and small children. *Oxfords* are suitable for older children. Sneakers with good arch supports are suitable for warm weather play.

Children's shoes should allow for growth and development. Growth varies with children. From the time a child walks until school age, the growth may be as much as a size

Discuss safety features of garments. Talk with mothers to determine if they have had problems with children falling because of certain types of clothing. Have they found parts of clothing in the babies' mouths? Report to class.

Collect pictures of two similar children's garments, one that is "cute" but would be uncomfortable for a child to wear and another that is attractive but also suitable for a little one. Be able to point out desirable and undesirable features of each.

With the group, plan a bulletin board or showcase display using examples of self-help features, add-a-year hems, and easy care features of children's clothing.

What was your favorite article of clothing as a little girl? Be prepared to tell why you remember it with pleasure.

every two months; from six years to ten years, about one size every three to four months; at ten years of age a larger size may be needed every four to six months.

When shoes are repaired, be sure they are not made shorter or narrower or changed in shape. When a child outgrows a pair of shoes, they should be discarded.

A child should have *overshoes* for cold or snowy weather and rubbers for rainy days.

SPECIFIC REQUIREMENTS FOR CHILDREN'S CLOTHES

CLOTHING FOR AN INFANT

A baby's clothing needs are limited to a few items which are necessary for his protection and comfort during the early months of life when his activities are basically eating and sleeping. It is better to have plenty of the few garments that need constant changing like shirts and diapers than to have a great variety of suits or dresses. Babies outgrow clothing very fast. Many dresses and suits given to a little one are outgrown before there is a chance to wear them.

Always select infants' clothes that open down the front or have a very large opening. A baby does not like to have his nose and mouth covered while clothes are being slipped over his head.

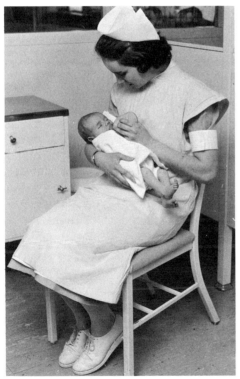

A newborn baby wears only a diaper and shirt. Here a small towel is wrapped around him for protection from possible drafts while he is being fed. Notice how the nurse protects her clothing from possible "burps" with a washable coverall.

Avoid any clothing that has a drawstring around the neck or a bonnet string that can get pulled tight. These can become dangerous if a baby rolls over and gets tangled in them. It is better to have tape or gripper fasteners than buttons that can come off and be swallowed or poked in a nose or ear.

Everything a baby wears needs to be washable. In fact, it is wise to wash everything a baby uses before wearing even if in a sealed package.

Suggested Layette. The United States Children's Bureau* lists the following items as the minimum a baby can get along with for his first six months:

Cotton shirts (long or short sleeve
    or sleeveless, depending upon
    the climate and season of the
    year).
Diapers (if diaper service is used,
    1 dozen will suffice.)   3 to 6 dozen
Nightgowns or wrappers   3 to 6
Sweaters   2 to 3
Light cotton blankets   3 to 6
Cap (a warm one to cover the
    ears), if weather is cold.   1
(Nice, but not necessary, are
    dresses and slips for special oc-
    casions.)

If you can provide more shirts and nightgowns, you will find the extra ones come in handy. Facilities for laundering make a difference in the amount of clothing needed as a mother with a convenient automatic washer and dryer may manage easily with the minimum.

Sizes. It may seem odd to select clothing sized "6 months" for a new born infant, but babies grow so fast

---

* Infant Care, Children's Bureau Publication No. 8, p. 31, 32.

that the 3 month size is good for only a short time. The 6 month size is usually comfortable for a small baby because of the style of infants' clothing. Most manufacturers base their sizes on a relationship of height and weight. The following chart gives standard measurements:

| Size | INFANTS AND BABIES | |
	Height in Inches	Weight in Pounds
3 months	24	13
6 months	26½	18
12 months	29	22
18 months	31½	26
24 months	34	29
36 months	36½	32

Diapers are the first item to be considered in a babies' wardrobe. If a diaper service is used, it is still wise to have a dozen for emergencies and later when the child grows out of diaper service but usually needs a few for night wear. It is essential that diapers be soft, absorbent, easily washed, and quick drying. The heavy flannelettes of grandmother's day, hemmed at home by hand, are no longer popular. Instead gauze and birdseye diapers are being used. Pre-shaped diapers are available but be certain they will fit a baby as he grows. Disposable diapers are preferred by some.

Protective panties are worn by most babies today to prevent bed clothing from becoming wet (or the clothes of the person holding the baby!). Heavy, inexpensive plastic pants may cause a rash to develop on the baby's buttocks. Select waterproofed silk or breathable plastic which may cost more but is washable and comforta-

A double-breasted undershirt that is easy to get on the baby and gives added protection across the chest. Notice the non-binding underarm seams and the diaper tabs.

WILLIAM CARTER CO.

A similar garment with no sleeves is available for warm weather wear.

ble. Soakers are liked by some mothers. These are wool knitted pants that go over the diapers and absorb excess moisture.

Undershirts are worn in most climates. In the summer many babies wear only diapers and undershirts for sleeping. Shirts that open the entire front and are fastened with gripper fasteners are the easiest to put on. Babies often object to anything going over their head. Ties are not as sensible, as babies like to suck them.

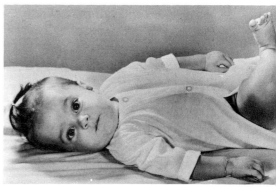

VANTA

Another simple garment opening down the front, made of cotton knit.

WILLIAM CARTER CO.

This baby has a well coordinated ensemble at his age! The teething bib and stretch pajamas are of soft terry cloth. The sacque and booties match the soft cotton knit sheets. Another means of fastening the bonnet other than ribbons would be desirable.

Nightgowns or wrappers can be used for both day and night wear for several months. Work is saved if they open all the way down the back. Then the edges can be spread apart so the gown won't be under the baby and have to be changed frequently. (If a baby sleeps on his stomach, the opening can be in the front.) Others prefer a nightgown with a drawstring in the bottom. This is permissible only if the gown is long enough so that the baby can move his legs freely and there is no danger of the string becoming loose. Wrappers and nightgowns are often made in pretty colors and designs so they can serve for most "dress-up" occasions.

In severely cold climates a *sleeping sacque* may be used. This is really an oversized nightgown of a heavy blanket material, usually a washable Orlon or Acrilan. Gripper fasteners are used with a soft knitted neckband. Often the hands are covered as well as the feet. Well-made ones provide room for the baby to kick freely.

Few babies wear *stockings* today,

as houses are kept warm and babies are wrapped in blankets when taken outside. When stockings and booties are used they should be soft and loose enough for active toes to wriggle.

Sweaters are a necessity. Many mothers put one on a baby when he sleeps, as a sweater will stay on and a blanket often does not. Sweater fabrics that are machine washable are preferred by many mothers who do not have time to hand wash delicate woolens.

Some babies are allergic to wool and must have cotton or acrylic fiber sweaters.

Bibs are necessary to protect a baby's clothing from soil, moisture, and drooling. Absorbent cotton fabrics such as terry cloth with a plastic underliner are wise choices. (A clean diaper serves the purpose until the little one can sit up.)

WILLIAM CARTER CO.

A garment for many uses; a hooded stretch "jamakin" snaps from neck to ankle for ease in dressing.

301

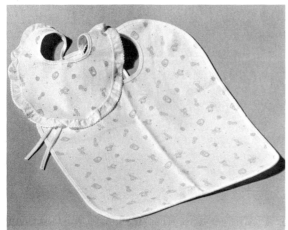

WILLIAM CARTER CO.

The smaller bib is a teething bib, worn most of the day during baby's teething months. The larger one is for feeding and is backed with a waterproof material.

Dresses and suits are fun to have for special occasions but are not necessary. Be sure they are comfortable so these occasions are not spoiled because the baby cries due to binding or scratchy garments.

CLOTHING FOR OLDER BABIES AND TODDLERS

When a baby starts to crawl and walk he has new clothing needs. He will probably wear soft shoes that lace high around the ankle. Socks that fit correctly will be needed. Undershirts for this age child usually slip over the head with special openings so no fasteners are needed. Training pants may help in the transition from diapers to regular pants. These are heavier and more absorbent than regular pants.

WILLIAM CARTER CO.

A terry cloth bib with a plasticized back for waterproofing is a mealtime necessity for infants and toddlers. Notice the crumb catcher at the hem and the snap closing at the back which is adjustable for several sizes.

A stretch denim knit romper with snap-fastened crotch and back is suited for little ones learning to crawl and walk.

WILLIAM CARTER CO.

Interview mothers of young babies. Ask their advice about layette items.

Estimate the cost of the layette suggested by the Children's Bureau on page 299.

Prepare an exhibit of garments that are suitable for the minimum layette. Local stores may be willing to lend garments to you or you may be able to borrow some from mothers whose children have outgrown them.

Investigate the availability and cost of diaper service in your community. Compare the cost with purchase and care at home. Include the use of disposable diapers.

Overalls are often worn, but they need to be large enough in the crotch to allow for diapers. *Jersey* shirts are a good choice. Babies starting to crawl get around easier in creeper type suits with short pants.

By the time a child is two years old he may want to dress himself. Then it is important to select garments with those features which are listed on page 288.

Clothing for toddlers is usually sized as follows:

	Height in Inches	Weight in Pounds
Size 1	31	25
Size 2	34	29
Size 3	37	34
Size 4	40	38

GARMENTS FOR PRE-SCHOOL CHILDREN

A child's age, especially in pre-school years, has very little bearing on the size that will fit. Note that patterns for home sewing are often sized differently from ready-made clothing, and therefore accurate measurements are particularly important. The following table lists the sizes followed by most clothing manufacturers:

	Height in Inches	Weight in Pounds
Size 5	43	44
Size 6	46	49
Size 6X	48	54

By the time a child is a preschooler, he may have definite preferences for color and style. Today girls and boys wear similar clothes for play. Shorts, slacks, and jeans are favorite play clothes for all but the most feminine girl. Even play shoes are similar, as oxfords and sneakers are preferred over other styles. Self-help features and sturdy, long wearing fabrics are very important at this stage, as well as comfort and safety features.

Little girls' dresses can be very attractive in a simple style with becoming lines and colors and simple trim. The fussy, starched clothes of yesterday are seen less today and little girls seem happier because of it. New fabrics make it possible for dresses to be feminine and also easily cared for.

Usually the style is for a little girl's dresses to end quite a bit above the knee. They should never be long enough so they are under the feet when she crouches to play.

Pockets for a hankie and a little girl's "valuables" encourage neatness and help provide a sense of self-importance. Patch pockets are easy to reach and less likely to tear if placed on the slant.

This three-year-old is dressed in clothing typical of little girls of 1900. High laced shoes, long heavy stockings, high-necked and long-sleeved dresses of stiffly starched materials. Adorable, but could she play as freely and dress herself as does a three-year-old today?

COTTON INCORPORATED

Little girls enjoy wearing long dresses for party times. This colorful skirt matches a sleeveless top and is dressed up by a velvet streamer-sash.

Similar garments for brother and sister. The only difference is the direction of the openings, and most young children do not notice this.

SIMPLICITY PATTERN CO.

304

Eight · Clothing for Children

Talk with mothers of pre-school children. What are their major problems about the clothing available to them? What things wear out first?

Collect pictures of garments worn by your grandparents when they were little children. (Or borrow actual garments if available.) How does the boys' clothing differ from today's? Is the girls' clothing the same? Which articles do you think children would prefer? What about mothers?

Construct a garment for a young child, following the suggestions for the child's comfort, safety, and pleasure. If you do not know of a small child, your teacher may be able to arrange to have a garment made for someone in a foster home.

Little boys enjoy dressing like their fathers or admired people. Do you think this young "man" feels bigger and braver in his army suit?

The Eton suit, a classic young boyish design, is given a festive look by the use of a bright coat with dark trousers. A collarless neckline provides for comfort, and a change of shirt can easily change the appearance of the suit. Sturdy oxfords and knee hose complete the neat look for a young man.

AMERICAN WOOL COUNCIL

Some girls like dress shoes and garments to be very feminine, preferring frilly petticoats and full skirts that make an "effect" when twirling. As little girls grow up, they enjoy having some clothes "just like mother's." Purses, blouses, and sport clothes can be like a favored adult's though most of a clothing wardrobe should be suited to the needs and activities of children.

Pre-school boys are seldom as fashion conscious as little girls but they want to dress like other boys as well as to be comfortable. When everyone else is wearing long pants, short pants may make some boys so uncomfortable they will withdraw from any activity. Other boys will enjoy the freedom and perhaps cause friends to copy them. Self-help features for little boys as well as sturdy construction are important. If trousers or overalls are all of the same style, self-help is easier and the small one feels more secure. Variety can be obtained by color and fabric differences.

Dual purpose garments. The turtle-necked sweaters shown here create a rather sportive look but with a change to an Eton shirt for the boy and a dressy blouse for the girl, they are ready for a party. The girl's gillie shoes are a change from the usual oxford.
AMERICAN WOOL COUNCIL

SIMPLICITY PATTERN CO.

Many mothers and big sisters enjoy making coats for little girls. This is a style enjoyed by the young miss and easily made with a matching hat.

Play clothes just like big brother's—surfer style sports shirt and pants with a matching striped jacket.
WILLIAM CARTER CO.

CLOTHING FOR THE ELEMENTARY AGE SCHOOL CHILD

Suitable clothing for the elementary school age child must meet the social and emotional needs of the group. Children from 6 to 12 years are anxious to gain acceptance from their peers. To conform to the gang or group is their way of belonging. If children dress very different from their classmates, they may become self conscious and possibly antisocial. Feelings of inferiority may result from something so seemingly insignificant as having to wear an odd-looking garment.

The younger child, 6 to 10, loves to wear the uniform of an organization such as Cub Scouts, Brownies, Campfire Girls, and similar groups. As children grow older the uniform may seem to be something worn by "sissies" unless it is for a special occasion.

Boys of early elementary age usually are very active and enjoy wearing clothes that look rugged—shirts hanging out, heavy shoes, and jeans are often popular. Girls may want to be like tom-boys or may prefer to dress in a more feminine manner. Most children want to select what they wear and resent suggestions from parents. Some mothers handle this when shopping by choosing two or three suitable items and letting the child make the final selection.

The child's age has little bearing on the proper size so it is wise to bring him along to be fitted whenever possible. Otherwise take along a garment that fits well when shopping or select clothing that can be taken out on approval. Never buy shoes without having them fitted on the child who will wear them.

DU PONT

A sensible washable jacket for a young man that can be worn much of the year. For very cold weather he adds a sweater for more insulative value. The hood can also fold flat as a collar.

307

Weather-wise miss is set for whatever weather develops while she is at school. Her coat and hood, which match her cotton canvas jumper and calico blouse, have been treated for water repellency.

Dark cotton plaids seldom show soil and wrinkles and are suitable for school activities. The pockets are handy for holding "treasures."

A sweater set, plaid-pleated skirt, and matching tights is a classic for winter school wardrobes in most climates.

The following charts may help in selection of proper clothing size. However, you will find that a child's proportions may not be like others and that the style of a garment may affect the size needed.

GIRLS

	Height in Inches	Weight in Pounds
Size 7	50	60
Size 8	52	67
Size 9	54	75
Size 10	56	83
Size 12	58½	95
Size 14	61	107

BOYS

	Height in Inches	Weight in Pounds
Size 7	48	54
Size 8	50	59
Size 9	52	65
Size 10	54	73
Size 11	56	80
Size 12	58	87
Size 13	59½	93
Size 14	61	100
Size 15	62½	107

Poor fit is the most frequent reason given by elementary age children for not wearing their clothes. The older elementary girl may select a garment on the basis of style even if it is not comfortable.

The same considerations for safety, easy care, growth allowance, and suitability to the shape and coloring of the child which were true of younger children are true of elementary age youth. Although they can manage tricky fasteners, they still appreciate easy-to-handle closures.

Make a survey of parents to find out the cost, length of time worn, and satisfaction derived from their children's shoes. Study consumers' magazines such as "Consumer's Reports" for points to check in buying children's shoes.

Collect children's garments which are outgrown but essentially wearable. Have a class discussion on how they can be freshened up and changed to appear different than when worn by big brother or sister. Select one and alter it.

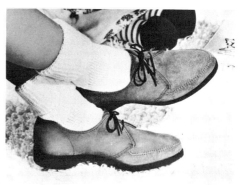

WOLVERINE SHOE CO.

Classic oxfords with three easy-to-lace eyelets are a favorite of school-age girls.

WOLVERINE SHOE CO.

For dressier occasions, side-buckle shoes are flattering.

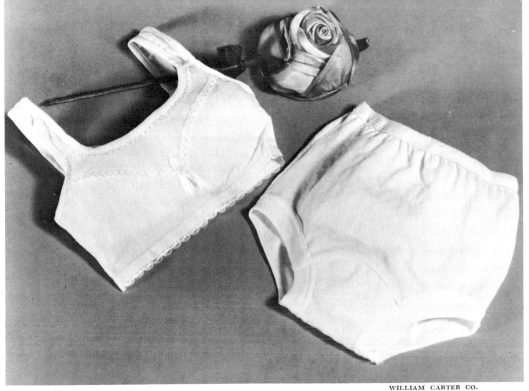

Another transition garment for the older elementary school girl is the rib-length stretch demisole and matching stretch pants.

Graduating from children's shirts and underpants, a youthful version of the "body-stocking" is a good choice. With stretch straps, it is knit of stretch nylon outside and absorbent cotton inside. There is a snap-open crotch and gently elasticized legs.

Each of these girls is the same age but her development is different. You can understand why it is not wise to select children's clothing by age alone.

Summary With Check-Up Questions

A child's self-image can be affected by the clothing he wears.
- *How will a child feel if he always wears out-grown clothing of his older brothers and sisters?*
- *What effect will constantly dressing a girl in dainty, delicate clothing have on her self-concept?*
- *If only the newest, most expensive clothes are bought for children, how will they regard themselves?*
- *How will a child feel if the clothes he wears are strange and different from those worn by others his age?*

Clothes for the pre-school child should be made to encourage him to dress himself and thus grow in independence.
- *Why are center zippers easier to handle than buttons?*
- *If buttons are used, what size should they be?*
- *How may a child react if he has to wait for adult help to get dressed or ready for the bathroom or undressed after playtime?*

Children can learn to take care of their own clothes when storage space is designed for their own abilities.
- *Why should a closet rod be at a height easily reached by a little child?*
- *How can drawers and hooks be labeled for a little one who cannot read?*

Clothing can contribute to the health and safety of children.
- *Why are bright colors wise for clothing to be worn in crowded areas or the country?*
- *What happens to buttons which easily become loosened?*
- *Necklines that anchor with drawstrings and hoods that are held on with ties under the chin are not wise for little ones. Why?*

Children's garments should be constructed so they can be made larger as children grow.
- *How can tucks be placed at the shoulders to allow for increased width?*
- *How can a waistline be made to allow for a few inches growth in length of a little girl?*
- *Are raglan or set-in sleeves better for growing children? Why?*

Children's clothing must be comfortable.
- *What effect do tight bands at the edges of puffed sleeves have?*
- *Clothing which is too large may be as uncomfortable as clothing which is too tight. Why?*
- *What effect do high necklines and tight bands at waistlines have on children?*

Wisely selected children's clothing is easy to care for and of sturdy material.
- *Will children enjoy playing in clothing that soils or tears easily?*
- *What fabrics are strong and seldom need ironing?*

Shoes are an expensive and important item for children.
- *Why should shoes never be passed on from child to child?*
- *When are sneakers suitable for wear?*
- *Why is it important to have a child's foot fitted correctly for shoes?*

Clothing needs change with the changing stages of children.
- *What are the major clothing items needed by infants?*
- *When children start to crawl and toddle, what clothes become important?*
- *What new things do you look for in pre-school child's garments?*
- *Starting school is a big step and clothing needs also change. Describe some of them.*

CHAPTER NINE

Other Family Members' Clothing Requirements

IN TODAY'S FAMILIES, parents as well as children should be attractively and appropriately dressed. A good appearance for all family members is important for their well-being and for those who associate with them. The American man is more clothes conscious than he was many years ago as his work involves meeting many people in situations where he is often judged at first by appearance alone. The American woman also has an increased interest in clothing as she works more and more outside the home—it is estimated that the average married woman can expect to work at least 25 years outside the home as well as maintain her role as wife, mother, and homemaker. Surely clothing can help her in her many duties. Besides selecting clothing for herself and her children, most wives consult with their husbands on their major clothing purchases and actually buy many of the accessories as socks, shirts, and underclothing. She may also be asked to help select clothing for elder members of her family who

are not able to shop for themselves or who appreciate someone else's views.

It is no longer sufficient that the American woman understand how to purchase clothing for herself alone—truly she is a purchasing agent for the entire family.

This chapter is concerned largely with clothing for men and special needs of the elderly. Information in every chapter that refers to clothing for young women is applicable for women of all ages.

MOTHER'S CLOTHING

Homemakers over 100 years ago were in quest of new conveniences to provide some relief from their multitudinous household tasks.

One winter evening during the Civil War in a modest home in the village of Sterling, Massachusetts, Ellen Butterick cleared away the supper dishes and spread her sewing on the dining-room table. After struggling over a gingham dress for her baby son Howard, she held it up to the light and said to her husband, "If we only had patterns to make our children's clothes, how much *easier* life would be!" Ebenezer, a man's tailor, translated his wife's request into a pattern for a man's suit, followed later by one for a baby's dress and a little boy's suit.

One day when Butterick's sales agent returned from a trip up in the country, he reported that a woman somewhere had urged Mr. Butterick to make patterns for ladies' garments. In reply to the request of another woman, Ellen Butterick's measurements were used for the first *wrapper* pattern, which was drafted on her dining room table.

It was a simple pattern, so planned that any housewife could use it; however it transformed feminine attire.

Pomeroy's *Democrat* of 1871 said: "The sewing machine has done more than the piano to 'happize' homes, and following the sewing machine came the *Butterick Pattern*."

At that time wrappers, in blue or gray calico print with large, matching, tie-around aprons, were the latest style trends in ladies' household attire. Their popularity continued with only minor changes until about 1908.

With the influence of color in homes and more leisure time for housewives came a yearning for a colorful, shorter, and semi-fitted household garment. Dress manufacturers, alert to the need, pioneered in the manufacture of a "house dress," which became the standard dress for homemakers' household activities.

PAYNE SISTERS

A housedress typical of 1905.

MCCALL'S MAGAZINE

A housedress of 1923. Notice how it follows the lines of other garments from the 1920's shown in Chapter One.

Our current culture includes many new household conveniences such as dishwasher, automatic washer, dryer, electric range, and convertible furniture—or dreams of these glittery contrivances! These things provide freedom for mothers, enabling them to indulge in creative hobbies, to have more time for their children, and to enjoy more neighborhood social life. There is scarcely a woman who does not have more choices than her mother did for spending leisure time.

The ideal wardrobe requirements of a housewife for whom homemaking is her only career includes garments suitable for her numerous activities,

as well as the services she renders her family. Her wardrobe contains several types of costumes. The popular house dress of the last decade no longer serves her needs. Substitutes for it include jeans, shorts, pants, coveralls, and dainty washable cotton frocks.

Women today have the opportunity and often the need to work outside the home. Many homemakers become wage earners to support the family or to supplement the family income. Their work may help provide education, better housing, and other family needs not always available with the earnings of one family member. The skills and abilities of women are needed not only by their own families but by society at large as well.

A shirtwaist worn with a long skirt is enjoyed by many mothers for social evenings, at home or away. The appearance of either the top or the skirt can be easily changed by different combinations.

PENDLETON WOOLEN MILLS

Today's mother finds a pants suit well adapted for homemaking activities. The addition of the jacket over a washable blouse makes it suitable for neighborhood shopping.

Nine · Other Family Members' Clothing Requirements

Whether a woman is serving on a P.T.A. committee, teaching, or engaged in any of the activities common today, a classic-style dress of an unusual woven fabric is suitable.

SIMMONS COLLEGE

CELANESE FIBERS

A multi-purpose dress such as this classic style is part of mother's wardrobe today. Suitable for informal entertaining, visiting, and other activities, it is of a wrinkle-resistant fabric which requires very little care. The gored skirt and shaped bodice flatter the fuller figure.

Although temporarily crippled by an accident, this mother cares for her family from a wheelchair. Since her dress buttons down the front, it is easy to put on without help. Three-quarter length dolman sleeves allow for ease of movement.

MARIAN S. PATMORE AND CLOTHING
RESEARCH AND DEVELOPMENT FOUNDATION

315

From old fashion magazines prepare a class report on the history of house dresses and work clothes.

Observe the activities of your mother for four different days to determine her clothing needs. Help her arrange her garments in outfits. Does her wardrobe supply her needs?

How do clothing needs of an older sister, who works in an office, differ from the needs of a working mother?

Make a picture collection of clothing and accessories for the mother of little children—for the mother who is active in club work—for the mother who must entertain her husband's business associates a great deal.

Interview homemakers to determine what clothes they prefer for housework with their reasons. Report your findings to the class.

The clothing requirements of a wage earning mother are similar to those of other business women but easy care is perhaps more important as her time is limited by home responsibilities.

MEN'S AND BOYS' CLOTHING

Becoming and appropriate attire gives a feeling of security and poise that helps a man in his daily business activities. The Men's Fashion Association, which is the educational arm of the male apparel industry, has taken polls and surveys of successful young executives, employment experts, and personnel people. All agree that a man's clothing and grooming do count in the world of business. They certainly count with prospective employers who must depend upon quick judgments of applicants and of others met in brief business contacts. A man who is well dressed for the occasion not only appears capable to others but feels more capable and confident himself.

A man's wardrobe must include clothes for *business, sports, leisure,* and *formal* wear. (For many a young man, school is his business.) What is considered proper in some geographical areas may not be suitable elsewhere. A dark suit is the only suitable business attire in some localities but sports coats and slacks are acceptable elsewhere. It is always well to find out the accepted dress for your school or business before planning a wardrobe.

Clothes must also be flattering to a man's *coloring* and *figure* as well as *suitable for the occasion. Design, fit, workmanship* and *fabric* should be considered when selecting men's clothing as well as the *cost.*

High school youths who learn the principles of good dress and clothing selection will have a better foundation for the future, whether it includes further schooling or an early career.

Women must usually learn about men's clothing as well as their own. They should be aware of the latest trends in fabrics and clothing and shoe styles. Their opinions are important in the selection of most garments. The sight of a wife accompanying her husband who is purchasing a suit is a common one. In many families, women take the responsibility for clothing care.

These suits and jackets feature wovens and knits with semi-soft shoulder tailoring. The lapels are wide and notched. Pockets get different treatments—frame patches with inlaid flaps (left), straight flaps (center), and bellows pouch patches with box pleats and scalloped flaps (right). Jackets have deep center vents, and trousers have subtly flared bottoms.

SUITABILITY

Some businesses have definite requirements concerning the color and type of clothing to be worn by their employees. It is always wise to ask an employment officer about the preferred clothing for the position you are undertaking. This will not indicate a lack of knowledge on your part but rather an awareness of the importance of the proper clothes for a situation.

Study the "Dress Right" code at the right. This code was adopted by thousands of high school student groups across the country during the 1960's. In the early 1970's, the code was declared unnecessary and an invasion against student rights. In what ways is this code inappropriate for today?

DRESS-RIGHT CODE APPAREL RECOMMENDATIONS * (*Boys*)
1968

RECOMMENDED:

1. Dress shirt and tie or conservative sport shirt and tie, with suit jacket, sport coat, or sweater.
2. Standard trousers, slacks or khakis; clean and pressed.
3. Shoes, clean and polished; white bucks acceptable.

NOT RECOMMENDED:

1. Dungarees or soiled, wrinkled khakis.
2. T-shirts, sweat shirts.
3. Extreme styles of shoes, such as hobnailed soles, sandals, boots.

NOTE: Standard dress while in school shops and laboratories should be determined by the school.

* *American Institute of Men's and Boys' Wear*

Colors

Personal coloring. Men do not think of their personal coloring as much as women do, but it is important when selecting clothing. Colors selected should be flattering to the man as well as currently in style. Borrow jackets in the basic colors such as dark blue, dark gray, light gray, brown, and a light tan. When you try them on, it will usually be obvious which shades and colors look best on you. You may not understand the reasons, but a study of color theory will explain them to you. See Chapter Three.

Wardrobe color plan. A wardrobe color plan requires time and effort but stretches your clothing dollar by adding only garments that fit into your wardrobe color scheme. When colors blend, many combinations of garments are possible.

A middle-weight fabric suitable for three-season wear. Fine light gray strips high light a dark background in a wrinkle-resistant fabric of wool. Notice the bottom button left open.

For example, a dark gray suit with black shoes, medium blue socks, and tie will take you almost any place you wish to go. Ties in other colors such as red, deep yellow, or gray and red stripes add variety, as will a soft yellow or soft blue colored shirt. A tweed sports coat can blend with the gray trousers, especially if the suit is a two-pants one. Try gray slacks in a lighter or darker value so there is a definite contrast.

Along with different colors, you'll become aware of different patterns and fabric finishes. They won't puzzle you if you remember to avoid combining two very unsimilar patterns such as striped trousers and a checked shirt or different fabric types such as a smooth gabardine with a hard, shiny surface, and a heavy tweed with a fuzzy surface.

As a person's color and texture sense develops, unusual combinations can be made which are suitable. In the meantime, the chart on page 320 will help you combine colors.

318

Sport coats are being accepted for casual wear, both summer and winter. The madras plaid at the left is a warm weather favorite as is the double-breasted denim blazer in the middle. A textured herringbone with bold paisley lining is worn in chillier weather.

FIGURES AND CLOTHES

Our better clothing manufacturers design a complete range of men's apparel for various types of figures. These include clothes specially cut and adapted for the following types: short, regular, tall, and portly. Do you know your figure type?

A *tall, thin* man can wear color contrasts in shirt and trousers, designed fabrics, soft pleats at the trouser waistline, and interesting pocket details. Horizontally patterned ties and shirts with a moderate collar spread are suitable.

For the *short, thin person* an outfit of one color is more becoming. Lightweight tweeds and single breasted suits of a patterned fabric are flattering as are shirt collars of the pinned tab and button-down style.

An *average* figure has a wide range of styles.

Vertical lines minimize the apparent width of a *stout* figure. Fabrics with rough surfaces and mixture fabrics increase the apparent size of a figure. A *short and stocky* man needs suits with little padding, shirts with low, sloped collars, and slim ties. A

319

COLOR COORDINATOR FOR MEN'S WEAR

SUIT	GRAY	BLUE	BLACK	BROWN	OLIVE
SHIRT Solid or Stripe	1. Blue 2. Off Wh./Yellow 3. Gray	1. Blue 2. Off White 3. Gray	1. Gray 2. Blue 3. Yellow	1. Tan 2. Off White 3. Blue	1. Gray 2. Blue 3. Off White
TIE	1. Red/Navy 2. Black/Gold 3. Green/Red	1. Red/Gold 2. Blue/Yellow 3. Blue/Green	1. Gold 2. Black/Blue 3. Black/Green	1. Brown/Red 2. Brown/Yellow 3. Green/Red	1. Gray/Green 2. Blue/Green 3. Red/Green
SILK SQUARE or SCARF	1. Blue 2. Black/Gold 3. Green or Red	1. Red/Gold 2. Yellow 3. Blue/Green	1. Gray 2. Blue 3. Green	1. Red 2. Yellow 3. Green	1. Gray 2. Blue/Green 3. Red or Green
JEWELRY	1. Silver Finish 2. Gold Finish 3. Gold or Silver Finish	1. Silver Finish 2. Gold Finish 3. Silver Finish	1. Gold Finish 2. Silver Finish 3. Gold Finish	1. 2. Gold Finish 3.	1. Gold or 2. Silver 3. Finish
BELT	1. Cordovan 2. Black 3. Brown or Black	1. Black 2. Cordovan 3. Black	1. Gray 2. or 3. Black	1. Brown 2. or 3. Cordovan	1. Black 2. Cordovan 3. Brown
SOCKS	1. Navy or Gray 2. Black 3. Green	1. 2. Navy 3.	1. 2. Black 3.	1. Brown 2. Brown 3. Green	1. Olive 2. Green 3. Brown
SHOES	1. Cordovan 2. Black 3. Brown or Black	1. Black 2. Cordovan 3. Black	1. 2. Black 3.	1. Brown 2. or 3. Cordovan	1. Black 2. Cordovan 3. Brown
HAT	1. Medium Gray 2. Black 3. Olive	1. Gray 2. Brown 3. Olive	1. Black 2. Gray 3. Olive	1. Brown 2. Green 3. Olive	1. Olive 2. Brown 3. Bronze
OUTERCOAT	1. Gray or Black 2. Black or Covert 3. Gray or Camel	1. Gray 2. Tan 3. Olive	1. Gray or 2. Black 3. Olive	1. Brown, Tan, 2. or 3. Charcoal	1. Gray/Olive 2. Olive or Brown 3. Olive or Tan
GLOVES	1. Gray Suede 2. or Black 3. Capeskin	1. Gray Fabric 2. or Brown 3. Cape or Mocha	1. Gray Suede 2. or 3. Black Cape	1. Brown Cape 2. Natural Pigskin 3. Olive Leather	1. Brown, Tan, 2. or Olive 3. Leather

HART SCHAFFNER AND MARX, CHICAGO

tall and heavy man looks better in suits of plain, subdued patterns, shirts with moderate to widespread collars, and ties of average width.

Take a good look at yourself in a full-length mirror. Could you improve your posture? Your figure determines the effect you produce in your clothes. Your appearance depends as much on the way you wear your clothes as the clothes themselves. The business suit fulfills Shakespeare's words, "The apparel proclaims the man." Are you making the most of your figure? Your success in life depends largely upon the way you look and impress people.

Suits and Top Coats

A suit is the most important wardrobe purchase for a man. The outer fabric for a suit affects its appearance and its durability. Most fabrics can be classified as either woolen or worsted. Woolens have a soft finish and are less firmly woven than worsteds. They do not keep their shape as well but they do not wrinkle easily. They are usually warmer because the napping holds in air. Worsteds are made from longer fibers and are generally closely woven with a hard finish. They wear well but those without a nap such as gabardines become shiny with wear and cleanings.

A fabric knit from polyester and wool is used for this suit, which features inlaid welt pockets and a deep center back vent in the jacket.

HART SCHAFFNER AND MARX

This suit is of a woven fabric of all wool. The pockets have wide flaps and there are side vents in the back.

321

Father and son have selected ties that contrast with their jackets—a plain tie for the son's plaid jacket and a boldly designed tie to go with the father's jacket of a subtly patterned double knit fabric. Notice how the shirt sleeve cuffs show a small amount below the jacket sleeves. The plaid in the boy's jacket is well matched—a sign of good garment construction.

Both worsted and woolen type fabrics are made of all wool fibers and blends of man-made and woolen fibers. Polyester fabrics such as Dacron and Fortrel are light in weight and very resilent. Many summer suits contain polyesters for these qualities and wool fibers for their comfort and appearance. Some of the man-made fibers are subject to pilling, static electricity, and glazing from improper pressing. Labels should help you understand the fabrics you select, as research is developing better blends every day.

Summer suits may be made of cotton and rayon. These fibers are cool and inexpensive but need wrinkle-resistant finishes for good service.

The amount of service and upkeep will depend upon color as well as fiber content. Mixtures are more practical than plain colors. They do not show spots, shine, or mends as readily. Dark shades usually require less upkeep than light tones.

Size and fitting of suits. Suits and coats are usually sized by chest measurement as well as general length such as short, average, tall, or portly. Measure over a shirt, just under the arms. But always try on a suit as the cut of the garment affects the actual sizing. (Did you know that the average size of suits worn by men in the United States in 1916 was 39? Today it is between a 41 and 42.)

Fit. No matter how well chosen suits are as to color, pattern, and style, they will not look well if they do not fit correctly. Here are some general rules to check. When you try on a garment, sit down, and walk around, and bend over. Put your wallet and other essentials in pockets because they can make a difference

in appearance. Wear correct fitting shirts when you purchase a jacket. Check to see that there is no strain on the buttons when the coat is fastened properly. Note: the bottom button is usually left open.

Jacket length. The bottom edge of the jacket can affect the appearance of the entire suit. How long should it be? Let your hands hang naturally at your sides. The bottom edge should be even with your knuckles or just cover the seat of the pants. During some seasons a change of length is more stylish so always check with a tailor or fitter before making a final decision.

Jacket collar. The collar should be low enough so that ¼ to ½ inch of a shirt collar shows at the base of the neck. Be sure the collar does not gap or stand away from the neck.

Jacket sleeves. Shirt sleeves usually show under the jacket sleeves about ½ inch.

Trousers are selected by both waistline and inseam measures. The waistline measure is taken around the waistline firmly but not tightly. The inseam measurement is the number of inches from the crotch along the inside seam to the bottom of the trousers. Therefore a fellow who wears a 30–32 trouser measures 30 inches around the waist and 32 inches down the inside seam of his pants.

Trousers should hang straight from the hips and just brush the top of the shoes. They should never be so long as to break or drag in back. Some seasons it is stylish to have trousers break a little over the shoes but this makes them look too large and they may wear out quickly as they rub against the shoes. Be sure the seat is comfortable but not baggy.

A casual tartan blazer, of the Prince Charles plaid, features side vents, flap pockets on the slant, and slacks which match one of the colors in the plaid.

A traditional topcoat, single breasted, of all wool tweed.

A worsted wool topcoat suitable for three seasons. The glen plaid fabric has a water repellent finish which supplements wool's natural resistance to moisture, and there is a zip-out warm lining.

Topcoats are bought less often than formerly. Today, men usually select a coat with a water-repellent finish and a zip-in lining that can be used for many types of weather. The water-repellent treatment provides protection from showers and some water-borne stains but a waterproof fabric is necessary for heavy rains. Buying points for a topcoat are similar to those for a jacket except for the need for a heavier fabric for warmth.

Why is there such a wide variation in prices? Two coats may appear the same with prices that differ greatly.

Why this difference? Quality usually makes the difference. Good quality fabrics are colorfast and pre-shrunk. In the very lowest-grade suits, the front interfacings are made of cotton fabric instead of resilient wool. In better quality suits, fabrics are cut accurately, the pattern is matched precisely, and hand tailoring is done skillfully. Stitching is close, and collars and lapels are neat and not flimsy. All these features of quality add to the original cost of a garment; however, they pay for themselves in comfort, service, and appearance.

If you want value for your money, always compare garments in different price ranges. Ask for fact tags that should give you information on the outer cloth, lining, coat front and collar interlining, pockets, workmanship, colorfastness, and shrinkage.

Characteristics of a well-made suit. Look for marks of good workmanship. One big difference between high and lower grade suits is in matching stripes and plaids. In the best suits the cloth is cut so the pattern matches precisely. In lower grade suits the pattern may not be matched at all or only in one direction. If you are looking for a moderate-priced suit, it is better to select a fabric with no pattern to be matched.

The way lining has been put in a coat is a point to notice. In fine quality suits the lining is smoothly fitted and finely stitched by hand. The lower edge of the coat is bound and fastened over the lining. A small pleat is left in the upper back for "give." Linings in poor quality suits are not always smoothly fitted. The machine stitching is coarse and may not match in color. No allowances for give is made, which may result in torn linings.

A type of coat suited for automobile driving and country wear. Shawl-collared with a pile fabric, the coat is of classic herringbone tweed.

In the coat pocket of many good suits you may find a booklet that explains many of the qualities you cannot see, and gives directions for proper care.

325

Examine the lining of a coat. A firm twill weave gives better service than a loosely woven plain fabric. Unlike women's suits, most men's jackets have a partial lining in the back.

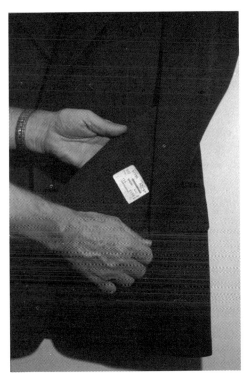

The fiber content and model number are given on a paper label sewn on the left sleeve. Remove the stitching carefully so as not to damage the fabric.

Crush the lapel. In a good grade suit, it will snap back in place.

Some good quality tweeds or loosely woven fabrics have trouser knees lined with closely woven fabric to lessen wear and prevent bagginess.

Interlinings can be as important as the fabric you see. They protect and reinforce the outer fabric and affect the drape of the collar and lapels. To get some idea of this hidden quality, grasp the coat front of a suit you know is high grade and pull your closed hand down over it. It will feel lightweight and soft, not stiff. The front will spring back into shape without a wrinkle when you let go.

In contrast, a poor quality suit will feel thick, bulky, and crisp. When you let go, you can feel the wrinkles left in the inside material.

Look at the trouser crotch. Is it pieced? Only better quality suits have legs that are not pieced at the crotches. It takes more material to make each leg in one piece and manufacturers of average and low priced garments cannot afford this. Piecing also affects comfort.

SHIRTS

When shopping for a *shirt*, look for details that provide long wear. Shirts vary little in style. The success of men's and boys' shirts is largely due to the type and quality of fabric used. To secure quality, always check the fabric, accuracy of cut, workmanship, fit, and comfort.

Broadcloth, madras, and *oxford* are popular for business shirts.

Dacron or other polyester fibers are used in a *tricot* or fine knit construction for easy-care shirts that never need ironing and that wear a long time. Shirts labeled "100%" polyester will not be as absorbent and will not carry away body moisture as rapidly as cotton but will dry quickly and require no ironing. The knit construction allows for easy evaporation of perspiration and thus these shirts are more comfortable than woven ones of polyester fibers.

Some broadcloths and oxford cloths are made from a blend of cotton and polyester fibers. These shirts will have the absorbency of cotton with the wrinkle resistance of polyester and will need touch-up ironing. There may be some problems with pilling and clinging of greasy soil.

Many 100% cotton shirts have finishes applied so that no ironing is required if washed properly. However, if shirts are sent to a commercial laundry, select cotton without finishes for best wear.

Few jackets can be bought without the need for some alterations. This jacket fits well, but the sleeves need shortening. Most stores will provide this alteration free of charge although it can be done easily by anyone who sews well. It helps, however, if the store fitter marks the suitable length.

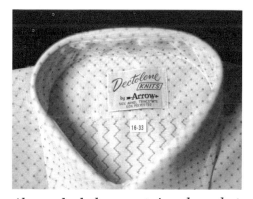

Always check the correct size when selecting shirts. The 16–33 shown on this label means this shirt will fit a man with a size 16 neck and a 33-inch sleeve.

APPEARANCE COUNTS!!!

POINTERS FOR PROPER CARING

- CLOTHES are aired and cleaned before seasonal storing.
- SHIRTS last longer when washed with collars turned up.
- TIES are hung unknotted and rotated between wearings.
- HANDKERCHIEFS are always pressed and changed daily.
- POCKETS are emptied and flaps straightened before hanging.
- JACKETS need periodic pressing and brushing.
- JACKETS are always hung unbuttoned.
- JEWELRY boxes keep male jewelry shining and unscratched.
- HATS need ample storage space and are boxed out of season.
- ROTATE clothes between wearings.
- PANTS need periodic pressing and are hung after each wearing.
- HOSE are changed daily and stored matched.
- SHOETREES, shoe horns and shoe polish prolong shoe life.

POINTERS FOR PROPER WEARING

- FACE the day clean and well shaven.
- SHIRTS are V-Tapered for a trim appearance.
- TIES accent wardrobe and reflect personality.
- HANDKERCHIEFS in breast pocket are casual but neat.
- LAPELS always lie flat against the jacket.
- SHIRT collars fit correctly and show a half inch at nape of neck.
- JACKETS allow for easy movement with well-fitted shoulders.
- SHIRT CUFFS end at wristbone, show half inch of linen.
- HATS flatter the face and complete the outfit.
- JACKET hems cover the seat, approximately thumb-tip length.
- PANTS fit smooth over the hips, neither baggy nor too tight.
- HOSE always keep bare legs from showing.
- SHOES need a good shine.

ELLEN JACOBSEN CO. FOR THE PHILLIPS-VAN HEUSEN CO.

It is important that fabrics for shirts be resistant to shrinkage, for even a small change in size can result in too tight a neck.

Cuffs are made in three styles—the French cuff which fastens with cuff links, the single or barrel cuff which buttons, and a combination type which buttons but can also be closed with cuff links.

Dress shirt sizes, usually printed inside the neckband, are indicated by circumference of the neck and by sleeve length. If the neck size needs to be checked, measure around the base of the neck, allowing slight ease for comfort. You can also take a comfortable fitting shirt and measure across the neckband from center of the top button to the center of the buttonhole. Measurements may be taken to the nearest inch or ½ inch, for example 14, 14½, 15, 15½ and up to 17. If the neck size falls between sizes, buy the larger one. For sleeve length, measure from the center back of the neck, across the shoulder over the bent elbow to the wrist. Sleeve lengths are available only to the nearest inch, for example, 32 inches, 33 inches and up to 35.

The body of some dress shirts may be tapered, reducing the waistline measurement by 4 to 7 inches for a trimmer fit. Note: Tapered shirts may be uncomfortable for the larger man. The polyester tricot shirts are made slimmer, as there is stretch or give in the material to allow for ease of movement.

Shirts for boys are sold by sizes based upon neck and chest measure, or upon chest and height measure.

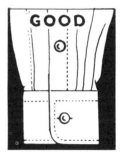
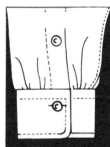

The best quality shirts have tucks placed near the sleeve opening. Gathers are a sign of a poorer quality shirt.

USDA

Neck size and sleeve length combinations commonly available in men's dress shirts:					
Neck size (inches)	14	14½	15, 15½	16, 16½	17
Sleeve length (inches)	32, 33	32, 33, 34	32, 33	32, 33	32, 33
			34, 35	34, 35	34, 35

Boys' sizes—regular:							
Size	6	8	10	12	14	16	18
Neck (inches)	11	11½	12	12½	13	13½	14
Chest (inches)	25	26½	28	29½	31½	33	34½
Height (inches)	46	50	54	58	61	64	66

Husky sizes for boys are also available.

important point: off the cuff

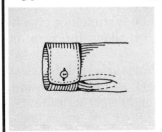

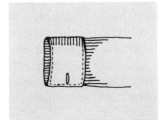

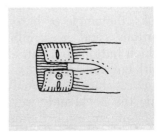

SINGLE — Also called "button" or "barrel" cuff. It fastens with a lap and an attached button.

FRENCH — Also called "double cuff". It is folded back and fastens with cuff links. A link cuff is a single fold French cuff which requires cuff links.

CONVERTIBLE — A "single" cuff with an extra buttonhole, to be worn with cuff links or as a regular buttoned cuff.

collar the correct style

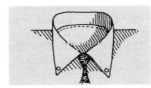

REGULAR—The most popular collar in existence; a classic that is becoming for all faces.

BUTTON-DOWN — Casual and youthful looking, for dress or sport. Goes well with sport jackets.

SPREAD —Width is becoming to long, thin faces as well as to average shapes.

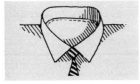

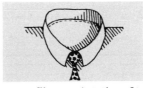

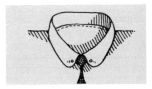

SHORT-POINT — Outstanding for the long-necked man; it gives a smart appearance.

TAB—Short-point that fits high on neck, looks well with average face. Flatters a full face. Snap-tab style needs no collar button.

ROUNDED — Another version of a short-point collar. Considered a dressy style, it's worn with a collar pin.

Woven sport shirts for men are marked by neck measure, under four basic sizes. The man who wears a 15½ dress shirt may find the medium size too small if the fabric shrinks some; the large may be too large if there is no shrinkage. Be sure to check labels for this.

Sport shirt sizes

Small . . . .(S) 14–14½ inches
Medium . . . .(M) 15–15½ inches
Large . . . .(L) 16–16½ inches
Extra Large . . . . .(XL) 17–17½ inches

Knit sport shirts have another system of measurement. To find the correct size, measure around the chest over a shirt. Keep the tape well up under the arms and over tips of shoulder blades. The resulting chest measure is the size required. Men's knit sport shirt sizes are divided into four major groups:

Small . . . .(S) 34–36 inches
Medium . . . .(M) 38–40 inches
Large . . . .(L) 42–44 inches
Extra Large . . . .(XL) 46–48 inches

A good quality dress shirt has smooth, firm fabric, is pre-shrunk and colorfast, with design or pattern match at collar, center front, and pocket. It has sharp collar points, firm, neat buttonholes, and four-hole pearl buttons sewed on securely. A *full-cut* shirt denotes good quality.

The design and workmanship of shirts affect the comfort, length of wear, and style which may be more becoming to one person than another.

AMERICAN INSTITUTE OF MEN'S AND BOYS' WEAR
Summer sport shirts are usually short sleeved cotton prints or knitted polo shirts with short neck openings.

AMERICAN INSTITUTE OF MEN'S AND BOYS' WEAR
Bold colors are popular for young men's shirts. On the left is a giant plaid cotton button-down sport shirt and on the right a wool flannel shirt which may be worn in or out.

331

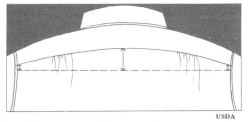

USDA

Shirts fit most comfortably if there are tucks or gathers over each shoulder blade. Gathers in the center are not as comfortable and produce a bulky appearance.

The *cut across the back* determines the comfort and length of service for a shirt. There should be sufficient fullness across the back to provide freedom of arm movement. Pleats or gathers over the shoulder blades are better than center gathers.

Sleeves in best-quality shirts are cut in one piece and are easier to iron and neater in appearance than if pieced. Sleeves in medium quality shirts are often pieced at the back of the arm to save material. This does not affect the fit, as the sleeves are the same size as those cut in one piece.

High school boys enjoy shirts with *convertible* collars and short as well as long sleeves. *Knitted shirts* are popular with boys for school and sportswear. *Polo shirts* slip over the head and have convertible collars. *T-shirts* have round, close necks, and perhaps an opening at the throat front.

ADDITIONAL ITEMS

Underwear. Men's underwear is usually of cotton or cotton blends for comfort, absorbency, and easy washability. Fit is also important to prevent discomfort from tight, binding garments.

Robes. Fabrics selected for robes should be serviceable, durable, and retain their shape and good appearance for the life of the garment. Soft, washable cotton fabrics are very popular; however lightweight wool makes a smartly tailored, long lasting, good appearing garment. Dacron robes in soft twill with a slightly lustrous surface are washable and retain their shape and appearance for a long time. Terry cloth robes are easily washed, warm, and absorbent.

A comfortable, serviceable robe is well tailored, with large, reinforced pockets, a shawl collar, and a belt of self-material. Well tailored, set-in sleeves are usually worn. The lap in front should be generous and the length right for walking and stooping.

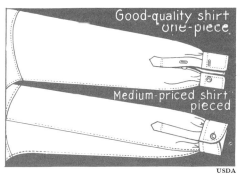

USDA

A good quality shirt has the sleeve made from one piece of fabric, which is easy to iron. A medium-priced shirt is pieced and although the fullness is the same, it is not as comfortable and is more difficult to care for.

332

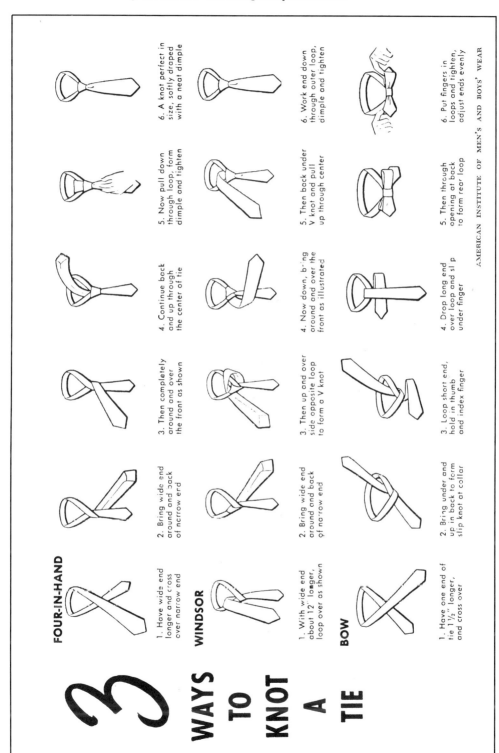

3 WAYS TO KNOT A TIE

FOUR-IN-HAND

1. Have wide end longer and cross over narrow end

2. Bring wide end around and back of narrow end

3. Then completely around and over the front as shown

4. Continue back and up through the center of tie

5. Now pull down through loop; form dimple and tighten

6. A knot perfect in size, softly draped with a neat dimple

WINDSOR

1. With wide end about 12" longer, loop over as shown

2. Bring wide end around and back of narrow end

3. Then up and over side opposite loop to form a V knot

4. Now down, bring around and over the front as illustrated

5. Then back under V knot and pull up through center

6. Work end down through outer loop, dimple and tighten

BOW

1. Have one end of tie 1½" longer, and cross over

2. Bring under and up in back to form slip knot at collar

3. Loop short end, hold in thumb and index finger

4. Drop long end over loop and slip under finger

5. Then through opening at back to form rear loop

6. Put fingers in loops and tighten, adjust ends evenly

AMERICAN INSTITUTE OF MEN'S AND BOYS' WEAR

Ties. Think twice before you select a matching tie and handkerchief to wear in a breast pocket. The tie attracts attention to the face but the matching handkerchief will distract from the face. A plain white or monogrammed handkerchief may be a better choice. The four-in-hand tie is the most common and is available in a wide variety of fabrics and patterns. Bow ties are worn in certain localities.

Gloves. The man who wears gloves while driving a car needs leather gloves or gloves with leather palms and finger grips. Leather with knit linings are generally preferred. Warm knitted gloves are in vogue wherever winter sports are popular. To select the correct size, place a tape measure around the knuckles with the fist

closed. The number of inches is the glove size.

Hats. Many employers regard going hatless, especially during cold or bad weather, as a sign of immaturity and irresponsibility and not appropriate for a business executive or one who hopes to be. The hat is an old symbol of stability. Select a brim and crown that will flatter your head shape, as well as the "latest" style. Even if "everyone" is wearing a narrow brim, it is possible to find slightly wider ones for the man who looks better in them. Measure the circumference of your head where a hat normally rests to determine the correct size. The chart below lists the corresponding hat size.

Circumference of Head	Hat Size
20½	6½
20¾	6⅝
21⅛	6¾
21½	6⅞
21⅞	7
22¼	7⅛
22⅝	7¼
23	7⅜
23½	7½

If a standard sized hat does not fit well, perhaps a special shape such as long oval is needed.

Socks and shoes. No man wants to attract attention to his ankles, and hairy legs are unattractive above short socks. Wear longer ones, tight enough to stay up. Although some men enjoy wearing bright colors, it is considered better taste to select dark socks that do not attract attention. Select fabrics and colors that can be thrown in with the wash without danger of shrinking or color damage to other fabrics. It's a wise man who

Du Pont

For sports wear a colorful ascot is a nice change from the traditional tie.

Classic shoe styles suitable for wear for all occasions. On the left, a plain-toe version in a smooth leather with a dressy pin dot sock. On the right is a scotch grain shoe with a tweedy executive length sock.

Many businesses provide uniform apparel for their employees. This man wears a red blazer-type jacket with the insignia of his company and a name plate. His tie and trousers are navy blue. (The woman's pants suit is of navy with bands of red and white. The company insignia is worn as a locket.)

buys three or more matching pairs so that a pair will always be available despite the sock gremlins who seem to live in many homes and hide one sock out of every pair!

Socks are sized by the number of inches from the point of the toe to the end of the heel. Most men select socks based on their shoe size, as shoes are usually carefully fitted. In general, sock sizes correspond with the shoe sizes as below:

Shoe Size	Sock Size
7–7½	10½
8–8½	11
9–9½	11½
10–10½	12
11–12	13

For a sure fit, you may choose stretch hose in the correct range for your foot. The fit of shoes is so important that it is essential to have them fitted by a capable, well-trained person. Sizes differ with shoe manufacturers, so you cannot always rely on what you have worn.

Formal wear. When the situation calls for it, there is no substitute for the rules of formal dress. A black tuxedo is the basis, with a cummerbund or formal vest. Black bow tie, black hose, and black polished calf or patent shoes are essential with the tuxedo. With "tails" a white tie, a pleated bosom shirt and special collar are usually worn. Midnight blue suits and other colors are in style from time to time. Ruffled shirts are a variation.

A white dinner jacket may be worn in our north temperate summer.

A dark suit, white shirt, and dark bow tie serve adequately for men who do not want to buy or rent seldom-worn formal clothes.

Wedding parties have clothing rules described in literature provided for the occasion.

Many shops rent formal clothes, if desired.

For summer formal wear, jackets are often more colorful than the traditional black. India madras is used here for this shawl-collared dinner coat. It is worn with a pleated-front dinner shirt, black cummerbund and bow tie, and black formal trousers.
AMERICAN INSTITUTE OF MEN'S AND BOYS' WEAR

WARDROBE TIPS FOR ALL MEN

1. Avoid extremes. Even though a certain style may be the rage, it may not necessarily look right on you.

2. Be bold about using color but don't go wild. This is simply a matter of good taste.

3. Favor the colors that favor you. For example, a blue shirt always looks good on a blue-eyed, fair-complexioned man.

4. Know your limitations. If you're on the portly side or on the road to more generous proportions, avoid tight-fitting garments.

5. Coordinate. Wear shirts, ties, handkerchiefs and hose that work with each other toward a more attractive complete picture, rather than a shirt and tie that seem to be at war with each other.

6. Keep well-groomed. Keep your fingernails neat and trim.

7. Be "hair-conditioned." Shave closely enough and frequently enough to avoid any show of stubble—and pay regular visits to your barber even if you don't appreciate his conversation.

8. Watch your linen. Are your handkerchiefs—the one in your rear trouser pocket and the one in your breast pocket clean and neat? Sloppy linen often suggests sloppy thinking.

9. Dry clean often. Even if you think dry-cleaning prices are out of line and would like to save a buck here and there, don't do it at the expense of your appearance. When a suit needs cleaning, have it done. This also is something worth keeping in mind if you don't particularly cater to moths as house guests.

10. Flatten your pockets. This is something many men are guilty of—avoid that unkempt look of pockets bulging with pencils and papers.

American Institute of Men's and Boys' Wear

Bring to class samples of several fabrics suitable for men's shirts for warm weather wear. What are the desirable and undesirable characteristics of each?

Bring to class samples of fabrics suitable for men's and high school boys' suits for winter wear. What are the desirable and undesirable characteristics of each?

Bring to class samples of fabrics suitable for men's and high school boys' suits for summer wear. What are the desirable and undesirable characteristics of each?

Plan a wardrobe for a high school boy in your school, with the assistance of a mail-order catalog. Figure the cost if the items are purchased during the present school year.

What clothes would he wear to church? To a formal party? To an informal party?

Select a color your father enjoys and plan a complete outfit using pictures from a mail-order catalog.

Borrow suit jackets of different colors as described on page 318. Arrange to have several boys with different skin and hair coloring come to class. Try the jackets on them and determine good and flattering colors for each boy.

Bring in pictures of men and boys in typical clothing worn since World War II. Notice how ties, hats, sport shirts, and width of trousers have changed.

Arrange to have a local retailer come to class to demonstrate proper fitting of a man's suit. Ask him to bring a top quality suit and one of moderate quality for comparison.

Plan a minimum wardrobe for a man starting college at your state university.

Helpful Hints on Clothes Care*

• Try not to wear a suit two days in a row. It will look better and last longer if given a rest between wearings. (The fibers return to shape . . . the day's wrinkles unwrinkle themselves.)

• Use a substantial hanger. (Not over a chair or by the neck loop. Both stretch the cloth.) Space the hangers a few inches apart: fibers need air to "breathe."

• See that the lapels and sleeves aren't twisted. Never put a suit away when damp.

• Brush your clothes as you take them off. This not only removes the day's dirt and grit but prevents it sandpapering the fabric. Occasionally brush out pockets and trouser cuffs.

• Remove spots as soon as possible. The longer they remain the harder to get out.

• Carry as little as possible in your pockets.

• When not in use, store (after cleaning) in sealed garment bags.

* Hart Schaffner & Marx, Chicago

Golden-agers enjoying a get-together. Notice the clothes they like to wear. The necklines are cut loosely so they do not bind, the fabrics are soft and often of a print design, and the skirts have some fullness. Necklaces and treasured brooches are favorite accessories.

OLDER FAMILY MEMBERS

Just as the young members of the family have special clothing needs, so do the older family members. The older person tends to keep the attitudes developed years ago regarding the proper type of clothing to be worn. Research shows they are more conservative and less readily accept fashion changes than younger people. Lowered income of many retired people results in more concern for price and durability.

Physical disabilities require that clothing have many of the characteristics for very young children—safety features, large openings, fasteners that can be easily closed, and fabrics that feel soft to the skin. Many elderly people have difficulty with back closures and with extending their arms over their head. Physical changes in body proportion result in frequently needed alterations on standard sized garments. Heavy clothes are not comfortable and lightweight fabrics with warmth are desirable. Acrylic and modacrylic sweaters and pile fabrics often provide needed warmth with lightness.

Personal coloring changes with the years. Yellow and brown are seldom attractive to aging skins. White hair makes it possible to wear colors that were not attractive when younger.

As more and more older people maintain their community activities, the clothing industry will develop clothing specially suited to their needs. In the meantime, careful shopping is necessary.

Suggest a clothing gift that would be suitable for an elderly man or woman. Describe it in detail and defend your choice.

Talk with elderly relatives and neighbors about their clothing problems. Determine the type of clothes they prefer and whether or not they have difficulty finding suitable items.

Design a dress suitable for an older woman who is not as "nimble" as she was when younger. Select a color flattering to gray or white hair.

Can You Explain These Terms?

business wear	*wardrobe color plan*	*French cuff*
sports wear	*woolen*	*single or barrel cuff*
leisure wear	*worsted*	*combination cuff*
formal wear	*waistline measure*	*"black tie"*
dress-right code	*shirt neck size*	*"white tie"*

Summary With Check-Up Questions

A good appearance for all family members is important for the well-being of each person and for others with whom he associates.

- *Why are children affected by the type of clothing worn by their parents?*
- *How will a child feel if he is proud of the appearance of his mother and his father? If he is not pleased?*

American men and women need to understand how to select clothing for all members of their families.

- *What percentage of men's clothing is selected by women?*
- *Do most men ask their wives' advice when purchasing coats and suits?*
- *When might men help to care for clothes of other family members?*
- *How often do women purchase clothing articles for elderly relatives?*

Clothing needs of women change as their family responsibilities change.

- *How will clothing needs of a young wife change from when she held a job outside the home without children and when she becomes a young mother?*
- *How will the clothing needs of a woman who works at home differ from those of a woman who commutes to a city to work?*
- *Mothers of teen-age children who work outside the home and also entertain their husband's associates have additional clothing needs. What are they?*

A man's clothing and grooming are very important in the world of business.

- *Does a man who is well-dressed feel more capable than one who knows he is not dressed correctly?*
- *How many business matters are often influenced by first impressions which include a man's appearance?*

Although few businesses and schools have specific clothing regulations, there are noticeable patterns of preferred clothing.

- *Why should one delay purchasing all clothing needed for college or a new job until one has been there a few weeks?*
- *Why are "Dress-Right" codes no longer desired by high school students?*

A man's wardrobe should be built around one or more basic colors flattering to him and that can be easily coordinated with accessories.

- *Why do some men look better in suits of dark shades rather than lighter values of the same color?*
- *What problems may arise in purchasing shoes if one selects a brown suit and a gray suit?*
- *How can one coordinate a dress suit, slacks, and sports coat so that the colors are not the same but harmonize when mixed?*

Men's clothing is usually made for four basic figure types: short, regular, tall, and portly.

- *What types of fabrics are suitable for a tall man that would not be wise for a short person?*
- *Should a short, thin man select a contrasting jacket and slacks or ones that match? Why?*
- *What is the effect of a double breasted suit on a short, thin man? A short, heavy man?*

Suits are usually made from fabrics of all wool or blends of wool and polyester fibers.

- *Why would wool and polyester be a suitable choice for a lightweight summer suit?*
- *Winter tweeds are usually made from all wool. Why?*
- *How can you determine the difference between a woolen and a worsted fabric by appearance? What will be the difference in wearing ability?*

Even the best quality suit will not be flattering if the fit is incorrect.

- *What is the correct length for the jacket?*
- *How much of the shirt usually shows at the bottom of the sleeve?*
- *How long should the trouser legs be?*
- *What is meant by a suit, sized 40, with trousers sized 36–30?*

Characteristics which help a suit hold its shape and wear well are hard to determine at first glance.

- *What can you learn about the quality of the suit from looking at the trouser crotch?*
- *What statements will you look for on a label?*

- *What happens when you crush the lapel of a good quality suit and a poor one?*

Men's shirts must be comfortable, fitted correctly, and easy to care for.

- *What is the difference between a shirt sized 15, 32 and one sized 16, 33?*
- *The shape of the collar can affect the appearance of the face. What is a suitable shape for a broad face? For a long narrow face?*
- *How can checking the fullness at the back yoke and the sleeve cuffs give a clue to quality of a shirt?*

No man's costume is complete without carefully selected shoes and hosiery.

- *What effect do run-down heels and shoes that need polishing have on the best looking suit?*
- *How can hosiery be held up so the bare leg does not show between the shoe and trouser bottom?*

Older family members have special needs for clothing, just as very young children do.

- *Why are safety features in clothing important for older persons?*
- *What types of closures are best for elderly people?*
- *Older people often feel the cold weather more intensely than when young, yet do not like heavy fabrics. What do you suggest to solve this problem?*
- *Why is it important that clothing for the elderly be attractive and in style as well as easy to care for and manage?*

PART 3

TEXTILE
FABRICS

CHAPTER TEN

Fibers for Fabrics

WHICH of the sweaters described on the next page would you buy for school? Would you buy a different one for your mother for a birthday gift? Would another one be better for your little sister? All of the sweaters are similar in style and all except A and D cost about the same. A and D are more expensive.

A few years ago a young woman would not have such a decision to make. A sweater was always of wool unless of cotton for summer. Fabrics today are fascinating and complex. No longer do we live in a time when we can go to a store and feel a piece of material and know from what fiber it is made and how it will wear. With the advent of man-made fibers and new finishes for natural ones, and blends of the two, wise shopping for fabrics has become a challenge which requires knowledge and thought. It can be satisfying to know that you have chosen wisely from the many items available and that you look well in your choice.

You are the person who can trans-

form a garment from the store shelves into something that makes you feel and look better when you wear it. You will be happy also if your choice does not involve too much care. You are the person who makes the final decision. Remember, the more you know and understand about fabrics, the wiser choice you will make.

To repeat, the study of fabrics is a fascinating one. In a way, it is a study of the history of man, as well as the application of science and art to everyday needs, to provide better clothing.

People have worn fabrics for many centuries. Earlier, probably just the skins of animals were worn as protection from bitter cold. Soon man learned to braid stems and leaves together to make a simple kind of fabric and later to weave them into cloth. Then he learned to make yarns from plant fibers and animal hair and to weave these into cloth—to protect him from cold, rain, and sun; to make him more attractive to himself and to others.

342

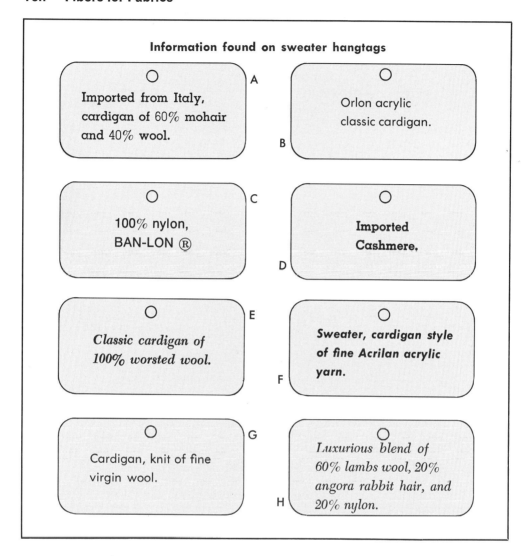

Information found on sweater hangtags

A ○ Imported from Italy, cardigan of 60% mohair and 40% wool.

B ○ Orlon acrylic classic cardigan.

C ○ 100% nylon, BAN-LON ®

D ○ Imported Cashmere.

E ○ *Classic cardigan of 100% worsted wool.*

F ○ *Sweater, cardigan style of fine Acrilan acrylic yarn.*

G ○ Cardigan, knit of fine virgin wool.

H ○ *Luxurious blend of 60% lambs wool, 20% angora rabbit hair, and 20% nylon.*

Today man can also create fibers from chemical elements, using sources such as coal, water, and gas. He can put finishes on some fibers that change them in both appearance and feel, so that they resemble other fibers. He can make the same fiber into either a delicate lace or a sturdy material for army tents! Truly, man has been able to provide for all his clothing needs.

But so many choices can create problems also. In order to choose wisely, you need a knowledge of the fabric and how to care for it. To understand fabrics you must understand *fibers, yarns, how fabrics are made,* and *finishes.*

In this chapter you will first read about the fibers readily available today. There are so many that you may think it an impossible task to understand them all. But when you realize that many fibers are related to others and have similar qualities, you will see that it is not too difficult.

343

CLASSIFICATION OF FIBERS AND COMMON TRADE NAMES*

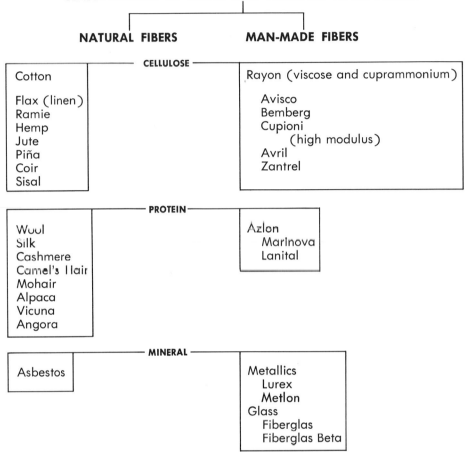

NATURAL FIBERS   MAN-MADE FIBERS

CELLULOSE

Natural	Man-Made
Cotton Flax (linen) Ramie Hemp Jute Piña Coir Sisal	Rayon (viscose and cuprammonium) Avisco Bemberg Cupioni (high modulus) Avril Zantrel

PROTEIN

Natural	Man-Made
Wool Silk Cashmere Camel's Hair Mohair Alpaca Vicuna Angora	Azlon Marinova Lanital

MINERAL

Natural	Man-Made
Asbestos	Metallics Lurex Metlon Glass Fiberglas Fiberglas Beta

THERMOPLASTIC OR HEAT-SENSITIVE
(MAN-MADE FIBERS)

CELLULOSIC	SYNTHETIC	
Acetate Celanese Estron Celaperm Chromspun Triacetate Arnel	Acrylic Acrilan Creslan Orlon Zefran Anidex Anim/8 Aramid Nomex Modacrylic Dynel Verel Nylon Antron Cadon Caprolan Qiana	Olefin Marvess Herculon Vectra Polyester Dacron Fortrel Kodel Terylene Trevira Spandex Lycra Vyrene Spandelle

* Note: Not all fibers are listed here as new ones are constantly appearing on the market.

There are just four major groups of fibers—cellulose, protein, thermoplastic, and mineral (and very few mineral fibers are used for clothing). But, you may ask, what about all the new man-made fibers that have appeared in the past ten to twenty years and others that are still to come? Even these belong to family groups and are related in properties.

Fiber families. There are many families of man-made fibers but several of these are not used for clothing, so you will not need to learn about them here. Each family or group has a generic name, which is like a family name. Each fiber has a specific name or trademark given it by its manufacturer, which is like a first name. For example, the polyester family has several members, including Dacron, Fortrel, and Kodel. Each one has slightly different properties but is generally similar to the others. When a new polyester fiber is introduced, it may have a strange first name but it will have "polyester" for a last name. You will then know that it is similar to Dacron and other members of the group that you recognize.

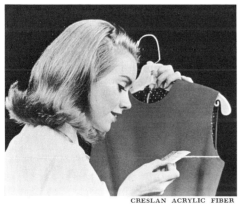

CRESLAN ACRYLIC FIBER

Study the tag accompanying each garment. The fiber content must be stated under federal regulations.

Write to the Federal Trade Commission for a copy of the Textile Products Identification Act. After studying it, prepare a display showing labeling requirements.

Our government has helped consumers to recognize fibers by passing a law in 1961 called the Textile Products Identification Act. This states that the generic name of the fiber must always accompany the trademark or manufacturer's name on a garment label or bolt of material. This law does not tell anything about the quality of the fabric. It does name the fibers and you have to decide if they have the characteristics desired. Fibers must be listed in order of weight and imported fabrics must be labeled as to country of origin.

Fiber Identification

Microscopic identification of fibers. Many common fibers can easily be identified with the aid of a microscope. Place a drop of water or glycerine on a clean glass slide. Place a few fibers on the drop of liquid and cover with a cover glass. If a yarn is used, untwist one end and place the loosened fibers on the slide. (It is very difficult to see individual fibers in a yarn or fabric.) After placing the slide in the microscope, focus under low power first. Later you may wish to examine the fibers under high power. Cotton, linen, and wool fibers can be easily identified. Compare with the photomicrographs of fibers on page 346. Most man-made fibers look alike and require more complicated methods for distinguishing them.

345

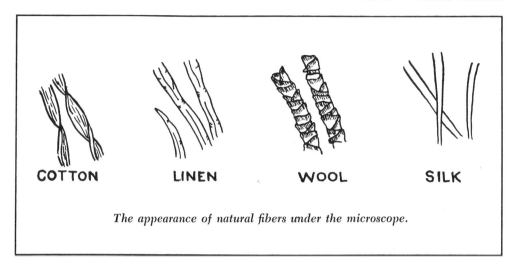

COTTON   LINEN   WOOL   SILK

The appearance of natural fibers under the microscope.

Fiber identification by burning. Many fibers can be easily identified by their burning behavior. When fibers are blended or have certain finishes added, the test is not reliable. However, it is worth learning how common fibers burn if one realizes that the test may not always be accurate. A simple burning test can often provide a clue of how to care for a fabric.

Take a piece of fabric a few inches square. Hold it carefully with tweezers or two large coins to avoid having your fingers burned. Slowly bring the fabric to the flame of a candle which has been set in a metal plate or piece of metal foil to catch any flaming fabric that may drop. First notice if the fiber continues to burn when re-

moved from the flame or whether it goes out (is self-extinguishing). Carefully note the odor, type of flame, and residue. After you have practiced with a piece of cloth, learn to do the test with groups of warp yarns and groups of filling yarns as fabrics are often a combination of fibers. Compare with the chart which appears on opposite page.

You do not wear fibers but rather fabrics, which are made up of many, many fibers. Fibers are first made into yarns and then into cloth and finally may undergo many finishing processes.

A few fabrics are made directly from fibers and others are made directly from chemicals. You will read about this in Chapter Eleven.

COTTON

Cotton is like an old friend that we take for granted. Because we know it so well and see it so often, we forget how important it is in our lives. Cotton is the most widely used fiber

today, despite the development of man-mades. It is found in almost every type of clothing as well as household sheets, towels, and curtains.

History

Cotton was considered tree wool in the early ages of mankind. It was thought that cotton was a type of "lamb" that grew on shrubs and bent down in the wind to graze on the land. Alexander the Great is given credit for bringing the first cotton to Europe and North Africa from India, where it had been grown and spun on looms for at least 2,000 years. Today some of the best cotton is still grown in the Nile valley of Egypt.

When the Spaniards came to this country, they found the Pima Indians in the Southwest growing cotton. After the American Revolution, the Southeastern states in this country became an important cotton producing area. Most southern plantations grew small patches of this plant for their own use.

The most tedious chore in preparing cotton for yarn was removing the seeds from the cotton fibers. After Eli Whitney invented his cotton engine (or "gin") to do this job in 1793, it became possible to produce cotton commercially. Today much of the cotton is grown in the Southwest where the climate and ease of irrigation are favorable to plant growth.

NATIONAL COTTON COUNCIL

Close-up of a cotton boll.

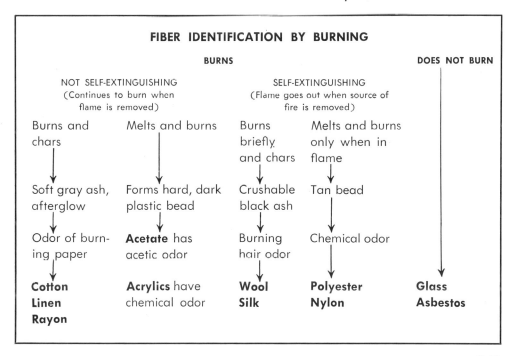

FIBER IDENTIFICATION BY BURNING

BURNS				DOES NOT BURN
NOT SELF-EXTINGUISHING (Continues to burn when flame is removed)		SELF-EXTINGUISHING (Flame goes out when source of fire is removed)		
Burns and chars ↓	Melts and burns ↓	Burns briefly and chars ↓	Melts and burns only when in flame ↓	
Soft gray ash, afterglow ↓	Forms hard, dark plastic bead ↓	Crushable black ash ↓	Tan bead ↓	
Odor of burning paper ↓	**Acetate** has acetic odor	Burning hair odor ↓	Chemical odor ↓	↓
Cotton **Linen** **Rayon**	**Acrylics** have chemical odor	**Wool** **Silk**	**Polyester** **Nylon**	**Glass** **Asbestos**

A mechanical picker harvesting cotton in a southern state.

4 feet high. When the blossom falls off after blooming, the seed pod or boll begins to grow. Inside the boll are seeds from which the fibers develop. When the boll is ripe, it splits open and fine white cotton hairs are ready to be picked, either by hand or by machine. Next it is sent to the cotton gin where the seeds and plant leaves are removed from the fibers. Cotton seeds are saved to be used for cottonseed oil and other products. The very short hairs, called linters, have many uses such as in the manufacture of rayon. (See page 375.)

After the fibers are cleaned, they are ready to be spun into yarn. The first major process is *carding*, which is much like combing one's hair. By this method the fibers are straightened by passing over a roller with metal teeth, and the very short fibers are removed. Cotton leaves the carding machine in a soft, untwisted rope called a *sliver*. Most of the fibers are then twisted into yarns and made into fabrics as described in Chapters Eight and Nine. Some long staple fibers go through an additional process called *combing*. This further straightens the fibers, combs out short ends, and makes the finished yarn smoother and more lustrous. See pictures of similar processing of flax fibers on page 354.

Varieties

There are many varieties of cotton, each serving a different purpose. Have you noticed the terms *Pima, Supima,* and *Egyptian* on labels of cotton fabrics? Each of these is the name of a *long staple* fiber. This means that the fibers are longer and finer than usual. They average between 1¼ and 2 inches in length and are also smoother and silkier than many other cotton fibers. The most common variety, *Upland,* which is used for most cotton articles, averages ½ to less than 1 inch in length.

Sources and Production

The cotton plant can be grown wherever long seasons of hot weather prevail. Today, leading producers are the United States, mainland China, southern Soviet Republic, and India. Some long-staple cotton is also grown in Egypt, Peru, and Brazil.

Cotton grows on bushes about 3 or

Properties

Cotton is classed as a cellulose fiber because it is derived from plant material. It has endless uses because of its good wearing qualities and its moderate cost.

- MICROSCOPIC APPEARANCE
  Each fiber has a natural twist. Short fibers can make strong yarns as the fibers tend to adhere together.

- BURNING BEHAVIOR
  Burns like paper, which is also cellulose. Will continue to burn when source of fire is removed. The odor is that of burning paper; there is a soft gray ash and an afterglow.

- STRENGTH
  Cotton is a reasonably strong fiber. It is not weakened by moisture.

- MOISTURE ABSORBENCY
  One of the major advantages of cotton is its absorbency. It will absorb water and other moisture such as perspiration. Therefore it does not make one feel clammy in warm weather. This quality is one of the reasons it is blended with man-made fibers. (Page 389.)

- NATURAL BODY
  Cotton is limp unless specially treated.

- RESILIENCY AND ELASTICITY
  Fabrics of cotton will wrinkle easily and need ironing after wear and laundering unless treated with a special finish.

- CONDUCTOR OF HEAT
  (This means that heat passes away from the body easily.) A fabric of cotton is comfortable in warm weather because it is a good conductor of heat.

- DIMENSIONAL STABILITY
  Shrinkage can be expected of all cotton cloth unless subjected to a shrinkage control process. Look for a label that tells you what the remaining shrinkage will be, not just that it has been preshrunk.

- WASHABILITY
  Fabrics of cotton can be easily washed in hot water with strong soaps. Bleach may be used on cloth that has not been resin treated. A hot iron can be used, but a very hot iron may scorch the fiber.

- STATIC ELECTRICITY
  Free from static electricity problems, cotton fabrics will not cling in cold, dry weather. Cotton clothes are safe for use in operating rooms and near oxygen tents as they do not generate sparks.

- SUSCEPTIBILITY TO MOTHS
      AND MILDEW
  Not affected by moths. Mildew will grow on cotton fabric if left moist in a warm place for a long time.

- OTHER PROPERTIES
  Cotton is weakened and will eventually disintegrate if exposed to strong sunlight. Perspiration and anti-perspirants can damage cotton, especially in the presence of heat. For this reason it is not wise to press a soiled garment.

Cotton bolls as they appear on the plant.
NATIONAL COTTON COUNCIL

Finishes

Several finishes have been developed that improve the appearance, hand or feel, and usefulness of cotton fabrics.

Mercerization is the process of soaking fabrics under tension in caustic soda, which results in less twist in the fibers so that more light is reflected. The yarns also become stronger, more lustrous, and easier to dye.

Sizing is a starch substance added to many cotton fabrics to give stiffness and gloss. This sizing may wash out and leave the fabric dull and sleazy. If a powdery substance falls from a cotton fabric when it is crumpled in your hand, it has probably

been oversized and will not hold up well.

Shrinkage control is possible for cotton fabrics to prevent excessive shrinking when washed. More than 2% shrinkage can seriously affect the fit of a garment. Sanforizing is a well-known process which guarantees that the fabric will not shrink more than 1%.

Napping is a process that raises the fiber ends. The fabric will feel warmer due to additional air spaces which hold in body heat. NOTE: Because cotton is not very resilient, the napping tends to flatten after use.

Easy-care finishes help cut down on wrinkling so that many cottons come out of the washing machine

Permanent press finishes added to 100 percent cotton may decrease fabric strength. As a result, cuffs and other places that receive considerable wear will fray more quickly than an untreated fabric. A consumer needs to decide when the ease of care gained is worth the shortened wear-life of the garment.

Cotton corduroy and cotton knit are used for comfortable, stylish sportswear.

The softness of cotton fabrics, their easy washability, and their comfort due to absorbency make cotton a first choice for little children's clothing.

needing little or no ironing. Many of these finishes are removed with excess heat, so washing should be done in luke-warm water. More details of these and other finishes applied to cotton fabrics are described in Chapter Twelve.

Care

Cotton does not need special care, as it is a sturdy fiber and can be washed easily. As noted, it should be protected from mildew. Fabrics with special finishes may be sensitive to chlorine bleach and high heat.

Uses

Cotton is a very versatile fiber. Cotton denim is used for heavy duty clothing and cotton batiste for the finest baby clothes. Voile is used for hot weather wear, and velveteen and corduroy for winter wear. Most children's and infants' clothing is made of the cotton fiber, as it can be washed easily. It is suitable for undergarments and sleepwear, as it is comfortable and absorbent. It takes colors well and may be glamorous enough for evening clothes or strong enough for utilitarian work clothes. Many man-made fibers are improved by the addition of cotton. See page 309. Many of the "paper" dresses are made from cotton or other cellulose products.

A fashion show of "paper" dresses (really non-woven cellulose fibers) is fun! Designs are as different as the idea of disposable dresses!

COTTON OR OTHER CELLULOSE FIBERS

Common fabrics made from cotton fibers are:

batiste	huckaback
birdseye	lawn
broadcloth	longcloth
calico	madras
cambric	muslin
canvas	nainsook
chambray	outing flannel
cheesecloth	percale
chintz	pique
cord	plissé crepe
denim	poplin
dotted Swiss	sailcloth
drill	sateen
duck	Tarpoon cloth
flannelette	terry cloth
gingham	ticking
Indian head	velveteen
	waffle cloth

These are described in Chapter Thirteen.

Secure a sample of a mercerized cotton fabric and one that has not been mercerized. Look at the fibers under a microscope as directed on page 345. How do they differ?

Experiment to determine whether cotton is strengthened or weakened by moisture. Take some cotton thread and moisten with your lips. Pull. Where does the thread break first? Repeat to be sure of your results. Do the same with yarns from a rayon fabric.

Prepare a bulletin board display on the cotton fiber. Secure a sample of a cotton boll if possible, and mount it with swatches of common cotton fabrics. Collect labels with terms that refer to cotton, such as Pima, combed, and others. Mount them with an explanation of the meaning of the terms.

LINEN

Now that you have read about cotton, you will discover that linen, another cellulose fiber, has many similar characteristics. However, it is not used as much as cotton for wearing apparel, as it is more expensive to produce and it cannot be used in as great a variety of fabrics.

History

Traces of treated flax have been found in pre-historic Stone Age ruins. The ancient Egyptians were the first to extract the long, tough fibers from the outer stem of the flax plant and to weave it into a fine cloth called linen. Egyptian mummies wrapped in linen fabrics can be seen in museums today.

In early days of the United States some linen was produced. The fabric, linsey-woolsey, was a combination of linen and wool, spun and woven by early colonists.

Sources and Production

Today, the flax plant is grown for fiber in Belgium, Ireland, U.S.S.R., Poland, Lithuania, and Germany. It is grown in the United States primarily for its seed, the source of linseed oil. A moderate climate with ample rainfall is needed for growing flax. Much of the linen grown in other parts of Europe is finished into fabric in Ireland, often called the linen capital of the world.

When flax is grown for fiber use,

Bundle of flax showing the seed pods from which linseed oil is made.

long. Very short fibers, called tow, are used only for less expensive fabrics.

The preparation of linen for spinning and weaving is a long and tedious process. In harvesting, the flax is pulled, never cut, as the fibers extend below the ground into the roots. The flax fibers must be separated from the stem by a process called *retting*. In the olden days this was done by spreading the flax bundles upon the ground and allowing the dew to act slowly on the plant. Today the plant is soaked in a special type of soft water to loosen the outer stalk. The stems are then dried and, by a process called *scutching*, rollers break and discard the useless, woody portions of the stalks, leaving exposed the long, smooth fibers.

the seeds are planted close together so the plant has no room to branch out and must grow tall to produce the long fiber which makes linen smooth. The fibers lie in bundles in the stem of the plant just under the bark. These must be loosened from the stalk before they can be combed to make ready for spinning. Most of the fibers are between 12 to 20 inches

The fibers are next *hackled*, a careful combing process, and finally arranged into a continuous broad ribbon called *sliver* for spinning. Once the purified fiber is obtained, the

The flax plant, which is sown in the spring and harvested in the summer, grows to a height of about 3 feet. Here you see the pulling of flax by hand. Although machines are being used on some farms, hand pulling still insures the longest unbroken fibers.

353

BELGIUM LINEN ASSN.

Here men are loading the bundles of flax into tanks filled with heated water. The soaking action loosens the outside flax fibers from the woody center stalk.

BELGIUM LINEN ASSN.

Either side of the River Lys in Belgium, piles of retted flax dry in the sunlight. In the concrete buildings the flax is retted (soaked) to loosen the outside fibers of the stalks for removal in processing.

BELGIUM LINEN ASSN.

The retting process finished, bundles of flax are stood upright in the fields and dried again—then retied and taken to be scutched, where rolls crush the straw separating the soft flax fibers from the harsh straw.

BELGIUM LINEN ASSN.

This combing machine draws flax over a series of teeth to separate waste, cleanse, and straighten the fibers. The pile of flax is ready to be fed into a machine where it travels from right to left to emerge as a wide "sliver."

process of making yarn is much like that used for other fibers, except that it must be kept damp constantly.

Because the natural color of linen is tan, it is usually bleached.

Properties

Linen is durable. It can be restored in appearance by washing and ironing. Its properties are similar to those of cotton, another cellulose fiber. Special characteristics are listed below:

- MICROSCOPIC APPEARANCE
  Flax fibers look like bamboo under the microscope. They have crosswise markings that appear like joints or nodes.

- FIBER STRENGTH
  Stronger than cotton, it is not affected by water. It is not elastic, so it may wear along folded lines.

- ELASTICITY AND RESILIENCY
  Linen is less elastic than cotton and therefore wrinkles easily. A crease-resistant finish is desirable.

- MOISTURE ABSORPTION
  Absorbs moisture even more readily than cotton. A good summer fiber because it feels cool.

- NATURAL BODY
  Good linen is crisp and leathery in feel and cool to the touch. Starching is seldom needed.

- WASHABILITY
  Washes like cotton except that it is best ironed quite damp with a hot iron.

Finishes

Beetling is a common finish for linen. The surface of the fabric is beaten

BELGIUM LINEN ASSN.

Emerging from the combing process, these long fiber wisps have passed over the series of graduated metal pins of the combing machine. A man gathers the glossy flax which now resembles switches of human hair.

IRISH LINEN GUILD

From flax to fabric—this picture shows the flax straw, the scutched or roughly combed fibers, and the fine smooth hackled fibers; the bleached yarn and finally the finished cloth.

with great wooden blocks which flatten the yarns so more light is reflected. The linen fabric therefore has great luster. Ironing on the right side maintains this luster.

Wrinkle-resistant treatments are common. Resin finishes cut down on moisture absorption and make the fabric warmer. However, most people prefer this to the usual wrinkling.

Shrinkage control treatments of several types are often applied to linen fabrics for clothing use.

Bleaching is necessary if white linens are desired. Bleaching always weakens a fabric somewhat, but linen is so strong that correct bleaching is not injurious.

Uses

Linen has many uses from the fine fabrics of church altar cloths to coarse, heavy crashes used for towels and slip covers. It is suitable for fine handkerchiefs, as it is smooth and can be easily washed and sterilized. Many summer dresses and suits are made of linen because it seems cool and comfortable.

Because linen is a moderately expensive fiber, a less expensive cloth made from cotton or rayon fibers resembling linen has been made. This rayon fabric with a special finish is often incorrectly called "butcher linen" and it does not wear as well.

Care

Linen needs no special care in washing and ironing as it is not affected by hot water or a hot iron.

• Most linen fabrics need to be ironed while quite damp on the wrong side, if a dull finish is desired. If a lustrous finish is preferred, iron on the right side.

Prepare a display for the linen fiber similar to that described for the cotton fiber on page 352.

Experiment to determine the effect of moisture on the linen fiber. Follow the directions on page 352.

• Linen will tend to crack and show wear along folds so it is best not to crease it sharply and to change the location of necessary creases from time to time.

Common fabrics made from linen fibers include batiste, crash, damask, huckaback, as described in detail in Chapter Thirteen.

Minor Cellulose Fibers

Perhaps you haven't heard of *jute, piña, hemp,* or *sisal,* but these are all cellulose fibers that are similar to cotton and linen.

COTTON INCORPORATED

Cotton and linen fabrics are especially suited for warm weather dresses as these fibers conduct heat away from the body, absorb perspiration so there is no clammy feel, and can be easily laundered.

Jute is used for making burlap, which has been fashionable for sportswear in some seasons. The fibers are taken from the jute plant much like linen is removed from the flax plant. Jute grows in many sub-tropical places but most of it comes from Pakistan. It is one of the cheapest textile fibers. It is not too strong, especially when wet. The rough texture makes it interesting for some types of clothes.

Piña would be a common fiber to you if you lived in the Philippines. Taken from the leaves of the pineapple plant, it makes sheer, lustrous fabrics. Dresses and shirts of piña are worn today for special occasions in the Philippines and some scarfs made of piña are sold in the United States. If you know anyone who has visited the Philippines, perhaps she can show you blouses or other articles made from this lovely fiber.

Talk with people who have lived or visited other countries. Do they have articles made from such interesting plant fibers as piña, hemp, or others uncommon to our country? Try to borrow them to bring to class. Take good care of them and return them promptly.

Using some references listed at the end of the book, list all the plant fibers used for clothing. Select one and prepare a report to the class.

Hemp and *sisal* are used largely for rope. These fibers grow in many parts of the world but the islands of the Caribbean and some African countries produce most today. Bags, summer play shoes, and occasionally belts and hats, as well as rugs, are made from these fibers.

WOOL

"Dyed in the wool," "All wool and a yard wide," "Don't let anyone pull the wool over your eyes," and similar expressions show how much wool is a part of our daily lives. Because wool is a protein fiber of animal origin, it has many properties which differ from those of the cellulose fibers.

History of Wool

No one knows when wool was first used for clothing but it was probably the first fiber that man learned to make into a fabric. At first early man draped the sheep skins over himself to provide warmth. Later he discovered that he could produce a fabric by matting the wool fibers together. By 3,000 B.C. the Babylonians were expert at spinning and weaving wool clothing. Sheep were especially valued during Biblical times as sources of both food and clothing as well as shelter, for tents were also made from wool fabrics.

In the early days of our country the British passed laws trying to force the colonists to buy wool fabrics from Britain. However, it was considered patriotic for the colonists to rebel and to make and wear their own woolen clothing. George Washington was inaugurated in a wool suit of American cloth.

Sources and Production

Almost every country in the world produces wool today, but the largest

Sheep grazing in the western United States.
PENDLETON WOOLEN MILLS

WOOL BUREAU, INC.

Machine shearing. The operator tries to get the entire coat off in one piece, which adds value to the fleece.

producers of wool for clothing are Australia, New Zealand, Union of South Africa, and the United States. (Wool used for carpets is a different type.) Wool is produced in every state in continental United States with Texas producing the largest amount. Because not enough wool is produced in this country to meet the needs of our people, it is necessary to import a large amount. Congress has enacted legislation which should encourage an increase in domestic wool production.

Wool is obtained from sheep, usually by shearing the live animal. Once or twice a year, depending upon the locality, trained shearers clip the fleece of the sheep so that it is kept in one piece. Some wool is obtained from animals raised for meat and is taken chemically from the skins after the animal is slaughtered. This wool, called *pulled wool*, is usually less alive and springy than fleece wool.

Experienced sorters judge the quality of wool from different sheep and different parts of the fleece. Notice how greasy the fleece looks as it comes directly from the sheep.

PENDLETON WOOLEN MILLS

Before being spun into yarn, the wool fiber is sorted, then scoured—a cleaning process which removes the natural oils or grease. This grease, called **lanolin,** is refined to be used in cosmetics. Wool is then carded, like cotton, and some long fibers are combed. The carding process straightens the fibers and lays them parallel so they can be spun into *woolen* yarns.

The longer fibers which will be used for *worsted* yarns are combed after carding. During this process, the fibers are straightened and the short fibers, called *noils,* are combed out. Yarns used for worsted fabrics are more tightly twisted than woolen yarns and result in fabrics which are smooth, firm textured, and lighter in weight than woolen fabrics.

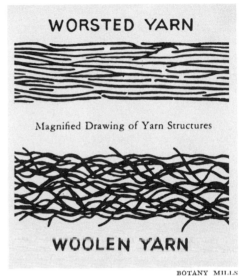

WORSTED YARN

Magnified Drawing of Yarn Structures

WOOLEN YARN

BOTANY MILLS

Woolen and worsted yarns under magnification. Notice how parallel the fibers are in the worsted yarn while the woolen yarn presents a fuzzier appearance.

Wool fibers passing through a detergent bath which removes the natural grease, a process called scouring.

PENDLETON WOOLEN MILLS

360

The fabric at the left, a combination of wool and nylon, was placed in an alkali solution. All the wool was dissolved, leaving the nylon as shown in the right hand picture.

The carding machine has rollers of sharp metal teeth. As the fibers are passed through the machine, the teeth straighten them and make them more nearly parallel.

PENDLETON WOOLEN MILLS

Wool Classification

Because there is not enough inexpensive wool to meet our needs, wool is *reclaimed* and used again. The Wool Products Labeling Act, passed in 1939, states that all wool fabrics must be classified into one of three types. This law affords some protection to the consumer but it does not offer any information about true quality.

Wool means that the fiber is being used for the first time in the manufacture of a wool product and that the fibers have not gone through any processes beyond the yarn spinning stage. The term *virgin wool* is a trade name that means that the wool has never been used in any way, not even converted into yarn. Noils resulting from the combing process may be used in new wool yarns but not in virgin wool.

Reprocessed wool is converted into a fibrous state from scraps and clips of never-worn woven and felted fabrics or from completed garments that did not sell for some reason. These fabrics are passed through a garnetting or shredding process which tears them down into fibers again.

Reused wool is made from fibers garnetted from fabrics that have been worn or used in some manner. It is commonly called shoddy.

Reused and reprocessed wool fibers show some evidence of damage in the garnetting process. Therefore they are not as springy and lifelike as when new. To cover their original colors, they are dyed a dark hue. This wool is suitable for garments that do not need to be soft and lovely. Many boys' jackets and camp blankets contain some reprocessed and reused wool.

Properties

Scientists, using X-ray techniques and special microscopes, have recently discovered that the wool fiber has an unusual structure which, under dry conditions, permits it to be extended when pull or pressure is put upon it and to return to its original form when the pull or pressure is released. Because of this, wool fabrics have unusual elasticity, resiliency, crease resistance, and abrasion resistance.

- MICROSCOPIC APPEARANCE
  The outer layers are a series of overlapping scales, like shingles on a house. These scales tend to hold the fibers together yet form tiny air spaces which act as insulators.

- BURNING BEHAVIOR
  Wool does not support combustion so, if the source of fire is removed, the flame will go out. It is a protein fiber and therefore has an odor of burning hair or feathers. A crushable black ash remains.

- MOISTURE ABSORPTION
  Wool is very absorbent. It can absorb up to 30% its weight and not feel wet. It also dries slowly. For this reason it is good for bathing suits and socks for athletes.

- ELASTICITY AND RESILIENCY
  A very resilient fiber, it bounces back to its original shape easily and therefore wrinkles hang out quickly. However, if wet, it will stretch and not return to shape. That is why wet garments must be handled with care.

- WASHABILITY
  Wool fabrics are subject to a unique type of shrinkage called felting. In

the presence of heat, moisture, and agitation, the scales tend to interlock and move in one direction. The fabric becomes smaller and the weave is less noticeable. This can occur each time the wool is subjected to these conditions. Therefore wool fabrics must be washed carefully in cool water with almost no agitation or rubbing. Many wool garments are better dry-cleaned.

• STATIC ELECTRICITY
Static electricity can be generated by wool but charges do not build up, as they are carried off by the moisture usually present in the fiber. Wool fabrics seldom cling in cold, dry weather, and dust particles can be brushed away.

• FIBER STRENGTH
The wool fiber is weak but wool fabrics are strong because of wool's resistance to abrasion and flexibility. However, wet wool is quite weak and must be handled with care.

• SENSITIVITY TO MOTHS
Moths and some beetles are attracted to wool fabrics and will eat the fiber. When buying wool fabrics, it is well to insist on mothproof finishes.

• SENSITIVITY TO CHEMICALS
Wool is fairly stable to acids but it is harmed by alkalies. Strong soap should not be used and fabrics should be well rinsed.

Almost all wool fabrics go through a *fulling* process in which heat, moisture, and pressure are carefully applied, causing the fibers to interlock and expand. The fabric shrinks a controlled amount from the woven size

PENDLETON WOOLEN MILLS

Wool fabrics undergoing a fulling process. Heat, moisture, and pressure are carefully applied to the fabric to "full" it or shrink it a controlled amount. This process closes in the weave and makes the fabric appear more compact. This man is measuring to determine if fulling has been completed.

and the weave closes in. The resulting fabric has a more finished appearance. Fabrics like meltons are heavily fulled, whereas challis is only slightly fulled.

Many wool fabrics are *napped* so that the tiny woolen fibers are raised from the surface of the fabric. This results in a warmer cloth which has a different appearance and feel. NOTE: Napped surfaces may show wear around buttonholes and sleeve edges, but the fabric is still strong.

Processes which make wool easily *washable* are in the development stage. Wool has been blended with other fibers for this reason, but now some all-wool fabrics can be made washable. Be sure to read labels carefully, as most woolens do not have this finish.

363

The wool fiber was selected for this pants suit because it tailors well, sheds wrinkles, and provides adequate warmth for autumn walks.

Care

Although wool is a long wearing, sturdy fiber, it does need special care. It does not soil readily but, when it does, the scales hold onto dust and odors. Woolen garments should be brushed and aired occasionally. They should be cleaned with care—either dry-cleaned or washed with mild soap in lukewarm water and with almost no agitation. Chlorine bleaches should not be used and soaps should be rinsed out well, as wool is sensitive to chlorine and alkali. It is also apt to sag when damp; therefore it is important to hang woolens on proper hangers.

Wool does stretch more than some fibers and tightly fitted skirts should

be lined with a firm fabric such as acetate taffeta to prevent the "back bulge." This same property makes it tailor easily. You will read more about sewing with wool in Chapter 17.

Uses

Wool is especially valued for its warmth and for its ability to take wear without noticeable wrinkling. For these reasons it is extensively used for coats, suits, skirts, winter dresses, pants, sweaters, scarfs, and mittens. Some lightweight wools are now being worn in the summer. Hats are often made from wool felt.

Common fabrics made from wool fibers are:	
bouclé	gabardine
broadcloth	jersey
challis	melton
covert	serge
felt	sharkskin
flannel	tweed
fleece	whipcord
zibeline	
These are described in Chapter Thirteen.	

Wool skirts, sweaters, pants, and jumpers worn with cotton blouses are almost a national uniform for school girls.

Prepare a display of the wool fiber as described on page 352.

Look at samples of the wool fiber under the microscope. Compare with samples of your own hair. Why is there a similarity?

Collect labels from fabrics that are made from new wool, virgin wool, reprocessed wool, and reused wool. Make a poster explaining the meaning of each term.

Wool and wool blends can be identified with the use of a strong alkali such as lye. With your teacher's supervision, place one tablespoon of lye in one pint of water in a glass or enamel pan. Heat to boiling, being very careful not to inhale the fumes. Place samples of fabrics containing all wool, no wool, and part wool in the solution. After a few minutes, use tongs to remove the fabrics. Notice how the wool is entirely disintegrated, after becoming slick and jelly-like at first. In a blend, the wool will dissolve and the other fibers will remain. The color of non-wool fabrics may change but the fibers are not affected. Rinse any residue carefully, using vinegar to help neutralize the alkali.

Wet a yarn of silk or wool with household chlorine bleach. These fibers turn yellow and after a while disintegrate from the action of the chemical. Compare with the effect on cotton or linen yarns.

Specialty Wools

Glamour or luxury wool fabrics are made from fibers such as *vicuna, cashmere, guanaco, camel, llama,* and *alpaca.* Their luxury stems from the fact that they are rare—coming from richly coated animals that live in such exotic places as the mountains of South America, India, Mongolia, and Tibet. Fabrics made from these fibers as well as those from the angora goat may be correctly labeled "wool," but usually they are called by their specific names because of prestige value.

The hair from almost any animal can be used as a fiber and made into fabrics but many hairs are not strong enough or pliable enough to be twisted into yarn. Raccoon, rabbit, deer, and other hair in small amounts is often added to wool fabrics for surface interest but has little effect on wearing qualities.

Goat Fibers

Goat hair is the most common of the specialty wools. Two members of the goat family produce fibers that make lovely fabrics—the angora goat which produces mohair and the cashmere goat which produces the cashmere fiber.

Mohair refers to the long fibers from the angora goat, so called because it has been produced in Angora, Turkey, for many centuries. Actually most of the mohair comes from goats raised in Texas. This fiber is long wearing with considerable luster but it needs special care. It is very resilient and is often blended with wool or other fibers to add wrinkle resistance. Because of its luster, texture, and ability to be dyed clear colors, it is used for high style sweaters and suitings.

Cashmere, one of the softest fibers to touch, comes from goats grown in Mongolia and Iran. Mongolia produces the finer quality. The finest cashmere garments are made from the soft underhairs of the goat but those from the coarse outer hairs may also be labeled cashmere. Therefore the term "cashmere" does not always indicate quality. True cashmere is a luxury fabric that cannot stand very much abrasion. It is not suitable for a coat that will be given any rough wear.

Camel Fibers

Many fabrics today are called "camel's hair" simply because they are the natural tan color of the camel, but true camel's hair comes from the Bactrian or two-hump camel that lives in Mongolia and Tibet. The hair is collected by a man who follows the camel caravans, picks up the hair that is shed, and places it on a basket carried by the last camel. In the morning he also gathers what the camels have shed while sleeping. Some of it is soft and lovely and some coarse. Therefore we have many types of camel's hair. It is especially valued for its warmth and light weight. A good quality coat of camel's hair will wear a long time.

Llama Fibers

The llama family of South America includes the alpaca, llama, guanaco, and vicuna. All these fibers are very expensive because of their rarity.

Collect articles made from specialty wools to show to the class.

Try to compare prices of the various specialty wool fibers. If there is a large store near you, price coats of comparable quality of wool, cashmere, camel's hair, and other fibers available. You may also do this with yard goods. Perhaps a store buyer can help you.

Vicuna and guanaco. Considered the world's most expensive fiber, vicuna often sells for more than $100 a yard. The price is due to the fact that the vicuna lives high, high in the Andes Mountains and is so difficult to capture that usually the animal must be killed in order to obtain the fleece. The diameter of the fiber is about half that of sheep's wool, so it is very fine and very soft.

The guanaco is a similar animal but less well known. Fabrics from both vicuna and guanaco fibers cannot take hard wear.

Llama and alpaca. Both the llama and alpaca also live in the Andes Mountains. Because of their warmth the Indians of South America use both fibers for ponchos, blankets, and rugs. Sweaters and mittens imported into the United States are valued for their warmth and interesting texture.

SILK

Silk has limited use today because of its cost and the development of many man-made fibers, but no other fiber has its luxurious appearance and feel.

History

The history of silk is fascinating. The

International Silk Association relates that silk was probably discovered by a teen-ager, a 14-year-old Chinese empress named Hsi-Ling-Shi. While walking in the garden one day she spied a small white cocoon growing on a mulberry bush. She brought the

Queen Elizabeth went "all out" in demanding silk and lace for her garments.

cocoon to her rooms and while examining it she accidentally dropped it into a basin of hot water. Suddenly a wispy filament began to unwind from the cocoon. Drawing it into the air, she found an incredibly slender strand of seemingly endless length. She thought this strange substance would make a beautiful robe. She called in the court weaver who gathered other cocoons and made the first silk fabric.

This was in 2,640 B.C. For nearly 3,000 years after that China was able to keep the secret of "sericulture," the cultivation of silk worms, and so monopolized the silk trade. Later, silkworm eggs were smuggled to Japan and the fiber became a success there. It is reported that silk finally arrived in Europe through two monks who, at the risk of their lives, smuggled out a supply of silkworm eggs in the handle of a hollow cane.

For many years silk was costly and was worn only by nobility. The Greeks wove their finest togas of silk. During Julius Caesar's reign it was almost worth its weight in gold. The royalty of Europe traditionally wore silk garments. Later the American colonists wore it as a status symbol.

During World War II almost no silk was available in the United States so that women became used to other fibers but after the war they again preferred silk for fine clothes. Stockings of silk, however, never regained their popularity.

Japan is still the leading producer of raw silk because mulberry trees grow well in its mild climate and the best quality silk comes from worms fed only on mulberry leaves. Silk is also grown in China, Italy, India, Korea, Turkey, and Brazil. No raw silk is produced in the United States due to the high cost of labor.

Silk is a filament spun by the silkworm when it is preparing its cocoon. When the *bombyx mori*, a medium sized moth, lays her silkworm eggs, they are about the size of a pinhead. Soon after a silkworm hatches from the egg into a caterpillar, it is fed its first mulberry meal. The silkworm eats continuously, day and night, until it is 10,000 times its original weight. (A lot of time and work is required to chop up the mulberry leaves for the worms.)

When the worm is about a month old it stops eating and moves its head back and forth, showing that it is ready to spin a cocoon. Twigs or grasses are provided, and it soon begins to spin. Below its mouth are two tiny holes. As the worm moves its body back and forth, the fluid is forced out of these tiny openings.

PHILADELPHIA COMMERCIAL MUSEUM

A silkworm on a twig.

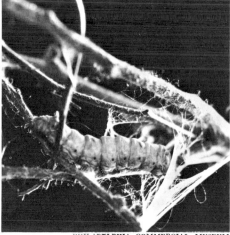

PHILADELPHIA COMMERCIAL MUSEUM

Here the worm is beginning to spin his cocoon, from which silk is made.

Upon reaching the air the filaments, or fibroin, are covered with a gummy substance, sericin, which holds them together. The worm spins the filaments at the rate of from 9 to 12 inches a minute, and the entire length of the continuous strand may be from 800 to 1,500 yards. It requires the worm about three days, moving its body back and forth in a figure-eight motion, to complete the cocoon.

After about two weeks of residing in the cocoon, the worm is transformed into a moth ready to come

out. If it emerges, it makes damaging holes in the silken cocoon. At this stage it is killed with hot water or dry heat, unless it is needed for reproduction.

The cocoons are placed in warm water so they will become soft and easy to reel. The single filament is too fine to use as a yarn so several cocoons are unreeled together. This formerly was done by hand but today most reeling is done by machines.

• When two silkworms set up housekeeping together, they produce a heavy yarn with slubs called *dupioni.*

• In some places, uncultivated silkworms live on oak leaves. The silk from these worms is called wild silk or *tussah,* a strong fiber which makes a rugged, rough-appearing cloth.

Spun silk is made from broken cocoons and other short lengths. It produces a fabric of good wearing quality but it is without luster and may become fuzzy with use. Often it is made into fabrics with the appearance of linen.

Because the silk fiber is really a yarn when created, it requires fewer processes at the factory than do wool or cotton. Many filaments are twisted together, depending upon the desired size of the finished yarn. The natural gums have to be boiled off so that the luster of the silk can be seen and the softness felt. In doing this, some of the weight of the silk is lost.

For many years it was customary to add metallic salts to the fabric to replace the weight loss, but this often resulted in a weak fabric with poor wearing qualities. In the United States, the Federal Trade Commission requires that any silk that contains more than 10% of weighting (15%, if black) must be so labeled.

368

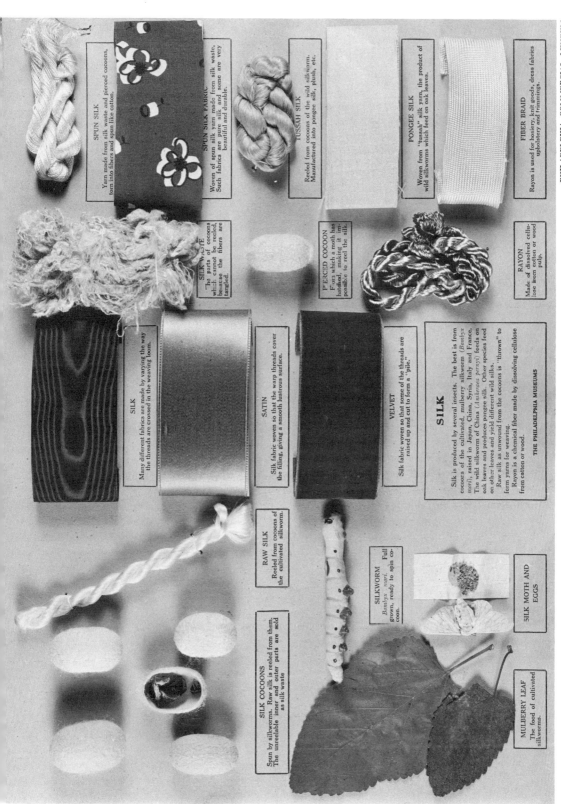

A chart showing the origin of silk and stages in transforming it to various typical fabrics.

Therefore any fabric labeled *all silk,* *pure silk,* or *pure dye silk* does not have excessive weighting. (The weighting is added with the dye and thus this term "pure dye"; it has nothing to do with the quality of the dye!)

Properties

Silk is more expensive than other fibers except the exotic fleeces. Reeled silk is smooth and lustrous, while spun, tussah, and dupioni silks are duller and more irregular in appearance. Silk is similar to wool in many ways, as both are protein fibers.

- MICROSCOPIC APPEARANCE
  The silk fiber appears as a straight, smooth, hollow cylinder. Silk fibers tend to shed dirt easily. The smooth yarns also tend to fray easily in fabrics.

- BURNING BEHAVIOR
  Burns like wool—another protein fiber—although often faster, as it is usually a finer yarn. Smells like hair and leaves tiny, crushable black beads. Weighted silk burns slowly and leaves the shape of the cloth due to the metallic content.

- STRENGTH
  Silk is a very strong fiber but, because it is usually made into fine materials, needs to be treated with care. It is weakened with age, sunlight, and perspiration.

- ABSORBENCY
  Very absorbent, like wool.

- WASHABILITY
  Silk itself is washable but fabrics are often made in such a way that dry-cleaning is necessary. Dyes used on silk are not always fast to washing.

- OTHER PROPERTIES
  Silk can be weakened by sunlight within a few months' exposure. Perspiration fades silk. It is a lightweight fiber. Age yellows white silk. It is not eaten by moths.

Common fabrics made from silk fibers are:

bengaline	organza
brocade	peau de soie
China silk	pongee
chiffon	satin
crepe	shantung
damask	surah
faille	taffeta
moiré	tussah
foulard	velvet

These are described in Chapter Thirteen.

Scarfs are often made from silk because of its luxurious, smooth feel and the manner in which it takes dyes so beautifully. This silk scarf is used for a turban effect.

370

BEST FOODS DIVISION CPC INT.

The scrunch method of dyeing a fabric was used for this silk satin blouse. The damp fabric was bunched into a bundle, secured with several rubber bands at random, and dyed in lukewarm water, suitable for silk fiber.

Finishes

Some *weighting* of silk does not seem to harm the fiber and does improve the hand and body of fabrics used for certain purposes. Overweighting weakens the fiber.

Many silk fabrics that are to be made into stiff cloths, such as taffeta, undergo a treatment which makes them crisp. This is called *scroop*.

Some silks water-spot but it is possible to buy fabrics today with a finish that is spotproofed against water.

Uses

Wedding dresses are traditionally made from silk fabrics as are many evening and cocktail-type gowns. Men's ties and women's scarfs are also made from silk as the colors have a lovely sheen and the fiber is resilient enough that knots do not make permanent creases.

Care

As a luxury fabric, silk should be treated with care. Preferably it should be dry-cleaned. If it is hand-washed, use lukewarm water and no chlorine bleach. Press with a slightly warm iron. Wild or tussah silks can be machine washed, as they usually make quite strong fabrics.

Prepare a display of the silk fiber as described on page 352.

MAN-MADE FIBERS

No one knows when man first began to dream of making a fiber that he could control. Natural fibers are subject to insects, windstorms, droughts, and other weather problems that man can do little about. As early as 1664 Robert Hooke wrote of the possibility of making artificial silk. By 1840 a crude spinneret had been made. This is a metal device, like a shower nozzle, with tiny holes through which the fiber forming substance can be pushed. Many men worked hard to develop a practical man-made fiber but Count Hilaire de Chardonnet is given credit for actually perfecting the process. At the Paris Exposition in 1889, where it was demonstrated, a famous chemist, Edwin Slosson, said, "At last man has risen to the level of the worm and can spin threads to suit himself." By 1910 a factory was started in the United States at Marcus Hook, Pa.

In the early stages of the development of this new fiber, the producers and general public thought that it had the characteristics of silk. As a result, it was called artificial silk. But it was a poor substitute for silk. It could be made into long filaments like silk but it was very shiny, did not have the feel of silk, and was different in many other ways. In 1919 silk was selling for $20 a pound while the new inexpensive fiber had been reduced to less than $3 a pound. When it did not appear as lovely as silk, many people thought it was a cheap imitation and an inferior product. Finally it was decided that the fiber needed a name of its own so that it would be appreciated for its own good points. In 1925 the Federal Trade Commission officially recognized the name "rayon."

When an acetate fiber was later developed, it was called acetate rayon —not because it was just like rayon but because it was also a man-made fiber. Consumers, not realizing that each fiber had very distinctive qualities, tried to treat rayon and acetate fabrics alike and were disappointed. Finally in 1952 the Federal Trade Commission realized that there would be many new fibers on the market and all could not be called rayon. As a result, they ruled that acetate should no longer be termed "rayon"; however, many people still confuse the two fibers.

In 1938 the Du Pont Company produced another new fiber called nylon. Everyone was excited about it as hosiery made from it was much sheerer and wore much longer.

Since World War II innummerable new fibers have been developed and more are yet to come. For some time it was felt that the new fibers were in competition with the older natural fibers, but they are really "complementers," not "competitors," as each has desirable qualities. The advent of new fibers has not reduced the quantity of natural fibers used, as the expanding population has caused an increased demand for all textiles.

The new man-made fibers do not duplicate all the desirable qualities of the natural fibers. The trend appears to be an increased use of blends in varying proportions for the best end use. (See page 389.)

Manufacture

Man-made fibers are of two types: (1) regenerated fibers and (2) truly synthetic fibers. *Regenerated* fibers are those made from natural fibrous substances such as cotton linters or wood pulp. The man-made fiber has

The raw material for man-made fibers is made into a liquid of viscous consistency before being forced through a spinneret.

the same chemical composition as the fibrous substances, but a different physical form. For example, rayon has the same chemical characteristics as the cotton and wood pulp from which it is made, but differs physically. *Synthetic* fibers are made from chemicals obtained from coal, air, water, sulphur, and/or natural gas.

By complicated processes, the raw materials are transformed into a liquid that is thick and syrupy. Then it is forced through a spinneret to form fibers. As the liquid comes from the spinneret in fine streams, it is hardened, either by air or a chemical bath, into a fiber. The filaments may be twisted together to form a continuous filament yarn or cut into short lengths and spun like cotton or wool.

Just as the length of a man-made fiber can be controlled, so can its thickness and shape.

FMC CORP., AMERICAN VISCOSE DIV.

Comparison of spinnerets used for filament fibers and tow from which short staple fibers are made. The smaller jet is for filament yarn and the large jet is for producing staple fibers.

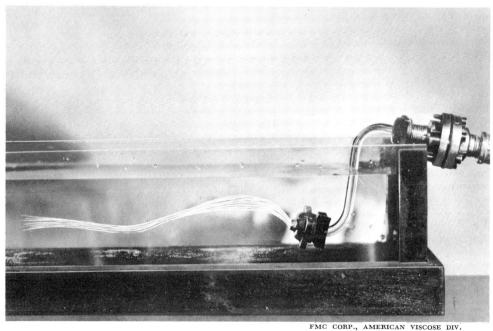

FMC CORP., AMERICAN VISCOSE DIV.

A viscose solution being forced through a spinneret into a sulphuric acid bath where it solidifies into fibers.

373

Filaments of yarn are collected as they emerge from the coagulating bath.

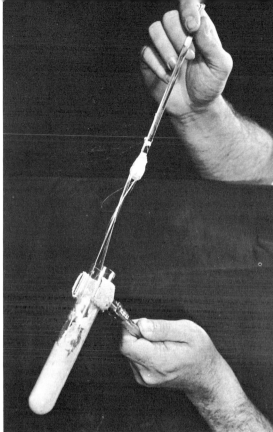

Here, in its most elementary form, is the "birth" of a man-made fiber in a research chemist's test tube.

Varying the size holes in the spinneret and the speed at which the solution is pushed through can result in fine or thick yarns. Other methods control the shape of the yarn. Crystal acetate is an example of this. It is a flat fiber forced through a narrow slit rather than through a round hole.

While the fiber is still in the liquid state, coloring materials may be added as well as chemicals which control luster. The dyeing, called *solution* or *dope* dyeing, results in color-fast fabrics.

Rayon—A Man-made Cellulose Fiber

The first fiber made by man was a regenerated cellulose—rayon. Even though man-made, it is classified as a cellulose fiber because its characteristics are similar to cotton and linen. Since its early stages of development, rayon has been improved in many ways. Now it can be made bright or dull or with any degree of luster desired. It can be made into long filaments like silk or cut into short, uniform lengths like cotton and wool and then spun into yarn. The fibers can be thick or thin, or thick *and* thin; some yarns resemble the natural thick and thin linen yarn and also dupioni silk. One type of rayon is strong enough for tire cords but this cannot be made soft enough for clothing. Other rayons are delicate enough to make the sheerest fabric.

374

Rayon can be made into thick and thin yarns that have the appearance of linen at lower cost. Special finishes keep the rayon crisp. This pants suit of rayon has a washable print blouse that will be comfortable due to its absorbency.

In use, rayon is the second major fiber in the world because of its low cost and versatility.

Source and Production of Rayon

A regenerated cellulose fiber means that it is cellulose in a different physical but the same chemical form. Most rayon in the United States today is made by the *viscose* process. Wood pulp or cotton linters are soaked in caustic soda and treated with other chemicals so the liquid can be forced through the holes of a spinneret into a bath of sulphuric acid which hardens the newly formed fibers. For smooth appearing fabrics, the filaments are wound directly on bobbins or cones. For cotton or wool-like fabrics, the filaments are cut into short lengths and spun into yarn much like those fibers.

Cuprammonium is another process which is similar to viscose, but usually results in a finer yarn.

Other more recently developed rayons are *polynosic* and *high-modulus*. Common trade names are Avril and Zantrel: These do not shrink or stretch in laundering and have a fine, silky feel. They are stronger than regular rayons. In many ways they are similar to cotton.

Properties

As said before, rayon is similar to cotton in properties, with a few exceptions.

- MICROSCOPIC APPEARANCE
  The fiber appears like a smooth rod. Therefore fibers tend to shed dirt easily and yarns will fray unless made from staple lengths and into spun rayon fabrics.

- BURNING BEHAVIOR
  Burns fast like other cellulose fibers, with an odor of paper and a soft, gray ash.

- STRENGTH
  Most rayons are moderately strong when dry but are weaker when wet. They need care during washing. (High modulus rayons are strong and not weakened by moisture.)

- RESILIENCY
  Wrinkles easily, so needs special finishing treatments.

- WASHABILITY
  May be washed like other cellulose fibers except some rayons lose strength when wet and need a short cycle when washed by machine. May be dried at any temperature and pressed with a medium-hot iron (almost as hot as for cotton). Will shrink unless given a shrink-resistant finish.

Burn samples of cotton and rayon yarns. Do you notice how similar they react? Now do the wet test described on page 352. Why are the results different this time for cotton and rayon fibers?

A *shrinkage control* finish is desirable, as rayons absorb moisture and can either shrink or stretch while wet. The polynosic and high modulus rayons are more dimensionally stable than the regular rayons and therefore do not shrink or stretch noticeably.

Wrinkle-resistant finishes are used to add body as well as to improve resistance to wrinkling and to minimize ironing.

Uses

Rayon is often known as the great imitator since it can be made to resemble fabrics of silk, cotton, linen, and wool. It is often blended with other man-made fibers to add absorbency, to cut cost, and because of the way it takes certain dyes so beautifully. Most "paper" fabrics are made from rayon fibers. New uses are expected as research continues.

ACETATE AND TRIACETATE

Developed about the same time as rayon, acetate, as previously noted, was called acetate rayon until 1952, when the Federal Trade Commission recognized that it had a different chemical composition and properties and ruled that it should not be called rayon but acetate. Triacetate was introduced in 1954 to serve slightly different needs, as it can be more easily washed. (Arnel is a trade name.)

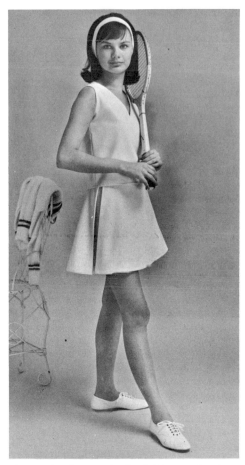

A tennis dress of sharkskin made from Arnel, a triacetate fiber. The short V-neck blouse and the inverted side pleats make it functional as well as attractive. The traditional tennis sweater is probably made from acrylic yarns which are readily washable.

Source and Production

Acetate is made from cellulose materials such as wood pulp, but the manufacturing process results in a fiber that is chemically different from rayon. The cellulose is combined with acetic acid to create a new chemical compound, cellulose acetate. When a solvent, acetone, is added, the cellulose acetate dissolves into a honey-like consistency, ready to be forced through the holes of a tiny spinneret. Fine filaments are produced and twisted together, then wound on a bobbin in the form of yarn.

Properties

Acetate is a thermoplastic fiber. This means that it is sensitive to heat. When it was new, many women did not realize this and found that a hot iron made the fabric soften, glaze, and even fuse and develop holes. It differs from newer thermoplastic fibers because it is not as strong but it is more absorbent.

- BURNING BEHAVIOR
  Continues to burn when removed from source of flame. May actually melt. Has a vinegar or acetic acid odor. Forms a hard, black plastic bead.

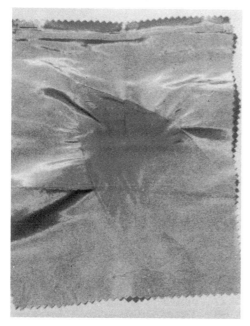

Effect of a hot iron on a heat-sensitive fabric.

- FIBER STRENGTH
  Not too strong, lacks abrasion resistance. For this reason it is considered a "beauty" fiber. Is weaker wet than dry.

- MOISTURE ABSORBENCY
  Absorbs less moisture than cellulose and protein fibers but more than other thermoplastics. Because of this it is less likely to shrink, will dry more quickly, and is more resistant to soiling than cellulose and protein fibers, but less than other thermoplastics.

- EFFECT OF ACETONE
  Acetone is a solvent. Fingernail polish remover which contains acetone will cause holes if spilled on any acetate fabric.

- COLOR FASTNESS
  Blue and green dyes on acetate fabrics will often fade due to gases in the air. Solution dyed fabrics, discussed on page 420, are permanently colorfast.

Triacetate was developed to serve needs other than acetate. It is stronger, can withstand higher temperatures, and is less likely to shrink or stretch. Originally used for tennis dresses because it washes well, stays white, and has a good body, it is well liked for knitted fabrics and many other easy-care garments.

Care

Clothing made of acetate should be hand washed in lukewarm water and rinsed well. Press on the wrong side while damp, with the iron at a low setting. Triacetate fabrics can be machine laundered and bleached if necessary. They can stand ironing at higher temperatures, preferably on

Experiment with the effect of acetone on acetate fabrics. Acetone may be obtained from any drugstore. Place some on a flat dish. Place a sample of a fabric that you know is acetate in the dish. Does it start to feel slick and then dissolve? Now place a sample of cotton or a rayon fabric in acetone. What effect do you notice? Try to test a sample of a combination of acetate and rayon fibers.

Determine the effect of a hot iron on acetate and rayon fibers. Select a sample such as taffeta. Set the iron control for "low" and test it on the acetate sample. Keep increasing the temperature until the fabric starts to "stick." Now determine how much hotter the iron can be before any damage is done to the rayon fabric.

the wrong side. Many acetate garments should be drycleaned.

Uses

Considered the beauty fiber, acetate has a pleasing hand and drape so it is often used for evening gowns and party frocks.

Triacetate is especially popular for jersey dresses, for travel wear, for summer pleated skirts, and other easy-care needs.

MAN-MADE SYNTHETIC FIBERS

The newer man-made synthetic fibers such as nylons, acrylics, modacrylics, polyesters, spandex, and olefins are similar in many ways. Characteristics common to these fibers will be listed here. Differences will

be discussed in the section on each specific fiber.

These fibers are *thermoplastic* or *heat-sensitive*. This means:

• They will glaze or melt from too much heat. Hot irons and hot dryers should not be used. Even a spark from a cigarette or match may cause a hole to develop.

• They can be heat set to hold embossed designs, creases, and durable pleats. Heat setting will also stabilize a fabric so it will not shrink or stretch, and knit garments will not need blocking.

These fibers are also *hydrophobic*, a word that means "water hating." Because of this, fabrics made from these fibers have the following characteristics:

• They do not absorb water or moisture so are quick to dry.

• They feel clammy and uncomfortable in humid weather.

• They build up static electricity charges which may cause fabrics to cling in cold, dry weather and attract lint and dust particles.

• They allow such stains as mud to be washed off easily. However, grease and oil stains are difficult to remove as the fabrics do not absorb the water which carries soap or a soil-removing agent.

• They require little or no ironing after wear and laundering.

• They are as strong wet as dry.

In addition, all these man-made fibers are resistant to moths and mildew. They are light in weight, yet are strong and long wearing. There is a tendency to pill, which is a balling up of tiny fiber ends on the surface of a fabric. They may discolor from heat, and gray due to static electricity holding onto soil particles.

Care of Man-made Synthetic Fabrics
The care of fabrics is discussed in detail in Chapter Seven. However, it is helpful to review a few of the major requirements for wise care. Most fabrics made from synthetic fibers are strong and can be machine washed with lukewarm and dried in the shade or tumble dryed at medium heat. Remove from the dryer when almost dry to prevent heat wrinkles from developing. High temperatures may set wrinkles which are hard to remove.

Bleach can be used in the correct amount, with the exception of spandex fabrics which are weakened by chlorine bleaches.

Because these fibers do not absorb water but do absorb oils, grease and oil stains are difficult to remove. Such stains should be pre-treated before laundering by applying liquid detergent directly onto the soiled spot, by rubbing in a paste made from powdered detergent, or by using a cleaning fluid before washing.

White fabrics, especially nylons, have a tendency to absorb other colors and should be washed only with other white garments. Thorough rinsing is necessary to remove soil and detergents and to prevent graying. An anti-static rinse or the use of a fabric softener in the last rinse will cut down on static problems and delay the accumulation of dust and lint.

NYLON—THE FIRST SYNTHETIC FIBER

With the advent of nylon, for the first time man could take plentiful raw materials and, through chemical processes, form long chain polymers to make synthetic fibers. A simple definition of a polymer is a long chain of molecules. Nylon is heat-sensitive and its properties are similar to other thermoplastics.

History
In 1939 the first nylon hosiery for women was marketed in limited quantities. Women found them to be stronger and sheerer than the silk hosiery they had been wearing. During World War II the supplies of nylon were sufficient only for military needs. Parachutes were made of nylon as were tents and many garments. After the war when nylon hose came on the market again, women were almost frantic to obtain them. Ask your mother about "nylon lines." Hours before opening time people would line up outside any store where it was expected that nylon hose would be sold. As the stockings were usually limited to one pair to a customer, women would enlist their husbands and children to stand in line with them. If their size was sold out when they finally reached the counter, they would buy any size available, as they knew some friend would be delighted to have them.

Since then nylon has become plentiful and is in demand for clothing and industrial uses. Today it is made by many companies throughout the world. In Germany it is called Perlon; in Great Britain it is called Bri-nylon, and in Mexico, Nyfil.

Source and Production
The term "nylon" refers to a whole group of fibers, not just one. Nylon is the generic term applied by the Federal Trade Commission for a group of protein-like chemical fibers. The method of fabrication depends upon

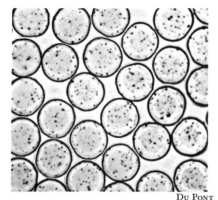

DU PONT
Cross section of conventional nylon.

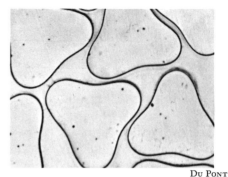

DU PONT
Cross section of Antron nylon (magnified 500 times). Because of the tri-lobal shape which is different from the usual round shape, Antron fabrics are more opaque and have a softer touch.

the intended use. The chemical elements present in petroleum, air, water, and natural gas are combined to form a nylon polymer which is processed in molten form and then pumped through a spinneret, air cooled, and solidified into filaments Nylon can be made into both filament and short, staple lengths. Of course, it can also be drawn in different fiber shapes. The original nylon had a cross section that was round but a new nylon called *antron,* has a trilobal shape. Because of this, antron is more opaque and has a more silk-like feel than regular nylon.

Properties

Like all thermoplastic fibers, nylon is lightweight and gives long wear, easy care, quick drying, wrinkle resistance, shrink resistance, moth and mildew resistance, and pleat and crease retention. It is especially valued for its unusual strength, its resistance to abrasion, and its light weight. Special characteristics are listed below.

- BURNING BEHAVIOR
  Nylon does not flame up but appears to melt. The odor is a chemical one. Hard, tan bead remains.

- STRENGTH
  One of the strongest of all fibers, it also has exceptional resistance to abrasion.

- EFFECT OF SUNLIGHT
  Nylon is weakened by sunlight. Should be dried in tumble dryer or in shade.

- SENSITIVITY TO CHEMICALS
  Not affected by most chemicals but sensitive to sulphuric acid which is present in soot and gases from chimneys. Specks of soot can cause holes in nylon fabrics.

Uses

Nylon is the leading yarn for lingerie and hosiery, as it is strong, sheer, stretches and returns to shape, and dries easily. Because of its strength and ability to be made into warm, windproof fabrics, it is used for ski clothes. Its strength and quick drying properties make it ideal for swimwear. It is often blended with other fibers to add abrasion resistance. Only a small amount blended with wool or cashmere can improve the wear at such stress points as sleeve edges, buttonholes, and collars.

380

This fragile looking robe is made from sturdy nylon yarns and maintains its appearance with easy washing and no ironing needed. (Notice the healthful midnight snack this wise teen enjoys.)

Care

Nylon needs little special care and should be machine washed, unless made into fabrics with delicate trim. Because of its heat sensitivity, it should not be subjected to hot water or high dryer heat. It is a so-called scavenger of colors, so it should be washed with only white fabrics. See page 262, Chapter 7, on ways to keep it from graying.

ACRYLICS

Orlon, Acrilan, and Creslan are trade names of acrylic fibers now on the market in this country.

History

The first acrylic fiber, trade-named Orlon and developed by the Du Pont Company, was produced in 1950. Since then others have been produced by different companies and the Du Pont Company has introduced special forms of Orlon such as Sayelle. Early acrylic fibers were difficult to dye so often were used only in pastel colors or blended with other fibers. Today most colors are available.

Production

Acrylics are so named because they are made from acrylonitrile, a chemical substance. Much like other man-made fibers, the semi-liquid chemical mixture is forced through a spinneret and hardened into filaments. Most acrylic fibers are cut into short staple lengths for sweaters or carpets, but some are used in long filament form for fabrics with the appearance of silk.

When weather is foul, this is one way to dress for it. The coat and tapered pants are made of a water-repellent and wind-proof fabric of nylon. Lightweight and sturdy, the combination provides unbeatable cover for watching football on a rainy day, or any activity in chilly, damp weather.

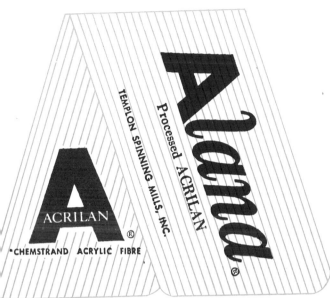

Zefran®

is The Dow Chemical Company's trademark for products including fibers, yarns, fabrics.

The Dow Chemical Company Textile Fibers Department Williamsburg, Virginia

Dow®

The acrylic fiber in this fabric is Zefran acrylic—the supernatural fiber because it combines the beauty of a superior natural with the performance of a superior man-made into one wonderful fiber. The like-new freshness and superb "touch appeal" of this fashion will delight you, wearing after wearing.

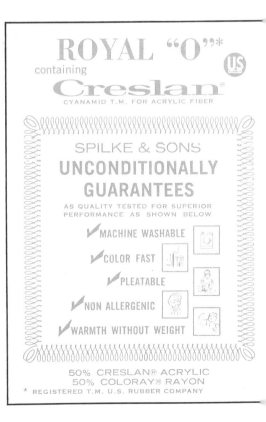

Acrylic fibers are made by several companies under different trade names.

Properties

Acrylics are similar to the other thermoplastic fibers. However, because they provide greater bulk with less weight than similar fibers, they are especially suitable for fabrics that are soft and warm. Other special characteristics are listed below:

- Burns very readily with a smoky, luminous flame, leaving a hard, dark ash.

- RESISTANCE TO SUNLIGHT AND CHEMICALS
  Very resistant to sunlight and chemicals. Used for awnings and for clothing of people who work with common chemicals.

- HAND (TEXTURE)
  Feels soft, much like wool.

Uses

Especially popular for sweaters, and other knit items, acrylic fibers have high bulk and can form air spaces to maintain warmth. These fabrics are soft, easy to wash, will not shrink, and are moth resistant. One of the major problems is that of pilling but research is underway to overcome this problem. They are also used for work clothing because of their resistance to many common chemicals.

MODACRYLIC FIBERS

Verel and Dynel are trade names of two modacrylic fibers. These fibers are similar to the acrylics but modified so there are special characteristics that make them suitable for long pile garments, as they look and feel like fur. Wigs, other than those of human hair, are made from Dynel.

BOBBIE BROOKS

Acrylics, because of their warmth and ability to maintain loft, are often used for sweaters. The girl's sweater is knit of acrylic fiber and her pleated skirt is a combination of wool and an acrylic fiber which helps the pleats stay sharp.

DU PONT

Another use for acrylic fibers is to make pile fabrics as shown in this jacket. The Orlon acrylic assures the utmost in warmth without weight.

The pile lining of this leather-look coat is made from an acrylic fiber, which adds warmth without weight. The plaid scarf and turtleneck sweater are also made from acrylics.

Because these fibers are very heat sensitive and are often difficult to iron at any temperature, they have not been used widely for clothing except for coats of a long pile, fur-like appearance. Modacrylics are non-flammable, which means they will burn, but as soon as the source of flame is removed the fabric will not flare up, drip, or melt. Concern for fire-resistant fabrics should result in greater use of modacrylics for children's sleepwear, shaggy rugs, and other items where ironing is not important.

POLYESTER FIBERS

Common polyester trade names are Dacron, Fortrel, Kodel, and Vycron.

History

The polyester fiber was developed in England. Its trade name was Terylene. The Du Pont Company bought the patent rights, did further re-

search, and in 1951 produced the first polyester in this country, which was named Dacron (*day*-cron). By 1960 Fortrel had been introduced by the Celanese Corporation and Vycron by the Beaunit Mill Company. Later Tennessee Eastman marketed Kodel. Others are being developed.

Manufacture

As with other man-made fibers, the manufacture is a complex chemical process involving many steps. The final step, again, is the forcing of a semi-liquid through a spinneret in order to form a filament. Like nylon, there are many types of polyesters, each serving a specific purpose. Polyester fibers are made in staple and filament forms and also as a film called Mylar. This plastic film is used for making "metallic" yarns.

Coat fabrics made with Dynel modacrylic fiber may be deep, shaggy piles such as seen in this parka or sleek, flat piles popular for dress coats.

UNION CARBIDE CORP., MAKERS OF DYNEL

MIKE'S MATERIAL MART

Polyesters and other man-made fibers can be used for fabrics of many designs and colors to meet almost any needs you may have.

Because polyester and nylon fibers are so strong, fabrics made from them may have a tendency to pill. The balls of fiber do not affect the wear of the garment, but they may be unsightly. Special care should be taken in home laundering and in wearing to prevent unnecessary rubbing of such fabrics.

Properties

The major advantage of the polyesters over other thermoplastic fibers, which they resemble, is their outstanding resistance to wrinkling, either dry or wet, and their ability to spring back to shape after wear. It has been said that a garment of a polyester fiber has the "come-to-work look at go-home time."

Uses

Polyester fibers are used alone in a wide range of fabrics from sheers to heavy suitings. Blended with wool, they improve crease and pleat retention, and wrinkle resistance, especially if wet. When combined with

SEARS, ROEBUCK AND CO.

A blend of polyester and cotton fibers is used for this shirt. The polyester adds wrinkle resistance so the shirt needs little or no ironing—a perfect match for the wrinkle-free polyester knit suit.

cotton, the polyester fibers add easy care to the absorbency and comfort of the cotton fibers. Neckties made of polyester fibers can be tied and retied without showing wrinkles. They can also be washed if desired.

OLEFIN FIBERS

Olefin fibers were unknown a few years ago but the introduction of Vectra hosiery with nation-wide advertising has made the American woman aware of this new fiber. Other olefin fibers include Herculon and Marvess.

These are unlike other fibers in that they absorb no moisture, are waxy in feel, and are lighter than water. They are inexpensive to produce and should find their place in many types of garments as well as carpets.

385

POLYESTER FIBERS

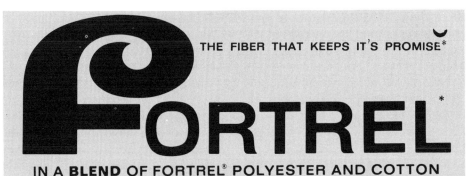

Polyester fibers are made by many manufacturers. Which others do you know of?

SPANDEX FIBERS

Spandex fibers are the most complex so far developed by man. They are similar to other thermoplastic fibers, but they have an unusual amount of stretch and will return to their original size. Therefore they are called elastic fibers. Lycra, Vyrene, Gospan, Spandelle, Blue "C" and Duraspan are trade names for this fiber but it will also be identified by the generic term, spandex.

These fibers are exciting as they serve the purposes of rubber but are more comfortable to wear, lighter in weight, and can be dyed pretty colors. At first, girdles of spandex fibers seemed so light that women could not believe they had any holding power, but experience proved they did. These fibers are quite strong and have good resistance to body perspiration, oils, and cosmetics. They can be washed but should not be subjected to high temperatures or bleaches.

Used extensively for foundation garments, spandex fibers are also used in swimwear, and blended with other fibers for many types of stretch fabrics such as hosiery and slacks. The fiber may be used alone (unsupported) or it may be a core around which other fibers are wrapped. Used in this manner, it has the appearance of whatever fiber is wrapped around it and yet it maintains its stretch properties.

ANIDEX

Anidex is the newest of the elastic fibers. Its exceptional resistance to sunlight, chemicals, and heat, and its ease-of-care properties make it possible to combine anidex successfully with both natural and man-made fibers.

AZLON—MAN-MADE PROTEIN FIBER

Several man-made protein fibers have been developed in the United States but none are now being made. Aralac and Vicara were the best known. Using protein from milk and corn, fibers were produced that had many characteristics of wool and cashmere, which are natural protein fibers. They were soft and warm but they were not very strong and were too expensive to produce.

METALLIC FIBERS

It is possible to make fabrics from strands of gold and silver but you will

New Lycra® Spandex with elastic properties gives foundation garments these important advantages:

LIGHTWEIGHT CONTROL

The greater elasticity of new, stronger "Lycra" spandex gives you the support desired in a foundation garment, yet makes possible bras and foundation garments up to one third lighter than conventional elastic yarn.

Comfort
Light "Lycra" spandex yarn brings you foundation garments in a new world of comfort and freedom.

Softness
Foundation garments elasticized with "Lycra" are extra soft, smooth to wear, and pleasing to the touch.

Life Span
"Lycra" resists detergents, body oils and perspiration that shorten the life of ordinary garments.

Ease of Care
Foundations made with "Lycra" can stand up to daily washing and wearing, yet lasts much longer than conventional garments.

Notice the qualities claimed for this fabric containing spandex fibers.

This coordinated sweater set features a diagonally striped acrylic knit cardigan over a diamond-pattern v-neck pullover. Both are in deep green and ivory and worn over an ivory cotton knit shirt.

What could be more luxurious than this shell and jacket of metallic yarns suitable for any evening affair?

seldom find them in local stores! Besides being very expensive to make, they are scratchy to wear and soon tarnish and have the unpleasant odor of tarnish.

Aluminum is used for yarns for decorative trim and to highlight certain fabrics. Strips of this metal are coated with either acetate or polyester films and, therefore, these yarns are rather heat sensitive. Those made with the polyester film coating wear longer and can stand higher temperatures in laundering and ironing than those with the acetate film.

Research is now underway which indicates that we may be wearing stockings of steel in the future. Incredible as it seems, very, very fine

strands of steel are soft and flexible and can be made into sheer looking hosiery which will give long wear. Experimental clothing for space explorers use several metallic fibers as they are strong and can withstand high temperatures.

MINERAL FIBERS

By now you have read of cellulose, protein, and thermoplastic fibers. There is another class of fibers, the minerals, that has not been mentioned. *Asbestos,* a natural fiber, and *Fiberglas,* a man-made one, are well-known. Both are used primarily for household articles and not for clothing. They are not flexible enough to be used for clothes that must take re-

3506
3506L

70% lamb's wool
20% angora rabbit fiber
10% nylon

Isn't this the softest, fluffiest blend you've ever found? We've added nylon to make it long-wearing as well!

hand washable

Turn sweater inside out. Wash in warm water, mild soap (no bleach). Knead suds through garment—don't rub or twist. Rinse well in cool water. Squeeze out excess moisture. Ease into shape. Dry flat away from heat or sun. Of course, you may dry clean if you prefer!

Notice the fibers used in the sweater from which this label was taken. The angora rabbit fiber adds extra softness to the lamb's wool and the nylon improves the strength of the fabric.

peated bending and machine washing. But who knows—perhaps some new improved process will be developed so that we will also be wearing mineral fibers. Beta glass yarns are more flexible than the original fibers and are being made into experimental clothing items.

FIBER BLENDS

Blended fabrics are made by blending together two or more fibers before

Answer the questions on page 342. Be able to defend your answer.

Make a collection of labels and advertisements that contain generic names of fibers. See if you can find at least one for each of the common generic groups and each of the basic natural fibers. What characteristics are claimed for each fiber? Discuss how these differ.

To determine the absorbency of fibers, cut strips of fabrics of different fibers into pieces about 1 by 8 inches. It is best if these fabrics have been washed so that any temporary finishes have been removed. Support each strip above a pan of water so that the edge of the sample hangs an inch in the pan. Pour red ink in the pan and measure the height to which the water rises on each strip after one, five, and ten minutes. A fabric is considered very absorbent if the dye has risen 5 to 6 inches at the end of 10 minutes; poor if only 2 to 3, and very poor if less than 2 inches. What conclusions can you make about the absorbency of different fibers?

they are spun into yarn. Desirable characteristics of each fiber are achieved if the blending is done correctly. For example, blends of cotton and polyester fibers produce fabrics which are absorbent and comfortable like cotton, and wrinkle resistant and easy to care for like polyesters. The exact proportions vary with the purposes for which the yarns are made —with some fibers almost 50% is needed to achieve distinctive purposes, and other fibers, such as spandex, can be used in smaller amounts.

Can You Explain These Terms?

generic	resiliency	worsted
trade name	abrasion	woolen
fiber	dimensional stability	noils
cellulose fibers	static electricity	virgin wool
protein fibers	mercerization	reprocessed wool
thermoplastics	sizing	reused wool
mineral fibers	napping	fulling
Pima cotton	flax	dupioni
Supima cotton	linseed	tussah
Egyptian cotton	retting	filament
upland cotton	hackling	scroop
long staple	beetling	weighting
short staple	wrinkle-resistant	spinneret
cotton boll	bleaching	synthetic fibers
carding	pilling	hydrophobic
combing	lanolin	polymer
sliver	fleece	blends

Summary With Check-up Questions

Everyone needs to understand fabrics today because of the increasing number of new fibers, the growing practice of blending fibers, and the many new fabric finishes and construction methods.

- *How many fibers were there in your grandmother's youth?*
- *How many fibers are on the market today?*
- *Can you tell by looking at a fabric how it will wear?*

You do not wear a fiber but a fabric.

- *What is the difference between a fiber and a fabric?*
- *Describe how a fiber becomes a fabric.*

There are four major groups of fibers: cellulose, protein, thermoplastic, and mineral.

- *To which group do cotton and linen belong?*

- *List two mineral fibers.*
- *What are some common protein fibers?*
- *To what group does rayon belong?*
- *List several thermoplastic fibers.*

The Textile Products Identification Act requires that almost all fabrics used for clothing must be labeled as to fiber content.

- *Does the fiber used in largest amount have to be stated first?*
- *Must a trade name be on the label or is a generic name adequate?*
- *What is the rule about imported fabrics?*
- *Must the label describe the quality of the fiber?*

Cellulose fibers include linen, rayon, and cotton. These fibers are absorbent, may shrink, will not hold creases, wrinkle easily, and are fairly strong.

- *Why do these fibers make fabrics which are comfortable to wear on warm days?*
- *How can you avoid buying a cellulose fabric or garment that will shrink?*
- *If you do not like to iron, what finishes will you request for these fibers?*
- *Why can these fabrics be washed without much special care? (In what ways does the conventional rayon differ from cotton and linen?)*

Protein fibers include wool, silk, and specialty wools such as cashmere, camel's hair, mohair and others. They are fairly expensive, resilient, absorbent, sensitive to chlorine bleaches, and need special care when washed.

- *Why are these fibers good for wear in cold weather?*
- *Although protein fibers can be washed, drycleaning is safer. Why is this?*
- *Why do wrinkles "hang out" from these fabrics?*

Man-made fibers are classified into generic or family groups. Although the members of each group may differ slightly, they are very similar in their characteristics.

- *Dacron belongs to the polyester family. Fortrel is also a member of this family. Will it be like Dacron in its properties?*
- *Why have consumers no need to know all generic groups?*
- *If a new fiber is produced that is similar to Orlon, to what generic group will it belong?*

Man-made fibers are not all synthetics; some are classified as regenerated fibers.

- *Why is it incorrect to call rayon a synthetic fiber?*
- *Acetate is made from raw materials similar to rayon, but it is not a regenerated fiber. Why?*

All natural fibers except silk are available only in short staple form; silk may be obtained in filament or staple form. Man-made fibers may be made in many forms.

- *How are multifilament fibers obtained?*
- *What is the difference in appearance of fabrics made from filament or staple lengths of the same fiber?*

Most of the man-made fibers are thermoplastic or heat-sensitive.

- *What effect will a hot iron have on such fabrics?*
- *Why will these fabrics hold their shape if properly heat-set?*
- *Pleats and creases may be long-lasting, almost permanent, in thermoplastic fabrics. Why?*

The majority of man-made fibers are hydrophobic.

- *Why do fabrics made from these fibers dry quickly?*
- *Why do such fabrics often feel clammy in hot, sticky weather?*
- *Why are these fibers as strong wet as dry?*
- *What can be done to control static electricity charges in such fabrics?*

Nylon is especially valued for its great strength and resistance to abrasion and its light weight.

- *Why is nylon often used as the outer covering of luggage?*
- *Sheer fabrics of nylon yarns can usually be washed in a machine and will wear a long time. Why?*
- *Why are ropes frequently made from nylon instead of hemp as in the past?*

Acrylic fibers are similar to the other thermoplastic fibers but they are especially valued for their soft hand (texture) and ability to maintain loft.

- *Why are sweaters often made from Orlon and Acrilan?*

- *Acrylic fibers are blended with woolen yarns for soft flannels rather than with worsteds. Why?*
- *Describe the different methods required to wash an acrylic and a woolen sweater.*

Spandex fibers have the unusual ability to stretch and to return to their original shape, and have other properties similar to man-made thermoplastics.

- *Why is spandex used more than rubber for foundation garments such as girdles?*
- *A small amount of spandex is often added to men's hosiery. What effect does this have?*

Modacrylic fibers are similar to acrylics but are specially made for man-made fur garments.

- *Why are wigs often made from modacrylic fibers?*

Mineral fibers are fireproof and have limited flexibility.

- *Very few clothing items are made from these fibers. Why?*
- *Why are curtains for schools, theaters, and other public buildings usually made from asbestos or Fiberglas?*

Fibers are often blended together to combine the desirable qualities of each.

- *What effect does adding rayon to acrylic fibers have?*

- *Why is a coat of wool and nylon stronger than one of wool alone?*
- *Why is a dress of cotton and polyester more comfortable and absorbent than one of 100% polyester?*
- *Why does a robe of cotton and polyester seldom need ironing?*

Polyester fibers are known for their outstanding resistance to wrinkling, wet or dry, and their ability to maintain a sharp crease.

- *Why are summer suits often made from a blend of wool and polyester fibers?*
- *No-iron fabrics of cotton often have polyester fibers added. Why?*
- *Travel garments are frequently made from polyester fibers. Why?*

The need for fire-resistant fabrics should result in greater use of modacrylics.

- *What will happen if a modacrylic is exposed to fire?*
- *Why is a modacrylic fabric a wise choice for children's sleepwear?*

The Wool Bureau has taken leadership in developing quality labels for garments made from wool.

- *What is the meaning of the woolmark?*
- *How does the woolblend label differ from the woolmark?*
- *Would you like to see similar labels on fabrics of other fibers? Why?*

CHAPTER ELEVEN

From Fiber to Yarn to Cloth

WHEN YOU LOOK AT A FABRIC, you will seldom notice the yarn from which it is made, but the appearance of the fabric and the wear expected from it depend a great deal upon the yarns.

FROM FIBER TO YARN

You can make a simple yarn by taking a small number of fibers, such as absorbent cotton, and twisting them together. This yarn will probably be bumpy and uneven because it has not gone through the straightening processes such as carding and combing, described on page 348 but it is stronger than a similar group of fibers, untwisted.

Hold a group of loose fibers between the thumb and forefinger of each hand and pull. Now twist these fibers together and pull. Do you notice how much more force or strength it takes to "break" the mass of fibers after they are twisted? If you make two yarns and twist them together, you will have an even stronger yarn.

Also, experimenting with the amount of twist, you will discover that the more tightly twisted the group of fibers, the stronger the yarn.

SPUN AND FILAMENT YARNS

The yarn you have just made by twisting short fibers is called a *spun yarn*. All cotton, linen, and wool yarns are spun this way as these fibers occur only in relatively short lengths. Silk and all of the man-made fibers can also be cut into short pieces and twisted or spun into yarn.

Another type is the *filament* yarn. It is made from very long fibers of silk and man-made fibers called filaments. Most filament yarns are made of many fine filaments and are called *multifilament*. A one-strand or *monofilament* yarn is used occasionally for sheer hosiery, laces, and other fine fabrics. Filament yarns are usually smoother, more lustrous, and less inclined to lint or pill than spun yarns. Fabrics of spun yarns are usually warmer than filament yarns, as more air is trapped by the short fibers.

The carding process. Bats of fibers come down the numbered bins at the rear of the room and pass over rollers of fine wire teeth. The fibers are straightened and emerge in webs of parallel fibers as seen in the foreground.

They also take longer to dry because moisture fills the air spaces.

Recently scientists have been able to make filament yarns that feel and look much like the spun variety. These are called *texturized* yarns because they have a rougher texture than the regular filament yarns. A common texturized yarn is the *high bulk* or loop, sold under such trade names as Taslan, Lofted, and Ban-Lon. A process involving jets of air as the filament leaves the spinneret creates loops on the surface of the yarn. Texturized yarns may give greater warmth with less weight and are resistant to pilling and abrasion because of fewer fiber ends.

Another process creates a yarn with a high degree of *stretch* and quick recovery. The yarns may have some bulk but they are used mainly for their stretch properties. Some examples are Helenca, Agilon, and Superloft. The individual filaments are

Close-up of a bobbin of cotton roving, a step between the loosely twisted sliver and the firmly twisted yarn.

Spools of roving are placed on the spinning frame. The ends of the roving are drawn through small rollers which draw the fibers out still farther. They are then wound onto revolving bobbins that apply a twist and create the finished yarn.

In large mills spinning methods vary according to the type yarn desired. Here fine linen threads are being spun for the weaving of sheer linens.

crimped, looped, or formed into little spirals before being heat-set. If properly done, these yarns will always return to their original shape after being stretched. A thermoplastic fiber such as nylon must be used so it can be heat-set but it may be blended with other fibers.

SINGLE AND PLY YARNS

A single yarn is the result of the first twisting of fibers. A *ply yarn* is made by twisting together two or more singles. When you twisted together two single yarns as described on page 393 you created a two-ply yarn. Twisting three yarns together makes a three-ply yarn. A ply yarn is stronger than a single yarn of the *same thickness and weight*. Ply yarns are often used for fabrics expected to take hard wear. Some lightweight fabrics are also made from ply yarns because very fine yet strong yarns are needed. The fabric voile is an example.

SHANTUNG

TWEED

SPUN RAYON FABRICS

LINEN-TEXTURED

COVERT

Fabrics made from yarns of short staple fibers.

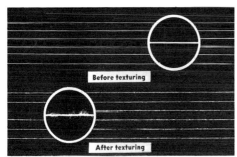

Du Pont

A multifilament yarn before and after texturing. Magnified sections of the untextured yarn are shown in the insets.

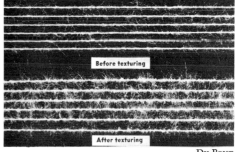

Du Pont

Taslan and other textured yarns.

A third twisting operation makes a *cord*, resulting in a very strong yarn. Some types of sewing thread are made this way.

Amount of Twist. Some yarns are barely twisted together and others are so tightly twisted that a ravel

from a fabric will appear kinky. The amount of twist influences the smoothness, stretch, shrinkage, and appearance of both yarn and fabric. Satins are made from yarns with little or no twist, so they produce a smooth, lustrous fabric. Crepe fabrics have very tightly twisted yarns and, when woven closely, will take hard wear

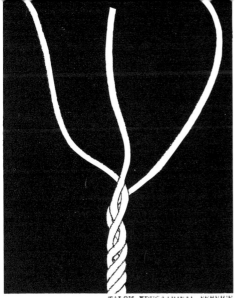

Example of three-ply thread—three single strands of yarn twisted together to form the thread. A two-ply thread would have two strands twisted together.

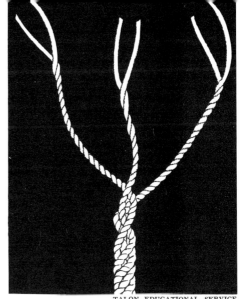

Example of a six-cord thread made by twisting two strands together; then two more and two more. The three coupled threads are twisted to form the thread.

but have a tendency to stretch or shrink. In between the smooth satin and the crinkly crepe are many variations depending upon the amount of yarn twist. The more tightly twisted the yarns, the greater strength, but the fabric will be firm and possibly scratchy.

To be correct, the term *thread* is used when a yarn is firmly twisted. In everyday usage, any yarn of fine diameter is called a thread.

Novelty Yarns

Yarns are made in different ways to add texture interest to fabrics. A single yarn may be varied in twist and diameter so that it appears as a *slub yarn*. Often two yarns are twisted together in such a way that *loops* are formed, as in bouclés. Yarns wound around a base yarn several times at one place produce a heavy *knot* effect.

Although novelty yarns add interest to a fabric and may help prevent wrinkling, they do affect the wear ad-

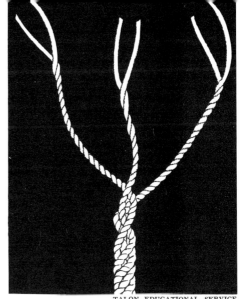

Close-up of a slub yarn. Used for crosswise yarns of shantung fabric pictured on page 396.

versely. Therefore, the smaller the novelty effect, the more durable the fabric. Novelty yarns can easily catch, pull, or show wear due to abrasion.

Yarn Size. The term *denier* is commonly used to describe yarn. It refers to the size of the yarn, that is, its thickness or diameter. The finer the yarn, the smaller the denier number. For example, nylon hosiery of 10 denier yarn is sheerer than 30 denier hosiery. Sewing threads are numbered differently. See page 511.

Secure samples of fabric with surface interest such as shantung, brocade, bouclé, and some novelties. Untwist the yarns and describe them. Can you draw a diagram showing how they are made? Explain why the type of yarn affects the appearance of the fabric.

Collect labels and advertisements of fabrics and threads that contain the terms "two-ply" or "cord." What type of garments are these used for? Why are these yarns used rather than single yarns?

Select a sample of a fabric that is smooth and lustrous like satin and another that is fuzzy looking like tweed. Unravel the yarns and measure the fiber length. What conclusions can you make about length of fibers and appearance of finished fabric?

Bring to class nylon hosiery made from filament yarns and hosiery made from staple yarns. What is the difference in appearance and feel? Why?

Make a collection of sewing threads available in the clothing laboratory. Read the specifications on the labels and be able to explain their meaning to the other class members. Notice the size numbers as well as other terms given. See if you can determine difference in thickness from those sized 50 and those with higher numbers.

Bring to class a well-washed stocking made from a stretch yarn such as Agilon. If you do not have one, perhaps the teacher will give you one that is no longer wearable. Examine its stretchability.

FROM YARN TO CLOTH

Almost all fabrics are made from yarns, usually by weaving or knitting but some by knotting, crocheting, or braiding. Look at the fabrics worn by your classmates. Until recently, most were woven. Today, knitted garments may be more common. Weaving is the interlacing of two or more groups of yarns. A simple example is making a basket from strips of paper.

THE WEAVING PROCESS

Weaving is done with a shuttle that interlaces yarns in a frame, called a loom, which originally meant only "tool." You will understand cloth better if you understand how a simple loom works. The loom is prepared with the lengthwise or warp yarns. Crosswise yarns are then inserted so they go over and under the warp to form a fabric. These crosswise yarns may be called either *woof* or *weft* but today they are usually called *filling* yarns, as they fill in a fabric. Handweavers often call the lengthwise threads "ends" and the crosswise threads "picks." The pick glass, shown on page 402, was named after these threads. As these yarns go back and forth, they go around the outer warp yarns at each edge and form a "self edge" which has become known as *selvage*. This finished edge or selvage is usually heavier than the rest of the fabric because warp yarns are placed closely together at the edges, or heavier end yarns are used for strength.

Look at the illustration on page 399. Can you see why the warp yarns are usually stronger than the fillings? They take more strain, as they must be held tightly in the loom. Most novelty yarns can be used for filling.

Starting a mat on a simple loom. Notice the warp yarns are in place and the shuttle is wound with coarse filling yarns. The stick shown is a shed stick which separates the warp yarns so that the fillings may be quickly inserted through without the tedious process of going over and under each separate warp yarn.

After yarns are wound onto large spools, they must be rewound evenly onto smaller bobbins. This woman is handling bobbins which fit into shuttles for weaving.

Preparation of the filling threads for weaving involves spooling or winding the yarn from large beams to smaller bobbins to carry the filling threads.

Warp threads are "dressed," wherein a sizing solution is added to warp threads to strengthen them through the stresses of weaving. This will usually be washed out before the fabric is finished.

399

A mammoth beam is being lowered onto a loom where it will provide the warp yarns needed for endless yards of cloth. It has already been wound with specially sized yarns.

DAN RIVER MILLS

400

A typical mill where fabrics are woven. Notice the large number of looms and the few people attending them. Once the loom is set up, it is completely automatic and needs human attention only for unusual problems.

DAN RIVER MILLS

After drawing each warp thread through an individual heddle, all the warp are now being tied or anchored to an empty roller which will hold the finished cloth when completed.

A "new" type of loom used for simple cotton fabrics. A large cone of thread is used instead of smaller shuttles and bobbins. Notice the warp threads coming from the back of the loom, the heddles which hold each individual warp yarn, the harnesses or racks which hold the heddles, and the completed cloth wound on the cloth beam in front of the loom. These looms are fast for simple fabrics but not for fancy or unusual fabrics.

401

Grain

When a pattern refers to the *lengthwise grain* of a fabric, it means the direction of the warp threads. The *crosswise grain* means the direction of the filling threads.

Thread Count

The number of threads in a fabric affects its durability. Usually, the more threads, the better the fabric quality. The thread count is always given as the number of threads per square inch of fabric. A high count fabric will keep its shape better, shrink less, be stronger, and usually look smoother than a low count fabric. For example, a cotton percale that has 60 warp and 60 filling threads per square inch will not be as durable as one that has 80 threads each way. A count stated 90 by 62 means that there are 90 warp threads and 62 filling threads. It is customary to state the number of warp threads first.

Sometimes a cloth is referred to as *balanced* or *square*. This is not as confusing as it may seem at first. An 80 square cloth means that there are 80 threads each way. This cloth is also "balanced," as the number of lengthwise threads is the same as the crosswise. Balanced fabrics usually wear better than those with a great difference between the lengthwise and crosswise count. However, interesting cloth textures can be achieved by unbalanced thread counts.

There is a special magnifying glass made for checking the thread count

Preparing to make thread counts of two different fabrics, these girls are using pick glasses or linen testers which have magnifying lens placed over carefully measured openings.

Pull a cotton fabric in the direction of the warp threads, the crosswise threads, and the bias. In which direction is there the most stretch? In which direction is there the least stretch? Can you explain why?

Secure a sample of a fabric which usually has a balanced thread count, such as percale, and one where the warp and filling count are different, as broadcloth. Do a thread count for each. A simple magnifying glass and ruler will be adequate if you do not have a pick glass.

of fabrics. It is called a *pick glass* or *linen tester*. To make counting threads easier, unravel about ¼ inch from both the lengthwise and crosswise sides of a small square of cloth. Place it on a surface of different color and carefully count the yarns seen through the opening in the pick glass. If the opening is ¼ inch, be sure to multiply the number of yarns you count by 4. If you do not have a pick glass, you can use a ruler.

The thread count of such fabrics as sheeting cloth is usually labeled. Mail order stores may state the thread count of some fabrics. Store buyers obtain such specifications when needed but most consumers must learn to judge these fabrics by their appearance.

Plain Weave. This is the simplest weave, sometimes called the over-one, under-one weave. As previously mentioned, it is similar to the way you may have made baskets when a child. The filling yarns go over one and under one warp yarn, alternating in the next row by passing under the threads that were passed over in the preceding row. This, the most common weave, is a good background for many designs. A fabric of plain weave is usually strong if the yarns are close together (and of good quality). Examples are organdy, gingham, percale, and Indian head.

Variations of the plain weave produce added interest and texture. The *basket weave* is made by passing two or more filling yarns over one or more warp yarns. Usually groups of 2 warps and 2 fillings or 4 warps and 4 fillings are used, as in monk's cloth. Oxford cloth is a modification with two warps passing over a single filling or a single filling passing over two warps. Fabrics of this weave are not as durable as the plain weave and may shrink more, but they are comfortable to wear—as air can easily permeate the cloth—and wrinkles show less, because the yarns can shift readily.

Other variations result when some yarns are heavier than others, as in grosgrain, faille, and dimity. Some of these fabrics have *crosswise rib effects* due to the use of heavy crosswise yarns and finer warp yarns. Broadcloth, faille, grosgrain, and bengaline are examples. These fabrics are not too durable, as the small yarns may break as they rub at the point where they cross the heavy yarns. They also tend to shrink lengthwise, since the large yarns swell when wet and stay slightly enlarged.

Other fabrics have lengthwise *cord* effects due to the use of heavy yarns at intervals as dimity and Bedford cord.

Sometimes heavy yarns are used both ways, at intervals, for crossbar dimity.

Plain weave fabric under magnification.

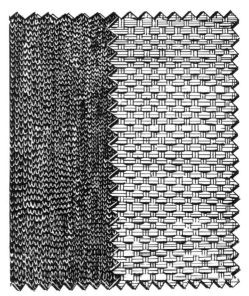

Drawing of a basket weave fabric and the tricot fabric which is used for a bonded lining.

Twill weave fabric. A right-hand warp faced twill. The diagonal moves from the lower left to the upper right and the warp threads predominate on the surface.

Twill weave. In the twill weave the filling yarns interlace with the warp yarns in such a way that diagonal lines are formed on the face of the fabric. It is possible to pack many threads into a twill weave, making it very strong and wear resistant. Gabardine, serge, some flannels, lining fabrics, and materials such as denim for work clothes are examples of the twill weave.

A twill that reverses its direction from time to time and makes a pattern like the bones in a herring is called *herringbone.*

Did you ever hear of a *lazy twill?* Usually fabrics are made with the diagonal line at the 45° angle. A diagonal line at a lesser degree is a lazy or reclining twill and one at a greater angle is a *steep twill.* Gabardine is an example of the latter.

Close-up of a herringbone variation of the twill weave.

Satin weave. In a satin weave, either the warp or filling yarns are floated across the surface, thus giving a smooth, apparently unbroken face which reflects light, produces luster, and has a smooth, almost slippery feel. The exposed parts of the yarns are called *floats* because they pass over several yarns. A long float may catch and break, thus causing a fuzzy surface. Satins with short floats can be very firm and durable.

When the warp yarns float over the surface, the fabric is considered true satin, and is usually made of filament fibers such as silk, acetate, or nylon. When the filling floats come to the surface, the fabric is called sateen which is usually made from cotton.

Because of the smooth qualities, satin weave is excellent for a coat lining that slips on easily. It is also preferred for formal wear, when a high luster is desirable.

Satin weave. Notice how the warp yarns float over four filling yarns.

FMC CORP., AMERICAN VISCOSE DIV.

Figure weaves. The figure weave may be simple or complex. Fabrics with a small, geometric pattern woven in as a regular pattern are produced with a *dobby* loom attachment. Bird's eye cloth, waffle cloth and some fancy shirting materials are examples. More elaborate woven designs—as in brocades, damasks, and some tapestries—are made on a loom with a complicated *Jacquard* attachment where each yarn is controlled separately.

Pile weaves. Pile weaves have an extra set of yarns in a three-dimensional effect. The word pile comes from a Latin word meaning fur, and pile fabrics do resemble natural furs in many ways. If the loops are not cut, the fabric will look like terrycloth. The loops may be on either side or on both. Uncut pile fabrics are very absorbent, since much yarn surface is exposed. They are also warm, since the loops hold in air pockets to act as insulators.

Examples of cut pile fabrics are velvet, velveteen, and corduroy. A long-wearing pile fabric will have a closely woven background cloth. Twill backgrounds are more durable than the plain weave.

Pile fabrics such as velvet are rich looking and drape nicely. It is important to remember that pile fabrics reflect light differently according to the direction of the nap. On page 585 you can read about this in greater detail.

Leno weave. Sheer fabrics with an open weave would not be very serviceable if made in the plain weave. Threads would shift and create the effect of holes. The *leno* weave is used to prevent this. Two warp threads are wrapped around each filling thread, holding it firmly in place.

A pile fabric. Notice how the pile stands at right angles to the background fabric. This is a long pile, often called a man-made fur.

The leno weave. The warp yarns twist around the filling yarns like a figure 8 and hold them tightly in place.

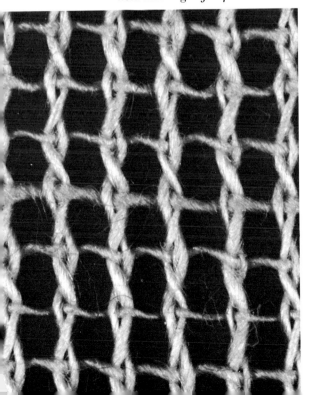

Chiefly used for sheer curtain material such as marquisette, you will also find this weave used in summer dress fabrics.

Novelty weaves. Combining different weaves produces novelties with an unlimited variety of interesting effects, contributing beauty rather than strength to a fabric.

Double cloth. Double cloth is not a separate weave but is an interesting way of weaving two fabrics together for reversible coatings, ribbons, and blankets. Any weave may be used but the yarns are interlaced in such a way that the top and bottom fabric are woven together at the same time.

KNITTING

Knitted fabrics slightly outnumber woven fabrics for clothing use. Increased demand for easy care and comfort plus new technological developments in fibers have resulted in a wide variety of knitted fabrics for clothing.

Knitted fabrics can be plain, ribbed, or of fancy patterns for making almost any type of garment, from sheer undergarments to heavy fleece outercoats. Knitted garments are comfortable because they "give" as one moves. They are generally warm since air is held in the fabric as an insulator. However, if they are loosely

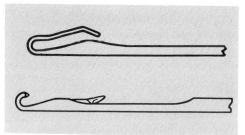
UNDERWEAR INSTITUTE
Special needles used for knitting machines.

DAN RIVER MILLS
A circular knitting machine.

knitted, they can be cool, especially when worn in windy weather.

Knitted garments stretch and shrink more than woven garments. If they are made of polyester, acrylic, nylon, or other heat-sensitive fibers, they will return to their original size in wear and cleaning if they have been properly heat set in the textile mill.

Snagging is a common problem. Sharp jewelry, rough purses, and laundering with hooks and eyes left open should be avoided. Some knits may run or ladder if a loop is broken. Pilling is common to many knit fabrics. See page 58.

Knitting is the looping of yarns together to form a fabric. There are two ways of doing this.

In a *filling or weft knit,* a single yarn travels round and round to form a tubular fabric or back and forth to create a flat fabric. Hand knitting is an example of a filling knit. This

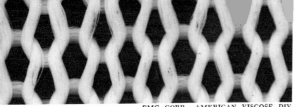

Filling knit fabric under magnification.

method creates a fabric that is very elastic and good for women's hosiery as well as most sweaters. The disadvantages are possible runs and stretching and sagging.

When a fabric is made on a flat machine, it can be shaped during the knitting process by increasing or decreasing the number of stitches in a row. Such a fabric may have a finished edge as in a woven fabric. If made on a circular machine, the fabric will be tubular. Home sewers will find it important to cut along a lengthwise row of loops, called a wale, and use this as a guide for the straight of grain.

There are many types of filling or weft knit constructions. Double knits have two interlocked layers, face and back, which cannot be separated. This gives the fabric built-in stability so it will not sag or stretch and yet will have comfort stretch and not wrinkle. It can be cut without a curling of edges. Textured filament yarns provide resilence and bulk to the fabric and spun yarns, especially wool, provide more snag resistance.

Single knits provide a thinner, lighter weight type of fabric that has excellent stretchability and is ideal for men's shirts and T-shirts. Single knits are often bonded to another fabric to prevent excessive stretching and to add more body to the fabric.

Interlock knits are a special type of weft knit fabric that is becoming popular for sweaters and underwear. These fabrics have a smooth surface on both sides and possess less elasticity than other weft knits.

In *warp knitting,* hundreds of parallel yarns are each passed through a separate needle on the knitting machine. Each needle creates interlocking loops along the length of the fabric. Warp-knit fabrics stretch primarily in the width.

Tricot warp knit fabrics are characterized by fine vertical ribs on the front and crosswise ribbings on the back. Tricot fabrics are usually runproof, snag resistant, and non-raveling. They resist bagging and creasing in wear. They do not provide enough stretch to be used for hosiery, which must fit the calf and ankle of the leg. Until recently, tricot fabrics were used largely for lingerie but new technological developments have made them appropriate for other uses. Pile knits and velours may also be made by warp knitting.

Raschel is a more complex knit. The raschel knitting machine can use any type of yarn. It produces a variety of fabrics from thermal underwear to dress fabrics and delicate lace.

Braiding. Some narrow fabrics are made by braiding. Three or more yarns are interlaced, usually for trimming, but these braids can be sewn together to make hats, summer purses, and other articles.

Crochet. A single strand of yarn is used with a special hook. A loop is made and another loop is pulled through this one until a chain is produced. Other loops are then made along this chain and a fabric results. Narrow edgings are often made by crocheting, but entire dresses and sweaters can be made.

Knotting. Knotting is the interlacing or interlooping of threads. The loops knot each step so that it cannot be unraveled. The fabrics are light in weight and have an open effect. Tulle, net, and many laces are knotted so uniformly that it is often difficult to tell whether the work is done by hand or by machine. Tatting is a similar method.

Nonwoven Fabrics

Not all fabrics are made from yarns; some are made directly from fibers. New nonwovens are attracting much attention, but one of the world's oldest fabrics is also nonwoven.

Felt. Felting, a very old process, was discovered accidentally, we are told. As men prepared for long journeys, they protected their feet by putting carded wool in the bottoms of their sandals. When they removed the wool it was a firm mass. They discovered that heat, moisture, and pressure from their feet made the wool fibers into a fabric. In the manufacture of felt today, heat and mois-

Warp knit (two bar tricot) fabric under magnification.

ture are applied to cause the wool scales to open; then pressure is applied to interlock and tighten the fibers into a mass. Felt may be made from fur, cotton, rayon, or other man-made fibers mixed with wool as well as all wool.

Gloves made by crocheting, which is the interlooping of threads into other loops. Quickly and easily made once the technique of crocheting has been mastered, these gloves are smart for many occasions.

Tatting is a form of lace-making with a shuttle and thread. It is used primarily for trimming handkerchiefs, children's clothes, and table linens but small motifs joined together can make blouses and teacloths. 409

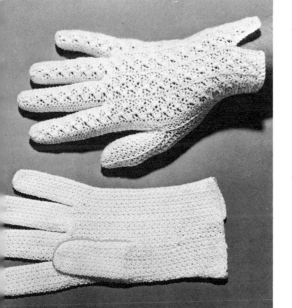

Practice making samples of the three basic weaves—plain, twill, and satin. You can use paper cut into strips or simple looms if available in your classroom.

If you know of someone who can make fabrics by tatting or other lace-making methods, arrange a demonstration in class.

A display of examples of various methods of making cloth is interesting and educational and can be a class project. List the various weaves and other methods of making fabrics such as warp knitting, filling knit, crocheting, and those listed in this chapter. Find a sample of each method and mount it under the proper label.

Make a list on your chalkboard of all the weaves and other types of construction methods (knitting, crocheting, etc.) used in garments worn by class members. Let each girl check her own garments and describe them.

Collect cotton fabrics of different textures such as gingham, voile, velveteen, corduroy, sateen, and others. The appearance and warmth of the fabrics differ although they are all cotton. Study the manner in which the weave makes a difference. Can you find some cotton knit fabrics? How do they differ? Explain why.

Secure a sample of nylon hosiery and nylon tricot knit as used for slips. One is a warp knit and one is a filling knit. Study the difference.

Felted fabrics are not as strong as those made by weaving, since the fibers are not as securely fastened together. Felts may also pucker when exposed to moisture and are seldom washable. They can be easily shaped for hats and slippers. Because there are no threads to ravel, felt is ideal for circular skirts and many household uses that do not require hemming or seam finishing.

Bonding is a modern process for making nonwoven fabrics. Fibers are laid out into sheets and adhesive substances are applied. Pressure and heat help the adhesives bond the fibers together. NOTE! Because the word "bonding" is often used to refer to two fabrics which are held together with heat or chemical adhesives as described in Chapter Twelve, the word "nonwoven" is a better choice for the fabrics described here. Bonding is a correct but confusing term to use for describing the method of creating fabrics directly from fibers.

Nonwovens have the feel of conventional cloth. They may be soft or stiff and can be printed or dyed. Inexpensive to produce, they are used for disposable items such as towels, napkins, draperies, and fun clothes.

Because there is no lengthwise or crosswise grain, interfacings of nonwoven fabrics have several advantages over woven materials. There is no need to consider grain of either inner or outer fabrics and therefore a nonwoven fabric may be cut out more economically.

"Paper" fabrics are really nonwoven fabrics made of a webbing of cellulose fibers, cotton or usually rayon, bonded together with various

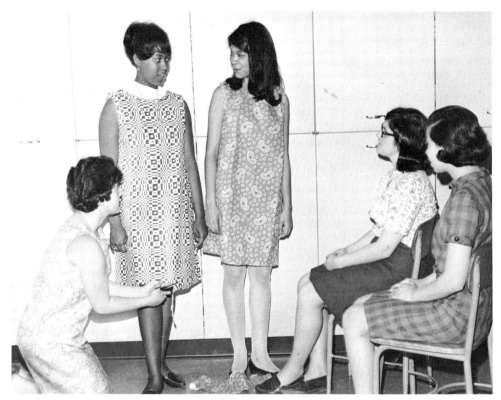

Dresses of nonwoven fabrics are fun and also easy to shorten. Because there are no yarns to fray, the "fabric" may be simply cut the desired length. These high school girls are getting the opinion of their classmates for the best length for these gay summer frocks.

materials. Occasionally nylon threads are placed at ½ inch intervals to add strength to the "paper fabric." If too much strain is not placed on these fabrics, they will last for a few wearings and are usually inexpensive enough to be disposed of with no regrets.

Needle-punch web fabrics. One of the newest fabric construction methods, needle-punching, is used for blankets and coatings. Fibers are laid out in a thick web effect but no bonding adhesive is required. Instead, barbed needles are worked up and down through the web in such a way that the fibers intermesh. This is a fast method that gives promise of making sturdy fabrics that are less expensive than the traditional ones which involve the making of yarns,

setting up of looms, and then actually weaving the threads into a fabric.

Obtain wool batting or a handful of wool fibers. Soak in hot water until thoroughly wet. Press with a hot iron and much force. Have you made a simple piece of felt? Why?

Make a collection of felt fabrics, ranging from very fine felts to heavy felts used for industrial uses.

Collect advertisements for nonwoven fabrics including needle-punch and "paper" garments. Notice the uses for which these fabrics are being recommended. Figure out the cost per wearing compared with a similar garment of woven fabric.

Can You Explain These Terms?

spun yarn	*denier*	*dobby weave*
staple yarn	*weaving*	*Jacquard weave*
filament	*loom*	*pile weave*
multifilament	*plain weave*	*leno weave*
monofilament	*basket weave*	*filling knit*
texturizing	*rib variation of plain*	*warp knit*
single yarn	*weave*	*double knit*
ply yarn	*thread count*	*knotting*
cord yarn	*twill weave*	*crocheting*
slub yarn	*pick glass*	*nonwoven fabrics*
loop yarn	*satin weave*	*felt*
knot yarn	*balanced*	*needle-punch web fabrics*

Summary With Check-up Questions

The appearance and wear of a fabric depends a great deal on the type of yarns used.

- *Will a fabric made from novelty yarns wear better than one from simple yarns? Why?*
- *For what fabrics are cord yarns selected?*
- *What effect has a two-ply yarn on the strength of a fabric?*

A spun yarn is made from short lengths twisted together.

- *Why are all cotton and linen fabrics made from spun yarns?*
- *How can spun yarns be made from nylon and other man-made fibers?*
- *Why will a spun yarn appear slightly fuzzy?*

A filament yarn is made from fibers of long length.

- *Why is silk the only natural fiber which can be made into filament yarns?*
- *Why can all man-made fibers be made into filament yarns if desired?*
- *How will a fabric made from filament yarns differ in appearance from one made from spun yarns?*

Fabrics made from spun yarns and those made from filament yarns of the same fibers differ in many ways.

- *Why are fabrics of spun yarns warmer than those of filament yarns?*
- *Why will fabrics of filament yarns dry faster?*
- *Why is pilling a greater problem with fabrics of spun yarns?*

Texturized yarns are filament yarns which look and act much like staple yarns.

- *Why are texturized yarns called by that name?*
- *What are various methods of making texturized yarns?*
- *Why is a heat-sensitive fiber necessary for making most texturized filament yarns?*

The most commonly used weave is the plain weave or some variation of it.

- *Why is it used so frequently?*
- *How does a basket weave differ?*
- *How are ribbed weave fabrics made?*
- *Fabrics with lengthwise cords such as dimity are variations of the plain weave. How are they made?*

Weaving is the interlacing of two or more groups of yarns done on a loom.
- *What are the lengthwise yarns called?*
- *What is the term for the crosswise yarns? What are other common terms?*
- *Can you give a simple explanation of how weaving takes place? Why is a selvage formed?*

Twill weaves are used for surface interest or for fabrics which require considerable strength as work clothes.
- *Why is it possible to make a stronger fabric with a twill weave than a plain weave?*
- *How is a herringbone fabric made?*

A satin weave is used when a very smooth surface is desired.
- *Why does a fabric made from a satin weave usually have a natural luster?*
- *A fabric with long floats may quickly become frayed looking. Why?*
- *What is the difference between a satin and a sateen fabric?*

Figured weaves may be simple or complex. A small, all-over woven design is made with a dobby attachment. A large, complex pattern is made with a Jacquard attachment which controls each yarn separately.

- *Why are damasks usually expensive to produce?*
- *How can you tell the difference between a woven design and a design that is embroidered?*

Pile weaves have an extra set of yarns in a three-dimensional effect.
- *What is the difference between an uncut pile and a cut pile?*
- *Why are pile fabrics more absorbent and warmer than plain weave fabrics?*
- *What effect has the background cloth on wearing ability of the pile fabric?*

Some fabrics are made directly from fibers without going through the yarn stage.
- *How is felt made? Why is some wool necessary in a true felt?*
- *Why are nonwoven fabrics less expensive than woven or knitted materials?*
- *What do you think is the future of nonwoven fabrics?*

Knitting is done by the filling-knit or the warp knit method.
- *Which method is more run-resistant?*
- *Which method makes a more elastic fabric?*
- *Why is ladies' hosiery not made from the warp knit method?*
- *Knit fabrics are being used for more and more types of garments. What are some of the reasons for this?*

The method of stating the size or diameter of yarn differs if it is a filament yarn or if it is made from short staple fibers.
- *Is a 10 denier yarn used for nylon hosiery thicker or thinner than a yarn of a larger number such as 30 denier?*
- *What is the difference between a size 50 and a 70 cotton sewing thread?*

Snagging is one of the most common problems with knitted fabrics.
- *What can be done when washing a garment with hooks and eyes to prevent snagging during laundering?*
- *What types of jewelry may cause snags?*

Some knit fabrics sag and loose their shape easily. Others maintain their shape well.
- *How will a polyester knit fabric differ from one made from cotton?*
- *What results will bonding with a closely woven fabric have?*
- *Why will a doubleknit be more stable than a single knit?*

CHAPTER TWELVE

From Cloth to Finished Fabric

HAVE YOU EVER VISITED A TEXTILE mill? If so, you were probably very disappointed when you first saw the cloth come off the looms or knitting machines. Instead of lovely, colorful material as you expected, you saw dull, limp, rough cloth marred with blemishes. In fact, the term used for cloth just off the loom is "gray." Only through many finishing processes does it become an appealing fabric that feels nice and has many functional uses.

Fabric finishes have many purposes, but mainly they are to make cloth *look better, feel better,* and *give better service.*

Routine finishes common to most fabrics are pictured on pages 414 and 415.

Many finishes are not visible to our eye, so it is difficult to tell what effect they will have on the finished fabric.

- Some finishes are not long lasting and will be destroyed through wear or improper, careless washing and use.
- Few finishes are permanent but, with proper care, finishes today

are *durable* and will last as long as you want to wear the fabric. Learn to read labels carefully so that you will know what to expect from the fabric and how to care for it properly.

Because gray goods are fairly stiff due to the presence of warp sizing, most fabrics are prepared for further finishing by washing. The fabric is placed on racks and dipped up and down in a cleaning solution.

PENDLETON WOOLEN MILLS

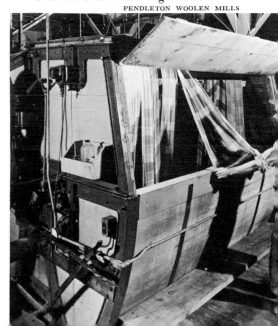

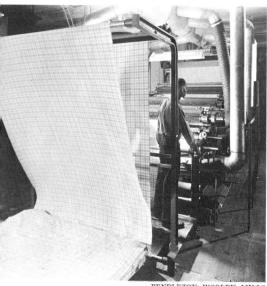

Shearing is a routine finish for many fabrics. After it has been washed and dried, the fabric is sheared to remove uneven surface fiber ends. Notice the circular blades in the rear similar to cutters in lawn mowers. The large tubes pull the lint away from the fabric to waste storage areas.

Framing machine stretches the processed cloth to a uniform width before it goes to the final finished stages.

Decating produces a smooth, wrinkle-free and lofty hand on woolen and worsted fabrics and blends containing wool fibers. The process is comparable to steam ironing. The dry cloth is wound under tension on a perforated cylinder. Steam is forced through the fabric. The moisture and heat cause the wool to become soft; then the tensions relax and the wrinkles disappear. The yarns become set in the shape as woven because of a cooling-off which is done with cold air.

After a final inspection, rolls of finished fabrics are ready to be wrapped and sent to retail stores for sale to consumers or manufacturers who will use them to make ready-to-wear garments.

Reliable fabric manufacturers continually test samples of their finished fabrics. The machine for testing the tensile strength of yarns and fabrics is shown at the far left. The man on the right is removing fabrics from the "fade-ometer" to determine the effect of artificial sunlight on their color and strength.

Look at the labels on page 146. After studying about fibers, perhaps you wonder how a linen fabric can be wrinkle resistant when you read that linen is non-resilient, or how cotton can be washed and worn with no ironing when you know that cotton is a naturally limp fiber, or how wool can be mothproof when you read that wool is a favorite food for moths. You have been told that cotton is an absorbent fiber and yet you see it being used in water-repellent fabrics for raincoats. The answer is that all of these things are possible through the uses of finishing processes which you will read about in this chapter.

First, however, how are fabrics finished to be colorful and decorative?

COLOR AND DESIGN

From historical records we know that early man tried to make his cloth

416

CIBA CORP., SUMMIT, N. J.

Early drawings show the process of using dyes from plants, berries, and roots. Indigo was used for blue and the root of the madder plant for red.

CIBA CORP., SUMMIT, N. J.

The Phoenicians were famous for a rich purple dye made from the milky secretion of a sea snail. More than 12,000 of the tiny mollusks produced one gram of dye— enough to color a man's shirt. Because it was so costly, it was used only for royal garments which gave rise to the term "royal purple."

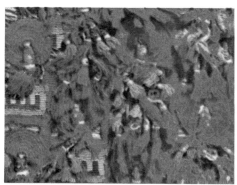

CIBA CORP., SUMMIT, N. J.

This brilliant section of a wool garment with tassels, an ancient Aztec fabric, was dyed with cochineal, a bright scarlet dye, made from the dried bodies of tiny insects found in Mexico and Central America.

CIBA CORP., SUMMIT, N. J.

Until the 19th century, brightly colored clothes were a mark of rank and wealth because dyeing was a costly and laborious process. The poor wore homespun in plain colors.

beautiful and distinctive through the use of color. He discovered that certain berries and plants would make colorful dyes if boiled in water and that fabrics would pick up these dyes.

- The Aztec Indians discovered cochineal, a red dye made by crushing the bodies of tiny insects that fed on cactus plants.
- The yellow pigment used for dying monks' robes in parts of Asia, even

today, is obtained from parts of the saffron plant.

- Indigo, obtained from the leaves of a plant in India, has become famous for its beautiful blue color.

CIBA CORP., SUMMIT, N. J.

In England in 1856, an 18-year-old boy named William Perkin was experimenting with chemicals and found a way to make the first chemical dye which has made it possible for rich and poor to enjoy color.

CIBA CORP., SUMMIT, N. J.

The chemical that Perkin had accidentally found to be a practical way to dye fabrics was called mauveine and was popular with Queen Victoria.

CIBA CORP., SUMMIT, N. J.

In the plants of world-wide organizations, research is constantly underway to create new products and to find better uses for the dyes and pigments already available.

- The fermented chips of certain trees produce the logwood dye which results in browns and blacks.
- One of the rarest dyes is the Tyrian purple color obtained from tiny sea mollusks. Over 12,000 animals are required to make a single gram of dye. Because of its expense and its scarcity, in the past its use was restricted to royalty; hence the term "royal purple."

Credit for developing the first synthetic dye is given to a 18-year-old English boy, William Perkin. As an assistant to a chemist he was trying to discover something else when he accidentally made a synthetic dyestuff. Since then there has been much research in this area, so that today we have dyes for almost any color.

Later, man also wanted designs on his material. Some painting on fabric was done, plus the creation of simple embroidery by using colorful threads. No one knows how long ago man learned to "print" designs, but in museums you can see fabrics that were printed by simple methods hundreds of years ago.

Carving pieces of wood into different shapes, applying paint on the parts of the wood that stood out, and then pressing this onto the fabric made a crude design. You may recognize this as *blockprinting*. Perhaps you have made a linoleum or wood block and printed cards or cloth.

It was discovered that by tying knots in cloth or wrapping parts of it with thread, these sections would resist the dye when the fabric was placed in the dye pot. This *tie and dye* method of color application is still used in many African countries, India, Malaysia and by young women in this country who like to

CIBA CORP., SUMMIT, N. J.

A special machine is used to test the fastness of color. It subjects the dyed cloth to rays similar to those of the sun. A few hours' exposure in this "fade-ometer" is equal to many days' exposure to the sun.

CIBA CORP., SUMMIT, N. J.

This swatch of fabric is made of 13 different fibers. It was immersed in a red dye suitable for nylon. Notice how the dye has almost no effect on acetate, arnel, and viscose, and produces a light red, or pinkish color on the other fibers. Finding dyes that are effective for each type of fiber is a real challenge to chemists.

create their own designed materials.

Later men found that a design painted with wax would not soak up the dye and that this wax could be removed later, leaving undyed sections. This *batik* method is recognized by a spidery effect caused by the wax cracking when placed in warm dye.

Hand blocked prints, tie and dye, and batik fabrics retain a charm of their own, that cannot be matched by modern methods, although today our machines and chemicals can quickly make designs on cloth that are different, beautiful, and permanent.

COLORFAST DYES

It is not possible to determine whether a color will be permanent just by looking at the cloth. It is necessary to read the labels carefully to understand their terms. The word "colorfast" is of little value unless you are told what the color will resist. Some colors will fade in washing but will be fast to sunlight, while others will change colors quickly in light and will come out of the wash look-

ing like new! Sunlight, drycleaning fluids, the heat of the iron, perspiration, and even the air can cause certain dyes to fade, or change color. It would seldom matter if a lovely evening gown made of taffeta was not fast to washing or sunlight as such a dress would not be exposed to these elements. A bathing suit, however, would need to be fast to salt and chlorine water as well as sunlight. Therefore, it is important that you learn to read the labels and to determine if the claims made suit your needs.

Vat dyes. When buying articles of cotton, linen, and rayon, you may often see the term *vat dyed*. This term originated a long time ago when a certain dyestuff had to steep in a large tub or barrel called a vat for several days. Today, this term refers to a specific type of dyestuff applied mainly to the cellulose fibers. It is considered the most colorfast of all dyes, but even very bright vat dyes may run or fade slightly.

419

STAGES IN DYEING

Textiles can be dyed at various stages in processing—from before man-made fibers are formed until after the cloth is woven. Whenever possible, cloth or piece dying is used, as it is cheapest, but dyeing at other stages may be necessary for certain finished effects.

Solution dyeing. Color substances can be put in the spinning solutions of some man-made fibers so that they emerge from the spinneret already colored. This is a true colorfast type of dyeing, as the color really becomes part of the fiber. The method was developed during World War II when the sailors were having difficulty with the black of their neckerchiefs rubbing off on their white uniforms. There were so many complaints that the Navy enlisted scientists to help solve this problem, and solution dyeing was developed. Not all colors can be created this way, as certain dyes will not react properly with the chemicals used to make the fibers. There are many trade names for fabrics dyed in

this manner, such as Celaperm, Jetspun, and Chromspun.

Stock dyeing. Some fibers are dyed while still in the loose fiber stage. Called stock, or fiber dyeing, this results in good dye penetration with a high degree of colorfastness. The yarns are very appropriate for heather effects as well as for some plaids and checks.

Yarn dyeing. Yarn is often dyed before being made into cloth. Yarn dyed fabrics also tend to have a high degree of colorfastness because the dye easily penetrates the yarn. This method is often used for plaids and checked fabrics. Yarn dyeing is less costly than stock dyeing but more expensive than piece dyeing.

Piece dyeing. Most solid color fabrics are piece dyed, which means the entire fabric is dyed after it is woven or knitted into cloth. Piece dyeing can result in colorfast colors. Heavy fabrics may not absorb the dye evenly and some color will be lost through wear and crocking (the rubbing away of color).

Stock dyeing—the fibers are dyed while in the loose fiber stage. The machine resembles a pressure cooker.

420

PENDLETON WOOLEN MILLS

Notice the plaid effect being created with the use of yarn-dyed warp and filling yarns at spaced intervals.

BELGIUM LINEN ASSOCIATION

Cross dyeing. Because certain fibers react only to certain dyes, it is possible to piece dye a fabric of two or more different fibers and have it emerge from the dye bath in different colors! For example, the red and white material pictured on this page is made of cotton and acetate fibers. When it was placed in a dye bath containing a red dye that "took" only on cotton, the acetate remained white so the effect of using two different colored yarns was achieved. Plaids and checks are often made this way.

Have you ever wondered why a fabric contains a large amount of one fiber and only a very small amount of another? There are many reasons, but sometimes it is for cross-dyeing purposes. For example, a fabric may be dipped in a blue dye that will be absorbed by some fibers only in a small amount, so a heather or other unusual effect results. You can see why fabrics made by the cross-dyeing method are cheaper to produce than by dyeing yarns separately at an earlier stage.

CIBA CORP., SUMMIT, N. J.

Special dyes are now available that will dye most fabrics satisfactorily in the home washer.

CIBA CORP., SUMMIT, N. J.

"Padding" is a relatively modern method of coloring fabric. The fabric is first run through the dye, then through pressure rollers which force the dye into the cloth. This process permits dyeing continuous rolls of fabric speedily and economically.

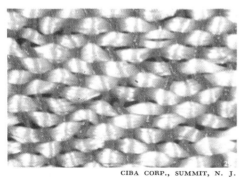

CIBA CORP., SUMMIT, N. J.

When a fabric is woven from fibers of different chemical composition—from cotton and acetate, for example, one fiber may accept a dye that the other refuses. In this fabric, the cotton fibers accepted the red dye and the acetate fibers remained unchanged. This is often called cross-dyeing.

CIBA CORP., SUMMIT, N. J.

Printing is another method used for coloring fabric.

Make a collection of labels and advertisements that make claims about the colorfastness of the dyestuffs used. Mount and explain the meaning of the terms used.

Bring to class fabrics that may have faded, or run, or bled, or crocked—where there was some problem with the coloring materials used. Explain to the class what happened and try to figure out how this could be prevented in the future. (Perhaps your neighbors or friends would lend you garments if you do not have any at home.)

Prepare a report for your class on the history of dyes. Encyclopedias and history books as well as geography reports furnish much information.

Prepare a display for your classroom tackboard of fabrics dyed at various stages: solution dyed, stock dyed, yarn dyed, fabric dyed, discharge dyed, and cross dyed. If you cannot find samples of fabrics dyed in all these methods, your class mates may be able to help you.

Experiment with resist methods of fabric dyeing. Select cotton or rayon fabrics which have been washed so no sizing remains. Tie off sections with heavy string or tie knots in the fabric . . . then dip in commercial dye solutions following directions on the dye packages. Rinse well under running cold water, untie, and press well. You may find that you can make scarfs, trimming for plain dresses, and other interesting accessories.

Prepare a demonstration for your classmates of the batik method of fabric dyeing and design. If you cannot find directions in art handcraft books in your library, most art supply stores can furnish information needed. Supplies can usually be obtained from grocery stores.

To determine the colorfastness of a fabric—select a colored fabric. Rub a white handkerchief over the fabric briskly. Notice whether some of the color rubs off. If so, this is an example of dry crocking. For wet crocking, try it with a wet handkerchief also.

Take a sample of fabric and cut in half. Mount one half carefully. Soak the other half in a solution of all-purpose detergent and water. Rinse; dry. Compare colors.

Cut a sample of fabric in half. Place one half of this in a dark place and put the other half on a window sill exposed to sun. Compare the two after a week or more.

To determine if a blouse or lining fabric will be affected by perspiration, you can do a simple test by wearing a piece of the fabric in your shoe for a few days. Sew it to a piece of white fabric and place it under your foot on the sole of the shoe. (You want a large enough piece to see any change of color but not so large it will be uncomfortable). Check to see if any of the color comes off on the white fabric. If so, you may have trouble with perspiration color change. You can also do this test in a laboratory by immersing a swatch of the test material and a white fabric in synthetic vinegar and keep at body temperature. Synthetic vinegar is close to human perspiration as it includes acetic acid.

PRINTING

Printing of fabrics is the application of color in the form of a surface design.

Roller printing. The most common method of printing today is with rollers. Thousands of yards can be printed this way in a short time. The design is engraved on a copper roller or cylinder. Each color requires a separate roller, continually supplied with color pastes. The fabric is fed through the rollers like a newspaper. Usually only one side of the fabric is printed. On sheer fabrics the color will penetrate and appear to be almost the same on both sides.

Occasionally the design is printed only on the *warp* threads, before the fabric is woven. When a solid color filling is put in, a shadowy design is made which is unusual and sought after for certain types of evening gowns. This is a rare, expensive method, as it is difficult to print on just the warp threads. Imitation warp prints may have a similar appearance but you can tell the true warp print by unraveling the threads. The filling threads will be a solid color and the print will be on the warp.

Fabrics can be roller printed to look like woven plaids and checks. These are satisfactory for many purposes but before buying it is important to be certain that the design is printed *on the grain.* If the printed lines are not parallel with the warp and filling threads, there will be many problems in sewing the fabric, as explained in Chapter 14.

Screen printing. When the design is too large to be placed on a roller or when only a small amount of fabric is to be made and it would not pay to engrave rollers, screen printing is

Dipping tied fabric into pots of various colored dyes. Notice how tongs are used to prevent burns.

used. A screen of fine silk, nylon, or other material is stretched on a frame. The screen is covered with a lacquer. A design is etched out or cut away and the color paste passes through only these openings onto the fabric. Many scarfs are made this way, as are colorful silks for blouses.

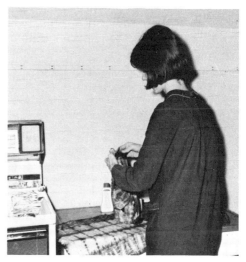

Untying the fabric is exciting as the finished fabric may have an unexpected design.

Discharge printing. Discharge printing is done on dyed fabrics and prints with a color-removing paste which removes or discharges certain portions of the color. The design is often white on dark backgrounds, such as polka dots, as it is hard to obtain dark colors even by printing. This must be carefully done so that the chemical in the color-removing paste does not eat away the fabric or weaken it for normal wear and laundering. Sometimes inexpensive bandanna-type handkerchiefs develop holes in the white areas for no apparent reason. These have probably been piece dyed red or blue and the color removed in the white areas. Some of the chemicals left on the fabric eventually weaken it.

Resist printing. A plain white fabric may have a paste design printed on it which will resist later dyeing. After dyeing, the paste is removed, leaving the design. This is similar to the batik method described on page 419 but is done by machines.

SPECIAL FINISHES FOR DESIGN AND TEXTURE

There are many other finishes which improve the design or texture of fabrics. Following is a description of some of these:

LUSTER FINISHES

Added luster can be created in many ways. Of course, luster obtained by fabric construction such as the satin weave is longer lasting than one produced by a finish. Sateen will retain its sheen longer than polished cotton.

NOTE. Fabrics with a finish applied to increase luster should be ironed on the right side to maintain the sheen.

Mercerization. You have already read about the mercerization process in Chapter 10. A slight luster is added to cellulose fibers when they are soaked in a caustic soda solution under tension.

Beetling. Linen fabrics are often beetled, which means that the fibers are pounded and flattened to reflect more light.

Calendering. Similar to the home ironing process, in calendering the cloth is run through polished, heated rollers under pressure so the surface is flatter, smoother, and glossier.

Glazing. Polished cottons and chintz fabrics have a glazed or shiny surface caused by the addition of resins or gums, sugars, or starches. NOTE: Synthetic resin gives the same effect as gums and starches but is more durable when it is washed.

THIRD DIMENSIONAL SURFACE EFFECTS

Some fabrics have third-dimensional surface effect caused by the type of weave used, such as velvets, brocades, and corduroys. Other special effects are created by finishing processes.

Moiré (more-ay). Great-grandmother probably had a Sunday dress of moire or watered silk. Moiré (a French word for watered) made it look watery, but the design usually disappeared with wear. Today most moire designs are permanent because the fibers used are heat-sensitive as acetate or nylon. As the heat melts the surface of the fabric in places, the design actually becomes part of the fabric. Thermosetting resins can be used with cotton fabrics to achieve similar effects.

Crinkle effects. Seersucker fabrics have a woven pucker, but plisse

American Indians used resist dyeing methods for fabric designs. The young man's shirt is an example of the use of matching blocks held firmly on either side of a fabric during the dyeing process to keep the color from penetrating the design area. Rosette knots were tied all over the girl's shirt before it was placed in the dye.

crepes and crinkle crepes are made by applying chemicals in stripes to plain fabrics. When subjected to special chemical applications, printed or striped parts of the fabrics shrink, leaving unexposed sections to crinkle.

Embossed designs. Embossed patterns may range from large roses that noticeably stand up from the fabric to simple, barely noticeable patterns such as embossed waffle pique. The design is carved on a roller and then thermoplastic fabrics are passed through, under steam and pressure. Resins added to cotton and rayon materials make it possible to emboss them. The embossing is permanent in nylon and other heat-sensitive fibers. NOTE: Follow the manufacturer's instructions for washing embossed cotton and rayon fabrics so as not to wash away the resins.

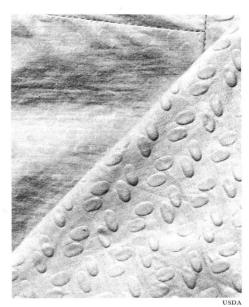

Embossed designs are permanent on heat-sensitive fibers. On fabrics of other fibers, the pattern may become less distinct with wear and laundering.

425

Flock printing. A design can be applied to a fabric with adhesive and then flocks—or short, fibrous particles—are dusted on. The resulting design is one that stands out from the fabric. It may or may not be permanent, depending upon the adhesive.

FINISHES THAT IMPROVE THE FEEL OR HAND OF FABRICS

Some fabrics are soft, others are crisp; some limp, others stiff. Many factors affect the feel of a fabric (spoken of as the hand), such as fiber content, type of yarn, finishes, and the fabric construction.

Sizing. Many people associate sizing with an inexpensive fabric used to make it look and sell better, but which is disappointing in use. Early sizings were largely of starch, gelatin, and waxes to make a fabric feel heavier and to have a smoother hand. The sizings filled in the openings in the weave and made the fabric appear to have a greater thread count. Even before being washed, many such fabrics lost much of their sizing through ordinary wear. After washing, the fabric became limp. Today permanent sizing is possible. Organdy can be made permanently crisp by an acid treatment. Other rayon and cotton fabrics can have resins added to create a stiffer or firmer effect which, with proper care, will last the lifetime of a garment.

Silk fabrics may be weighted as described in Chapter 10.

FINISHES FOR IMPROVED PERFORMANCE

Today many of the most important finishes cannot be seen. They change the properties of a fabric but they do not change the appearance or the feel. Because of these developments, we have raincoats made from cotton, shirts ready to wear right from the dryer, woolens safe from moths, and household fabrics that shake off spilled liquids.

SHRINKAGE CONTROL

You may not think shrinkage control very exciting, but you will appreciate it if you ever have a favorite dress that is too small to wear after one or two washings. Because fabrics shrink for many reasons, there are many different types of finishing processes to control shrinkage.

Most thermoplastic fabrics will not change their size as these fibers do not absorb moisture and have usually been heat set to a correct size during their manufacture. However, woolens and cellulose materials, if not properly treated, can shrink so that a garment may be no longer usable.

Many labels state that a garment is *preshrunk*, but this term is of little value. What you need to know is how much *more* it will shrink. Less than 1% residual or remaining shrinkage will not have any noticeable effect upon size, but more than 2% can affect the comfort and fit of a garment.

Some fabrics which have resin finishes added for improved crease resistance or water repellency will hold their original shape as long as the resin finish is intact. Improper washing (too much heat and too long agitation) may remove it and then you may find that a dress has become too small "all of a sudden."

NAPPING

Some fabrics are napped simply to improve the appearance, but this

426

finish serves generally to improve the *performance* of the material. By mechanical means such as the use of wire brushes or teasels (natural burrs), the ends of the fibers are roughed up or pulled to the surface to produce a downy or fuzzy effect, as in blanket cloth and flannelette.

Since napping pulls out fibers from the body of the fabric, it is important to examine a napped fabric carefully to see that the process has not weakened it. Hold the cloth up to the light to see any thin spaces. Rub the fabric between the thumb and forefinger to determine the firmness of both weave and nap. If the nap remains as part of the fabric, the cloth may be considered durable. If the nap comes off, the fabric may not prove serviceable.

Teasel.

Fabrics that have been napped are warmer, as air is trapped among the fibers and makes the fabric a good insulator. The material may appear softer and more attractive.

Conversely, the nap is not resistant to abrasion and may show early wear at the edges of sleeves, collars, and buttonholes.

• Sometimes napping conceals loosely woven cloth. Unfortunately, in such a case, the nap soons wears off and the base fabric appears.

• Some long-napped fabrics may shed.

• In sewing, garments must be cut so the nap goes in one direction, for example with fleece.

EASY CARE

When nylon, the polyesters and other thermoplastic fibers first came on the market, women experienced the joy of clothes that did not need ironing after every wearing or washing. They were used to having wrinkles hang out from woolen clothes, but wool was not suitable for all uses. To answer the demand for less ironing of all fabrics, chemists developed finishes for cotton, linen, and rayon which were first called *wash and wear*. So many problems developed that women began to think of these finishes as *"wash and beware."* Although *wash and wear* is still used, the term *easy care* is more accurate. The fabrics may need a little touchup after washing, but no longer is it necessary to sprinkle, starch, and laboriously iron every one.

Fabrics that have the terms *wash and wear*, *wrinkle-resistant* and *easy care* on their labels are made in a similar manner. Chemical substances, often resins, are applied to fabrics in different ways. These resin particles penetrate fibers more or less uniformly or are permanently cross-linked with the fiber molecules. Cross-linked fibers act much like a spring in a screen door —they return to their original shape when the strain is released. Just as a spring makes it harder to open the screen door, it is harder to wrinkle fabrics that are cross-linked or have resin finishes.

Resin finishes make the fibers less absorbent and therefore such fabrics will dry more quickly. They are warmer to wear, and may be less comfortable in warm, humid weather.

Many cotton fabrics lose strength when reacting to these chemical treatments and have a lower tear strength. Such cottons are often blended with polyesters or nylons for more strength. Others have an unpleasant odor, especially when moist.

One type of resin will react with chlorine in a chlorine bleach. This resin is called "chlorine retentive." Sometimes the fabric will turn yellow immediately; in other cases it will turn yellow after washing and being pressed with a warm iron. Eventually the concentrated chlorine will disintegrate the fabric. The tag on most fabrics bearing this finish has the words, *Do not use bleach.* However, it is wise not to use a chlorine type bleach on any fabric that claims to have an easy-care finish unless the label states that it may be bleached.

All such fabrics should be washed in cool or luke-warm water unless otherwise stated. Hot water may remove the resins, and then the fabric will no longer have its easy-care properties.

Some oily stains are difficult to remove from these finishes, especially if allowed to become set. "Come Clean" and "Soil Off" are examples of special finishes to release oily soil easily. It is advisable to remove all stains as soon as possible and never to press stained clothes of any kind.

Despite problems created by the finishes, women naturally prefer these fabrics as they are easy to care for and retain their appearance well. But remember, easy care does not mean *no care.* Follow directions on the label.

PERMANENT PRESS

The crease, the wrinkle, there isn't much doubt,
Are alike in a number of ways,

But the crease is the one that so quickly comes out,
While the wrinkle's the one that stays.

Courtesy of Richard Amour and
The Saturday Evening Post

No longer need this poem be true. Permanent press provides easier clothing care than ever before available. A garment that has been given this finish comes through automatic washing and drying smooth, ready to put on without a stroke of ironing. It will keep its shape and retain desired creases or pleats throughout the life of the garment. Many of the garments made with easy-care fabrics were disappointing because the sewing threads and the facing materials required ironing, although the fabric did not. The latest process is to treat a fabric with special resins but not to cure it until the garment is completely finished. The finish is set or cured by baking the garment in a factory oven at a temperature suited to each fiber used. The garment develops "memory" for the way it is set and will always return to this shape, provided any heat applied does not exceed that of the oven.

Blended fabrics have taken the lead in permanent press. Almost all permanent press processes involve the use of cross-linking chemical finishes that react only with the cellulose components (cotton or rayon) in the fabric. Because these chemicals also weaken cellulose, making it brittle and less resistant to abrasion (35% to 50% less strength), man-made fibers as nylons and polyesters are used to reinforce the fabric. The thermoplastic synthetics also aid in shape-setting when pressed with high-temperature presses.

Some permanent press garments

are made of 100 per cent man-made fibers—polyesters, nylons, or acrylics —by simply using the high-temperature presses and increased pressure.

Permanent press garments are difficult to alter, as seams can't be let out or hems lengthened without showing the original seam line. Therefore, check for correct fit when you buy. Proper care is also important, as most of the fabrics perform best if washed in warm (not hot) water, rinsed in cool water, removed from an automatic dryer when barely dry, and hung up properly. Line drying may require some ironing touch-up.

Stains need pretreating and chlorine bleach can create problems. Other problems sometimes present are color changes due to high temperature curing.

The joy of having blouses that always look neat, pants that maintain knife-sharp creases, and shirts that keep their crispness despite the weather offset the special care needed by this finish.

WATER AND STAIN-REPELLENT FINISHES

Few fabrics are waterproof unless they are of plastic film or fabrics with a plastic coating. Coats made of these materials are waterproof for heavy downpours but are not comfortable for frequent wear. No body moisture can escape and the wearer may become damp from perspiration rather than from the rain.

Water-repellent finishes have been developed which help fabrics resist wetting, and which can be penetrated only by continuous exposure to water. Chemicals are used that interact with the surface of individual fibers in such a way that water is

DOW CORNING

The effect of a drop of grape juice on fabrics treated with a water-repellent finish and an untreated fabric. Which fabric has been treated?

repelled. The spaces between the fibers are not closed and thus air and water vapor can move through for comfort. Some finishes are nondurable and need to be replaced after every cleaning; others are durable, will withstand proper laundering and dry-cleaning.

An easy test for water repellency is to place a drop of water on the flat surface of a fabric. If the drop flattens out, it has wet the surface and the cloth is not water repellent. If it takes on a spherical or round shape, it has not wet the surface and will probably roll off.

(SYLMER) DOW CORNING

Effect of water spilled on a loosely woven fabric treated with a water-repellent finish.

joyed without fear of stains, such as party clothes, upholstery materials, tablecloths, ties, and trousers, some finishes offer resistance to both oily and water-borne stains.

These finishing materials are applied in a bath or by spray as one of the final steps in fabric finishing. An invisible chemical shield formed around the fibers repels watery and oily substances.

Again, easy care does not mean *no care*. Stains should be removed as soon as possible by blotting, not rubbing. Stains that are allowed to remain become difficult to remove. More detailed directions are in Chapter 7. There are many trade names for water-repellent finishes such as Cravanette, Scotchgard, Sylmer, and Zepel. Look on the label to see if the finish is durable or non-durable and if resistant only to water-borne stains or also to oily stains.

In order to retain water repellency, clothes must be properly rinsed after cleaning. Because soaps and detergents are wetting agents, they cause water to penetrate which is *not* desired in a water-repellent fabric.

Garments which are machine launderable may need an extra cycle of rinsing. Ironing also helps maintain water repellency.

Soil and stain resistance. Water-repellent finishes will also repel water-borne stains so that such common spills as black coffee, tea, and soft drinks can be rolled off or blotted up before being absorbed to create a spot. Most water-repellent finishes will absorb oily materials so that coffee with cream will stain but black coffee will not. To meet the need for fabrics which can be en-

FIRE RETARDANTS AND FLAMEPROOFING

Some fibers are naturally fireproof. Mineral fibers such as asbestos and fiber glass cannot support combustion. Protein fibers and some thermoplastics are fire retardant, as they ignite slowly and burn only a very short time. However, thermoplastics melt as they burn; this melted substance can cause a severe burn if it sticks to the skin.

The Flammable Fabrics Act of 1957, amended in 1967, prohibited the sale of garments considered dangerously flammable.

Because of the growing concern for consumer safety, new federal standards for safe fabrics are being developed. Children's sleepwear, sizes 0–6x, sold after July, 1973, must meet standards for flame resistance. Some states have raised this requirement to sizes 14 and under.

Approved fabrics are not fireproof, but they are flame-resistant. They will not spread a fire and will not melt or drop a hot residue. Because many of the finishes may be destroyed by improper laundering, it is essential to follow directions given on labels of fire-resistant fabrics.

You can apply a temporary finish, especially valuable for children's costumes and holiday decorations. For a home treatment, the United States Department of Agriculture recommends that you purchase 3 ounces of boric acid and 7 ounces of borax from a drugstore. Dissolve these in 2 quarts of warm water. After the fabric has been soaked thoroughly in this solution and dried, it will be considered fire retardant. This finish needs to be renewed after every fabric washing or cleaning.

MOTH-RESISTANT FINISHES

Some fibers are naturally mothproof, as moths are not attracted to them. Wool and fabrics containing wool can now be made moth resistant through the use of fabric finishes. Certain chemical substances added during laundering or drycleaning will protect the fabric for several months, as described in Chapter 7. By the addition of chemical substances during cloth manufacture, wool fabrics can be made immune to moth damage for life. This finish adds only a little to the cost but is a valuable asset for sweaters or other articles that may be stored for long periods of time. *Mitin* is one trade name for a long-lasting finish.

HYGIENIC OR ANTISEPTIC FINISHES

Clothing fabrics may be treated with antibacterial finishes to retard the growth of bacteria and fungi. Such treatment helps prevent the spread of infection, reduces perspiration odor, and delays mildew attacks.

INSULATING FINISHES

A metallic coating on the back of a lining fabric provides warmth or coolness, depending upon the weather. In cold weather the body heat remains close to the body and in summer the sun rays are reflected away. The quality of the fabric to which these coatings (usually aluminum flakes) are applied determines the performance of the finish. A common insulating finish is known by the trade name *Milium*.

A flame-resistant treatment has been applied to this fabric.

DU PONT

BONDED FABRICS

Although not technically a finishing process, the technique of bonding one fabric to another is an important step in the completion of a finished fabric. Bonding is the process of permanently sealing one fabric to another. The first appearance of such fabrics was made in 1963 and since then fabric bonding has developed into a multi-million dollar market and is used for almost all purposes.

The first bonded fabrics used a polyurethane foam for the backing but today most fabrics are backed with a tricot of acetate or nylon. Fabrics of any type may be used for backing as well as for the face.

How are fabrics bonded together? All tricot and some urethane foam backings use a chemical adhesive as the bonding agent. The adhesive is coated or sprayed on the surface of the foam or fabric underlining and the fabrics are joined together with light pressure from rollers. Heat is needed to melt the surface of some adhesives; in others the adhesive has holding power by itself.

In some cases, the foam is bonded to the outer fabric by fusion. The surface of the foam is slightly melted by a gas flame so that it adheres to the outer fabric when brought next to it.

Bonding can be long-lasting but there is no way the consumer can tell by appearance or feel whether or not the fabrics will separate. Very smooth, slick surfaced fabrics such as satins and taffetas may not hold the bonded fabric as well as those with rough surfaces or those woven from short fibers. In these cases, the invisible network of tiny fiber ends helps hold the two fabrics together. Although most bonded fabrics will wear well, it is important to purchase them from reliable retailers who will stand behind their products.

• *Urethane foam.* Foam laminates consist of one sheet of foam which may vary from $\frac{1}{32}$ to $\frac{1}{8}$ inch thick. The foam is applied by adhesive or a heat method. These fabrics may be washed or drycleaned. If pressing is needed, press on the fabric side with a low heat or steam setting.

Advantages of foam bonded fabrics are:

Added warmth due to insulating qualities of air held in many tiny cells of the foam.

Lightweight.

Protection against stretching in knitted and loosely woven fabrics.

Added resistance to wrinkling.

Adds new feel and plumpness.

• *Tricot lining.* Tricot, a warp knit fabric, is usually made of acetate for lining bonded fabrics. If washability is essential, nylon is preferred. Advantages of tricot-bonded fabrics are:

Controlled degree of stability with some elasticity or "give."

Resiliency.

Crease-resistance improved.

Good drapability.

Easier to sew—less seam fraying and raveling or curling.

Can be pleated by heat setting when outer fabric may not allow such pleating.

Use of unusual fabrics such as very loosely woven or knitted ones because the backing provides stability.

Garment has comfort of soft lining but is more easily made without need for separate lining, which can creep and bunch up.

Many fabrics have an improved hand and drape and a more elegant appearance.

432

COMFORT-STRETCH

Many stretch fabrics are made with the use of yarns which are elastic, either because of inherent stretch properties as those that contain spandex fibers or those that are texturized and heat set for stretch described on page 394. However, a finishing process known as slack mercerization is also used to provide comfort—stretch, a term used for a small amount of stretch which provides for "give," for comfort in routine wear or mild activity. This finish is applied to fabrics, usually cotton.

Fabrics are soaked without tension in a bath of sodium hydroxide—the same chemical used in mercerizing cotton. This causes the fabric to shrink and although it will stretch when worn, it will return to its original shape. These fabrics often stretch only in the cross-wise direction. The resulting fabric not only is more comfortable to wear but it is more wrinkle-free as there is less strain because the fabric gives with body movement. Special sewing care is needed for comfort-stretch fabrics as described in Chapter 17.

Make a collection of labels and advertisements that contain trade names of various finishing processes. Underline the names and terms describing the finishes. Be able to explain what they mean.

Wash a simple cotton percale fabric. Cut it in half. Prepare the fire retardant finish described on page 431. Dip half of the cloth in this solution and let dry thoroughly. Carefully hold the untreated cloth with tweezers or forceps to candle flame and observe. Do the same for the fabric treated with the fire retardant finish. What difference do you notice?

Secure samples of fabrics that are labeled stain or water-repellent. Place drops of water, coffee, and salad oil on them. Notice the effect of these liquids. How accurate are the labels?

Select embossed cottons such as plisse crepe and those with other designs. While wet, iron firmly. What has happened to the design? Formulate rules for care of fabrics with embossed designs.

To determine the effect of ironing on the sheen of a fabric, select a dark-colored cotton. Iron one half with a hot iron, pressing hard. Leave the other half unironed or iron it on the opposite side. Compare the appearance of the ironed section. Mount and label as to effect of ironing on the right side.

Test cellulose and protein fabrics for potential shrinkage. Secure a 5 or 10 inch sample of cotton fabric and one of wool that have not been labeled pre-shrunk. Carefully mark a 4 or 9 inch square with waterproof ink or with basting threads on each sample. If the fabric frays badly, you may need to overcast the outer edges. Wash with a regular load of laundry in a machine with all-purpose soap or detergent and dry as usual. Do not iron. Carefully measure the dried samples. Figure the shrinkage per yard by multiplying by 9 if you had a 4 inch sample, or by 4 if your sample measured 9 inches. Do the same with a sample of fabric guaranteed not to shrink. Compare results.

Can You Explain These Terms?

gray cloth	*resist printing*	*easy care*
block printing	*luster*	*wash and wear*
tie and dye	*mercerize*	*permanent or durable press*
batik	*beetling*	*chlorine retentive*
color fast	*calendering*	*wrinkle resistance*
vat dyes	*glazing*	*crease resistance*
solution dyeing	*moire*	*waterproof*
stock dyeing	*embossing*	*water repellent*
yarn dyeing	*flock printing*	*water-borne stains*
piece dyeing	*resins*	*oily stains*
cross dyeing	*sizing*	*fireproof*
crocking	*preshrunk*	*fire retardant*
roller printing	*residual shrinkage*	*insulating finish*
screen printing	*dimensional stability*	*bonded fabrics*
discharge printing	*nap*	*comfort-stretch*

Summary With Check-up Questions

Fabrics which have just come off a loom or knitting machine are seldom ready for use. Finishes must be applied to make the cloth look better, feel better, and/or to give better service.

What is the purpose of finishes that:
- *Make the fabric more water repellent?*
- *Apply color to a fabric?*
- *Smooth a fabric?*
- *Make a fabric resistant to shrinkage?*

Trade names of finishes are too numerous to memorize and new ones are introduced often. The consumer must learn to read labels and understand the purposes and claims for various processes.
- *Why is it important to save the labels of garments?*
- *Why must a consumer notice carefully whether a label states, for example, that a garment is waterproof or water resistant?*

Dyeing of fabrics can take place at various stages from before the spinning of man-made fibers until the fabric is completely woven.
- *What is the term for dyeing fibers in loose fiber stage?*
- *What is the term for dyeing a woven fabric one color?*
- *Why is it possible for a fabric to be dipped in a one color dye and the resulting fabric emerge in two colors?*
- *What does solution-dyed mean?*

The term "colorfast" means many different things, as colors may be affected by sunlight, water, detergents, perspiration, fumes in the air, chlorine, and other chemicals.
- *What is the difference between a color that fades and one that "runs?"*
- *Why are some fabrics colorfast to laundering but fade when worn in swimming pools or the ocean?*

- *How does crocking differ from fading?*

Printing is the application of color to a fabric in the form of a design.

- *What are the advantages of roller printing compared with screen printing?*
- *Why are fabrics with large amounts of dark, solid colors and small amounts of light-colored designs such as polka dots usually created by the discharge method?*
- *Why are yarn-dyed plaid fabrics usually of better quality than those with printed plaid designs?*

Built-in fabric designs created by construction methods nearly always last longer than those created by finishes added to the fabric.

- *Luster created by a satin weave is longer-lasting than one created by the addition of glazing materials as starches or resins. Why?*
- *Why do patterns in fabrics created by figured weaves outlast those created by embossing methods?*

Shrinkage control finishes are desirable on fabrics made of cellulose and protein fibers.

- *Why do hydrophobic fibers seldom shrink?*
- *Of what value is the term "preshrunk" on a label? What is a preferred term?*

Fabrics which have been napped are warmer, feel soft, and have an interesting appearance.

- *Why are napped fabrics warmer than similar unnapped fabrics?*
- *Why is it difficult to notice when poor quality yarns have been used in napped fabrics?*

The term "wash and wear" is primarily concerned with fabrics while the terms "durable" and "permanent press" are concerned with completed garments.

- *Why do garments made from wash and wear fabrics often need touch-up ironing along seam lines, facings, and other details?*
- *Why are alterations difficult to make on durable-pressed garments?*

"Permanent press" fabrics are either heavyweight cotton fabrics or blends of cellulose and nylon or polyester fibers.

- *What is the effect of the chemicals used for this process on the strength of cellulose fibers?*
- *Why are polyesters and nylons desirable fibers to blend with cotton for durable-pressed fabrics?*

Stain-resistant finishes may resist water type stains, oily stains or both. When stains do penetrate the finish, they should be removed as soon as possible before being absorbed by the fabric.

- *Water-repellent finishes repel some staining materials as well as light rain.*

  Stain-repellent finishes may resist both water and oily stains. Why is this type finish necessary for many fabrics?
- *Why are fabrics with water-repellent finishes not suitable for wear in heavy rains?*

Bonding one fabric to another is an important process in the finishing of fabrics.

- *When are polyurethane foams desired for backing purposes?*
- *When would acetate tricot materials be desirable?*
- *What are the advantages of nylon tricot over acetate tricot backings?*

CHAPTER THIRTEEN

Fabrics for Clothing

FABRICS FOR CLOTHING can be of an infinite variety due to variations in fiber content, methods of construction, design, and finish. However, there are certain fabrics which are used commonly every year. The informed person needs to know the proper name for these frequently used materials. To call a piece of cloth "cotton" is of little meaning because it may be as fine as batiste, as heavy as canvas, or as luxurious as velveteen. The same can be true of fabrics made from other fibers.

A fabric called by its fiber content only is assumed to be of plain weave, medium weight, with no distinguishing characteristics. Whenever possible, learn the proper name of a fabric and use it.

Fabrics can be classified in various ways as many are similar; in fact, it is difficult for even a textile expert to distinguish between certain fabrics, such as between a heavy broadcloth and a fine poplin. However, it is of value to know as much as possible about each fabric classification and each specific fabric so you will select, sew, and care for fabrics wisely.

Fabric popularity goes in cycles. Some basic fabrics are always in wide use while others tend to disappear from common use for a few years and then reappear with great interest for a time until others take their place. Some years "fashion" calls for garments made from heavily textured yarns; then bouclés, crashes, and even burlap fabrics are popular for clothing. As the consumer tires of these fabrics, other types will gain in popularity until they, too, are replaced by the "latest." During the years when a popular fabric is in great demand, fabric departments will feature many, many bolts and varieties. Other years only the largest stores will carry even a small amount of this fabric. Some seasons a "new" fabric appears on the market which is a basic one simply called by an appealing name.

In this chapter fabrics will be grouped by common characteristics, usually in order of finest to heaviest or a similar manner. On page 437 there is an alphabetical listing of fabrics for easy reference, even if you are unsure of its classification.

FABRIC INDEX

PLAIN WEAVE FABRICS

Plain weave fabrics are made on a two-harness loom and are the least expensive to produce. Unless there is a printed design or a surface finish, there is no right or wrong side. Fabrics that are balanced (have approximately the same number of threads going in each direction) wear better than unbalanced fabrics where there is a great difference between the number of warp and filling yarns. Plain weave fabrics with strong yarns and a high count (many threads per square inch) wear better than those of lesser quality and fewer yarns.

Sheer fabrics are very thin, lightweight, and transparent. They may ravel considerably and seams which will show through the fabric need to be of uniform width and carefully finished. Lightweight zippers and other fastenings should be used. Facings and interfacings can create problems as plain material showing through the outer fabric may cause it to appear differently as will the use of the same fabric, especially if figured. It is better to line the entire bodice of such a garment than to try to face the neckline and other openings. Undergarments must be chosen with special care for their appearance. Sheer fabrics are cool but if heavier undergarments are necessary, they may be warmer than expected. Thread slippage can create problems unless of high count or made from the leno weave as described on page 406.

• *Middleweight* fabrics of the plain weave are probably used in the largest quantity. These materials take their charm from their color and applied design.

• *Heavyweight* fabrics have coarser yarns and a medium thread count.

Special heavy duty threads are needed when sewing with such heavy fabrics as canvas.

• *Lightweight* plain weave fabrics with no special distinguishing characteristics include the following:

Cheesecloth. Thin, loosely woven cotton of carded yarns. Originally used for wrapping cheese. Fine grades used for covering hotbeds and tobacco fields, bandages and costumes. Typical thread count varies from 20 to 12 to 44 x 40.

Batiste (baa-TEEST). Soft, sheer cotton fabric, finer than nainsook and softer than lawn. Long-staple, combed fibers used. Usually mercerized. Also made from blends of polyester and cotton. Used for lingerie, infants' wear, and blouses.

Lawn. Lightweight, thin plain weave cotton of combed or carded yarns, not mercerized. Finish may be soft or fairly stiff. Used for curtains, linings, handkerchiefs, and women's clothing. Liberty lawn is a well-known fabric from Great Britain.

Longcloth. Lightweight, unfinished bleached muslin free from starch or sizing. Used for underwear and linings.

Nainsook. Fine, soft, white cotton with a slight polish on one side. Longcloth and nainsook are identical before finishing. Finer grades may be mercerized. Used for infants' clothing, lingerie, blouses.

Voile. Thin, transparent fabric. Slightly crisp feel due to tightly twisted yarns. Best quality made from 2-ply combed yarns with hard twist; poorer quality yarns become fuzzy. Used for summer dresses and blouses.

China-silk. Plain weave, lightweight fabric used for scarfs.

• *Medium weight* plain weave fabrics include the following:

Percale. (per-kale). Very common cotton fabric, usually printed but may be white or dyed. Checks and plaids may be printed to simulate gingham. Good quality often called 80 square, meaning approximately 80 warp and 80 filling threads per square inch. May be carded or combed. Used for dresses, blouses, sleepwear, children's clothes, and sheets.

Muslin. Firm, plain weave cotton fabric, stronger and heavier than longcloth and percale. Little sizing used except in poor grades. May be bleached, semi-bleached, or unbleached. Muslin is a term often applied to any plain-weave, balanced fabric ranging from lawn to bed sheeting. It is a specific term for medium weight fabrics which are stronger and heavier than longcloth and percale and are starched or given a slightly crisp finish. Used for sleepwear, dresses, children's clothes, and sheets.

Indian Head. Trade name for a plain weave cotton fabric, white or

Indian Head.

vat-dyed, or printed with a smooth, durable finish. Used for a variety of household purposes and many types of garments.

Calico. Term refers to small, all-over old fashioned print on plain weave cotton of medium weight. Used for household fabrics and dresses.

Challis (shall-ee). Lightweight dress fabric of wool made of soft, smooth yarns, often printed but may be of plain colors. Usually woven 27″ wide. Used for dresses and robes.

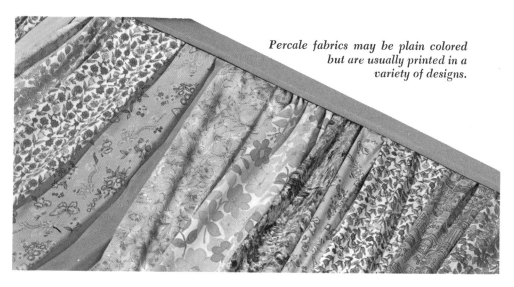

Percale fabrics may be plain colored but are usually printed in a variety of designs.

Challis may also be made of rayon spun yarns, used for nightwear. Often printed with a delicate, dainty design.

Sharkskin. Firm, medium weight smooth fabric of dull acetate or Arnel filament yarns. Used for tennis dresses, summer skirts, and sportswear. Differs from men's sharkskin suiting.

Taffeta. See rib-weave fabrics.

• *Heavyweight* plain weave fabrics include the following:

Canvas. Heavy, firm plain weave cotton or linen cloth. Ranges from lightweight used for interfacings to heavyweight used for tents. Some weights are called duck or sailcloth.

Burlap. Coarse canvas made of jute fibers in natural tan; may be dyed. Low grades for gunny sacks and furniture webbing; better grades for draperies and novelty clothing.

YARN-DYED PLAIN WEAVE FABRICS

A few fabrics are differentiated from similar plain weave ones because of the use of colored yarns in certain patterns. For example, a medium weight fabric with a printed plaid would be called a percale but if the plaid design is produced by the use of different colored yarns, it would correctly be called gingham. Examples include:

Chambray. Plain weave with lengthwise and crosswise yarns of different colors. The filling threads are often white and the selvages will appear all white. Occasionally there are woven-in stripes. Heavy weight used for men's work shirts. Other weights for sports clothes and dresses.

Gingham. A yarn-dyed plain weave fabric in checked or plaid pat-

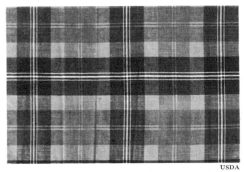

USDA

Gingham, a woven plaid, plain weave fabric.

terns. Fine ginghams are of combed and mercerized yarns; lower grades are carded. (Tissue gingham is a finer weight fabric.) Used for dresses, blouses, sport shirts, children's wear, and curtains.

Madras (mad-dress). A type of gingham woven in India of yarns which will bleed or run in washing, resulting in a soft, muted appearance. Used for sport shirts, summer jackets, and dresses. Madras with a woven pattern is a different fabric.

Tarpoon. A trade name for a yarn-dyed woven pattern poplin. Usual design is small tartan plaids. Used for children's snowsuits, men's golf jackets, walking shorts, and general sportswear.

CRISP, SHEER PLAIN WEAVE FABRICS

Fabrics may be stiffened with the addition of sizings which add body, stiffness, and weight. Temporary sizings are starch and gelatin and durable finishes are made by the addition of resins or cellulose solutions. Examples are:

Tarlatan. Thin, open fabric of plain weave, highly sized. About as coarse as cheesecloth but stiff. White or colors. Does not launder well. Used for costumes and Christmas stockings.

Crinoline. Stiff, open, plain weave fabric highly sized with a dull finish. Used for interlinings, petticoats, and bookbindings. Usually only white, gray, or black.

Buckram. Two-ply cotton fabric stiffened with glue or other sizing for hat frames, interlinings for purses and fabric details. Seldom washable.

Organdy. Thin, stiff transparent fabric of cotton in plain weave with fine combed yarns. Low grades are coarse, wrinkle easily, and soften with wear. Better grades have durable crisp finish. Used for dresses, curtains, blouses, and collars.

Organza. Sheer fabric of silk in plain weave. Slightly stiff because of silk gum. Resembles organdy but softer drape. May be made of rayon or synthetic fibers with finishes.

LENO WEAVE FABRICS

The leno weave is used to provide firmness and strength for sheer, low count fabrics. Each pair of warp yarns is crossed around one filling yarn and this prevents slippage of yarns. May be combined with other weaves for novelty, open effects in shirtings and dress fabrics. Often used for bags for laundry and vegetables, and for mosquito netting. The major clothing fabric is described below:

Marquisette. Made from cotton, linen, rayon, or any man-made fiber. Usually used for curtains or formal gowns. Always distinguished by leno weave.

PLAIN WEAVE, BASKET WEAVE VARIATION FABRICS

Basket weaves are made with two or more adjacent warp yarns woven as one and with two or more adjacent filling yarns woven as one. The most common basket weaves are 2 x 2 or 4 x 4, but other combinations are used. Variations are made by using two yarns in the warp direction and one in the filling direction, as in oxford cloth.

Usually the thread count is not high and the resulting fabric is porous and very pliable. Wrinkles "hang out." The fabric is absorbent and comfortable in humid weather.

Common basket-weave fabrics are:

Monk's cloth. Rough material made of heavy cotton yarns. Usually natural color, may also appear to be oatmeal color due to ply yarns, one natural and one dyed brown. Used mainly for draperies, scarfs, or novelty clothing items.

Hopsacking. Somewhat porous but strong basket-weave cloth made of cotton, linen, or wool. Used primarily for coats and suits.

Duck, canvas, and *sailcloth* may be made with a basket weave but are plain weave fabrics of plyed yarns.

Oxford cloth. A 2 x 1 fabric made of combed cotton yarns with the warp yarns much finer than the filling yarns. It has a flat appearance because the two warp yarns occupy the same space as the one filling yarn. White or yarn dyed. Used for men's shirts, blouses, and dresses.

PLAIN WEAVE, RIB VARIATION FABRICS

Ribbed fabrics are made with a plain weave with many more warp than filling yarns. The result is a crosswise rib or ridge. The warp yarns often completely cover the filling yarns which may be the same size or much larger. Ribbed fabrics are always unbalanced, having a ratio of two warps to one filling or greater.

Ribbed fabrics have more body because there are more interlacings per square inch than in balanced plain-weave fabrics. The heavier the fabric, the more body it has and it will be more suitable for a bouffant silhouette. An exception is broadcloth, a fine, mercerized fabric which is softer and has better drape than percale.

In a fabric where the warps may cover the filling yarns, warp yarns may wear out first, resulting in crosswise breaks. Slippage of warp yarns across the filling yarns may occur in filament fabrics of medium to low quality. Some fabrics may shrink excessively in the lengthwise direction, because the heavy filling yarns swell when wet and cause the lengthwise yarns to draw up or shorten to cover them. When dry, the warp yarns tend to maintain their drawn-up length.

Broadcloth. The finest crosswise rib, often difficult to notice. Unless examined closely, may be mistaken for percale, but thread count is different; combed broadcloth may be 144 x 76 and carded cloth 100 x 60. Often mercerized to increase luster. Used commonly for men's shirts, blouses, uniforms, and pajamas. May also be made from silk or nylon. Wool broadcloth has a slight nap brushed in one direction. See p. 447.

Faille.

Poplin. Heavier crosswise yarns so that fine crosswise ribs are noticeable. Usually cotton fibers, often mercerized. Used for nurse's uniforms and summer jackets.

Faille (file). Soft, ribbed fabric of silk, rayon, or synthetic fibers. Lighter and flatter ribs than bengaline. Used for women's dresses, men's ties, dressy blouses.

Bengaline. Crosswise ribs heavier than faille. Filling yarns often of cotton fibers and covered completely by warp yarns of silk or synthetic filament fibers. Used for dresses, suits, summer coats.

Grosgrain (GROW-grain). Firm, stiff, pronounced ribbed fabric. Filling yarns usually cotton and warp yarns of rayon, silk, or synthetics. Often woven in narrow width for ribbons.

Ottoman. Heavy corded silk, rayon, nylon, or wool fabric with a cotton cord filling. Broad flat ribs alternate with smaller ribs. Used for dressy suits and coats.

Rep. Resembles poplin but has a heavier and flatter rib effect. May be of cotton or silk or synthetic fibers. Used for men's ties, suits, or in heavy weight for upholstery fabrics.

Moire (mor-RAY). Lustrous, watery design embossed on a faille fabric. Design is permanent only on thermoplastic fibers.

Taffeta. Taffeta has a crosswise rib that is flatter and less noticeable than other rib fabrics. It has a crispness or body, often applied by special finishes. Made of filament fibers, it may vary from a fine, lightweight (tissue) to a medium-weight fabric. The term taffeta is confusing as it may refer to a balanced plain-weave fabric as well as a ribbed fabric. Used for formal gowns.

CORDED FABRICS

Cords are vertical or warpwise ridges and are not to be confused with ribs as in faille and bengaline that go crosswise. Examples include:

Pique (pea-KAY). Has warpwise corded effect due to extra filling yarns on the back and stuffer warp yarns under each cord. May be pin wale or wide wale. Usually of mercerized cotton yarns, but may be of almost any fiber. Variations include *birdseye* pique where the cords are made in such a way that they come together and then separate to form a birdseye effect. This fabric is not reversible as is birdseye diaper cloth.

Bedford cord. Coarser and heavier than pique but made in a similar manner. Corded material first made in New Bedford, Massachusetts; hence the name. Today usually called just "cord." Made of wool or cotton yarns or blended with man-made fibers. Used for suits, sports clothes, uniforms.

Dimity. Sheer and crisp cotton fabric made of combed or carded yarns. Warp-wise cords made by weaving two or more yarns as one and separating them with areas of plain

Can you find examples of the following fabrics in this illustration—lace, dotted Swiss, tricot, lamé, brocade? Would you call any of these fabrics by other names?

weave. Used for little girl's dresses, summer wear.

TWILL WEAVE FABRICS

A twill weave is one in which each filling yarn floats across two or more warp yarns with a progression of interlacings of one or more to the right or left to form a distinct diagonal line, or wale.

Twill fabrics vary in the prominence of the wales, the direction of the twill line, the degree of angle of twill, and the type of floats on the surface of the cloth. (A float is that portion of a yarn which goes over two or more yarns.)

The prominence of a twill line or wale is increased with long floats and hard twist yarns.

Printed pique. Notice the lengthwise ridges.

The direction of the twill wale usually slants up to the right in wool fabrics while in cotton fabrics the twill line goes up to the left. This fact may help determine the right or wrong side of a fabric.

The degree of angle of the twill depends on the ratio of warp to filling yarns. A regular or even twill has the twill line at a 45 degree angle. If a fabric is folded so a warp thread parallels a filling thread, an even twill line should be exactly on the bias. A steep twill has an angle greater than 45 degrees and a reclining twill (sometimes called lazy twill) is less than 45 degrees.

Twill fabrics are seldom printed because the surface already has an interesting texture due to the wales. Some silk twills are exceptions. A twill weave makes it possible to pack more yarns into a given space than a plain weave, and to create a very strong fabric. Because of fewer interlacings, so the yarns can move more freely, twill fabrics are softer and have better wrinkle recovery than a comparable plain weave cloth.

Twill fabrics do not have an up and down unless there is a design or heavy nap applied. (Turn the fabric upside down and examine the direction of the twill line; it always goes the same way!) Except for even twills where the filling thread goes over two warps and under two warps, there is a right and wrong side to the fabric. In a few fabrics the filling threads float on the surface of the fabric but in a majority the warp yarns come to the surface more often.

Twill fabrics present few problems in use except for those with prominent wales such as gabardine which may become flat by improper press-

ing or wear. The result will be a shiny appearance, especially in dark colors. Occasionally the direction of prominent twills will appear different on coat lapels and will necessitate special cutting of a pattern. Common twill weave fabrics are:

Serge. Even 2x2 twill, reversible, usually of worsted yarns but may have woolen or acrylic yarns one way for softness, becomes shiny with hard wear. Used for uniforms and men's suits.

Gabardine. A warp-faced twill with a very pronounced distinct steep twill line. It has a 60 degree or greater angle. The wrong side does not appear to be a twill weave. Hard, yet smooth and very little nap. Made of cotton, rayon, wool, or blends for jackets, slacks, shorts, and raincoats.

Covert (COE-vert). Made of cotton with a mottled effect due to two-ply yarns of different colors. Finer yarns for children's wear; heavier weight for uniforms. If made of wool fibers, usually of worsted yarns.

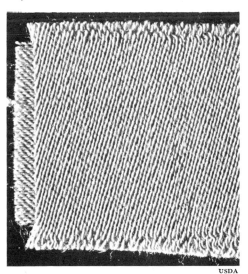

Gabardine. The steep twill line is from lower left to upper right.

Looks like gabardine but is coarser. Often has a flecked appearance. Durable, long-wearing. Used for suits, uniforms, coats, and riding apparel.

Whipcord. Steep twill similar to gabardine but heavier. Worsted, woolen, or heavy cotton; solid color; for riding habits, uniforms, and outdoor garments.

Sharkskin. A worsted twill men's suiting material. Light and dark yarns alternate lengthwise and crosswise. May be plain, striped, or patterned. Neat, sturdy, and practical; good for office wear. Spots and mends do not show readily. Differs from plain weave sharkskin used for women's clothing.

Denim. Heavy right-hand twill made of coarse cotton yarns. Heavier than jean cloth, less coarse than drill. Colored warp yarns and white or light filling yarns. Comes in various weights. Used for work clothes, sportswear, and slipcovers.

Drill. Cotton material resembling denim. May be bleached, unbleached, or piece-dyed. Lightweight drill is often called jean cloth and used for play clothes. Khaki colored drill used for uniforms.

Foulard. Soft, lightweight silk fabric, always printed. Occasionally of cotton or rayon. Used for neckties, linings, dresses. May be called "tie silk."

Surah. Slightly firmer than foulard. Silk, nylon, acetate, or rayon in twill weave plain or printed; for dresses, linings, kerchiefs, and ties. May be called "tie silk" also.

PILE FABRICS

Pile fabrics are three-dimensional fabrics with tufts or loops standing up from a basic cloth. An additional set of warp or filling yarns is woven into the basic cloth structure (plain or twill weave) to make loops or cut ends on the surface.

Quality and durability are determined by the thread count. The higher the count, the denser the pile and the more durable the cloth. A close weave increases the resistance of looped pile fabrics to snagging and of cut-pile fabrics to shedding and pulling out.

Pile fabrics are warmer than flat fabrics because they entrap more body heat. If the pile is worn next to the body instead of on the outside, more heat is entrapped. Pile fabrics are absorbent (if the fibers used are absorbent) because more yarn is exposed. This explains why most bath towels are of a looped pile weave.

Cutting and sewing of pile fabrics requires special consideration. Pile fabrics have an up and down, even if made of one all-over color. Light reflects differently from each direction of the pile. The fabric looks richer as one looks into the pile, so that most garments are cut with the pile directed up. The important thing is to cut all pieces with the pile going in the same direction. Otherwise, it may appear as if fabric of two different colors is used.

Common pile fabrics are described below:

Terry cloth. A highly absorbent fabric made from cotton or rayon yarns with loops on one or both sides. Fabric does not have an up and down direction as cut pile does. Needs very little ironing. Used for bath towels, beach robes, and sportswear.

Velveteen. A filling-face pile fabric

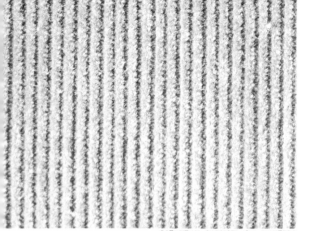

Blow up of pinwale corduroy (*usually 16 ribs to the inch*).

Blow up of midwale corduroy (*usually 14 ribs to the inch*).

Some corduroy fabrics are printed and may resemble other fabrics at a distance.

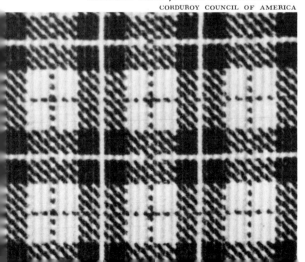

woven of soft, mercerized cotton yarns which form floats which are later cut and brushed to form a short pile. May be washed with care. Used for formal wear, robes, and children's dresses. Has more body and less drapability than velvet.

Corduroy. Short pile formed into lengthwise ribs or ridges. Wide wale has 3 to 10 ribs per inch: medium wale has 14 ribs; pinwale has 16 ribs. A combed pinwale may be as fine as 21 ribs per inch. Needs little or no ironing, especially if dried in tumble dryer. Used for children's clothing, bedspreads, sportswear, and heavier weights for coats.

Velvet. A warp pile fabric formed by the weaving of two fabrics together with a 5th set of yarns. The two fabrics are cut apart and the pile brushed up. Pile is usually $\frac{1}{16}$ inch or shorter. May be made of silk, rayon, or synthetic fibers. More lustrous and drapable than velveteen. Used for formal gowns and evening coats.

Velour. Fabric with a short pile, heavier than velveteen, usually of cotton and used for upholstery purposes. Wool velour is heavily napped to resemble a pile fabric and is used for coats. Another velour is a felt which has a close nap and is used for hats.

Plush. A cut-pile fabric with a deeper pile than velvet or velour, usually greater than $\frac{1}{4}''$. It may be made from cotton, wool, silk, or man-made fibers. Used for coats, upholstery, powder puffs, and coat collars.

Fur-like fabrics. Resemble plush but may be finished by curling, shearing, or printing to resemble real fur. Often made of blends of modacrylic and acrylic fibers.

446

NAPPED FABRICS

A finishing process for many fabrics is napping which is pulling loose fibers to the surface of the fabric. The raised fibers form a downy surface on the fabric and change its appearance and texture. Loosely twisted yarns are needed in at least one direction to provide for easy exposure of fiber ends. Napped fabrics should not be confused with those made with a pile weave although at first glance they may appear the same. Napping may flatten or wear off but the three dimensional quality of the pile fabrics is built-in.

Napped fabrics are warmer than flat fabrics because the fibers form air pockets which insulate and retain the body warmth of the wearer.

Because the napping hides the original yarns of the fabric, it is difficult to determine the quality of the yarns used. The nap of low quality yarns may wear down quickly around the edges of a coat, under buttons, or any place that is subject to abrasion. Although the fabric is still strong, it will appear "worn."

Napped fabrics made of cotton and rayon fibers flatten under pressure and have less insulating value than wool because cellulose fibers are less resilient. Fibers are shorter so there may be more shedding.

Common napped fabrics are:

Flannel. The word flannel is closely associated with the napping finish. Flannel fabrics may be of wool, rayon, acrylic, or other man-made fibers in a plain or twill weave but all are napped to some extent. Used for suits, coats, robes, and sportswear.

Suede cloth. Woven or knit of cotton, rayon, or wool and closely napped to resemble chamois leather. For sports coats, gloves, and slippers.

Duvetyn (dōō-ve-tēn). Made of various fibers in plain or twill weave with a napped surface but softer than suede cloth. Used for dresses and sportswear.

Broadcloth. When made of wool, broadcloth has a nap that is pressed in one direction to add luster. May be of several weights. Used for coats, suits, and dresses.

Fleece. A coat weight fabric with a long brushed nap. Do not confuse with plush or pile fabrics. May be of loosely twisted yarns. Used for winter coats and sportswear.

A

B

USDA

Twill weave fabric (A) before napping and (B) after napping. Notice how the raised fibers make it difficult to observe the weave.

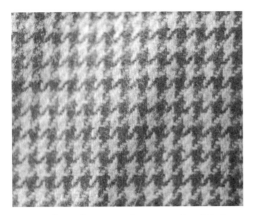
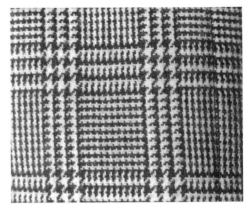

Flannel in two designs. The fabric on the left is a shepherd check design and the one on the right is commonly called a Glen plaid.

Flannelette. Soft cotton fabric, napped on one side, usually striped or printed. Used for sleeping garments, interlinings, and shirts.

Outing flannel. A white or yarn-dyed cotton fabric napped on both sides. Used for same purposes as flannelette.

Canton flannel. Heavy cotton material with twilled weave showing on one side and long, soft nap on the other. Bleached, unbleached, or piece-dyed. Used for work gloves, sleeping garments, and interlinings.

Zibeline. Heavy woolen coating with long shaggy nap pressed in one direction. Often a lustrous appearance.

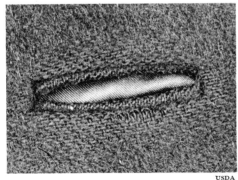

USDA

Wool fleece, showing wear around button-holes.

448

Melton. Thick, smooth woolen fabric, heavier than broadcloth; resembles felt but is woven; much felted, napped, shorn close, and dull finished. Uses: overcoats and cold-weather jackets.

FABRICS WITH A HIGH LUSTER

Fabrics can be made with a high amount of luster by the use of long floats of the satin weave or by the addition of finishes which provide a glossy appearance.

Long floats which reflect light are part of the satin weave. Yarns are usually of low twist and often made from lustrous filament fibers. No twill effect should be visible on the surface except in low count fabrics where there may be a slight twill line. The long floats of satin fabrics completely cover the surface so crepe filling yarns can be used to give softness and drapability. Inexpensive yarns may also be used to reduce the cost. A satin for upholstery purposes may have silk face yarns for appearance and cotton filling yarns for strength and lower cost. There is a definite right and wrong side to fabrics with a high luster.

Other lustrous fabrics are made from the plain or twill weave with the addition of finishes which add a glazed or glossy surface.

Examples of *lustrous* fabrics made with the *satin weave* are:

Satin. Made of silk, rayon, or any filament fiber in a weave that has long, lengthwise floats. The warp yarns float over at least four filling yarns or as many as seven. High count satins are durable. Low count satins will fray easily, pull at the seams, and rough-up during wear. Used for coat linings because the smooth fabric slips easily over other fabrics. Also for formal gowns, lingerie, and sleepwear.

Sateen. Made from cotton or similar staple yarns with the filling yarns coming to the surface as floats. If you smooth a sateen in the direction of the shine, you will find the fabric is shiny crosswise—just the opposite direction from a rayon or silk satin. Often mercerized for added luster. Used for linings and dresses.

Ticking. A cotton fabric with a satin weave where the warp yarns float in such a manner that the result is a lustrous twill. Stronger and heavier than sateen because of a higher warp count. Heavy weights used for mattress and pillow covers. Other weights used for sportswear.

Chino is a medium weight lustrous cotton fabric with warp floats, used for skirts, slacks, and sportswear.

Fabrics that obtain a *luster* through the use of *finishing materials* are:

Chintz. Usually a plain colored cotton fabric of plain weave but it may be printed. Treated with starch or resin layer on the surface to add smoothness and gloss. Glazed finishes

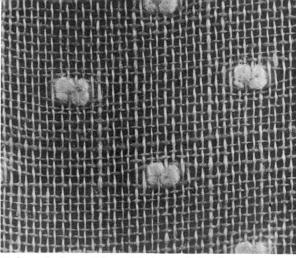

Enlarged photo of dotted Swiss made by the clipped dot method. Notice how the filling threads separate to allow for the heavier crosswise yarns (used for the dots) to interlace.

may disappear in first washing, or may be long lasting, depending on materials used. Used for drapery materials and also summer dresses and robes.

Polished cotton. Term applied to cotton fabric, usually of plain weave but may be a sateen weave, with a surface layer of resin to add gloss. Thinner layer than for chintz and fabric is more apt to wrinkle. Used for dresses.

Cambric. Usually a loosely woven fabric of plain color that is stiff and glazed. Will not wash. Used for costumes and decorations. (Do not confuse with linen cambric used for handkerchiefs . . . often called handkerchief linen.)

FABRICS WITH DOTS AND DESIGNS

Dots and small designs may be woven into fabrics with the use of additional yarns which interlace with some yarns and then float across the back of the fabric before interlacing with other yarns. When the fabric is finished, the floats are cut off. The most common fabric made this way is described as follows:

Dotted Swiss. Name given to fine, sheer fabric similar to organdy or lawn with woven-in dots, usually made by the clipped-spot method. Heavier extra filling yarns are interlaced with some warp yarns, then float across the back before interlacing with other yarns. Later the extra threads are cut off, leaving cut, fuzzy ends on one surface of the fabric. Some dots are made with a swivel attachment in which extra warp yarns are twisted around some of the ground fabric at intervals. The yarn is sheared off between the dots and the cut ends are on the back of the fabric. Swivel dots are not as easily pulled out as clipped spots. Dots may also be made of paste. These stick to a hot iron and are usually used on nylon or polyester sheers that require little ironing.

Schiffli fabric. Term applied to many fabrics that are embroidered with a machine called a "Schiffli" which creates more intricate designs than the swivel or clipped dot method. Many embroidered organdies, eyelet batistes, and linen fabrics are embroidered by Schiffli.

Fabrics With Unusual Yarns

Some fabrics are identified by distinctive names because of the use of unusual yarns. Examples include:

Bouclé (boo-CLAY). Term applied to any fabric made entirely of boucle yarns (see page 397 for description) or combined with smooth warp yarns. The occasional loops on the surface of the yarn results in a dull textured appearance. May be knit or woven of wool or any fiber. Especially preferred for sweaters and sport suits.

Crash. Term given to many plain weave dull fabrics with coarse, uneven yarns. Fabric may vary from dress linen weight to that of toweling or heavy drapery fabric. Usually of cotton or linen yarns.

Pongee. Plain weave of silk yarns that are irregular in size and usually of natural color. Duller than shantung and lighter weight. May be imitated with acetate or other manmade fibers. Used for luxury robes, blouses, and dresses.

Shantung. Plain weave fabric of subdued luster with crosswise yarns that have occasional long slubs. May be of silk with natural irregular yarns or of synthetics. Used for dresses and dressy women's suits. "Body" or stiffness may need to be restored after cleaning.

Honan. A silk, similar to shantung but the slub yarns are in both warp and filling. Used for dresses and luxury robes.

450

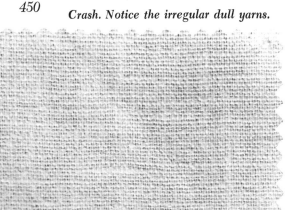

Crash. Notice the irregular dull yarns.

Shantung.

USDA

Tweed. Rough textured woolen fabric, stock or yarn dyed. May be plain or twill weave of medium to heavy weight. Has a prickly texture and a hand-crafted appearance and usually a mottled color due to the use of mixtures of colored yarns or fibers. Used for coats, winter suits and skirts. May also be made from cotton and man-made staple fibers for lighter weight suits.

FABRICS OF KNOTTED THREADS

Fish nets are made by tying knots into yarns to form a mesh-type fabric. Finer fabrics for clothing can be made, plain or figured, in a similar manner by hand or machine. Examples include:

Net. A sheer mesh made by twisting threads around each other in order to produce hexagenal (six-sided) meshes which appear round at a distance.

Macrame. A knot-tied textile with two yarn ends locked around one another. It can be used as a basis for an allover knotted fabric or a knotted fringe.

Tulle. A fine net, used in bridal veils and ballet costumes.

Lace. Laces have two parts; a ground fabric similar to net, and a design which varies from simple dots to elaborate floral patterns. May be narrow for delicate edgings or wide for dress material. Kinds of lace include Alencon, Chantilly, Cluny, Irish Crochet, Rose Point, Val, and Venetian Point.

FABRICS WITH WOVEN-FIGURED DESIGNS

Designs may be woven into fabrics by alternating the type of weave used or by changing the direction of the floats. Other patterns may be made by using additional yarns which interlace with the basic fabric in several ways.

Small figures are made on a *dobby* loom which provides for 20 to 30 different arrangements of warp yarns. This means that the figure must be complete with 20 to 30 yarns. Usually it is a simple geometrical form; however it may be a small floral or other pattern. Besides adding design interest, small figures increase absorbency because of the exposure of more yarn surface, as in huckaback and birdseye diaper cloth.

Fabrics with small woven figures include:

Huckaback (or huck). A pebbly surface with irregular filling floats which give added absorbency. Made of cotton or occasionally linen. Used primarily for hand towels and as a background for Swedish embroidery.

Birdseye diaper cloth has a diamond-shaped pattern that resembles the eye of a bird. Reversible. Made of cotton.

Madras. True madras is a soft cotton fabric with a woven design on a plain background; cord stripes, checks, small figures. Usually mercerized. Used for men's shirts or women's blouses. Not to be confused with the plaid madras which is described on page 440.

Large woven figures are made on a *Jacquard* loom where each thread is controlled separately so that any pattern is possible. If the figures involve long floats, the fabric may be easily snagged. Sewing elaborate brocades with smooth filament yarns requires skill because the smooth yarns are not interlaced closely and may fray.

Examples of fabrics made with a Jacquard weave are:

Damask. Made of variations of the satin weave. The design is distinct on both sides. Usually the flat figure has filling floats forming the design and the background is made up of warp floats. Made of cotton and linen for tablecloths or of silk and synthetics for blouses, robes, and formal gowns.

Brocade. Similar to damask in pattern, the design is slightly raised and the yarns used are usually silk, nylon, or other man-made filament ones. The fabric is not reversible. Elaborate brocades for formal wear may have a definite raised design with the addition of metallic threads (Lamé).

Matelasse. See description under crepe fabrics as appearance is usually more of a heavy crepe than of definite figures, although it is made on a Jacquard loom.

KNITTED FABRICS

Knitted fabrics are made by either the filling or weft knit, or a warp knit method which is described on pages 407.

Common knitted fabrics include.

Jersey. A true jersey fabric is made in a stockinet' stitch, a type of weft or filling knit. Wool jersey does not run due to the fuzziness of the wool yarns that causes them to cling together. May be bonded with a tricot knit fabric to increase fabric firmness. Made from wool, cotton, rayon, or almost any of the synthetics. Used for underwear, cool weather dresses, and infants' wear.

Tricot (TREE-cot). Tricot is a warp-knit fabric which keeps its shape better than a filling knit. Usually made of filament yarns, it is a more compact fabric than jersey. Does not stretch or run as easily. Many warp-knit fabrics made of syn-

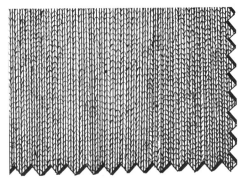

Drawing of tricot knit fabric.

thetic filament yarns as triacetate (Arnel) are wrongly called jersey as they are technically a heavy tricot fabric. Used for underwear, sleep wear, dresses (especially travelwear), and as backing for many bonded fabrics.

Double-knit. A term given to many types of knit fabrics that are made from two sets of needles. Has more firmness and durability than single knits. Fabric appears reversible. Used for suitings and dresses.

Raschel. A term describing a large variety of knit fabrics with designs that resemble lace. Often knit very loosely with tricot backing for stabilization.

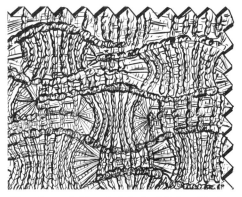

Drawing of Raschel knit fabric. Designs vary but all are loosely knit and resemble lace.

CREPE FABRICS

Crepe (crape). Refers to a fabric with a crinkly surface made with crepe yarns (true crepe) or with a puckered surface (crepe effects).

True crepe is created by the use of yarns that are tightly twisted, often in alternating directions. When wet, crepes tend to shrink because of the high twist yarn. Their stretchiness makes them difficult to press. May be made of silk, rayon, cotton, and wool.

Crepe-appearing fabrics of acetate, nylon, polyesters, and other synthetic fibers are usually made in a "crepe weave" with floats of irregular length which give the appearance of a crinkled surface. These fabrics do not have the potential shrinkage of true crepes. They are easier to press as they are not stretchy and the crinkled effect cannot be pressed flat.

Examples of these fabrics include:

Crepe. Yarns tightly twisted to produce a crinkly surface. Vary from a flat crepe which is only slightly crinkly to crepe de chine which is very crinkly. Soft, graceful drape, usually a soft luster due to yarn twist.

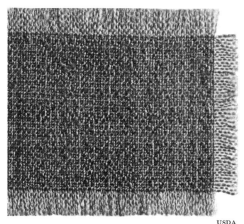

Wool crepe. Crinkled effect is due to highly twisted yarns.
USDA

FABRIC RESEARCH LABORATORIES, INC.

Oxford cloth as it appears under magnification. Notice that two fine warp yarns occupy the same space as one filling yarn. The use of white filling yarns and yarn-dyed warps is common.

Used for linings, dresses, and blouses.

Chiffon. Soft, very sheer, almost filmy fabric that drapes well. Has a slightly creped appearance. Used for scarfs, dresses, and formal gowns.

Another crepe-appearing fabric is "*Whipped Cream*," a trade name for a fabric of heat-sensitive fibers such as polyesters which has a slight all-over crinkled appearance due to embossing. A raised design is pressed into the cloth by an engraved roller. The design is permanent when heat-set. Easy to sew and care for, it is not considered a true crepe.

Matelasse (mat-las-say). Matelasse is a French word for cushioned or padded, which is the appearance of this fabric. Made as a double cloth with two sets of warp and two sets of filling yarns that interlace in a pattern effect. Classified as a crepe effect fabric because the appearance is usually more of a heavily crinkled one than one of definite figures. Made of silk, rayon, nylon, or several other synthetic filament yarns.

453

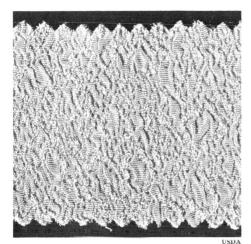

Matelassе.

USDA

Some fabrics have a crinkled appearance in stripes, alternating with smooth sections of fabric. Examples are:

Seersucker. True seersucker is made by a slack-tension method where there are two warp beams. The yarns on one beam are held at a regular tension while those on the other beam are at a slack tension. As the fabric is woven, the slack yarns crinkle. The stripes are always in the warp direction. If the fabric is raveled, the warp yarns in the crinkled stripe will be longer than in the flat section. Heavier than plisse crepe, it is used for dresses, summer suits, and men's sport jackets. If made of cotton, it will be cool but wrinkle easily; blended with polyester or acrylic fibers it will keep its trim appearance better.

Plisse crepe (plee-SAY). Plisse is made from lawn or similar material by printing sodium hydroxide in the form of stripes on the cloth. The caustic soda causes the fabric to shrink in the treated areas which results in the untreated areas becoming puckered. Plisse can be distinguished

from seersucker by pulling it flat. With a little tension it becomes flat but will resume its crinkle when tension is removed. Softer than seersucker, it is used for sleepwear, infants' wear, and summer dresses.

NONWOVEN FABRICS

Some fabrics are made directly from fibers without being made into yarns, as described on page 409. Examples are:

Felt. True felt is made of all or part wool fibers treated with heat, moisture, and pressure so the fibers interlock and form a fabric. Thickness, weight, and texture vary according to such uses as hats, skirts, pennants, and blackboard erasers. The name "felt" should not be used if fabric does not contain wool fibers or if it is held together with adhesives. Felt may look like melton but one can unravel lengthwise and crosswise yarns from melton. Felt does not have as much strength as fabrics made of woven yarns.

USDA

Plisse. The smooth stripes are where the chemicals were applied, causing the untreated sections to pucker.

454

Pellon. A trade name for a non-woven fabric used for interlinings and made from a combination of such fibers as nylon, cotton, rayon, or others. Because it was one of the first nonwoven fabrics, the term "Pellon" has been applied to many nonwoven interfacings but should not be used for fabrics made by other companies. All-bias pellon is made from fibers that are individually texturized so that there is a "give" to the fabric similar to the bias direction of woven fabrics.

Visit a fabric store or a yard goods department. Prepare a report on fabrics that are being featured. Perhaps you can arrange to speak to a buyer about the fabrics currently being featured.

Prepare an exhibit of closely related fabrics, pointing out the similarities and differences. For example, you may select pile fabrics and include corduroy of different type wales, velveteen, velvet, and other pile fabrics; or select dotted Swiss made with clipped spot dots, swivel dots, or paste dots.

Collect advertisements for clothing articles. Underline the fabric names. Write a description of the fabric mentioned in each advertisement. If possible, find a small sample and mount it.

Which fabrics are featured for warm weather wear and which are mainly for cold weather use? Obtain a winter copy and a summer copy of a mail order catalog. Look through the fabric section and list fabrics which appear in only one issue.

Prepare a "How can you distinguish" quiz for class review. Select fabrics closely related such as broadcloth and poplin, ottoman and bengaline, batiste and percale, and others. Form two teams and ask opposing team members one question from a list you have prepared.

If the answer is not given by the person asked first, ask one of the opposing team members.

Keep score.

Summary With Check-up Questions

A fabric should be called by its correct name and not by its fiber content.

- *How would a cotton voile fabric differ from a cotton velveteen?*
- *If a fabric is correctly called by its fiber content only, how would you expect it to be made?*

Plain weave fabrics that are balanced (with approximately the same number of threads in each direction) usually wear better than unbalanced fabrics.

- *Why is an 80 square percale a better choice than a percale with a 90 x 60 thread count?*

Some fabrics have names different from similar plain weave ones because of the use of colored yarns in certain patterns.

- *How does gingham differ from percale?*
- *Chambray may be the same weight as muslin but it is correctly called another name. Why?*

455

The leno weave is used to provide firmness and strength for sheer, low count fabrics.

- *Why is the leno weave a good choice for laundry and vegetable bags?*
- *Why does marquisette wear quite well despite its sheerness and low count?*

Basket weaves are made with two or more adjacent warp and/or filling yarns woven as one.

- *How does the weave of oxford cloth cause it to be absorbent and comfortable in hot, humid weather?*
- *Why does monk's cloth seldom wrinkle?*

Ribbed fabrics are made with a plain weave with many more warp than filling yarns so that a crosswise ridge results.

- *Why do most rib weave fabrics have more body than similar plain weave fabrics?*
- *Why are poplin, faille, and bengaline often mistaken for each other?*

Cords are vertical or warpwise ridges and should not be confused with crosswise ribs as in faille or grosgrain.

- *How does the direction of ridges in pique differ from faille and other ribbed fabrics?*

A twill weave has a diagonal line or wale formed by the progression of interlacings of warps and fillings. Twill fabrics vary in the prominence of the wale, the direction of the twill line, the degree of angle of the twill, and the length of floats.

- *Is gabardine a steep or lazy twill?*
- *How does serge differ from gabardine?*
- *What is the direction of the twill line in denim?*

Pile fabrics are three-dimensional with tufts or loops standing up from a basic cloth. Napped fabrics have loose fibers pulled to the surface.

- *Why are pile and napped fabrics warmer than flat fabrics?*
- *Why are most towels made in a pile weave?*
- *How does velveteen differ from a fleece?*

Fabrics with a high amount of luster can be made with long floats in the weave or by the addition of special finishes.

- *Why do the long floats of the satin weave cause the fabric to appear lustrous?*
- *How does the direction of the floats in satin and sateen differ?*
- *Why will cotton sateen probably retain its luster longer than polished cotton?*

Figured designs may be woven by the dobby or the Jacquard method.

- *Why are Jacquard fabrics usually more expensive than plain or twill weave fabrics?*
- *How can a dobby design be distinguished from a Jacquard design?*

Dress fabrics may be made in the same manner as fish nets, by knotting yarns together.

- *How do net and lace fabrics differ?*

Crepe fabrics have a crinkly surface caused by the use of crepe yarns or by finishes which produce a puckered surface.

- *What is the basic difference between true crepe fabrics and crepe-appearing synthetics?*
- *Why are true crepe fabrics often difficult to sew and press?*

PART 4

CLOTHING CONSTRUCTION AND ALTERATIONS

457

CHAPTER FOURTEEN

Combining Pattern and Fabric in Creative Construction

IF YOU LEARN TO SEW WELL when you are young and enjoy it, you will have a satisfying and profitable skill that will serve you all your life. You will be able to:

- express your own personality by making your own clothes, by combining the pattern, fabric, and trimmings you prefer.
- have more and better-wearing clothes for your share of the family budget.
- alter your clothes so they will fit well and remain in style.
- make simple repairs to keep your clothes looking like new . . . and save money on dressmaker fees.
- make clothing and gift items for other family members.
- make your home more attractive by creating curtains, draperies, decorative pillows, and other household accessories.
- judge the workmanship in ready-made clothing.
- improve ready-made clothing, both in workmanship and fit.

- have a creative hobby, a personal means of expression.
- use your skills in a career, either full or part-time.

Not everyone can learn to sew easily . . . some take longer than others and get discouraged at times, but all can learn to sew well enough for personal needs. Perhaps you do not really care to learn to *make* clothes because you prefer to buy your clothing ready-made. You will find that the time and effort spent now in learning to sew a few basic garments will pay off in wiser selection later—you will know what to look for. When you learn how, you may enjoy sewing so much that you will surprise yourself and others by making some attractive garments.

Some get discouraged when they do not make a Paris creation the first day. Remember when you learned to read? You started with simple books but gradually you had a choice of more interesting ones. Students who type remember the first few days

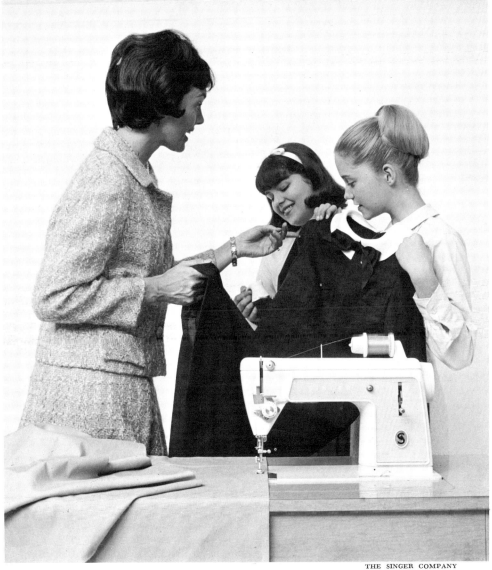

There is a special satisfaction in being able to express your own personality by making your clothes. Combine the pattern, fabric, and trimming you especially like to create the dress you want.

typing was tedious and inaccurate but the learning time paid off as you became more proficient and able to type for personal needs and possibly for a job.

Your first project may actually cost almost as much as a ready-made garment and not look as nice but remember, you are learning priceless skills; learnings you will use all your life. Soon you may be creating garments

of which you can be truly proud.

Deciding what to make at first may not always be easy. You will want to make something you can use but it is more important to *learn* basic skills within your ability and achieve success. Your teacher can guide you in pattern and fabric selection as she can judge your skill and is aware of the time and equipment available for a class project.

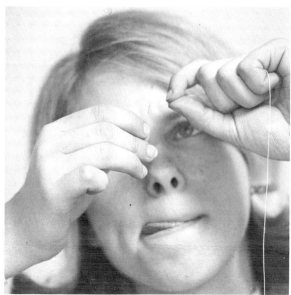

Just threading a needle can seem difficult when one is beginning to learn to sew—but soon it will become easy and so will other aspects of sewing.

It is often a good idea to select a quick project that may seem very simple if you have sewn before. However, it will give you an opportunity to get used to the machines and other equipment in your laboratory and will help your teacher to judge your abilities and weaknesses. Soon you will want to select a project using a commercial pattern as almost all the clothing you will make in later years will involve understanding the use of patterns. When you have mastered the sewing machine and know how to use a pattern well, you will want to select projects that involve more difficult construction methods and unusual fabrics, and you will want to perfect your fitting techniques.

When you have decided what to make, the first step is to select a pattern correctly sized for you and in a flattering style. While you are decid-

460

ing on the fabric and trimming you wish, which may take a little time, it is wise to practice the use of the sewing machine and other equipment. (Chapter Fifteen.) When you have your pattern, study it carefully and make any needed alterations as described later in this chapter. After the fabric is prepared for cutting by preshrinking, if necessary, and straightening the grain, you are ready to pin the pattern onto the fabric and cut it out. Pattern markings need to be transferred to the fabric.

Before starting to sew, plan ahead so you will know how to proceed easily and quickly to a lovely, finished garment. Read the guide sheet carefully to learn the general procedure. Plan a time chart so you will be finished when expected and will know how you are progressing.

Aprons can be a good choice for a first project. You will learn to use the sewing machine and to understand fabric grain and simple pattern markings. (The fabric and pocket can express your individuality.) In a very short time, you will have something you can use and will feel secure enough to start a more ambitious project.

Interview men and women to learn how they use their sewing skills. What clothing articles do they make? What type of mending do they do most frequently? Do they do any fitting or make other alterations to ready-made clothing? What do they make for their home? Report your findings to the class.

With the advice of your teacher, select pictures of suitable patterns for a beginning project for your class. Place them on the bulletin board for class comments.

Make a chart listing the necessary steps in preparing a pattern and fabric for sewing. Include the name of each class member and determine some means of checking progress.

A suitable project for a beginner. The jumper may be worn over a blouse or as a sleeveless dress. Pocket flaps at waistline may be omitted for an easier pattern.

PATTERN SELECTION AND ALTERATIONS

After you have decided what you want to make, which do you select first—the pattern or the fabric? Either one may be the inspiration for your new pants, shirt, skirt, or whatever you have decided on. Usually, it's best to select the pattern first; one that is appropriate for your figure, your activities, the fabric you wish to use, your sewing ability, and the time available.

SELECTING A SUITABLE PATTERN STYLE

If you are learning to sew or are getting used to new equipment, you'll achieve success easier if you do not select a complicated pattern. The simpler patterns are often labeled, "Easy To Sew"—if in doubt, look at the diagram of pattern pieces. A pattern with few pieces is usually easier to make than one with many pieces.

Sometimes a pattern seems to have many pieces but some are optional. Gussets, welt pockets, and unusual yokes are usually too complicated for a beginner. For the pattern shown on page 467 the collar and pocket welt may be omitted and the dress can be with or without sleeves.

A very slim skirt is harder to fit than one with a medium amount of flare.

Be sure the pattern design flatters your figure. Regarding this, you may want to reread Chapter Two.

The pattern picture may make a pants leg or skirt seem fuller than it really is. Check the width listed on the pattern envelope with the measurements.

In some schools your teacher may select a basic pattern suited to your ability and the course requirements. You may have an opportunity to add some distinctive details. Each pattern you use should have new learnings for you as well as repeat skills in which you need more practice.

JUNIOR

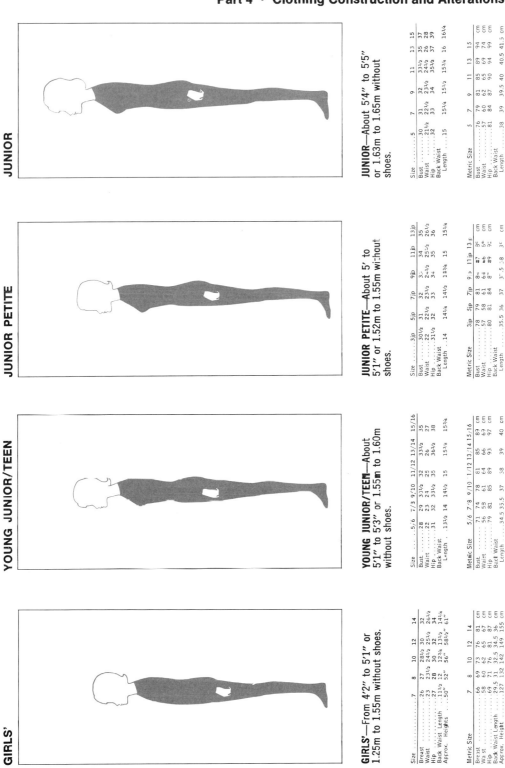

JUNIOR—About 5'4" to 5'5" or 1.63m to 1.65m without shoes.

Size	5	7	9	11	13	15
Bust	30	31	32	33½	35	37
Waist	21½	22½	23½	24½	26	28
Hip	32	33	34	35½	37	39
Back Waist Length	15	15¼	15½	15¾	16	16¼

Metric Size	5	7	9	11	13	15	
Bust	76	79	81	85	89	94	cm
Waist	57	60	62	65	69	74	cm
Hip	81	84	87	90	94	99	cm
Back Waist Length	38	39	39.5	40	40.5	41.5	cm

JUNIOR PETITE

JUNIOR PETITE—About 5' to 5'1" or 1.52m to 1.55m without shoes.

Size	3jp	5jp	7jp	9jp	11jp	13jp
Bust	30½	31	32	33	34	35
Waist	22	22½	23½	24½	25½	26½
Hip	31½	32	33	34	35	36
Back Waist Length	14	14¼	14½	14¾	15	15¼

Metric Size	3jp	5jp	7jp	9jp	11jp	13jp	
Bust	78	79	81	84	87	89	cm
Waist	57	58	61	62	64	67	cm
Hip	80	81	84	87	89	92	cm
Back Waist Length	35.5	36	37	37.5	38	38	cm

YOUNG JUNIOR/TEEN

YOUNG JUNIOR/TEEN—About 5'1" to 5'3" or 1.55m to 1.60m without shoes.

Size	5/6	7/8	9/10	11/12	13/14	15/16
Bust	28	29	30½	32	33½	35
Waist	22	23	24	25	26	27
Hip	31	32	33½	35	36½	38
Back Waist Length	13½	14	14½	15	15⅜	15¾

Metric Size	5/6	7/8	9/10	11/12	13/14	15/16	
Bust	71	74	78	81	85	89	cm
Waist	56	58	61	64	66	69	cm
Hip	79	81	85	89	93	97	cm
Back Waist Length	34.5	35.5	37	38	39	40	cm

GIRLS'

GIRLS'—From 4'2" to 5'1" or 1.25m to 1.55m without shoes.

Size	7	8	10	12	14
Breast	26	27	28½	30	32
Waist	23	23½	24½	25½	26½
Hip	27	28	30	32	34
Back Waist Length	11½	12	12¾	13½	14¼
Approx. Heights	50"	52"	56"	58½"	61"

Metric Size	7	8	10	12	14	
Breast	66	69	73	76	81	cm
Waist	58	60	62	65	67	cm
Hip	69	71	76	81	87	cm
Back Waist Length	29.5	31	32.5	34.5	36	cm
Approx. Height	127	132	142	149	155	cm

MISS PETITE

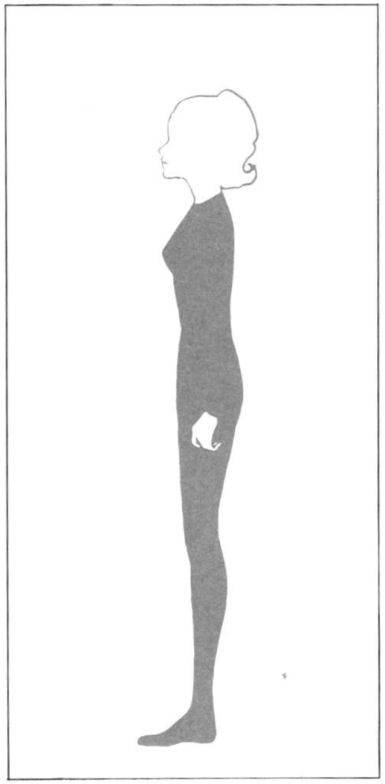

MISS PETITE—About 5′2″ to 5′3″ or 1.57m to 1.60m without shoes.

Size	6mp	8mp	10mp	12mp	14mp	16mp
Bust	30½	31½	32½	34	36	38
Waist	22½	23½	24½	26	27½	29½
Hip	32½	33½	34½	36	38	40
Back Waist Length	14½	14¾	15	15¼	15½	15¾

Metric Size	6mp	8mp	10mp	12mp	14mp	16mp	
Bust	78	80	83	87	92	97	cm
Waist	60	62	65	69	73	78	cm
Hip	83	85	88	92	97	102	cm
Back Waist Length	37	37.5	38	39	39.5	40	cm

MISSES'

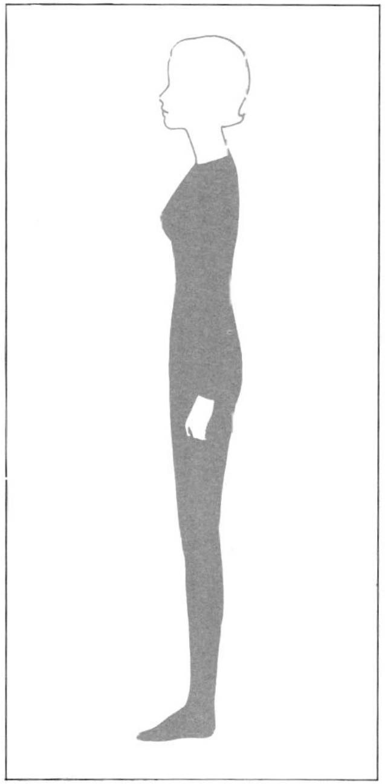

MISSES'—About 5′5″ to 5′6″ or 1.65m to 1.68m without shoes.

Size	6	8	10	12	14	16	18
Bust	30½	31½	32½	34	36	38	40
Waist	22	23	24	25½	27	29	31
Hip	32½	33½	34½	36	38	40	42
Back Waist Length	15½	15¾	16	16¼	16½	16¾	17

Metric Size	6	8	10	12	14	16	18	20	
Bust	78	80	83	87	92	97	102	107	cm
Waist	58	61	64	67	71	76	81	87	cm
Hip	83	85	88	92	97	102	107	112	cm
Back Waist Length	39.5	40	40.5	41.5	42	42.5	43	44	cm

HALF-SIZE

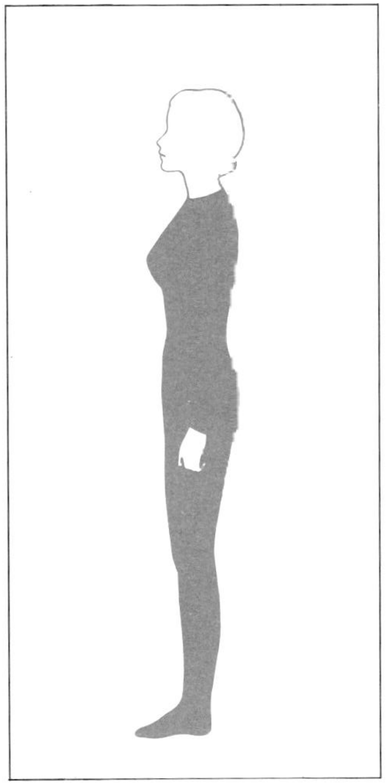

HALF-SIZE—About 5′2″ to 5′3″ or 1.57m to 1.60m without shoes.

Size	10½	12½	14½	16½	18½	20½	22½	24½
Bust	33	35	37	39	41	43	45	47
Waist	26	28	30	32	34	36½	39	41½
Hip	35	37	39	41	43	45½	48	50½
Back Waist Length	15	15¼	15½	15¾	15⅞	16	16⅛	15¼

Metric Size	10½	12½	14½	16½	18½	20½	22½	24½	
Bust	84	89	94	99	104	109	114	119	cm
Waist	69	74	79	84	89	96	102	108	cm
Hip	89	94	99	104	109	116	122	128	cm
Back Waist Length	38	39	39.5	40	40.5	40.5	41	41.5	cm

WOMEN'S

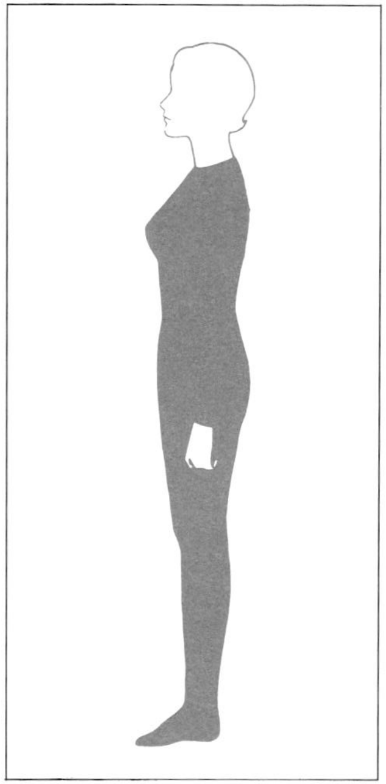

WOMEN'S—About 5′5″ to 5′6″ or 1.65m to 1.68m without shoes.

Size	38	40	42	44	46	48	50
Bust	42	44	46	48	50	52	54
Waist	34	36	38	40½	43	45½	48
Hip	44	46	48	50	52	54	56
Back Waist Length	17¼	17⅜	17½	17⅝	17¾	17⅞	18

Metric Size	38	40	42	44	46	48	50	
Bust	107	112	117	122	127	132	137	cm
Waist	89	94	99	105	112	118	124	cm
Hip	112	117	122	127	132	137	142	cm
Back Waist Length	44	44	44.5	45	45	45.5	46	cm

SIMPLICITY PATTERN CO.

The same pattern but each girl's individual choice of fabric and trim makes the dresses appear very different.

CORRECT SIZE AND TYPE

Patterns come in many figure types and sizes. Selection of a correct pat-

tern size can prevent many fitting problems later. Your age or the size you select in ready-to-wear clothes seldom is a guide to proper pattern size or type. You will need to have accurate measurements taken to determine your best choice.

The major pattern companies follow the same set of body measurements for the bust, waist, hip, and back waist length. However, they may differ in shoulder width and slant, shape of armhole and neckline, and slant of the underarm. The amount of ease may also differ (p. 468). Because of these variations in pattern shape and seam allowance, one brand may fit you better than another. Use the four basic measurements as a guide but try different

---

PATTERN SIZES FOR TEEN BOYS AND YOUNG MEN

Buy by size, not by age.

Coats and Jackets: Measure around the fullest part of the chest.

Shirts: Measure around the neck and add ½″ for the neckband (or buy pattern by ready-made shirt size).

Sleeve Length: Measure from back base of neck along shoulder to wrist.

Trousers: Measure around waist over shirt (not over trousers). Be sure to measure at natural waist as this determines size even if trousers are designed as hip-huggers.

Hip (seat): Measure around fullest part of hip.

Check the body measurements on the back of the envelope of the style you select, *before* purchasing pattern.

Size	TEEN-BOYS'				YOUNG MEN'S					
	14	16	18	20	34	36	38	40	42	44
Chest	32	33½	35	36½	34	36	38	40	42	44
Waist	27	28	29	30	28	30	32	34	36	39
Hip (Seat)	32½	34	35½	37	35	37	39	41	43	45
Neck	13½	14	14½	15	14	14½	15	15½	16	16½
Height	61	64	66	68						
Sleeve Length					32	32	33	33	34	34

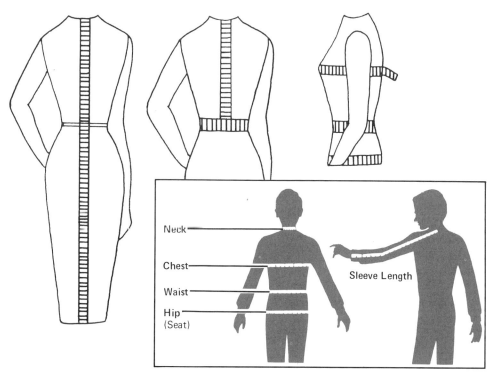

brands of patterns to find the one that fits you best, to keep alterations to a minimum.

Patterns are made in several figure types to fit differently proportioned figures. *Girls'* patterns are designed for a growing, constantly changing figure that is not yet developed. The *Young Junior/Teen* type (for a girl who is no longer flat chested but is not yet fully developed) is short waisted, small across the back and around the waist. *Junior* patterns are for the fully developed figure but shorter in waist length than a miss. *Misses'* patterns are for the taller figure with an average developed bustline, waistline, and hips. Don't let age fool you as some grand-mothers wear junior patterns while the half-size pattern provides a good fit for some young women.

The difference between teen-boys' and young men's sizes is described on page 464.

To select your correct type and size, have a friend measure you. It is almost impossible to take accurate measurements on yourself. The im-portant measurements are the *bust, waist, hip,* and *back waist length.* You will also need to know your *height* which you probably know from school examinations. For some gar-ments you may need to know your arm length (taken from shoulder to wrist bone) and the desired finished length of dress or coat. Experienced sewers may use the shoulder, upper arm, and other measurements to aid in fitting, but these measurements are seldom needed for most sewing.

How to take accurate measure-ments. For accurate measurements,

465

wear your usual undergarments and shoes. Measurements may be taken over a lightweight dress but be sure to remove a bulky sweater or heavy skirt. Stand erect but at ease. If you can stand in front of a full length mirror, check to see that the measuring tape is in a correct position across your front as your friend helps in back.

Take these four measurements:

- BUST—measure around the body at the fullest part of the bust, high under the arms, and straight across the back.
- WAIST—measure around the body at the natural waistline (where the body bends.)
- HIP—measure around the body— 9 inches below the natural waist for Misses, Women, and Junior.

7 inches below the natural waist for Half-sizes, Junior Petite, and Young Junior/Teen.

- BACK WAIST LENGTH—measure from the top of the prominent bone at the base of the neck to the natural waistline.

To obtain the *arm length*, measure from the shoulder over the elbow to the wrist with the arm bent. Place your hand on your hip to get the proper arm position.

If you don't know your height, stand without shoes with your back against a flat surface. Have a friend place a book or ruler on your head, parallel to the floor, and mark your height, then measure with a yardstick to the bottom.

Write down your measurements. Copy a chart like the one on page 468. Now study the pattern chart and compare your measurements. Determine your *figure type* first and then your *size*. A blouse or dress pattern is selected by bust measure as it is easier to alter the lower part of the garment, if necessary, than the upper part. Full skirts are selected by the waist measure but straight or semi-fitted skirts, and pants must fit over the hips. Select a pattern that fits the hips and plan to alter the waistline if necessary.

You can learn a lot from studying the pattern envelope. What answers can you find to the following questions from the back of the pattern envelope shown on page 467?

1. How wide a hem is allowed?
2. What fabrics would be suitable?
3. Which view is sleeveless?
4. Can this dress be easily made from checked or plaid fabrics?
5. How long a zipper is needed?
6. How wide is the dress at the lower edge? Does it differ for different sizes?
7. Would you need to purchase interfacing for view 1? For view 2 or 3?
8. If this dress is made from corduroy or any fabric with a one-way design, will more fabric be needed?
9. How much plain material will you need to buy for size 12, misses, if the fabric is 36″ wide? How much will you need if it is 44″ wide? If you select a wool or similar fabric that is 54″ wide, how much will you need?
10. How long is the finished dress, size 12, misses?
11. If you have a 2½ yard piece of fabric 44″ wide without a design, will that be enough for this dress in size 12, misses?

Special Fabric Advice
Before selecting plaids, one-way or napped fabrics, read this section.

Fabric Yardage
To find out the amount of material needed, circle the *view* you are making, the *width* of your fabric, and the pattern *size*. Draw a line across from the width and down from the size for the yardage needed.

Clue to Skirt Fullness

Other Material Needed
Don't forget linings, interfacings, trimmings

Measurement Chart
Check your measurements with those on the pattern envelope. Buy the right size so only minor adjustments are needed.

Necessary Notions
Buy zipper, thread, buttons and other notions when you buy your fabric so you will be ready when needed.

Garment Description
Read the description to learn of details you haven't noticed or cannot see from the picture.

Fabric Suggestions
Fabrics that suit the pattern style are listed here.

Back Views
Check to see if style and details are what you want

A PATTERN FROM SIMPLICITY'S "HOW-TO-SEW" SERIES

Extra fabric required for one-way designs.   Use nap yardage and layouts for one-way design.
Not suitable for stripes, checks, plaids and obvious diagonal fabrics.

		SUB-TEENS				TEENS				MISSES				
Fabric required	Sizes	8s	10s	12s	14s	10t	12t	14t	16t	12	14	16	18	
View 1 Dress														
35" or 36" with or without nap		2¼	2¼	2⅜	2⅜	2⅜	2½	2½	2¾	2⅝	2⅝	2⅞	2⅞	Yds.
44", 45" with nap		1⅞	2	2⅜	2⅜	2⅜	2½	2½	2½	2⅝	2⅝	2⅝	2⅝	"
44", 45" without nap		1½	1⅝	1⅞	2⅛	1⅝	2¼	2¼	2¼	2⅜	2⅜	2⅜	2⅜	"
54" — " "		1⅜	1⅜	1⅝	1⅝	1⅜	1⅝	1¾	1¾	1¾	1¾	1¾	1⅞	"
View 2 Dress														
35" or 36" with or without nap		2¼	2¼	2⅜	2⅜	2⅜	2½	2½	2⅞	2⅝	2⅝	2⅞	3	"
44", 45" with nap		1⅞	2	2⅜	2⅜	2⅜	2½	2½	2⅝	2⅝	2⅝	2⅝	2⅝	"
44", 45" without nap		1⅝	1⅝	1⅞	2⅛	1¾	2¼	2¼	2¼	2⅜	2⅜	2⅜	2⅜	"
54" " "		1⅜	1⅜	1½	1½	1½	1⅝	1⅝	1⅝	1⅜	1⅝	1¾	1¾	"
View 3 Dress														
35" or 36" with or without nap		2⅜	2⅜	2½	2⅝	2½	2⅝	2¾	3	2¾	2⅞	3	3⅛	"
44", 45" with nap		1⅞	2	2⅜	2⅜	2⅜	2½	2½	2½	2⅝	2⅝	2⅝	2⅝	"
44", 45" without nap		1¾	1¾	2⅛	2⅛	2	2¼	2¼	2⅜	2⅜	2⅜	2⅜	2⅜	"
54" — " "		1⅜	1½	1⅝	1¾	1½	1¾	1¾	1¾	1¾	1⅞	1⅞	1⅞	"
Width lower edge dress	44	45	47	49	45½	48	50	52	48½	50½	52½	54½	Ins.
View 2 Interfacing — ¼ yard of 25", 32", 35", 36" woven or non-woven fabric.														
View 3 Interfacing — ⅜ yard of 25", 32", 35", 36" woven or non-woven fabric.														
STANDARD BODY MEASUREMENTS	Bust	28	29	31	33	30	32	34	36	32	34	36	38	Ins.
	Waist	23	24	25	26	24	25	26	28	25	26	28	30	"
	Hip	31	32	34	36	32	34	36	38	34	36	38	40	"
Back length — neck base to waist			13½	13¾	14	14¼	14¾	15	15¼	15½	16	16¼	16½	16¾	"
Finished back length dress		35	36	37	38	38	39	39¾	40½	41	41½	42	42½	"

Notions — Thread, bias seam binding (opt.), neck type zipper: 18" for sizes 8s thru 14s; 20" for sizes 10t thru 16t; 22" for sizes 12 thru 18. V. 2 and 3: Tailored shoulder pads (opt.).

SUB-TEENS', TEENS' AND MISSES' ONE-PIECE DRESS (INCLUDING TISSUE LESSON-CHART . . . "How to apply a neckline facing and collar"). Dress with slightly lowered round neckline has back zipper. V. 1 is sleeveless. V. 2 has welts and short set-in sleeves. V. 3 with collar and short set-in sleeves has welts and top-stitching trim.

Suggested fabric types — Cottons and blends; pique, sailcloth, cotton knit, velveteen, linen. Silks, synthetics and blends; textured silks, cotton homespun. Wools and blends; crepe, flannel.

Printed in U. S. A.
© 1966 Simplicity Pattern Co. Inc., 200 Madison Avenue, New York, N. Y.
In Canada: Dominion Simplicity Pattern Ltd., 120 Mack Ave., Scarborough, Ont.
In Great Britain: Simplicity Patterns Ltd., 39-45 Tottenham Court Rd., London, W. 1., England.

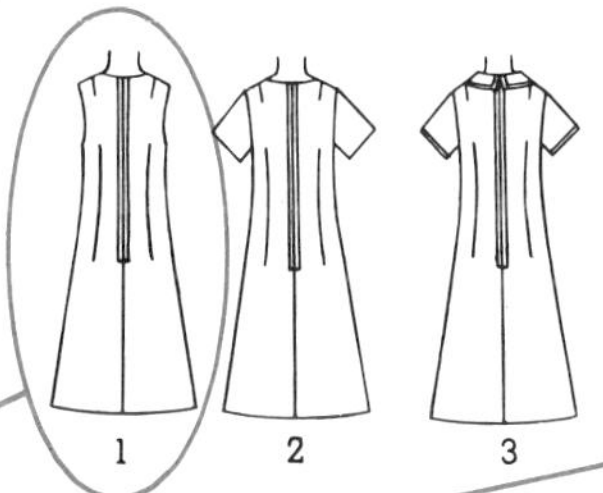

DRESS   9 PIECES GIVEN

E BACK NECK FACING

D FRONT NECK FACING

K COLLAR VIEW 3

C BACK   B SIDE FRONT   A FRONT

F ARMHOLE FACING VIEW 1

H SLEEVE VIEW 2-3

G WELT VIEW 2-3

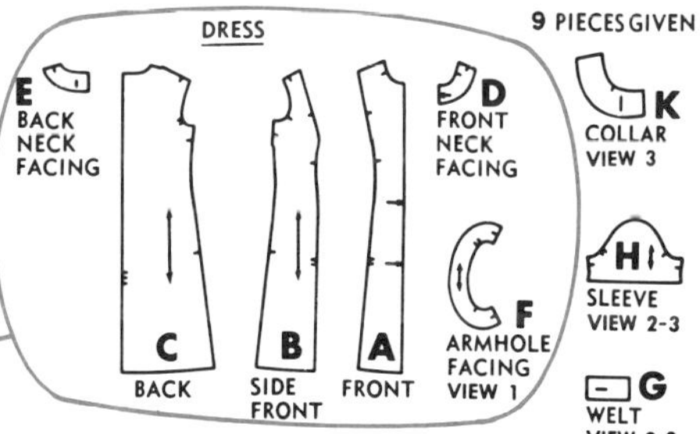

2-1/4" HEM IN DRESS

Pattern Pieces
Look at the number and shape of pieces . . . which are needed for the view you selected?

SIMPLICITY PATTERN CO.

Look for this information on the pattern envelope back.

If you can't find the right size for your figure type, purchase the next size larger and make necessary alterations. It is easier to make a pattern smaller than to enlarge it. If a store is out of your correct size, do not accept another size but seek one elsewhere or ask to have the correct size ordered for you. Alterations are not difficult but it is best not to do any more than necessary.

If your school has pattern shells available, you are fortunate as you can readily determine your pattern type and size. If not, perhaps some advanced students can help make them or they may be purchased.

Ease. The pattern size refers to the body measurements for which the pattern is made, not to the actual pattern measurements. Most garments are larger than body measures to allow for ease or comfort as you move about. A size 32 dress will probably measure 35 to 36 inches around the bust. The amount of ease varies with the particular pattern style. In a Misses' basic style with fitted bodice, set in sleeve and waistline seam, the ease at the bustline is about 3 inches. A bodice with raglan sleeves will have more ease; a strapless evening dress, less. The ease allowance for the waistline is about ¾ of an inch; for the hips it will average 2½ inches.

Checking on pattern size. If you have not used a pattern recently and are not sure that you have chosen the correct size, check the pattern to make sure it will fit correctly. Then any needed alterations can be made in the paper pattern, eliminating serious fitting problems later. There are several methods for testing a pattern:

• The easiest way is to *compare your own measurements* with those stated on the back of the pattern envelope.

Sample Chart

MY MEASUREMENTS COMPARED TO THE BODY MEASUREMENTS FOR WHICH MY PATTERN IS DESIGNED

	My Measurements	Body Measurements for My Pattern	Changes Needed
Bust	34	34	None
Waist	24½	25½	Subtract 1"
Hips	37	36	Add 1"
Back waist length	16	16¼	¼" or none
Finished back length of dress or skirt or other garment	37	41	Shorten 4"

Pattern type I should select ___Misses___
Pattern size I should select ___12___

BLOUSE ALTERATIONS

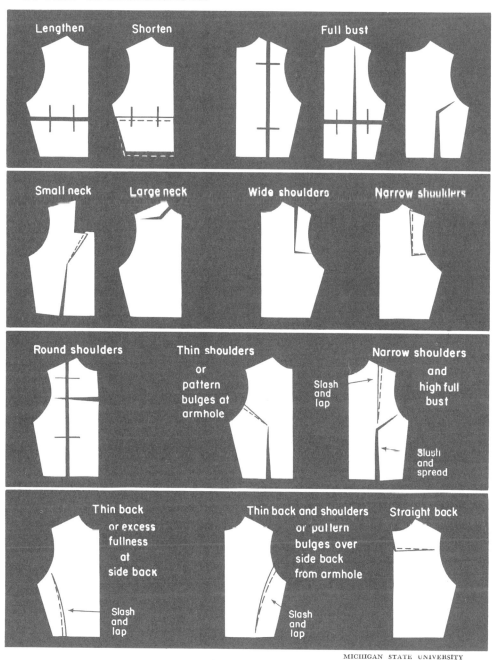

Blouse alterations.

MICHIGAN STATE UNIVERSITY

SLEEVE ALTERATIONS

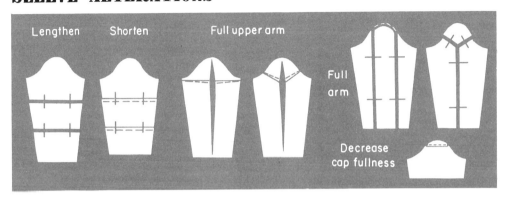

SKIRT ALTERATIONS

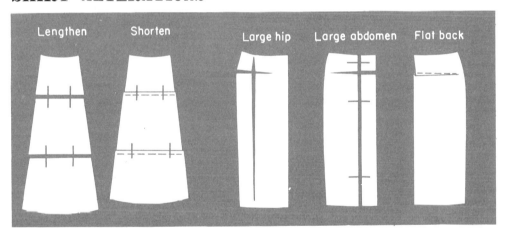

SLACKS and SHORTS

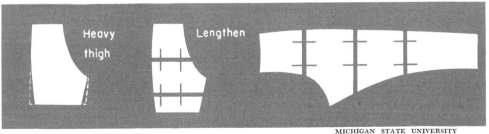

MICHIGAN STATE UNIVERSITY

Sleeve, Skirt, Slacks and Shorts alterations.

470

Prepare a demonstration of the proper way to measure for selecting a pattern. Present it to the class before other members start to obtain their measurements.

Determine the most common bust measurement in your class. Check other measurements carefully to learn if different figure type patterns are needed. Be prepared to give the reasons for selecting each figure type.

Compare the skirt lengths preferred by most class members with those planned for the patterns used.

Copy the chart on page 468 and complete it for yourself after your partner has helped you take your measurements.

If these correspond, no pattern alterations should be necessary. If there are variations, copy the chart on page 468—make a note of any changes needed.

• Another method is to *pin the pattern together and try it on*. Pin all darts, tucks, and pleats according to the marks on the pattern and pin the seams together on the seam allowance. Place pins parallel to the edge of the pattern on the stitching lines. You will have only half of the pattern to try on so be careful to place the center front and center back correctly. Remember that paper does not act like fabric so you cannot fit too closely.

Skirt lengths change so frequently it is wise to check the pattern length. This can be done by holding the skirt pieces to your waistline. Be sure to place the waistline seam mark at your waist, not the pattern edge. If a pattern seems to be a little short, add an inch or whatever seems needed. If it is much too long, it is sensible to shorten it now.

• Experienced sewers may want to *measure the pattern pieces* to determine if alterations are needed. This is difficult if you do not know how much ease is desirable for differing pattern styles. If you do select this method, be certain to measure from seamline to seamline, not seam edges. You will also need to subtract darts, tucks, and the details which may affect the pattern size.

UNDERSTANDING PATTERN MARKINGS AND DIRECTIONS

When you have your pattern, take some time to study it. You can learn a lot from the pattern envelope and the direction sheet. Look at the back of the envelope first. Circle the view you are making and notice the pattern pieces needed for that view. Take the pattern pieces out of the envelope. Study them carefully to identify them. Are there choices for such details as cuffs, collars, and pockets? Select the ones you wish to use and put the others back in the envelope. You may wish to refer to these pieces or to use the pattern another time.

Study the markings on the pattern pieces. Now is a good time to learn the meaning of the terms and symbols used by most pattern companies. There are two types of pattern markings. One is called *cutting* directions —these help you cut the pattern correctly; the other is to help you put the material together and these are called *construction* markings.

Simplicity PRIMER

Guide for Cutting — Sewing — Detailed Dressmaking

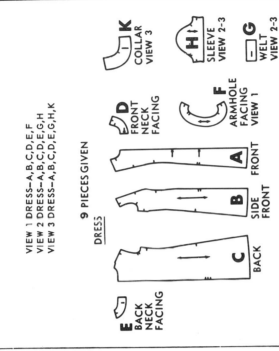

1

2

3

FOLLOW YOUR PROGRESS FROM START TO FINISH

put a ✓ in the ☐ after finishing each step

☐ **1. SELECT THE PATTERN PIECES** for the view you are making.

VIEW 1 DRESS—A,B,C,D,E,F
VIEW 2 DRESS—A,B,C,D,E,G,H
VIEW 3 DRESS—A,B,C,D,E,G,H,K

9 PIECES GIVEN

DRESS

C BACK

B SIDE FRONT

A FRONT

E BACK NECK FACING

D FRONT NECK FACING

F ARMHOLE FACING VIEW 1

K COLLAR VIEW 3

H SLEEVE VIEW 2-3

G WELT VIEW 2-3

☐ **2. PRESS THE PATTERN PIECES.**

☐ **3. COMPARE YOUR BODY MEASUREMENTS** with those on the back of the envelope.

Caution: Do not measure pattern tissue, for in addition to body measurements, ease is allowed in the pattern for garment style and comfortable wearing.

4. IF ALTERATIONS ARE NECESSARY, they should be made in the pattern before placing on fabric. Pattern pieces show where to make simple alterations such as:

To Lengthen. Cut pattern on printed line. Place paper underneath. Spread pattern the necessary amount and pin to paper.

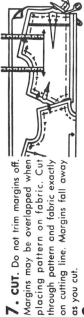

To Shorten. Crease on printed line. Pin a pleat as deep as half the amount to be shortened (i.e. 1/4" deep to shorten 1/2")

5. PREPARE FABRIC. Press creases out of fabric. Unless fabric is preshrunk, sponge or shrink before cutting.

To Straighten End. Snip selvage and pull a crosswise thread. Cut on this line. Some fabrics may be straightened by tearing.

To Straighten Threads. If crosswise threads of fabric are not at perfect right angles to the selvage, pull the fabric on the bias in the opposite direction until crosswise threads are straight and squared with the selvage. Fabric with permanent finish cannot always be straightened.

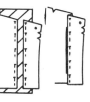

6. CUTTING PREPARATION.

a. Circle in pencil the cutting layout for the **view, size** and **fabric width** you are planning to use.

b. If pattern is to be cut on **double thickness** of fabric, fold fabric with right side inside and place pattern on wrong side. For **single thickness,** place pattern on right side of fabric.

c. Guides for using your pattern:

→ This **grain line** arrow indicates straight grain of fabric. Place pattern with ends of arrows an even distance from selvage or a straight thread.

↓ These **fold lines** indicate fold of fabric. Turn **margin under** on **printed line** before placing on **fold** of fabric.

◆ **Notches** mark seams to be joined.

d. Follow your cutting layout when placing pattern pieces on fabric. Pattern may be placed on fabric with printed side up or against fabric, as shown in layout.

---

e. When duplicate pieces are cut one at a time, **reverse the pattern for the second piece** or turn fabric over. On cutting layouts, **duplicate pieces are shown by broken lines.** When a pattern piece extends beyond fold of fabric, cut out all other pattern pieces, then open fabric and cut that pattern piece.

7. CUT. Do not trim margins off. Margins may be overlapped when placing pattern on fabric. Cut through pattern and fabric exactly on cutting line. Margins fall away as you cut.

8. MARK FABRIC. Construction details must be marked on the fabric. Mark center front and back with a clip at top and bottom.

Tailor's Tacks. Use long double thread without knot. Take 2 small stitches thru pattern and both fabric layers, leaving long loop. Cut top loops and remove pattern. Separate fabric, clip threads between fabric layers, leaving thread tufts on both layers.

TRACING WHEEL AND DRESSMAKER'S TRACING PAPER. Markings should be made on wrong side of fabric. Use ruler to guide straight lines; mark curves freehand.

For doubled fabric: lay one piece of tracing paper face up under fabric; a second piece, face down directly under pattern. Do not remove all pins.

For single thickness: lay one piece of tracing paper face up under the wrong side of fabric.

DO NOT REMOVE PATTERN UNTIL READY TO WORK ON EACH PIECE.

SIMPLICITY PATTERN CO.

PATTERN CONSTRUCTION SYMBOLS

Shown here are the most-used symbols and
instructions found on Simplicity pattern
pieces for guiding your cutting and sewing.
Sometimes other pattern pieces may have
additional, less-used symbols.

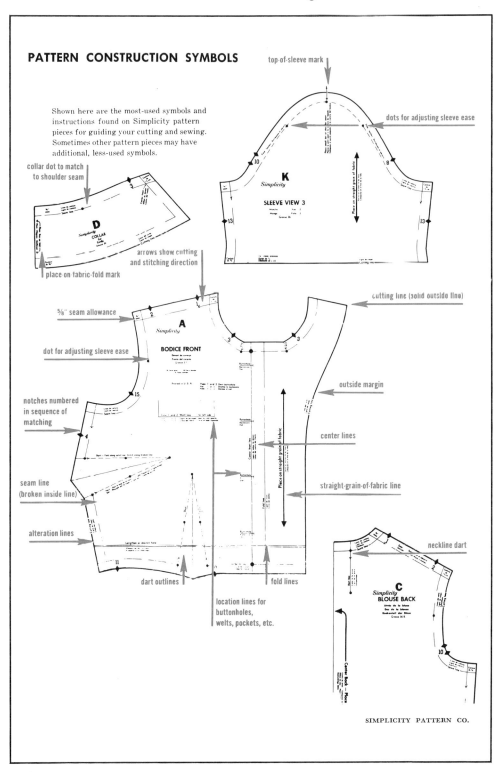

top-of-sleeve mark

dots for adjusting sleeve ease

collar dot to match
to shoulder seam

arrows show cutting
and stitching direction

place on fabric-fold mark

cutting line (solid outside line)

⅝" seam allowance

dot for adjusting sleeve ease

outside margin

notches numbered
in sequence of
matching

center lines

seam line
(broken inside line)

straight-grain-of-fabric line

alteration lines

neckline dart

dart outlines

fold lines

location lines for
buttonholes,
welts, pockets, etc.

K *Simplicity*
SLEEVE VIEW 3

D *Simplicity* COLLAR

A *Simplicity*
BODICE FRONT

C *Simplicity*
BLOUSE BACK

SIMPLICITY PATTERN CO.

Cutting line. Pattern pieces are printed on large sheets of tissue paper stacked together and then cut apart by machines. When many patterns are cut at once, it is difficult to cut the edges of tissue paper accurately, so the printed line, which is always accurate, is used as the cutting guide. On some patterns it is shown by a single line. On others it is a double line and the cutting is done between the two lines. It is a waste of time to cut off the margins. At a fold edge you may find it helpful to trim or turn back the paper margin right to the fold line. When placing the pattern on the material, overlap the pattern edges but not the cutting lines.

Grain line or straight of the goods. Usually indicated by a long straight arrow, every pattern piece will have a mark that indicates the direction of the straight of the goods, also called the lengthwise or crosswise grain. If this arrow line is not placed along a thread going in the right direction, the garment will sag and not hang well.

Fold. Some pattern pieces are made to be placed on a fold of the fabric so the finished piece will be twice the size of the pattern tissue. The fold is usually indicated by arrows pointing to the fold edge. Be very careful to place the pattern fold line, not the margin, right on the fold. If you are a little careless and place a blouse center about ½ inch away from the fold, the entire front will have a neckline 1 inch too wide. And if you are careless with the back piece, your blouse will be 2 inches too large and the neckline will surely gap! Do *not* cut along the fold edge. Unless otherwise indicated, the fold line is the straight of the material.

Seam allowance. The seam lines on a pattern are indicated by broken lines. The major pattern companies have agreed on a ⅝ inch seam allowance for most seams. Occasionally you will find a narrower seam so read directions carefully.

Direction of stitching. Some patterns include arrows in the seam allowance marking. Stitching is to be done in the direction of the arrows to maintain correct fabric grain. (See p. 545.)

Notches. The triangle markings found along the cutting lines of the pattern indicate where pattern pieces are to be joined together. On some patterns the notches are numbered to indicate the sequence of matching seams.

Center front and center back. There are several ways to indicate the center front and center back. If not along a fold or a seamline, these lines will be shown on the pattern by a printed line or dots.

Waistline. One-piece dresses and long overblouses have a marking which indicates the normal waistline.

This will help in fitting darts or other means of shaping the waistline.

Dots, circles, lines. Special details such as location of pockets, the beginning or ending of an opening, or the place to match the shoulder seams to the top of the sleeve are indicated in many ways. Check your pattern carefully now to learn what these markings mean.

Alterations lines. Some patterns indicate places to make simple alterations. After you have studied your pattern, answer the questions on page 476.

(Copy this chart on a separate piece of paper and complete the questions after studying your pattern.)

HOW WELL DO YOU UNDERSTAND YOUR PATTERN?

Name_____ Class_____

Pattern brand_____ Size and Type_____ View selected_____

1. Can you identify each pattern piece?
2. What pieces will you need for the view you have selected?
3. What pieces are to be cut from trimming or other material?
4. Have you read everything on each pattern piece?
5. How is the lengthwise grain marked?
6. How is the seam allowance marked? Is there any place where the allowance is more or less than ⅝ of an inch?
7. How are the darts marked?
8. How are gathers, pleats, or tucks marked?
9. How is the waistline marked?
10. How wide a hem is allowed?
11. How are the center front and center back marked?
12. How is the top of the sleeve or the armhole facing marked where it should meet the shoulder seam?
13. What is the purpose of the notches? If they are numbered, why?
14. Which pieces are planned to be cut on a fold of the material?
15. What marks help you in the placement of pockets?
16. What mark indicates the end of an opening as where a zipper is inserted?
17. How are buttonholes and the placement of buttons indicated?
18. What pieces are to be placed on the crosswise grain of the fabric?
19. What pieces will be cut on the bias of the fabric?

ALTERING YOUR PATTERN

If you discover that your pattern is too big or too small, too long or too short for you, you can correct it easily before cutting out your fabric. As you gain experience, you should be able to alter a pattern so that it will fit individual figure irregularities. Directions for detailed fitting alterations are given in Chapter 17.

Beginning clothing construction projects are usually selected so that very little fitting is required as you should first learn how to use equipment, fabrics, and patterns. As one gains experience, it is natural to select patterns that give a greater knowledge of fitting. Because of this, simple pattern alterations are described here and more detailed directions are given in Chapter 17. You may wish to refer to them now if you have special fitting problems.

Some commercial patterns have printed alteration lines on the major pattern pieces for your convenience. Always keep these grain lines straight by making tucks or slashes to alter the pattern parallel or at right angles to the lengthwise grain lines.

Make alterations within the boundaries of the pattern if possible so the original shape of each pattern piece is preserved.

To make pattern pieces longer, cut the pattern apart and insert the required amount of tissue or other paper. Pin or tape it in place. Try not to make the cut where it will interfere with any details as darts or tucks. (Don't forget to lengthen *both* front and back and also matching facings.)

To make a pattern shorter, pin a tuck in the pattern tissue. The width of the tuck should be one-half the amount to be removed—a one-inch tuck will shorten the pattern two inches. Skirts can usually be shortened by trimming the required amount off the lower edge. A full skirt will have less width at the bottom but a short person does not usually want as much. If you want to maintain the original skirt width, alter the pattern just below the hip line and even up the side edges.

The length of pants is checked in two places, the crotch depth and the leg length. Any needed crotch adjustment must be made before cutting the pattern as it is almost impossible to correct it once the fabric is cut. Take your crotch measurements by measuring the distance from your center front waistline to the chair, while sitting erect. Add ¾" for ease. On the back pattern piece at the side seam, measure up from the depth of the crotch line to the waistline seam. (Crotch line is fullest part of pants.) Compare this with your own measurement, plus ¾". Lengthen or shorten as needed on the alteration line between the waistline and depth-of-crotch line. Make this alteration on the front pattern piece also.

It is important to alter patterns for slacks, shorts, and pants-type garments before cutting the material. This adjustment is difficult to make later.

To determine your crotch length, measure the distance from your waistline to a chair, while sitting. Add ¾" for ease.

To determine the crotch length of your pattern, measure along the side seam from the crotch line to the waistline seam mark.

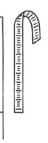

477

HOW TO TAKE BODY MEASUREMENTS
FOR PANTS AND SHORTS

Stand evenly on both feet. Measure snugly over undergarments you usually wear with pants. Side length is from waist to desired finished length.

Select patterns for skirts, pants, and shorts by waist measurement. For hip-hugger patterns OR if hips are much larger in proportion to waist, select size by hip measurement.

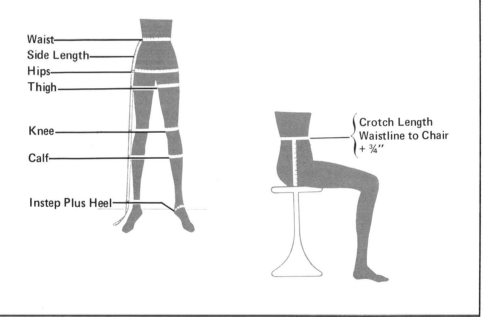

For leg length, measure from the waistline down the side of the leg to the point where you want the finished pants to end. After adjusting the crotch length, compare with pattern measurements and make needed adjustments at the alteration line or lines between the crotch and lower edge.

A one-piece dress may need to be shortened or lengthened both above the waistline and below it. If you make all the changes at the lower edge, you may find the waistline is too low or too high.

A long sleeve usually needs to be shortened or lengthened above and below the elbow to keep the elbow fullness at the proper place.

To make a pattern narrower or wider, divide the amount to be taken out by the number of pattern pieces —one-half inch off each gore of a four-gore skirt will make the pattern two inches smaller.

If your teacher has a sample pattern similar to that used by your class, prepare a bulletin board display of the meaning of the pattern markings.

Copy the questions on page 466 and complete them. Hand the paper to your teacher for checking or go over the questions in class.

Answer the questions on page 476 and hand to your teacher for checking before proceeding with your sewing project.

Working in small groups appointed by your teacher, prepare brief demonstrations of the common alterations listed in this chapter.

SELECTING YOUR FABRIC

An important step is deciding on your fabric—will it be suitable for your figure, the pattern selected, your wardrobe needs, and your ability?

Wise fabric choices for the beginner. The beginner will find it easier to learn basic sewing techniques if an easy to handle fabric is selected. Many beautiful fabrics are also easy to work with. As you gain experience, you will want to work with increasingly difficult fabrics so you can learn to handle successfully many types of materials.

In general, fabrics that are firm and closely woven are more easily handled than loosely woven or knitted fabrics. Fabrics made from cotton and linen or blends of cotton and synthetics are easier to handle than those of wool or 100 per cent synthetics which may stretch and ravel easily and are often slippery. It is often difficult to see your stitching on black and very dark colors. White fabrics can become so soiled that the finished garment is disappointing. Plaids and large designs that need to be matched take a lot of time and create problems in cutting and sewing.

Before selecting a sewing project, consider the types of fabrics with which you want to work and their characteristics.

S. PHILADELPHIA HIGH SCHOOL

THE INNES COMPANY, WICHITA, KANSAS

When you find a fabric that you like, check to be certain that it is suitable for your pattern.

Good choices for beginners are plain fabrics which are of medium color and have small, all over designs. Crooked stitching shows more on plain fabrics than on small patterns. However, the fact that there is no right and wrong side on a plain fabric makes it preferable for beginners. Some suggestions are broadcloth, chambray, percale, Indian Head, sailcloth, poplin, homespun, and blends of polyester and cotton.

Just because a fabric is easy to sew does not mean it must be dull or uninteresting. You will find lovely colors and different texture effects in easy to sew fabrics.

Fabrics which take more skill and time to sew are:

Stripes and plaids. (Always avoid printed plaids.)

Designs that must be matched.

Pile fabrics such as corduroy and velvets. (Fur fabrics are more difficult to sew than short pile fabrics.)

Plastic and vinyl fabrics.

Satins and crepes which stretch or ravel easily and are slippery.

Sheers.

Stretch fabrics and knits.

Very loosely woven cloth.

Fabrics with nubby and unusual yarns.

See Chapter 17 for suggestions for sewing with these fabrics.

Match the fabric to the pattern. When a pattern designer planned a pattern, he had certain fabrics in mind. There is usually a list of suggested materials on the back of the pattern envelope. You do not need to limit yourself to these suggestions but if you do the fabric will surely be suitable for the pattern.

Look at the pattern picture. Does the fabric act as the pattern suggests? If there are pressed pleats, form the material into pleats. Do they hold nicely or do they sag? If there are soft gathers shown in the pattern, check to see if your material falls in soft folds and does not stick out harshly.

A print may lose its effect if it is cut into small pieces. Also, construction details like welt seams may not be noticed in a print.

Select good quality fabric. You will want to buy a good quality fabric but it does not need to be the most expensive. Seldom does it pay to buy a poor quality fabric even if it is inexpensive.

SIMPLICITY PATTERN CO.

Would you believe that these smart dresses are made from patterns planned for beginners? Dress A is made from an easy to sew all-over floral print with lace trim at the neckline. The yoke trim which looks like hand smocking on Dress B is ready-made and easily applied to add a distinctive note. The use of cross-stripes for the yoke in Dress C requires very little matching. Stripes again appear in the simple sleeveless blouse (D) but are easily handled because of the absence of details that require matching. The A-shaped skirt is a good learning project. Dress E is made from a printed upholstery-type cotton that looks elaborate but is really very easy to sew. (The back of the pattern envelope for this style is shown on page 467.) Notice how different each dress looks, because of individual use of fabric and trimming even though the patterns are similar. Which dress will make a girl look taller? Shorter? Heavier? More slender?

The time and effort to make a custom made garment is wasted on a poor quality fabric which will not wear well nor show your good workmanship. The most expensive material may cost a lot because of unusual threads or design, not because the quality is the best.

Study the information printed on the label at the end of the bolt of a fabric. This will give the manufacturer's name and details on fiber content, width, price, and information on finishes. Do not take the salesperson's word that the fabric will not shrink or fade, but look for such information on the label itself.

Be certain to get a permanent care label for your fabric. Check to see that the code number on the label is the same as the one that appears on the bolt of the fabric.

The large designs in the printed fabrics used for both of these robes would not be as effective if the patterns were made of many pieces, such as a princess style.

Check to see if the design has been printed off grain or if there are flaws in the fabric. A small flaw which shows only on the wrong side is not serious but others may create problems in cutting.

Loosely woven material ravels and pulls apart at the seams. It will also stretch out of shape and be difficult to sew well. One way to tell if the material is firmly woven is to push it between your thumbs and forefingers. Place the material over both thumbs and under your first fingers. Push the

thumbs upward and together. If the material is firmly woven, the threads will remain in place. If the threads slip or actually break, the fabric will create problems both in sewing and in wear.

Fold the fabric in half lengthwise with the selvages together. If the raw ends of the fabric meet or do so within one inch, the fabric has been finished correctly. If there is a great deal of difference, you will have to straighten the material as described on page 488.

The stunning tuck detailing in this dress would be almost unnoticeable if made in a printed fabric.

A fabric with the design printed off grain is almost impossible to use for an attractive, well-fitted garment. If the grain is correct, the design will seem crooked and if the design appears straight, the fabric will be off grain and the garment will not hang evenly.

Which of these fabrics will shrink so little, if any, that it will not be noticeable? Would you recommend preshrinking any one of these fabrics? Can you explain your answers?

Look at the design and see if it is printed along the actual fabric threads. Don't go by a cut edge, which may be off grain, but by a crosswise thread.

If the fabric frays on examination in the store, you can be sure it will fray when you are working with it at home.

If you have selected a print, stand away from it about five feet. Do some colors seem more noticeable than you expected? Is there a definite direction to the fabric so that it must be handled as a striped fabric? Does the print appear busy at a distance?

Fabric to suit your figure. What effect will your fabric choice have on your figure? Clinging fabrics will reveal any figure problems. Heavy and bulky fabrics make a figure appear larger. Shiny fabrics also make you appear larger, but dull fabrics may make you appear smaller. Refer to Chapter Two for more suggestions on how fabrics affect your appearance.

Before you purchase your material, ask yourself these questions:

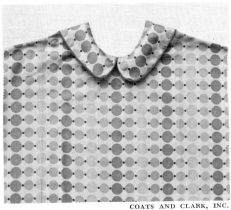

COATS AND CLARK, INC.

An example of an all-over print that must be handled as a plaid. Notice the placement of center front on the line of dominant color dots and the careful attention given to the crosswise lines.

- Will the fabric texture and design flatter my figure?
- Is the fabric suitable for my pattern?
- Is the fabric suited to my sewing ability?
- Will the fabric blend with other items in my wardrobe?
- Is the fabric of good quality?
- Can I provide the care this material needs to keep it looking nice?

TLC FOR YOUR FABRIC

Have you ever seen a home-sewn garment that looked "tired" and worn before it was even completed?

Your garment will look new if you give your fabric the tender loving care (TLC) it deserves. Don't crush and wad your fabric into a small sewing box after every sewing class. If you must put it away in a box, fold it carefully.

Keep the fabric off the floor. Tables should be dusted and hands washed. It is wise to wear an apron if you have on a dark skirt which may be linty. Always check to be sure there is no excess oil on the sewing machine. You may want to keep light colored fabrics wrapped in a clean cloth when not being worked upon.

Don't put undue strain on the fabric. Stretching and waving it in the air or pulling it around behind you will result in a tired, sad piece of cloth.

Watch lipstick and perspiration stains when fitting clothes. Biting threads may also mean lipstick damage as well as dull teeth.

As soon as your garment is stitched together, keep it on a hanger in an uncrowded place, if possible. Pin the neck edges together so they won't stretch.

Using samples available in your classroom and pictures of fabrics, arrange a display of fabrics suitable for beginning projects, and fabrics that should be used when one has more experience. Prepare labels stating why certain fabrics are not suitable for beginners.

Find pictures of patterns and fabrics that do not complement each other. For example, large prints that prevent one from seeing construction details or soft, clinging fabrics that would not be suitable for crisp pleats.

Find woven and knit fabrics that are of good quality and easy to sew. Find similar fabrics that are of poorer quality and more difficult to handle. Mount and explain the differences.

When pressing, be sure the iron and press cloth are clean. The steam iron should have fresh clean water.

AMOUNT OF MATERIAL TO PURCHASE

Buy enough for your garment. Follow the suggestions of the pattern company for fabric width and pattern style as well as your size. If you are taller than average you may need to purchase more fabric. Discuss this with your teacher beforehand. Even if you are quite short you may still need to buy the recommended amount because of the way the pattern must be cut. As you gain experience, you may be able to purchase a different amount than stated, but at first it is better to have a little too much than too little. If your fabric has not been preshrunk, you may need to buy an additional $\frac{1}{4}$ yard.

(Copy this guide on a separate sheet of paper. Complete the left-hand column before you shop for your material. As you purchase each item, enter the cost in the right-hand column. When you finish, total all expenditures to determine the complete cost of your project.)

MY SHOPPING GUIDE

NAME _____   CLASS _____

Article to be made	Cost of material
Pattern number, type, and size _____	Cost of pattern _____
Amount of fabric required _____	Cost per yard _____
Width of fabric _____	Total cost of fabric _____
Number of spools of thread needed	Cost per spool _____
_____	Total cost of thread _____
Size and type of zipper _____	Cost of zipper _____
List other notions needed (for example, buttons, seam tape, interfacing, snaps, etc.) _____	Cost of each additional item _____

_____ Total cost of supplies for garment __ _____

The width of the fabric usually makes a difference in the amount needed but with some patterns, especially one piece dresses or jumpers, you may need the same amount of 36-inch wide fabric as a 54-inch width.

SELECT NOTIONS AND TRIMMING WHEN YOU PURCHASE YOUR FABRIC

Buy the thread, zipper, interfacing or lining material, and any other items needed to complete your garment when you buy the fabric. You will save time by making all your purchases at once but more important, your work will not be delayed because of the lack of a necessary item. See Chapter Fifteen for suggestions for purchasing notions.

PREPARATION OF FABRIC FOR CUTTING

Before laying out the pattern, you will need to be sure that your fabric is preshrunk and that the grain is straightened.

Determine the right side of the fabric. Cotton and linen fabrics are usually folded right side out. Woolens and wool type fabrics are folded with the right side in. In napped fabrics, the nap is thicker and heavier on the right side. In twill fabrics, the twill is more distinct on the right side. Satins and sateens have longer thread floats and more sheen on the right side. The selvage may appear more finished on the right side. Sometimes there may be slight mends and flaws on the wrong side. If you can't determine the right from wrong side, no one else will either, so relax and use either side.

Preshrinking a fabric

If the fabric is washable and the label states that it will not shrink more than one per cent, or if it is made from nylon, acrylics, polyesters or other fibers which do not shrink, you can forget about preshrinking. However, if you are unsure, it is wise to "relax" the fabric. Many cottons, linens, rayons, woolens and blends are subject to relaxation shrinkage. This means that the fabric was stretched during the finishing process and when it is put in water, it will "relax" into its original shape—we say that it shrinks! Preshrinking can help avoid fitting problems later and keep the garment looking new.

To preshrink cotton fabrics, thoroughly wet them and allow to dry without strain. Fold the material loosely and place it in a sink with warm water until thoroughly wet. Drain and pat out excess moisture. Then hang it up over a shower rod or two or more clotheslines. Such a fabric will seldom need to be pressed before use. Cottons for garments which will be machine dried later are best dried in a dryer. Machine dryers often shrink materials more than other methods of drying and it is wise to subject the fabric to such stress before cutting. Fabrics dried this way may not feel as "new" to work on as those drip dried, but they are less apt to shrink later.

Woolens may be preshrunk in different ways. Some you may want to send to a cleaner who will preshrink them for a small charge. Other woolens, especially those to be hand washed, can be soaked in warm water in a bathtub and then dried flat without strain before being steam pressed. The safest way is to wring a sheet out in water until damp, but not wet. Lay the wool material over the sheet. Usually you will fold it lengthwise

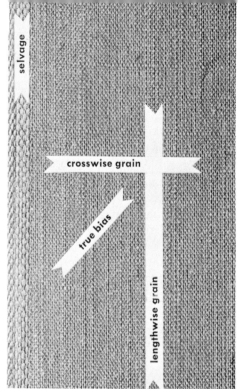

When you use a pattern, you will note a marking "straight of the goods." This mark must be placed on a thread parallel with the selvage (the lengthwise grain). The lengthwise threads (warp) are parallel with the selvage; this is the lengthwise grain or "straight of goods." The crosswise threads (weft, woof, filling) running from selvage to selvage is known as the crosswise grain.

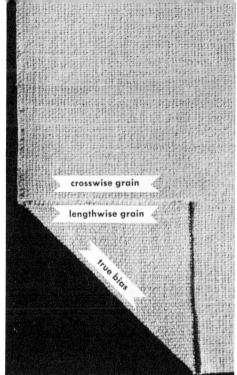

The bias direction or grain of a fabric is the one that furnishes the most give or stretch. The true bias is the diagonal direction across two grain lines. This direction is located by folding the selvage or any lengthwise thread along a crosswise thread. The fold gives the direction of the true bias. Diagonals at other angles, although they are called bias, are not true bias but are merely off grain and stretch very little.

with the ends and selvages pinned together with rustproof pins. (First be sure you have the ends cut along a crosswise thread.) Begin at one end and fold or roll the damp sheet and fabric loosely together. Cover with a towel to keep in the moisture. Leave it for several hours or overnight. Unroll the wool fabric, smooth out the wrinkles and let it dry flat. If the fabric needs pressing, press on the wrong side with a steam iron or use a damp press cloth.

NOTE: A steam iron seldom provides enough moisture to shrink a woolen fabric.

Why a fabric needs to be straightened. When a fabric is woven, the lengthwise threads are at right angles to the crosswise threads. During the finishing processes the threads are often pulled askew but, after wear and washing, the threads will return to their original position. Therefore, if you cut a cloth off grain, it will relax during use and the garment will sag and hang off grain. A skirt may pull to one side, a blouse may twist, or a collar may not lie flat. *To straighten the cloth* means to get the crosswise threads at right angles to the lengthwise threads. Fabrics that have had resin finishes added, such as wash and wear fabrics, will not shift in direction. The finish holds the threads in position.

487

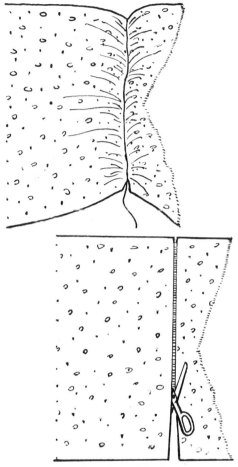

After a crosswise thread is drawn out, the cloth is cut along the line left.

How to tell if the fabric is grain perfect. First, have the raw ends of the fabric cut along a crosswise thread. Some fabrics can be torn crosswise and, if so, tear along a crosswise thread. If this is not possible, cut along a thread if you can see one. Otherwise you will have to pull out a thread and cut along the line which is left. If the thread breaks as you are pulling it, cut to this place and pick up the thread again. When you have true crosswise threads at both ends, you can check to deter-

mine if the fabric is straight in one of three ways.

(1) Place it so the selvage lies along the edge of a table. If the crosswise cut end lies perfectly along the adjacent table side, at a 45-degree angle, the fabric is straight. (An L square can also be used.)

(2) Another way is to fold the fabric in half lengthwise with the selvages along a table edge. If the two selvages come together and the cut ends of the material are together and even with the end of the table, the material is straight. If the two ends do not come together, the material will have to be straightened.

(3) If you are in doubt, take time to pin the edges together across one cut end and along the selvage. If the pinned fabric lies flat and smooth on the table, the fabric is grain perfect. If the fabric is skewed or there are large bubbles, the fabric needs straightening. If the fabric is off ½ inch, it is not too serious, *but* some fabrics are off as much as three or four inches and need straightening.

To straighten the fabric

If the fabric is slightly off grain, you may straighten it by pulling. When material is pulled on the bias, it stretches. Always pull the corners of the shorter edges, moving your hands over a few inches each time you give the material a good, firm pull. Check from time to time to see if you have evened the material so you don't pull too far in the opposite direction. Keep on trying until the two selvages and two ends of the material come together and are even with the corner of the table. You may need to have your partner pull the opposite end.

A better way is to use moisture to

To straighten the cloth, pull the corners of the shorter edges.

relax the fabric. If you need to preshrink the fabric, you can combine this process with straightening as just described. Fold in half lengthwise, pin edges together or machine baste across the ends and along the selvage. Place in warm water about 30 minutes until thoroughly saturated. Remove and unfold but do not take out the pins or basting. Let the fabric drip dry across a shower rod or several rows of clothes line.

If the fabric is still off grain, it has probably been set permanently by a finish and will not change shape in washing.

(Copy these questions on a separate sheet of paper and answer the questions. Your teacher may want to check your answers before you start to place your pattern on the fabric.)

ARE YOU READY TO CUT OUT YOUR PATTERN?

1. Have you circled the pattern layout you will use? Have you checked to be sure you have selected the correct one for your pattern size, fabric width, pattern view, and if the fabric has a nap or not?
2. Have you made the needed alterations in the pattern tissue?
3. Have you put back in the envelope all the pattern pieces not needed for this view?
4. Is your fabric preshrunk, either by you or by the manufacturer?
5. Is the grain in correct alignment?
6. Does your fabric have a nap or up and down design? If so, what adjustments will you make in cutting out the pattern?
7. Are your fabric and pattern pressed carefully? (If needed.)
8. Will your fabric be folded lengthwise or crosswise or in another manner?

9. Are there shaded pieces in your pattern layout? If so, what do they mean?
10. Are there dotted lines in your pattern layout? If so, what do they mean?
11. Which pattern pieces are cut on a lengthwise fold? Are there any to be cut on a crosswise fold?
12. Which pieces are cut only once?
13. Which pieces are to be cut more than twice?
14. Are there pieces to be cut separately and reversed for the other side?
15. Do you know which pattern pieces are used for any needed facings?
16. If there is a belt, is there a pattern for it? If not, how is it cut?
17. Will you need to allow material for bias bindings or other uses?
18. What special problems will you have in cutting out this pattern and fabric?

Find examples of fabrics printed off grain as well as those printed on the grain. Display and describe the problems that would occur if fabrics printed off grain are used for a typical fitted garment.

Copy the questions on page 489 and complete them before starting to cut out your pattern. Have your teacher check your answers.

It is a good idea to check while in a store and to refuse to purchase fabric finished off grain. Manufacturers will be more careful if consumers refuse to buy such fabrics.

Now be sure the fabric is well pressed before placing the pattern on it. The center fold may need special attention as it is often difficult to press out.

PLACING PATTERN ON MATERIAL FOR CUTTING

Now is the time to decide on the recommended pattern layout for your material and pattern. *You will need to consider the size, width of material, and pattern view.* If your material has a one-way design or nap, select the directions for cutting such fabrics. Circle the correct layout so you can refer to it easily.

Lay the material on a large table. A chair or smaller table will hold any surplus to keep it off the floor and to keep strain off the material. If you do not have a large enough table, special cutting boards may be purchased which can be folded when not in use. A very clean floor may be better than a table which is too small.

Place the material as the pattern indicates. If the directions call for lengthwise folded material, fold it right sides *together* along a lengthwise thread. This will allow for easier marking and some pieces will be ready in the correct position for sewing. A crosswise fold occurs on a crosswise thread and the selvages are brought back on the selvages. If the pattern layout shows the fabric as a single layer of material, place the fabric right side up.

Pupils who are making a similar pattern watch a demonstration on proper pattern layout.

S. PHILADELPHIA HIGH SCHOOL

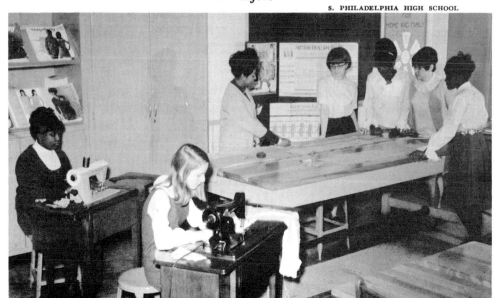

GENERAL NOTE: WHEN PATTERN PIECES EXTEND BEYOND FOLD OF FABRIC CUT OUT ALL PIECES EXCEPT PIECES THAT EXTEND;THEN OFEN OUT FABRIC AND ON SINGLE THICKNESS CUT EXTENDING PIECES ON RIGHT SIDE OF FABRIC IN POSITION SHOWN.

Cutting Layouts

View 1 DRESS

35" 36" Fabric With Or Without Nap
Sizes 8s, 10s, 12s, 14s
Sizes 10t, 12t, 14t
Sizes 12, 14

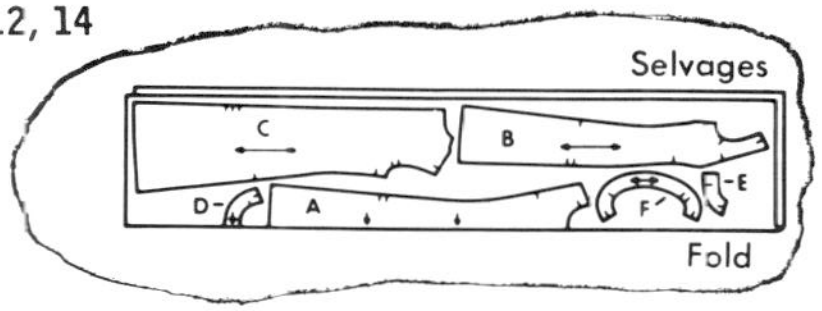

35" 36" Fabric With Or Without Nap
Size 16t
Sizes 16, 18

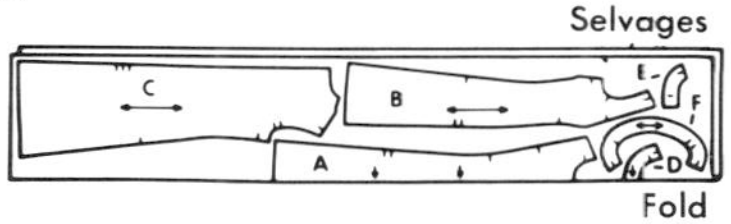

44" 45" Fabric With Nap
Sizes 8s, 10s

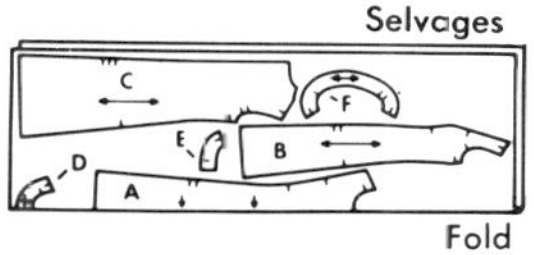

44" 45" Fabric With Nap
Sizes 12s, 14s
Sizes 10t, 12t, 14t, 16t
Sizes 12, 14, 16, 18

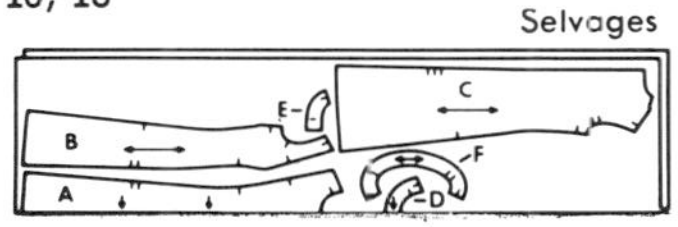

54" Fabric Without Nap
Sizes 8s, 10s
Size 10t

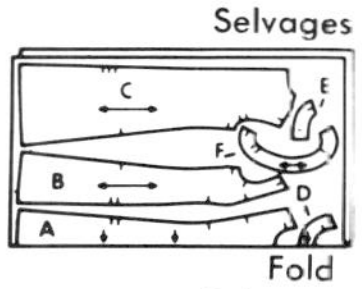

54" Fabric
Without Nap
Sizes 12s, 14s
Sizes 12t,14t,16t
Sizes 12,14,16,18

44" 45" Fabric
Without Nap
Size 12s

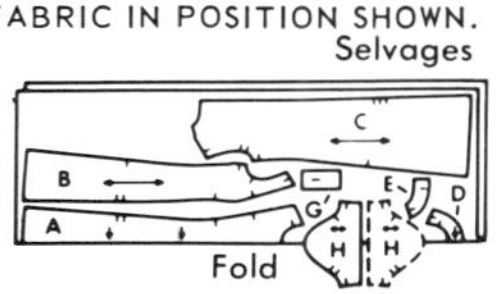

44"45" Fabric
Without Nap
Size 14s
Sizes 12t,14t,16t
Sizes 12, 14, 16, 18

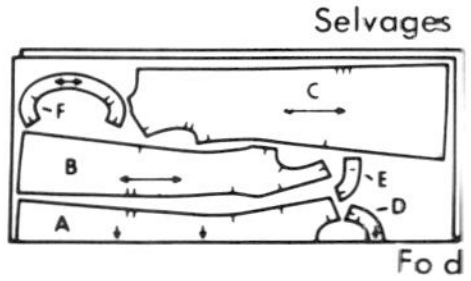

View 2 DRESS

35" 36" Fabric With Or Without Nap
Sizes 8s, 10s, 12s, 14s
Sizes 10t, 12t, 14t
Sizes 12, 14

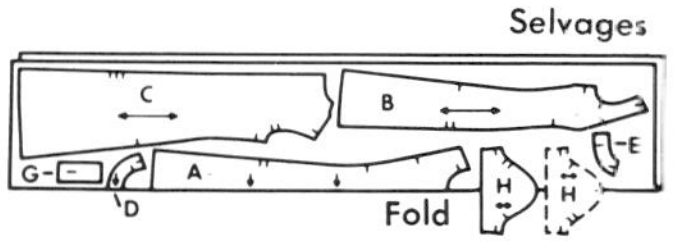

35" 36" Fabric With Or Without Nap
Size 16t
Sizes 16, 18

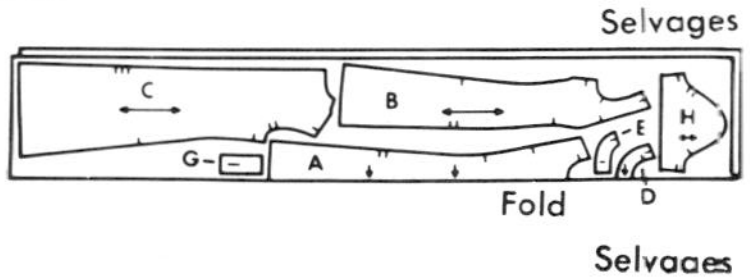

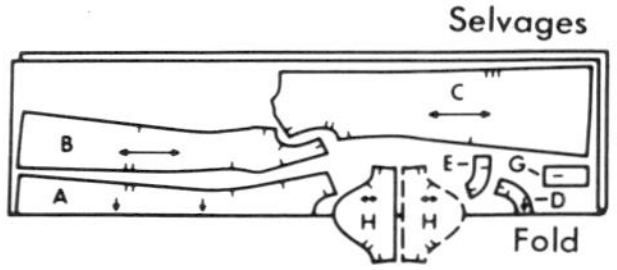

54"Fabric Without Nap
Sizes 8s, 10s, 12s, 14s
Sizes 10t, 12t
Size 12

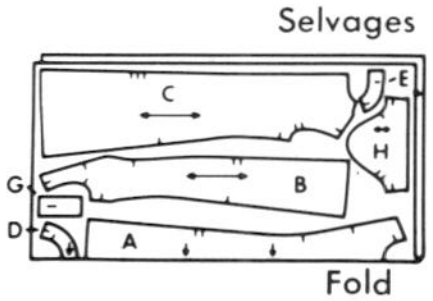

54" Fabric
Without Nap
Sizes 14t, 16t
Sizes 14, 16, 18

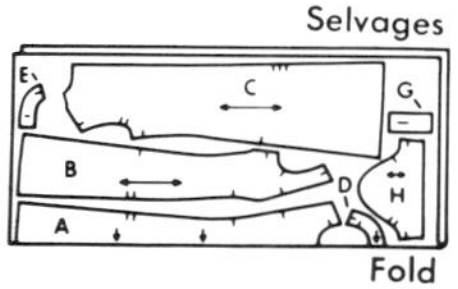

View 2 INTERFACING

NOTE: NECK–Cut 1 on fold by D and 2 by E, less 3/8" on inner unnotched edges.

25" 32" 35" 36" Fabric
All Sizes

SIMPLICITY PATTERN CO.

Find the correct cutting layout for your pattern view, size, and width of fabric. If your material has a one-way design or a nap, you may need a special layout. A girl who wears a size 12 is making View 1 from plain material that is 36 inches wide. Did she circle the correct layout to use?

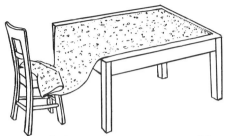

Use a chair to support excess material.

Do you see a pattern piece marked with a dotted or broken line? If so, this piece will have to be cut twice. If your pattern calls for cuffs, you will need four pieces—two for the outside of the two cuffs and two to face the inside. If you cut out one pattern piece on folded material, you will have only two cuffs. For a beginner or for anyone who is matching designs, it is a good idea to cut another pattern piece from plain paper to use in placement.

Follow the pattern layout directions. These have been prepared by experts and will insure good results. When you have more experience, you may be able to change the layout to suit your particular needs.

Sewing is fun if you have a partner to help you with some details. Helping her at other times gives you additional experience.

Note carefully on the layout which edge is the selvage and which is the fold.

Place the large pattern pieces on first. Pin them loosely, matching the grain lines. Two pins should hold each piece in place.

Do not cut any piece of material until you are certain that all pattern pieces are properly placed. If the pattern layout calls for one part to be cut on a lengthwise fold and another on a crosswise fold, you may have to do some juggling to check all the pieces but it is worth the effort. Mistakes made in sewing can often be corrected but once material is cut, there is little that can be done to correct an error except to buy more material. Not only is this a needless cost, but the material may not be available.

To be certain each pattern piece is on the grainline or straight of the material, place the arrow along a lengthwise thread. If your material has a woven design or coarse threads, you may be able to see the lengthwise threads and you can place the arrow directly over a lengthwise thread. Usually you will need to use the fabric selvage as a guide. If the lengthwise grainline is parallel to the selvage, it will have to be on a lengthwise thread (if you straightened the material first). You can check this by using a yardstick—be sure the distance from the top arrow to the selvage is the same as the distance from the bottom arrow to the selvage. If one distance is greater, you will need to move the pattern until both measure the same. Cut facings in the same direction as the pieces to which they are applied. It may take more material this way but facings will lie more smoothly. If your fabric has a one

492

This teacher is using the overhead projector to stress the importance of laying the pattern on the grain.

way design, follow directions for placement on nap fabrics (Page 588).

If the pattern piece is to be placed along a fold, pin it first along the fold before placing other pins.

When you are certain you have all the pieces correctly placed, smooth out each pattern piece and place pins to secure it for cutting. If the pattern pieces are straight and the material is firm, pins need be only four inches apart. On curved edges and slippery materials you will need to pin more closely. If you place pins inside the cutting line at right angles to the pattern, it will be easier to cut a smooth edge and the shears will not be dulled on the pins.

Before cutting, check your chart to be sure that you have not forgotten any needed pieces. It is wise to have your teacher or an experienced person check your pattern now.

CUTTING YOUR FABRIC

Cut with long, even strokes except at curves and details where short cuts are needed. Short, choppy strokes result in jagged edges which are difficult to match with other edges. Keep the material flat on the table. Lifting the cloth will cause it to slip and seam edges will not be accurate.

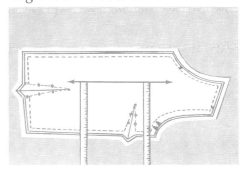

If each end of the lengthwise grain line (indicated by arrows) is the same distance from the selvage, one can assume that the arrow line is placed correctly.

Hold your shears correctly. Place the thumb in the smaller hole and two or three fingers in the larger one. Be sure the larger hole is close to the table.

Remember, pinking shears do not cut a pattern accurately. The uneven edges make it very difficult to put pieces together.

Cut in the *direction of the grain* whenever possible. Cutting with the grain keeps the threads in proper position and prevents stretching. The arrows on some patterns are guides. Otherwise, cut from the largest part of a pattern to the narrowest.

Walk around the table to cut. Do not move the fabric any more than is necessary.

Notches should be cut *away* from the pattern. They are easier to see and less likely to ravel into the seamline. Double and triple notches can be cut in one piece—up, across the top of two or three notches and down. The size of the notch clues you for proper matching.

Keep pattern pieces pinned to the fabric until you have transferred the marks from the pattern to the cloth. It is better not to unpin a piece until you are ready to sew it. Neatly lay aside the scraps for machine test stitching and for trying new processes. Fold your pattern and material carefully.

Refer to the section on Shortcuts (Chapter Seventeen) if you have had considerable experience in sewing and want to learn faster methods.

TRANSFERRING PATTERN MARKINGS TO THE FABRIC

Marks that appear on the pattern, which give directions for putting the garment together, have to be trans-

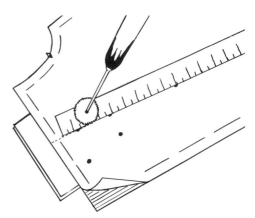

Marking a dart with tracing paper and a tracing wheel.

ferred to the fabric. This is done after all the pieces have been cut and before the pattern tissue is removed. The seamlines need not be marked if you have a gauge on the machine which you use as a guide. (Do not transfer cutting marks such as straight grain or alteration lines.) Can you think of other pattern marks that do not need to be transferred to the material?

The method used for transferring pattern marks will depend upon your fabric and how fast you will be able to complete the garment, as explained in the following section. You may need to take more time marking the fabric when you are learning to sew than when you have more experience. Be certain to mark accurately as it is a waste of time to check pattern pieces to figure out marks that you forgot in the first place.

Tracing Wheel. If you use a tracing wheel and dressmaker's carbon paper for transferring pattern markings, your markings will be accurate. (Note: This is not the carbon paper used for typing.)

Select a carbon close to the fabric color but one that you can still see (marks do not always come off). For double thicknesses of material, place one sheet of tracing paper face up under the lower layer of the fabric and another sheet face down between the pattern and upper layer of fabric. One long sheet folded over may also be used. For a single thickness, place the carbon paper with marking side against the wrong side of the fabric.

Trace along the lines. A ruler will help on straight lines. At the ends of darts and pleats use a short horizontal line to mark the ending. A dot and other markings can be marked with an X.

Whenever possible, omit the carbon paper. Many materials will hold tracing wheel marks long enough for construction.

Pins and chalk. To transfer such markings as the center front, button-holes, and pocket placement to the right side, machine or hand baste along the marking line. A faster but less accurate way is to use pins and chalk. Place the pins through the pattern and both layers of the fabric. Chalk the fabric at each pin on the wrong side. Carefully remove the pattern as you chalk-mark pins on the top fabric layer.

If a garment is to be made at once, marking with pins alone may be adequate. However they are easily lost if you must stop work and put your fabric away often.

Iron marking. Another method for quick fabric construction is iron marking. This can be used on firm fabrics that take a crease well. With the pattern piece still attached to the fabric, lay the garment piece on the ironing board pattern side down. Fold back on stitching lines and

JOHN DRITZ AND SONS

A ruler aids in making straight lines when using a tracing wheel.

press. Repeat the pressing process for opposite stitching lines. Remove the pattern and stitch darts or tucks along creased lines.

Tailor's tacks. Tailor's tacks show on both sides of the fabric and are necessary for heavy fabrics and those harmed by a tracing wheel. They do take time to make and mark only certain points of a line, not the entire line. Use a long, double thread without a knot. Take two stitches through the pattern and both layers of the fabric at each symbol, leaving a one-inch loop. Remove the pattern carefully, separate fabric layers gently and clip threads between layers. A tuft of thread is left on both fabric pieces.

See section on Shortcuts (Chapter Seventeen) for other marking ideas to use when you have experience in sewing.

Unless the grain of the fabric is easily seen because of fabric design or yarn size, it is wise to mark the cross-wise fabric grain above the bust line and at the hip line for easier fitting.

HOW WELL DO I WORK IN THE CLASSROOM?

	Always	?	Seldom
1. Do I have a suitable box or basket in which to keep my equipment? Do I keep it in good order?			
2. Do I protect my fabric while I work by keeping my hands clean? by dusting the table and machine when necessary? by keeping the fabric off the floor?			
3. Do I maintain good posture while hand and machine sewing?			
4. Do I utilize my time to the best advantage? by avoiding unnecessary talking with my neighbors? by planning ahead so I will not need to wait for the use of equipment? by asking for help only when necessary? by putting my work away carefully so it will not need unnecessary pressing? by walking around the room only when necessary?			
5. Do I cooperate with the other girls by sharing the use of school supplies and equipment? by returning everything to its proper place after use?			
6. Do I help the appearance of the room by picking up pins, needles, and fabric scraps that fall to the floor? by putting my chair back in place at the end of the class? by closing the sewing machine if it is my turn to do so?			

The lengthwise grain should also be marked if it is not the same as the center and back front line. Hand baste in contrasting thread with stitches far apart.

YOUR NEXT STEP

You are almost ready to start putting together the pieces of your garment. In Chapter Sixteen you will find descriptions of general construction processes, plans for the unit method of construction, and detailed directions for the most used construction techniques.

Mark a dart on practice fabric with a tracing wheel and dressmaker's carbon paper and also with tailor's tacks. Be prepared to state when each method is a good selection and which you prefer.

Working in small groups, adapt the work habits chart shown on page 496 to your classroom situation. Prepare enough copies of the revised chart for everyone in your class and check it when directed by your teacher.

Summary With Check-up Questions

Clothing construction is a means of expressing one's creativity and obtaining personal satisfaction.

- *How do you feel when someone compliments you on an article you have made yourself?*
- *Is a garment for which you selected the pattern, fabric, and trimmings more personal than one bought ready-made?*

The ability to sew is a valuable resource worth money to those who possess it.

- *Why is it possible to make garments for less than it costs to buy them ready-made?*
- *How can the ability to sew and make repairs to clothing articles be worth money?*
- *What job opportunities are open to a person who can sew? (See Chapter Eighteen)*

Anyone with limited sewing ability and who is pressed for time will be more successful if a pattern that is easily made is selected.

- *Is it natural to get discouraged if you are trying to do something that is very difficult and time consuming?*

- *Is a pattern labeled "Easy-to-Make" a good choice for a beginner?*
- *If a pattern is not labeled, how can the number of pattern pieces be a clue to its difficulty?*

Patterns are made in many figure types and sizes.

- *Will a very short girl wear the same figure type pattern as a tall girl, even if bust and hip measurements are the same?*
- *How does a pattern planned for the Teen-Boy compare with one in the Young Men's figure type?*
- *Why do some older women find that the Misses pattern type is best for them and some young girls may need to select a pattern in the Women's type?*

Accurate measurements are essential for a wise selection of pattern size and type.

- *What are the four most important measurements for selecting a pattern size?*
- *What additional measurement helps in selecting pattern figure type?*
- *How will the fit of a garment be affected if you select a pattern based on inaccurate measurements?*

Choosing the correct pattern type and size saves time and effort later.

- *If your pattern needs alterations, will you be able to start sewing as soon as someone whose pattern fits well?*
- *What will happen if you cut your fabrics from a pattern that is too small or too short for you?*
- *If you selected a pattern too large to be "safe," what will happen if you cut your fabric without altering the pattern?*

Whenever possible, make needed alterations on the pattern before cutting out the fabric.

- *What will be the result of cutting out a pattern that is too short for you?*
- *How can you alter a dress that is too narrow across the hips? Would it have been easier to make the changes in the pattern tissue?*
- *Will a dress that is too large and has to be made smaller by making deep seams fit as well as when the proper alterations are made in the pattern tissue?*

Anyone with limited sewing ability or time will be more successful if a fabric that is easy to handle is chosen.

- *Will it be more time consuming and difficult to sew with a slippery fabric that frays easily or a firm, sturdy fabric?*
- *What are the advantages of a plain fabric?*
- *Why is white or black not the best choice for a beginner?*
- *If a plaid or striped fabric is selected rather than an allover print, what will be the effect on sewing time and patience needed?*

The fabric should be matched to the pattern selected.

- *If a fabric is stiff, like taffeta, will it be suitable for a pattern with gathers at the yoke?*

- *How can you determine if a pattern will work up well in a plaid design?*
- *Experienced sewers often have their pattern with them when selecting their fabric. What are the advantages of this?*

Purchasing the pattern, the correct amount of fabric, and all necessary sewing supplies in one trip is a good plan to follow.

- *Why will it save time to select all items at once?*
- *If you do not purchase enough fabric at one time, can you be sure you will be able to obtain more later?*
- *How can the lack of a seemingly small item such as correct color thread, a zipper, or buttons cause a major delay in the completion of a garment?*

Fabrics are seldom ready for cutting when purchased.

- *Are all fabrics preshrunk?*
- *How will you know if you need to preshrink a fabric?*
- *Why do some fabrics need to have the grain "straightened" before use?*

Different fabrics require different methods of preshrinking.

- *What is the best way to preshrink woolen fabrics?*
- *How are cotton, linen, and rayon fabrics best preshrunk?*
- *Will you preshrink a fabric made from only polyester or acrylic fibers?*
- *Should you preshrink a fabric that is drycleanable only?*

Select the correct pattern layout for your material and pattern size and view.

- *How will the width of your fabric affect the way the pattern pieces are placed on it?*
- *Why is it important to select the layout planned for the pattern view you have selected?*
- *If your fabric has a nap or one-way design, will a special layout be needed?*

Cutting out a pattern correctly makes the actual sewing easier and more successful.

- *What will be the appearance of seam edges if you hold the fabric away from the table during cutting?*
- *Why is it important to cut notches away from the pattern, into the excess fabric?*
- *If the grain line is not placed correctly, will your garment hang correctly?*

The method used for transferring pattern markings will depend upon your fabric, and how fast you are able to complete your garment.

- *On what fabrics is a tracing wheel and carbon paper suitable?*
- *Why are tailor's tacks needed for heavy wools and delicate silk and silk-like fabrics?*
- *Marking with pins is seldom satisfactory for a class project. Why?*

Can You Explain These Terms?

pattern alteration	*basic waist length measurement*	*center front and center back*
girl's pattern type	*cutting line*	*TLC for fabrics*
young junior/teen pattern type	*seam line*	*preshrinking wool*
junior pattern type	*fold line*	*preshrinking cotton*
misses' pattern type	*straight of the goods*	*to straighten a fabric*
women's pattern type	*seam allowance*	*tracing wheel*
bust measurement	*direction of stitching*	*dressmaker's carbon*
waist measurement	*notches*	*iron marking*
hip measurement		*tailor's tacks*

METRIC SYSTEM

Since the United States is planning to go on the metric system, the following chart of metric equivalents for inches, feet, and yards will be of help in adjusting to new terms.

1 inch	. . . .	25 millimetres
1 foot	. . . .	0.3 metre
1 yard	. . . .	0.9 metre
1 millimetre	. . . .	0.04 inch
1 metre	. . . .	3.3 feet
		1.1 yards

CHAPTER FIFTEEN

Selection and Use of Sewing Equipment

Y OU CAN MAKE GARMENTS for your-self with old scissors from the kitchen drawer, pins gathered from around the house, and measuring aids borrowed from a friend—but the results will probably look amateurish, you'll be frustrated as you work, and your friends may not be happy to see you coming. It is very discouraging to try to cut cloth with dull scissors, to try to use a thimble that is too tight or falls off, or to search for a needle whenever you need one. Select your sewing equipment carefully and keep it in good condition in one place. You will find sewing more enjoyable and your finished product better looking.

Select a few essential items and add to them gradually. If you take good care of your sewing tools, you will gather a good selection that will serve you for many years. Label them with your name and use them ONLY for sewing.

The wise selection of sewing equipment and supplies is important for the success of any project. Can you name each item in this picture?

RISDON MANUFACTURING CO.

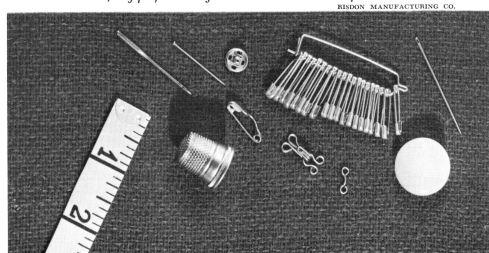

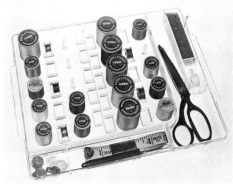

JOHN DRITZ AND SONS, INC.

A plastic tray with compartments for common sewing equipment makes it easy to keep everything ready for use.

SEWING EQUIPMENT

Sewing box. First of all, you need a place to keep your equipment. Perhaps there is a tote drawer at school for you. This is handy but you will also need a container for your small equipment to keep it from getting lost among your fabric and pattern pieces. You can buy a simple plastic tray or an elaborate sewing box or you can use a candy or shoe box. Be sure your choice is durable. If it is also attractive so that you get a lift every time you use it, you will find it easier to keep it neat.

A basket, a cigar box covered with attractive paper, or a sewing tray will keep your small equipment convenient and in good condition.

Shears and scissors. Your very own pair of shears or scissors is a good investment—one that you use only for sewing. Cutting paper, string, and other materials may dull and nick the blades. Look at the pictures on page 502. Do you know which are shears and which are scissors? Why are the handles bent?

Technically, *shears* usually measure six inches or more in length and have a small opening in one handle for the thumb and a larger opening in the other for two or more fingers. Shears are used for heavier cutting than scissors. Bent handle shears make it easier to cut out fabrics as one needs scarcely lift the fabric from the table when cutting. *Scissors* are six inches or less in length and have small matching holes in the handles.

One pair of dressmaking shears, about six inches long, with sharp, close-fitting blades will handle most cutting needs. Be sure they cut evenly to the very tips of the blades. Two pairs are better, one pair of shears about 7 or 8 inches long for cutting out fabrics and a pair of scissors 3½ to 4 inches for snipping threads and clipping to corners.

If you are left-handed, you may find left-handed shears easier to work with.

Pinking shears are not for cutting fabrics as it is difficult to get an accurate edge with them—they are *finishing* shears to use for finishing seam edges. *Scalloping* shears are also available. They will give a ravel resistant seam finish as well as an attractive edging for such nonwoven fabrics as felt, vinyl, and interfacings. See the picture on page 503 for the proper use of these shears.

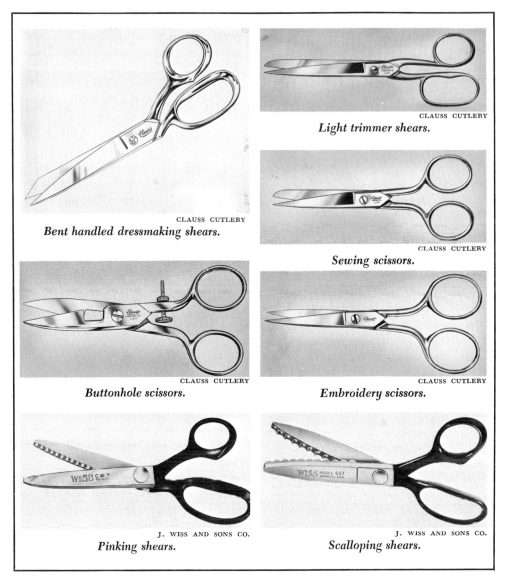

CLAUSS CUTLERY
Light trimmer shears.

CLAUSS CUTLERY
Bent handled dressmaking shears.

CLAUSS CUTLERY
Sewing scissors.

CLAUSS CUTLERY
Buttonhole scissors.

CLAUSS CUTLERY
Embroidery scissors.

J. WISS AND SONS CO.
Pinking shears.

J. WISS AND SONS CO.
Scalloping shears.

Buttonhole scissors make straight, uniform buttonholes without creasing the fabric. A thumbscrew regulates and controls the length of the cut. *Embroidery* scissors have short blades with sharp points.

CARE OF SCISSORS

Like other tools, shears and scissors need proper care. The following directions will keep them like new.

- Keep them for sewing ONLY. If you cut cardboard, string, pins or anything but cloth, the blades may become dull and nicked.
- Keep them clean. Wipe away the lint. You may need to place a drop of sewing machine oil at the screw occasionally.
- The tips are for cutting fabrics, not as a substitute for a screw driver or a tack lifter.

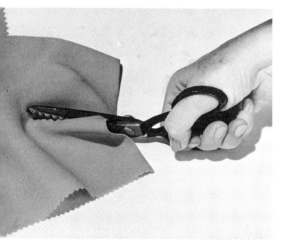
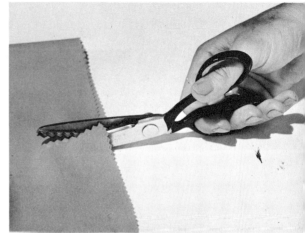

A

B

Do you know how to use pinking shears properly? (A) This girl is squeezing the blades together by putting opposing pressure on the handles. This results in a shaggy, not completely cut line. (B) The correct way: Let the shears do the work for a cleanly pinked slash.

- If hung, scissors and shears should be suspended by both finger rings with blades together.
- When not in use, store with blades closed and protected. Leather or plastic cases slide over the blades for safety and protection.
- When they get dulled, have them sharpened by someone who knows the correct method. Pinking and scalloping shears must be sent back to the factory for sharpening.

Pins. Good pins for sewing use are made of brass or steel and are sold by weight in a box, or in a paper. *Dressmaker* pins are of medium diameter and are suitable for most sewing. *Silk* pins are very slender with a needle point to be used on very fine fabrics. Needles can be used as pins for very delicate fabrics that may be easily marred. Pins with colorful plastic heads are attractive and easy to see, but they may melt close to a hot iron.

NOTE: Always buy many more pins than you think you will need. It is amazing how many pins you will use.

Pincushion. A box is a convenient place to store pins but boxes do manage to get upset, usually on the floor! A wrist pincushion helps keep pins out of your mouth and is readily available if you need pins while being fitted or at the ironing board. Some girls prefer to pin a large pin cushion to their skirt as they work.

Thimble. Smart sewers find that a thimble protects the finger, especially if sewing for long periods of time or working on heavy materials. Be sure a thimble fits the middle finger of the hand with which you sew. Thimbles come in many sizes. Try one on to see that it fits snugly but not too tightly. Metal ones may be more effective than bulky plastic ones. NOTE: A thimble may feel awkward at first but when you have learned to use it, you will appreciate its help.

NOTIONS REF

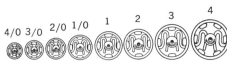

SNAP FASTENERS

Brass, rustproof; Studs and sockets have guide holes for easy placement on garment. White or Black.

THIMBLES

Chromium plated brass thimbles will not tarnish. Extra deep dimples prevent needle from slipping. Each thimble is stamped for size. Available in boxes or on cards.

HOOKS, EYES & LOOPS

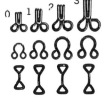

SKIRT HOOK & EYE
Skirts, shorts, trousers—jackets. Special snap-catch prevents accidental opening. Nickel and Black. Brass, rustproof.

COAT HOOKS & EYES
White or Black Brass, rustproof

REGULAR
Brass, rustproof, "Third wire" hook holds eye or loop securely in place. White or Black.

SAFETY PINS

BLANKET PIN
Size 6

Extra stiff wire-Brass, rustproof

PINETTE

perfect for fastening Gripper® Cover Buttons

SAFETY PINS
00

BABY-SAFE DIAPER PIN

BABY SAFE
Stainless Steel Wire— Stainless Steel Lined Plastic Caps won't crack or fall off. 4 colors—pink, blue, white & maize

2

0

1

3

Size No. 00 & 0 are Brass, rustproof; Nos. 1, 2 & 3 come in Stainless Steel, Brass or Steel.

SNAP FASTENERS

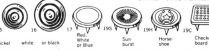

15 16 17 19S 19H 19C
Nickel white or black Red. White or Blue Sun- burst Horse- shoe Checker- board

Simply tap them on or use Gripper Pliers for even easier application of 16, 17 & 19 Round.

15-16...very popular for baby's clothes

17-19S-19H-19C...perfect for decorative uses —Western shirts, casual clothes

COVER BUTTONS

Unique design assures a wrinkle-free cover in just 3 simple steps with the flexible "Button Maker" supplied in each kit, and there are no sharp, irritating prongs to snag material or fingers. Buttons are made of rustproof aluminum— washable, dry cleanable.

14/20 14/24 14/30 14/36 14/45 14/60

ERENCE GUIDE

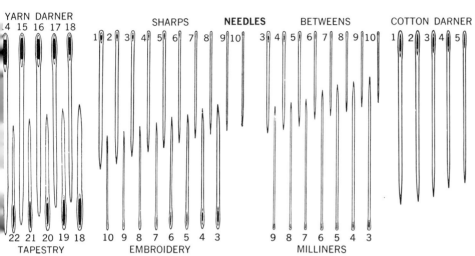

YARN DARNER
4 15 16 17 18

SHARPS

NEEDLES

BETWEENS

COTTON DARNER

22 21 20 19 18
TAPESTRY

EMBROIDERY

MILLINERS

For any given size needle, the smaller the size number, the longer & thicker the needle. All Needles except Tapestry & Yarn Darners have gold plated eye for easy threading, & to prevent fraying of thread. English Needles—Sheffield steel—Nickel plated.

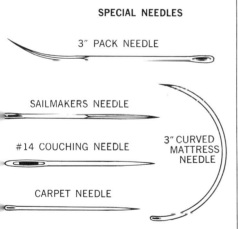

SPECIAL NEEDLES

3" PACK NEEDLE

SAILMAKERS NEEDLE

#14 COUCHING NEEDLE

3" CURVED
MATTRESS
NEEDLE

CARPET NEEDLE

Pack Needle—For sacks & string sewing
Sailmakers Needle—For canvas awning
Couching Needle—For embroidery—Heavy threads
Carpet Needle—For rugs, carpets, heavy fabric
Curved Mattress Needle—For upholstery, car seat

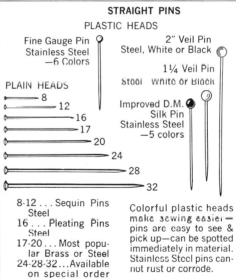

STRAIGHT PINS

PLASTIC HEADS

Fine Gauge Pin
Stainless Steel
—6 Colors

2" Veil Pin
Steel, White or Black

1¼ Veil Pin
Steel, White or Black

PLAIN HEADS

8

12

16

17

20

24

28

32

Improved D.M.
Silk Pin
Stainless Steel
—5 colors

8-12 . . . Sequin Pins
Steel
16 . . . Pleating Pins
Steel
17-20 . . . Most popular Brass or Steel
24-28-32 . . . Available on special order only Brass or Steel

Colorful plastic heads make sewing easier — pins are easy to see & pick up—can be spotted immediately in material. Stainless Steel pins cannot rust or corrode.

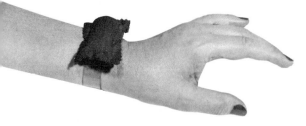

A wrist pin-cushion can be bought or made by attaching an elastic to a small pin-cushion.

Needles. Hand sewing will be easier if your needle is the correct size for the fabric and thread you are using. There are several types of needles. Choose the one that you find easiest to use. *Sharps* are average length needles with a small eye and are most commonly used for hand sewing. *Crewel* or *embroidery* needles have large eyes that are easy to thread. They are used for embroidery and can also be used for regular sewing. *Betweens* are short needles with a small eye. They do not bend as eas-

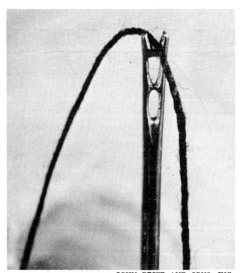

An easy to thread needle. Line up the thread with the needle eye and a slight pull results in a threaded needle.

ily as a large needle and may be suitable for you if your hands are small.

Needle sizes vary from a coarse 1 to a fine 12. Heavy fabrics need coarse needles, and fine needles work best on delicate fabrics. Number 7 or 8 is a good size for most sewing. You can buy a package all one size or one of assorted sizes. (Number 5 to 10 is a good selection.)

Curved and *double pointed* needles are also available for special sewing tasks. As you undertake more advanced projects, you may want to consider their use. Plan to store needles in a pin cushion or the papers in which they came. An emery bag is often used to sharpen and clean needles but if they are left in the emery bag, they will rust.

Do you have difficulty threading a needle? Select a split needle so the thread can be pulled down into position or use a needle threader. A wire is inserted easily into the needle eye; the thread is put into the larger loop and pulled through the needle.

Measuring tools. A *tape measure* is essential. Many inexpensive ones stretch so they are not accurate and the ends fray. Select one that is firm with clearly printed numbers, and a metal tip on the short end. Some students find that numbering which begins at opposite ends of the two sides is more convenient to use. Others find that they measure inaccurately if they twist this type of tape measure so they prefer the same numbering on both sides. One with metric measurements on one side is a good choice.

A *yardstick* is helpful for measuring hems as well as general marking. Be sure the one you use is smooth so it won't snag your fabric.

A *small ruler,* four to six inches long, is useful for marking straight lines and for measuring buttonholes and hems. A combination ruler and gauge is a convenient item. A clear plastic ruler is a good choice as pattern lines and fabric are visible through the ruler and measurements can accurately be made.

A *hem marker* is more accurate for most girls to use than a yard stick. There are many types available. One type has a ruler mounted on a base with a clamp attached which may be adjusted for the proper hemline. Another person is needed to mark the hemline with pins. One type you can use yourself is a ruler on a floor stand with a container of powdered chalk which marks a line when you squeeze a rubber bulb.

Other Equipment. Marking equipment such as a tracing wheel and dressmaker's carbon is usually available in the classroom. Be sure to choose the correct type wheel; some have long, sharp points for thick woolen fabrics and others are more suitable for fine fabrics. If possible, select a carbon that will wash out of a washable fabric. A *dress form* is handy for fitting and trying out different style effects. Experienced sewers find them convenient. If you do not have a large table where you may cut out fabrics, a folding *cutting board* may be worth having. A *stitch ripper* is useful for small cutting jobs and for ripping out unwanted stitches. It is specially designed with a cutting edge at the center of the blade and a sharp point to slip under a stitch. It can also be used to slit open buttonholes and is much safer than a razor blade. Browse through the sewing equipment sections of

UNIQUE DISTRIBUTING CO.

A dressmaker's form makes it easy to measure your own hem length. A hem marker is more accurate than a yardstick, whether you use it on a dressmaker's form or someone else marks the hem for you.

local stores to learn what is available. Many items are gadgets which you will seldom use, but others may prove to be helpful to you and worthy of purchasing. Pressing equipment is described on page 527.

507

A dress form is helpful for women who sew a great deal. This one is adjustable to fit members of the family who may be of different sizes. Draping fabrics over the form helps one visualize the effect of the finished garment. It is often easier to fit a garment on a form than on oneself.

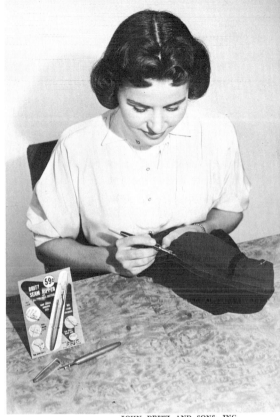

A stitch ripper being used to quickly and safely remove unwanted hemming stitches.

508

A cutting board provides protection for your table and a secure work surface. This board has one-inch markings in all directions to aid in cutting out fabrics. It can be folded and stored in a small space.

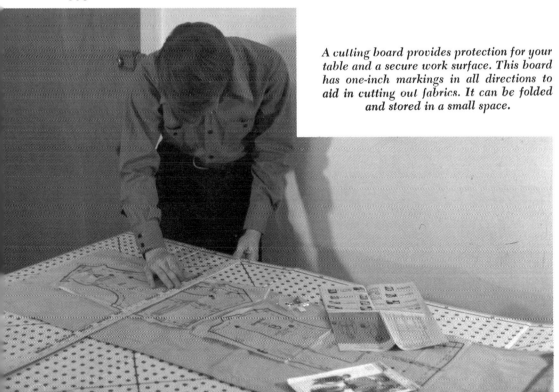

Practice using pinking and other shears correctly. Demonstrate to the class how to let the shears do the work.

Arrange a display of good and poor sewing equipment. Try to find a frayed tape measure and one that has stretched, shears that do not cut well, blunt needles, and bent pins to contrast with good equipment.

Prepare an exhibit of different kinds of needles for hand sewing. Which length is most comfortable for you? Compare with those selected by girls whose hands are larger or smaller. What conclusions can you make?

Try on several thimbles of different sizes. Which one is most suitable for you? Copy the size on your chart of needed equipment so you won't forget it.

Make a list of safety precautions to observe when using small equipment such as scissors, shears, needles, pins, and other articles.

Visit a store that sells a large variety of sewing equipment. Make a list of each type of item seen on display. Include the purpose for each item. (You will find it listed on the package or label.) Report to the class. Perhaps you will compare your list with that of someone who has "shopped" at another type of store.

Plan a day when each student will bring to class a sewing aid that she or a family member or friend finds very useful. Be prepared to tell why it is liked.

Describe the best way to mark each piece of your equipment with your name.

Investigate equipment for marking hems. Evaluate them as to: (a) ease of operation, (b) cost, (c) durability. Give your information as a special class report.

SEWING SUPPLIES AND NOTIONS

The correct choice of sewing notions and supplies is as important as the selection of fabric or equipment. Read the back of your pattern envelope to determine what you need.

Thread. Do you know that there are many types of threads available? Most girls notice the large display of mercerized cotton thread, size 50, in fabric stores and do not look for another type of thread which may be more suitable for their needs.

Mercerized cotton thread, size 50, is used for almost every type of sewing. Over 150 colors are available. The mercerization process gives the thread added luster and strength.

Plain cotton thread comes in many sizes, from number 8 which is very coarse to number 70. White thread can be obtained in sizes up to 100 which is extremely fine and used only for the most delicate sewing.

Heavy duty cotton thread is recommended for sewing sports clothes, slip covers and other items that need strong seams.

If you are sewing on silk or woolen fabrics, you will find that *silk thread* is especially suitable. It has more stretch than cotton thread but is not as heat sensitive as synthetic threads.

SEWING EQUIPMENT CHECKLIST *(Copy on another sheet of paper and check your needs)*				
	Available in Classroom	I need now	I would like to have	
			Now	Later
Sewing box or basket				
Shears—8″				
Scissors—5″				
Pinking shears				
Needles—size 7 or 8				
Emery cushion				
Pins				
Pin cushion				
Thimble				
Small ruler or gauge				
Yardstick				
Tape measure				
Seam ripper				
Tracing wheel				
Carbon paper				
Chalk				
Sewing machine				
Iron				
Ironing board				
Seam roll				
Tailor's ham				
Hem marker				
Others				

Polyester threads are used with knits, bonded fabrics, and others that stretch and require more give than is possible with cotton thread. A dual-duty or core-spun thread is made of polyester filaments wrapped with cotton fibers and can be used as an all-purpose thread for most fabrics. Linen thread is very strong, although not readily available.

Very heavy cotton thread is called button and carpet thread. This is used for hand sewing of buttons, heavy mending, and reinforcements. *Buttonhole twist* is a silk thread that is used for making handmade buttonholes and for decorative stitching as along lapels and collars.

Basting thread is soft and inexpensive and comes in large spools. Most girls prefer to baste with left over cotton thread that contrasts in color with their fabric for easy removal.

Slide fasteners. There are many weights and types of slide fasteners or "zippers." The pattern envelope usually states the correct length. The length refers only to the teeth—not the tape. Select one that matches your fabric in texture as well as color.

COATS AND CLARK, INC.

Sewing threads are available in many sizes. No. 50 cotton thread is most commonly used. White is available from a heavy 8 to a fine 100. Black is available from size 8 to size 70.

Zippers with metal teeth are not as fine as those made of nylon or other synthetic materials. Nylon zippers may disintegrate if pressed with a very hot iron. Some nylon zippers are available with covered teeth so as to be less heat sensitive.

Snaps and hooks and eyes. Snaps are used for fastening where there is little strain. They are available in black and a silver color and in different weights or sizes. *Hooks and eyes* are used where there is strain on an opening and also come in various weights. You will notice that each hook has a round and a straight eye. The straight eye is used to fasten edges that lap over each other as with a skirt waistband, but the round eye is used to fasten edges that just meet each other.

Buttons. Buttons are available in many sizes. If your garment is to be drycleaned, select those that will not dissolve in the drycleaning fluid. It is wise to purchase an extra button to have in case one is lost.

Seam tapes, bias and decorative trims are usually used on washable fabrics and should be preshrunk at the factory. If they are not, soak them in water until thoroughly wet and allow to dry flat before using.

SEWING MACHINE USE AND CARE

All home sewing was done by hand before Elias Howe invented and marketed the sewing machine in 1846. His first machines were awkward and moved slowly as compared with the modern ones. However, they were a sensational advance. Louis Antoine Godey, original editor of the old *Godey's Lady's Book,* said, "Next to the plough this is perhaps humanity's most blessed instrument." Mahatma Gandhi, the late Indian leader, exempted the sewing machine from his ban on Western machinery. He said, "It is one of the few useful things invented.

More ornamental than sewing efficiency is characteristic of this 19th century model. Sewing is guided with left hand only as right hand is needed to turn the wheel.

511

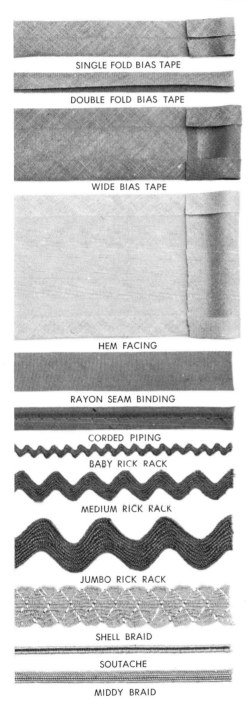

SINGLE FOLD BIAS TAPE

DOUBLE FOLD BIAS TAPE

WIDE BIAS TAPE

HEM FACING

RAYON SEAM BINDING

CORDED PIPING

BABY RICK RACK

MEDIUM RICK RACK

JUMBO RICK RACK

SHELL BRAID

SOUTACHE

MIDDY BRAID

COATS AND CLARK, INC.

It pays to learn the proper names of trimmings you may wish for your garment so you can ask for them by name at the store.

Certainly for the amateur seamstress the sewing machine is the most helpful piece of equipment. It increases the speed and niceness of your work. Yet the machine is also the most expensive and complicated piece of equipment you will use. Its good features should not be wasted. Your ability to turn out well-made clothes with a minimum of effort will depend largely on the skill you develop in using the sewing machine.

HOW A SEWING MACHINE WORKS

The principles underlying every machine are the same; however, different makes vary in minor points. Some machines are portable to be used on a table and others come in a variety of cabinets. Some machines produce the regulation lock stitch only and others also do zig-zag, chain stitching, and other decorative stitches. Each machine comes with a book of instructions as a source of information on its operation. This book has been carefully written with clear diagrams to help you get the best use from your machine. Study it carefully and keep it in a machine drawer or handy place for frequent reference.

Regardless of what machine you use, you will need to learn how to *open and close the machine,* to *start and stop it,* to *thread it,* to *stitch straight lines, curves, corners,* and to *anchor threads.* Most important, you will have to *learn control* over the machine—how to start it, slow and stop it. This takes practice. Later you will want to *recognize machine problems* so you will know when to seek help from your teacher. As you gain experience, you will be able to take care of many problems and to *clean and oil a machine* yourself.

HINTS ON THE USE OF THREAD

- Use a contrasting color thread for hand basting.

- Use thread one shade darker than fabric—thread appears lighter when stitched.

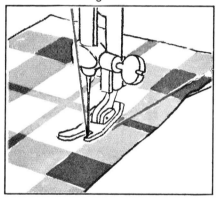

- For multi-color plaids or prints select predominant color OR use one color on top and another on bobbin.

- Select correct type of thread according to fabric weight.

TALON EDUCATIONAL SERVICE

THE SINGER COMPANY

Modern sewing machines may be portable to be stored away after each use or may be mounted in a simple console cabinet or a more elaborate one that looks like a desk with storage drawers.

Check to see that the sewing machine light shines on the needle area. Sewing is easier and safer when the needle area is well lighted.

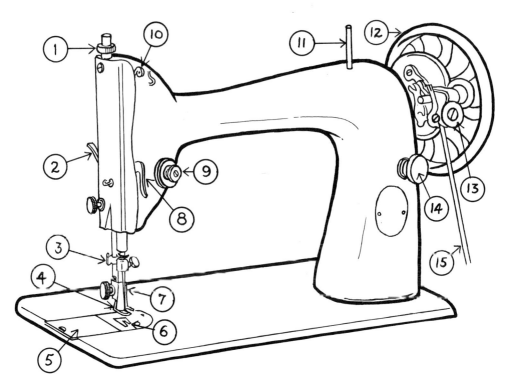

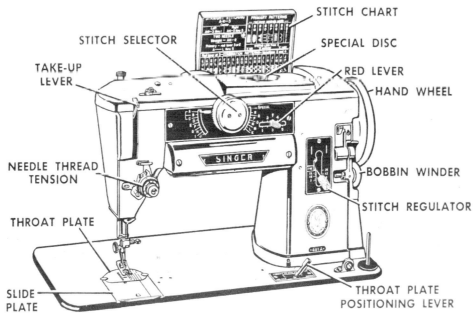

STITCH CHART

STITCH SELECTOR

TAKE-UP
LEVER

SPECIAL DISC

RED LEVER

HAND WHEEL

NEEDLE THREAD
TENSION

BOBBIN WINDER

STITCH REGULATOR

THROAT PLATE

SLIDE
PLATE

THROAT PLATE
POSITIONING LEVER

THE SINGER COMPANY

*Parts of an older sewing machine and a recent automatic one are similar. How
many can you name?*

You should learn the *names* of the common parts of the machine so you won't call everything a thingamajig or a whatsit.

Names of machine parts. A good place to start learning how to use the machine is to learn the names of the parts. As you study them you will learn their function and this will be a good foundation for sewing. Study the diagrams on page 514 and compare them with the machine you are using. The spool of thread is placed on a *spool pin* and passes through a *thread guide* on its way to the *tension.* This part regulates the "tension" or pull on the upper thread to keep a balanced stitch. It is important that you treat this part with respect. If it is not adjusted correctly, your machine is unusable and may not be easily fixed. Be sure the thread goes through the little discs and under the

THE SINGER COMPANY

Close-up of the upper tension. Be certain the thread goes between the discs and under the hook for proper tension.

hook because if it passed behind or in front of them, there will be no tension on the thread. After going through another thread guide, it must go through the *take-up* lever which syncronizes the thread as it goes in and out of the material. After passing through one or more thread guides, it passes through the *needle.* It is very important that the thread go through the needle in the correct direction. Some machines thread from left to right, some from right to left, and many new ones from front to back. If the needle is placed correctly, the thread enters the eye from the long groove side of the needle.

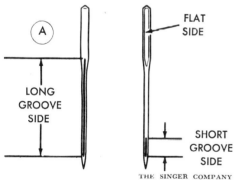

THE SINGER COMPANY

(A) Look at the needle and feel it with your fingernail to find the long groove, (B). To replace needle, loosen the needle clamp screw with your right hand while you hold the needle with your left. Pull down on the needle to take it out. To put in a new needle, hold the needle in your left hand and insert it with the long groove in the proper position. On most new machines it will be towards you . . . on others it is usually on the same side as the last thread guide. After inserting it up as far as it will go, tighten the needle clamp screw.

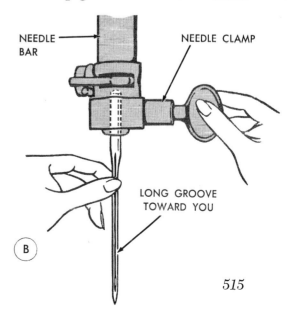

515

Usually the last thread guide is also on the side from which the thread enters the needle.

The needle passes between the *presser foot* (each side is called a *toe*). Under it is the *feed dog* which has sharp teeth to help push the material along as you sew. Under the *throat plate* is the *bobbin* which contains the lower thread. The two threads unite to form a stitch called the lock stitch. The *bobbin winder*, if needed, is usually on the right of the machine. Nearby you will also find the *stitch regulator* which controls the length of each stitch. The numbers on it usually refer to the number of stitches per inch. Moving the lever to the upper part often reverses the stitch direction. The *balance wheel* is that wheel on the right which goes around as the machine is powered. The *stop motion screw* is in the center and is loosened when winding a bobbin. Most machines today run on electricity and have either a *knee* or

foot lever. A treadle receives its power from your foot motion which engages a belt to turn the balance wheel.

Behind the needle is a *thread cutter* which is handy for cutting threads after stitching. The presser foot is lowered and raised by the *presser bar lifter* located in the back of the machine. At the top of the machine you will find a *presser bar control*. This screw regulates the amount of pressure placed on the presser foot and is changed only if you are working on very heavy or very thin material.

Be sure you have good light on your sewing. The machine light should be used every time you are using the machine. Additional lighting is necessary and should usually come over your left shoulder. In some homes and schools the lighting is so even that this may not be important.

LEARNING TO STITCH ON A MACHINE

For a *correct position*, place both feet on the floor, sit well back in your chair and bend slightly forward from the hips only. Be sure the chair is the correct height for the machine you are using . . . if you feel awkward, try a different height chair.

Use the left hand to guide but not to pull the fabric. The right hand should be free to be placed on the balance wheel to control the machine as needed.

To start to sew, lower the presser foot. Start the machine by applying pressure on the knee or foot lever. Most beginners start off very fast or barely move. Practice until you can control the machine and maintain the speed you wish. Slow stitching is harder than fast. You may find it

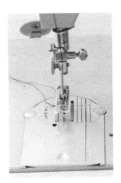

COATS AND CLARK, INC.

Throat Plate—A round hole in the throat plate of your sewing machine is essential for most straight stitching. The wider oval hole of zig-zag machines allows the fabric to be drawn into the hole, and the seam becomes puckered. If you have a zig-zag machine, you can buy an alternate plate with a round hole from your sewing machine dealer.

helpful to practice on paper that has straight and curved lines drawn on it.

To turn a corner, stop with the needle in the paper close to the corner. Raise the presser foot, turn the paper (pivot), drop the presser foot and continue stitching. If the needle is out of the cloth when you turn, the corner will not be square.

Stitching is seldom done by looking at the needle or the line where you are going to stitch but by keeping your eye on a point a distance from the needle.

Most machines have numbered guide lines in the throat plate. The numbers indicate the distance, in eighths of an inch, from the needle. If you want a ⅝ inch seam, for example, line up your fabric edge with line 5. If your machine does not have these marks, you can make or purchase a gauge or a magnet, or a piece of tape can be placed the correct distance from the needle.

The outer edges of the toes of the presser foot are also used as guides for small seams or for top stitching. The distance from the needle to the outer edge of one toe is usually ¼ inch and the other is ⅛ inch.

To stop, place your right hand on the balance wheel. The needle must be at the highest point when you remove the material so the threads will not jam up the bobbin case.

To prevent dust damage it is best to keep a machine closed when not in use. Lower the head carefully. Practice doing this so you won't lose control of the head and cause damage by dropping it. Be sure the electric cord is wound around the head of the machine so it will not get jammed.

On paper or a double thickness of a firm fabric, practice starting "stitching," and stopping an unthreaded machine.

As soon as you feel in control of the machine, thread it following the diagram for the machine you are using. Reread the section on page 515.

To keep thread from knotting when you begin to stitch, first bring the bobbin thread up through the hole in the throat plate. To do this, hold the end of the top thread loosely with the left hand while the balance wheel is turned once (direction varies with the machine). Pull the top thread to draw the bobbin thread up through the hole in the throat plate. Now pull the bobbin thread up and place both threads back of and under the presser foot.

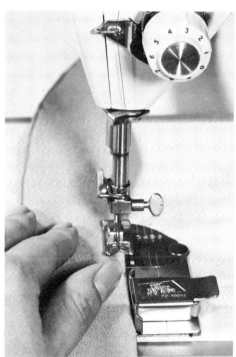

JOHN DRITZ AND SONS

A magnetic seam gauge holds onto any machine. Although this machine has marks on the throat plate, the gauge is needed for a narrower seam.

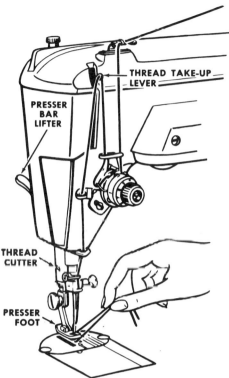

THE SINGER COMPANY

Typical upper threading. Be sure to follow specific directions for the machine you are using.

Always have material under the presser foot when stitching on a machine that has thread in the needle. Otherwise a thread jam may form underneath and it will be difficult to remove. Because most sewing is done on two pieces of cloth, it is wise to practice on a double thickness. Be sure you have the correct size thread for the needle and fabric being used.

Removing material from the machine. The needle should be at the highest point when the material is removed. Raise the presser foot and draw the material back of it until the threads are about 6 inches long; then cut them in the middle so at least 3 inches of thread remains.

Fastening machine stitching. To *tie threads,* pull thread on the wrong side of fabric until you can catch the loop of the upper thread; then pull the upper thread through and tie the two threads together in a square knot. *To fasten stitching by retracing,* stitch to the fabric edge. Raise stitch level to top and backstitch to reinforce end of seam. If machine does not reverse stitch direction, leave needle in material, raise presser foot, turn the material around and retrace the first stitching *To fasten by locking stitches,* raise the presser foot slightly and stitch several times in the same place to lock the threads

SIZE OF STITCHES. The correct size of the stitch will vary. If you want to machine baste or gather fabrics, you will use the largest stitch possible, about 6 stitches per inch. Twelve to 15 stitches per inch is suitable for seams on medium weight fabrics. Very small stitches, about 18 to 22 stitches per inch, are good for fabrics which require stretch and strength. (A smaller, short stitch is more elastic than a larger one.) If your machine does not move when you start it, perhaps you have the stitch regulator set at such a small stitch that it gets no place!

TENSION. Stitching done with a tension improperly adjusted will either pucker or perhaps fall apart easily. The upper and lower tension need to be balanced so that the interlocking of the threads is even. If loops are noticeable on one side, one tension is looser than the other. If the tensions are too tight, the stitching will pucker. Always do your test stitching on a sample of double thickness material.

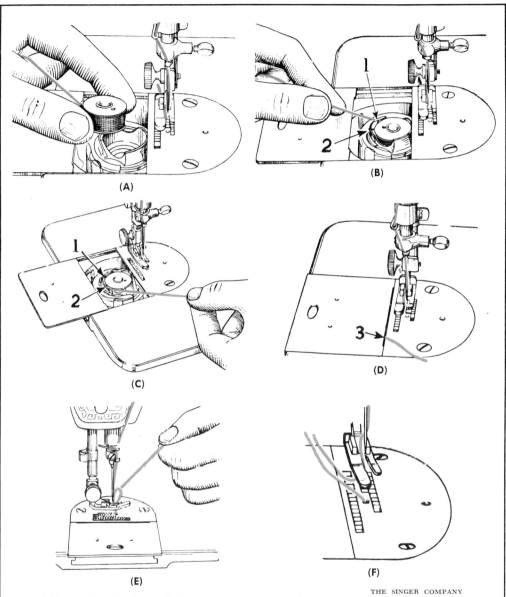

THE SINGER COMPANY

(A) *To thread a lower bobbin case, have the take-up lever at its highest point. Open the slide plate. Place the bobbin in the base.* (B) *Draw the thread into slot 1 and under spring 2.* (C) *Draw the thread into the notch on the case. Pull out at least 3 inches of thread across bobbin.* (D) *Close slide plate and allow thread to enter notch on slide plate.* (E) *To get the thread up, hold the needle thread lightly with your left hand. Turn the hand wheel until the needle has gone down and up and the take-up lever is at its highest point. Pull the needle thread, and a loop of the bobbin thread will come to the surface.* (F) *Put your finger through the loop and pull the end of the bobbin thread up. Place the needle thread between the toes of the presser foot and pull threads back as shown, ready for stitching.*

FABRIC, THREAD, NEEDLE, AND STITCH LENGTH TABLE

FABRICS	THREAD SIZES	NEEDLE SIZES	STRAIGHT STITCHES PER INCH
DELICATE—tulle, chiffon, fine lace, silk, organdy, fine tricot	Fine Mercerized 100 to 150 Cotton Synthetic Thread	9	15 to 20
LIGHTWEIGHT—batiste, organdy, jersey, voile, taffeta, silk, crepe, plastic film	50 Mercerized 80 to 100 Cotton "A" Silk Synthetic Thread	11	12 to 15 (8 to 10 for plastic)
MEDIUM WEIGHT—gingham, percale, pique, linen, chintz, faille, satin, fine corduroy, suitings	50 Mercerized 60 to 80 Cotton "A" Silk Synthetic Thread	14	12 to 15
MEDIUM HEAVY—gabardine, tweed, sailcloth, denim, coatings, drapery fabrics	Heavy Duty Mercerized 40 to 60 Cotton	16	10 to 12
HEAVY—overcoatings, dungaree, upholstery fabrics, canvas	Heavy Duty Mercerized 20 to 40 Cotton	18	8 to 10

THE SINGER COMPANY

If the upper tension is tighter than the lower, more of the lower thread will be drawn to the upper part of the fabric. The upper thread will not interlock, but will lie flat on the top of the fabric. In this case, the upper tension needs to be loosened or the lower tension tightened. Usually the adjustments are done from the top. The instruction book that comes with your machine will give specific information for adjusting your machine.

Too tight a tension will result in a puckered seam or one where stitches break with stress. If you pull the fabric in the direction of the seam, and one or more threads break, the tensions are too tight for your fabric.

There must be enough pressure on the presser foot to keep the fabric in control, but not so much that it can't travel smoothly through the machine. A screw, usually at the top of the machine above the presser foot, can be adjusted for pressure—most thick fabrics need less pressure and thin fabrics more. If the fabric seems to go slowly or stitches pile up, or if the fabric seems to jump, change the adjustment on the screw and test again.

Cleaning a machine. When a machine is not kept clean, dust may cause the oil to become thick and the machine to run heavily. Loose

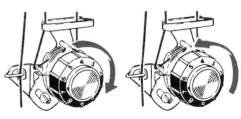

INCREASE   **DECREASE**

THE SINGER COMPANY

Tension Dial . . . Turn right to increase, left to decrease.

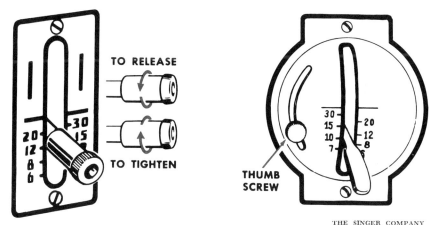

THE SINGER COMPANY

How to change stitch length on different kinds of sewing machines. Turn thumb screw or thumb nut to left to loosen . . . move lever to number for stitch length . . . tighten screw.

threads caught in or around the bobbin may slow down or stop the machine. Use the brush that comes with the machine to remove lint from the bobbin case and tension discs.

Oiling. All machines need to be oiled at least twice a year or more often if used a great deal. If you have a machine of your own, read the manual to determine when oiling is recommended. Mark the date on your calendar to remind you of the job. (Consult your manual to determine oiling procedure.) Use a good quality oil made only for sewing machines. The motor requires a special lubricant. After oiling, stitch on paper or practice cloth until the excess oil disappears.

Solving simple machine problems. Many times the answer to the complaint, "There is something wrong with this machine" is that it is not threaded properly or that it is not plugged in!

If the machine does not seem to work right, check first to see that it is threaded correctly top and bottom, that the needle is straight and in correct position. If this does not seem to help, check the points listed below.

Read through this chart now to notice common machine problems and then refer to it as they develop for you and your classmates. You will soon learn to prevent many from happening and to recognize what to do about others.

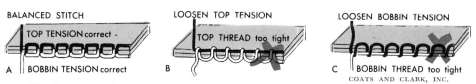

COATS AND CLARK, INC.

Check your stitching to see if the tension is regulated correctly. A balanced stitch with both top and bottom tension correct will appear as in A. If the top thread lies loose along the top and does not interlock with the lower threads, the top tension is too tight (B). If the lower thread lies flat along the lower fabric, the bobbin thread is too tight (C).

MACHINE SEWING

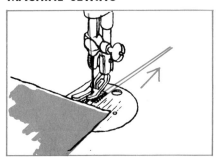

- Both thread ends should be pulled towards back of presser foot before stitching.

- Thread should be wound evenly on an empty bobbin.
- For perfectly balanced stitch use identical type thread for both upper threading and bobbin.

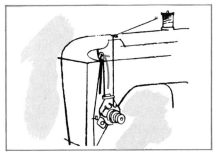

- Before and after stitching be sure take-up lever on machine is at highest point. This prevents thread from slipping out of needle, jamming or breaking.

If thread breaks in sewing machine— Check:

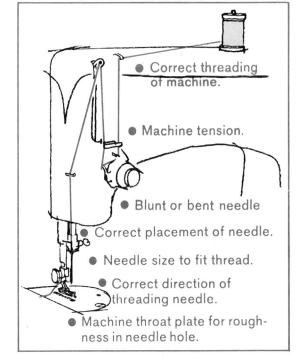

- Correct threading of machine.
- Machine tension.
- Blunt or bent needle
- Correct placement of needle.
- Needle size to fit thread.
- Correct direction of threading needle.
- Machine throat plate for roughness in needle hole.

- Lower the needle into fabric before stitching to eliminate thread jamming.

TALON EDUCATIONAL SERVICE

SOLVING SIMPLE MACHINE PROBLEMS

COMMON PROBLEMS	POSSIBLE CAUSES
Stitches uneven in length or fabric doesn't feed through	• Incorrect pressure on presser foot • Feed dog needs adjustment • Stitch-length regulator set for too small stitches
Machine runs hard	• Lack of oil or gummed oil • Thread wound around wheel or bobbin case • Bobbin winder against wheel or belt during stitching
Upper thread breaks	• Threaded incorrectly (especially needle) • Needle set wrong side out or bent • Rough or sharp places along thread pathway or needle hole in throat plate • Upper tension much too tight • Poor quality or rotten thread • Thread wrapped itself around spool pin
Lower thread breaks	• Bobbin case or shuttle threaded incorrectly • Lower tension much too tight • Rough or sharp edges on throat plate • Bobbin wound unevenly, too tightly or loosely, or too full • Dirt or lint in shuttle cavity so bobbin can't turn freely • Poor quality or rotten thread
Needle breaks	• Needle wrong size or improperly placed • Pulling on fabric while stitching • Sewing over pins • Failure to raise needle before removing fabric • Attempting to remove fabric with threads between toes of presser foot
Skipped stitches	• Needle too long or short • Needle too small for thread • Needle bent • Needle threaded incorrectly • Too little pressure on presser foot • If zipper foot is used, not close enough to needle • Thread take-up (check spring) on upper tension, or loop taker on lower tension not properly adjusted
Looped stitches (top or bottom)	• Tension (top or bottom) adjusted improperly

GENERAL SUGGESTIONS FOR SEWING MACHINE USE

Let the machine do the work . . . don't push or pull the fabric through.

Have needed equipment handy at the machine so you will not have to be getting up and moving about too often.

Do not stitch over pins. The presser foot may be flexible, but stitching over pins may result in a crooked place in the seam, a longer stitch that weakens the seam, or a broken or bent needle.

Always test-stitch on a fabric sample of two thicknesses to check the tension, stitch size, and threading before starting to sew.

Support the weight of a fabric well. Large pieces may need to have a chair placed near the machine to hold the weight.

Learn to use the seam gauge. Only a very skilled person can stitch an even seam without a gauge.

SAFETY. A sewing machine is not to be feared but it *is* a machine . . . If the needle should go through your finger, do not panic or pull your finger away from the machine. Hold it still and raise the needle out of your finger (use your hand on the balance wheel to control this). It is wise to check with your school nurse if this happens.

SEWING MACHINE OPERATOR'S TEST

Purposes: To help you and your teacher determine if you can
- thread your machine correctly
- stitch a straight seam
- recognize an average length stitch
- change the size of stitches
- use a seam gauge
- turn a square corner
- tie thread at ends of a seam
- retrace thread at seam ends
- lock stitch thread at seam ends

Directions: Fold a piece of cotton cloth, 9 x 12 inches or larger, in half. Cut one edge on a curve as pictured. Using a ruler, draw lines as pictured. Thread the machine yourself. Follow directions as they are listed here.
1. Stitch along line 1 with average length stitch, tie thread ends.
2. Stitch line 2 with a smaller size stitch, retrace ends.
3. Stitch line 3 with the largest stitch, lock stitch ends.
4. Stitch line 4, turning square corners, average size stitch. Clip thread ends.
5. Stitch along curved edge, using a seam gauge, ⅝ inch from the edge.
6. Print your name on the cloth and give it to your teacher to be checked.

Did you pass? If not, you need more machine practice before starting to sew on your garment.

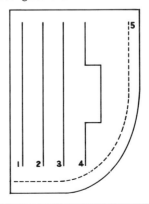

Sewing Machine Attachments

Slow, tedious handwork of the past has been speeded through the use of many interesting attachments available for almost every sewing machine. Some machines have these built in as part of the basic machine. Dainty narrow hems, gathering, buttonholes, binding, and decorative stitches are easily made when you have learned to handle the attachments skillfully. Your first attempts will probably not have the results you prefer but don't give up. Read the directions carefully and practice with suitable material and thread—soon you will be pleased with the help these sewing aids can give you.

A zipper foot is almost essential for

The custom details of this little girl's dress were made on a modern sewing machine. Directions for the applique trim and the cording are given in the instruction book for most machines.

PFAFF INTERNATIONAL

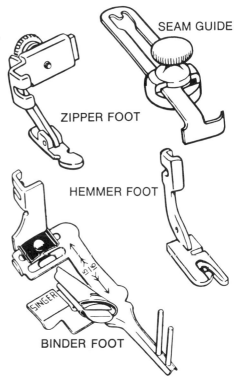

SEAM GUIDE

ZIPPER FOOT

HEMMER FOOT

BINDER FOOT

THE SINGER COMPANY

Common attachments.

making any garment. It can also be used for applying cording and piping trim.

The binder foot is used to apply bias binding as a trim and for some seam edges that ravel.

The hemmer foot stitches a narrow hem without basting or pressing.

A buttonhole attachment will make either slot-type or keyhole buttonholes in many different sizes. Interchangeable templates are available for many sizes.

Other attachments of interest are the blind stitcher, the zigzag or decorative stitcher, and the ruffler.

Detailed instructions are available from most sewing machine companies and other references listed at the end of the book.

UNIQUE ZIPPER CO.

A special presser foot, available for most sewing machines, is needed to insert invisible zippers correctly.

THE SINGER COMPANY

Close-up of a buttonhole attachment. The template shown at the left controls the length and shape of the buttonhole and the dial on the attachment controls the width of the stitches. This picture shows a keyhole buttonhole being made.

Practice the driver's license test on scrap material. When you feel that you can use the machine well enough to pass the test, follow the directions on page 524.

Examine a machine to locate the places where oil should be used. How will these places be cleaned before and after oiling?

Clean and oil a machine at school, following the instructions given in the machine booklet of instructions.

Practice the following operations: (1) Change the length of stitch. (2) Adjust the upper tension. (3) Place a needle correctly in a machine.

Assume the responsibility for the care of the sewing machine at home.

Check your posture at the sewing machine. Practice sitting properly at a sewing machine.

GREIST COMPANY

A blind stitch hemmer attachment.

JOHN DRITZ AND SONS

PRESSING EQUIPMENT AND PRESSING TECHNIQUES

Pressing well is as important as stitching well. A garment that is not pressed until the last step will surely look "homemade" and one that is only carelessly done after each step can never look as professional as desired.

PRESSING EQUIPMENT

Good pressing equipment is as important as a good sewing machine and needles and pins.

Ironing boards. An ironing board should be smoothly padded with a scorch resistant cover that fits snugly. Cotton blankets or sheet wadding make satisfactory pads as does plastic foam specially made for this purpose. Most ironing board covers on the market have been treated so they will not scorch or burn and some are made to reflect heat to the underside of the piece being pressed. An adjustable ironing board is a good choice for people of different heights and for ironing while seated. It can also be used for additional sewing work space.

A small board, easily made and padded at home, is adequate for most pressing of seams and small details before the garment is completely finished. This can be placed on a table near a sewing machine for easy access. A sleeve board, which is essential for pressing sleeves and other hard-to-press places, will also serve for detail pressing.

Irons. A combination steam and dry iron is the most helpful type of iron for general pressing. For the type of water follow directions for the iron you are using. In hard water areas distilled water is often neces-

A folding sleeve board, double sided, is handy for ironing sleeves and other hard-to-reach areas, as well as darts and small sewing details.

sary to avoid clogging the iron. Some irons also have a spray attachment for heavy dampening of details.

Keep the soleplate clean and smooth. Avoid ironing over pins which can scratch the soleplate. Some plastics such as buttons and heat sensitive zippers will melt from a hot iron. Select the correct temperature for each fabric. Blends must be ironed at the temperature of their most heat sensitive fiber.

A press cloth is used between the iron and the zipper. The ironing board cover is a metallized fabric to reflect iron heat evenly. The combination steam and dry iron also has a spray attachment.

JOHN DRITZ AND SONS

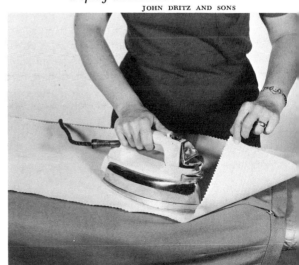

A double pressing cloth, wool on one side and cotton muslin on the other. The wool side is placed next to the garment to prevent shine. The cotton side retains moisture. Notice that this experienced sewer uses a seam roll when pressing a zipper so that the tape edges will not leave an imprint on the right side of the fabric.

When leaving the iron even for a few minutes, it is a good idea to unplug it (pull on the plug itself, don't jerk the cord). The thermostat is usually effective in controlling the temperature so it will not overheat but the iron may fall on the floor or touch some other material that is affected by its heat.

Pressing cloth. A good pressing cloth is made from a light-colored piece of wool flannel and a piece of medium weight muslin the same size. Stitch the two pieces together at one end. To use, soak the cotton piece in water; then wring out. Place the cotton over the wool press cloth and steam press from the cotton side. This will produce steam without the possibility of too much heat which may harm the fabric or cause undesired shine.

A transparent cloth such as cheesecloth or a specially made non-woven one is handy for pressing details you wish to see.

Seam board or roll. When some fabrics are pressed, the seam edge will show through the right side of the garment. A seam board or roll helps prevent this. Long skirt seams are also given the proper curvature when pressed over a seam roll. You can make a roll by cutting a rolling pin in half lengthwise to make it lie flat. It need not be covered. Or you can roll a magazine tightly and tie with strong thread. The roll should be about two inches in diameter. Several thicknesses of muslin may be wrapped around it.

A seam board or roll may also be purchased.

Needle board or velvet board. A needle board or velvet board is used to press pile fabrics such as corduroy, velvet, velveteen, and some fleeces.

A transparent press cloth lets you see details you may be pressing. This type of cloth is not suitable for fabrics sensitive to heat and which shine easily.

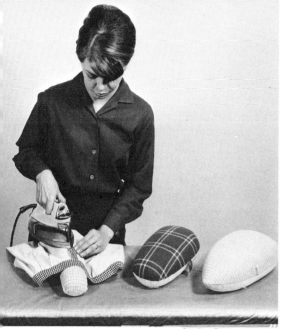

This girl is giving a demonstration to her class on the use of professional pressing equipment also used by home sewers who want a professional look for their garments. She is using a seam roll to prevent an imprint of seam edges on the right side of the garment. The tailor's hams (don't they have the shape of one?) will be used for pressing curved areas.

This board has fine metal teeth. The pile of the fabric is placed against the board while ironing and does not mat down. This is an expensive item for most homes where it is seldom used. A piece of firm pile fabric placed face up on an ironing board serves almost as well.

Tailor's cushion. The tailor's cushion, often called a ham because it is shaped like one, is used for pressing curved surfaces such as blouse fronts, sleeve tops, and hip areas where the curved shape is desired, especially in wool fabrics.

Wooden clapper. A wooden clapper is used to obtain a sharp well-creased edge such as on the hem of a skirt or a pleat edge, especially in wool fabrics. Beating with a wooden clapper while the fabric contains steam will flatten creased edges and remove press marks. This is used primarily in tailoring.

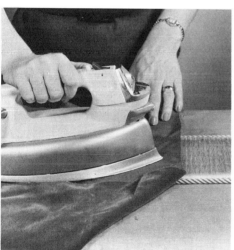

A needle-board for pile or high nap fabrics. This board is a bed of needles angled carefully for the pile of the fabric to fall between them, so the pile will not be flattened when pressed. It is useful for velvets and napped fabrics as fleece and camel's hair.

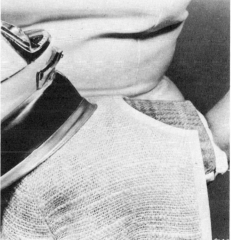

Can you see that this girl has a pressing mit on her hand? Convenient for hard-to-reach and rounded areas such as the shoulder of a garment or children's clothes. The wrist length pockets protect the girl's hands from the steam.

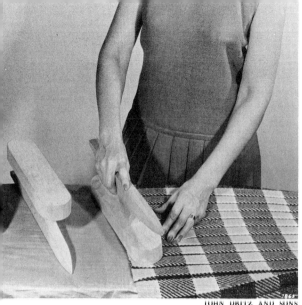

JOHN DRITZ AND SONS

*The pleats of this wool skirt are being flat-
tened after steaming by the use of a pounding block, also called a tailor's clapper. The
other side of this two-in-one pressing aid is a
point presser, used for pressing open seams
of points on collars and lapels. A clapper
can be easily made at home from a block of
wood by rounding the edges and sanding
until smooth.*

PRESSING TECHNIQUES

Pressing is not ironing. To press, lift
the iron and set it down in a different
place. Always follow the grain of the
fabric. Press every seam and dart before crossing with another row of
stitching. The failure to press a garment at each step in its construction
is the prime reason why it may appear ill-fitted and poorly made. Be
sure the soleplate of the iron is clean
and smooth. Select the proper temperature for the fabric being pressed.
If a steam iron is used, be sure the
steam is flowing. Although thermo-
stats are usually reliable, it is wise to
test the iron on a scrap of the material first. The amount of heat, moisture, and pressure required depends
upon the kind of fabric being
pressed.

Always press in the same direction
that a seam or detail was stitched.

Directional pressing is as important
as directional stitching (see page
544).

Fabrics should be pressed on the
wrong side whenever possible. The
final pressing on the right side may
require the use of a press cloth to
prevent fabric shine.

Don't overpress—too hot an iron,
too many times, or pressing until a
fabric is bone dry—will result in a
"tired" or shopworn look!

Cotton, linen, and rayon fabrics
may be pressed with a hot iron. They
are usually dampened before pressing although a steam iron may add
enough moisture. Linen needs to be
quite damp. Resin or wash-and-wear
finished fabrics require a warm, not
hot, iron.

Silk fabrics can scorch and be
weakened with too much heat, so use
a warm iron. These fabrics often
waterspot so check carefully before
pressing with a steam iron. Use a
damp cloth placed over a dry cloth
and press on the wrong side whenever possible.

Synthetics such as acetate, nylon,
acrylics, and polyesters may become
glazed if pressed with too much heat.
Use a low temperature and steam to
help prevent a shiny appearance.
Blends should be pressed as you
would for the most sensitive fiber in
them. If in doubt, test a sample of the
fabric.

Wool fabrics need moisture to prevent dry iron scorch but too much
moisture may cause shrinkage. A
steam iron may be adequate but
smooth finished fabrics such as gabardine and serge require a press
cloth between the iron and the wool.
Place a damp cloth on the wrong side
of the fabric with a dry cloth on top

and press with a moderately hot iron until the cloth is almost dry. On dark materials use a dark colored pressing cloth to prevent lint. If a shine occurs on wool, it may be made less noticeable by pressing first on the right side with a cloth dampened in vinegar (one tablespoon of vinegar to one cup of water) and finished on the wrong side using a damp cloth. Press until the fabric is almost dry; then brush the right side.

When it is necessary to press wool on the right side, as for a patch pocket, use a heavy dry cloth directly over the material.

Avoid flattening *pile fabrics* as velvet, corduroy, velveteen, and some woolen fleeces when pressing. Place them face side down on a needle board, a turkish towel or an extra piece of a pile fabric. Steam press from the wrong side, using a very light touch of the iron. You may also steam seams open by placing a steam iron on end and running the material and pressing cloth across it. Wring a wet pressing cloth as dry as possible, pick up the velvet by one seam allowance. Hold a damp cloth right over the seam and pass lightly across the iron. Turn the garment, hold by the other seam allowance and repeat the procedure.

Fluff the nap by steaming with the iron held one-half inch above the fabric. While the fabric is still damp, brush the nap or pile with a soft-bristled brush.

Many garments of pile fabrics can be freshened by hanging over a tub of steaming water or placing in a bathroom with the door shut and a warm shower running. In all cases, allow the fabric to dry slowly before moving it or wrinkles will set in.

Steaming a seam on napped material.

CONSTRUCTION DETAILS

Seams are usually pressed open. To get a sharp seam, press seam edges together first and then open. If the edge of the seam allowance leaves a mark on the right side of the garment, use a seam roll. Placing pieces of plain paper between the seam allowance and fabric may also prevent this "show through."

Darts are pressed to one side unless very large or of heavy fabric. Bust and elbow darts that are horizontal are pressed down. Waistline and shoulder vertical darts are pressed toward the center front or center back. Deep or bulky darts are slashed up to one inch of the point. They are pressed open over a ham.

Plackets are pressed on the right side with a press cloth. The cloth prevents metal teeth from scratching the iron, or nylon teeth from being melted from the heat. Always press a zipper closed to keep its shape.

Pleats are basted in place before pressing. Press with the grain.

Hems are pressed along the fold line in an upward direction with the warp threads. If a hem is pressed around, it may be stretched out of shape. When there are pleats and seams where the portion of the seam above the hem is not pressed open, clip the seam at the top of the hem so the part inside the hem may be pressed open to prevent bulkiness.

531

Iron basting can be used for creasing a narrow hem. Turn the raw edge, creasing it with an iron as it is turned; then make the second turning and press. The iron should hold it in position for hemming, either by machine or hand.

Iron marking is a quick way to mark many pattern details. See the Shortcut Section in Chapter 17.

TO KEEP AN IRON LIKE NEW

- When changing from a higher setting to a lower one, ALWAYS wait for the iron to cool before ironing synthetic fabrics.

- Follow fabric temperature guide to eliminate accidents.

- If fabric or starch sticks to the soleplate, it may be removed with a fine grade (00) steel wool. Avoid getting soap into the steam vents.

- Steam vents may be cleaned with cotton tipped swabs (such as Q-Tips).

- To remove melted synthetic fabric from the soleplate, heat the iron on the lowest setting until the residue softens somewhat. Scrape off as much as possible with a thin piece of wood. (A wooden tongue depressor is fine). Then use fine steel wool (grade 00) to completely remove the rest.

- Always empty a steam iron after each use while it is still hot. Store it on its heel until it is cool. Never store the iron face down when moisture is in the tank as this can cause damage to the soleplate.

WESTINGHOUSE

Study the direction book for the steam iron used in your classroom. Give a demonstration on the use and care of it.

Prepare a chart on the proper care of the iron used in your classroom. Place it near the ironing board where it will be of help to all using it.

Make a seam roll from a magazine or rolling pin.

Prepare a demonstration of pressing wool correctly. References listed at the end of the chapter will be of help.

Experiment with the effect of dry and moist heat on samples of various wool fabrics. Place a hot iron directly on half of the wool sample and press the other half with a damp pressing cloth. Observe the difference. (It is wise NOT to experiment with synthetic fibers— some of the fibers may melt and stick to the iron, and they are very difficult to remove.)

Can you obtain an iron that has a stained soleplate? If so, try cleaning it with directions on this page and report your results.

Obtain an adjustable ironing board. Experiment with different heights until you find the one that is most comfortable for you. Measure the distance from the floor to the board. Have other classmates of different heights find the best height for them. Record their preferences. Is the preferred height more closely related to one's overall height or to the distance from one's elbow to the floor? Explain the reasons for your answer.

ST. CHARLES MANUFACTURING CO.

A well arranged clothing laboratory. Discuss how you could arrange your sewing area at home.

BE A GOOD MANAGER OF YOUR TIME

When a sewer manages her time well, she can sew more easily and also achieve better results.

Select equipment that does a good job and is comfortable for you to use. Select as good quality equipment as your budget permits. Store it in a suitable place so you can avoid hunting for needed articles and accidents may be prevented.

Just as a well arranged kitchen helps a cook, a convenient sewing center can speed up work and make it easier. Consider a U-shaped arrangement with a sewing machine at the center of the U. On one side have a card table or similar work surface for laying out, cutting and hand sewing and on the other an ironing board or place for pressing. Be sure your lighting is adequate and glare-free. You will need good overall room lighting and also a lamp that directs bright light on your work. The sewing machine bulb helps for work at the machine but it is not enough.

533

Most girls find the extra lamp most helpful if it is placed in back and slightly to the left of the needle. Remember that dark fabrics and night sewing require more light than usual.

Maintain a good posture when sewing and ironing. Learn to sit at your machine to do most of the work.

At school, plan ahead to avoid waiting for help. When it is your turn, ask ahead for help for several steps. In clothing labs there are seldom enough sewing machines or ironing equipment for every student. Therefore you may need to wait occasionally. Plan ahead for jobs you can do while waiting.

Learn to make one trip with all equipment. Avoid unnecessary talking at school. At home you may find that music helps you sew faster.

Keep your work space clean and free for work. Place books and purses where they belong and not on your sewing table.

Avoid unnecessary difficulties at the machine by learning to use it well. Avoid ripping and doing over by practicing new processes first on scrap material.

Select patterns and materials that are suitable for your ability and the time you have available. Learn to eliminate some processes when you can. Know when to pin baste and when it is necessary to hand baste.

Plan ahead first—don't plunge in. Read the pattern envelope and guide sheet carefully to be certain you have everything on hand when needed. Make a plan for proceeding. Perhaps the one on page 535 will be of help.

SAFETY PRECAUTIONS IN THE SEWING WORKROOM

For safety, sewing equipment needs to be kept in good condition and in place. Accidents are caused in a school or home sewing room when operators do not handle equipment correctly. Sewing machine needles cause accidents when one does not give undivided attention to her task. The handles of a pair of scissors should always be turned toward the person to whom you are handing them. Razor blades are seldom safe for ripping. Keep needles and pins in a cushion.

Electrical appliances with faulty wiring or badly worn cords are responsible for many fires and painful burns. The first rule for safety in sewing is to keep electrical appliances in perfect repair. If you receive a shock, if an electric iron or electric sewing machine shorts or becomes overheated, your safety is endangered. Use common sense about electrical cords—don't cause them to become frayed or unplug them by pulling the cord—use the plug itself. Watch that cords are not in the way so that girls can easily trip over them.

To reach high shelves, use a firm, solid stepladder. Avoid such "booby traps" as chairs or other furniture or boxes piled on chairs or table tops.

In case of an accident, even a minor one, be sure to report it to your teacher.

Name _____ Class _____

PLAN FOR CONSTRUCTING A GARMENT

Date supplies needed _____ Time alloted for making _____

Check those you will need:

1. Pattern	5. Shears	9. Trimming
2. Material	6. Tape rule	10. Box for supplies
3. Thread	7. Thimble	11. Others _____
4. Pins	8. Needles	_____

WEEKLY PLAN FOR CONSTRUCTING A GARMENT

Week	What I Plan To Do This Week	What I Actually Did This Week
1		
2		
3		

Note: The Plan will include the number of weeks allotted for garment.

DAILY ACCOMPLISHMENT RECORD

What I Plan To Accomplish Today	What I Actually Did	What I Must Do Before Tomorrow in Order To Follow My Schedule
Monday		
Tuesday		
Wednesday		
Thursday		
Friday		

List the sewing equipment available in your school laboratory. Develop a chart dividing responsibility for daily care of sewing equipment at school. Include the machines, irons, and small equipment. Don't forget the need to clean scraps and pins from the floor.

With your teacher and other students, make plans for using and storing personal and departmental equipment so that everything will be easily obtained and kept in good order.

Notice the posture of your classmates as they sew at their desks. Describe comfortable posture for hand sewing.

Summary With Check-up Questions

The wise selection and proper use of sewing tools is important for the quality of one's work, ease of construction, and appearance of the finished garment.
- *What effect will dull shears have on cutting out a garment and later putting the seams together?*
- *Why is it better to use fine, sharp pins rather than dull, thick ones on delicate fabrics?*
- *Does it make any difference if you use a needle too short or too long for your hands?*
- *What effect will a thimble that is too loose or too tight have on your sewing? (and your disposition?)*

Equipment properly stored will be easy to find when needed and will be in better condition and cause fewer accidents than if carelessly stored.
- *What could happen if you rummage in a box full of many items while searching for a pair of shears?*
- *Why is it best to hand shears in such a manner that the blades are closed and not open?*
- *Will pins and needles stored in a pincushion or box be as blunt and bent as those "left around"?*
- *What may happen to a steam iron if the water is not drained after use?*

The correct choice of sewing notions and supplies is as important as the selection of fabric or equipment.
- *How will the wrong shade of thread affect the appearance of a dress?*
- *Why is it important to match the weight of a zipper to the weight of a fabric?*
- *How will the appearance of a garment be affected if trimmings shrink after laundering?*

The basic principles of all sewing machines are similar although they differ in some details.
- *What percentage of all sewing is straight sewing that can be done on almost any machine?*
- *Can attachments duplicate most of the fancy stitching effects of machines with built-in zigzag equipment?*
- *If you can control the speed of your machine, holding the fabric, and stop and start stitching, will you find it easy to handle another machine?*

Machine stitching is most attractive and strongest when the machine is adjusted to provide an even tension and the correct sized stitch for the fabric being used.
- *Will a smaller or longer stitch provide more stretch?*

- *How will a seam appear if the tensions are too tight?*
- *How will a seam appear if one tension is too loose?*

Pressing as you go avoids the homemade look.

- *It is not necessary to press every seam as soon as completed. Why is it necessary to press seams before they are crossed with another line of stitching?*
- *What is the best way to press wool?*
- *Why does a tailor's ham give a more professional appearance to curved areas of garments than the straight board?*

Time is saved if equipment is used as intended and kept clean and in good condition.

- *Will it take longer to cut out a garment with dull shears that bind than with a pair that are sharp and cut easily?*
- *How will your sewing progress be affected by a machine that needs adjustment or will not work at all?*
- *Failure to clean an iron as soon as it becomes soiled may make it more difficult to clean later. What could happen to your fabrics if you use a soiled iron?*

Can You Explain These Terms?

shears	*lock stitches*	*tension*
scissors	*zipper foot*	*take-up lever*
needles—sharps	*binder foot*	*presser foot*
needles—betweens	*hemmer foot*	*feed dog*
needles—crewel	*buttonhole attachment*	*throat plate*
silk pins	*seam board or roll*	*bobbin*
thimble	*needle or velvet board*	*stitch regulator*
mercerized thread	*tailor's cushion*	*balance wheel*
heavy duty thread	*clapper*	*stop motion screw*
buttonhole twist	*spool pin*	*thread cutter*
slide fasteners	*thread guide*	*presser bar lifter*
retracing		*presser bar control*

CHAPTER SIXTEEN

Basic Construction Techniques

T HE MAKING OF ANY GARMENT is divided into two major parts— (1) the preparation that is needed before sewing can be started, and (2) the actual putting together or construction of the garment. Both parts are important; if the selection and preparation of a pattern and fabric have been carelessly done, the best workmanship will still result in a garment of poor appearance. You may want to review the preceding two chapters and check to see that your pattern and fabric are ready for use and that all the supplies you need are at hand. Also be sure that you have some skill in using a sewing machine and other sewing equipment.

USE OF A PATTERN GUIDE SHEET

No attempt is made in this book to provide directions for putting together a specific type garment as a skirt, jumper, blouse, or dress. Styles vary greatly and change frequently as fashion changes. Construction methods also change as new fabrics and sewing supplies become available.

Whenever you purchase a pattern, you will find a pattern direction or guide sheet enclosed with it that is planned specifically for that pattern. The guide sheet is prepared by an expert in sewing who understands the pattern well. She works with artists who make drawings of many of the techniques for further clarification. The directions are planned for the type of fabric selected by most people for the particular pattern. The methods suggested are those that can most easily be used by the majority of sewers with satisfactory results. If you follow the procedure suggested, you will have an acceptable garment.

However, the fabric you select may handle differently from the one for which the directions are written. You may prefer other methods because they are easier for you or you like the finished appearance better. Because fitting problems vary so much, most directions omit any mention of them. In addition, the guide sheet directions must be brief because of space limitations. Therefore, you will need to know more about

538

SEWING DIRECTIONS

1. READ INSTRUCTIONS printed on each pattern piece as you work.

2. WORK IN UNITS according to the sewing directions.

3. STAY-STITCHING is a line of regular machine-stitching (in one thickness of fabric) on, or close to the seam line within the seam allowance. It prevents stretching. Stitch with grain.

Stay-stitching will be shown **only the first time** a section or unit of garment is illustrated in the instructions.

4. SEAM ALLOWANCE is $5/8''$ unless otherwise stated.

5. TO JOIN SEAMS, match notches with same numbers, 1 to 1, 2 to 2, etc.

6. STITCHING DIRECTIONS are shown by arrows on printed seam lines. Press each seam before it is joined to another. Press in same direction as it was stitched. *Note:* We suggest machine-basting, using longest machine stitch.

SIMPLICITY PATTERN CO.

Example of general sewing directions found on pattern guide sheets.

---

construction techniques than can be provided by the most complete guide sheet. In this chapter, techniques common to the making of most garments are described in detail so you will understand how to use them, and also be better able to judge which method to use. For example, your guide sheet may suggest a plain seam but after reading about seams, you may decide that a flat fell seam is better for your material.

To summarize, when you are inexperienced in sewing, follow the procedure given on a pattern guide sheet and refer to more complete directions as needed. As you gain experience, you will find other methods you prefer. However, a wise person always reads through the pattern directions to determine if there are procedures or details which are new to her.

Plan Ahead

After reading the general directions for making your garment, it is wise to make a plan of procedure. The first few times you will need to write it down but later you will be able to plan in your head.

Consider the steps to be done. Actually list them on a plan sheet to help you organize your time and equipment. If you have to wait for help or the use of some equipment, you can look ahead and start another step. (It helps to know if you are keeping up with your work on a school project that usually has to be completed in a definite period of time. When you are sewing at home, you will probably not need a time plan.)

If all of the students in your class are making similar garments, you may work together to develop a procedure and time plan. Be sure to include fitting and pressing, both of which are often omitted from pattern guide sheets. You may need your teacher's help at first. If time is not too important, you can simply check each step as it is completed.

Hand sewing, machine sewing, pressing, and fitting—with so many activities underway at once in a busy classroom, it is important that each class member share equipment according to a plan made for the class. Helping one's partner with fitting problems is a learning experience as well as doing your share as a group member.

PLAN SHEET FOR 4-GORE SKIRT			
Steps	**Date to be finished**	**Date completed**	**If completed later than planned, give reasons**
Stay stitch as needed	Oct. 1	Oct. 1	
Baste seams and darts	Oct. 3	Oct. 4	
First fitting	Oct. 4	Oct. 6	Partner absent, others busy
Stitch seams and darts	Oct. 5		
Press	Oct. 5		
Insert zipper	Oct. 8		
Apply waistband (baste)	Oct. 9		
Second fitting	Oct. 10		
Sew waistband	Oct. 10		
Press	Oct. 10		
Attach hooks and eyes	Oct. 10		
Put up hem	Oct. 12		
Final pressing	Oct. 13		
Complete garment evaluation.	Oct. 19		

This is a plan sheet for a simple skirt developed by a high school girl who has done some sewing. Do you think her plan is workable?

UNIT METHOD OF CLOTHING CONSTRUCTION

One of the first directions given in the pattern guide sheet is to work in units. (See directions for the jumper on pages 542 and 543.) The unit method of clothing construction is a good procedure for beginners. This method means completing as much work as possible on one unit or section of a garment before going on to the next. For example, if you are making a dress, you will complete the waist front first, then the back waist, then attach the two together before starting the skirt. A unit is a part of a garment but it may involve more than one pattern piece. A waist front may have pockets attached and perhaps interfacing.

The unit method has many advantages over other methods of clothing construction. Because you work on one section at a time, you can see clearly what you are doing. Much of the detailed work can be completed while the pattern pieces are flat and more easily handled. Because the pieces of the garment which go together are assembled in units that are easily identified, each piece receives a minimum of handling. Excessive wrinkles, stretching, and a shopworn appearance are avoided.

This is an efficient method when you have short periods of time for work, as class periods. One unit can often be completed during a period and laid aside until you are ready to attach it to another unit.

If you anticipate fitting problems, you may find it necessary to leave some units basted so that you can try on the whole garment before the final sewing, but this is seldom necessary for patterns selected by beginners.

When you make your sewing plan, organize your work into units. If you have to wait for help or the use of equipment, you can start on another unit but you will want to complete each unit in order whenever possible.

Notice the jumper plan on page 542. The front is completed first and then the back. The front is attached to the back and the neck facings and neck edge are finished before the armhole is faced. After stitching the side seams, the hem is completed. It is a logical plan so that a beginner can see exactly what she is doing and understand what to do next.

EXPLANATION OF COMMON SEWING DIRECTIONS

Many terms are used in pattern guide sheets and are not explained because they are common to most sewing processes and sewers soon learn their meaning.

DIRECTIONAL STITCHING

By now you are aware of the need to keep the fabric grain perfect. Always stitch in the direction of the grain to prevent stretching the fabric.

Stitching directions are shown on some patterns by arrows along the printed seam lines. If in doubt, rub your finger along the seam edges. The direction that smoothes the threads so they stay in place is with the grain; the direction that roughs up the threads is against the grain.

Another simple rule that is usually true is to stitch from wide to narrow. This means from the bottom of the skirt to the top. When stitching around a neckline, stop stitching in the center and start again at the other end, moving into the center from the opposite direction.

SUGGESTIONS FOR MAKING A JUMPER

1. Select pattern in correct size.
2. Select fabric, interfacing, thread, zipper, and seam tape.
3. Fit and alter pattern if necessary; prepare fabric for cutting.
4. Pin pattern on fabric and cut; transfer pattern markings in best way for type of fabric.
5. Preshrink zipper if necessary.
6. Check sewing machine stitch and tension adjustment on sample of fabric.

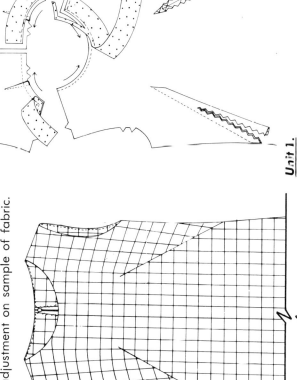

Unit 1.

1. Stay-stitch front neck edge.
2. Baste interfacing to front neck edge. Trim interfacing ⅝" at shoulder seam. Trim interfacing ⅜" from neck edge.
3. Stitch front darts. (Baste and fit if unsure of fit.) Trim excess material and press open.

Unit 2.

1. Stay-stitch back neck edge.
2. Attach interfacing as for front.
3. Stitch back darts, press towards center back.
4. Stitch center back seam to notch. Machine baste seam up to neckline.
5. Apply neckline type zipper, using lapped method.

Unit 3. Neck facings

1. Stitch neck facing seams together. Turn outside edge under ¼", stitch.

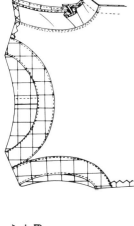

2. Baste neck facing to jumper. Stitch, trim seams, clip curve.

3. Understitch neck seam by turning all seam allowances toward facing and top stitching close to seam through seam allowances.

4. Turn facing to inside, baste neck edge, press. Tack facing to shoulder seams. Turn in and hem back edge of facing along zipper.

4. Stitch side seams of jumper and press seams open. Slip-stitch the facing to jumper.

Unit 4. Armhole facings and underarm seams.

1. Stitch armhole shoulder facing seams together. Press open. Turn outside edge under ¼", stitch.

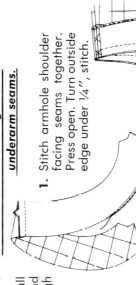

2. Baste facing to armhole, stitch. Trim seam, clip curve.

3. Understitch armhole facing. Baste armhole edge, press.

Unit 5. Hem

5. Mark correct hem length, trim to even width. Stitch seam tape to hem and slip-stitch to inside of jumper.

543

If you continue to go all around the neckline in one direction, you will tend to pull the threads on the last half out of shape. This may not matter once the neckline is staystitched (p. 545) or a facing is attached as previous stitching should hold the grain in place. But if in doubt, stitch in the direction of the grain. The little extra time it takes will be saved in easier matching of parts and will certainly result in a more professional looking garment.

DIRECTIONAL PRESSING AND PRESS AS YOU SEW

Pattern guide sheets seldom mention pressing as it is assumed that the importance of pressing after each step is understood. Pressing after each seam is made may not be efficient unless the ironing equipment is handy to the sewing machine, but it is most important that no seam or detail be crossed by another seam until it is correctly pressed. Detailed directions for pressing various fabrics are found in Chapter Fifteen. Waiting to press a garment until it is completed can only result in a homemade appearance.

Always press in the direction of the fabric grain. Pressing off grain may result in stretched and puckered areas and can make it very difficult to match seams evenly. Refer to page 487 for a more complete discussion of fabric grain. Arrows on a pattern indicating direction in which seams should be sewn are also guides for the direction of pressing.

FITTING

The success of any garment is judged by its appearance on the wearer. Nothing is more important than fit.

The pattern guide sheet may not mention when it is necessary to fit a garment. But even if you have selected the correct size pattern and made needed alterations, you may have some changes to make in the garment itself. Fabric does not fit like paper and while your measurements may be the same as those the pattern is planned for, your weight may be distributed in different places. (A heavy back and a small bust will measure the same as a slender back and a large bust but require different fitting techniques.)

Fitting is an individual matter as some girls are content to wear garments that bulge while other girls are insistent that there be no unnecessary wrinkles, bulges or binding areas. When you are learning to sew, you will probably be content with garments that fit as well as those you buy, but as you gain experience, you will want to improve your fitting ability so that your clothes will have a custom-made appearance. (See Chapter Seventeen for specific fitting suggestions.)

• KEEP YOUR WORK NEAT

If you wait until your garment is finished to trim excess threads, pull bastings, and trim seams, you will probably have a frustrating experience while sewing, as you will not be able to see clearly what you are doing and threads will get all tangled up. Clip your threads, trim seams when you are certain they are accurate, and keep the fabric clean as you go along so you will not have to launder it before wearing your garment.

RIPPING

No one likes to rip a seam she has just made and too much ripping can cause a fabric to appear frayed and worn. However, if you have made a mistake that can be easily corrected, don't be afraid to rip. Just as pencils have erasers, a seam ripper belongs in every sewing box. You will have to learn when to rip (your teacher can help you judge this) and when to leave a slight error, remembering to improve on the next project.

Too much ripping means that something needs to be improved. Are you careless and stitch before knowing what you should do, have you selected too complicated a pattern or fabric for your ability, or do you need to practice on sample fabric first?

STAY-STITCHING

Because of the nature of a fabric, any edge that is cut on a bias or slightly bias direction may stretch as soon as the pattern is removed. The purpose of stay-stitching is to keep the bias edges of a garment from stretching and to ensure that the fabric will retain the exact shape and measurement of the pattern. For example, a curved edge such as a neckline can be stretched just by handling during the sewing of side seams and darts. Then when it is time to put on the collar, the neckline will be too big.

To stay-stitch, use a regulation machine stitch with matching thread through a single thickness of the fabric. Place the stitching ½ inch from the seam allowance so it will not show when the garment is completed. On a neckline or deep curve you will have to stitch right on the seam line for best control.

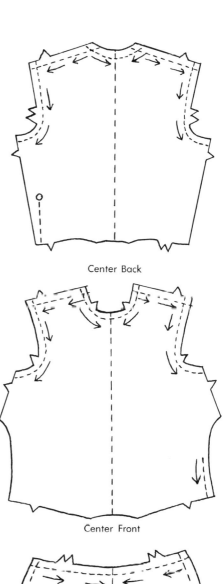

Center Back

Center Front

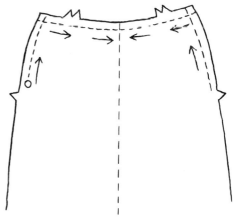

PELLON CORPORATION

Stay-stitching. The arrows show the direction of stitching in order to maintain the fabric grain.

Center Back

Stay-stitch at places where needed as soon as you have unpinned a pattern to prevent stretching from handling. Stitch in the direction of the fabric grain. Never stay-stitch a true bias seam as found on some flared skirts. The remainder of the bias fabric around the seam will stretch and the garment will not hang gracefully if the seam does not stretch also.

Experienced sewers often omit most stay-stitching because they have learned how to handle fabric without straining it, but they will still need to use it at deep necklines and other large curved areas.

There is no need to stay-stitch edges cut on the lengthwise or crosswise grains as these edges seldom stretch. The bottom edge of a skirt is not stay-stitched either as the hemming holds it in place.

BASTING

Directions on pattern guide sheets seldom include basting as it is assumed the garment will fit. However, many parts may need to be put together temporarily to be checked for proper fit before being stitched permanently. Having to rip a dart or seam sewn with a regulation-sized stitch is unpleasant and hard on the fabric—releasing a row of basting is quick and the fabric is not harmed.

Reasons for basting. Besides holding sections of a garment together for a fitting, basting is needed to hold two pieces of fabric together to keep them from slipping during machine stitching. The top layer of the fabric often tends to push forward due to the action of the presser foot. This is especially true if the fabrics are of different weights as when corduroy is stitched to percale. Only a very

skilled person can attach a pocket or cuff or other detail that is not basted to the garment without it slipping out of the proper position.

Some lines need to be marked on the right side of the garment so they can be referred to easily during sewing. Examples are the center back and front lines, and the location of buttonholes and pockets.

Basting is also needed to aid in pressing. Pleats and the finished edges of some collars and facings are basted to be kept in proper place until the final thorough pressing.

Baste only when necessary. Firm fabrics and straight seams that do not require fitting can be machine stitched directly, with perhaps the aid of a few pins. Slippery fabrics and complicated details need to be basted by even the most experienced sewers to ensure professional results.

Basting takes time although it may save time if it prevents needless ripping. Too much handling of the fabric while sewing results in a finished garment that does not have a new, fresh appearance. Learn to control your fabric and the sewing machine so that basting is used only when necessary.

Methods of basting. Before basting, you will need to pin the seams, darts, or other details in position. Large pieces should be placed flat on a table. Place pins first at each end and at any marking point such as notches. (Pins are placed at right angles to the seam line.) Then continue to pin only as close as necessary; every 4 or 5 inches is adequate for firm fabrics but slippery ones may need pins placed as close as 2 inches.

PIN-BASTING is a quick method that is suitable for details that do not have to be fitted too accurately and that can be quickly completed. (Pins may fall out if a garment is frequently put aside as at the end of each class period.) Pins are placed parallel to and directly on the stitching line.

MACHINE-BASTING is another quick method suited for firm fabrics and those that do not hold needle marks. It is sturdy and accurate, especially if a seam gauge is used. Use the longest machine stitch or a chain stitch if

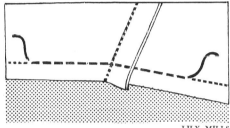

LILY MILLS

To machine-baste, use the longest regular stitch or a chain stitch.

your machine can be set this way. Don't tie the thread ends. Stitch directly on the seam line with matching thread if you are quite sure the stitching will not have to be removed. Otherwise use a contrasting color and place it ⅛″ from the final stitching lines for easy removal later.

Baste ⅛″ from the seamline in the seam allowance so the basting stitches can be easily removed.

HAND-BASTING. Custom dressmakers use hand-basting frequently but most of the garments made by home

sewers can be pin or machine basted satisfactorily. Use a single thread of a contrasting color. This is a good way to use leftover thread. If your fabric will show thread marks, silk or nylon thread is preferred.

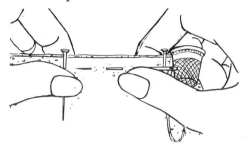

Position for the hands in basting. Notice the use of the thimble.

There are three kinds of basting stitches—even, uneven, and diagonal. *Even* basting is a long running stitch that is the same length on both sides of the fabric. A few backstitches oc-

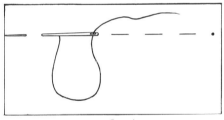

Even basting.

casionally will hold it firmly. It is used to hold a collar to the neckline and in other places where there is strain. *Uneven basting* is a long stitch with a short space between stitches.

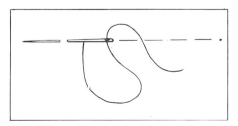

Uneven basting.

547

It is used as a guide line for center of a garment section or where there will be little strain in fitting. Place the long stitch on top and the short stitch underneath. *Diagonal basting* is made by taking a diagonal stitch on the right side and a short vertical stitch on the underside. It is used to baste linings to outside fabrics.

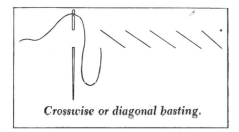

Crosswise or diagonal basting.

TOP-BASTING or SLIP-BASTING is essential for matching plaids, stripes, and other designs, and for many alterations. It takes a little time but results in a professional appearance in which you can take pride. Work from the right side of the fabric. Crease or press one edge along the seam line. Lap it over the remaining edge to meet the seam line. Pin along the seam line, matching the fabric design very carefully. Slip-baste pieces together. Slip the needle through the upper, folded layer of the fabric, then pick up a few stitches in the lower layer, and slip the needle again through the upper, folded layer. Lit-

tle children call this the tunnel stitch —the train goes through the tunnel, comes out and picks up a few passengers, and then goes back through the tunnel! When you open the seam, you will find a line of stitches on the wrong side that will serve as a guide for machine stitching.

EASE

Don't confuse the term "ease" with gathering. To ease means to push in a slight fullness so no puckers or gathers are noticeable on the seam line. You may wonder how you can put two seams together if one is a little longer than the other, but fabric has "give" and the extra fullness can be pushed into place and evenly distributed. Don't make the mistake of cutting off the extra length along one side if the pattern has planned ease allowance.

Ease-stitching. Ease-stitching helps distribute fullness evenly. This is often used for the sleeve cap and a circular hem. Use 10 stitches per inch; do not fasten the thread at the ends. If fullness is slight, pin as shown on this page pulling up threads gently at intervals to work ease in smoothly. (If there is more fullness than desired, pull up thread from both ends. Press carefully and the tiny gathers will disappear.)

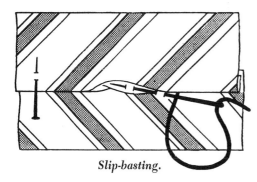

Slip-basting.

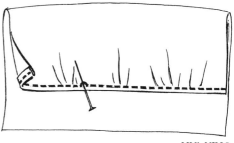

LILY MILLS

Ease-stitch.

Whenever one edge of a seam is slightly longer than the other, it must be "eased in" to fit without puckers or gathers. The shoulder seam is an example. Make a line of ease stitching (about 10 stitches per inch) on the seam line of the longer edge. When pinning the seam, pull up the ease thread slightly and distribute the extra fullness along the seam. As you gain experience, you will be able to do without the ease stitching by holding the fullest side toward you and pinning at intervals.

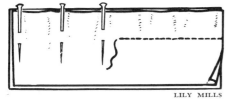

LILY MILLS

How to stitch an eased seam.

UNDERSTITCHING

Whenever there is a seam line to be turned to the inside such as with cuffs and facings, understitching will help make a sharp edge and help keep it sharp. It is really a row of top-stitching done on the right side of the facing close to the seam line. Place the facing and both seam allowances away from the outer fabric. Stitch through both seam allowances and the facing but NOT the outer fabric. This may seem confusing and unnecessary but it is one of the most important and helpful steps in clothing construction. Practice until you understand it.

SLASH

Slash may mean to make a clean cut with shears up to a certain mark or it may mean to cut open. A curved dart is slashed open so it lies flat.

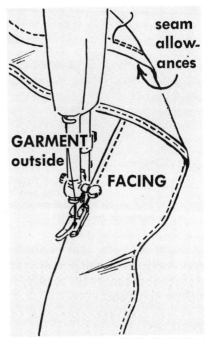

COATS AND CLARK, INC.

Understitching keeps a facing from rolling forward and insures a crisp, sharp edge. It consists of stitching facing to seam allowances as follows: Open out facing and place work on machine, right side up and all seam allowances under facing. On facing, make a line of stitching very close to the seam, through all thicknesses. Don't understitch into or around corners.

TRIM

Trim means to cut away excess fabric. Trimming occurs most often in seams where the excess seam allowance is cut away; for example the inside of curved collars. Corners are trimmed diagonally by cutting across the point close to the stitching.

CLIP

Many pattern directions state to clip seams. To clip means to make a short snip in a seam allowance up to but not into the stitching, with the point of the scissors at an angle to the seam. Curved seams are usually clipped so they will lie flat when turned. The outer seam edge is often shorter than the actual seam line and clipping allows room for expansion.

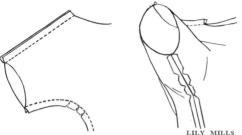

LILY MILLS

Clipping curved seams makes it possible for the seam to lie flat.

Selvages that are heavier than the fabric itself and which may shrink are clipped at intervals so they will not draw up or curl.

TOP-STITCH

Top-stitching is done for decoration or to hold a seam edge in place. Patch pockets are top-stitched in place. The finished edges of a waistband, collar, and cuff are often top-stitched as is the yoke seam. Use a regular stitch. Stitch on the outside of the garment, through all thicknesses of the material.

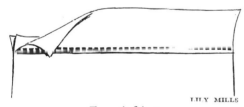

LILY MILLS

Top-stitching.

The toe of the presser foot may serve as a guide for straight stitching. The stitching is usually close to the seam line (1/8 or 1/4 inch), but it may be farther away for decorative purposes.

HAND SEWING

Before the days of the sewing machine, everything was sewn by hand. Today you can still make a dress or suit or any article entirely by hand

550

SIMPLICITY PATTERN CO.

Top-stitching makes an interesting trim along the front, bottom, edges and collar of the jacket.

Understitching helps keep the neck trim standing up and the facings in place. Which sleeve detail do you prefer?

SIMPLICITY PATTERN CO.

THREADING NEEDLE

- Hold needle against white surface for clearer sight of needle eye.

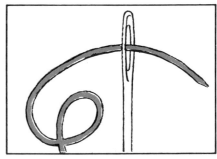

- Select a needle with eye large enough for thread to pass through freely.

- When threading needle brace one hand against the other to steady needle.

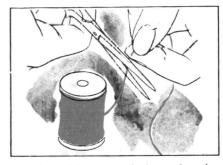

- Cut thread from spool, do not break or bite.

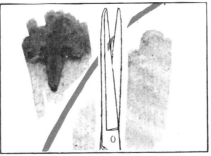

- Cut thread on a slant.

TALON EDUCATIONAL SERVICE

but there is no need to do so. Machine sewing is faster, stronger, and often as attractive in appearance. It is necessary to learn how to use a needle and thread, however, for handbasting, sewing on buttons and other fasteners, finishing most hems, and for many decorative stitches.

Select the correct type of thread and needle size for the fabric you are using. The chart on page 520 is a guide. If you thread the needle before you cut the thread, it will kink less. Keep the loose end of the thread fastened in the slit on a spool for a neat sewing basket.

HAND SEWING

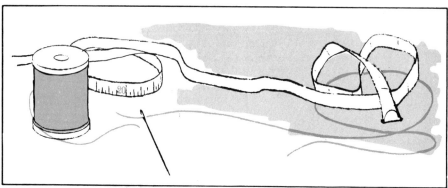

To prevent tangles or breaks:

- Use no longer than 20" length of thread for hand sewing.
- Thread the needle with the same end that was cut from the spool; this same end should be knotted.
- Use single strand of thread.
- If a double strand of thread is used (for sewing snaps, hooks, eyes) adjust position of thread through needle eye after sewing each snap, etc., to prevent breakage caused by friction.

TALON EDUCATIONAL SERVICE

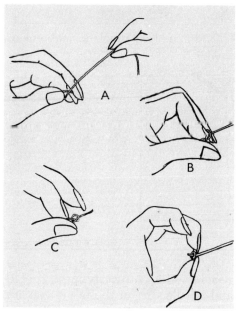

Making a knot in thread for hand sewing. (A) Wind the thread around the end of the little finger. (B) Roll the thread tight between the thumb and first finger. (C) Slip the loop off the end of the finger. (D) Make a small knot by drawing the thread tight.

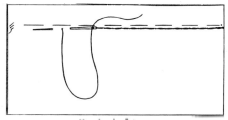

Backstitching.

Making a knot in the end of the thread takes a little practice. Follow the directions on this page.

Basic stitches are the running stitch and the backstitch. To make a *running stitch*, weave the needle in and out of the fabric several times before pulling the thread through. The *backstitch* is firmer and used wherever there is strain on a seam. Take one stitch at a time, always beginning just inside the end of the preceding stitch.

Overcasting is a slanting, evenly spaced stitch used to keep cut edges from raveling. Do not pull tight.

552

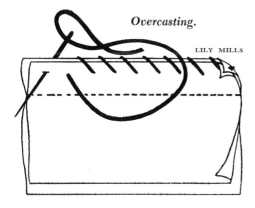

Overcasting.

LILY MILLS

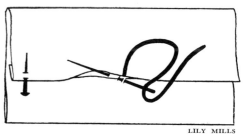

LILY MILLS

Slip-stitching.

The **catchstitch** is used for finishing hems, especially on stretchy fabrics, and for tacking facings. Start at the left. Insert the needle from right to left, first in the hem and then in the garment. Bring the needle out at the lower left, take a backstitch on the upper line a little to the right. Keep the thread below the needle.

stitch for hems and should be invisible from the right side. Take tiny stitches, even slanted, fairly far apart. Catch just one thread in the under layer of the fabric.

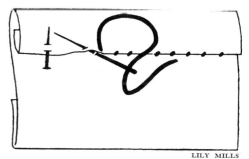

LILY MILLS

Blind-hemming.

Seams and Seam Finishes

When two pieces of cloth are stitched together, the joining line is usually called a seam. Choose the type of seam best suited to your fabric and its location in the garment.

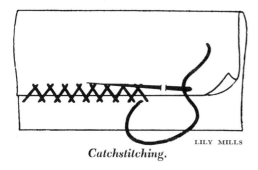

LILY MILLS

Catchstitching.

Take a backstitch on the lower line a little to the right. Keep the thread above the needle. Repeat.

Slip-stitching is used for finishing hems and facings with almost invisible stitches. Bring the needle through the fold of the hem, pick up a thread of the fabric at the same point, and return the needle into the fold of the fabric. Stitches are usually 1/2 inch apart but can be longer on hems and facings where there is no strain.

Blind hemmings is the most-used

To pin a seam, lay the two pieces of material on a flat surface. Place the longer edge toward you so that the fullness will be held toward you as you pin. Pin the edges together, placing the pins at right angles to the seam line and about two inches apart. Baste if desirable. Each seam should be stitched, finished, and pressed before another seam crosses it. It is especially important to press each seam as it is finished because pressing helps avoid the homemade look.

Keep the seam allowance an even width. Patterns are planned for an allowance of ⅝ of an inch. Learn to use a seam gauge as described in Chapter Fifteen. If you vary the width of the seam allowance, you will have difficulty putting together the pattern pieces. Stitching a sleeve seam with a ¾″ allowance and the cuff seam with ⅜″ allowance may not seem like a serious error but the cuff will be almost an inch too wide for the sleeve and obviously will not go on easily.

Secure the ends of stitching as described on page 518. If a seam is crossed by another row of stitching, there is usually no need to secure the threads. Just clip the ends to keep a clean finish. (Where the seams cross, trim corners of seams diagonally.)

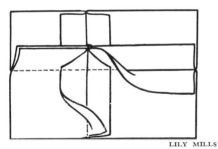

How to stitch seams that cross.

To avoid puckered or stretched seams, check the sewing machine tension. If you share a machine with others, it is always wise to first test stitch a few inches on a folded piece of your material.

Very soft and sheer fabrics may need to have tissue paper placed under the seam, over the feed dog. This is easily pulled off when the seam is finished.

Plain seam. The plain seam is the most used and simplest seam. Right sides of the fabric are placed to-

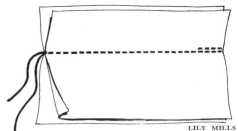

LILY MILLS

Plain seam. The right side has been secured by retracing.

gether and the seam is stitched with the usual seam allowance. Be sure to match the end of the pattern pieces at the seam lines, not at the pattern edges.

SEAM FINISHES FOR THE PLAIN SEAM. Firmly woven materials need no finishing of seam edges although you may want to apply one for a better appearance. If the material frays easily, it will be necessary to finish the seam to prevent this.

A *pinked edge* is attractive and helps prevent fraying but is not suitable for loosely woven fabrics. Use pinking shears and do not cut too closely to the stitching.

LILY MILLS

Pinked finish.

Overcasting or a zigzag stitch is suitable for fabrics that fray easily. Each edge is overcasted separately if the seam is to be pressed open. Over-

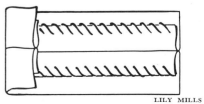

LILY MILLS

Overcast seam finish.

554

cast the two edges together when the seam will not be pressed open, as for an armhole or skirt and waist joining. If done by machine, use the zigzag attachment or adjustment, being careful not to pull the edges too tightly.

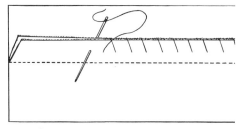

Seam edges overcast together.

A *clean finish* is also called a *turned and stitched edge*. This is a neat seam finish for unlined jackets and for lightweight fabrics that ravel. It can be quickly done and is long lasting. Press the seam open. Turn under each edge about ⅛ inch. Machine stitch close to the edge.

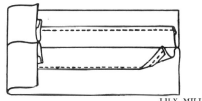

LILY MILLS

Clean finish or stitched and turned.

Bound seam edges are suitable for heavy fabrics that fray easily and for jackets, coats, or robes that are not lined. Bias tape or seam binding may be used. Crease it just off center.

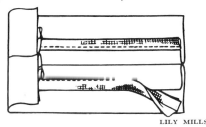

LILY MILLS

Bound seam.

Place it over each seam edge with the wider part of the binding inside. Beginners may need to baste before machine stitching.

A *double-stitched seam* is a good, easy finish for sheer fabrics. After stitching the plain seam, make a second row of stitching in the seam allowance, about ⅛ inch from the first. Trim close to the second row of stitching.

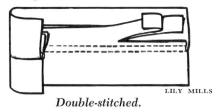

LILY MILLS

Double-stitched.

OTHER SEAMS

A *French seam* is a seam within a seam. The raw edges are completely covered. It is suitable for undergarments, blouses, and dresses of sheer materials. Place the *wrong* sides of the material together and stitch about ¼ inch from the edge. Trim edges ⅛ inch from stitching. Press seam flat and fold right sides together and crease. Stitch ³⁄₁₆ of an inch from the edge.

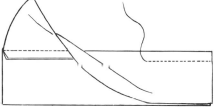

French seam.

A *flat fell seam* is used where a durable, tailored finish is desired as in a tailored blouse or trouser-type garment. It is also used on robes or smocks where raw edges are not desirable. It takes more time to make than other seams but it is durable, no other seam finish is needed, and it is easy to iron. Stitch the seam with the *wrong* sides together, with the usual allowance. Trim the under seam allowance close to the stitching. Press both seam edges together toward the garment back or downward. Turn the edge of the top seam allowance about ¼ inch and fold over the lower seam edge. Top stitch close to edge.

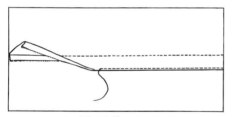

Flat-fell seam.

A reverse flat fell seam may be made from the wrong side of the garment so that the bulk is on the wrong side and only two rows of stitching show on the right side.

Lapped seam. A lapped seam may be used on curved or pointed seams where stitching from the inside is difficult. It is often used for a decorative effect. Turn under and baste the seam allowance of the top piece of material before placing it over the seam allowance of the under piece or

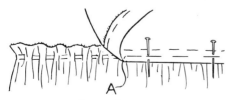

Lapped seam.

stay-stitch along the seam allowance. Turn under the top piece on this line and press.

Pin over the other piece, matching the seam lines. Then top-stitch close to the folded edge.

Handling Special Type Seams

• *To stitch a bias edge to a straight edge,* keep the bias edge on top. Baste or pin carefully, easing in any fullness in the bias edge. Stitch on the usual seam line.

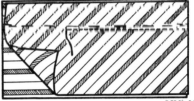

LILY MILLS

How to stitch a bias edge to a straight edge.

• *To stitch a napped fabric to a plain,* stitch with plain fabric on top so napped surface always faces up.

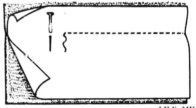

LILY MILLS

How to stitch a napped fabric to a plain.

• *To tape a seam* that may stretch, for accurate waistline seams, and for front edges of coats and jackets, baste tape which has been preshrunk to one side of a seam. (Keep

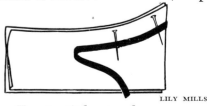

LILY MILLS

How to stitch a taped seam.

the edge of the tape just over the seam line.) Then pin both seam thicknesses together and stitch seams and tape along seam line.

For a decorative *piped seam,* use bias fold tape, a fabric strip of pure bias, ribbon, or braid. Fold down the center. When pinning the seam, place the trim between seam edges so that the fold extends beyond the seam line toward the garment. Stitch on the seam line.

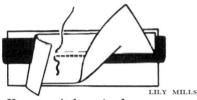

LILY MILLS

How to stitch a piped seam.

DARTS

Darts help shape the fabric to your figure or add decorative lines. One of the first sewing techniques you will need to learn is to make a dart that tapers to a smooth, puckerless point.

Darts vary in length and width and may be made horizontally, vertically, or diagonally. The dart should always point to the fullest part of the body but not go beyond it. One of the most common changes necessary in fitting a garment is to change the direction of the dart. See page 602.

Darts are clearly marked on a printed pattern. (A) The different type darts are all made in basically the same manner. To sew, follow the pattern instructions. (B) Be sure you have transferred a cross line at the point so it is easier to see when you fold the dart. If you have used tailor's tacks, connect them with tailor's chalk. (C) Fold on the center line with the right sides together so the slanted lines meet. Pin. If you are not

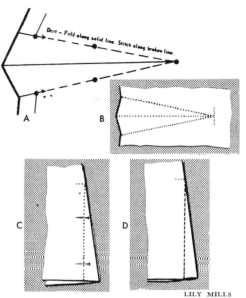

LILY MILLS

How to stitch darts.

certain of the fit, baste and check. (D) Stitch the dart, tapering to nothing at the point. The grain line is preserved if you stitch from the wide part to the point, but you may have better control if you start at the pointed end, where you can carefully place your needle to catch just one thread of fabric for the first stitch.

Press waistline and neckline darts toward the center front or back. Underarm and sleeve darts are pressed downward. When pressing over a rounded surface, a tailor's ham helps to keep the contour of the fabric.

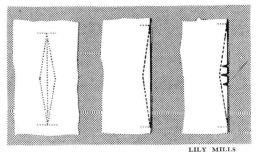

LILY MILLS

Double-pointed dart.

557

In heavy materials, the dart may be cut open along the fold and pressed open. If the edges fray, they may be overcast.

A *double pointed dart* is often used at the waistline of a one-piece dress. After folding on the center line, stitch from either point to the other on the stitching line. Clip at the center, up to but not into the stitching, so the dart will press smoothly.

A *curved dart* is used for some design details. After stitching, slash the fold almost to the point and press the dart open. Excess material may be trimmed off.

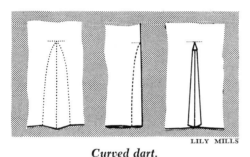

LILY MILLS

Curved dart.

The *back neck dart* is so narrow that it is usually marked only by a line of the pattern. Fold the dart on the marked line. Stitch, tapering from the point to ⅛ inch at the neck edge.

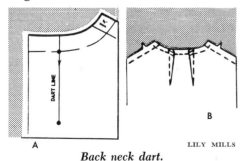

LILY MILLS

Back neck dart.

TUCKS

Tucks are another means of providing fullness or decoration. (A) Mark

558

the sewing line. (B) Bring the corresponding lines together. (C) Stitch, taking care to fasten end of the tuck carefully. Retracing is usually necessary to anchor the stitches. Be sure that all tucks are the same length. Press tucks to one side as shown in the pattern. (D) If tucks are made on the wrong side, only a line of stitching and the released fullness will be seen.

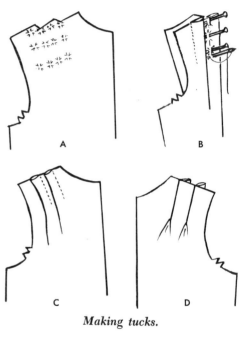

Making tucks.

GATHERS

A third means of controlling fullness or adding decoration is the use of gathers. Gathering may be done by hand or machine.

To gather by hand, use a row of running stitches along the seam line. Anchor securely at one end and pull to the desired length.

Machine gathering is much faster and more secure. Using the largest stitches possible on your machine, stitch two parallel rows, one about ⅜ inch from the seam edge and one on

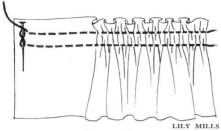

LILY MILLS

Machine gathers.

COATS AND CLARK, INC.

Finish for bottom of blouse to be worn over a skirt or tucked in. It is flat and raw edges are finished. The double folded hem is stitched close to the fold and to the bottom edge of the blouse.

the seam line. Leave the thread ends free. To gather, twist one set of thread ends around a pin in a figure 8 manner. Pull up the bobbin threads until the gathers are the desired length. If you wrap both threads around your finger, you will be able to have even tension as you pull. Anchor the other ends around a pin to secure for seam-stitching.

HEMS

Almost everything one sews has a hem of some type. A good hem is flat, has stitches that are invisible on the right side and is sturdy so it won't loosen easily.

Blouse Hems

A blouse hem is easy to make as rarely do you need to measure an exact length. If the blouse is to be worn tucked under skirt or slacks, it

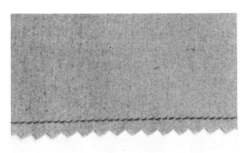

COATS AND CLARK, INC.

Finish for bottom of blouse to be worn tucked under a skirt or slacks. A row of regulation machine stitching is ¼ to ½ inch from the raw edge and the edge is pinked.

should be as flat as possible so there is no ridge to destroy the smooth line.

Firm material can be finished by a row of machine stitching about ½ inch from the edge, and by pinking the edges. A row of zigzag stitching also secures the edges satisfactorily. Fabrics which fray will need to be turned under once or twice and stitched about ¼ inch from the fold.

An overblouse may have a hem as deep as one inch but ¼ inch is more common. Machine stitching is the usual method although you may prefer to use hand stitches on a dressy blouse.

Scarf Hems

The edges of a scarf, and collars of single thickness are finished in a narrow hem. The edge is rolled and slip-stitched. If the material is hard to handle, the edge may be turned and stitched on the machine. The edge is turned again and whipped or slip-stitched down. (See next page.)

559

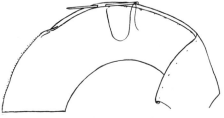

Rolled slip-stitched hem.

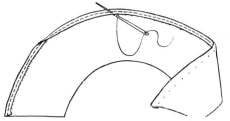

Edge turned, stitched, turned again, and whipped down.

MAKING A PANTS OR SKIRT HEM

Allow pants or a skirt to hang awhile to allow for any possible stretching. A skirt with bias seams will need to hang for a few days. The fabric will stretch before you put up the hem.

Decide on the distance from the floor you prefer for your hem. You will have to consider the current style but also your own figure and preferences. A full skirt may be slightly shorter than a straight skirt.

The easiest way to determine the desired length is to try on a garment of the length you like and measure that. Keep a record of your length.

You will find it easier to mark a hemline if you have a partner to help you. It will be more accurate if you stand on a table or fitting platform so your partner can work at eye level. Wear the undergarments and shoes you will wear with the garment being measured. Stand straight and relaxed and keep your arms still. It is better for your partner to move around you than for you to turn. (Sometimes the

skirt design is such that an evenly measured skirt will appear crooked; however, the most important thing is the appearance, so adjust it as needed.)

(1) With a skirt marker (see page 507 for description of types available) or a yardstick, have your partner *mark the hemline* or the bottom edge of the garment. Marks need be only 4 or 5 inches apart on straight skirts but should be closer for full skirts.

(2) Take your skirt off. Lay it on a table and *check to see if the pins are straight and form an even curve.* If an occasional pin is out of line, move it but if the entire row is jumpy, it is wise to try it on and re-mark it now.

(3) Another way to check is to fold the skirt in the center front and center back with the side seams together. Check to see if the pins make an even curve.

(4) *Fold the hem* on the line of pins, or chalk marks *placing pins perpendicular to the fold.*

(5) *Baste ¼ inch* from the folded edge.

(6) Now is the time to *determine the width of the finished hem.* A very full skirt requires a narrower hem than a straight skirt. A wide hem in a circular skirt creates problems as the excess fullness makes it almost impossible to produce a flat hem. Unless you are allowing for growth, a 1 inch hem is suitable. If the skirt is not too full, a width of 2 to 3 inches is usually correct. However, if you are growing fast or anticipate a style change next season, you may want a wider hem. A full skirt in sheer material, if cut straight, is often 6 to 8 inches deep for appearance and to help hide the bottom edge of a slip.

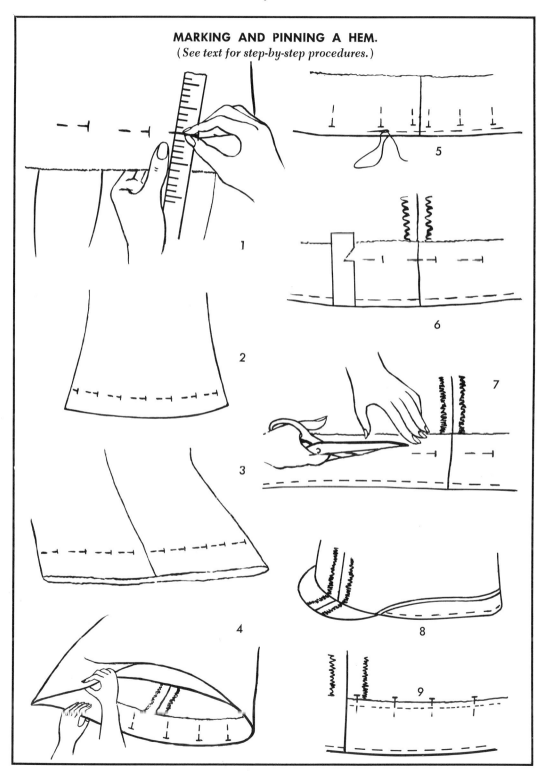

MARKING AND PINNING A HEM.
(See text for step-by-step procedures.)

A hem gauge is convenient for measuring the width of the finished hem before you trim it. You may buy one or make it from cardboard. Go around the entire hem, marking it with chalk, pins, or pencil.

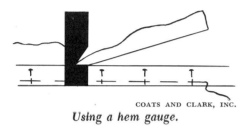

COATS AND CLARK, INC.

Using a hem gauge.

(7) *Cut along the marked line,* being careful not to cut into the garment itself.

(8) *Decide how to finish the raw edge.* A firmly woven woolen, jersey, or a bonded fabric may have a *row of machine stitching* placed about ¼ inch from the raw edge to stabilize it. The edge may be pinked if desired.

On a lightweight cotton or washable fabric, turn the raw edge under once and *edgestitch.* This row of stitching provides a base for hand hemming stitches.

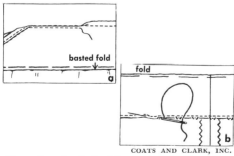

COATS AND CLARK, INC.

Turned and stitched hem. (a) Make a line of machine stitching ¼ inch from cut edge through hem fabric only. (On a curving hem, ease fullness with pin.) Turn edge under on stitching line; topstitch. (b) Pin or baste hem to garment about ¼ inch below top-stitching. Sew hem with inside hemming or with slip stitch as shown.

Seam tape is used for fabrics that ravel easily and are too heavy to have the raw edge turned under. The tape can be applied by top-stitching or by seam-stitching. Top-stitching makes a flatter hem but seam-stitching may be easier for beginners whose stitching is a little shaky.

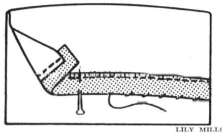

LILY MILLS

Seam-taped hem, top-stitched.

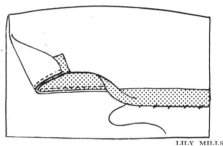

LILY MILLS

Seam-taped hem, seam-stitched.

(9) Now straighten skirt out on a table. Pin the hem edge to the skirt, placing pins at seam lines and center back and front. Distribute extra fullness.

Slight fullness in the hem is easy to smooth out with a line of ease-stitching at the raw edge. For a seam-taped hem, ease-stitch the tape on. Match hem to garment at seams and center back and front. Adjust fullness along the ease thread by drawing up the stitches gently at intervals. Steam press to shrink ease out.

Hems in circular skirts have too much fullness to ease out. To make a hem as flat as possible, ease-stitch the raw edge and pull up the bobbin thread from both ends. Space gathers evenly; steam press to shrink out as much fullness as possible. Stitch tape over the edge.

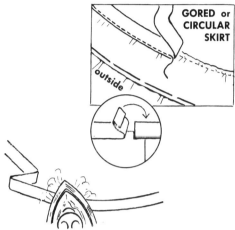

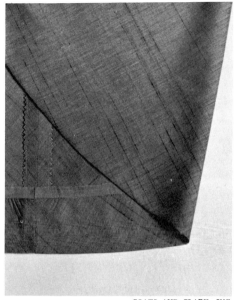

COATS AND CLARK, INC.

Hem with seam binding, completed.

COATS AND CLARK, INC.

Hem with seam binding. On a circular skirt, machine stitch with large stitches ¼ inch from cut edge. Pull up to fit under part of skirt. Steam press seam binding to follow curve of the hem. Topstitch binding, easing gently, to right side of fabric about ¼ inch from edge, overlap turned-under end.

There are many types of hemming stitches. It is wise to try different methods so you will know which you prefer.

The *slip-stitch* is a common method as is the *blind hemming stitch*. These are described on page 553. The *catch-*

stitch is suitable for stretch fabrics and knits.

A *tailor's hem* is used for firmly woven fabrics. The raw hem edge may be finished in any method. Baste or pin hem in place about 1″ from the edge. Use inside hemming. Turn the hem edge back about ¼″ and sew the underside of the hem to the skirt. Catch only one thread in the skirt. Stitches may be placed quite far apart because they are protected by the hem itself.

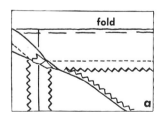

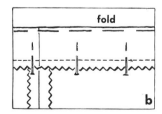

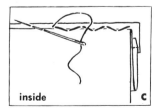

COATS AND CLARK, INC.

Tailor's hem. (a) Make a line of machine stitching through one thickness of fabric about ¼ inch from cut hem edge. Pink, scallop, or overcast the edge. On a gored or circular skirt, reduce the fullness. (b) Pin or baste hem to garment about ¼ inch below stitching line, as shown, matching seams. (c) Sew hem with inside hemming stitch.

COATS AND CLARK, INC.

Inside hemming. Turn hem back against right side of the garment, making the fold in the outer fabric even with machine stitching on a tailor's or clean finished hem or about ⅛ inch below edge of hem with seam binding. Pick up one thread in garment fold, then take a stitch through machine stitching or seam binding.

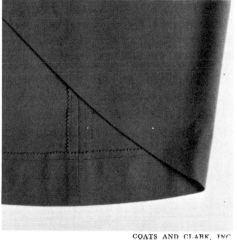

COATS AND CLARK, INC.

Tailor's hem, completed.

A *blind hem* may be made on the sewing machine so that it will be almost invisible and also durable. The fabric needs to be firm and the hemline straight or only slightly full. It takes a little practice to perfect the technique but once learned, it will be a quick and sturdy method for many garments, curtains, and other household items. Follow the directions on page 564. The blind attachment for a machine does this automatically.

For a hem where a seam comes in a pleat, clip the seam allowance to the seam line at the top of the hemline. Press the seam to one side above this and open below it. Between the finished hemline and the raw edge, trim the seam allowance narrower for a layered-finished effect.

Pockets

Pockets are added to a garment for convenience or for design purposes or for both. There are many styles—pockets may be applied to the outside of a garment, set in a seam, or set in as a welt pocket.

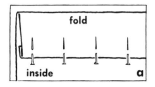

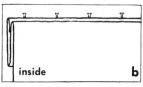

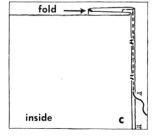

COATS AND CLARK, INC.

Machine finished blind hem. (a) Turn in raw edge of hem ½ inch and crease, turn up hem on marked hemline and press a sharp crease. (b) Fold entire hem back against right side of garment with hem edge extending about 1⁄16 inch beyond fold. (c) Machine stitch on extending edge of hem (10–12 stitches per inch) for 5 stitches, ending with machine needle up. Then pivot fabric slightly, put needle down into body part of garment once, and bring needle up; again pivot fabric so that you are working on extending edge and repeat as shown.

Top stitching outlines the patch pockets and other details of this brushed denim jacket, which could be made by a high school student.

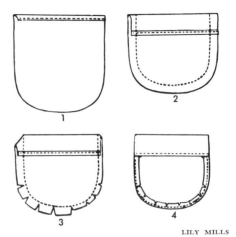

LILY MILLS

Patch pockets, four basic steps.

Patch pockets are applied to the outside of a garment and may be round, square, or pointed in shape. It is important that the top edges be secured firmly so the pocket will not pull loose, nor tear the fabric.

There are four basic steps in applying a rounded or patch pocket. (1) Turn the upper edge ¼″ to the inside. Stitch along the edge. (2) Press the top hem to the outside. Stitch on the seam line all around the

pocket (threads do not need to be anchored—clip ends). (3) Trim the corners diagonally to get rid of excess material so you can get a sharp corner. Trim the seam. On round pockets clip seam allowance to stitching, in V-shapes. This cuts out the extra fullness and keeps the curved edge smooth when the pocket is turned. (4) Turn the hem to the inside. Press the seam allowance to the inside along the stitching line. You may want to slip-stitch or top-stitch the hem in place. Now the pocket is ready to be stitched in place on the garment.

On pointed pockets and square pockets all corners must be mitered. Clip excess fabric at corners by cutting diagonally across.

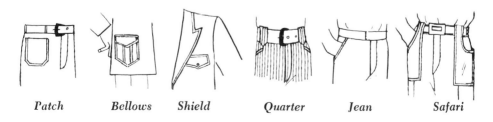

| Patch | Bellows | Shield | Quarter | Jean | Safari |

Pocket Styles

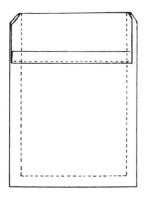 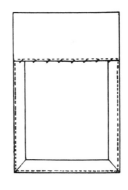 

Square pocket with flap.

Mark the position of pocket on the garment. A mark for the location of each top corner is all that is needed if you keep the fabric grain correct.

At top corners, reinforce pocket as shown on page 275. Top-stitch pocket in place.

A square pocket with a flap is made in a similar manner except the top hem is a deeper fold that flaps over to the right side. You may find it easier to get even corners if you stitch to the end of the pocket, using a seam gauge and then start across the bottom again. Because of the depth of the flap facing, it must be hemmed in place. The flap will hide the stitching on the right side.

A Side Seam Pocket

Pockets are often placed in a side seam for convenience. They are in-

tended to be inconspicuous. Stitch the side seam of the skirt to the mark indicated on the pattern. Press the seam open. (1) With right sides together, pin pocket pieces to skirt front and back, matching notches. Stitch with a 3/8" seam. (2) Turn pocket pieces to the inside. With right sides together, stitch the pocket together. Start from the exact bottom of the 3/8" seam and around the pocket, using a 5/8" seam. (3) Press the pocket to the inside of the skirt and towards the front. Press on the 5/8" seam line to conceal the pocket seam. Baste the top of the pocket to the skirt waistline.

Front Hip Pocket

A front hip pocket can be decorative as well as practical, especially if made from a contrasting fabric that

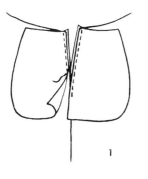  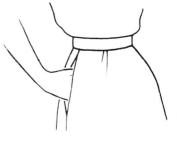

Side-seam pocket.

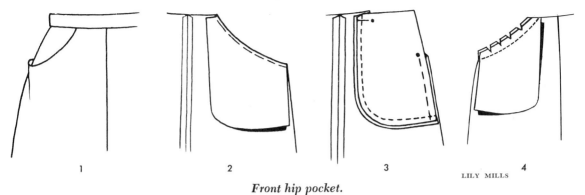

1   2   3   4

LILY MILLS

Front hip pocket.

matches other trim used on the garment. (1) With right sides together, stitch the pocket facing to the skirt front as shown. Trim the seam and clip the curve. (2) Turn facing to inside. Understitch the facing and seam allowances together. (See page 549). (3) Again, with right sides together, stitch pocket to pocket facing along the curved edge shown. Stitch only as far as side edge. Baste or pin the side edges of the pocket to the side seam of the skirt and the top edge to the waistline. (4) When the side seams of the skirt are stitched, your pocket will be finished.

BINDINGS

A binding is an edge finish which shows equally on the right and wrong side of the material. It often serves as part of the decoration of the garment as well as a finish for raw edges. It is usually narrow and cut on the bias rather than on the straight.

CUTTING BIAS STRIPS. Take a piece of fabric and straighten the edges both lengthwise and crosswise. Fold the material so that the crosswise thread lies parallel to the lengthwise or selvage. Crease the diagonal thus formed. Mark the strips the desired width. Measure carefully, using a ruler. Cut, making sure the ends of the strips are straight with the thread of the material.

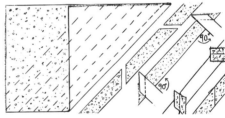

Cutting and joining bias strips.

JOINING BIAS STRIPS. Place right sides of two strips together either crosswise thread to crosswise thread or lengthwise thread to lengthwise thread. Baste, stitch, and press seam open. Clip projecting corners.

Bias bindings may also be purchased in several widths.

Applying a Single Bias Binding

Select a bias strip twice the width of the finished binding, plus seam allowance on each edge. Sew one edge of the binding to the edge of the garment, right sides together.

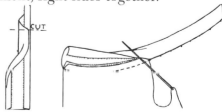

Applying single bias binding.

567

Turn binding to inside; turn under seam allowance and hem to position.

Applying a Double Bias Binding

Select a bias strip four times the width of the finished binding, plus seam allowance on each edge. Fold strip through the center and press.

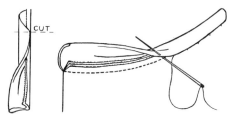

Applying double bias binding.

Sew raw edges of binding to garment, right sides together.

Turn binding to the inside and hem the folded edge to position.

The binding attachment for a sewing machine is another means of applying a bias binding.

FACINGS

A facing is an edge finish which is visible only on one side of a garment. It may be used as a finish to necklines, sleeves, blouse fronts, hems, and plackets. The facing may be turned to the wrong side so it is invisible or it may be turned to the right side and used as a means of decoration as well as an edge finish.

A facing should be cut on the exact grain as the piece that is to be faced or else cut on the bias. A crosswise grain placed on a warpwise grain may pull out of shape with wear and laundering and should be done only for design purposes as with contrasting stripes.

When a garment edge that is to be faced is curved or on the bias, stay-stitch it before beginning work. Also

PFAFF

Bias binding can be applied quickly and accurately with a binding attachment. For a variation, rickrack can be inserted at the same time.

stay-stitch the facing edge if the garment fabric is loose or stretchy.

Pin the facing to the garment, right sides together and stitch, using a regular size stitch except at corners where the stitches should be smaller for reinforcement.

On a curved seam, grade or layer the seam and clip the seam allowance.

On a square edge, layer the seams and clip the corners, just to the stitching.

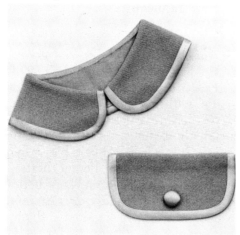

COATS AND CLARK, INC.

Satin binding applied to collar and pocket edges of a wool dress. The button is covered to match.

COATS AND CLARK, INC.

A facing of contrasting fabric cut on the bias and brought to the right side for decorative purposes.

Turn the garment to the wrong side and press the layered seam toward the facing, being certain the facing is all the way out from under the seam. Turn the garment to the right side and understitch. (Page 549.) Then turn facing to wrong side, being sure the seamline stitching does not show. Tack free edges of facing to garment seams or slip-stitch loosely to garment if needed.

Linings, Underlinings, Interlinings, Interfacings

Before you have done much sewing, you will encounter these words. Is there a difference? Yes, indeed. A *lining* is used to cover inside seams, make the garment slip on smoothly, prevent possible irritation from

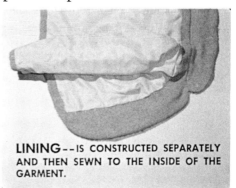

LINING--IS CONSTRUCTED SEPARATELY AND THEN SEWN TO THE INSIDE OF THE GARMENT.

PELLON CORP.

rough, outer fabric, and make the inside attractive. Most patterns provide a pattern for the lining which is constructed separately and then sewn to the inside of the garment.

An *underlining* is often called a backing and has the purpose of making a fabric appear firmer.

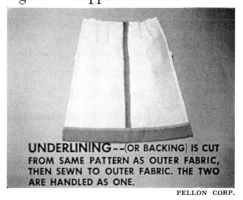

UNDERLINING--(OR BACKING) IS CUT FROM SAME PATTERN AS OUTER FABRIC, THEN SEWN TO OUTER FABRIC. THE TWO ARE HANDLED AS ONE.

PELLON CORP.

Often the underlining may be permanently attached to the fabric at the mill in a bonding process. If it is, you can treat the fabrics as one. If you decide to underline with a separate fabric, select a firm, closely woven one made for that purpose. Cut it with the grain exactly matching the top fabric or use a nonwoven fabric. Baste the two together and handle the fabrics as one. You may prefer to make a few details separately such as darts in bulky fabrics.

Interfacing is placed between the facing and outer fabric. It gives body and shape to collars, lapels, necklines, cuffs, pocket flaps, and waistbands.

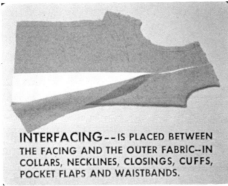

INTERFACING -- IS PLACED BETWEEN THE FACING AND THE OUTER FABRIC--IN COLLARS, NECKLINES, CLOSINGS, CUFFS, POCKET FLAPS AND WAISTBANDS.

PELLON CORP.

Interlining provides additional warmth. Warm fabrics as wool, quilted or napped cotton, or urethane foams are cut the same as the outer fabric. Darts are often cut along the stitching line and the edges barely overlapped to prevent undue bulkiness. Sometimes the interlining is handled as one with the lining; this is easier to do but does not result in as professional an appearance of the finished garment.

FASTENERS

Buttons and Buttonholes

Buttonholes may be worked with thread, by hand or machine, or bound with self or contrasting fabric. The choice is largely a matter of personal preference. (Machine-made ones are especially suitable when time is limited and bound buttonholes are usually found on better quality ready-made dresses and coats.) Machine or handmade thread buttonholes are often used for washable garments.

Where to place buttonholes. Buttonhole locations and sizes are clearly marked on commercial patterns. However, if you have made any alterations, you may need to change the location of some of the buttonholes. On a blouse or garment top, keep the top buttonhole and the one at the waistline; then evenly respace the remaining ones between top and bottom. On a skirt that buttons down the front, keep the top buttonhole where shown on the pattern; locate the best location for the bottom one

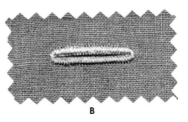

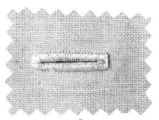

COATS AND CLARK, INC.

A

B

C

(A) *Bound buttonhole.* (B) *The hand-worked buttonhole* (C) *Machine-worked buttonhole.*

570

in relation to the hem, and respace evenly those in between.

If there is strain on the closing, buttonholes should be made at *right angles to the edge of the closing*. If not, they may be cut parallel to the edge or even on the bias for decorative purposes. Be sure to place them so the button will be placed exactly on the center line of the garment. Because of this, buttonholes start ⅛″ away from the vertical center line, toward the opening edge. The exact length of the buttonhole depends upon the length and the thickness of the button. Usually it is ⅛″ longer than the button but first cut a trial buttonhole for size to be sure.

Directions for machine-made buttonholes are available in the instruction booklet for the attachment you will be using. Read them carefully. If you are making hand-worked ones, one row of machine buttonholing makes a good base for the hand stitches.

Bound buttonholes require some practice so make a sample one before starting on your fabric. Follow the directions on page 572.

Snap Fasteners

Snaps are used on flat surfaces where there is little strain. They should be placed close enough together to prevent gapping. They should be invisible but placed near enough the opening to keep it smoothly closed.

• SEWING ON SNAP FASTENERS

1. Mark the position of the ball part on the wrong side of the upper edge of the opening.

2. Using a single heavy thread, fasten it with several small stitches.

3. Sew the ball in place with several small overhand or buttonhole

stitches in each hole. Slip the needle under the snap and between the two thicknesses of material to pass from one hole to the other. Fasten thread with several small stitches.

4. Close the placket and mark the position for the socket with pins or chalk on the imprint left by the ball. Sew socket in same manner as ball.

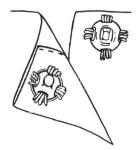

Sewing on snap fasteners.

Hooks and Eyes

Hooks and eyes are used to fasten openings which will have considerable strain. There are two kinds of eyes, round and straight. The round eye is used where the edges of the opening just meet. The straight eye is used on edges that lap and is placed back from the edge. Thread loop may replace straight eye if the closing does not receive much strain and a very flat closing is desired.

• SEWING ON HOOKS AND EYES

1. Place the hook in position on the wrong side of the upper edge of the opening.

2. Use a single thread and the overhand or buttonhole stitch and sew the hook at three places: around each ring and under the prong.

3. Close the opening and locate the position of the eye.

4. Sew around each ring of the eye, using the overhand or the buttonhole stitch. Fasten thread securely with several small stitches.

BOUND OR FABRIC BUTTONHOLES

There are several methods to make these. Experiment and use easiest one for you. Fabric for this type buttonhole may be cut on a true bias or on the lengthwise grain. Machine stitch buttonholes with a small stitch to strengthen the sides and corners (18 to 20 stitches per inch). Cut a lengthwise strip of fabric 1½ inches wide and twice the length of all the buttonholes.

A

(A) Baste stitch parallel lines down each side of strip ½ inch down from cut edges.

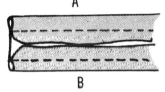

B

(B) Fold strip to wrong side on stitched lines. Press folds and remove stitching. Baste stitch ⅛ inch from folds. Cut strip into buttonhole length plus 1 inch.

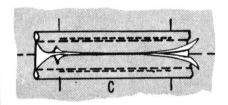

C

(C) Right sides together, place one folded edge ¼ inch above marked buttonhole. Stitch over baste-stitching through both folds the length of the buttonhole. Fasten threads.

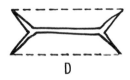

D

(D) On wrong side, start at center on marked line and slash through garment and strip ¼ to ⅜ inch from ends. Clip diagonally to corners.

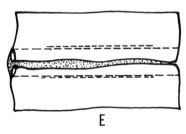

E

(E) Turn strip to wrong side through slash, pulling ends to straighten. Turn to right side of garment and hand baste the bound edges together loosely. Press lightly.

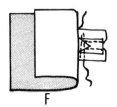

F

(F) At end of buttonhole, fold back garment and put ends of strip and triangular piece under needle. Stitch across both close to end of buttonhole several times. After facing is put on, slash facing as for buttonhole and finger hem to buttonhole.

LILY MILLS

How To Sew On Buttons The Right Way

For added security and neat appearance, it is recommended that buttons be sewn on in the following manner:

A. To find the right position for the button, pin the garment closed as if it were buttoned. Place a pin at the outer end of the buttonhole into the fabric underneath. The center of the button is placed at this point.

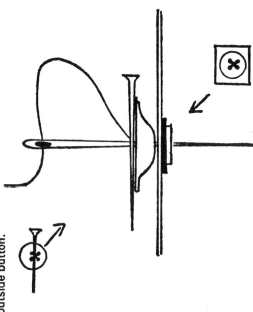

(Sew button here)

B. When sewing on button, use heavy thread or buttonhole twist. Make a stitch on right side of fabric where button is to be placed. Bring needle through button—place a pin across top of button to allow for extra "play"—then bring needle through button back into fabric.

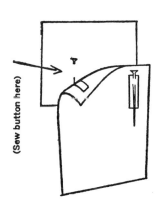

C. If button is to be under strain, it should be reinforced by sewing a small square of fabric or a small button on inside of garment under the outside button.

D. To sew on a shank button, bring needle through fabric and shank, then back through fabric. Make small stitches. If shank button requires extra "play," sew in same manner as **B**, except that the pin is placed directly on fabric underneath the button shank.

Continue sewing back and forth over pin. Remove pin and wind thread firmly around threads under button forming a shank. Draw needle to wrong side of fabric and fasten with several stitches.

LA MODE BUTTONS, B. BLUMENTHAL & CO., INC.

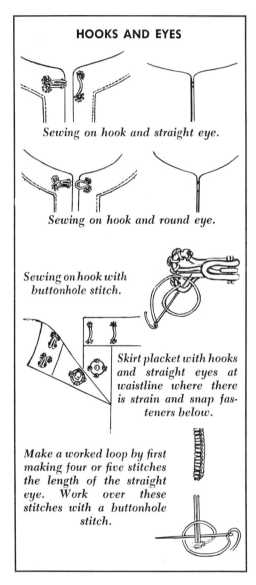

HOOKS AND EYES

Sewing on hook and straight eye.

Sewing on hook and round eye.

Sewing on hook with buttonhole stitch.

Skirt placket with hooks and straight eyes at waistline where there is strain and snap fasteners below.

Make a worked loop by first making four or five stitches the length of the straight eye. Work over these stitches with a buttonhole stitch.

ZIPPERS

A slide fastener, commonly called a zipper, is used to close openings in many different types of garments, including skirts and dresses.

Check your pattern envelope for the type and length of zipper. If you are very tall or very short, you may prefer a different length but the suggested length is a wise choice. (The length is measured from top to bottom of the teeth or coil, not the tape.) Try to find a color that matches your fabric; otherwise consider tinting the tape to match. Zippers are made with either metal teeth or coils of nylon or polyester that mesh together. The coils are usually finer and preferred for lightweight fabrics but the choice is a matter of personal preference. Remember to keep a hot iron away from the heat-sensitive coil type, or buy the type with the coil covered with fabric.

Zipper applications are either lapped or centered. In *lapped* applications, one side of the opening forms a lap over the zipper, concealing it. Often this method is called a concealed zipper. In the *centered* application, the two edges of the opening meet over the zipper which is centered directly under the opening. The centered application is used most often for a neck placket or the front opening of a sports jacket. The lapped method is used for skirt and dress plackets. Your choice of method will depend upon your pattern, your fabric, and your own preference.

Detailed directions for application are on the package accompanying the zipper. These directions are planned for the particular zipper you have purchased and should be read carefully, even though you may prefer to follow another method.

Remember, a zipper foot (page 525) is essential for a neat, smooth placket because some of the stitching must be very close to the metal teeth or the coil. Zippers are usually sewn by hand in such pile fabrics as velvet and velveteen. The seam will not be as strong but the stitches will show less and the pile will not be matted.

How To Put in a Concealed Zipper

When joining bodice and skirt at waistline, start and end seam stitching ¼ inch above actual seam line at placket (a). Stitch on a slant to where side seam line and waist seam line meet; then continue stitching on waist seam line. Press seam up. Machine baste placket edges together on seam line. Press seam open.

Working on the inside of your dress place the fastener face down on the back seam allowance, with end of metal chain at lower end of placket. Place left side of fastener teeth against closed seam line. With left edge of the presser foot against the chain, stitch the tape to the back seam allowance from bottom to top. When the foot reaches the slides at the top of the fastener chain, either open the fastener and continue stitching or stitch slightly wider to allow more space for the slides (b).

Remove presser foot and put on zipper foot. Fold the zipper to the right, with the right side up. Make a fold (about ⅛ inch) on the back seam allowance, bringing the edge of the fold close to fastener teeth. Stitch the fold to the fastener tape from the bottom to the top (c).

Spread garment flat with fastener face down over front seam allowance. A small pleat will form in back seam allowance at bottom and top of fastener. Stitch through all thicknesses across the bottom, up the side close to the chain, and across the top (d). Draw upper threads to the underside at the lower and upper edges of the placket and tie by hand.

Remove baste stitching from the underside of back seam allowance. Press finished placket on right side. (e) Shows outside of dress placket.

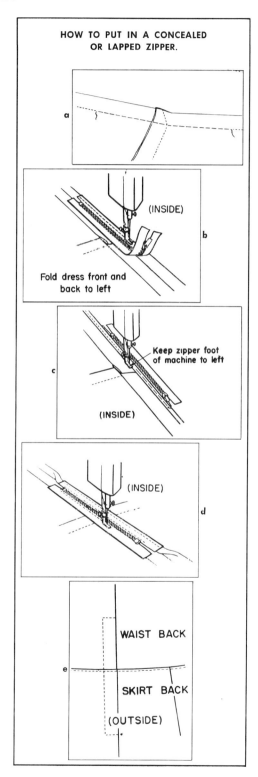

HOW TO PUT IN A CONCEALED OR LAPPED ZIPPER.

a

b — (INSIDE)
Fold dress front and back to left

c — Keep zipper foot of machine to left
(INSIDE)

d — (INSIDE)

e — WAIST BACK
SKIRT BACK
(OUTSIDE)

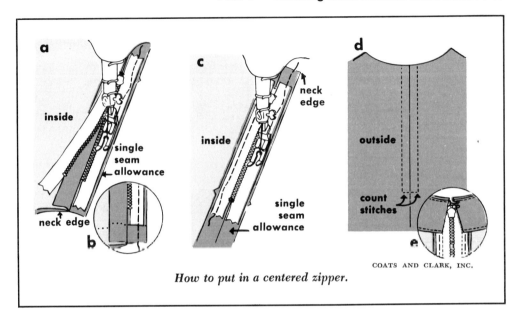

How to put in a centered zipper.

COATS AND CLARK, INC.

Centered Application

When inserting a zipper in a skirt or neck opening, using the centered method, be sure the opening is the length of the zipper plus the seam allowance needed for the neck edge or the waistline seam. Machine baste seam closed. Clip basting at 2″ intervals for easy removal later.

Working on the inside of the garment, open the zipper. With the *bottom of placket* away from you, extend right-hand seam allowance as shown in diagram. Place one tape on it face down, with the bottom stop at bottom mark and teeth or coil against seam line. Starting at the bottom, use regular presser foot and machine baste along the edge of tape (a) until you are about an inch from neck seam line. Stop and trim off tape-end at seam line. Then continue stitching to edge of garment (b). On a skirt or dress placket, the tape is not trimmed.

Close zipper. On a neck placket, trim off second tape-end even with

first. With top of placket away from you, extend free seam allowance and free zippper tape under presser foot. Starting at neck edge, machine-baste along edge of tape (c).

Change to zipper foot and regular size stitch.

Work on outside, with garment spread flat as shown (d). Mark bottom of zipper with pin. Starting at top of placket, stitch down along one side of zipper. Just below bottom, pivot on needle. Stitch slowly across bottom, counting stitches to seam line. Count same number of stitches on other side of seam line, pivot again and stitch along other side of zipper to top of placket.

Take out machine basting, working from right side. Press placket. Finish neck facing and add hook and eye (e).

PLEATS

Pleats are usually marked on a printed pattern with solid and broken lines, plus arrows which show the direction of the pleats. If you are marking with tailor's tacks, the use of two colors of thread is helpful; one color for the folded edge of the pleat and another color for the line to which it is brought.

Pleats should be made from the right side unless otherwise directed. Place pins at right angles to the pleat edges and baste in place. Baste the entire length of the pleat except for about 6 inches at the bottom to allow for hemming. Leave the basting in place until the garment is finished. Baste across the top edge to hold pleats in place, keeping the top edges even. Machine stitch from the bottom up to keep the grain in proper position.

Knife pleats all run in the same direction. They usually lap from right to left so a pleat will cover the side placket.

Box pleats are two pleats turned away from each other.

Inverted pleats are two pleats turned toward each other.

A *vent pleat* or a kick pleat is planned to allow fullness at the lower edge of the skirt for walking. Stitch across the top of inverted or vent pleat through all thicknesses to hold it firmly in place.

Inverted and vent pleats may be made with a full length underlay or a shorter one just where the extra material is needed. If the material extends to the waistband, the pleat will hang neater but it will be bulkier. Most pleats are top stitched close to the folded edge. If they are stitched from the wrong side, the appearance is smoother. Be sure to fasten the ends of the stitching securely—retracing or lock-stitching is wise.

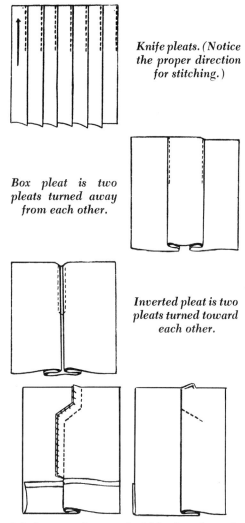

Knife pleats. (Notice the proper direction for stitching.)

Box pleat is two pleats turned away from each other.

Inverted pleat is two pleats turned toward each other.

Stitch across the top of a kick pleat through all thicknesses to hold it firmly in place.

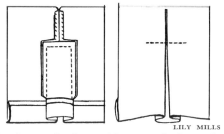

An inverted pleat with an underlay only under the pleat should be stitched across the top through all thicknesses to hold it in place.

SLEEVES

Although there are many sleeve styles, for construction purposes there are four basic types—set-in sleeve, raglan, kimono and tailored sleeves as in a man's shirt.

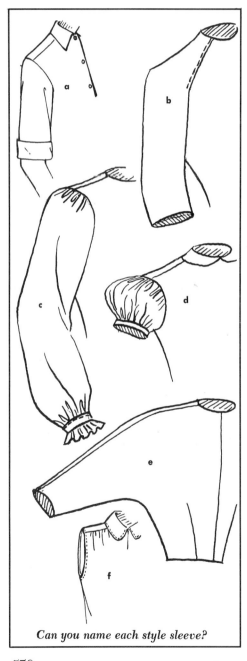

Can you name each style sleeve?

A *kimono* sleeve is an extension of the waist front and waist back. The underarm seam needs to be reinforced with tape so it will not pull out easily. (See page 275). Gussets allow more freedom of movement.

A *raglan* sleeve is easy to insert. (a) With right sides together, stitch the sleeve to the front and back of the garment, matching notches. Clip the curves so the seams will lie flat. Press seams open unless otherwise directed. (b) Join the underarm and sleeve in one continuous seam.

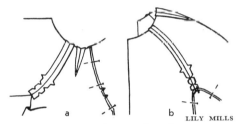

LILY MILLS

How to set in a raglan sleeve.

To set in a *tailored* sleeve, (a) join the seam to the armhole, wrong sides together, matching markings. Make a flat fell seam. Trim sleeve seam (not blouse seam) to ¼". Press seam toward sleeve. Turn under the blouse seam and lap over the trimmed edge. Top-stitch the turned blouse seam in place. (b) Stitch the underarm seam and sleeve seam in one continuous seam, using a flat fell seam also.

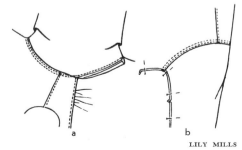

LILY MILLS

How to set in a tailored sleeve.

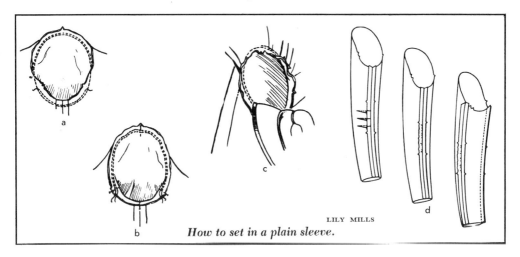

LILY MILLS

How to set in a plain sleeve.

Set-in sleeves have extra fullness or ease in the sleeve cap for proper fit. This ease allows for easy arm movement. Therefore, the top of the sleeve edge is larger than the armhole. The fullness can be eased in so there will be no puckers or gathers.

Before stitching the sleeve seam together, stitch with large stitches along the seam line around the sleeve top between notches. Stitch again 1/4" from the first stitching, within the seam allowance. Turn the sleeve right side out, garment wrong side out.

(a) With the right sides together, pin the sleeve in the armhole at the underarm seams, notches, and top of sleeve mark. Pull ease threads until the sleeve fits the armhole. Adjust the ease evenly, leaving the one-inch plain at the top.

(b) With a little practice you can stitch the sleeve in directly but most sewers find it easier to use sufficient pins to hold the sleeve firmly.

Stitch the sleeve in the armhole. Start just above one notch and stitch toward the underarm, continuing around the sleeve. When the starting point is reached, stitch again around

to the next notch 1/8" from the first stitching to reinforce the underarm.

(c) Press seam open to shrink out as much fullness as possible. Then lightly press seam toward sleeve. Exception: for a softly rolled shoulder line, as for jackets and coats, press the seam away from the sleeve. If the seam edges fray, overcast to keep them neat.

(d) Long sleeves must provide fullness for elbow and arm movement. This is done with darts which come at the elbow, with ease, or a two-piece sleeve. If the fullness does not come at your elbow, make the necessary alterations.

WAISTBANDS AND WAISTLINE SEAMS

It is important to reinforce a skirt waistband and the waistline seam of a dress to prevent stretching during wear.

A waistband is preferably cut on the lengthwise grain as it will stretch the least in that direction. In addition, it is interfaced with a firm fabric that will not stretch. The sewing directions for a skirt or pants pattern will help you apply the interfacing correctly.

579

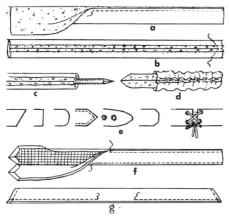

Making flat and tie belts.

BELTS AND SASHES
Flat and Tie Belts

(a) Cut a piece of material twice as wide as the finished belt plus seam allowance, and long enough to lap the desired distance. A belt may be cut lengthwise or crosswise of the fabric according to the design requirements. Place the right sides together and stitch the length of belt. With fingers inside the open belt at each end, adjust so seam comes to the middle on one side of the belt. This is important! Press belt flat.

(b) Stitch across one end to give shape to the buckle end of the belt leaving the other end open.

(c) Place the eraser end of a pencil at the center point of the cross stitching and, working the two pressed layers loose between thumb and finger, push the end of the pencil against the stitching turning the belt inside itself.

(d) Continue pushing with pencil and sliding top layer of belt until the belt is entirely turned. Use a pin to pull out the point of the belt; then press belt.

(e) Eyelets of buckle prong may be made with a stilletto and buttonholed.

(f) For a wide belt or one made of limp material, it may be necessary to cut an inner belt of canvas or other stiffening fabrics. Belts with stiffening may be made by several methods. Make no seam allowance when cutting this inner belt. Fold the belt piece and crease, cut the buckle end in the desired shape, turn under the seam allowance all the way around, and baste in place, clipping at corners. Lay edge of canvas along crease inside of belt and baste the turned-down edges. Stitch around outside close to edge.

(g) If the belt is to be tied, stitch, leaving a space open in the center. Turn the belt from both ends through this opening. Press and close with slip-stitches. Wear the belt with this side down.

Belt Loops or Carriers

Thread loops are easy and fun to make. They are placed on the garment at the side seams, half above and half below the waistline.

Using double thread, insert the needle through the side seam below the waistline, bringing the thread to the outside. Take a small stitch for reinforcement. Take another stitch, but instead of drawing it up, leave a loop as shown. Reach through the loop with your forefinger and make a tight crochet chain, continuing until the chain is 1/4" to 1/2" longer than the belt is wide. Pull the thread through the last loop, pulling the thread tight. Anchor the chain in the seam above the waistline.

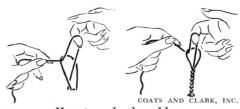

COATS AND CLARK, INC.
How to make thread loops.

CHECK UP

Whenever you complete a garment, take a little time to evaluate it. It helps to get the opinions of your classmates. Learn what you have done well and what you need to improve in future sewing. Completing a checklist like this may help you better understand your progress.

HOW WELL DID I DO?			
	Very Good	Satis- factory	Needs Improvement
How does my garment appear on me?			
Does it fit well?			
Is the color and line flattering?			
Does it have a neat, well-pressed appearance?			
Did I make a wise pattern selection?			
Did I select the fabric wisely?			
Are the notions and trimmings suitable?			
How well did I accomplish the following construction processes? Seams			
Darts, tucks, or gathers			
Pleats			
Collar or other neck edge finish			
Sleeve or other armhole finish			
Zipper			
Buttons, buttonholes, other fasteners			
Waistband or waistline seam			
Hems			
Other construction details			
What did I do especially well? What improvements do I need to make the next time I sew?			

Summary With Check-up Questions

The preparation of pattern and fabric before sewing and the actual putting together of a garment are equally important.

- *If a fabric is cut off grain, can it be corrected in sewing?*
- *What effect will irregular stitching have on a well-fitted garment?*
- *Will the best quality fabric maintain its appearance if it is frequently ripped and resewn?*

An inexperienced sewer will find it wise to follow the procedure given on the guide sheet accompanying the pattern. An experienced person may use other methods but should read the guide carefully before starting to sew.

- *By whom is the pattern guide sheet prepared?*
- *Do new styles call for different ways of putting together pattern pieces?*

It is wise to have a general plan, written or in mind, of the general procedure for putting a garment together.

- *Will such a plan help you be aware of the time available for your project?*
- *Can you think of a situation when you may sew some detail before it should be done because you did not plan ahead?*
- *If you have forgotten to obtain all needed materials, will a plan help remind you of missing items?*

Keeping a garment neat and clean while you sew helps in the final appearance.

- *When should excess threads and seam edges be trimmed?*
- *What difference does it make if an unfinished garment is tossed into a sewing drawer or hung up correctly on a hanger?*
- *Why is it easier to sew on a garment that does not have dangling threads and bulky seams?*

The unit method of clothing construction is a good approach for beginners.

- *Is it less confusing to complete as much as possible on one unit before proceeding to another?*
- *Why is the unit method efficient when short periods of time are available, as class periods?*
- *What are the units in a simple skirt? In a blouse?*

It is important to keep the fabric grain perfect to stitch and press in the direction of the grain.

- *What may happen to the appearance of a garment if the grain is not kept perfect?*
- *Why are the arrows printed on the seam lines of many patterns?*
- *What may happen to a neckline if it is stitched in a continuous direction?*

The success of a garment is judged by its appearance on the wearer. Nothing is more important than proper fit.

- *If a garment does not fit well but is beautifully made with neat, even seams and other details, will it flatter the wearer?*
- *Why may it be necessary to check the fit of a garment while sewing even if the pattern was carefully altered to fit?*

Basting is used to hold garment sections together temporarily for a fitting, to keep fabric from slipping when machine stitching, as an aid in pressing, and as a means of making some pattern marks visible on the right side.

- *Why are the center front and center back lines often hand or machine basted?*
- *When is pin basting suitable and when is hand basting desirable? What are the advantages of machine basting when it will not leave marks on the fabric?*

582

To ease means to push in a little fullness so no puckers or gathers are noticeable on the seam line.

- *How do "ease" and "gather" differ?*
- *Why is it necessary to ease one seam to another, as for example, back shoulder seam to front shoulder seam?*
- *When easing a longer seam to a shorter one, which is held on top?*

Use the proper type seam and seam finish for the fabric and location of seam.

- *Why is a flat fell seam often used for tailored shirts and sports garments?*
- *Why would a French seam be a good selection for a side seam in a sheer fabric?*
- *A firm fabric that does not fray easily is usually made with plain seams. How would you finish the seam edges?*

It is important to understand the difference between a lining, an interlining, an interfacing, and an underlining.

- *When the main purpose is to provide additional warmth as in a coat or jacket, which is selected?*

- *Why is the underlining often permanently attached to a fabric at the factory?*
- *What is the purpose of interfacing?*

The purpose of stay-stitching is to keep the bias edges of a garment from stretching and to ensure that the fabric will retain the exact shape and measurements of the pattern.

- *Why are straight edges cut on the lengthwise grain not stay-stitched?*
- *Why is it important to stay-stitch a neck edge immediately after removing the pattern from the fabric piece?*
- *If one garment piece stretches more than another before sewing, will it cause difficulty in putting the pieces together?*

Understitching helps make and keep a sharp edge whenever a seamline is turned to the inside.

- *Why does understitching, for example, a facing, save on basting and pressing?*
- *Why doesn't understitching show on the right side?*

Can You Explain These Terms?

pattern guide sheet	understitching	gathers
unit method of clothing construction	slash	tailor's hem
	trim	blind hem
directional stitching	clip	patch pocket
directional pressing	top-stitch	binding
lining	running stitch	facing
underlining	overcast	concealed zipper
interlining	catchstitch	centered zipper
interfacing	slipstitch	knife pleat
stay-stitching	blind hem	box pleat
even basting	plain seam	inverted pleat
uneven basting	French seam	vent pleat
diagonal basting	flat fell seam	kimona pleat
top or slip-basting	lapped seam	raglan sleeve
ease	darts	tailored sleeve
ease-stitching	tucks	set-in sleeve

CHAPTER SEVENTEEN

Advanced Clothing Construction and Alterations

ONCE YOU HAVE LEARNED to make attractive garments from fabrics that are easy to handle and from patterns that are not complicated, you will want to learn to work with *unusual fabrics* that require more understanding of machine adjustments and skill in handling.

By selecting the correct size pattern and making a few simple adjustments, you will have a garment that fits as well as most ready-to-wear clothing you can buy. However, as you develop skill in sewing, you will probably want to *improve your fitting methods* so your clothing will appear custom-made for you. In addition, the patterns you select will probably require more detailed fitting.

Improving ready-made clothing, both old and new, may not seem like an advanced technique but it is. (Alterations can be more difficult than making a new garment. It makes sense to learn to make a few simple garments before attempting much clothing alteration. You will find it easier when you understand clothing construction from the inside out.)

When one is driving in a strange neighborhood, it is safer and usually quicker to follow established routes but when one is familiar with a place, *short-cuts* are usually available which save considerable time. The same is true in sewing; a beginner will find it quicker in the long run to follow directions planned for the inexperienced but as one begins to feel at ease with sewing, there are many short-cuts which may be helpful.

Many of the *short projects* and the ideas for *gifts and accessories* given in this chapter are easy enough for anyone to make; others are complicated. They are included in this section because most students will concentrate on their own clothing (at first) and, with experience, will be ready to make specialty items.

SEWING WITH FABRICS THAT REQUIRE SPECIAL CARE

Many fabrics require special handling because of unusual designs, fiber content, or finishes. These are often referred to in sewing as special fabrics, although they are quite commonly used. It is wise to learn to sew first on fabrics that are easy to work with before selecting fabrics that require special handling . . . although once accustomed to them, they are not difficult to use and you can create unusual and distinctive effects. A beginner can make a satisfactory garment with these fabrics but the need for special attention to details may try one's patience. Once you have mastered the use of the sewing machine and can make a garment from firm fabrics with no matching problems, special fabrics are a challenge and the effect obtained by their use can be rewarding.

Pattern directions often refer to fabrics with nap; technically nap refers to a special type of finish (page 426) but the term is commonly used to refer to any fabric design or finish that requires handling the fabric as if it were a one-way design. Plaids, stripes, nap finishes, pile weaves, or one-way prints are examples.

Because most special fabrics are not easy to alter once sewn, it is especially important to select a pattern that fits, and to make any needed alterations before cutting the fabric. Usually a pattern with few intricate details allows the fabric to be shown to greater advantage. Before stitching, always test the sewing machine setting on a folded scrap of the fabric you will be using. Be certain the needle size, type of thread, and stitch length are suitable. Adjustments may need to be made in the tension and the pressure on the foot.

Bulky seams that will be enclosed, as inside a collar or facing, should be

Once you have learned to make dresses, skirts, and simple garments, you may want to learn to make tailored garments as these 4-H members have done. References for tailoring techniques are listed at the end of the chapter.

graded or *layered*. This means that one seam is trimmed narrower than the other one. The uppermost seam allowance should be the widest to prevent a bulky ridge from showing after pressing.

NAPPED AND PILE FABRICS

Napped and pile fabrics differ in the way in which they are made, although sewing directions are similar. A napped fabric has surface threads raised while a pile fabric has an extra set of threads woven so the fabric has a three-dimensional quality. In construction directions, the word "nap" is used to refer to both types of fabrics because each reflect light differently, depending upon the direction of the nap or pile. If you ignore the difference, you will end up with a garment that appears to be made of two different colors—not different enough to be smart but different enough to appear odd.

SIMPLICITY PATTERN CO.

A plaid three-piece outfit planned for the girl with sewing skill and patience. Notice the careful placement of bound buttonholes and pockets.

Making a bathing suit which fits well can be an easy project with today's stretch fabrics and zigzag sewing machines.

VIKING SEWING MACHINE CO.

SIMPLICITY PATTERN CO.

The dress is made of a heavy diagonal twill, underlined to hold its shape. The coordinated checked jacket makes the dress into a costume.

An imaginative use of a large checked fabric. The yoke of the dress and matching jacket are cut on the bias. Notice the careful attention to proper fit.

SIMPLICITY PATTERN CO.

Fabrics which require special care in sewing.

CROMPTON-RICHMOND CO.

Notice how the extra threads in a pile fabric stand away from the surface to form a three-dimensional quality.

CROMPTON-RICHMOND CO.

Stroke the surface. If you rough it up, you are going against the grain. If it feels smooth, you are stroking in the direction of the grain.

CROMPTON-RICHMOND CO.

The preferred direction of the nap or pile is upwards. Notice how the color appears richer and darker in that direction.

The best way to determine the direction of the nap is by feel. Place the fabric flat on a table. Run the palm of your hand along the length of the fabric. If it feels smooth and lies flat, the nap is running in the direction of your hand movement. But if it feels rough and resists you, the nap direction is running opposite to your hand.

A richer color is obtained by using the nap running up. Nap running downwards appears lighter and shinier. It is generally preferred to use pile fabrics as velvet and velveteens with the nap running in an upward direction to take advantage of the richer color. Corduroy may be used either up or down, whichever appearance you prefer. Long napped fabrics as fleeces and zibelines always run down, similar to the direction of natural fur. (Fabrics like flannel and flannelette which are slightly napped are handled like plain fabrics.) *Just be certain that the nap on all garment pieces runs in the same direction.*

Once you have decided which way the nap runs, chalk-mark arrows on the wrong side of the fabric.

587

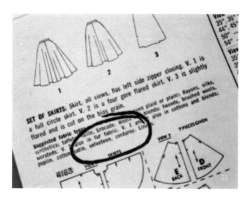
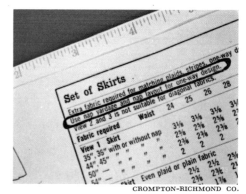

Check the pattern envelope to see if the list of suggested fabrics include pile and napped fabrics. Notice also if there is a special cutting layout.

Pattern layout. Follow the pattern layout for nap fabrics. Place all pattern pieces on the fabric so that the tops of the pieces are in the same direction. Be sure to have the pile side up as you work with the fabric. If a fold is needed, be certain it is lengthwise.

The width of some pattern pieces makes it necessary to place the pattern with the fabric flat rather than folded lengthwise. Do not fold the fabric crosswise for a double thickness as the nap of the section cut

from the top layer of the fabric will run in the opposite direction to that of the bottom layer. To cut two thicknesses at one time, measure the

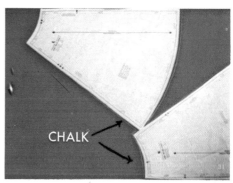

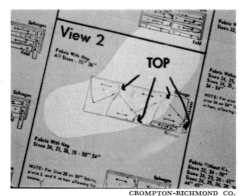

When the pattern pieces are to be laid out on a single thickness, the layout shows some of the pieces in solid lines and some in broken lines. The broken lines in this diagram indicate that the pattern pieces are to be turned over before being placed again.

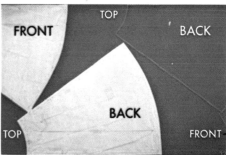

When pattern pieces are cut singly, it is wise to place them first and chalk around them. Then move the pieces to the other location and pin in place. Adjustments in placement can be made, if needed, which could not be done if an error was discovered after the first pieces were cut.

588

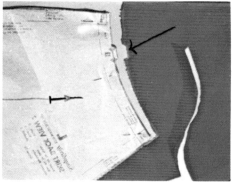

CROMPTON-RICHMOND CO.

Cut with sharp shears. Notches are more easily seen if they are cut in groups. For two or three notches, cut up at the first one, across the top to the last one, and then down.

CROMPTON-RICHMOND CO.

In securing a pattern to corduroy, always pin along the wales.

length of the fabric needed to cut one thickness and cut your fabric crosswise at this point. With right sides together, reverse the second layer so the bottom edge becomes the top. Check the direction of the arrows you chalk-marked on the wrong side of the fabric. The nap on both pieces will then run in the same direction.

Marking and cutting. Tailor's tacks, pins, or tailor's chalk are suitable ways to mark pile and heavily napped fabrics. Tracing wheel marks are difficult to see. Since regular size notches may fray, cut notches slightly larger than usual.

Use sharp shears and cut with the grain. Fine velvets mar easily so use needles or fine pins for holding the pattern on the fabric.

Very wide wale corduroy is often treated as a striped fabric and the ribs should be matched. See the rules for matching stripes.

Stitching. Napped and pile fabrics have a tendency to slip in stitching so it is best to baste the seams first. A longer than average machine stitch is needed (10 to 12 stitches per inch.)

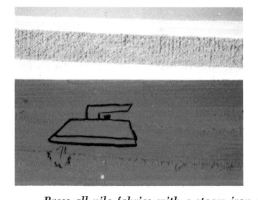

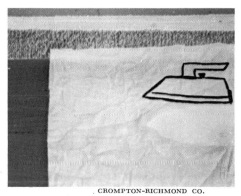

CROMPTON-RICHMOND CO.

Press all pile fabrics with a steam iron or a damp pressing cloth. Place fabrics face down on a terry cloth towel or a velvet board. The steam iron is placed very gently on the place to be pressed, then lifted and moved to the next position.

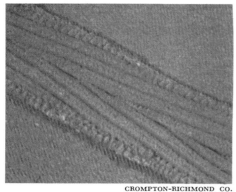

The best method for finishing seams on pile fabrics is overcasting, either by hand or machine

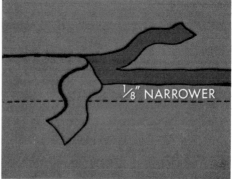

Trim and layer seams whenever they are enclosed in a collar, cuff, waistband, or facing seam. Trim one edge ⅛" narrower than the other to blend the edges and prevent a bulky appearance.

The pressure on the presser foot may need to be lessened. Experiment on scraps of the fabric until you find a stitch that looks well.

When pressing, be sure to follow the instructions on page 527.

The tailor's hem, with or without seam tape along the raw edge, is a good choice.

FUR-LIKE FABRICS

Fur-like fabrics are sewn in much the same way as pile fabrics. The direction of the nap is downward, as in fur. If the pile is thick and long, it is better to cut from the wrong side without cutting into the pile threads. This may be done with sharp shears or a razor blade. Baste firmly and try to brush the pile away from the seam line. Use a medium long stitch and a loosened tension. Work the pile out of the seams with a pin after you have completed the stitching.

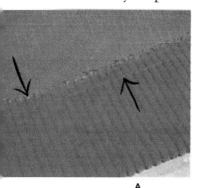

A

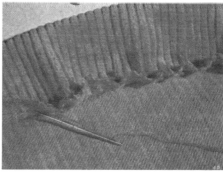

B

C

A tailor's hem is suitable. (A) Pin the hem up, matching ridges of the corduroy fabric. For hems and facings on pile fabrics, first overcast the edge and then stitch ¼" from the edge, in an ease stitch. (B) To take up the hem ease, pull up the stitching thread with a pin at intervals. Turn the hem edge back about ¼" and catch to the skirt by inserting the needle in the underside of the hem and picking up one or two threads in the underside of the hem, and then in the garment itself. (C) A sturdy, inconspicuous hem is the result.

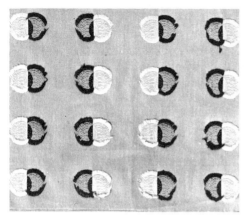

An all-over design that must be handled as a fabric with crosswise and lengthwise stripes for the most satisfying appearance.

PLAIDS AND STRIPES

It is fun to learn to sew with plaid and striped fabrics. Although it is more difficult than using plain or all-over design fabrics, you can create many individualized effects.

Pattern selection. Select a pattern that is suitable for plaid or striped fabrics. Although it is possible to make almost any pattern in a plaid or

Sewing with plaid fabrics takes more patience and skill than plain fabrics. For a first project, select an even plaid, such as this one. Notice how well the plaid matches at the lapels and collar ends.

striped fabric, the wrong type of pattern will require a great deal of time, skill, and the results may not be satisfying. If the garment pictured on the pattern envelope is shown in plaid or stripes, you know it is suitable for such fabrics. Read the pattern envelope. Often there will be a statement that a pattern is NOT suited for certain fabric designs.

If in doubt, select a pattern with few seams and a minimum of intricate detail.

Fabric selection. Did you know that plaids and stripes can be either uneven or even? Look for an even, balanced stripe or plaid design unless you are prepared to spend extra time in matching designs. To determine the type of design, these three questions should be answered:

1. Does the fabric have a right and wrong side?
2. Does the design have an up and down effect?

Notice how the large check was used to advantage by cutting the yoke on the bias. Not only does it add design interest but it also eliminates the need to match lines, which can be difficult at this location.

3. Does the design have a right and left effect?

If the answer to all these questions is no, the plaid or stripe is an even, balanced design.

But first, how do you determine the correct answers to these three questions? Select the center vertical line or bar in the plaid or stripe design and check the colors and spaces to the right and to the left of this bar.

Uneven or one-way direction stripe design. On which stripe would you place the center front and center back pattern marking?

If the right and left readings are different, the fabric has a right and left in design. This can be noticed in the fabric above. If the wide black line is considered the center line, the spaces to the left read wide grey, white, narrow grey, black, medium grey, and white, but the spaces to the right read white, wide grey, narrow black, and so on. Select any vertical line in this illustration and it will be found that the spaces to the left read differently than the spaces to the right. Thus this is an uneven design with a right and left.

The plaid shown in lower right on page 591 is an example of an even

plaid; the design is the same both up and down and right to left.

Whenever possible, select an even plaid or stripe. You can usually find one that pleases you. If you are making a full skirt with gathered or unpressed pleats, the type of plaid does not matter but it can be very time consuming and frustrating to match seams and details with an uneven design.

Buy only woven stripes or plaids; it is almost impossible for a manufacturer to print crosswise stripes so they will match along seamlines.

A plaid is usually more complicated than a stripe to work with because the matching must be done in two directions rather than just one. The following directions refer to plaids but also apply to stripes; if there is a difference, it will be stated.

Amount of fabric to buy. Usually you will need to purchase additional fabric to match any design. The pattern envelope may indicate how much more is needed if the pattern is planned for such fabric. The size of the plaid makes a difference as a large plaid may require ¾ yard extra, and ½ yard will be sufficient for a small plaid. You can determine this yourself if you count every place where the design must be matched and then measure the number of inches needed for each plaid repeat. Multiply the number of matching places by a repeat measurement. For example, a two-piece skirt that must be matched at only one set of notches and a plaid fabric that repeats every 2 inches will require an additional 4 inches. However, if the plaid design is 6 inches for each repeat, you will need 12 additional inches.

Pattern layout. The visual effect is

the most important consideration when working with plaids and stripes. It is one of the few times when appearance is as important as grain.

Before starting to pin the pattern to the fabric, look at it carefully and visualize it when completed. Will you want to emphasize one color or line in the plaid? The dominant stripe may be the largest, the strongest color, or any one you prefer.

- Place the center front and the center back on the dominant bar or a space between it. (Decide which you prefer.) Remember to use the center front marking and not the seam allowance edge.
- Determine where the crosswise stripes or plaid bars should be placed. Plan from the hem up—so the fold of the hem falls at the lower edge of the dominant bar at the center front. Check your skirt length with the pattern and mark the length on the tissue—then place this marking on the bottom of the dominant crosswise bar.

If there are pleats, parts of the design will be folded in. Find the most pleasing arrangement to you and make adjustments in the pattern if needed.

Planning. Hold the fabric up to you and experiment with placement of crosswise bars. Avoid a dominant bar at the fullest part of the bust if possible. Will a yoke affect the placement? Usually the dominant crosswise bar should run across the garment just below the shoulders or high on the chest. Try, if possible, to avoid placing darts on the most noticeable crosswise or lengthwise plaid bars.

Don't be afraid to let the design work for you. Consider a chevron ef-

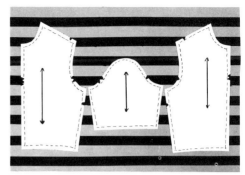

To carry a major stripe across the chest, sleeve top, and back, place matching notches of the sleeve cap and the armhole seam on the same stripe. It is not possible to match the sleeve, back, and front for more than a few inches because of the armhole curve and extra ease allowed in the sleeve. The shoulder seams will also match nicely. Notice that the underarm notches are also on the same stripe.

fect at a seam, a bias binding, or horizontal stripes for a yoke on a vertically striped dress. Pockets can be cut in any of three directions; lengthwise, crosswise, or bias.

First place the pattern correctly for the center front and center back. Then locate desired crossbars if using a plaid or horizontal stripe. Now match the bars at the *side seam* notches. It is not possible to match all seams because of darts and other details; only the most noticeable parts are important. Place the *waist* so the underarm notches fall on the same location of the design. (Remember to match at the seam line, not the pattern edge.) The upper part of the seam will not match if there is an underarm dart but this is not noticeable.

Match *skirt side notches* and line up the most pleasing lower edge pattern. Place the center of the *collar* pattern on the center of the same vertical bar used for the center back.

Check to see how the bars will appear at the front collar edges. Uneven designs will need a seam made in the center back of the collar and the fabric reversed so the front collar edges will be the same.

Place the dominant stripe down the center of the *sleeves*, starting at the shoulder marking. Remember to center the dominant stripe on cuffs unless you wish to place them on the bias or opposite grain for design purposes. Sleeves cannot match all around the armhole because of the ease allowance. The best effect results when the sleeve front is matched to the waist front at the underarm notch. This way the plaid continues across from the front straight around the sleeve to match with the black plaid. (See p. 593)

If you are in doubt about matching certain pattern pieces, lightly pencil the desired design on the tissue and then you can see immediately if you are matching the needed lines as you move the pattern about on the fabric.

One-way plaids create many problems. Always lay the pattern pieces in the same direction. You may need to make a center back and front seam if there is none so the stripes on one side of the center will be a mirror image of those on the other side. Place the fold line in the center of the dominant stripe and allow an additional 5⁄8″ for seam allowance when cutting.

For the sake of appearance, the placement of *buttonholes* may need to be changed from the one suggested on the pattern. On vertical stripes, they should be aligned on the same stripe. Bound buttonholes may be cut on the bias, vertical, or crosswise grain. For large, wide stripes,

match the color of each buttonhole to the stripe on the garment. Each buttonhole may be a different color but the total effect will be a smooth one.

Once the pattern is placed, the garment is put together in much the same manner as plain material.

Marking may be a little more difficult as tracing paper may not show evenly on multi-colored fabrics.

Joining seams. Seams will have to be pinned more carefully and often top-basted as shown on page 548. Seams sewn with thread in two colors of the fabric—one for the bobbin and one for the top—may be less noticeable.

BORDER PRINTS

Prints with a wide border require a special cutting layout that is always included in a pattern showing a bordered print on the envelope. The border runs along the lengthwise grain of the fabric. Therefore, the pattern is placed on the crosswise grain of the fabric if the border is placed at the lower edge of the skirt. The top of a garment may be cut from plain matching material, or from the border, reversed to form a yoke effect.

LARGE PRINTS

If the print has a one-way design, the pattern must be cut as directed for a napped fabric. Some large prints may be matched at the seamline or at least the dominant color sections placed adjacent to similar sections. It is important to plan the location of prints to balance colors and motifs. Often a certain design is selected for the center back and center front. Be especially careful about the part of the design placed at the largest part of the bust and hips.

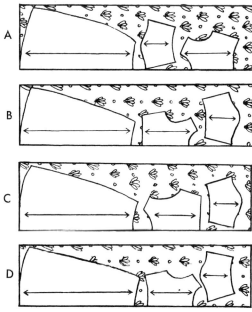

Which diagram is correct?

BONDED FABRICS

Bonded fabrics are made by permanently fusing a backing fabric to the outer or face fabric. The added body provides built-in shape retention and wrinkle resistance. Seams will not stretch or fray and little if any interfacing or underlining is needed.

The backing may be a tricot, taffeta, plain cotton, or similar fabric or it may be a layer of synthetic foam. The foam provides warmth without bulk or weight and is used primarily for outerwear. The tricot backing adds comfort and an "instant" lining to many fabrics.

When purchasing the fabric, check for a straight grain as these fabrics cannot be easily straightened. Select a pattern without intricate seams and details. Try to cut the facing and garment all in one to eliminate a seam.

Bonded fabrics seldom shrink so there is no need for preshrinking at home. Mark with tailor's tacks, chalk, or extra notches as a tracing wheel may leave marks.

Ripping may leave marks so hand baste when in doubt and fit carefully whenever necessary. If foam sticks to the machine or another fabric, place tissue paper next to the foam. Seams usually do not lie open easily. If the design is appropriate, press them open and top stitch close to the seam line. On slacks, shorts, unlined coats and jackets, a flat fell seam is used. Trim off the backing fabric close to the seam line before folding under the top section.

After stitching at seams and darts on bulky fabrics, separate backing and face fabric and trim off backing fabric close to stitching.

For bound buttonholes, remove backing fabric from buttonhole strip and use face fabric only.

Make a tailor's hem or top stitch seam binding to edge. Hem to backing fabric only, if it is of tricot. Foam will not hold the stitches.

STRETCH FABRICS

Stretch fabrics "give" with movement. Specially constructed yarns that stretch when pulled and then bounce back into shape are used. These fabrics add comfort to garments, hold their shape better and wrinkle less. They are not planned to restrain a person or to be made into a tight garment that must stretch to fit.

Some fabrics are woven with the stretch on the crosswise grain, from selvage to selvage; others, with stretch on the lengthwise grain. Crosswise stretch adds comfort and ease of movement as one bends forward, sits down, or moves one's shoulders. Lengthwise stretch fabrics are used for neat appearing pants.

Trousers of this type are kept in place with straps under the instep. Two-way stretch fabrics are also available but are used primarily for manufactured garments as swim suits and foundation garments.

When purchasing fabric. Since the stretch characteristic has been added to fabrics primarily for comfort in action plus slimness of fit, the direction in which the stretch is used in a garment is important as explained before. Pants can be made from crosswise stretch if the fabric is wide.

Be certain to relax the fabric before cutting it. It may have been rolled on a bolt in a stretched manner. Stretch the fabric gently and lay it smooth on a flat surface to relax for 24 hours. It is best to pre-shrink it if this has not been previously done.

Do not line or interface the garment with regular fabric—use stretch linings.

Pattern selection. Select your usual size pattern. You may not need as much ease as usual so the garment can be fitted a little closer to the body but a smaller size will be too tight. Patterns that require many seams defeat the purpose of the stretch as the seams make it firm.

Pattern layout and cutting. Lay the pattern pieces on the fabric in the direction of the desired stretch. Be certain that facings go in the same direction as the pieces to which they will be attached. Belts and waistbands should be placed in the non-stretch direction.

When cutting, do not allow the fabric to hang over the edges of the cutting table as it will be distorted. Avoid stretching the fabric as you work. Place pins at right angles to the direction of the stretch.

Machine stitching. Stitch with a balanced tension using small stitches, stretching fabric very slightly while stitching. Avoid heavy pressure as this distorts the natural relaxed tension of the fabric. A zigzag stitch is desirable, in most cases, however a textured nylon thread may be used with a regular stitch.

Seams not on the "stretch" direction are stitched in a conventional manner. Seams on the stretch direction require special handling. Clip the basting at 4-inch intervals. As you stitch, stretch the fabric by holding it behind and in front of the presser foot. In other words, the fabric must be held under tension while it is being stitched. Medium or slow speed is required. Seams stitched in this manner will recover their original dimension when pressed; yet, when stretched to the maximum capacity of the fabric, they will not break.

Zippers can be sewn in the conventional manner. Do not stretch the fabric as the zipper tape will not stretch. Buttonholes are made in the non-stretch direction. A small patch of iron-on or closely woven interfacing is needed to stay them.

Hems. The use of regular seam binding will destroy the stretch properties and result in a rigid look. Zigzag the raw edges, overcast by hand, or use bias seam binding. Sew in place loosely with catch or slip stitches.

SHEERS

Sheers may be soft as chiffon, crisp as organdy, or in-between as voile, lawn, and dimity. Sheers are easily handled, with the exception of chiffon, but they require special finishing techniques to maintain their airy, feminine appearance.

Pattern and fabric selection. Choose a pattern with as few seams as possible. Each seam appears darker than the fabric itself and detracts from the total appearance. A full gathered or pleated skirt can be cut from the crosswise grain if the fabric hangs nicely in that direction. You may want to purchase additional fabric to allow for a wide or double hem which adds body and a dressmaker finish to full skirts.

Crisp sheers need no special care when *machine sewing* but soft sheers slip easily. Basting is often necessary and tissue paper may need to be placed under the seams during stitching. It can be easily removed.

Seams should be as invisible as possible with no raw threads showing. Narrow French seams are desirable. Another method is to make a plain seam and place a second row of stitching ⅛″ from the seamline. Trim the seam allowance close to this stitching.

Eliminate *facings* whenever possible. A binding of self material makes a neat edge, or the entire bodice may be lined with the same fabric if it has no design.

A *double hem* is preferred, with the raw edge in the bottom fold. Turn the hem up the desired width, then turn it up again so the raw edge is in the fold. Slip stitch loosely to the garment. A deep hem of 8″ or more may be flattering if the skirt is cut full and straight.

Another hemming method is to make a very narrow hem, similar to a hand rolled one. (See p. 560.) Fold the fabric to the wrong side ⅛″ outside the marked hemline and press. Stitch as close to the edge as possible. Trim off excess fabric close to the stitching. Turn the stitched edge to the wrong side again, press, and stitch close to the edge.

DURABLE PRESS

The terms "durable press" and "permanent press" are used interchangeably to describe finishes applied to fabrics to eliminate the need for ironing after laundering. Durable press fabrics available for home sewing are not the same as those used in ready-to-wear fashions. Garments you purchase have been treated in special ovens to permanently form pleats, creases, seams, and hems. This process is not available to home sewers.

Advantages of the fabric available to home sewers is that alterations can be made when necessary, but commercially set garments cannot be changed.

There are no complicated sewing techniques involved but a few differences between fabrics with and without these finishes are apparent. No amount of pulling, steaming, or pressing will straighten off-grain fabrics so check the printing of any designs before purchasing the fabric. If the print is not on grain, the finished appearance will not be correct. Preshrink all interfacings, underlinings, and trim unless you are certain they will not shrink. Permanent press fabrics do not shrink and if attached to fabrics that do, the smooth appearance will be lost.

Machine sewing may result in puckering if the tension and stitches are not adjusted properly for the fabric being used. Select mercerized cotton thread or a cotton with polyester core thread.

The tension may need to be loosened when sewing with wash-and-wear and durable press fabrics. If a ripple forms as in A, loosen presser bar screw. If the seam is puckered as in B, loosen top tension and bobbin screw. Make adjustments until you have a smooth seam (C) that forms no ripple.

Medium to long stitches with a slightly loose tension will result in less puckering if the thread shrinks when washed. Use a fine needle with a sharp point. A regular throat plate with a small round hole rather than the oval hole used for zigzag stitching is necessary.

Durable press fabrics ravel little, if at all. Pinking is usually a good finish for seams, hem, and facing edges. If garments will be laundered frequently, a row of straight or zigzag machine stitching close to the seam edge will prevent fraying.

Understitching of facings helps keep them from rolling to the outside.

Worked buttonholes (machine or hand) are more satisfactory than bound.

Zipper tapes must be preshrunk. (Zipper tapes have a tendency to shrink and cause puckering in the seam line.) To shrink, soak in very hot water for 10 minutes. Allow to dry without stretching; or wash and dry in automatic washer and dryer. When inserting the zipper, ease the tape slightly in the seam.

During sewing, use an iron set at low or synthetic for touch-up pressing. When garment is finished, give it a final press with hot or cotton setting and steam or use a damp press cloth. Fabrics are often heat sensitive so be sure to test first on a fabric scrap.

KNITTED FABRICS

Knitted fabrics are adaptable to almost any type of use. For those with a bonded lining, refer to page 595 for additional suggestions. Because of the amount of stretch in knit fabrics, avoid a circular or bias cut skirt unless your fabric has a bonded lining. Look for a pattern with few seams and simple lines.

To determine the lengthwise grain, locate a continuous wale or rib and mark it with chalk or a basting stitch. To locate the crosswise grain follow a row of loops across the width of the fabric. If the fabric is made in a tubular form, cut it open along a lengthwise rib. Do not use the fold line which is usually off grain.

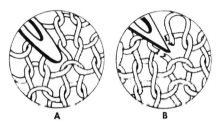

A   B

Use a ball point needle, which pushes aside the fabric threads (A). A regular needle may pierce them (B). A fresh needle for each garment minimizes snags and skipped stitches.

Use a throat plate with a small hole for straight stitching to keep fabric from getting caught as the needle passes through it.

For most knits, you can use a straight stitch, 12–15 per inch. Use a second line of stitching alongside the first for areas of stress such as a crotch seam. Use narrow zigzag stitch for stretchable knits.

Stay-stitching is important with these fabrics, unless bonded. Reinforce shoulder and waist line seams with twill tape or seam binding.

Let the garment hang at least 24 hours before marking the hemline. The tailor's hem gives an inconspicuous seam finish.

Vinyls and Plastic Films

Vinyls and plastic films can be made into many professional-looking garments and articles for the home. The waterproof quality of vinyl makes it a natural for rainwear and the novelty appearance makes it popular for accessories of all types. There are three types of vinyl on the market—transparent film, opaque with a knit backing, and a vinyl-coated fabric. All are sewn in a similar manner with a few exceptions.

Simple, straight lined patterns are best. Vinyl cannot be eased in seams and darts. Knit-back vinyl is more flexible than the others, so with care it is possible to set in sleeves. Raglan and kimono sleeves without an underarm gusset are easiest to handle.

Make all alterations before cutting out the pattern. Ripping to change the fit will leave marks. Keep in mind that pins also will leave marks that will not disappear, so either pin only in the seam allowance, use masking tape, or hold pattern pieces in place with weights. Markings can be made with chalk or grease pencil.

Machine stitching should be 8 to 10 stitches per inch; vinyl will tear if sewn with small stitches. Place double-faced cellophane tape between layers to be stitched or join them with masking tape or paper clips on the outside. Vinyl often sticks to itself or other surfaces so use a strip of tissue paper between the vinyl and the metal throat plate of the sewing machine.

You cannot press vinyl with an iron. Finger press (rub edges with your fingernail or the dull edge of a shears) and plan to make top-stitched or welt seams. Rubber cement will also hold back seam allowances if the seam must be pressed open.

Handworked buttonholes or machine-made ones are possible. (Knit-back vinyl may stretch with the use of a buttonhole attachment so practice on a sample first.)

Select one of the special fabrics listed in this chapter. Obtain samples and experiment with seams and machine adjustments. Demonstrate to the class effective ways to work with this type of fabric. It is a good idea if each class member selects a different type of fabric so you can learn from each other's report.

Visit a fabric store or the fabric section of a large department store. Talk with the buyer or a salesperson about the latest fabrics on the market which may require special handling. Report to the class.

Underlinings and interlinings are usually eliminated. Remember that vinyl cannot be drycleaned so if lining is used, be sure it is washable.

Hems may be held up with tape or glued in place. Top-stitching, ½ to 1 inch from the fold, makes a good finish for some hems. Knit-back vinyl and some vinyl coated fabrics can be hemmed with hand stitching. Pick up one or two threads in the backing, and use a tailor's hem method. (See p. 563.)

Excess seam allowance must be trimmed away and layered whenever possible to lessen extra bulk.

LEARNING TO FIT A GARMENT

Much of the satisfaction with your finished garment depends upon how well it fits. If it is too large or too tight, it can make you appear larger. It can call attention to or de-emphasize figure irregularities. It can make a garment appear fashionable or out-of-style, smart or dowdy. No matter how good the stitching is, a garment which does not fit will not make a good appearance. It may also be uncomfortable to wear and it is difficult to appear poised and well dressed if a garment binds or pulls. If you will take time to learn how to fit your blouse or skirt, you will be better able to fit other clothing articles you may make or buy in the future.

Learn to recognize fitting problems of others in your class and how to solve them. Few people stay the same size or shape as most change with age and new fitting problems develop. Do not let your partner be the only one to learn how to fit you properly. Someday you will be on your own.

Learn to make alterations on the pattern before cutting whenever possible. If the pattern has been altered properly and the grain line kept in place through correct cutting and stitching, fitting alterations will be kept to a minimum. Because a paper pattern does not handle or drape on the body exactly the same way as fabric does, you can expect minor fitting problems.

Experts often cut a pattern of an inexpensive fabric like muslin and machine baste it together to check the fit. After altering the muslin to fit, they use it as a pattern for the garment fabric.

WHEN TO FIT

How often you will need to check the fit of a garment while sewing will depend upon the style of the garment and your own figure problems. A fitted skirt should be checked before sewing the seams but a gathered or circular skirt will not need to be fitted until it is time to apply the waistband. Another fitting will be needed for the correct hem length.

It is wise to check the placement of underarm or waist darts before stitching them permanently. Check the total fit of the waist before the sleeves and collar are attached. When making a dress, baste the bodice to the skirt and check for final total fit before completing the garment and inserting the zipper and other fasteners.

Some styles are so complicated that the entire garment must be basted together in order that the effect and fit can be correctly judged. This is seldom necessary for today's fashions.

As you come to know your own figure and how to select patterns wisely, you will learn when you need to check the fit of a garment before proceeding. Fitting too often can be time consuming and result in a tired looking garment but on the other hand, not fitting when necessary may result in tedious ripping and a garment that does not appear to be made for you. Consider your special needs and the garment style as you plan when to check the fit of the garment.

How to Check for Proper Fitting

- Wear the type of undergarments and shoes you will wear with the garment. A dress or pants fitted in stocking feet will hang differently when worn with shoes.
- Fit before a large mirror—a triple mirror is desirable. Have a partner help you whenever possible but learn what adjustments she makes so you will know what to do in the future.
- Pin the openings together along the seam line or the center front line. Do not fit with just one sleeve in or

with just one side seam sewn . . . the entire garment will be pulled out of line.

- Before checking for the hem length, let the garment remain on a hanger for a day or more to give the bias parts a time to adjust. This is also a wise precaution before fitting the skirt to the garment top.

- Don't cut off any fabric until you are sure you are correct. It is best to fit, pin the changes, rebaste, and try on again to check before you cut. Once the cloth is cut, you can't put it back in case you are wrong.

- Try the garment on, right side out. Almost no one is equal on both sides of the body and if you try on the garment wrong side out, you are fitting the fabric to the wrong side of the body. For example, if your left hip is one inch larger than your right hip and you try on the skirt wrong side out, you will end up with a skirt that is two inches too large for the right hip and too small for the left hip. It may be easier to change the seams if the garment is inside out but the final results will not be accurate.

- *To fit a garment right side out . . .* Pin the new seam or darts from the right side. Then mark the pins with chalk on both sides . . . remove the pins and match the chalked lines. Rebaste and try on.

Another method is to slip-pin. Turn under one side along the desired seam allowance and pin the fold down over the other side, meeting the new seamline. This may sound confusing but it is easy with practice. Then you can slip baste the seam together (see page 548) and later stitch on the machine from the wrong side.

WHAT SHOULD YOU LOOK
FOR IN FITTING?

- Check the grain line. Crosswise yarns are parallel to the floor at the bust and hip line, unless there is an unusual style detail. If the crosswise grain droops, an alteration is needed. The lengthwise yarns should go straight up and down and not off to an angle. The lengthwise yarns in the sleeve cap lie in the direction of the arm when it hangs straight at the side. Usually the crosswise yarns of the top of the sleeve are also parallel to the floor. Straighten your grain lines, vertically and horizontally on the figure and you will have corrected your fitting problems. (Can you think of patterns where the details make an exception?)
- Are the seams crooked? Do they slant to one side or do they appear to wiggle?
- Are there unwanted wrinkles or too much fullness?
- Is the center front or center back out of line?
- Next check the placement of the darts—do they point to the fullest area of the body and not extend beyond it?
- Does the garment seem tight and restricting or is it too loose? Is there room enough across the shoulders for you to bend over without pulling out the seams? How does the skirt behave when you sit down?
- Check the fit of the shoulders. Does the fit conform to the prevailing fashion? Sometimes narrow shoulders are in style and other times wide shoulders are preferred.
- Check the neckline—is it tight and binding or is it sagging? If it seems too snug in a pattern or unfinished garment, it may be because of the width of the seam allowance which will be taken up in the seam.

HOW TO CORRECT COMMON
FITTING PROBLEMS

- Determine what is wrong.
- Analyze what causes the undesirable effect.
- Decide upon a remedy based on changes in seams, darts, or tucks that can correct grain lines and restore desired smoothness and fit to the garment.
- Use the simplest method for alteration.
- Try to decide how you could have avoided this in pattern alterations so you will not have this problem in the future.

Lengthwise wrinkles usually mean the garment is too wide.

Crosswise wrinkles indicate too much length.

Diagonal wrinkles indicate the need for shoulder, sleeve, or underarm alterations. Follow the diagonal to locate the problem areas.

One of the most common adjustments necessary is in direction of the *underarm or waist dart*. It should point to the fullest part of the bust but not extend beyond it.

The easiest way to change the location of a dart is to tip the point. Use the same marks at the seamline but pin the dart to the new tip.

If this results in a downward slant to the dart, it will give a drooped effect to the bustline. Then it is better to relocate the dart and draw in a new dart location. Draw a line through the center of the dart to be moved. Then draw another line parallel to the first at the location to which the dart is to be changed. This is the center of the new dart. If the stitching lines of the dart are straight, you can measure them at their widest part, transfer this measurement, and draw the new stitching lines at each side of the new center dart line. If the stitching lines are curved, they can be traced from the original dart

and then retraced around the new center dart line.

Shorten the waistline dart if it is too high toward the bustline.

See illustrations of common fitting problems and the suggested adjustments on pages 603 to 607.

A GARMENT FITS WELL WHEN

- There is ample room throughout with no unnecessary wrinkles or bulges.
- The center front and center back grain lines hang perpendicular to the floor.
- Crosswise yarns are parallel to the floor at the center front, back shoulder, and hip lines.
- Side seams hang straight down and do not swing to the back or front.
- The waistline seam encircles the body at the smallest part of the waist with 1″ ease. It dips slightly in front following the natural waist curve.
- Armhole seams are vertical from the top of the shoulder to halfway down the armhole unless the style calls for an extended shoulder.
- Lengthwise grain in center of sleeve is perpendicular to the floor and does not swing forward or backward.
- Neckline lies close to the body: it does not bind or gap.
- Bustline darts point toward the bust but end before the fullest part.
- Some folds will form in a dress when the wearer moves, but when she sits or stands still, there will be no unbecoming folds.
- A properly fitted garment is comfortable when the wearer stands, sits, and moves around. It is snug where fashion demands but never feels tight or strained.

Common Fitting Problems

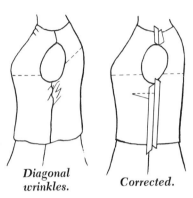

Diagonal wrinkles.   *Corrected.*

Diagonal wrinkles fall from shoulder blade to underarm. The blouse pulls up in the center back and at the lower edge. The front neckline may be pulled back. Round shoulders and prominent shoulder blades may cause this difficulty. Rip the shoulder seams until the grain of the fabric is straight across the upper back. Let out the seam at the neckline and take it in at the armhole. Rip the underarm seams and trim out the armhole. If there is not enough fabric, you may need to add a back shoulder yoke.

Lower edge of skirt pokes out in front. The side seams swing forward and diagonal wrinkles extend from the center front of waistline to the hem. The blouse may be so short in the front that it pulls up the grain of fabric in the skirt. To correct this difficulty, rip the side seams and the front waistline seam. Lift the front of the skirt at the sides until the grain of the fabric is straight across the hipline

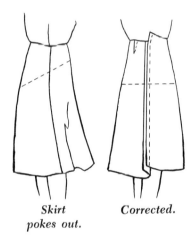

Skirt pokes out.   *Corrected.*

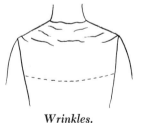

Wrinkles.

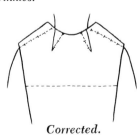

Corrected.

Wrinkles across the back of neck. The back of the dress across the shoulders is too tight or the neck may be too high. A full neck may cause the difficulty. Cut the neckline deeper at the back, and put darts in the neckline. It may be necessary to open the shoulder seam and take up more of the back seam near the neckline and less at the armhole. Notice the improvement in grainline direction the alteration has made.

COMMON FITTING PROBLEMS
(Continued)

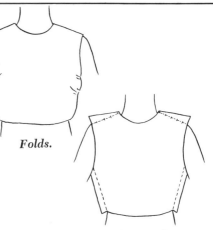

Folds.

Corrected.

Folds at the armhole in front near the underarm seam. A person with a hollow chest, flat bust, or round shoulders is often shorter between the shoulder and front waistline than the pattern. Therefore the dress sags below the bust. Do NOT try to take off excess length by cutting off the waistline, thus destroying the crosswise grain.

Twist.   *Corrected.*

Skirt seams twist to one side. Skirt seams may twist to the side for either of two reasons or a combination of both. If the skirt hem is uneven on one side, the problem is probably caused by one hip being larger or higher than the other. To correct this, first take off the waistband. Then lift the skirt up on the smaller side until the seams hang straight. Pin in the seams until the skirt fits smoothly at the waist and hips. Tie a cord around the natural waist and mark a new waistline all around. Replace the waistband and re-hem the skirt. Another reason is that a part of the skirt may not have been cut on the straight of the goods. The only way to alter this is to recut the skirt, if the style permits.

Skirt wrinkles across small of back. If the skirt wrinkles across the small of the back, it may be too tight across the hips or too long from the waist to the hips. Try letting out the side seams at the fullest part of the hip and see if this corrects it. Otherwise, rip the waistband across the back from side seam to side seam. Lift the skirt until the wrinkles disappear (the grain will probably straighten also). Mark the new waistline location with pins or chalk and replace the waistband.

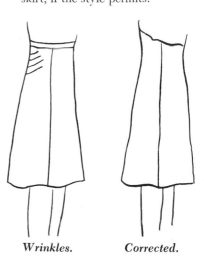

Wrinkles.   *Corrected.*

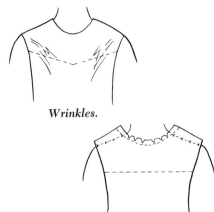

Wrinkles.

Corrected.

Diagonal wrinkles from shoulder to center back or front. The shoulder seam stands up from the shoulder near the base of the neck. The shoulders are too square for shoulder line of garment. Rip the shoulder seam and lift it at the neck until the wrinkles are removed. Slope the seam to the shoulder tip. If this is a high necked dress and this adjustment makes the neck a trifle too small, clip the neckline. Avoid clipping into the seam line.

Wrinkles from the side of the neck toward armholes. The wrinkles form because the base of the neck is large or the shoulders slope more than the pattern provided. Clip the neck edge in a few places. Or if the shoulder seam is deep enough, let it out at the base of the neck and take a deeper seam as it slopes to the tip of the shoulder. If the armhole is too tight under the arm, alter.

Wrinkles.

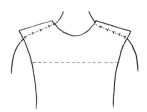

Corrected.

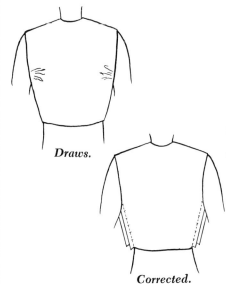

Draws.

Corrected.

Blouse draws at underarm seam just below the armhole. The pattern may be too small at the bust line, or the person have a large muscle across the back near the underarm. Rip the underarm seams, and let them out until the width across the back is comfortable. Do not change the front seam allowance. It may be necessary to change the shoulder seams. Lift the sleeve edge of the shoulder seam.

COMMON FITTING PROBLEMS
(Continued)

Diagonal wrinkles from bust line to underarm waistline. The lower front edge of the blouse swings out and up. The underarm seam swings forward. This may be caused by a prominent bust or a very erect figure. When there is sufficient length, rip open the underarm and shoulder seams. Taper the seam allowance on the front shoulder to ¼ inch at the neck edge. Add one or more small darts at the underarm.

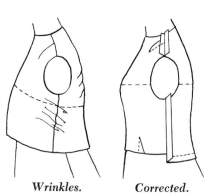

Wrinkles.   *Corrected.*

 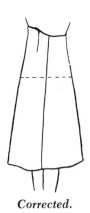

Cups.   *Corrected.*

Skirt cups in the back and side seams swing forward. The side of the skirt may be too long between the waist and hips, permitting the grain of the fabric to drop at the hipline. Raise the skirt at the waistline until the grain of the goods is straight across at the hips.

Lower edge of the skirt swings out at the back. The side seams swing back. This may be caused by a sway-back and large hips. Rip the skirt and waist apart, and lift the front and side gores of the skirt until the crosswise grain of the goods is straight all around the hip line. Trim off extra fabric at the waistline.

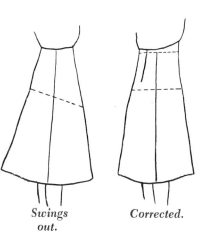

Swings out.   *Corrected.*

Each garment you make is an exciting challenge, because the results are so close to your heart. You can go slowly until you have mastered each new experience and learn the best ways to start more difficult projects. But even simple garments can do ever so much for you—if you "let" them!

Sewing requires *more than skill* in construction processes. Take an inventory of your personal qualities or personality traits. *Eagerness* will carry you along over the rough spots to the completion of the garment. *Imagination* will help you visualize the finished portions of the garment as well as the entire garment. *Cleverness* in contriving some individual finish or trim will make your garment distinctive and help you anticipate each construction process. *Carefulness* will help you triumph over the little problems.

There are a few fundamental processes with which a beginning seamstress should be familiar and use until she becomes experienced. Pinning and basting will be important, even if you do not always use them with shortcut methods. You will learn many construction techniques whose mastery will determine your progress. As you sew, you will acquire devices and methods which will secure specific effects or results you desire. Different methods will be used for various fabrics and various styles of garments.

There is always more than one way to do a task. What is easy for you may be difficult for another girl. If you are willing to learn other methods than those you have always followed, you may discover the real joy of wearing fine, handmade garments.

Home sewing takes time and energy. But so does shopping for and altering ready-made clothing. A simple garment can often be made in the time it takes to shop several stores to find the right combination of style, fabric, and size. In addition, research studies have shown that the time needed for making most garments can be reduced by almost half and the finished results will be as satisfactory as with former time consuming methods. As you learn to sew, try to use the method which is the fastest but which also gives the results you desire. Few women have as much time as they want, and need, and learning to sew as quickly as possible will result in more time to spend with your family or in other activities.

What Is a Shortcut?

A shortcut in sewing is a device or technique that should save time and energy and produce a neat finish. But experience, that makes a short cut possible for a professional seamstress, may be lacking for you. Accurate methods do not seem like a short cut, yet they are! The girl who sews accurately and never has to rip out or correct many other mistakes may finish her garment before a girl who uses clever "shortcuts" but makes errors. Remember, you can spend more time ripping machine stitches than needed if you were more accurate.

• FABRICS

The right selection of a fabric is a major time saver. Don't waste your time on a poor quality fabric. Choose firmly woven cloth that does not ravel easily, that will stay in place, and not be slippery to handle.

Select preshrunk fabrics that are grain perfect and ready for use.

Avoid plaids, large checks, and prints that are difficult to match. Avoid fabrics that are printed or finished off grain and those that will need additional seam finishing that takes time.

• PATTERNS

Patterns labeled easy-to-sew can usually be made quickly. Select a pattern with few pieces and avoid time consuming details as underarm gussets, welt pockets, and unusual plackets. Select the right size to cut down on alterations. If you make two or more garments from the same pattern at the same time, you can work faster and if the fabrics selected are different, no one but you will know the pattern is the same. Select fabrics that use the same color thread so that you will not lose time rethreading the machine.

• EQUIPMENT

Learn to use your equipment well and keep it in good repair. If you have to search all over the house for your shears, only to find them too dull to cut easily, much of the time saved by other methods will be lost. Any sewing machine, old or new, can help you save time if it is in good repair. Keep the dust and lint removed and oil it as needed to keep it in good condition. "Press as you sew" is important so arrange to have ironing equipment easily available. Arrange your large sewing equipment so that you can sit in one place and machine sew, hand sew, and press. See suggested arrangement, on this page. A seam gauge is essential so that seam allowances will be the

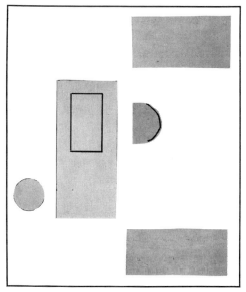

A well arranged sewing center with the sewing machine in the center of the U, a work surface for cutting out and hand sewing on one side, a pressing surface on the other, and good light close by. Supplies are kept in drawers at hand.

same thus ensuring easy matching . . . it can also be used for guide lines for many sewing methods as explained later.

A pin cushion attached to your machine is helpful as is one worn on your wrist. For the ripping that is necessary despite careful work, have a seam ripper available.

• PATTERN CUTTING AND MARKING

Time must be taken in correct placement of pattern pieces. Some sewers prefer to anchor the pattern with small weights rather than pins.

Notches, center front and center back, fold lines, and the dart markings that come along seam lines can be quickly marked with a short clip into the seam allowance. Do not use this method for fabrics that fray easily or until you are skilled so you will not cut too far.

Cutting a small outward notch at these places is also a quick way to mark the fabric which will have meaning when you understand patterns well. These methods can save marking time and also sewing time as the clip or notch is clearly visible from both sides of the fabric.

Press marking may be used to mark straight lines, such as hems, darts, tucks, and pleats on firmly woven fabrics. (See page 495.)

• STAY-STITCHING

The time spent stay-stitching bias edges to prevent stretching is a short cut as it simplifies further construction processes. (See p. 545.)

• SEWING

Learn the value of understitching facings, cuffs, collars and at other places. Not only is the edge kept in place, but pressing may not be necessary.

Many seams can be pressed open by pulling them over a firm edge as that of a table or the machine.

Learn to secure thread ends, when necessary, with lockstitching. (See p 518.) Tieing threads and retracing are time consumers. Use the machine thread cutter to keep excess threads cut. Whenever possible, stitch several pieces right after each other and clip the threads between them later.

Neck and sleeve facings can be held in place without hand sewing by stitching along the shoulder and underarm seamline on the right side.

Use your seam gauge and large stitches to mark the turning line for yoke and pocket edges. A quick stitching along these edges without tieing thread ends provides an accu-

Investigate time-saving equipment and time-saving construction methods other than those listed in this book which do not sacrifice quality. Question women who sew and read current literature on the topic. Report your findings to the class. Perhaps you will want to prepare a demonstration of one or more ideas.

rate line for turning under the edges. The stitching can be left in the fabric if the thread matches.

Straight hems in many fabrics can be stitched inconspicuously and quickly using the blindstitch attachment or the blind-hemming method on a traditional sewing machine. See page 564.

Most important *plan*, before you begin to sew! First, plan the *entire construction* of your garment. Then you can decide how you will proceed with each unit.

Remember, the time spent on choosing a design that will please you cannot be "cut short," and all careful planning takes time. Otherwise, short-cut construction methods do no good, because you would not like the finished garment.

IMPROVING READY-MADE CLOTHING, NEW AND OLD

Seldom can you find a ready-made garment that fits perfectly, has good lines for you, is of the right fabric and color, has good workmanship, all for the price you want to pay. You may have to compromise . . . you can't change the color or style of fabric very easily but you can improve the fit, workmanship, and make simple design changes to suit you. If you are able to make needed alterations, correct careless workmanship, or change buttons or other trim to improve the garment, you will more often have just what you want. Knowing how to do these things is helpful to any person. A tailor is not always available and the cost of these services may be more than the garment is worth to you; if you can make these changes yourself, you can have your purchases ready for use sooner and you will save the alteration money to be used for additional clothing or other purposes.

Not everyone will have the time or desire to construct garments, but most people are responsible for selecting and caring for clothing for themselves and their families. One of the major reasons for learning to sew a simple garment is to be better able to judge good workmanship and know how to make needed changes in ready-made clothing. You can learn to make these improvements without learning how to make a garment. However, constructing one or two simple articles helps in understanding how ready-made garments are made and what changes can be sensibly made; and the skills you learned in making garments are similar to those used for improving or remodeling ready-made clothing.

Even if a garment fits you perfectly when it is bought, figures and styles change and you may need to make adjustments in size and hem length later. Buttons pop off, seams split open, hems become loose, and holes develop. Very few people can afford to discard garments just because of these minor problems and few would want to stop wearing a favorite dress for these reasons. Some clothing is no longer wearable because of fashion changes or becomes tiring due to frequent wear. Many of these can be easily rejuvenated or made over for other family members, freeing money for other uses. You will also experience a feeling of creativity and satisfaction. A wise woman knows how to improve ready-made clothing as well as how to renovate clothing no longer in use.

IMPROVING READY-MADE GARMENTS BEFORE WEARING

Manufacturers design and construct most clothing for the mass market. This means that the style, fit, and cost must be suitable for many people and cannot be planned to suit individual figure variations or design preferences. (Very expensive clothing is occasionally made in limited quantities to meet individual needs.)

Improving the design. Often the only difference between an expensive and a less expensive garment is the trim. If the basic garment is what you want, you may find it worthwhile to replace the buttons with the design and quality you prefer. Scarfs of unflattering color or designs can be discarded for new ones. Consider replacing belts of poor material. Unless you can obtain a dress at a reduced price, it doesn't make sense to change major design elements.

Improving the workmanship. Because so many garments are made at a time, it is difficult for manufacturers to inspect for loose buttons, split seams, or dangling threads. Repairing this workmanship and making reinforcements when needed will result in a better appearing garment and may prevent repairs later.

Check over your ready-made garments before wearing them. Even on the most expensive garments the *fastenings and trimmings* may need to be sewn on more securely. Buttons, snap fasteners, and hooks all need to be checked. On thin or loosely woven fabrics, add a piece of fabric tape for reinforcement on the underside of the garment under buttons.

Frayed buttonholes may need to be reinforced or a few stitches taken at the end so they will not gap.

Replace missing or poorly made *belt loops* with new ones made from matching thread. (See p. 574.)

Narrow or loosely stitched *seams* pull out easily with wear or washing. Strengthen by machine stitching on the original seam line. If the fabric is also fraying, another row of stitching near the cut edge helps. Or you can do some rapid overcasting by hand or with a zigzag machine attachment.

Reinforce raglan or kimono underarm seams with tape as shown on page 275.

Secure *dangling threads* by pulling to the inside of the garment and tieing. Clip excess threads for a neat finish.

Washable *collars and cuffs* that have been basted in place will be easier to care for if they are removed and snap fasteners applied.

Lingerie tapes with a snap at one end attached to shoulder seams of wide-necked dresses hold lingerie straps out of sight.

Labels which show through sheer fabrics or which pop up at the back of the neckline should be clipped out. If they contain helpful information for the care of the garment, resew them in a less noticeable place.

Overcast or stitch down any loose or fraying edges of a *placket* since these might be easily caught in a zipper.

Reinforce with extra stitching or tape any *points of strain* to prevent stretching. Examples are pocket corners and slits or pleats in narrow skirts.

Improving the fit. Fitting changes are necessary or desirable in a large percentage of garments which are bought ready-made. Garments are made to fit the average person and although your general measurements may be similar to those for which a particular garment is sized, you may be longer or shorter waisted, prefer your skirts a different length, or have some figure irregularity so that an adjustment in the fit of the garment will improve its comfort and enhance its appearance.

Many stores provide an alteration department for this service at an extra fee. However, even though you plan to alter a garment yourself, often a fitter will pin-fit it for you without charge. If in doubt about whether fitting changes are possible, the fitter may be able to advise you.

Learn to recognize which alterations are simple and which are impossible to attempt. Some alterations require more time and skill than is practical except for the very skilled person. Avoid changes that involve the neckline, shoulder seam, and armhole. Generally, the skirt is easier to change than the waist.

Some alterations are not possible. You can not let out seams with narrow or clipped seam allowances nor can you let out a dart that has been clipped or slashed. Some fabrics such as those with a permanent press finish are permanently marked by stitching or pressing so the original seam lines will always show.

Some changes are easily done such as shortening a skirt or leveling an uneven hemline. Letting out seams, changing darts, or resetting zippers are more difficult but can be done successfully.

Usually, it is easier to take in than to let out.

Remember, it is often harder to alter a ready-made garment than to make a new one. Consider whether or not the time and effort spent is worth it.

To change the skirt length, first rip out the present stitching. Press the lower part of the skirt flat, following the fabric grain. Then put skirt on, decide on the desired length, mark the distance from the floor, and re-hem as if you were making the skirt. (Page 561) You may have to remove the seam tape if the hem is uneven or too wide, and replace it at the correct location.

Do not attempt to turn up the hem only in certain places. The result will be a botchy, poor appearance.

If the hem width is too narrow, you may need to face it.

To change the fit of a skirt band, do not attempt to move the buttons or hooks and eyes unless only a very small amount of change is needed. A gap or fabric bulge will result at the closing which is not attractive. The band should be removed, fitted, and either taken in or made longer. (A piecing can often be added which will not show if in the underpart.) Refit the skirt seams and darts as needed and reapply the waistband. If adjustments have to be made on the zipper placement, see pages 575 and 576.

To change the location of a waist-line dress seam, check to see if there is enough material at the lower edge for lengthening. If it needs changing in only one place as the small of the back or the center front, tie a tape around your waist and mark with chalk the desired waistline location. Rip the waistline seam a few inches beyond where the change needs to be made so there will be a smooth transition from the former to the new location. Restitch the seam.

It it needs shortening all around, rip out the zipper and the waistline seam. Try on the bodice and determine the correct location of the waistline. Restitch the seam and reset the zipper.

To change the hip size, rip the skirt from the top of waistband. Fit carefully and make identical changes in the seams on both sides, unless your hips differ in size. Trying to make all the changes on one side to avoid removing the zipper will result in a skirt that does not hang properly. You may be able to make adjustments in the center front and center back seams if the skirt has a side zipper. Sometimes all the adjustments can be made below the waistline so that it will not be necessary to remove the waistband or waist top.

To alter a waistline size, it may not be necessary to remove the zipper. If only minor adjustments are needed in size, it may be possible to rip the waistline seam where the darts are located; let out or take in as needed, or restitch the seam. Waistline darts are often located near skirt pleats and these also can be adjusted easily in size.

Visit a department store with an alteration service. Secure a list of the cost of common alterations. Report to the class. You may also want to talk with the fitter about fitting changes she does not recommend and those that she feels are sensible. Find out how long a time is required to complete each alteration.

Bring to class a new garment that you or a family member has recently purchased. Look it over to determine how the workmanship can be improved before wearing to prevent major repairs later and to help its appearance.

Come to class prepared to tell others about some garment you or someone you know has purchased and improved by slight changes.

To re-set zippers. Seldom is there a need to change a zipper although occasionally one may "break" in some manner and will have to be replaced. Because of other alterations however, the zipper often is removed and then replaced. For directions, see pages 575 and 576.

Other alterations are described on page 281.

BRINGING MY WARDROBE UP TO DATE

Do you want more clothes than are possible on your clothing budget?

The clothing needs in many families often exceed the clothing budget. You may have discovered this when you tried to balance the gaps in your wardrobe with the money available for new clothing. Instead of daydreaming about the many clothes you would like to have, consider how your wardrobe may be increased by

remodeling garments now out of circulation.

Fortunately there are many ways of reconditioning old garments to make them smart and serviceable again. Except for certain drastic years of change, fashion usually provides us with styles that lend themselves to renovation. Check your wardrobe inventory and take a second look at those garments which cannot be worn in their present condition and yet seem too good to discard. Older garments may be remade for a younger member of your family, or you may restyle them for your use.

Are there some garments that may be brought up-to-date with minor changes or with the addition of new accessories by using your energy and ingenuity?

Your previous training in construction and in judgment will help you to increase your wardrobe and stretch your clothing budget.

What changes will be made?

You may have some garments that cannot be worn unless you refit them, change some parts; or rip them apart, redesign, and remake. Perhaps others merely need to be worn in different combinations. The skirt you have never enjoyed may be satisfactory when worn with a different blouse or sweater.

Make a list of the garments you do not wear. Try on each garment before a full-length mirror, and observe the style, fit, becomingness, durability, and neatness of the fabric. *Keep a record* of suggested changes for each garment.

Analyze each garment carefully to find the features that give it an outmoded look. Then check current

614

fashion magazines and window shop for attractive style trends. A successful remodeled garment will be becoming to the wearer in line, color, and fabric texture.

A garment that *does not fit well* may require redesigning. Restyling a garment *for yourself* will take less time than remaking it *for a smaller person*. However, there may be worn places that make it undesirable for you. Then redesigning the garment for a smaller person is practical.

BRINGING CLOTHES UP-TO-DATE WITH MINOR CHANGES

Often only minor changes or the addition of accessories will bring many garments up-to-date. Simple alterations such as changing a hemline, or belt, adding a neckscarf, collar and cuffs, or costume jewelry may be all that is needed for a new look.

Changing the trimming. Some garments are unattractive because there is too much trimming or the wrong type. As you try on your clothes, ask yourself if each piece of trimming is needed and appears to belong to the garment. Tired flowers or bows can ruin a perfectly good dress.

New trimmings can add new life to other garments. Braids and rickrack of many styles are available in a variety of designs, and can change the appearance of clothing. Alteration lines such as places where hems have been let down can be covered with braids or decorative machine stitching. Coats often show wear along the front edges and sleeve bottoms. These can be easily covered with braid especially made for such purposes.

You will be surprised how a change in *buttons* can change a garment. Many dresses can be made suitable for either sports or dress wear just by the type of buttons used. Why not try crocheting buttons to match some of your clothes to give a more custom made look? Perhaps you can cover buttons to match a scarf or other accessory worn with your outfit.

Old belts can be brightened up and new ones made for little money. If you have extra material, you can make a matching belt from a kit available in fabric stores or by covering cable cord; or you may want to make a contrasting belt to match another accessory item.

The same dress with a change of accessories.

SIMPLICITY PATTERN CO.

615

COATS AND CLARK, INC.

Braids and other trim are available in many patterns and materials. They are attached with one or two lines of machine stitching, usually close to each edge or are blind-stitched by hand. Which of the trims shown is baby rickrack, jumbo rickrack, sequins, middy braid, Chanel-type folded braid? Which of the woven trim designs do you like?

PFAFF INTERNATIONAL

With an automatic sewing machine you can make attractive borders rapidly and easily to cover old stitching lines or transform commonplace garments into distinctive ones. By using different colored threads, twin or triple needles, and by inserting ribbon, rick-rack, and lace, many types of borders can be made.

SUGGESTIONS FOR APPLYING TRIMS

Sequins are attached, as shown, so the thread is hidden by the overlapping sequin. A single sequin is held in place with a bead.

Rickrack may be sewn by hand, with each tip caught, or machine stitched. An interesting trim can be made by interlocking rickrack, either the same or contrasting colors.

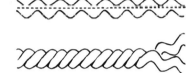

Chinese ball button can be made with soutache braid or corded tubing. Loop as shown. Sew down ends on the wrong side.

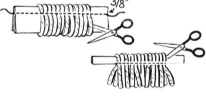

Yarn fringe is made by folding paper to width of fringe desired plus ½" for heading. Wind the yarn around. Stitch ⅜" from one edge. Cut fringe as shown, remove paper at perforations formed by stitching. Remove other end of fringe.

Fabric fringe is made by trimming away any selvage first. Then draw out threads as shown. On a loosely woven fabric, machine stitch along the base of the fringe.

A tailored bow can be made from ribbon or flat tubing. Cut one piece three times the size of the bow and one short piece for the center. Fold the long piece and tack as shown. Wrap the short piece around the center and sew.

COATS AND CLARK, INC.

A suit jacket with an unattractive neckline, torn buttonholes, or worn edges can be quickly converted to a Chanel-type design. Cut a new front in a shape that pleases you. Experiment with paper to make a pattern that you can use as a guide. Select a braid that harmonizes with the suit material and is made for binding suit edges. Apply with machine or hand stitching, whichever is suitable for the fabric. This girl released the top stitching of the pockets, added some braid, and then restitched the pockets.

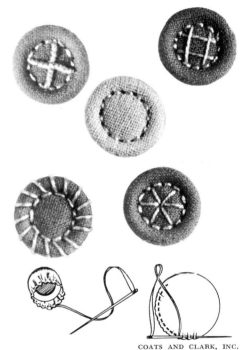

COATS AND CLARK, INC.

Covered buttons made from bone rings. Cut circles twice the diameter of the rings. Gather the edge, using doubled thread. Draw up over the ring, fasten securely. To trim, use embroidery thread and make stitches as shown. Attach with a thread shank.

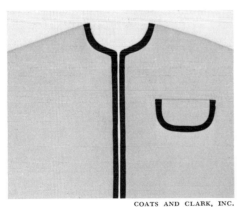

COATS AND CLARK, INC.

Braid is available in many colors and widths. Applied to worn edges of jackets and coats, the result is a fresh, new appearance. If collars and lapels are cut off for a new neckline shape as shown here, enough material is available for a pocket flap.

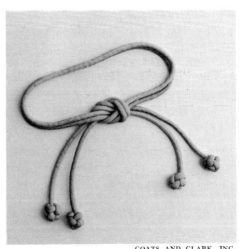

COATS AND CLARK, INC.

Belt made by covering tubing with bias fabric strips. Ends are knotted in an oriental manner.

Another idea is to select a wide piece of grosgrain ribbon, sew a narrow ribbon of contrasting color down the center, and fasten with a bow from one of the colors used. You may wish to use some of the ribbon to trim a collar or pocket.

A dress which is too short for use may be cut off and used as a blouse with a jumper or skirt.

Sleeve changes are another way of making a garment appear new. Long sleeves can be easily shortened. Cuffs may be used to add length as well as a new look. A dress that is too plain or shows wear under the arms may be given a new look by adding new sleeves of contrasting material. A new collar or neckline piping to

Dresses with worn or unattractive sleeves and necklines can easily be converted into jumpers which can be worn with a variety of blouses. If there is not enough available material from the sleeves for facings, wide bias binding can be purchased in almost every color. If the belt shows signs of wear, replace it with one worn with another garment or a new one that harmonizes with the fabric color and texture.

A smart at home outfit made from two dresses; the blouse was a dress too short to be used and cut off to a blouse length . . . the jumper was another dress with the sleeves and collar removed.

match the sleeves coordinates them with the original design.

You may want to remove the sleeves and make a sleeveless dress or jumper. Facings for the armhole can be easily made from the old sleeves.

Changing the neckline of an old dress may be just what is needed to make it more becoming and stylish. Perhaps a scarf can be worn in an interesting manner. A new collar or dickey may be needed or perhaps you would prefer to remove the collar and face the neckline so that jewelry or scarfs can be worn. A neckline that is too low can be made higher by adding a band or ruffle around the edge. It can also be filled in with a dickey made from a discarded blouse or even a man's shirt.

AMERICAN WOOL COUNCIL

Another idea for a new look from an old garment. Remove sleeves and cut a low neckline (experiment with patterns cut from paper first.) Face the openings and you have a stylish addition to your wardrobe.

Too low a neckline to please you? Fill it in with a dickey you can wear with other garments also. You may want to cut the neckline lower so the proportion of the dickey to the entire blouse is pleasing. Bind the neckline edge in a matching color.

Do you have a light-colored dress in your closet you seldom wear because the sleeves make it uncomfortable on hot days? Remove the sleeves and bind the edges with fabric cut on the bias from the sleeve parts. A button-front dress can serve as a beach cover-up as well as a summer dress.

Another way to make an attractive garment from one with a neckline too low or not flattering. Cut it into a low V-neck and insert a piece of contrasting or matching striped fabric. Make a band, similar to a belt, and add narrow braid to match the stripes. Start the band at the shoulder seams to avoid shaping it for the back neckline.

Slip-over *sweaters* can be changed to cardigan sweaters quite easily. Mark the center front along a rib of the knit with basting thread. Stitch carefully on the machine on each side of this mark. Cut along the mark. Bind the cut edges with grosgrain ribbon or fabric from a dress with which you may wish to wear the sweater. Buttonholes can be made with a machine attachment if desired. A few small holes in a sweater can often be covered with an appliqued decoration available in fabric stores.

Costume jewelry can be made from odds and ends for almost noth-

A "good" but seldom used sweater can be transformed easily into a distinctive one with the addition of various trims. This sweater has a trim made of jumbo rickrack and ribbon.

Make a coordinated outfit from a skirt and a sweater that is "good" but doesn't complement anything in your wardrobe. Cut it up the front, following directions given above and bind the opening with grosgrain ribbon to match the skirt. Insert a zipper for quick and easy fastening.

ing. Besides, you will have fun making it. Try painting old wooden beads in popular colors. Some beads can be colored with household dyes. Two or more old necklaces can be braided together with black velvet ribbon to make a stunning new one. Rickrack can be used to make earrings and pins that resemble a variety of flowers and can complement the colors in your outfit. Look at the jewelry counters of local stores and in craft booklets and you will find many ideas that can easily and inexpensively give your wardrobe the lift it needs.

To shorten a dress or pants, let down the old hemline. Don't be tempted to fold the present hem up as the results will not be satisfactory. Re-hem, using the method described on page 561.

621

To lengthen a hemline is more difficult, especially if you do not have a deep hem or if the original hemline cannot be pressed out. Braid and other trim can be stitched over hemline marks, as suggested before. Repeat the braid some other place in the garment. Why?

If the hem is not wide enough for the length needed, a bias facing or wide binding may be purchased for this purpose. A narrow hem, stitched several times on the machine, is often attractive. The width between the rows of stitches will depend upon the other stitching on your dress. A skirt may also be lengthened by adding a ruffle, band, or wide braid to the bottom. Often the skirt may be slashed at an attractive place and another piece of fabric inserted. (Read Chapter Two on proportion again.) A yoke at the waistline or a set-in belt is another way to lengthen a skirt. Whatever method you decide to use will depend upon the type of skirt and the current fashion.

To *refresh slips and nightgowns,* tint them and add lace at the top and lower edge. If the top of a slip is worn and the skirt is good, a half slip can be made from it.

Often garments that are too small can be fitted by letting out seams and taking in darts.

Pockets can be used to cover a tear if it is in a location where a patch will be suitable. Patches can be used as part of the design as well as covering up worn elbows and other places. Old leather gloves make good patches for sports garments.

REMAKING GARMENTS

Some garments cannot be easily brought up-to-date just with simple changes but may need to be remade, at least in part. You may be able to use the skirt or the blouse section as is, but usually it is necessary to rip the entire garment and remake it.

After you have decided the changes to be made, many questions should be considered, as:

• Do I have the patience and ability to produce a successful garment?
• Is the fabric strong enough to justify remodeling?
• Is the remodeled garment needed or would my time be better spent doing something else?
• Will it cost as much or more to remodel the old garment than to buy a new one?
• Will the remodeled garment be becoming or will it look made-over?
• Am I sure that I have enough material to make the desired changes?

Remember that more imagination and skill are needed to remodel a garment than to make one from a new fabric.

Preparing the fabrics for remaking. Fabrics must be in good condition to make a satisfactory garment. The seams should be ripped and well brushed. The fabric should be laundered or drycleaned. If you press seam lines with a damp cloth, the holes left from former stitching will usually disappear. If you have enough material, it will save time to cut off the seams rather than to rip them.

Some fabrics may need to be tinted to renew the color or dyed to change it. Commercial dyes are successful if directions are followed carefully.

Some fabrics are woven so either side may be used for the right side. If so, use the wrong side as it will show less wear, be less faded, and appear newer. Remember to shrink all new fabrics used in remade garments.

Your own wardrobe may not be the only source of material for such remodeling. Investigate cast-offs of family members. You may discover fabrics of much better quality than you can afford to buy at present prices. The old garments will provide opportunities to work out your own ideas in styling. However, do not attempt it without a commercial pattern to use as a guide. Remodeling calls for knowledge of the construction processes which you have studied in this chapter.

Selecting a pattern for remodeling. As you select a commercial pattern, consider the original lines of the garment and the size and shape of the pieces as well as the fabric. The chart on the pattern envelope will help you decide whether the pattern pieces will fit your fabric. Look for opportu-

nities for piecing, in in pleats, panels, and gathers. Whenever possible, use the original closing.

Before you start cutting, check to see that you have enough material to make the pattern selected. This may be done by spreading all of the pieces of material you have on a table. Make sure they are turned the right way and that you can determine the grain line of each one. (You will probably not have a selvage for a guide.) Place the largest pieces of the pattern on the largest pieces of the material and continue in this manner until all pieces have been placed. If it is necessary to piece the material, plan so the piecing will come where it will not show as under the arm, in a pleat, or in gathers. Perhaps the piecing can become part of the design as a yoke.

A man's suit will provide adequate fabric for a suit with a narrow skirt and a vest type of jacket. Use a commercial pattern and cut the skirt from the trousers. You may need to piece the jacket in the back or under the arms. A novel buckle closure adds a distinctive touch and is a wise choice when there is not enough fabric for an overlap for buttonholes.

This girl's suit was made from a dress of her mother's. The dress had hung in a closet for three years, seldom worn because it did not fit properly. She ripped the dress seams and pressed the fabric. A pattern suited to her figure was selected. The jacket and skirt were underlined with fabric her mother had. She selected a white blouse from her wardrobe for contrast of value and texture. The price of the "new" garment was the cost of the thread, zipper, and pattern.

BOISE JUNIOR COLLEGE

Quickly made from a full skirt no longer liked by big sister. Trimmed with left-over materials or parts of a dress too short for this growing girl.

Pep up your wardrobe by making a sleeve-less overblouse to match a favorite skirt. Only a small amount of fabric is needed—perhaps you can find a remnant that is attractive. Removing the sleeves and collar from a "tired" or outdated suit results in a smart outfit when worn over a matching checked shirt.

One way to stretch the fabric from a make-over is to plan a yoke and sleeves from a harmonizing fabric. Bands at the bottom of the sleeves and matching collar add style and tie it together. Perhaps two dresses could be combined in this manner.

Do you have a suit with a good skirt but an out-grown or out-of-style jacket? Select a simple checked fabric in matching colors and make a new jacket, binding the edges with bias strips cut from the old jacket. This collarless style is easy to make although the curved, bound pockets take a little extra time. You could substitute patch pockets, piped to match the skirt.

Make a plan for remodeling one of your seldom worn dresses into a child's garment: a man's coat into a jacket; a dress into a jumper, or a blouse. Include a picture or drawing of a suitable pattern, if needed.

Analyze your wardrobe to determine what clothes you have on hand that are not worn and can be remodeled. Figure the cost of remaking a garment and the amount of satisfaction it would give to determine whether the result would be worth your time and energy.

Prepare a display of inexpensive ways of making belts, buttons, and costume jewelery.

Demonstrate the quickest and safest methods for ripping garments.

Bring to class one or more garments that you or another member of your family never wear. Conduct a contest by having each girl list as many suggestions as possible for restoring the garment to use.

You may be able to cut the facings from another material that matches. When the garment is cut, make it according to the pattern directions.

Many articles of clothing too small for older members of the family can be made into "new" garments for children. Daddy's or Mother's old coat will provide enough wool fabric for a child's topcoat. A coat with button-front, collar, raglan sleeves, and patch pockets can be quickly made. Boys' trousers are more difficult to make and fit but an Eton suit coat is easily made from Daddy's old suit and can contrast smartly with purchased trousers. Girls' dresses can be made from a variety of clothes.

Suggestions for Renovation Projects

From man's shirt to child's dress, blouse, apron, dickey.

From dress to child's dress, jumper, skirt, blouse, bolero, apron.

From man's suit to skirt, jumper, boy's suit.

From coat to child's coat, short coat, boy's suit.

From towel to bibs, wash cloths, pot holders, beach bags.

From sheets to crib sheets, curtains, aprons, child's dress.

SHORT PROJECTS

Short projects can meet a need for creative expression and for sewing practice. If you finish work on your garment early or must wait for a sewing machine or teacher assistance, you may enjoy making a short project. At holiday time you will be elated to discover the gifts you can create at little or no cost—a perky hat for mother, a scarf for sister, a poncho for a favorite friend. For Dad and brother, a vest or tie or barbecue apron will be welcome. Hoods, tote bags, and aprons are delightful to construct. And who doesn't enjoy stuffed toys and decorative pillows? Don't forget yourself—smart accessories to match or contrast with other garments are fun to make and to wear.

Many of these can be made from materials left over from your garments or from remnants often available at little cost. Others require special fabrics. Some can be made at home by hand if you do not have a sewing machine. All offer an opportunity for creative stitchery and to improve your sewing skill.

SIMPLICITY PATTERN CO.

The kind of hat that goes anywhere. It's a six-sectioned brimmed hat made with matching or contrasting brim. A good project for learning how to stitch as the brim is usually reinforced with rows of machine stitches.

SIMPLICITY PATTERN CO.

A tote bag and matching hat can be quickly made from small amounts of fabric, to match or contrast with your costume.

SIMPLICITY PATTERN CO.

Ponchos can be made almost instantaneously. Facing the neckline and stitching on fringe to trim the edges is all that is necessary to complete this attractive coverup for beach and sports wear.

SIMPLICITY PATTERN CO.

Perhaps you will enjoy making and wearing a fringed madras head scarf.

In a very few hours you can knit a turtleneck dickey suitable for either a young man or a girl to wear under a shirt.

SIMPLICITY PATTERN CO.

JOHN DRITZ AND SONS

A novel apron uses an apron hoop instead of a waistband. Hem the bottom, making a casing at the top, and insert the hoop. This apron has ball fringe used as a trim on the hem edge.

627

Fabric scraps left over from sewing were used to make this hand-appliquéd wall hanging showing a fishing village in the Caribbean. Why not try making a similar wall hanging of a local scene.

Fun to make for little children, both the girl's dress and the boy's overalls are easy for mother to care for as they open flat for ironing. The little boy can dress himself because of the long front zipper opening. Both children enjoy the gayly colored pockets for keeping treasures.

SIMPLICITY PATTERN CO.

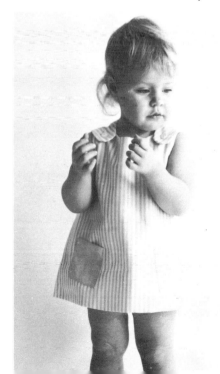

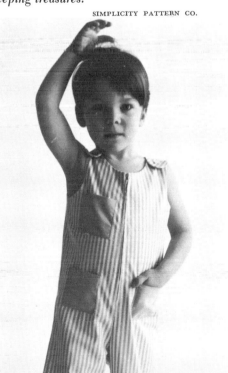

Macrame is a hobby enjoyed by people of all ages. Why not make a bag to coordinate with an outfit you have made or as a gift?

Accessories for tennis and other sports can be made easily. The tennis racket cover has an attached pocket for balls. The tote bag by itself has many uses.

SIMPLICITY PATTERN CO.

Stuffed animals—decorative and practical—delight all ages. Stuff them with polyester filling or well-washed nylon hose, and they will be washable.

SIMPLICITY PATTERN CO.

Embroidery Stitches

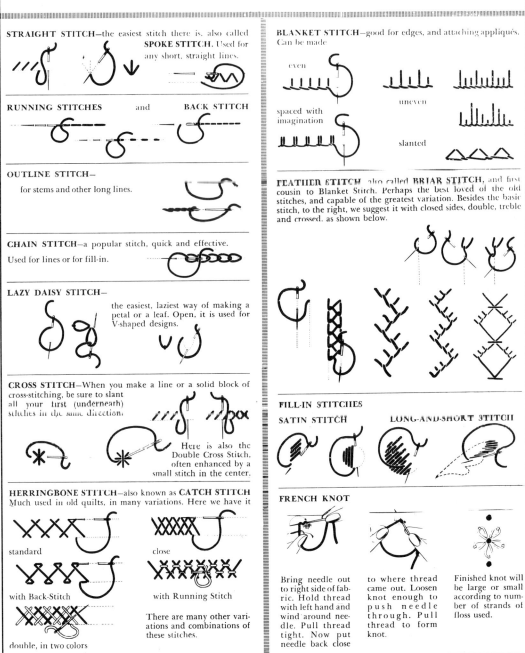

STRAIGHT STITCH—the easiest stitch there is, also called **SPOKE STITCH**. Used for any short, straight lines.

RUNNING STITCHES and **BACK STITCH**

OUTLINE STITCH—
for stems and other long lines.

CHAIN STITCH—a popular stitch, quick and effective. Used for lines or for fill-in.

LAZY DAISY STITCH—
the easiest, laziest way of making a petal or a leaf. Open, it is used for V-shaped designs.

CROSS STITCH—When you make a line or a solid block of cross-stitching, be sure to slant all your first (underneath) stitches in the same direction.

Here is also the Double Cross Stitch, often enhanced by a small stitch in the center.

HERRINGBONE STITCH—also known as **CATCH STITCH** Much used in old quilts, in many variations. Here we have it

standard

close

with Back-Stitch

with Running Stitch

double, in two colors

There are many other variations and combinations of these stitches.

BLANKET STITCH—good for edges, and attaching appliqués. Can be made

even

spaced with imagination

uneven

slanted

FEATHER STITCH also called **BRIAR STITCH**, and first cousin to Blanket Stitch. Perhaps the best loved of the old stitches, and capable of the greatest variation. Besides the basic stitch, to the right, we suggest it with closed sides, double, treble and crossed, as shown below.

FILL-IN STITCHES

SATIN STITCH

LONG-AND-SHORT STITCH

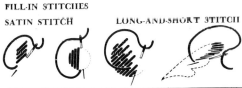

FRENCH KNOT

Bring needle out to right side of fabric. Hold thread with left hand and wind around needle. Pull thread tight. Now put needle back close

to where thread came out. Loosen knot enough to push needle through. Pull thread to form knot.

Finished knot will be large or small according to number of strands of floss used.

COATS AND CLARK, INC.

Commercial patterns are available for many gift items or directions are often found in needlework and craft booklets. Check the references at the end of the book for more suggestions.

EMBROIDERY[*]

Embroidery, one of the oldest and most satisfying arts, has again become fashionable. A number of the best known and most used stitches are described and illustrated on the preceding page. Practice them until they become automatic and then enjoy the fun of creating designs of your own.

Embroidery threads and fabrics. The choice of threads and fabrics depends upon the item to be made. Fabric of almost any kind, cotton, linen, wool, burlap, and blends may be used if they are of good quality. Six strand floss thread is made especially for light weight fabrics. It comes in wide variety of colors and may be separated when a finer thread is needed. It is exciting to experiment, however, with a wide variety of threads and yarns. Try heavier cottons, metallic threads, linen, raw silk, and wool. Don't forget that fishing and butcher twine and cord make unusual effects.

Embroidery needles. The best needles for embroidery are crewel needles. They are about 1¾ inches long and have a long eye slightly larger than the thread to make an opening in the material for the thread to slip through. If a blunt point is needed, use a tapestry needle.

Scissors and thimble. It is very difficult to embroider without a thimble. It must be lightweight and fit the middle finger. You will find your work easier if you have two pairs of

Exhibit easy to make articles. Ask class members to bring any they or others have made.

Make a list of short projects, or use the items on display, and compare each article's cost, use, and appearance with a similar ready-made article.

Visit an accessory section of a large store and a gift department. Note articles that could be easily made from left-over fabric or remnants.

Gather together left-over fabric from a recent sewing project. What can be made from this fabric?

very sharp scissors—a 3½″ size and a 4 to 5″ size.

Hoops. Hoops come in a variety of sizes and in two shapes, round or oval. Select a hoop the size and shape of the area being worked so the fabric is taut and will not pucker.

Finishing. Embroidery should be neat and attractive on the wrong side as well as the right. Avoid using knots or continuing thread from one completed motif to another. Always begin stitches by making a few running stitches along the line to be embroidered. End stitches, or start a new thread, by securing it on the wrong side of the work by weaving it in and out of the last stitches.

Pressing. When embroidery is finished, it should be pressed on a board that is thickly padded so the raised face of the embroidery can sink into the padding and not be flattened by the iron. Place article right-side down and press with a damp cloth. Remove cloth and press dry.

[*] *"Learn How," Lily Design Book No. 206*

Summary With Check-up Questions

The ability to alter and remodel garments can be a financial asset as well as contribute toward comfort and attractiveness.

- *When can an old garment be remodeled or altered to fit for very little effort and money?*
- *How can the ability to alter the fit of a garment contribute to one's appearance and comfort?*

Judgment is necessary in knowing when and how to remodel garments.

- *If the fabric is weak, is it worthwhile remodeling a garment?*
- *Will you enjoy wearing a remodeled dress if the design is spoiled by the alterations?*
- *If you create a remodeled garment that suits your wardrobe needs and that you enjoy wearing, is it worth the time and skill spent?*

Many fabrics require special handling because of unusual designs, fiber content, or finishes. It is wise to delay using these fabrics until one has experience with easy to handle materials.

- *Why is a plaid fabric more difficult to sew than a plain fabric?*
- *Pattern directions refer to "nap fabrics" as needing special pattern layouts and additional yardage. Give examples of these fabrics and explain why special care is needed.*

Ready-to-wear garments must be suitable for many people and cannot be planned to suit individual figure variations or design preferences, nor can manufacturers afford to inspect for all workmanship defects.

- *What can the buyer do to improve workmanship before wearing a garment?*

- *How can the design be made to suit the individual without expensive changes?*
- *What types of fitting problems can be easily overcome by the average sewer?*

Much of the satisfaction of a garment depends upon how well it fits.

- *Why is it necessary to fit a garment to the individual who will wear it rather than make it for "average" measurements?*
- *Does it matter if a dress is too tight or too loose if it is a lovely color and design and is well made?*

Research studies have shown that the time needed for making most garments can be reduced considerably with short-cut methods and the results will still be satisfactory.

- *How can the arrangement of sewing equipment affect time spent on sewing?*
- *Give an example of two similar fabrics, one which will make up quickly and one which will take considerable time.*
- *Why are many short cuts suitable only for the experienced sewer and not for a beginner?*

Can You Explain These Terms?

special fabrics	border print
graded seam	bonded fabric
nap fabric	stretch fabric
pile fabric	durable press
even plaid	sewing short-cut
one-way plaid	clothing renovation

PART 5

LOOKING AHEAD

CHAPTER EIGHTEEN

Careers in Dress

NOW IS THE TIME to look ahead to your future and make plans for a career that will be meaningful.

Until recent years, men planned for careers without much consideration for the effect their work would have on their personal, home, and family lives. Most women expected to work at "almost any job" until they were married. There was always the possibility they would get a job again when the children were grown. However, seldom was any planning done ahead of time to prepare for these jobs.

It is now recognized that most young people will work outside the home most of their lives. The likelihood is great that a young woman will combine two careers—a homemaker and a paid worker—at various times in her life. Estimates made by the U. S. Bureau of Census state that the high school girl of today will work outside her home about thirty years. Most men will work until they retire, close to age 65.

While you are in high school is the time to seriously consider your abili-

ties, your interests, and your goals. What do you enjoy doing most, what do you do well, what do you want to do with your life? How can you get the education and training needed

Dreaming about the future? While you are in high school is the time to give serious thought to your future career and to make plans to achieve your goals.

634

for a job suited to you and your future life? As a young person, you will want to consider the effect of your career on your personal and home life. Some women prefer to concentrate on their family when the children are young. On the other hand, some prefer to work part-time while others prefer to spend all their energies on a career. A man will discover that the quality of his personal and home life is greatly affected by the type of job he has and the satisfaction he finds in his career. Both men and women will find their career plans affected by the type of job their marriage partner has, the number of children they decide to have, and the region in which they live.

You may want to select a career area that can serve you, both as a homemaker and as a wage earner. Any aspect of home economics helps you prepare for a better personal and home life as well as an interesting and rewarding job outside the home. The relationship is twofold as experience in running your own home can be an asset to your career.

Whatever career you enter, knowing how to dress appropriately and attractively and how to be well groomed will be helpful in securing a position and in advancement. The study of home economics while in high school is also of direct benefit to girls who enter many career areas, as noted on pages 636 and 637.

However, if you like fashions and fabrics and beauty, there are many careers available to suit your personal interests. Some can be entered directly after high school; some require a year or two of post high school training. Others require a bachelor's degree from a college and if you have the interest and ability to consider graduate study, there are many openings for women with a master's or a doctor's degree.

In this chapter you will read of the many types of career opportunities open to young women who enjoy working with textiles, fashion, and helping others appear at their best. Because the opportunities for jobs and training differ in each part of our country, you will want to talk with guidance counselors in your school, personnel in your nearest state employment office, those already at work, and also read as much as possible about the jobs that interest you. References listed at the end of the book may be of help to you.

RETAILING

As a high school graduate, there are a variety of careers for you in department stores, specialty shops, and other retailing establishments. Opportunities for the high school graduate to advance to section head, floor manager, buyer, or an executive position in personnel or advertising are good. The best opportunities are in large stores specializing in women's clothing and accessories. Retailing is one of the few remaining fields where employees without a college degree can advance to executive positions although a college degree often helps in advancement.

Basic and advanced training in merchandising, marketing, and distributive education is offered under the public school vocational program in many localities. Department stores and other retail establishments often cooperate with schools and offer full-time employment to students upon graduation.

Comments made by former Arkansas high school students now engaged in various kinds of occupations concerning the value of their home economics study*

- *Billing clerk and junior bookkeeper.* Being honest, doing the best work I know how, being on time at work, dressing appropriately for work, keeping my desk and work neat and in order, and showing respect to my supervisors are things I learned in homemaking courses.

- *Garment factory worker.* The sewing that I had in the home economics classes helped me a great deal in doing a good job for my employer. The factory where I worked made dresses, and I worked on what is called "first operation"—sewing the shoulders of dresses together and putting on collars. I liked it very much. My reason for quitting was a transfer in my husband's job and to raise a family. I might add that I have two little daughters that benefit greatly from my sewing experience and are proud to say "Mommy made my dress."

- *Presser.* From studying homemaking, I learned first how to do a good job no matter what the job is. Knowing about home laundry has helped me hold my present job as a presser. Learning about food and nutrition, how to serve foods, keep house, how to plan and manage money have proved very helpful to me on other jobs as cafeteria work, domestic work and managing the home for myself and others.

- *IBM data processing clerk.* My homemaking courses were the beginning of my overcoming a terrible inferiority complex. It was in those classes that I began building my self-confidence. Also, I learned many helpful pointers in the field of grooming and fashion.

- *Fashion model.* My job as a model requires eating the right foods, being well dressed and knowing how to meet people. I learned this from my homemaking courses.

- *Secretary and receptionist.* Our studies in personality, good grooming and poise helped me in obtaining my jobs. Our studies about budgeting, home management, cooking and sewing enable me to run my home while working out.

- *Personal shopper.* By taking home economics in school, I learned about fashions which has helped me in my work, and I learned about being well groomed; I also learned about home work and balanced diet, which helps when you have a family to take care of.

- *Recorder.* For the type of work in which I am presently engaged, my homemaking courses aided me in knowing the proper dress for office work—cleanliness, neatness, and also office etiquette.

- *Salesperson—department store.* My knowledge I obtained as to correct fitting, selection of clothes, choice of colors, correct ways of sewing, how to follow recipes have been most valuable in my work and running a home. I don't need domestic help if I manage well, so that's money earned. While working, good grooming and good manners are important.

- *Seamstress.* My course in homemaking has been a great value to me in managing my home and caring for my young daughter. In college I sewed for myself and others. At present I'm self employed as a seamstress and have been offered work in a dress shop making alterations.

- *Beautician's assistant.* My study of face types and cosmetics for various skin types has been of great help to me on my present job. I know how to keep myself looking neat and attractive. All of this I learned in home economics classes.

- *Physical education teacher.* Proper etiquette, good grooming habits, introduction to the biological and social development of children, colors and their stimulation of various responses have been helpful to me in my public school teaching work.

- *Airline stewardess.* As an airline stewardess I found numerous things helpful to me that I had learned in home economics such as good posture, grooming, how to meet people and to sum it up—just to be a good, gracious hostess.

* *Determining Kinds of Gainful Employment in Which Former Homemaking Students from Arkansas Secondary Schools Engage, and What Knowledge and Skills Homemaking Curriculums May Contribute to These Gainful Occupations.* (*University of Arkansas, College of Education, February 1966*).

- **Secretary.** I learned in my home economics class how to dress properly for office work and how to use different accessories. The fellowship with girls at FHA meetings helped me in meeting people with different personalities and therefore, now helps me associate better with my co-workers. Home economics also taught me about budgeting money and it now comes in pretty handy.

- **Bank clerk.** Homemaking helped me to learn to speak well, develop a pleasing personality, dress correctly, be neat and clean, and to know the correct way of doing things.

- **IBM key-punch operator.** I think what has been most helpful were our good grooming and personality units. Homemaking helped us learn the importance of cleanliness and being able to get along with all kinds of people and being able to put ourselves on a schedule in which we would have time to do the things we need to do.

- **Homemaking teacher.** All the information learned in homemaking has been helpful in planning my program of work for my homemaking classes.

- **Seamstress.** During college I worked part-time for the drama department in making costumes. Also one summer I worked part-time for a theatrical costumes company. The knowledge of sewing gained in home economics was mainly responsible for my obtaining this particular employment.

Stockgirl. Many high school girls enter merchandising as stock clerks. They keep stock in order in the stockroom and on the selling floor, take inventory of the supplies on hand, check incoming orders against invoices, and replenish merchandise on sales counters and tables.

Advancement may lead to becoming head of the stock department or salesperson.

Salesperson. The Department of Labor reports over a million and a half women are employed as sales workers. Duties of a salesperson in a self-service department store consist of writing out sales slips, ringing up sales, making change, and packaging purchases. Merchandise must be arranged in an orderly way and displays made up from time to time.

A sales position in fashions, furs, or fabrics is more demanding. This salesperson is expected to be informed about the merchandise carried and have a knowledge of materials and current fashions. Customers may want suggestions on various styles, colors, or models, and may need help in coordinating their clothing purchases.

Most stores conduct brief training sessions for all new sales people. The training may consist of making out sales slips and using the cash register or it may be more extensive and include instruction concerning the merchandise as well as store policy.

The standard work week differs in each store. Employees usually work on Saturday, a busy day for sales, and have another day off during the week. They may also work a few nights a week. Many part-time or temporary jobs are available in selling during holiday seasons.

The work of a salesperson is varied and offers many opportunities for working with people, as well as clothing and fabrics.

Buying for any store is an important position and specialized training as well as experience is desirable preparation. This future buyer is justifying her selections in a buying class and will learn from her fellow students' comments.

Advancement for a salesperson may be to a supervisory position as section head or department manager. Outstanding salespersons may become assistant buyers and then buyers, although more and more these positions require some college or post-high school study in merchandising and business administration.

Buyer. A merchandiser is a better term than buyer to describe all the functions of a buyer, since these include buying merchandise to be sold as well as receiving it, pricing it, promoting its sale, selling it, and handling complaints about it. Time is divided between the selling floor, the stockroom, her desk, and buying trips to the "market." One must sense what

FASHION INSTITUTE OF TECHNOLOGY

Sales promotion is an important part of merchandising. Department personnel work together on effective ways to interest others in buying their merchandise.

Top management positions involve decision making based on a thorough knowledge of current business and fashion trends and resources available to the company.

DOWNEN ZIER KNITS

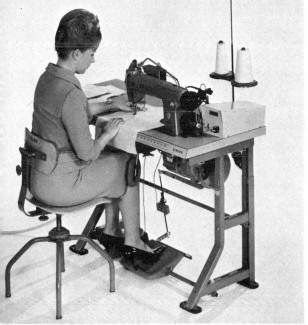

A power stitching machine. The operator heels the machine treadle to position the needle down—a touch of the knee or toe switch positions it up and trims top and bottom threads neatly under the throat plate. Another foot pedal controls the speed of stitching.

A power stitching machine used for chain-stitching on knitwear and foundation garments. Notice the careful attention given to proper chair position.

will sell and understand the wishes of those who shop in the department. Outstanding buyers may become merchandise managers and be in charge of several departments.

Fashion coordinator. A fashion coordinator is usually a former buyer who has a high sense of color, design, and fashion. Responsibilities include coordinating fashion throughout the store, arranging for fashion shows, teen-age fashion boards, and other promotion ideas.

FACTORY WORK

Workers who operate the machines used in manufacturing and drycleaning are called operatives. A high school education is not required for most of these jobs but it is helpful for advancement to highly skilled or supervisory work. You must be at least 16 years of age to work in a factory and 18 years of age before you are allowed to operate machines considered hazardous. Federal and state laws set these requirements for your protection. In many states, a person under 18 must obtain a work permit in order to work in a factory.

In industries manufacturing clothing and textiles, a large percentage of the operatives are women. Many women operatives belong to labor unions and are covered by collective bargaining agreements which establish working conditions, pay rates, and fringe benefits.

Power machine operator. A power machine operative works with fabrics at a power sewing-machine that is somewhat different from a home sewing machine. Many trade and vocational schools offer courses in power-sewing machine operation. In some areas, programs established under the Manpower Development and Training Act provide training for those who are able to meet the requirements of the act. Training may also be given on the job.

Power-sewing machines are used widely in the garment industry and also in making draperies and stitching together the upholstery sections for furniture and automobiles.

In the garment industry, power-sewing machine operators usually start as single needle machine operators. An operator on men's shirts, for example, may do facing, hemming, or a more difficult operation, such as collar or pocket setting. In the women's dress industry, she may stitch together all of the parts of the dress.

Some specialties require a high degree of skill and versatility, for example, the operation of a power-driven embroidery machine. In some of these machines the needle is housed in a revolving shaft and can be made to sew in any direction by manipulating a hand control. Artistic ability is important for this work and an expert can create intricate designs. Usually an experienced power-sewing machine operator must take special training in a technical school.

Power-sewing machine jobs are concentrated in certain localities where there are industries that employ operators with this skill. Garment centers of large cities and communities in the South with large mills are examples.

Inspector, examiner. Some plant experience, or on-the-job training is needed to become inspectors or testers. This work consists of examining parts of the finished product for flaws and separating perfect from imperfect products.

Assemblers in a factory folding pillowcases prior to their packaging. The women at the rear of the room are inspecting the pillowcases and pressing those that need it.

THE SPRINGS COTTON MILLS

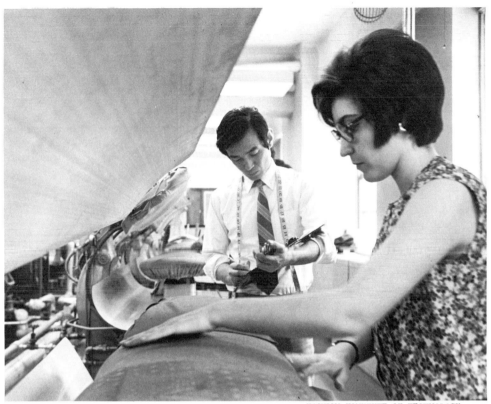

A management engineering student analyzes methods of molding fabrics with pressure, heat, and moisture. This knowledge is needed by many workers in the fashion industry as well as those who operate cleaning establishments.

Assembler. Factory workers who bring together parts are called assemblers. In the textile and clothing field, employees are needed to fold textile items and to package them.

COMMERCIAL LAUNDRY AND DRYCLEANING ESTABLISHMENT

There are many positions in commercial laundry and drycleaning establishments. *Pressers* and those who operate other machines are considered operatives and are often covered by state laws for such work.

The *checker* receives garments and must be able to work well with customers. The *sorter* decides how each garment can be best cleaned. One of the most skilled jobs is that of *spotter;* this person must understand fibers, finishes, and stain removal methods. Training may be obtained by working with a skilled spotter or through special courses offered by the International Fabricare Institute. The *inspector* may also make minor repairs. In a small concern one person may do several jobs; in a large establishment there is more opportunity for specialization.

FASHION OR APPAREL DESIGN

The clothing industry is the second largest industry in the United States and the largest in New York City.

An inspector in a drycleaning plant examines all garments for standards of cleaning, spotting, finishing, and needed repairs.

Talented and trained apparel designers find positions in this industry as designers, assistant designers, or stylists.

The designer creates new ideas. This is often done by draping materials over a dress form or a live model. Sketches are made of new creations. The *assistant designer* may help design clothes but usually helps by finishing routine steps, running errands, and visiting showrooms to select needed trimmings and fabrics. A *sample-maker* or sample hand does the actual sewing. The dress is then worn by a live model and its merits judged. The production manager helps decide what it will cost to produce the design. If the design is approved, a pattern maker prepares a set of paper patterns. The dresses are then produced by the power machine operators, the finishers, and the pressers.

Center of the garment industry is New York City. This is a frequent scene on 7th Avenue.

An important part of studying fashion design is learning to drape garments directly on a body form.

Both men and women find employment as fashion designers. Here a design is being draped in muslin before being made up in the final fabric.

An interest in clothing design and in social service can be combined in the development of garments suitable for handicapped persons. This girl is modeling a culotte type dress with an easy-to-handle side closure suitable for wear while confined to a wheel chair.

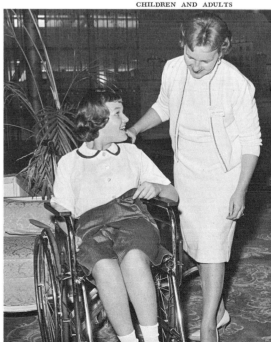

A fashion design course of study in a post-high school program includes achieving the ability to sketch the original design, to interpret these ideas by means of draping and flat patterns, to select fabrics, and to actually construct the garment. The ability to develop original ideas from the creative thought to the completed garment is essential. A designer or stylist seldom does the actual construction but must understand how garments are put together and must supervise those who do the actual sewing.

Textile Design

If you have artistic ability and a love of color and design and fabrics, the textile design field offers many opportunities. As part of class requirements, students in post-high school programs design with paint for printed and woven fabrics, design on the hand loom, create screen printed patterns, study color fundamentals, fashion, textile science, and other aspects of the fashion industry. Graduates of post-high school programs in textile design find employment in the application of art to printed, woven, and knitted fabrics; they create designs, style lines, and direct studios.

Fashion Illustration And Advertising Design

High school graduates who are proficient in drawing and who demonstrate artistic ability, creative imagination, and an interest in art and fashion may be interested in enrolling in programs in Fashion Illustration and Advertising Design in many types of post-high school and college programs.

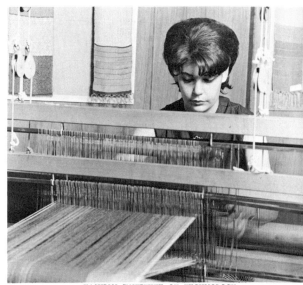

FASHION INSTITUTE OF TECHNOLOGY

Creating designs on a hand loom is an important part of a textile design course.

FASHION INSTITUTE OF TECHNOLOGY

Textile designers work in many ways; this one is using paints to develop a unique fabric design.

645

Planning the layout for a fashion advertisement, this illustrator uses her ability to draw, her creative imagination, and her knowledge of fashion.

Ability to sketch and an interest in fashion is necessary for a successful career in fashion illustration.

Initial opportunities as illustrators, layout artists, and assistant art directors are available after professional preparation. There is opportunity for advancement as you gain experience.

CLOTHING MAINTENANCE SPECIALIST

The Manpower Development and Training Program developed by the U. S. Office of Education recognized the need for clothing maintenance specialists to help families. Under the employer's supervision, the clothing maintenance specialist alters, cleans, presses, repairs, and stores the clothing of individuals and families. Training programs are available in many areas in the United States where there is a demand for this type

of service. If you are interested in such a program, contact your local or state vocational and technical education office.

Unless a family is very large, the services of a clothing maintenance specialist are needed for only a few days each week. Therefore, this position may be a part-time one for a busy homemaker who cannot work full time or she may serve two or more families for full time work.

HOME LAUNDRY

In many communities, some people cannot do their own laundry. They may not have time or may be in poor health, but they like to have their laundry done by home methods. If you enjoy seeing clothing looking like new and find pride in seeing a soiled, stained garment freshened with your ability and knowledge, you may be interested in developing a home laundry service. You will need good laundry facilities and the means to deliver the finished laundry to your customers, although some may be willing to come to you. If you are able to do simple mending you will be more in demand.

You should understand basic business practices such as customer relations and bookkeeping.

ATTENDANT IN SELF-SERVICE LAUNDRY OR DRYCLEANING ESTABLISHMENT

Many self-service laundries and drycleaners have an attendant who works with the customers, helping them use the equipment effectively. If you enjoy meeting people and helping them with their clothing problems, you may be interested in this type of work.

BEAUTY OPERATOR

If you have nimble fingers and a sense of style and enjoy seeing people at their best, you may be interested in the beauty field as a hairdresser, cosmetician, or beautician. Beauty operators shampoo, cut, style, set, straighten, or tint their customers' hair and give permanent waves. They may give manicures and facials. They make appointments, sterilize tools, and help clean the shop and equipment. In large shops they may specialize in one aspect.

A state license is required. You must fulfill the minimum age requirements, complete an approved course or apprentice training, pass an examination on theory and practice, and present a health certificate. Many public vocational high schools offer courses to meet state licensing requirements. These may lead to a high school diploma or be taken as a postgraduate course. There are also a large number of private schools where the requirements can be met in 6 to 9 months.

DRESSMAKING

If you have a liking for dressmaking and the ability to sew well, you may find employment in the clothing industry making designers' samples, working as an alteration hand, or you may prefer your own business.

Alteration worker. Large department stores and speciality shops usually have an alteration department employing several alterationists who are able to alter the fit of ready-made garments and to make simple repairs to articles damaged from handling in the store. A few speciality shops have a custom dressmaking section where garments are made to order.

If you have a basic understanding of sewing, you may be able to work as an assistant in a large alteration department and learn more on the job. Specialized training is available in many vocational schools, usually located in large cities.

Home dressmaking. Establishing a dressmaking and alteration business of your own is not easy but it can lead to a satisfying income and pleasant work. A knowledge of trade skills, short-cuts, professional techniques, and the ability to time your work are important. A good way to start is to gain experience as an assistant in an alteration department for six months to a year.

You may work in a department store or a tailor shop. Specialized training in a vocational school will also provide you with an opportunity to learn the needed skills and gain some experience. Don't start your own business until you are proficient because a poor reputation will be difficult to overcome.

You will need a room kept solely for this purpose—an extra bedroom, a sunroom, a reconstructed garage—anywhere that is light and airy and large enough for a cutting table, pressing board, sewing machine, storage, and a curtained try-on area. You will also need good quality equipment.

Others must know you are in business. You will need cards printed to advertise. You should get acquainted with local store personnel who may refer customers to you. You will need to understand business and tax requirements and be able to maintain a businesslike approach to your customers, many of whom will become friends.

You may prefer to specialize in alterations or custom dressmaking or in home decoration items such as draperies and slip covers. Some people have developed good businesses by specializing in such areas as wedding gowns or children's clothing or special costumes.

In some communities you may be asked to teach adult groups in adult education or recreation programs, where a college education is not a requirement.

MILLINER

A small but important speciality is that of millinery. If you are handy with a needle and have a good sense of design, you may be interested in designing and making hats. A good way to learn is to work as an assistant to a competent milliner.

TECHNICIAN AND RESEARCH

In these days of technological progress, many young people discover they have an interest and aptitude for technical work. Textile laboratories often employ men and women technicians. There is a wide range in the skill requirements for technician jobs. Some relatively unskilled jobs can be filled by high school graduates, especially if they have had courses in mathematics and physical sciences that emphasize laboratory work. Special training, however, is becoming increasingly important for all but the most routine work. If this type of work interests you, it is wise to investigate the requirements and plan to get all the training possible.

Textile laboratory aide. Firms in the textile industry employ laboratory aides to work with chemists and others doing testing and research. They may assemble equipment, make computations, tabulate and analyze results of experiments, and test products against specifications.

Research workers. A career in research is open to you if you have a bachelor's degree and if you have had careful training in research procedures and methods.

If you are considering research as a career, you need the following personal qualities: fondness for work with hands and head, willingness to improve your skills and abilities, imagination, persistence, interest in details, common sense, curiosity, cooperation and a willingness to give of yourself. A research worker must be able to interpret and report his re-

Typical of the many activities involved in fabric testing and research, this technician has saturated samples of colored fabric with artificial perspiration. She will place them in an oven at body temperature for 48 hours and then determine the amount of staining.

sults clearly. *Textile* and *clothing research* problems include the uses of fibers, fabrics, and finishes. Another research area is clothing and its relation to economic status and social participation. Positions are available in universities, government agencies, industries, and in private testing agencies.

TEACHING

If you enjoy imparting your knowledge and enthusiasm to others, you should consider teaching. You are probably aware of the work of a high school teacher and know that she may teach only in the area of clothing and textiles or she may teach many areas of home and family living. An elementary or junior high school teacher usually teaches many aspects. In junior colleges and universities, the work will be more spe-

There are many opportunities for teaching in the areas of clothing and textiles. This teacher is helping high school girls select clothing suited to the wearer and the occasion.

cialized and the teacher will concentrate on clothing and textiles.

A bachelor's degree in home economics and education is necessary for most public school teaching positions. If you elect to major in clothing and/or textiles, you will usually take basic courses in family living, child development, management, design, and foods and nutrition as well as your major subjects. Advanced study is necessary for teaching positions in junior and senior colleges—a master's degree is required and a doctorate is preferred.

Learning to design clothing, both by draping on a dress form and by flat pattern drafting, is part of a college major in clothing. This student is using a half-size scaled form to find the best effect for the fabric she intends to use.

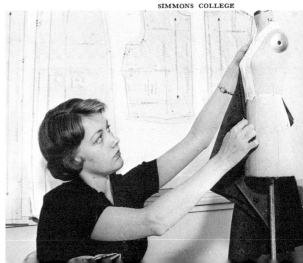

BOSTON CENTER FOR ADULT EDUCATION

Working with adults who want to learn to design their own clothes is rewarding. This teacher is a graduate of a three-year program in fashion and design and is employed in a designer's studio. She teaches several evening fashion classes for adults.

"WHAT'S NEW IN HOME ECONOMICS"

Extension home economists work with women in many ways to help them become better homemakers and consumers. This home demonstration agent has presented a demonstration lecture on selecting clothes for the family at a Business and Professional Women's Club meeting. Two club members are seeking special information from her after the meeting.

In many communities there are positions available in adult education programs for those who may not have attended college but who are skilled in clothing construction and related areas and who finds satisfaction in helping others learn.

Teachers in fashion, design, and retailing in post-high school courses must have had successful experience in these fields. A college education is not always required.

EXTENSION SERVICE

Extension service provides an opportunity to work informally with young people or adults in their homes and communities. The cooperative extension service employs college educated home economists as county representatives of state universities, land grant colleges, and the U. S. Department of Agriculture. The county extension home economist, often called a home demonstration agent or a home agent, is often a generalist

but finds that clothing and textiles are of major concern to the families in one's locality and thus has many opportunities to use one's knowledge and ability in this subject. In each state there is a clothing specialist who coordinates clothing programs. Usually experience as a county home economist and additional specialized study are needed.

The extension home economist may work with young people in 4-H clubs or with adults, individually and in groups. Radio, television, and newspapers are used to furnish information to families in the county. Local leaders of groups are trained and one is continually trying to find better ways to teach families new principles, techniques, and how to apply research findings to improve home and family life. One must be able to work independently, plan time well, and work with other people.

Business

A home economics college education offers opportunities for a variety of interesting occupations to the person who wishes to accept the challenges and benefits of a business career. There are always new futures in business as home economists tell others about the products of a manufacturer and interpret consumer needs and wants back to businessmen.

Sales promotion and education. Working for a sales promotion or education department of a pattern or textile manufacturer is the beginning job of many business home economists. One must study consumer needs, develop and promote new products, and plan educational materials and programs. Many of the bulletins used in high school home economics classes are prepared by a home economist. Often, one will travel throughout one section of the country presenting fashion shows and other educational programs to 4-H clubs, schools, and other community groups. The company's product will be demonstrated—how to use it and how to care for it. One may work with photographers to help them present the best picture possible of the product or write for a magazine or newspaper. Testing products, equipment, and fabrics and writing directions for their use is also done.

Fashion photography is another career field for those who are interested in relating art and design to fashion.

FASHION INSTITUTE OF TECHNOLOGY

A home economist for a utility shows consumers the right methods for clothing care as well as proper care of equipment.

Utility company representative. Most gas and electric companies employ home economists as their representatives to teach consumers the use of equipment and appliances so they will want to purchase . . . and to build good will for the company. In the past much of the work was with food; therefore, ranges, refrigerators, and small cooking appliances were of major interest. With the increasing complexity of textiles today and the increased use of automatic washers and dryers, fabrics have also become a focal point. Considerable knowledge of textiles is necessary to help others give clothing the proper care.

The utility company home economist gives demonstrations to large groups, works with individual homemakers in their own homes, answers telephone and mail inquiries, tests new equipment and teaches salesmen how to use it, writes directions to accompany some equipment, and may help plan advertising and other publicity activities.

Equipment company representative. A home economist interested in clothing and fabrics may be employed by a manufacturer of sewing machines, other sewing equipment, or laundry equipment. The work of each one is different but the major purpose is to promote the correct use of the equipment to the consumers and to help the company understand the needs and wishes of consumers. Many of the job responsibilities are similar to a utility home economist but the audience is often nationwide.

Communications. Radio, television, newspapers, and magazines provide opportunities for employment for those who are skilled in presenting ideas, either through writing or direct presentation, and who has a special-

FASHION INSTITUTE OF TECHNOLOGY

Journalism offers many possibilities for those interested in fashion. Writing for newspapers, magazines, and fabric companies can be a satisfying experience. These students are comparing styles of leading fashion magazines for a class report.

ized knowledge of a subject of wide interest such as textiles and clothing, or knows how to find the needed information quickly.

Work on newspapers, magazines, and broadcasting staffs is highly competitive. Opportunities also exist for communication specialists in educational associations, manufacturing, advertising, and public relations firms; government agencies; and trade journals.

JORDAN MARSH AND CO.

The job of a fashion editor of a large nation-wide magazine is varied. Meeting with teen fashion boards of large department stores is one of her many activities.

List the added responsibilities of a homemaker who works outside the home. Discuss how training in home economics can help her.

Compare the responsibilities single and married men have concerning their clothing today with those of men a few generations ago. Why have these changes taken place?

Consult your school guidance office for recent reference materials on careers related to fashion and fabrics that are open to the high school graduate and to the person with a college education. Arrange a display of bulletins and pamphlets on your classroom bulletin board.

Ask a representative of your nearest state employment office to talk to your class about requests received for workers in clothing related occupations.

Prepare a report on part-time jobs open to teenagers which can help prepare for future careers.

Select a career related to clothing and fabrics that interests you. Prepare a report and present it to the class. If possible, interview people who are working at this career and include their experiences with a summary of your readings.

Visit a college or university to learn of the home economics majors offered. If such a visit cannot be arranged, invite a college representative to talk with your class. Another group may wish to visit vocational and technical schools with majors in clothing and textiles, and compare the programs and employment opportunities.

Interview a tailor or custom dressmaker to determine how this work differs from that of an alteration hand. Visit the alteration department of a large clothing store to learn of the work of those employed there. Find out the most common alterations.

Prepare a report on the cost of establishing a home dressmaking business. Find out the skills necessary and the personal qualities essential to success in such a business.

Make a list of specialty items suitable for home manufacturing. Select an article which might be made at home. Purchase the material, make the item, and display it in class. How long did it take to make it, how much did it cost, how would you sell it, and how much would it sell for? Draw conclusions about home manufacturing of clothing and gift items. Compare possible profits from selling homemade items with probable wages from factory work. What are other advantages of each type of work?

Discuss the pros and cons of selling in a large department store. Interview a personnel officer to determine the qualities desirable in a salesperson. Determine the usual wages and other fringe benefits.

With a committee, compile a list of occupations at which a mother can work at home either full or part time when her children are little. Find out the training needed for these occupations.

Determine the opportunities available in home economics for those who have advanced college degrees (master's and doctor's). What types of work are available, what are the usual salaries, and what are the specific requirements?

Summary With Check-up Questions

It is important for students to consider their future goals and career wishes when selecting high school courses.

- *How will your interests affect your choice of high school courses?*
- *Why is a realistic understanding of your abilities necessary for a wise choice of a high school major?*
- *If you discover that you have not taken the necessary courses for entrance into college or post-high school training programs, how can they be made up?*

There is a continually increasing demand for trained home economists and salaries and working conditions are very attractive.

- *Why are jobs in the business area of home economics increasing?*

- *How do salaries of workers in home economics related occupations compare with those of other jobs?*
- *Why are there many opportunities for advancement in home economics related careers?*

A home economics education helps prepare for one's personal and home life as well as for a rewarding career.

- *In what ways does a home economics high school and college education help in one's personal and family life?*
- *What career opportunities are there for those who have majored in home economics?*
- *Why is it often possible to combine a career in home economics and home-making more easily than other careers?*

CHAPTER NINETEEN

Looking Ahead to the Future

HOW WILL A STUDY OF DRESS help you in the future, regardless of the career you select? Today's teens can expect to live independently for part of their life and will need to know how to select and care for their own clothing. Since most will marry, much of their adult life will be spent living in a family group. Many of those who do not marry will maintain their own homes or help care for other family members.

Everyone should know how to choose and care for clothing, be well groomed, and understand the relation of clothing to other needs and wants. Adults, however, have increased responsibilities and often must know how to select clothing for children and other family members. They need to understand line, design, and hues suitable for different figure types and natural colorings other than their own.

Caring for clothing becomes more complex when one is responsible for the clothes of family members of differing ages, in terms of needs and desires. Also, despite less time available for personal care, adult family members need to be well groomed and attractively dressed as a family may be judged by the appearance of its members. Most people enjoy seeing others looking attractive. Adults should be an example to younger family members so they can learn to experience the self confidence that comes from ·good grooming and an attractive appearance.

Almost every day a homemaker must make decisions concerning how to spend the family money and the use of time and energy. It takes a super shopper to sort the large number of items on the market into the few the family really needs and wants. How much of the family income to spend for clothing and the proportion for each family member are major responsibilities of the homemaker. Because the needs change with changes in age, social activities, and occupational level, a homemaker must continue to reassess the family's clothing decisions.

Many men share in the responsibilities and pleasures of making a home for themselves and their families. A knowledge of clothing selection, use, and care can aid in this aspect of living.

Sewing is a hobby enjoyed by many women, either alone or with friends.

Home sewing can satisfy the creative use of leisure time for many homemakers as well as help furnish items for the family wardrobe. Knitting and needlework as well as sewing draperies, slipcovers, and other articles for the home are enjoyed by many people. Being able to alter clothes to fit growing children and to meet style changes can stretch the clothing budget so that more money will be available for other needs and desires.

If you have studied clothing in high school, you are fortunate, for you will find your role as an adult easier because of your knowledge and skills. There are many opportunities available to you after high school so that you can acquire additional needed information and use your abilities better.

Schools often have adult education programs which include classes in basic sewing, tailoring, children's clothing, millinery, knitting, and other areas related to clothing. Many

of these are free or available for a very small fee. If your local school system does not have information available on such classes, you can obtain it from your state education office located in your capital city. Community organizations, such as the YWCA or YWHA and private adult education groups, frequently offer day and evening classes which include clothing and related topics.

The Cooperative Extension Service sponsors sewing groups, lectures, and makes available helpful leaflets on the selection, construction, and care of clothing for all family members. Certain booklets have been listed in the references at the back of the book. Headquarters for local extension groups are usually in your county seat and the state headquarters at the land grant university.

Other sources of help are booklets and demonstrations, often made available at department stores by pattern companies and fabric manufacturers. Consumer magazines can also help you keep abreast of new fabrics, fashions, and other clothing ideas.

Visit an adult education class in clothing if available in your school system. Learn the requirements for joining the class. Observe projects being made and talk with members about their reasons for coming to class. Report to your classmates about the opportunities available to them for further study when they have completed high school.

Talk with the home economist from your local Cooperative Extension Service office (usually located in the county seat.) Ask her about the clothing programs planned for the year. Obtain copies of bulletins about clothing selection and construction which are available to homemakers in your county. Prepare a display for your classroom or school exhibit case.

Visit your town library. Make a list of recent books about clothing, fashion, grooming, and design that you believe would be of interest to a homemaker. Report to your class.

Select one or two adults to interview who have no children at home, or have pre-school children, or older children. Ask them what clothing items they have bought or helped a family member select within the past month. Find out what sewing they have done. What types of clothing repairs are most common in their home? Do they have any clothing care problems other than the usual laundering? Compare your finding with those of other students who have interviewed adults with different types of families.

SELECTED STUDENT REFERENCES

Chapter One

Books

Bigelow, Marybelle S. *Fashion in History.* Burgess Company, Minneapolis, Minn., 1970.

Horn, Marilyn. *The Second Skin.* Houghton Mifflin Company, Boston, Mass., 1968.

Lester, Katherine M. and Rose N. Kerr. *Historic Costume.* Charles A. Bennett Co., Inc., Peoria, Illinois, 1967.

Payne, Blanche, *History of Costume,* From Ancient Egyptians to the Twentieth Century. Harper and Row, Publishers, New York, 1965. Reference book with many illustrations.

Roach, Mary Ellen and Joanne Bubolz Eicher. *Dress, Adornment, and the Social Order.* John Wiley and Sons, Inc., New York, N. Y., 1965. College reference concerning the reasons men and women use dress and adornment.

Leaflets and Other References

J. C. Penney Company, 1301 Avenue of the Americas, New York, N. Y. 10019—"Forum" available twice a year from manager of local J. C. Penney store or New York office; "Clothing Communicates," filmstrip.

Tom McAn Shoe Company, 67 Millbrook Street, Worcester, Mass. 01606—"Shoe Fashions Today and Through the Ages," filmstrip available on loan.

Chapter Two

Books

Beitler, Ethel Jane and Bill Lockhart. *Design for You.* John Wiley and Sons, Inc., New York, 1961.

Kefgen, Mary and Touchie-Specht, Phyllis. *Individuality in Clothing Selection and Personal Appearance.* Macmillan Company, New York, N. Y., 1971.

Pankowski, Edith and Pankowski, Dallas. *Art Principles in Clothing.* Macmillan Company, New York, N. Y., 1972.

Sturm, Mary Mark and Edwina H. Grieser. *Guide to Modern Clothing.* McGraw-Hill Book Co., New York, 1968. Chapter 2, The Color and Design of Your Clothes.

Leaflets and Other References

The McCall Corporation, Dept. S. S., Dayton, Ohio 45401—"To Plan the Perfect Costume, Use Optical Illusion."

National Urban League, 55 E. 52nd Street, New York, N. Y. 10022—"Charm by Choice," filmstrip available for purchase.

Chapter Three

Books

Beitler, Ethel Jane and Bill Lockhart. *Design for You.* John Wiley and Sons, Inc., New York, 1961. Chapter 6, Color Sounds Off.

Pollard, L. Belle. *Experiences With Clothing.* Ginn and Company, Boston, 1961. Chapter 6, Style and Fashion.

Rathbone, Lucy et al. *Fashions and Fabrics.* Houghton Mifflin Co., Boston, 1962. Chapter 4, The Colors You Wear.

Spears, Charleszine. *How To Wear Colors With Emphasis on Dark Skins.* Burgess Publishing Co., Minneapolis, Minn., 1965.

Sturm, Mary Mark and Edwina H. Grieser. *Guide To Modern Clothing*. McGraw Hill Book Co., New York, 1968. Chapter 2, The Color and Design of Your Clothes.

Todd, Elizabeth and Frances Roberts. *Clothes for Teens*. D. C. Heath and Co., Boston, 1963. Chapter 5, Selecting Garments Which Are Becoming and Well Designed.

Leaflets and Other References

Educational and Consumer Relations, J. C. Penney Company, Inc., 1301 Avenue of the Americas, New York, N. Y. 10019—Color bibs available for purchase.

Interchemical Corporation, 67 West 44th Street, New York, N. Y. 10036—"The Color Tree."

Chapter Four

Books

McDermott, Irene E. and Florence W. Nicholas. *Homemaking for Teen-Agers*, Book 1. Chas. A. Bennett Co., Inc., Peoria, Illinois, 1966.

Pollard, L. Belle. *Experiences With Clothing*. Ginn and Company, Boston, Mass., 1961. Chapter 1, Your Wardrobe.

Rathbone, Lucy et al. *Fashions and Fabrics*. Houghton Mifflin Co., Boston, Mass., 1962. Chapter 6, Planning Your Wardrobe.

Sturm, Mary Mark and Edwina H. Grieser. *Guide To Modern Clothing*. McGraw-Hill Book Co., New York, 1968. Chapter 4, Planning Your Wardrobe.

Todd, Elizabeth and Frances Roberts. *Clothes for Teens*. D. C. Heath and Co., Boston, Mass., 1963. Chapter 4, Planning a Wardrobe.

Whitcomb, Helen and Rosalind Lang. *Charm*, The Career Girl's Guide to Business and Personal Success. Gregg Division, McGraw-Hill Book Co., 1964.

Leaflets and Other References

Cooperative Extension Service, University of Arizona, Tucson, Arizona 85721—"Clothes for the Places You Go."

Good Housekeeping Bulletin Service, 57th Street at 7th Avenue, New York, N. Y. 10019—"How To Plan a Wardrobe."

Household Finance Corp., Prudential Plaza, Chicago, Illinois 60601—"Your Clothing Dollar."

International Ladies Garment Workers Union, 22 West 38 Street, New York 10008—Free leaflets include "The Long and Short of It," "A College Wardrobe," "Fashion and You," "How To Be Well-Dressed," "Travel in Style," "Your Dream Wardrobe."

McCall Corporation, Dept. S. S., Dayton, Ohio 45401—"To Choose the Perfect Costume—Consider Your Wardrobe" and "Wardrobe Planning Guide Charts."

Sears, Roebuck and Co., Consumer Information Division, Chicago, Illinois 60601—Free booklet, "Selecting Fashions." Filmstrip, "Teen Fashion," available on loan.

Celanese Fibers Marketing Co., 522 Fifth Avenue, New York, N. Y. 10038—"Winning Wardrobes for Young Women," "Clothing for Young Men."

Chapter Five

Books

Lane Bryant. *Know Your Clothes*. Lehigh Brooks, 45 W. 57 Street, New York, New York 10019.

Rathbone, Lucy et al. *Fashions and Fabrics*. Houghton Mifflin Co., Boston, Mass., 1962. Unit 3, Shopping for Clothes.

Sturm, Mary Mark and Edwina H. Grieser. *Guide To Modern Clothing*. McGraw-Hill Book Co., New York, 1968. Chapter 5, Buying Your Clothes.

Todd, Elizabeth and Frances Roberts. *Clothes for Teens*. D. C. Heath and Co., Boston, Mass., 1963. Chapter 6, Shopping for Ready-made Garments.

Wingate, Isabel G., Karen K. Gillespie, and Betty G. Addison. *Know Your Merchandise*. Gregg Division, McGraw-Hill Book Co., New York, 1964.

Selected Student References

Leaflets and Other References

Consumers Union, 256 Washington Street, Mt. Vernon, New York 10550—"Consumer Reports," monthly magazine.

Consumers' Research Inc., Washington, New Jersey—"Consumers' Research Bulletin," monthly magazine.

Government Printing Office, Washington, D. C. 20402—"Buying Women's Coats and Suits," Home and Garden Bulletin No. 31.

Household Finance Corp., Prudential Plaza, Chicago, Illinois 60601—"Your Clothing Dollar" and "Money Management."

Manager of local J. C. Penney store or Educational and Consumer Relations, J. C. Penney Co., Inc., 1301 Avenue of the Americas, New York, N. Y. 10019—"Consumer Buying Guide for Gloves." Other buying guides include "Fabrics," "Foundation Garments," "Hosiery," "Slips," "Shoes," "Sweaters," "Swimwear," "Hairpieces," and "Men's Dress Shirts."

Leather Industries of America, 411 5th Avenue, New York, N. Y. 10016—"Stay on Your Toes," and "Tips on How to Buy Shoes."

Cooperative Extension Service, Michigan State University, East Lansing, Michigan 48823—"Saving with Sense at Sales," Extension Bulletin No. E-396.

Cooperative Extension Service, New York State College of Home Economics, Ithaca, New York 14850—"Shopper's Handbook, Labeling, Fabric Facts, Clothing Care," E-1093.

Division of Home Economics, Federal Extension Service, U. S. Department of Agriculture, Washington, D. C. 20250—"Be a Good Shopper."

Chapter Six

Books

The Look You Like, Answers to Your Questions About Skin Care and Cosmetics. 1967. American Medical Association, 535 N. Dearborn St., Chicago, Ill. 60610.

Archer, Elsie. *Let's Face It,* A Guide to Good Grooming for Negro Girls. J. B. Lippincott Co., Philadelphia, Pa., 1959.

McDermott, Irene E. and Florence W. Nicholas. *Homemaking for Teen-Agers,* Book 1. Chas. A. Bennett Co., Inc., Peoria, Illinois, 1966. Chapter 5, Look Your Best Through Grooming.

Whitcomb, Helen and Rosalind Lang. *Charm,* The Career Girl's Guide to Business and Personal Success. Gregg Division, McGraw-Hill Book Co., New York, 1964.

Leaflets and Other References

Avon Products, 30 Rockefeller Plaza, New York, New York 10020—"The Beauty of You."

Bonne Bell, P.O. Box 6177, Cleveland, Ohio 44101—"The Great Looks Book."

John H. Breck Inc., Springfield, Massachusetts—"The Story of Beautiful Hair."

The Cleanliness Bureau, 40 East 41st Street, New York, N. Y. 10017—"Help Yourself to Better Looks, a Better Home, Better Future, and a Better You."

The Gillette Company, 100 Charles River Plaza, Boston, Massachusetts 02114—"Neat is Not a Dirty Word."

National Dairy Council, 111 N. Canal Street, Chicago, Illinois 60606—"A Girl and Her Figure" and "Posture on Parade."

National Urban League, 55 E. 52nd Street, New York, N. Y. 10022—"Charm by Choice," filmstrip available for purchase.

Food and Drug Administration, U. S. Department of Health, Education, and Welfare, Washington, D. C. 20250—"Facts for Consumers—Cosmetics."

Chapter Seven

Books

Lyle, Dorothy Siebert. *The Clothes We Wear.* Department of Home Economics, National Education Association, 1201 16th St. N.W., Washington, D. C. 20036.

Pollard, L. Belle. *Experiences With Clothing.* Ginn and Company, Boston, Mass., 1961. Chapter 3, Extending the Service of Clothing.

Rathbone, Lucy et al. *Fashion and Fabrics.* Houghton Mifflin Co., Boston, Mass., 1962. Unit 4, Taking Care of Your Clothes.

Sturm, Mary Mark and Edwina H. Grieser. *Guide To Modern Clothing.* McGraw-Hill Book Co., New York, 1968. Chapter 6, Caring for Your Clothes.

Todd, Elizabeth and Frances Roberts. *Clothes for Teens.* D. C. Heath and Co., Boston, Mass., 1963. Chapter 2, Keeping Clothes Neat and Clean.

Leaflets and Other References

Cooperative Extension Service, University of Arizona, Tucson, Arizona 85721—"Darning on a Simple Machine," Folder 121.

Association of Home Appliance Manufacturers, 20 N. Wacker Drive, Chicago, Illinois 60606—booklets on home laundry.

Best Foods Division, CPC Int., 1137 W. Morris St., Indianapolis, Indiana 46206—"Tie-Dye," "Fancy Fabrics."

Textile Fibers Department, Technical Service Divison, E. I. duPont de Nemours and Co., Inc., Wilmington, Delaware 19898—"Home Laundering of Garments Containing Dacron."

Cooperative Extension Service, University of Massachusetts, Amherst, Mass. 01003—"Ideas for Extra Storage," Pub. 324.

Cooperative Extension Service, Michigan State University, East Lansing, Michigan 48823—"Textile Care—Keeping Clothes in Service," Ext. Bulletin No. E-404.

Home Service Department, The Maytag Company, Newton, Iowa 50208—"The Bride's Guide to Home Laundry," "Know Your Laundry Recipes" and "Removing Spots and Stains."

International Fabricare Institute, P.O. Box 940, Joliet, Illinois 60434.

Procter and Gamble, Cincinnati, Ohio 45201—"About Detergents," "About Soaps," "Focus on Family Wash," "Washday Wonders."

Pendleton Woolen Mills, Portland, Oregon—"How to Press Wool," "Sweater Sense," "Wool Responds Beautifully to Easy Care."

Cooperative Extension Service, Washington State University, Pullman, Washington 99163—"Plan a Workroom for Laundry and Other Activities," Bulletin 562.

U. S. Department of Agriculture, Washington, D. C. 20250—"Clothing Repairs," H. & G. Bulletin 107; "Detergents for Home Laundering," H. & G. Bulletin 49; "Home Laundering, the Equipment and the Job," H. & G. Bulletin 101; "How to Prevent and Remove Mildew," H. & G. Bulletin 68; "Protecting Woolens Against Clothes Moths and Carpet Beetles," H. & G. Bulletin 113; "Removing Stains from Fabric," H. & G. Bulletin 62; "Sanitation in Home Laundering," H. & G. Bulletin 97; "Home Planning Aids—Bedrooms and Clothes Closets," Misc. Pub. 1004.

Chapter Eight

Books

Tate, Mildred T. and Oris Glisson. *Family Clothing.* John Wiley and Sons, Inc., New York, 1961.

Leaflets and Other References

International Ladies Garment Workers Union, 275 7th Avenue, New York, N. Y. 10001—"How to Dress Your Little Girl."

Cooperative Extension Service, South Dakota State University, Brookings, South Dakota 57007—"Buying Clothes for Tots" and "Buying Patterns for Children's Clothing."

Community Program Coordinator, 3M Company, Bldg. 224–62, St. Paul, Minn.—booklets on safety.

Children's Bureau, U. S. Department of Health, Education, and Welfare, Washington, D. C.—"Infant Care" and "Prenatal Care."

Selected Student References

Chapter Nine

Books

Tate, Mildred T. and Oris Glisson. *Family Clothing.* John Wiley and Sons, Inc., New York, 1961.

Leaflets and Other References

Men's Fashion Association of America, 1290 Avenue of the Americas, New York, New York 10019—write for most recent educational booklets.

Educational Services Department, The Arrow Company, 530 Fifth Avenue, New York, N. Y. 10036—"What Every Woman Should Know About Men's Shirts."

Cooperative Extension Service, North Dakota State University, Fargo, North Dakota 58103—"Mr. Senior Citizen, Look Your Best," and "Mrs. Senior Citizen, Look Your Best."

Cooperative Extension Service, New York State College of Home Economics, Ithaca, New York 14850—"Shopping for Shirts," H. E. Leaflet No. 33; "Young Man, Take a Clothes Look," E-1092; "Making Shirts for Men of the Family," S-26.

Manager of local J. C. Penney store or Educational and Consumer Relations, J. C. Penney Company, Inc., 1301 Avenue of the Americas, New York, N. Y. 10019—"Consumer Buying Guide for Young Men's Slacks," "Men's Dress Shirts" and "Men's and Boys' Sport Coats."

Home Economists Service Bureau, Phillips Van Heusen Corp., 417 Fifth Avenue, New York, N. Y. 10016—"What Everyone Should Know About Men's Fashions."

U. S. Department of Agriculture, Washington, D. C. 20250—"Men's Suits, How to Judge Quality," H. & G. Bulletin 54; "Clothes for the Physically Handicapped Homemaker, with Features Suitable for All Women," Home Economics Research Report No. 12.

Chapter Ten

Books

American Home Economics Association. *Textile Handbook.* The Association, 2010 Massachusetts Avenue, N.W., Washington, D. C. 20636, 1971.

Denny, Grace G. *Fabrics.* J. B. Lippincott, Philadelphia, Pa. 1962.

Potter, M. David and Bernard Corbman. *Fiber To Fabric.* Gregg Publishing Co., McGraw-Hill Book Co., New York, N. Y. 1967.

Hollen, Norma and Saddler, Jane. *Textiles.* Macmillan Company, New York, New York, 1973.

Joseph, Marjorie L. *Introductory Textile Science.* Holt, Rinehart, and Winston, 1972.

Leaflets and Other References

American Fabrics, 24 E. 38th Street, New York, N. Y. 10016—"American Fabrics," quarterly magazine.

The Wool Bureau, 360 Lexington Avenue, New York,—"Beauty Secrets for Your Wool Wardrobe" and other student booklets.

Celanese Fibers Marketing Company, Consumer Education Department, 522 Fifth Avenue, New York, N. Y. 10036—"Fibers for Contemporary Fabrics," filmstrip on free loan with accompanying booklet.

Belgium Linen Association, 280 Madison Avenue, New York, N. Y. 10016— Write for list of current booklets.

E. I. duPont de Nemours and Co., Inc., Textile Fibers Dept., Product Information, Centre Road Building, Wilmington, Delaware, 19898—Booklets on Dacron, Nylon, Orlon, Lycra, and other man-made fibers.

Irish Linen Guild, 1271 Avenue of Americas, New York, N. Y. 10016—"Linen for Modern Living Kit."

Man-Made Fiber Producers Assoc., Inc., 350 5th Avenue, New York, N. Y. 10001—"Man-Made Fiber Fact Book."

Cooperative Extension Service, New York State College of Home Economics, Ithaca, New York 14850—"Shoppers Handbook, Labeling, Fabric Facts and Clothing Care."

Manager of local J. C. Penney store or Educational and Consumer Relations, J. C. Penney Co., Inc., 1301 Avenue of the Americas, New York, N. Y. 10019—"Textile Cartoons," "Consumer Buying Guide on Fabrics," and "Fashions and Fabrics."

U. S. Bureau of Standards, "Fibers and Fabrics" (1970), Superintendent of Documents, Washington, D. C. 20402.

Chapter Eleven

Books

See references for Chapter Ten.

Leaflets and Other References

The Underwear Institute, 468 Park Avenue, New York, N. Y. 10016—"Knitting, a Booklet of Knitting Facts and Information."

Talon Educational Service, 41 E. 51st Street, New York, N. Y. 10022—"Learning About Thread."

Chapter Twelve

Books

Birrell, Verla. The Textile Arts. Schonkin Company, New York, New York, 1973. Also see references for Chapter Ten.

Leaflets and Other References

Dyes and Chemical Division, Dept. A., Organic Chemical Dept., E. I. duPont de Nemours and Co., Inc., Wilmington, Delaware 19898—"Zepel."

Extension Service, New York State College of Home Economics, Ithaca, New York 14850—"Fabric Finishes for Beauty, Service, and Protection," Bulletin 1126.

Cooperative Extension Service, South Dakota State College, Brookings, South Dakota 57007—"Fabric Finishes," FS-163.

U. S. Department of Agriculture, Washington, D. C. 20250—"Making Household Fabrics Flame-Resistant," Leaflet 454.

Chapter Thirteen

Books

Denny, Grace G. Fabrics. J. B. Lippincott, Philadelphia, 1953.

Focus on Fabrics. National Institute of Drycleaning, Silver Spring, Maryland, 20910.

Leaflets and Other References

Cooperative Extension Service, South Dakota State University, Brookings, South Dakota 57007 —"Fabrics Worth Noting: Deep-Pile Fabrics," "Foam-Backed Fabrics," "Knits," and "Stretch Fabrics."

Kandel Patterns for Knits, 4834 N. Interstate, Portland, Oregon 97217—booklets on sewing with knits.

Chapter Fourteen

Books

Bane, Allyne. Creative Clothing Construction. McGraw-Hill Book Co., Inc., New York. 1966.

Bishop, Edna Bryte and Marjorie Stotler Arch. Bishop Method of Clothing Construction. J. B. Lippincott Co., Philadelphia, Pa., 1962.

Selected Student References

Dunn, Lucille. *Steps in Clothing Skills.* Chas. A. Bennett Co., Inc., Peoria, Illinois, 1970.

McDermott, Irene E. and Florence W. Nicholas. *Homemaking for Teen-Agers*, Book 1. Chas. A. Bennett Co., Inc., Peoria, Illinois, 1968. Chapter 7, Learning To Sew.

Schrieber, Joanne. *Good and Easy Sewing.* Betty Crocker Home Library, General Mills, Inc., Minneapolis, Minn. 55440.

Leaflets and Other References

Butterick Pattern Service, 161 6th Avenue, New York, N. Y. 10013—Write for most recent student educational aids on pattern selection and clothing construction.

Simplicity Pattern Co., Inc., 200 Madison Avenue, New York, N. Y. 10016—Write for most recent student educational aids.

McCall Pattern Co., Educational Department, P.O. Box 9119, Manhattan, Kansas 66502.— Write for most recent student educational aids.

Vogue Pattern Service, 161 6th Avenue, New York, N. Y. 10013—Write for most recent student educational aids.

Chapter Fifteen

Books

See books for Chapter Fourteen.

Leaflets and Other References

Coats and Clark, Inc., 430 Park Avenue, New York, N. Y. 10022—"A Story of Thread."

General Electric Co., Housewares Division, Bridgeport, Conn. 06602—"Press as You Sew for Professional Results."

Griest Manufacturing Co., 446 Blake Street, New Haven, Conn. 06515—"How to Use the Narrow Hemmer and Ruffler."

Singer Company Educational Department, 30 Rockefeller Plaza, New York, N. Y. 10020— Write for most recent student booklets on use of sewing machine.

United States Department of Agriculture, Washington, D. C. 20250—"Buying Your Home Sewing Machine," H. & G. Bulletin No. 38.

J. Wiss and Sons Company, 33 Littleton Avenue, Newark, New Jersey 07107—"Story of Shears and Scissors."

Chapter Sixteen

Books

Johnson, Hildegarde. *Sewing Step by Step.* Ginn and Co., Boston, Massachusetts, 1969.

Also see Chapter Fourteen.

Leaflets and Other References

Coats and Clark, Inc., 430 Park Avenue, New York, N. Y. 10022—"Sew Your Zipper 1-2-3."

Pellon Corporation, 1120 Avenue of the Americas, New York, N. Y. 10036—"The Importance of Shape," filmstrip with accompanying booklet.

Unique Zipper Co., 161 Sixth Avenue, New York, New York 10013—"Unique Zipper Handbook."

Also see Chapter Fourteen for pattern companies listing.

Chapter Seventeen

Books

Bane, Allyne. *Tailoring.* McGraw-Hill Book Co., New York, New York, 1968.

Beck, Doris May. *Custom Tailoring for Homemakers.* Charles A. Bennett Co., Inc., Peoria, Illinois, 1964.

Also see references for Chapter Fourteen.

Leaflets and Other References

Better Homes and Gardens, Meredith Publishing Co., Des Moines, Iowa 50303—"Pattern Adjustment," "Professional Sewing Tips," "Sewing Casual Clothes," "Tailoring Suits and Coats."

Coats and Clark Inc., 430 Park Avenue, New York, N. Y. 10022—Write for most recent student educational aids.

Corduroy Council of America, 15 East 53rd Street, New York, N. Y. 10022—"How to Sew with Corduroy."

Retail Fashions Fabrics Co., Hoechst Fibers, 1515 Broadway, New York, New York 10036—"How to Sew a Knit."

Simplicity Pattern Co., 200 Madison Avenue, New York, New York 10016—"Sewing for Men and Boys."

Dan River Mills, 111 West 40th Street, New York, N. Y. 10018—"Secrets of Sewing with Stripes and Plaids."

Lily Mills Co., Shelby, North Carolina, "Learn How to Crochet, Knit, Embroider, Tat, Weave."

McCall Corp., 230 Park Avenue, New York, N. Y. 10017—"Needlework and Crafts," published twice a year.

William E. Wright and Sons, West Warren, Mass.—"How-To" leaflets on use of trimmings.

U. S. Department of Agriculture, Washington, D. C. 20250—"Changing the Hem in a Dress," PA-756; "Fitting Coats and Suits," H. & G. Bulletin 11; "Fix New Clothes to Make Them Last Longer," PA-766; "How to Tailor a Woman's Suit," H. & G. Bulletin 20; "Making Pants Longer or Shorter," PA-768; "Making the Waistline Fit on Pants," PA-755; "Pattern Alterations," H. E. Research Report 32; "Simplified Clothing Construction," H. & G. 59; "Tapering Pants," PA-754.

Chapter Eighteen

Books

Jabenis, Elaine. *The Fashion Director.* Wiley Books, New York, New York, 1972.

McDermott, Irene E. and Jeanne L. Norris. *Opportunities in Clothing.* Chas. A. Bennett Co., Inc., Peoria, Illinois, 1968.

Phillips, Velma. *Home Economics Careers for You.* Harper and Brothers, New York, N. Y., 1962.

Tate, Mildred T. *Home Economics As a Profession.* McGraw-Hill Book Co., New York, N. Y., 1961.

Leaflets and Other References

American Home Economics Assoc., 2010 Massachusetts Avenue, Washington, D. C. 20636—"Home Economics Has a Career for You in Textiles and Clothing."

Fairchild Publications, Inc., 7 E. 12 Street, New York, New York 10003—"Women's Wear Daily" and booklets on retailing careers.

Manager of local J. C. Penney store or Educational and Consumer Relations, J. C. Penney Co., 1301 Avenue of the Americas, New York, N. Y. 10019—"It's an Exciting Career—Home Economist in Business," filmstrip. "Job Opportunities in Retailing for Young Men and Women," "Completing a Job Application," and many other career materials.

Sears, Roebuck & Co., 512 Burlington, LaGrange, Illinois 60502—"A Department Store in a Classroom."

Chapter Nineteen

See references for Chapter Eighteen.

INDEX

Index

Index